792.0922

D1389139

JOY RIDE

ALSO BY JOHN LAHR

BIOGRAPHY

Tennessee Williams: Mad Pilgrimage of the Flesh

Honky Tonk Parade: New Yorker Profiles of Show People

The Diaries of Kenneth Tynan (editor)

Show and Tell: New Yorker Profiles

Sinatra: The Artist and the Man

Dame Edna Everage and the Rise of Western Civilization: Backstage with Barry Humphries

The Orton Diaries (editor)

Coward the Playwright

Prick Up Your Ears: The Biography of Joe Orton

Notes on a Cowardly Lion: The Biography of Bert Lahr

CRITICISM

Light Fantastic: Adventures in Theatre

Life-Show: How to See Theater in Life and Life in Theater
(with Jonathan Pryce)

Astonish Me: Adventures in Contemporary Theater
Acting Out America: Essays on Modern Theatre
Up Against the Fourth Wall: Essays on Modern Theater
A Casebook on Harold Pinter's The Homecoming
(edited with Anthea Lahr)

NOVELS

Hot to Trot
The Autograph Hound

PLAYS

Elaine Stritch at Liberty (with Elaine Stritch)
The Manchurian Candidate (adaptation)
The Bluebird of Unhappiness: A Woody Allen Revue (adaptation)
Diary of a Somebody (adaptation)
Accidental Death of an Anarchist (adaptation)

JOY RIDE

LIVES OF THE THEATRICALS

JOHN LAHR

B L O O M S B U R Y

LONDON · OXFORD · NEW YORK · NEW DELHI · SYDNEY

Bloomsbury Publishing

An imprint of Bloomsbury Publishing Plc

50 Bedford Square	1385 Broadway
London	New York
WC1B 3DP	NY 10018
UK	USA

www.bloomsbury.com

BLOOMSBURY and the Diana logo are trademarks of Bloomsbury Publishing Plc

First published in Great Britain 2015

© John Lahr, 2015

John Lahr has asserted his right under the Copyright, Designs and
Patents Act, 1988, to be identified as Author of this work.

All rights reserved. No part of this publication may be reproduced or transmitted
in any form or by any means, electronic or mechanical, including photocopying,
recording, or any information storage or retrieval system, without
prior permission in writing from the publishers.

No responsibility for loss caused to any individual or organization acting
on or refraining from action as a result of the material in this
publication can be accepted by Bloomsbury or the author.

British Library Cataloguing-in-Publication Data
A catalogue record for this book is available from the British Library.

ISBN: HB: 978-1-4088-6863-8
ePub: 978-1-4088-6864-5

2 4 6 8 10 9 7 5 3 1

Book Design by Chris Welch
Printed and bound in Great Britain by CPI Group (UK) Ltd, Croydon CR0 4YY

To find out more about our authors and books visit www.bloomsbury.com.
Here you will find extracts, author interviews, details of forthcoming
events and the option to sign up for our newsletters

To

GEORGEANNA MOTTS

Guardian Angel

CONTENTS

Introduction   xv

PART I: PLAYWRIGHTS   1

1. ARTHUR MILLER   7
   A View from the Bridge   23

2. AUGUST WILSON   28
   Gem of the Ocean   61
   Joe Turner's Come and Gone   65
   Seven Guitars   68

3. TONY KUSHNER   75
   Angels in America   102
   Caroline, or Change   110

4. DAVID MAMET   115
   The Cryptogram   143
   Glengarry Glen Ross   151

5. SARAH RUHL   152
   Eurydice   165
   Stage Kiss   168

6. CLIFFORD ODETS   173
    Golden Boy   188

7. DAVID RABE   192
    Hurlyburly   207

8. HAROLD PINTER   209
    Moonlight   225
    The Room and *Celebration*   232

9. WALLACE SHAWN   236
    The Designated Mourner   250
    Grasses of a Thousand Colors   256

10. NEIL LABUTE   261
    The Mercy Seat   277

11. SAM SHEPARD   281
    True West   294

12.   WILLIAM SHAKESPEARE   298
    John Barton   298
    Hamlet   311
    The Winter's Tale   317
    Othello   324
    Macbeth   328
    King Lear   331

PART II: PRODUCTIONS   333

    Arcadia   339
    The Pajama Game   346
    The Retreat from Moscow   349

Private Lives   353

Company   358

Sweeney Todd: The Demon Barber of Fleet Street   361

Me, Myself & I   365

Oklahoma!   369

The Light in the Piazza   374

Orpheus Descending   378

The Rose Tattoo   383

Carousel   387

PART III: DIRECTORS   399

13. NICHOLAS HYTNER   407
The History Boys   422

14. INGMAR BERGMAN   425
Madam de Sade   452
The Misanthrope   460

15. SUSAN STROMAN   469
The Producers   493

16. MIKE NICHOLS   499
Death of a Salesman   539

Acknowledgments   545

Index   547

We must risk delight. We can do without pleasure,
but not delight. Not enjoyment. We must have
the stubbornness to accept our gladness in the ruthless
furnace of this world . . .

—Jack Gilbert
"A Brief for the Defense"
Refusing Heaven

INTRODUCTION

In my half century of theatergoing, I've seen grown-ups stand on their seats to cheer, keel over into the aisle after a punch line, throw coats onto a horseshoe stage for the parading star to step on, stuff handkerchiefs in their mouths to keep from laughing, and even briefly lose consciousness and collapse between seats. That last ecstatic guy was me, blindsided by one of Dame Edna Everage's illiberal salvos. Part of the theater's big magic is its ability to exhilarate; it has the power to put us beside ourselves, to banish gravity, to call out of us our most buried feelings, to make the moment unforgettable, to kill Time. That's its joy ride.

Nowadays, theater criticism is on the decline. The media's obsession with lifestyles and celebrity has hijacked the discussion of the dramatic craft and process. Thumbs up or down are hardly good compasses by which the public can get its bearings on a writer and the work. As a result, the theatricals and the cultural history to which they contribute are largely left out of the public conversation. ("Who is Marlon Brando?" a twenty-something college-educated fact-checker at *The New Yorker* asked me a while ago.) If we see a play today, it's usually in the context of no context. This depletes the audience's pleasure, as well as its sensibility. The more we know about the artists, the more we can appreciate their art. If we need better plays—and we do—we also need better audiences. As Tallulah Bankhead once told an avid would-be actress, "If you really want to help the American theater, don't be an actress, *dahling*, be an audience."

Since my mid-twenties, I have spent a good part of my professional life as an audience member. I grew up in the theater; I've written for the theater; I've helped to manage theaters. I have an abiding affection for the derring-do of actors, who are, in my eyes, athletes of the spirit. Ever since my sister, Jane, and I hung out between shows in my father's dusty Broadway dressing room, playing among the costumes and props in the murk of backstage, the theater has been associated in my mind with fun, mystery, and adventure. It's where I go to think, to travel to places and times I've never imagined, or to inhabit psychological situations that I would otherwise run a mile to avoid. Theater is where I can ponder the past and imagine the future. If I'm honest, it's also where I preserve the memory of my parents and their show-biz roots.

Theater is an artisanal industry in a technological age. Everything about it goes against the grain of our distracted, fast-moving cultural moment. A play requires the audience to work, to contend with eloquence and with ambiguity, to think. In a film, the audience sees what the director wants it to see; with a live production, the audience must take more responsibility for meaning. The fact that theater is a minority art form doesn't minimize its cultural importance. Theater is still the only popular entertainment in which you can hear a writer's individual voice in stories undiluted by corporate agreement; in which language, in all its vulgar and vivacious permutations, is continually brought up to date; in which you can feel the carnal wallop of actors as they turn themselves inside out in the greatest show on earth, which is the show of human emotion.

In a movie or on television, performances are repeatable and unvarying; they don't require an audience. By contrast, in the theater, the spectator's attention can make a significant difference to the quality of the event. "The play was good but the audience was a dismal failure," George Bernard Shaw kidded on the square. The audience's job is to be open and alert to the world onstage; the actors' job is to be open and alert to the world of the play. In a real sense, the audience is a partner in the play-making. Every performance is different, and so is every audience. Each night of a play is a new dance to the same tune. This dynamic exchange of energy is theater's particular piquancy. The synergy is humanizing; the paying customer enters as an individual but becomes part of a communal event, a sort of entangled collective, in which both sides of the theatrical equation learn from the other's response. "Your audience gives you everything you need," the legendary comedienne Fanny Brice once observed. "There's no director who can direct you like an audience."

In a time of terror—such as our time—the theater's promotion of ideas and feelings takes on a significant extra social valence. The terrorist's ambition is not just to kill people but to kill thought; to divide the society against itself and, in doing so, force it to implode from within. As the general mood of retreat and the many political false steps of current Western democracies indicate, the strategy of terrorism is working better than we like to admit. Terrorism makes a spectacle of absurdity, in which pain unmakes the world. Theater, which attempts to understand our pain, makes a spectacle of meaning and coherence. Now, more than ever, theater is not only a demonstration of courage but an engineer of it.

Joy Ride: Lives of the Theatricals is my rearguard action to address the problem of the context of no context. The aim here is to bring the theatergoer up close and personal with the artists and their processes, with the plays and the playwrights, with what they seek to express, and how they express it. One section of the book deals exclusively with specific theatrical productions; in these cases, the critical task is to bring some sense of theater history to an appreciation of the event under consideration. In an ideal world, this volume would also include profiles of actors and of the makers of American musical theater, but the size of such a book was judged prohibitive for the pocketbooks of both the aficionados and the publishers. Tennessee Williams, Oscar Wilde, Noel Coward, and Barry Humphries (Dame Edna Everage)—some of the supremos of the modern stage—are conspicuous by their (almost complete) absence. Because I've written extensively about them in other books, the decision has been to cede their spots to other accomplished playwrights, directors, and productions that have also corrupted me with pleasure. Taken together, what remains comprises many of the high points of my stint at *The New Yorker*.

I was fifty in 1992, when during a transatlantic phone call, I told the magazine's new editor, Tina Brown, that I was "hot" to be *The New Yorker*'s senior drama critic. "I like the word 'hot'," she said, and hung up. I felt "the air brighten," as Seamus Heaney said, in "Fosterling," a poem about his own coming of literary age at fifty. "Time to be dazzled and the heart to lighten," he added. I know the feeling. Until Tina's call, like all veteran freelancers, I'd bounced around from gig to gig. I'd never had a regular job or a regular paycheck. I remember in September, of that same year, flying to New York from London, where I live, for a half-hour meeting with Tina. In the end, she had time for only ten minutes. My job, we agreed, was to write a new kind of criticism: to bring the reader as far as possible into the theater world, to take it, so to speak, out of the reading room and into the rehearsal room. I was to start the following month. I knew what I was being handed. I told myself not to waste a minute, and I didn't.

I walked away from the building and ambled a few blocks west on Forty-Third Street to Broadway, which looked the worse for wear in the midday sun. I remember thinking that this was now my patch; I was somehow connected to, and responsible for, the theatrical world, which my father, as a comedian, had dominated decades before. I gave myself five years at the job. By the time it ended—December 10, 2012—I had been at the magazine for twenty-one years, published the best part of a million words, and written more than forty profiles. (I continue to write profiles for the magazine.) My run as senior drama critic was the longest in *The New Yorker*'s history. (Wolcott Gibbs, who took over from Robert Benchley in 1940 and spent eighteen years on the aisle, was second.) As I always saw it, my job was to keep the theater in the public discourse, to use the platform of the magazine, to give theatergoers not just a sense of the play but a sense of the history out of which it came. I loved writing for *New Yorker* readers, an audience that grew, under the editorship of David Remnick, to more than a million a week. I never had one bad day on the job: it was my joy ride too.

At the end of this book, as a kind of envoi to the happiest years of my writing life, I have reproduced a photo of my office, that twelve-by-ten-foot windowless warren on the twentieth floor of the Condé Nast Building, where for two weeks of every month for more than two decades, I spent much of my time. In this home away from home, I surrounded myself with photographs of my beloveds: my wife, my son, my sister, my dad (the laminated cover of *Time*, with him as a grimacing baseball player in the revue *Two on the Aisle*; another with his policeman's hat askew in his burlesque cop act), Richard Avedon, and the film director and my dear friend Karel Reisz, kissing my then-infant son. There, studded among the books, were postcards from playwrights (Stoppard, Mamet, Albee, Miller); a photo of "Millie," the huge trout I caught in New Zealand (and, in honor of its tenacity, named after my mother); a photo of me under the Broadway marquee of *Elaine Stritch at Liberty*, which I co-wrote; a framed invitation to *The New Yorker Pocket Revue*, which I devised and which was staged at the Hudson Theatre for the magazine's seventy-fifth anniversary.

With books piled almost to the ceiling on shelves on either side of my desk and with Paul Davis's ravishing theater illustrations in front of me, I sat at my computer monitor in a sort of valley of theatrical lore and literature. This little cave of consciousness was where, for the first time, I felt free to be myself in print. Part of that freedom was knowing that my deft editor, Deborah Treisman, was only seven paces away in her airy corner office. I could go out on any narrative limb, take any kind of linguistic risk; if I fell or floundered, Deborah was there to catch me and get me back on track. I could write without fear—a liberation!

My habit was to write over the weekend, when the office was quiet, except for the occasional strolling security guard. If the writing flowed, I'd finish on Sunday, in time for sushi and the evening NFL game at the local *boîte*. If I was struggling, I'd push through without dinner until around midnight. The review was always on Deborah's computer when she walked in at ten o'clock Monday morning, with her cup of tea and a muffin. For the next couple of hours, she practiced her forensic voodoo, what we came to call, with some justification, "a shampoo and blow dry." By noon, Deborah's proof was finished and on my chair. After her initial edit, our adjustments took maybe five minutes. (Profiles, of course, required more extended conversations and more rewrites.) But, short or long, the mind-meld never lost its thrill. On the edited page, you are still you, but somehow brighter, clearer, smoother, almost glamorous. Your words dip and swing with their proper music; your hard-won meanings land with their intended clout. No wonder the relationship feels so intimate and so joyous. You are being given the greatest of gifts: to be your best self in print. Among the things that Deborah has pinned to the cork wall above her desk is a Xeroxed photo of me as a tweedy ten-year-old posed with my sister and our parents at our Stork Club table for Easter lunch. I like it that the photo is there, on the same wall that features the drawings and avowals of love from her daughters. In some magical way, I'm watching over Deborah, just as she, in a very real, meaningful way, has watched over me these many years.

The last thing I took from my *New Yorker* office before I closed the door on it forever was a snatch of dialogue from Tom Stoppard's

The Invention of Love, which I'd typed out many years before to give myself heart, and which still gives me heart back in London, where it is taped to the mantelpiece of my study. "Only to shed some light," Stoppard writes. "It doesn't matter where on what. It's the light itself against the darkness. It's what's left of God's purpose when you take away God."

J.L.

London

November 4, 2014

PART I
PLAYWRIGHTS

In every pitch letter I write to a potential subject of a *New Yorker* profile, I mention two things: that I have no tabloid intentions and that, in order for this three- to four-month exercise to yield good results, it has to be a collaboration. My goal is to bring the reader as close to the person and the craft as I can. The result is long and detailed, a sort of mini-biography of six to ten thousand words; to produce it, I generate a binder of about a thousand pages of interviews with my subject, as well as with subsidiary witnesses to the life and art. Out of this raw material, rather as if I were panning for gold, I grab what I hope are the choice nuggets to build the story. The reading experience is meant to feel effortless, but the writing experience isn't: it requires a literary juggling act of interpretation, observation, and concision.

Writing a profile has a lot in common with the art of tailoring: the more sittings, the better the fit. Access, emotional availability, and trust are crucial to the result. By agreeing to sit for a portrait, the subject is also agreeing to play the profile's psychological game, which I spell out in advance. Only once, in my early days of researching the David Mamet profile, when the bolshie playwright refused to talk about his late father, who was crucial to the formation of his character and, as it happens, to his style, did I turn off the tape recorder and suggest we call it quits. (Mamet broke the impasse by agreeing that his sister could talk about their father.)

The first biography I wrote, in 1969, was of my father, the comedian Bert Lahr, whose career spanned fifty years of American show
business; when I began my research, I was shocked to discover that,
in half a century of rave reviews and millions of published words,
very little light had been shined on his personality or his comedy.
My Dad had lived most of his life in the spotlight, but he was never
really seen. My book on my father, and my books on other theatrical
figures—Joe Orton, Barry Humphries, Noel Coward, and Tennessee Williams—were attempts to redress what I saw as this narrative
lacuna: to bear better witness, to change the discourse about theatricals, who are, after all, "the abstract brief chronicles of the time,"
as Hamlet says about actors.

When I arrived at *The New Yorker* in 1992, the magazine offered a
treasure trove of new opportunity: it gave me space and the support
of fine editing and fact-checking, which allowed me to make deeper,
more accurate, more elegant forays into the worlds of theater and
film. The magazine also served as a kind of magic carpet, providing
unique entrée into the lives of my subjects. My brief, as Joe Orton
would say, has been infinite. I have been more or less free to follow
my enthusiasms and my curiosity. I could go to Sweden to track Ingmar Bergman, to Africa in pursuit of the filmmaker Mira Nair. I
sat in with a team of TV sitcom writers to profile Roseanne, walked
the streets of Pittsburgh with August Wilson, saw Tony Kushner
through the anguish of a Broadway first night, and even schlepped
into the Connecticut woods with Arthur Miller to find the cabin he
built in order to write *Death of a Salesman*. The *New Yorker* profiles
also provided another, more personal opportunity: they allowed me
to study the mystery of talent and the price of fame, two issues that
bedeviled me as a child growing up in the household of a star.

In my mind, I am writing a sort of Lives of the Theatricals, doing
for show people what my literary hero Dr. Samuel Johnson did for the
poets of his day, commingling biography and criticism. Although my
subjects are in the public eye, because of the superficiality of most

popular discussion, they are rarely, if ever, interpreted. Not every subject wants to get up close and personal. "I love what you do, John," Mel Brooks told me over the phone. "I just don't want you doing it to me." But for many of the people I have profiled, as well as for me, the scrutiny of their art took on a surprising piquancy. "It was also a great inspiration to me to go through the process with you and see the results," the film director Ang Lee wrote. Al Pacino, notoriously tight-lipped and unbiddable with the press, fired off more than forty lengthy e-mails in an attempt to explain his career and his process.

What I try to do is listen, and let the personality and the circumstances in which the individual allows himself or herself to be seen play on me. I dig where my subject leads me. The process is both analytic and intuitive. The goal is to surrender myself to the subject and to the world of his or her work, by treating each as a metaphor for the other. By the time I meet my subjects, I've read all their press interviews, I know their work, and I know their official stories. Those things aren't what I'm looking for; or, if they're offered, not what I report. I'm listening for what shaped their expression and what they seek to *express* in themselves. With playwrights, the clue to their metabolism often lies in the rhythms of their prose—Tennessee Williams's floridness, Sarah Ruhl's lightness, Mamet's defensive ferocity—spiritual smoke signals that point to something beyond their practiced facades. Over time, if all goes well, I can ask the forbidden questions, and get answers. In the profiles included here, for instance, you will hear Tony Kushner link his heroic theatrical endeavor to the fierce, frustrated artistic ambition of his mother; David Mamet explain how his uncanny ear for dialogue developed in the midst of threatening family dinner-table conversations; and August Wilson trace his literary obsession back to his humiliated childhood heart. These singular revelations can emerge only from a singular relationship, a climate of mutual regard, which cannot be faked and which sometimes feels almost like love.

1
ARTHUR MILLER

On a crisp April weekend in 1948, Arthur Miller, then only thirty-three and enjoying the first flush of fame after the Broadway success the previous year of *All My Sons*, waved good-bye to his first wife, Mary, and their two young kids, in Brooklyn, and set off for Roxbury, Connecticut, where he intended to build a cabin on a hillock just behind a Colonial house he had recently purchased for the family, which stood at the aptly named crossroads of Tophet (another name for Hell) and Gold Mine. "It was a purely instinctive act," Miller, who long ago traded up from that first forty-four-acre property to a four-hundred-acre spread on Painter Hill, a few miles down the road, told me recently. "I had never built a building in my life."

Miller had a play in mind, too; his impulse for the cabin was "to sit in the middle of it, and shut the door, and let things happen." All Miller knew about his new play was that it would be centered on a travelling salesman who would die at the end and that two of the lines were "Willy?" "It's all right. I came back"—words that to Miller spoke "the whole disaster in a nutshell." He says, "I mean, imagine a salesman who can't get past Yonkers. It's the end of the world. It's like an actor saying 'It's all right. I can't speak.' " As he worked away on his cabin, he repeated the play's two lines like a kind of mantra. "I kept saying, 'As soon as I get the roof on and the windows in, I'm gonna start this thing,' " he recalls. "And indeed I started on a morning in spring. Everything was starting to bud. Beautiful weather."

Miller had fashioned a desk out of an old door. As he sat down to it his tools and nails were still stashed in a corner of the studio, which was as yet unpainted and smelled of raw wood. "I started in the morning, went through the day, then had dinner, and then I went back there and worked till—I don't know—one or two o'clock in the morning," he says. "It sort of unveiled itself. I was the stenographer. I could hear them. I could hear them, literally." When Miller finally lay down to sleep that first night, he realized he'd been crying. "My eyes still burned and my throat was sore from talking it all out and shouting and laughing," he later wrote in his autobiography, *Timebends*. In one day, he had produced, almost intact, the first act of *Death of a Salesman*, which has since sold about eleven million copies, making it probably the most successful modern play ever published. The show, which is being put on somewhere in the world almost every day of the year, celebrates its fiftieth anniversary next month with a Broadway revival from Chicago's Goodman Theatre, directed by Robert Falls and starring Brian Dennehy as the fanatical and frazzled drummer Willy Loman.

"He didn't write *Death of a Salesman*; he released it," the play's original director, Elia Kazan, said in his autobiography, *A Life*. "It was there inside him, stored up waiting to be turned loose." To Miller, there was a "dream's quality in my memory of the writing and the day or two that followed its completion." In his notebook for *Death of a Salesman*—a sixty-six-page document chronicling the play's creation, which is kept with his papers at the University of Texas at Austin—he wrote, "He who understands everything about his subject cannot write it. I write as much to discover as to explain." After that first day of inspiration, it took Miller six weeks to call forth the second act and to make Willy remember enough "so he would kill himself." The form of the play—where past and present coalesce in a lyrical dramatic arc—was one that Miller felt he'd been "searching for since the beginning of my writing life." *Death of a*

Salesman seems to spill out of Willy's panic-stricken, protean imagination, and not out of a playwright's detached viewpoint. "The play is written from the sidewalk instead of from a skyscraper," Miller says of its first-person urgency. But, ironically, it was from the deck of a skyscraper that Miller contemplated beginning his drama, in a kind of Shakespearean foreshadowing of Willy's suicidal delirium. The notebook's first entry reads:

> Scene 1—Atop Empire State. 2 guards. "Who will die today? It's that kind of day . . . fog, and poor visibility. They like to jump into a cloud. Who will it be today?"

As Miller navigated his way through the rush of characters and plot ideas, the notebook acted as ballast. "In every scene remember his size, ugliness," Miller reminds himself about Loman on its second page. "Remember his own attitude. Remember *pity*." He analyzes his characters' motives. "Willy wants his sons to destroy his failure," he writes, and on a later page, "Willy resents Linda's unbroken, patient forgiveness (knowing there must be great hidden hatred for him in her heart)." In Miller's notebook, characters emerge sound and fully formed. For instance, of Willy's idealized elder son, Biff, who is a lost soul fallen from his high-school glory and full of hate for his father, he writes, "Biff is travelled, oppressed by guilt of failure, of not making money although a kind of indolence pleases him: an easygoing way of life. . . . Truthfully, Biff is not really bright enough to make a businessman. *Wants everything too fast*." Miller also talks to himself about the emotional stakes and the trajectory of scenes:

> Have it happen that Willy's life is in Biff's hands—aside from Biff succeeding. There is Willy's guilt to Biff re: The Woman. But is that retrievable? There is Biff's disdain for Willy's character,

his false aims, his pretense and these Biff cannot finally give up
or alter. Discover the link between Biff's work views and his anti-
work feelings.

Although the notebook begins with a series of choppy asides and
outlines, it soon becomes an expansive, exact handwritten log of
Miller's contact with his inner voices. For instance, it reveals the
development of Charley, Loman's benevolent next-door neighbor,
whose laconic evenhandedness was, in Miller's eyes, partly a projection of his own father. Charley speaks poignantly to Biff at Willy's
graveside ("Nobody dast blame this man"); what appears in the last
scene as a taut and memorable nine-line speech, a kind of eulogy,
was mined from words (here indicated in italics) that were part of a
much longer improvisation in the notebook:

> A salesman doesn't build anything, *he don't put a bolt to a*
> *nut* or a seed in the ground. A man who doesn't build anything
> must be liked. He must he cheerful on bad days. Even calamities
> mustn't break through. Cause one thing, he has got to be liked.
> *He don't tell you the law or give you medicine.* So there's no rock
> bottom to your life. All you know is that on good days or bad, you
> gotta come in cheerful. No calamity must be permitted to break
> through, Cause one thing, always, you're a man who's gotta be
> believed. You're way out there *riding on a smile and a shoeshine.*
> *And when they start not smilin' back,* the sky falls in. *And then*
> *you get a couple of spots on your hat, and you're finished. Cause*
> *there's no rock bottom to your life.*

Here, as in all his notes for the play, Miller's passion and his flow
are apparent in the surprising absence of cross-outs; the pages
exude a startling alertness. He is listening not just to the voices
of his characters but to the charmed country silence around him,
which seems to define his creative state of grace:

Roxbury—At night the insects softly thumping the screens like a blind man pushing with his fingers in the dark. . . . The crickets, frogs, whippoorwills altogether, a scream from the breast of the earth when everyone is gone. The evening sky, faded gray, like the sea pressing up against the windows, or an opaque gray screen. (Through which someone is looking in at me?)

On a bright-blue December afternoon last year, Miller, now eighty-three, returned to the cabin with his third wife, the photographer Inge Morath. Although she has lived with Miller for more than three decades, only one mile away from the *Salesman* studio, she had never seen the place. "The main house was occupied by people I didn't know. They were sort of engineer people. Very antipathetic," Miller said, swinging his red Volkswagen into the driveway of the new, friendly writer-owners. In a tan windbreaker and a baseball cap, he looked as rough-hewn and handy as any local farmer. (The dining-room tables and chairs in his current, cluttered 1782 farmhouse are Miller's handiwork, produced in his carpentry workshop.) After a cursory inspection of his old home, Miller, who is six feet three and stoops a little now, set off toward the cabin, up a steep hump that sits a few hundred paces from the back of the house. "In those days, I didn't think this hill was quite as steep," he said.

The cabin, a white clapboard construction in somewhat urgent need of a new coat of paint, stood just over the top of the rise, facing west, toward a thicket of birch trees and a field. "Oh, it will last as long as it's painted," Miller said, inspecting what he had wrought. "See, if a building has a sound roof, that's it, you'll keep it."

"I didn't know it was so tiny," Morath said. She snapped off a few photos, then waved her husband into the foreground for a picture before we all crowded into what proved to be a single high-ceilinged room. Except for a newly installed fluorescent light and some red linoleum that had been fitted over the floorboards, what Miller saw was what he'd built. He stepped outside to see if the cabin had been wired for electricity. (It had.) He inspected the three cinder blocks on which it was securely perched against the side of the hill. "I did the concrete," he recalled. Leaving, he turned to take a last look. "I learned a lot doing it," he said. "The big problem was getting the rafters of the roof up there alone. I finally built it on the ground and then swung them up." He added, "It's a bit like playwriting, you know. You get to a certain point, you gotta squeeze your way out of it."

Where does the alchemy of a great play begin? The seeds of *Death of a Salesman* were planted decades before Miller stepped into his cabin. "Selling was in the air through my boyhood," says Miller, whose father, Isidore, was the salesman-turned-owner of the Miltex Coat and Suit Company, which was a thriving enough business to provide the family with a spacious apartment on 110th Street in Harlem, a country bungalow, and a limousine and driver. "The whole idea of selling successfully was very important." Just as Miller was entering his teens, however, his father's business was wiped out by the Depression. Isidore's response was silence and sleep ("My father had trouble staying awake"); his son's response was anger. "I had never raised my voice against my father, nor did he against me, then or ever," wrote Miller, who had to postpone going to college for two years—until 1934—because "nobody was in possession of the fare." "As I knew perfectly well, it was not he who angered me, only his failure to cope with his fortune's collapse," Miller went on in his autobiography. "Thus I had two fathers, the real one and the metaphoric, and the latter I resented because he did not know how to win out over the general collapse."

Death of a Salesman is a lightning rod both for a father's bewilderment ("What's the secret?" Willy asks various characters) and for a son's fury at parental powerlessness ("You fake! You phoney little fake!" Biff tells Willy when they finally square off, in act 2). After the play's success, Miller's mother, Augusta, found an early manuscript called "In Memoriam," a forgotten autobiographical fragment that Miller had written when he was about seventeen. The piece, which was published in these pages in 1995, is about a Miltex salesman called Schoenzeit, who had once asked Miller for subway fare when Miller was helping him carry samples to an uptown buyer. The real Schoenzeit killed himself the next day by throwing himself in front of the El train; the character's "dejected soul"—a case of exhaustion masquerading as gaiety—is the first sighting of what would become Willy Loman. "His emotions were displayed at the wrong times always, and he knew when to laugh," Miller wrote. In 1952, Miller, rummaging through his papers, found a 1937 notebook in which he had made embryonic sketches of Willy, Biff, and Willy's second son, Happy. "It was the same family," he says of the twenty pages of realistic dialogue. "But I was unable in that straightforward, realistic form to contain what I thought of as the man's poetry—that is, the zigzag shots of his mind." He adds, "I just blotted it out."

Every masterpiece is a story of accident and accomplishment. Of all the historical and personal forces that fed the making of *Death of a Salesman*, none was more important than a moment in 1947 when Miller's uncle Manny Newman accosted him in the lobby of the Colonial Theatre in Boston after a matinee of *All My Sons*. "People regarded him as a kind of strange, completely untruthful personality," Miller says of Newman, a salesman and a notorious fabulist, who within the year would commit suicide. "I thought of him as a kind of wonderful inventor. There was something in him which was terribly moving, because his suffering was right on his skin, you see. He was the ultimate climber up the ladder who was constantly being stepped on by those climbing past him. My empathy for him was immense. I mean, how could he possibly have succeeded? There was no way." According to Miller, Newman was "cute and ugly, a bantam with a lisp. Very charming." He and his family, including two sons,

Abby and Buddy, lived modestly in Brooklyn. "It was a house without irony, trembling with resolutions and shouts of victories that had not yet taken place but surely would tomorrow," Miller recalled in *Timebends*. Newman was fiercely, wackily competitive; even when Miller was a child, in the few hours he spent in Newman's presence his uncle drew him into some kind of imaginary contest "which never stopped in his mind." Miller, who was somewhat ungainly as a boy, was often compared unfavorably with his cousins, and whenever he visited them, he said, "I always had to expect some kind of insinuation of my entire life's probable failure."

When Newman approached Miller after that matinee, he had not seen his nephew for more than a decade. He had tears in his eyes, but, instead of complimenting the playwright, he told Miller, "Buddy is doing very well." Miller says now, "He had simply picked up the conversation from fifteen years before. That element of competitiveness—his son competing with me—was so alive in his head that there was no gate to keep it from his mouth. He was living in two places at the same time." Miller continues, "So everything is in the present. For him to say 'Buddy is doing very well'—there are no boundaries. It's all now. It's all now. And that to me was wonderful."

At the time, Miller was absorbed in the tryout of *All My Sons* and had "not the slightest interest in writing about a salesman." Until *All My Sons*, Miller's plays had not been naturalistic in style; he had "resolved to write a play that could be put on," and had "put two years into *All My Sons* to be sure that I believed every page of it." But Miller found naturalism, with its chronological exposition, "not sensuous enough" as a style; he began to imagine a kind of play where, as in Greek drama, issues were confronted head on, and where the transitions between scenes were pointed rather than disguised. The success of *All My Sons* emboldened him. "I could now move into unknown territory," Miller says. "And that unknown territory was basically that we're thinking on several planes at the same time. I wanted to find a way to try to make everything happen at once." In his introduction to the fiftieth-anniversary edition of *Death of a Salesman*, Miller writes, "The play had to move forward not by following a narrow discreet line, but as a phalanx." He continues, "There was no model I could adapt for this play, no past history for the kind of work I felt it could become." The notebook for the play shows Miller formulating a philosophy for the kind of Cubist stage pictures that would become his new style:

> Life is formless—its interconnections are cancelled by lapses of time, by events occurring in separate places, by the hiatus of memory. We live in the world made by man and the past. Art suggests or makes the interconnection palpable. Form is the tension of these interconnections: man with man, man with the past and present environment. The drama at its best is a mass experience of this tension.

At first, the Manny Newman encounter inspired in Miller only the intimation of a new, slashing sense of dramatic form. The play's structure is embedded in the structure of Loman's turbulent mind, which, Miller says, destroys the boundaries between then and now. As a result, "there are no flashbacks, strictly speaking, in *Death of a Salesman*," he says. "It's always moving forward." In this way, Miller jettisoned what he calls "the daylight continuity" of naturalism for the more fluid dark logic of dreams. "In a dream you don't have transitional material," Miller says. "The dream starts where it starts to mean something." He continues, "I wanted to start every scene at the last possible instant, no matter where that instant happened to be." He picked up a copy of his play and read me its first beats: " 'Willy?' 'It's all right. I came back.' 'Why? What happened? Did something happen, Willy?' 'No, nothing happened.' " He added, "We're into the thing in three lines." His new structure jump-started both the scenes and the stage language, whose intensity Miller called "emergency speech"—an "unashamedly open" idiom that replaced "the crabbed dramatic hints and pretexts of the natural." Willy dies without a secret; the play's structure, with its crosscutting between heightened moments, encouraged the idea of revelation. The audience response that Miller wanted to incite, he said, "was not 'What happens next and why?' so much as 'Oh, God, of course.'"

When, early in 1948, Miller visited his cousin Abby Newman to talk about the blighted life of his late father, Miller himself had just such an epiphany. Newman told Miller, "He wanted a business for us. So we could all work together. A business for the boys." Miller, who repeated Newman's words in the play, wrote in his autobiography, "This conventional, mundane wish was a shot of electricity that switched all the random iron filings in my mind in one direction. A hopelessly distracted Manny was transformed into a man with a purpose: he had been trying to make a gift that would crown all those striving years; all those lies he told, all his imaginings and crazy exaggerations, even the almost military discipline he had laid on his boys, were in this instant given form and point. I suddenly understood him with my very blood."

Willy Loman is a salesman, but we're never told what product he lugs around in his two large sample cases. Once, a theatergoer buttonholed Miller and put the question to him: "What's he selling? You never say what he's selling." Miller quipped, "Well, himself. That's who's in the valise." Miller adds, "You sell yourself. You sell the goods. You become the commodity." Willy's house echoes with exhortations to his two floundering sons about the presentation of self ("the man who creates personal interest is the man who gets ahead. Be liked and you will never want") and the imperialism of self ("Lick the world. You guys together could absolutely lick the civilized world"). In his notebook Miller writes, "Willy longs to take off, be great," and "Willy wants his boys prepared for any life. 'Nobody will laugh at them—take advantage. They'll be big men.' It's the big men who command respect." In Willy's frenzied and exhausted attempt to claim himself, Miller had stumbled onto a metaphor for a postwar society's eagerness to pursue its self-interest after years of postponed life. In Willy's desperate appetite for success and in the brutal dicta offered by his rich brother Ben ("Never fight fair with a stranger, boy. You'll never get out of the jungle that way"), *Death of a Salesman* caught the spirit of self-aggrandizement being fed by what Miller calls "the biggest boom in the history of the world." Americans had struggled through the Depression, then fought a world war to keep the nation's democratic dream alive; that dream was, broadly speaking, a dream of self-realization. America, with its ideal of freedom, challenged its citizens to see how far they could go in a lifetime—"to end up big," as Willy says. (In the play, Ben, whom Willy looks to for answers—the notebook points to him as "the visible evidence of what the boys can do and be. Superior family"—is literally the predatory imperialist who at seventeen walked into the African jungle and emerged four years later as a millionaire.) Miller was not the first to dramatize the barbarity of American individualism; but, in a shift that signalled the changing cultural mood, he was the first to stage this spiritual battle of attrition as a journey to the interior of the American psyche. "In a certain sense, Willy is all the voices," Miller said later. In fact, "The Inside of His Head" was Miller's first title for the play; he also briefly toyed with the idea of having the proscenium designed in the shape of a head and having the action take place inside it.

In the economic upheavals of the thirties, social realism reflected the country's mood; plays held a mirror up to the external world, not an internal one. But in the postwar boom Tennessee Williams's *The Glass Menagerie* (1945) and *A Streetcar Named Desire* (1947), written in what Williams called his "personal lyricism," suddenly found an audience and struck a deep new chord in American life. The plays were subjective, poetic, symbolic; they made a myth of the self, not of social remedies. Indeed, the name "Willy Loman" was not intended by Miller as a sort of socioeconomic indicator ("low man"). Miller took it from a chilling moment in Fritz Lang's film *The Testament of Dr. Mabuse* (1933) when, after a long and terrifying stakeout, a disgraced detective who thinks he can redeem himself by exposing a gang of forgers is pursued and duped by them. The chase ends with the detective on the phone to his former boss ("Lohmann? Help me, for God's sake! Lohmann!"); when we see him next, he is in an asylum, gowned and frightened and shouting into an invisible phone ("Lohmann? Lohmann? Lohmann?"). "What the name really meant to me was a terrified man calling into the void for help that will never come," Miller said.

Willy Loman's particular terror goes to the core of American individualism, in which the reputable self and the issue of wealth are hopelessly tangled. "A man can't go out the way he came in," Willy says to Ben. "A man has got to add up to something." Willy, who, at sixty, has no job, no money, no loyalty from his boys, is sensationally lacking in assets and in their social corollary—a sense of blessing. "He envies those who are blessed; he feels unblessed, but he's striving for it," Miller says. Although Willy's wife, Linda, famously says of him that "attention must be paid," he feels invisible to the world. "I'm not noticed," he says. Later, Linda confides to the boys, "For five weeks he's been on straight commission, like a beginner, an unknown!" As Miller puts it now, "The whole idea of people failing with us is that they can no longer be loved. You haven't created a persona which people will pay for, see, experience, or come close to. It's almost like death. You have a deathly touch. People who succeed are loved because they exude some magical formula for fending off destruction, fending off death." He continues, "It's the most brutal way of looking at life that one can imagine, because it discards anyone who does not measure up. It wants to destroy them. It's been going on since the Puritan times. You are beyond the blessing of God. You're beyond the reach of God. That God rewards those who deserve it. It's a moral condemnation that goes on. You don't want to be near this failure."

Death of a Salesman was the first play to dramatize this punishing—and particularly American—interplay of panic and achievement. Before *Salesman*, Eugene O'Neill's *The Iceman Cometh* (1946) raised the issue in the eerie calm of Harry Hope's bar, whose sodden habitués have retreated from competitiveness into a perverse contentment; as one of the characters says, "No one here has to worry about where they're going next, because there is no farther they can go." But in Willy Loman, Miller was able to bring both the desperation and the aspiration of American life together in one character.

Willy is afflicted by the notion of winning—what Brecht called "the black addiction of the brain." He cheats at cards; he encourages his boys to seek every advantage. Victory haunts him and his feckless sons. In a scene from the notebook, Biff and Happy tell Willy of their plan to go into business. "Step on it, boys, there ain't a minute to lose," Willy tells them, but their souls are strangled by their father's heroic dreams, which hang over them like some sort of spiritual kudzu. In another notebook entry, Biff rounds fiercely on Willy: "I don't care if you live or die. You think I'm mad at you because of the Woman, don't you? I am, but I'm madder because you botched up my life, because I can't tear you out of my heart, because I keep trying to make good, be something for you, to succeed for you."

In dramatizing the fantasy of competition, Miller's play was the first to dissect cultural envy in action—that process of invidious comparison which drives society forward but also drives it crazy. "You lose your life to it!" Miller says of the envy that feeds Willy's restlessness. "It's the ultimate outer-directional emotion. In other words, I am doing this not because it's flowing from me but because it's flowing against him." He goes on, "You're living in a mirror. It's a life of reflections. Emptiness. Emptiness. Emptiness. Hard to go to sleep at night. And hard to wake up." In his mind, Willy is competing with his brother Ben; with Dave Singleman, a successful old salesman who could make a living "without ever leaving his room" and who died a placid, accomplished death on a train to Boston; with his neighbor Charley, who owns his own business; and with Charley's successful lawyer son, Bernard. "Where's Willy in all this?" Miller asks. "He's competed himself to death. He's not existing anymore, or hardly."

In his notebook Miller wrote, "It is the combination of guilt (of failure), hate, and love—all in conflict that he resolves by 'accomplishing' a 20,000 dollar death." In death, Willy is worth more than in life. His suicide is the ultimate expression of his confusion of success with love and also of his belief in winning at all costs. As a father, he overlooked Biff's small childhood acts of larceny—taking sand from a building site, stealing basketballs, getting the answers for tests from the nerdy, studious Bernard—and Biff has continued his habit into adulthood, out of a combination of envy and revenge. A notebook citation reads, "It is necessary to (1) reveal to Willy that Biff stole to queer himself, and did it to hurt Willy," and "(2) And that he did it because of the Woman and all the disillusionment it implied." In the final version of the play, Biff, admitting in passing that he spent three months in a Kansas City jail for lifting a suit, tells Willy, "I stole myself out of every good job since high school!" At first, Miller saw the twenty thousand dollars of insurance money as cash to put Biff on the straight and narrow. " 'My boy's a thief—with 20,000 he'd stop it,' " he wrote in the notebook. Instead, Willy's suicide—the final show of force and fraud, in keeping with his demented competitive fantasies—is pitched on a more grandiose and perverse note. In an early draft of the terrific penultimate scene, where Biff exposes Willy and calls it quits with him and his dream, there is this exchange:

> BIFF (to him): What the hell do you want from me? What do
>   you want from me?
> WILLY: —Greatness—
> BIFF: No—

In Miller's final draft, Willy, who will not accept his son's confession of thievery, takes Biff's greatness as a given as he visualizes his own suicide. "Can you imagine that magnificence with twenty thousand dollars in his pocket?" he says to Ben. He adds, "Imagine? When the mail comes he'll be ahead of Bernard again." When he goes to his death, Willy, in his mind, is on a football field with Biff, and full of vindictive triumph ("When you hit, hit low and hit hard, because it's important, boy"). "He dies sending his son through the goalposts," Miller says. "He dies moving." Miller pauses. "I think now that Kazan had it right from the beginning. He said, 'It's a love story.' "

On the last page of his notebook, Miller scribbled a short speech to give to the original cast after its members had read the play in galleys: "I want you all to know now that the cannons are quiet that this production has been the most gratifying I have known. I believe you are the finest ever gathered for any play and I am exceedingly proud and gratified not only for myself but for the American theater." (The original cast included Lee J. Cobb as Willy, with Mildred Dunnock, Arthur Kennedy, and Cameron Mitchell.) In its passage to greatness, *Death of a Salesman* was enhanced enormously by the poetic set design of Jo Mielziner, who created a series of platforms, with Willy's house as a haunting omnipresent background. However, as Elia Kazan pointed out in his autobiography, "The stage direction in the original manuscript that Art gave me to read directly after he'd finished it does not mention a home as a scenic element. It reads, 'A pinpoint travelling spot lights a small area on stage left. The Salesman is revealed. He takes out his keys and opens an invisible door.' " Kazan continues, "It was a play waiting for a directorial solution." It got it. *Death of a Salesman* also got its share of bad suggestions. Kazan's then wife, Molly Day Thacher, who was a playreader for the Group Theatre and had some influence over Kazan, tried to get Miller, as he remembers it, "to cut out Uncle Ben, all the memory scenes, and simply make it a realistic little narrative." And the co-producer, Kermit Bloomgarden, nervous of a play with "Death" in its title, took a poll among theatergoers which asked, "Would you go to see a play called *Death of a Salesman*?" Nobody would. "They had a list of about fifteen titles," Miller says. "One was 'Free and Clear.' I'll never forget that."

In the intervening half century, the surface of American life has changed, but its mad competitiveness hasn't. "I'm not aware of any change in the way people look at this play," Miller says, but he admits that Willy's complaints about loyalty from the head office ring strange to contemporary ears. "Workers now—not just workers but management—know that nobody will have much pity for them." Last year, in a poll taken by the Royal National Theatre of eight hundred English theater professionals, Miller was voted the greatest contemporary playwright; but in America, where in some quarters he's seen as a kind of Jeremiah, Miller is not accorded quite the same honor. He ascribes his decline in popularity to the erosion of the "unified audience" that came with the rise of the avant-garde in the early sixties. "The only theatre available to a playwright in the late forties was Broadway," Miller writes in the fiftieth-anniversary edition of *Salesman*. "That theatre had one single audience . . . catering to very different levels of age, culture, education, and intellectual sophistication." He continues, "One result of this mix was the ideal, if not frequent fulfillment, of a kind of play that would be complete rather than fragmentary, an emotional rather than an intellectual experience, a play basically of heart with its ulterior moral gesture integrated with action rather than rhetoric. In fact, it was a Shakespearean ideal, a theater for anyone with an understanding of English and perhaps some common sense."

But there was nothing Shakespearean in the response to "that damned disturbing play," as Kazan called it, on the night of its debut, February 10, 1949, in Philadelphia. "The curtain came down and nothing happened," Miller says. "People sat there a good two or three minutes, then somebody stood up with his coat. Several men—I didn't see women doing this—were helpless. They were sitting there with handkerchiefs over their faces. It was like a funeral." He continues, "I didn't know whether the show was dead or alive. The cast was back there wondering what had happened. Nobody'd pulled the curtain up. Finally, someone thought to applaud, and then the house came apart." ▪

—January 25, 1999

A View from the Bridge

The revival of Arthur Miller's 1955 play *A View from the Bridge* (deftly directed by Gregory Mosher, at the Cort) is a singular astonishment: a kind of theatrical lightning bolt that sizzles and startles at the same time, illuminating the poetry in the play's prose and the subtlety in its streamlined construction. *A View from the Bridge* may not be Miller's best play, but this is one of the best productions of his work that I've ever seen.

In John Lee Beatty's moody set, the action emerges from the chilly shadows of the brown warrens of Red Hook, a working-class Italian enclave on the seaward side of the Brooklyn Bridge. "This is the gullet of New York swallowing the tonnage of the world," Alfieri (the compelling Michael Cristofer), a lawyer, who serves as a kind of chorus for the tragic tale, says at the opening. He adds, "I am inclined to notice the ruins in things, perhaps because I was born in Italy." The ruin in question is the longshoreman Eddie Carbone (Liev Schreiber), a palooka with no purchase on language or on his own psyche, who is destroyed by his unexamined desire for his teenage niece, Catherine (Scarlett Johansson), whom he and his wife, Beatrice (Jessica Hecht), have raised. When Catherine falls in love with one of the two illegal immigrants that they put up—cousins from the Old Country—Eddie's only way to keep her from getting married is to report the cousins to the Immigration Bureau. By dropping the dime, Eddie betrays his wife, his niece, his relatives, himself, and, by extension, his entire tribe. The story's symmetry is elemental and terrifying; it hurtles to its conclusion, propelled by Schreiber's uncanny, incandescent performance.

Saturnine and strapping, Eddie enters in a cloth cap and an overcoat as rumpled as the world he inhabits. He is driven by feelings that he can neither fathom nor control, and which he hides beneath a show of paternal concern. "Listen, you been givin' me the willies the way you walk down the street, I mean it," he tells his curvaceous niece, taking in her hourglass figure from the comfort of his easy chair. "Catherine, I don't want to be a pest, but I'm tellin' you you're walkin' wavy." Of the many gifts that Schreiber brings to the role—a swift mind, a pitch-perfect ear for the sludge of the demotic, a reservoir of restrained aggression, an ability to listen—the most important, it seems to me, is a sense of his own unresolved nature, an inchoate longing that makes him a perfect emotional fit for Eddie. There's a loneliness and an agitation in Schreiber that are at odds with his technical command; this combination of fragility and force makes him seem both mysterious and dangerous, and therefore compelling to watch.

As Catherine, Johansson is a superb object for Schreiber's ambivalent desire. In a robin's-egg-blue sweater and a form-fitting gray skirt, she glows with ripeness and an alertness to life. The top student in her high-school graduating class, Catherine, in the opening scene, gets word that she has been offered a fifty-dollar-a-week job at a local plumbing company. Eddie, who has bigger dreams for her, balks at the idea, before finally conceding. "You wanna go to work, heh, Madonna?" he says. "All right, go to work." Tearfully, Catherine throws herself into his arms, then bustles happily around the threadbare apartment. "I'm gonna buy all new dishes with my first pay!" she says. Catherine's world is opening up; Eddie's is closing down. Onstage, Johansson is more resourceful than most of her film roles have allowed her to be; her face is a detailed map of Catherine's internal climate—her loyalty, her gratitude, her eagerness, her rebelliousness against Eddie's petty tyrannies, and her insistence on her own desires, in particular for the happy-go-lucky blond cousin, Rodolpho (the excellent Morgan Spector), whom Eddie thinks is "a weird," because he sings, cooks, and sews.

"You married too?" Catherine asks Rodolpho when he arrives with his brother, Marco (Corey Stoll), a family man with three children to feed. "I have no money to get married. I have a nice face, but no money," Rodolpho says, laughing. By the time he has finished singing a jazz version of "Paper Doll"—"Leave him finish, it's beautiful," Catherine says when Eddie tries to interrupt—Catherine is under his spell. At a stroke, she is claimed by romance and Eddie by envy: when he first goes to see Alfieri about putting a stop to the relationship, he claims he's been robbed ("He . . . puts his dirty filthy hands on her like a goddam thief"). "I'm tryin' to bring out my thoughts here," Eddie tells Alfieri. In fact, everything in this ravishing production demonstrates the opposite: Eddie staunchly refuses to think. All the negative is projected into other people. Drunk at Christmas, Eddie arrives home to find Rodolpho coming out of

Catherine's bedroom. In an electrifying moment—superbly staged by Mosher—the two men lunge at each other. Schreiber seems to throw the full weight of his melancholy into the tackle, which sends them sprawling across the kitchen table. In front of Catherine, Eddie plants a taunting kiss on Rodolpho's lips. As Catherine tries to pull him away, Eddie grabs her and kisses her hard on the mouth. The horror of the scene is immediately erased from Eddie's mind by the sound of his own righteousness. "Don't lay another hand on her unless you wanna go out feet first," he says to Rodolpho as he exits. Even at the finale, when Eddie faces off against Marco, who is being deported, he insists on his honor. "Wipin' the neighborhood with my name like a dirty rag! I want my name, Marco," he says.

"Something perversely pure calls to me from his memory," Alfieri says of Eddie in an elegiac epilogue. "Not purely good, but himself purely, for he allowed himself to be wholly known." In both style and content, this weasel-worded speech seems to contradict the play: Eddie never allows himself to be known; he hides even from himself. So what is going on? About whom is Miller speaking? Miller had heard the Carbone story from a longshoreman around 1950, when he was writing a screenplay about the waterfront for Elia Kazan—which he withdrew from production in 1951, as the House Un-American Activities Committee hearings loomed. (Kazan testified, controversially, as a friendly witness.) Miller thought of that murky first draft as a "probe"; he entitled it "An Italian Tragedy" and put it away. By the time he came back to the story, in 1955, he had fallen in love with Marilyn Monroe, whom he would soon marry; he was in the process of divorcing his wife of sixteen years and breaking up their family. He was, he said, in "psychological country strange to me, ugly and forbidding." Betrayal had become part of Miller's story, as well as Kazan's. In his movie *On the Waterfront* (1954), Kazan attempted to justify his decision to testify by depicting an informer as a heroic victim of systemic corruption. *A View from the Bridge*, by contrast, depicts the informer as a deluded victimizer. "It would have been nice if Art, at this moment, while expressing the strong disapproval he felt, had acknowledged some past friendship—or even written me a few words, however condemnatory," Kazan, who had directed the Broadway productions of Miller's *All My Sons* and *Death of a Sales-man*, wrote in his autobiography. Instead, it seems to me, Miller replied to Kazan from the stage. Alfieri's ambivalent envoi is a rueful way of forgiving Kazan his trespasses, and, by extension, allowing Miller to forgive himself his own. "And so I mourn him—I admit it—with a certain . . . alarm," Alfieri says as the curtain falls. ■

—February 1, 2010

2
AUGUST WILSON

If anybody asks you who sang this song
Tell 'em
It was little Jimmy Rushing,
He's been here and gone.

The playwright August Wilson lives in a leafy, genteel part of Seattle intended by the city's founding fathers to be the site of the state capitol, and so named Capitol Hill. He moved here in 1994, with Constanza Romero, a Colombian-born costume designer who is now his third wife, and they share a rambling turn-of-the-century house with Azula, their three-year-old daughter. Azula has her father's ear and number, as well as total control of the living room, which, apart from a jukebox and a piano—props from Wilson's productions—hasn't a stick of adult furniture. Wilson, who doesn't drive, is more interested in the inner terrain than the external one; writing, he says, "is for me like walking down the landscape of the self. . . . You find false trails, roads closed for repairs, impregnable fortresses, scouts, armies of memory, and impossible cartography."

Wilson does most of his pathfinding below the living room, in a low-ceilinged basement, lit by neon bars, where he goes to sneak cigarettes, listen to records, and wait for his characters to arrive. He writes standing up, at a high, cluttered pine accounting desk, where he can prop his legal pad and transfer his jottings to a laptop computer. Pinned on a bulletin board, just beside where he stands to write, are two quotations, as bold as street signs: "TAKE IT TO THE MOON" (Frank Gehry) and "DON'T BE AFRAID. JUST PLAY THE MUSIC" (Charlie Parker). When Wilson looks up from his desk, at the dingy wall with its labyrinth of water pipes, he sees honorary degrees from the University of Pittsburgh, his home town, and from Yale, where his career as a playwright began, in 1982—just two of twenty-three he has accumulated so far, which is not bad for a fifty-five-year-old writer who quit school when he was fifteen.

For years, about two steps behind Wilson's writing table, an Everlast punching bag was suspended from the ceiling. When Wilson was in full flow and the dialogue was popping, he'd stop, pivot, throw a barrage of punches at the bag, then turn back to the work. Recently, however, during a particularly vigorous rewrite of his new play, *King Hedley II*, which opens on Broadway this month, Wilson knocked the bag and its ceiling hook down, and it now rests mournfully in the corner. Wilson has a retired boxer's heft—thick neck, square shoulders, wide chest—and a stomach whose amplitude is emphasized by suspenders that bracket his belly like parentheses. Wilson is the product of a mixed marriage, but, he says, "the culture I learned in my mother's household was black." He has a handsome face that is dominated by a wide forehead and a concentrated gaze. He exudes a very specific sense of gravity. He gives away nothing at first, or even second, glance. But when his guard is down, and especially when he's telling a story, you feel what his wife calls "the sizzle."

Wilson, who was originally named Frederick August Kittel, after his German father, says that his model for manhood—"the first male image that I carry"—is not his father but an old family friend, "the brilliant Hall of Fame prizefighter" Charley Burley. Archie Moore called Burley the best fighter he'd ever faced, and Sugar Ray Robinson refused to box him, but after his glory days as a pugilist were over Burley became a garbageman in Pittsburgh and lived across the street from the impressionable young Wilson. In Burley's Friday-night regalia—hundred-dollar Stetson, cashmere coat, yam-colored Florsheim shoes—Wilson saw something iconic. Burley was one of those black men, Wilson writes, who "elevated their presence into an art. They were bad. If only in an abstract of style."

Burley was known as "the uncrowned champion"; Wilson is known as "the heavyweight champion"—a nickname given to him by the director Marion McClinton, who is staging *King Hedley II*. McClinton explains, "It's August's language—the rhythm of hurt, the rhythm of pain, the rhythm of ecstasy, the rhythm of family— which sets him apart and is why we call him the heavyweight champion." Between 1959, when Lorraine Hansberry had a hit with *A Raisin in the Sun*, and 1984, when Wilson made his sensational breakthrough with *Ma Rainey's Black Bottom*, a play about black musicians' struggle with their white bosses in the twenties, the number of African-American plays to succeed on Broadway was zero. (There were, of course, many other black playwrights during this time—Amiri Baraka, Ron Milner, Phillip Hayes Dean, Richard Wesley, and Ed Bullins, among them—who won critical praise and a coterie following.) *Ma Rainey* ran for ten months. Almost immediately, Hollywood came calling, mostly with offers for bio-pics of Louis Armstrong, Muhammad Ali, and the like; Wilson wasn't tempted. He asked the Hollywood nabobs why so many black playwrights had written only one play. "I go, 'Where is Lonne Elder? Where is Joseph Walker?' They go, 'They're in Hollywood.' And I go, 'Oh, I see,' " he says. "I wanted to have a career in the theater."

Wilson's success also triggered what McClinton calls "one of the more major American theatrical revolutions." His audience appeal almost single-handedly broke down the wall for other black artists, many of whom would not otherwise be working in the mainstream. His plays were showcases for an array of first-rate performers, such as Charles S. Dutton, Samuel L. Jackson, Courtney Vance, Angela

Bassett, Ruben Santiago-Hudson, and Laurence Fishburne. And the opportunities for African-American playwrights also increased. "What's happened since 1984 has been incredible," McClinton says. "A lot of black writers had doors opened to them basically because August knocked them open. So then you start seeing Kia Corthron, Suzan-Lori Parks, Keith Glover, Robert Alexander, Lynn Nottage, Sam Kelley, Carlisle Brown, Charles Smith, Michael Henry Brown—I could keep going. American theater now looks toward African-Americans as viable members."

Wilson followed *Ma Rainey* with six critically acclaimed plays in a row—*Fences* (1987; Pulitzer Prize, Tony Award), *Joe Turner's Come and Gone* (1988), *The Piano Lesson* (1990; Pulitzer Prize), *Two Trains Running* (1992), *Seven Guitars* (1996), and *Jitney* (2000). He actually had drafts of *Fences* and *Joe Turner's Come and Gone* in his trunk before *Ma Rainey* made it to Broadway, and sometime after the success of that play, he has said, it dawned on him that each play he'd written so far was "trying to focus on what I felt were the most important issues confronting black Americans for that decade." Wilson gave himself a mission: to continue to chronicle, decade by decade, the "dazed and dazzling" rapport of African-Americans with the twentieth century. *King Hedley II* is set in the 1980s, which leaves only the first and last decades of the century to be written. The plays form a kind of fever chart of the trauma of slavery. Their historical trajectory takes African-Americans through their transition from property to personhood (*Joe Turner's Come and Gone*); their struggle for power in urban life (*Ma Rainey*); their dilemma over whether to embrace or deny their slave past (*The Piano Lesson*); the broken promise of first-class citizenship after the Second World War (*Seven Guitars*); their fraught adaptation to bourgeois values (*Fences*); stagnancy in the midst of Black Power militancy (*Two Trains Running*); and their historical and financial disenfranchisement during the economic boom (*Jitney* and *King Hedley II*).

"The average struggling non-morbid Negro is the best-kept secret in America," Zora Neale Hurston wrote in 1950. Wilson has put that man—his songs, his idiom, his superstitions, his folly, and his courage—on the stage. His plays are not talking textbooks; they paint the big picture indirectly, from the little incidents of daily life. "People can be slave-ships in shoes," Hurston said. Wilson's characters are shackled together by something greater than poverty; their bondage is to the caprices of history. "We's the leftovers," Toledo, the piano player and only literate member of Ma Rainey's band, tells the other musicians. "The white man knows you just a leftover. 'Cause he the one who done the eating and he know what he done ate. But we don't know that we been took and made history out of."

Wilson's work is a conscious answer to James Baldwin's call for "a profound articulation of the Black Tradition." He says he wanted to demonstrate that black American culture "was capable of sustaining you, so that when you left your father's or your mother's house you didn't go into the world naked. You were fully clothed in manners and a way of life." In the past, playwrights such as Dubose Heyward, Paul Green, and Eugene O'Neill made blacks and black culture the subject of drama; Wilson has made them the object. "When you go to the dictionary and you look up 'black,' it gives you these definitions that say, 'Affected by an undesirable condition,' " Wilson says. "You start thinking something's wrong with black. When white people say, 'I don't see color,' what they're saying is 'You're affected by this undesirable condition, but I'll pretend I don't see that.' And I go, 'No, see my color. Look at me. I'm not ashamed of who I am and what I am.' "

Wilson's characters often scrabble desperately, sometimes foolishly, for an opportunity that rarely comes. But when opportunity knocked for Wilson he seized it with a vengeance. He has tried to live his writing life by the Buddhist motto "You're entitled to the work but not the reward"; nevertheless, he has become a very rich man—in 1990, he was the most produced American playwright—and he is only getting richer. After *Seven Guitars*, he and his co-producer, Ben Mordecai, formed a joint venture called Sageworks, which allows Wilson to exercise unusual control over the destiny of his plays—and also to take both a writer's and a producer's share of their profits. A Wilson play has a gestation period like no other in the history of American theater, and no other major playwright—not Arthur Miller, Tennessee Williams, Eugene O'Neill, or David Mamet—has negotiated the latitude to work so freely. Before a play arrives on Broadway, Wilson refines his story through a series of separate productions. In his rehearsal mufti—black turtleneck and cloth cap—he sits beside the director for almost every hour of every production, and, since *Seven Guitars*, he's taken to "writing in the heat of the moment." By the time *King Hedley II* reaches New York, the play, which shows the fragmented life of a Pittsburgh ghetto during the Reagan years, will have been seen, digested, reconceived, and rewritten after productions in Seattle, Boston, Pittsburgh, Chicago, Los Angeles, and Washington. This long reworking, like a brass rubbing, brings the play's parameters and its filigree of detail into bold relief until the drama emerges, as Wilson puts it, "fat with substance."

"When I was writing *Joe Turner*," Wilson says, "I realized that someone was gonna stand up onstage and say the words, whatever the hell they were. That's when I realized I had a responsibility to the words. I couldn't have the character say any old thing. There couldn't be any mistakes." To achieve this sort of focus requires the kind of appetite for victory that is epitomized, for Wilson, by a breed of championship racehorses, which in order to win "bite their own necks to get more oxygen." He began his own extraordinary endeavor late, at about forty, and his time is valuable. He does not spend it on the telephone, or watching television, or going to movies (between 1980 and 1991, he saw only two, both directed by Martin

Scorsese—*Raging Bull* and *Cape Fear*). His work requires a lot of "doing nothing" to generate "brain space." So Wilson, whom Azula calls "the slippery guy," is usually to be found puttering in the crepuscular gloom of his basement, where he communes with himself and, if he's lucky, taps into what he calls "the blood's memory," that "deepest part of yourself where the ancestors are talking." To do so requires a kind of ritual preparation. "Before I write something, I wash my hands," he says. "I always want to say I approached it with clean hands—you know, a symbolic cleansing."

Wilson's plays, filled as they often are with visions and visionaries, have a kind of hoodoo of their own, which can seem strange to white viewers, who are often critical of his use of the supernatural. He is a collagist, making Afro-Christian parables, and his plays are best when the real and the spiritual are wedded (*Joe Turner*, *Seven Guitars*, *The Piano Lesson*), in order, as he says, "to come up with a third thing, which is neither realism nor allegory." Then, his intensity and his natural eloquence—what Henry Louis Gates Jr. calls "an unruly luxuriance of language, an ability to ease between trash talk and near-choral transport"—most effectively highlight another comparatively unsung quality of his writing: the ability to unfetter the heart. Under his focussed gaze, characters take on uncanny, sometimes awesome, life, and, unlike most contemporary male playwrights, he can write memorable roles for women as well as men. Wilson's work is not much influenced by the canon of modern Western plays, almost none of which he has read or seen. "I consider it a blessing that when I started writing plays in earnest, in 1979, I had not read Chekhov. I hadn't read Ibsen. I hadn't read Tennessee Williams, Arthur Miller, or O'Neill," he says. By then, he had been writing poetry for fifteen years and had read all the major American poets. "It took me eight years to find my own voice as a poet. I didn't want to take eight years to find my voice as a playwright." To this day, as incredible as it seems, with the exception of his own productions and a few of his friends', Wilson has seen only about a dozen plays.

In the age of the sound bite, Wilson is that most endangered of rare birds—a storyteller. A Wilson tale takes about as long as a baseball game, which is to say a good deal longer than the average commercial play. Although audiences will happily watch sports contests into double overtime, the play of ideas and characters is another matter. In this arena, they are accustomed to what Shakespeare called the "two hours' traffic," and Wilson has taken a lot of flak for his capaciousness. According to *The Oxford Companion to American Theatre*, his plays "lack a sense of tone and a legitimate, sustained dramatic thrust." This criticism is, to my mind, unjust, but it reflects a distinctive cultural and artistic difference. Virtually all the seminal white postwar plays—*The Glass Menagerie, Long Day's Journey into Night, Death of a Salesman*—revolve around the drama of American individualism; they mark a retreat from exterior into interior life. Wilson, however, dramatizes community. "Community is the most valuable thing that you have in African-American culture," he explains. "The individual good is always subverted to the good of the community." Wilson's plays are distinctive—and longer—because society, not just a psyche, is being mediated. They demonstrate the individual's interaction with the community, not his separation from it.

In Wilson's plays, the white world is a major character that remains almost entirely offstage; nonetheless, its presence is palpable—its rules, its standards, its ownership are always pressing in on the black world and changing the flow of things. "I look around and say, 'Where the barbed wire?' " Hedley says, observing that as a slave he would have been worth $1,200, and now he's worth $3.50 an hour. "They got everything else. They got me blocked in every other way. 'Where the barbed wire?' " To which his sidekick replies, "If you had barbed wire you could cut through. You can't cut through having no job." "Blacks know the spiritual truth of white America," Wilson says. "We are living examples of America's hypocrisy. We know white America better than white America knows us." Wilson's plays go some distance toward making up this deficiency. For white members of the audience, the experience of watching a Wilson work is often educational and humanizing. It's the eternal things in Wilson's dramas—the arguments between fathers and sons, the longing for redemption, the dreams of winning, and the fear of losing—that reach across the footlights and link the black world to the white one, from which it is so profoundly separated and by which it is so profoundly defined. To the black world, Wilson's plays are witness; to the white world, they are news. This creates a fascinating racial conundrum, one first raised by Baldwin: "If I am not what I've been told I am, then it means that *you're* not what you thought *you* were *either!*"

II

August Wilson was born in 1945 in Pittsburgh's Hill District. Although it was just four minutes by car from downtown, the Hill—known then as Little Harlem—was a lively, flourishing, self-contained universe, with its own baseball teams, nightclubs, businesses, and newspaper, and its own people, some of them legends who had left its one square mile to sing their distinctive songs to the world: Lena Horne, Erroll Garner, Ahmad Jamal, Earl (Fatha) Hines, Billy Eckstine, George Benson. When Wilson was a child, the Hill had a population of fifty-five thousand; since then, as a consequence of the 1968 riots, urban renewal, and competition from white neighborhoods, to which African-Americans now have putative access, the Hill's boundaries and its buoyancy have shrunk. Today, its rows of small, decrepit houses sit on the sloping land like a set of bad teeth—irregular, decaying, with large gaps between them. Beside one such desolate, littered vacant lot, at the rear of 1727 Bedford Avenue, Wilson grew up. You have to bushwhack your way through a tangle of branches that covers the ten steep steps to the boarded front door of the forty-dollar-a-month apartment where Wilson, the fourth of six children, lived with his mother, Daisy Wilson, and his siblings, Freda, Linda Jean, Donna, Richard, and Edwin.

Daisy ran a structured household that was centered on family activities. "Monday at seven, the Rosary came on the radio, so we said the Rosary," Wilson recalls. "Art Linkletter's *People Are Funny* was Tuesday. We played board games. Then there was the Top Forty. Everyone got to pick a song. If your song got to No. 1, you got a nickel." The backyard, where Daisy planted flowers and played dodgeball and baseball with her children and, on summer evenings, sat around a card table for games of Tonk, is blocked off now and difficult to see, but in the set for *Seven Guitars* Wilson preserved the ramshackle solace of the place so exactly that when his sister Linda Jean first saw the show she burst into tears. At the core of Wilson's personality is a kind of truculent resolve, which comes, he says, from his mother's example. (Daisy, who planned her own funeral, down to the gown she'd wear, died of lung cancer in 1983; for the past eighteen years, Wilson has returned to Pittsburgh on her birthday to gather with his family and visit her grave.) She was a tall, strong, handsome homebody, who had left school after the seventh grade and lived by the gospel of clear-eyed common sense and competitiveness. For Wilson, the best example of Daisy's brand of bumptious integrity is an incident that took place around 1955. She was listening to a quiz program that was offering a new washing machine to anyone who could answer a question correctly. Daisy knew the answer, and knew that, with six children, a washing machine would be a blessing. But when she won the contest and the promoters found out that she was black, they offered her instead a certificate to the Salvation Army to get a used washing machine. "Mother said she wanted the new machine or she didn't want any," Wilson says. "I remember Julie Burley"— Charley Burley's wife—"saying to her, 'Oh, Daisy, you got all them kids, what difference does it make? Take the washing machine.' And my mother said, 'Something is not always better than nothing.'"

Wilson's sense of his own uniqueness came, at least in part, from his mother's adoring gaze, what Baldwin called "the crucial, the definitive, the all-but-everlasting judgment." Wilson was Daisy's much longed-for first son. "My mother said she would have had eleven girls—she didn't care—she would have kept trying till she had a son," says Wilson's sister Donna, who remembers being told of her father's disappointment at her own birth. " 'Another split-ass,' he said." Freda says, "Mother seemed to have a need for a male in the house to show leadership. She clearly felt that August was the best and smartest of us, so he should be given the duty of going downtown at the age of ten or eleven to pay the bills. It wasn't just about paying the bills. Her underlying reason was to prepare him for the world." "She made me believe that I could do anything," Wilson says. He adds, "I wanted to be the best at whatever I did. I was the best dishwasher in Pittsburgh. I really was. I got a raise the first day I was there. When I sit down and write, I want to write the best play that's ever been written. Sometimes that's a fearsome place to stand, but that's when you call on your courage."

Wilson had a high IQ; he also had a gift for language. In kindergarten, he was already entertaining the class with his stories. By the sixth grade, he was turning out love poems for the girls he fancied: "I would I could mend my festering heart / Harpooned by Cupid's flaming dart / But too far the shaft did penetrate / Alas, it is too late." At his Catholic grade school, Wilson's intellectual overreaching drove the nuns crazy. "When they said no one could figure out the Holy Trinity, I was like, 'Why not?' I instantly wanted to prove it could be done," he says. As Wilson grew into adolescence, even his friends acknowledged a certain grandiosity in him; his nickname was Napoleon.

Wilson's hankering to be spectacular was fed not only by his mother's expectations but by his father's abdications. Fritz Kittel considered himself German, although when he had immigrated to America, with his three brothers, in 1915, he was an Austro-Hungarian citizen. The first time he met Daisy, at a neighborhood grocery store, she was shy. At the urging of her grandmother, the next time she saw him she was more flirtatious. They married, but by the time Wilson was born, Linda Jean says, Fritz was staying at the house only on weekends and living in a hotel during the week. Wilson remembers him as "mostly not there," adding, "You stayed out of his way if he was there." Fritz was, Wilson says, "an extremely talented baker," who worked for a while at New York's Waldorf-Astoria. He was also a wine drinker—"Muscatel by the gallon"—and couldn't keep a job.

The only father-son experience Wilson remembers was being taken downtown by Fritz in a blizzard to get a pair of Gene Autry cowboy boots. "He gave me a bunch of change, about seventy-five cents, and told me, 'Jingle it.' To let them know I had money." Otherwise, his memories focus on his father's hectoring abuse. Wilson refers to ferocious arguments, which sometimes ended with Fritz outside heaving bricks at their windows. "We knew to hide," Freda says. "We ran together, we'd fall behind the bed together, then, obviously, someone would sneak up to the window and look down." If Wilson closes his eyes to conjure up his father, he sees a tall man singing a German song to himself as he comes home from work with three-foot-high brown bags full of baked goods. "When he got angry, the next thing you know, Dad was just throwing the bags on the floor and stomping and crushing all the doughnuts and things in the bag," Linda Jean recalls. "And we needed those morsels." One Thanksgiving, in a tantrum, Fritz pulled the door off the oven and Daisy had to prop it back up with a stick so the turkey could finish roasting. Fritz's tranquil moments could be as tyrannical as his outbursts. "He believed in reading the papers," Freda says. "We had to sit down. We were not allowed to talk. We were not allowed to play. It was complete silence." Freda saw him as a displaced person, "an off-the-boat-type person." She says, "I don't think he ever fit here in America. I don't think he ever accepted black people. Or the culture. I think for my whole family there's a deep sense of abandonment." By 1957, when Wilson was twelve, Daisy had divorced Kittel and taken up with David Bedford, a black man whom she later married. "I loved the man," Wilson says of Bedford, an avid reader who was a community leader, and who, Wilson learned, after his death in 1969, had spent twenty-three years in prison.

Wilson inherited his father's volatile temperament. "He was a kid with a temper," Freda says. "And a sorry loser, because, in his mind, if he played to win he should win because he should have figured out whatever strategy was needed to win. And not figuring out that strategy was just highly unacceptable to him." In this regard, Wilson hasn't changed much over the years. "My goodness, when he got emotional he was mad scary," says the professor and playwright Rob Penny, who was one of Wilson's closest friends on the Hill. "You'd think he was gonna snap out, attack you, or beat you up or something. He was very intense." When he was about twenty, Wilson cuffed his sister Donna and broke her jaw. I asked Constanza Romero what she had found most surprising about Wilson after she married him, and she said, "His temper—his temper scared me." She referred to an explosion over a misplaced telephone number. "He went crazy, absolutely bonkers," she said. "He starts speaking very strongly, cussing himself out. He really doesn't allow himself any mistakes, any leeway."

"I just always felt that the society was lined up against you," Wilson says. "That in order to do anything in the world you were going to have to battle this thing that was out there. It wasn't gonna give you any quarter." For Wilson, the battle began in earnest when he was a freshman at Central Catholic High School, where he was the only black student in his grade and was placed in the advanced class. "There was a note on my desk every single day. It said, 'Go home nigger,'" Wilson says. The indignities—the shoving, the name-calling, the tripping—were constant; so was Wilson's brawling. The Christian Brothers frequently sent him home by taxi. "They would have to walk me through a gantlet of, like, forty kids. I would always want to say to them, 'But you're not saying anything to these forty guys. You're just escorting me through them as though they have a right to stand here.'" Then, one day when Wilson was in his early teens, a student standing in front of him during the Pledge of Allegiance made mention of the "nigger" behind him. "I said, 'OK, buddy,'" and, at "liberty and justice for all," Wilson punched him. "We go down to Brother Martin's, and he's ready to send me home. I said, 'Hey, why don't we just do this permanently? I do not want to go to school here anymore.'" Wilson went next to a vocational school, where the academic content was "I swear, like fifth-grade work." When his shop teacher, angry that Wilson had knocked in a thumbtack with a T-square, punched Wilson so hard that he knocked him off his chair, Wilson lunged at the teacher and "bounced him off the blackboard." "Give me a pink slip," he said. "I'm leaving this school."

At fifteen, Wilson ended up at Gladstone High School, taking tenth-grade classes but still officially in the ninth grade. He sulked in class, sat in the back, and refused to participate. Then, in an effort to redeem himself in the eyes of a black teacher, who ran an after-school college club Wilson wanted to join, he decided to take one assignment seriously. It was an essay on a historical figure, and Wilson chose Napoleon. "The fact that he was a self-made man, that he was a lieutenant in the army and became the emperor, I liked that," Wilson says. He researched it; he wrote it; he rented a typewriter with money he'd earned mowing lawns and washing cars; he paid his sister Linda Jean twenty-five cents a page to type it; and then he handed it in.

"The next day, the teacher asked me to stay after class," Wilson says. On the paper the teacher had written two marks—A-plus and E, a failing grade. "I'm gonna give you one of these two grades," he told Wilson. Suspecting that one of Wilson's older sisters had written the paper, he asked, "Can you prove to me that you wrote this?" Wilson remembers saying, "Hey, unless you call everybody in here and have all the people prove they wrote them, even the ones that went and copied out of the encyclopedia word for word, I don't feel I should have to prove anything." The teacher circled the E and handed the paper back. "I tore it up, threw it in the wastebasket, and walked out of school," Wilson says.

Every morning for the rest of the school year, rather than tell his mother he'd dropped out, Wilson walked three blocks to the local library. Over the next four years, by his own estimation, he read three hundred books, spending as many as five hours a day in the library. He read everything—sociology, anthropology, theology, fiction. "The world opened up," he says. "I could wander through the stacks. I didn't need anyone to teach me. All you had to do was have an interest and a willingness to extract the information from the book." It was about this time that Wilson began to see himself as a kind of warrior, surviving unapologetically on his own terms. The first person with whom he had to do battle was Daisy, whose dashed dreams for her son made her a furious opponent. "She told him he was no good, that he would amount to nothing," Linda Jean says. "It was relentless. It was an agony for him. He suffered many indignities. He was often denied food. She would take the food out of the refrigerator, put it in her bedroom, lock the door, and then go out. He was made to live in the basement for a while. She said he was dirty. She didn't want him in the house upstairs."

By the time Wilson was banished to the basement, he had decided to become a writer. "I was like, 'OK, I'm gonna sit here, I'm gonna write some stories. I'll show you,'" Wilson says. "I was gonna demonstrate my worth to her. I negotiated cooking privileges. I'd get fifteen cents and go buy me three pounds of potatoes. I was gonna demonstrate that I could feed and take care of myself." He lasted a week. "My mother was very disappointed," Wilson says. "She saw a lot of potential that I'd squandered, as far as she was concerned." To get out of the house, Wilson joined the Army. He took the Officer Candidate School test and came in second in his battalion, just two points behind the leader. Then, as often happens in Wilson's plays and in his life, he came up against the rules: to be an officer, you had to be nineteen; he was seventeen. And, if he couldn't be an officer, he wasn't interested.

Wilson headed across the country to California, where he worked in a pharmacy, until his father's terminal illness brought him back to Pittsburgh. Wilson and Linda Jean visited their father, who told them stories about being in the Army and the battle of the Argonne Forest. "Then he suddenly looked up and said, 'Who are you?'" Wilson says. "He basically chased us out of there, but for a couple of hours we had a great time." On his deathbed, Wilson's father called for his son "Fritz." Afterward, Wilson wrote a muted memorial, "Poem for the Old Man," which begins by evoking his father in his prime ("Old Fritz, when young/could lay a harem") and ends with Wilson himself ("his boxing boy/Is hitting all the new places/Too soon to make a mark").

Wilson took refuge in the African-American community, and it, in turn, nurtured him and contained him and his rage at his father's abandonment. "He's so faithful to the blackness. He's faithful like a father—that represents fidelity to him," says James Earl Jones, who starred in *Fences*. Wilson found another father figure in Chawley Williams, a black drug dealer turned poet, who became his protector on the street. "August wasn't really black. He was half-and-half," Williams says. "He was too dark to be white, and he was too white to be dark. He was in no man's land. I knew he was lost. I was lost. Kindred brothers know one another. We were trying to become men. We didn't even know what it meant." In time, Wilson would write himself into the center of modern black American history. But when he hit the streets he had no money, no marketable skills, no proven talent. He was, he says, "searching for something you can claim as yours."

On April 1, 1964, Wilson walked into downtown Pittsburgh to McFerron's typewriter store and put twenty dollars on the counter for a heavy black Royal Standard in the window. He'd earned the money by writing a term paper—"Two Violent Poets: Robert Frost and Carl Sandburg"—for Freda, who was then at Fordham University. He lugged the typewriter up the Hill to the basement apartment he'd rented in a boarding house, placed the machine on the kitchen table, put a piece of loose-leaf paper in it, and typed his name. Actually, he typed every possible combination of his name—Fred A. Kittel, Frederick A. Kittel, Frederick A. Wilson, A. Wilson, August Wilson—and settled finally on the last because it looked best on paper. He then laboriously typed a batch of poems. He'd heard that *Harper's* paid a dollar a line, so he sent the poems there. "They came back three days later," Wilson says. "I said, 'Oh, I see. This is serious. I'm gonna have to learn how to write a poem.' I wasn't deterred by that. I was emboldened." But because he "didn't like the feeling of rejection," Wilson didn't send out another poem for five years. (His first published work was "Muhammad Ali," which appeared in *Black World* in 1969.) "It was sufficient for me to know that I wrote poetry and I was growing as an artist," he says.

Most sightings of Wilson on the Hill were in restaurants—the White Tower, Eddie's Restaurant, the B & W, Moose's—bent over, scribbling on his tablet or on napkins. Decades later, Wilson would walk through the neighborhood and people would stop him and ask, "You still drawin'?" "I found out later people thought I was a bum," Wilson says. "The thing that sustained me was that my idea of myself was different from the idea that society, my mother, and even some of my friends had of me. I saw myself as a grand person." He adds, "I saw the pictures of Richard Wright, Langston Hughes—all of them always had a suit on. I thought, Yeah, that's me. I want to be like that." At a local thrift shop, he bought white shirts for a dime, the broad ties he favored for a nickel, and sports coats for thirty-five cents. In the poetic sphere, he'd come under the influence of Dylan Thomas, and he went through the Black Power movement with a coat and tie and a pipe, intoning poetry in an English accent. "People thought he was crazy in the neighborhood," Chawley Williams says. He adds, "When I met August, I was in the drug world. Here come August. He's sensitive, he's articulate, he has talent, he's trying to write. And the hustlers of the streets is at him. They could get him to do things, 'cause he wanted to belong. He would allow them to come to wherever he stayed at to eat, to get high and shoot their dope, to lie up with different women. They were trying to get him to get high. I put a halt to that."

Fish love water, it is said, and are cooked in it. But although Wilson swam in this predatory world he never felt threatened. If you ask him now to imagine the street back then, a smile crosses his face; he holds out his big right hand and trembles it. "A shimmy," he says. "The avenue shimmered. Hundreds of people on the sidewalks. Life going on." The vibrancy ravished him. Once, riding up Center Avenue in a friend's convertible, Wilson heard gunshots. "I hopped out of the car and ran down to where the gunshots were," he says. "There's this woman chasing the man around the car, and—*boom!*— she shot him. He was bleeding, and he asked this guy, 'Man, drive me to the hospital.' The guy said, 'You ain't gon' get all that blood in my car!'" Wilson adds, "I remember one time I didn't go to bed for damn near three days because every time I'd go to bed I felt like I was missing something."

Although Little Richard, Frankie Lymon and the Teenagers, Chuck Berry, and other rock and rollers had spilled over the backyard fences of Wilson's childhood, it wasn't until this time that he first heard the blues. For a nickel at a St. Vincent de Paul charity shop, he bought a bootleg 78-rpm record on whose tattered yellow label he could make out the words "Bessie Smith: 'Nobody in Town Can Bake a Sweet Jelly Roll Like Mine.'" Smith's impudent, unabashed sound stunned him. "The universe stuttered and everything fell to a new place," he wrote later. Like James Baldwin, who wrote that hearing Bessie Smith for the first time "helped to reconcile me to being a 'nigger,'" Wilson saw the moment as an epiphany: "a birth, a baptism, and a redemption all rolled up into one." Wilson played the new record twenty-two times straight. "Then I started laughing, you know, 'cause it suddenly dawned on me that there was another record on the other side." He adds, "It made me look at the world differently. It gave the people in the rooming house where I lived, and also my mother, a history I didn't know they had. It was the beginning of my consciousness that I was the carrier of some very valuable antecedents."

Wilson considers the blues "the best literature we have." As a way of preparing the emotional landscape for each play of his cycle, he submerges himself in the blues of the period. For *Hedley*, for instance, he's asking himself, "How'd we get from Percy Sledge's 'Warm and Tender Love' to 'You My Bitch'?" Even the structure of his sentences—the frequent reiteration of themes and words—owes much to the music's repetitions, its raucous pitch and improvised irony. From *Two Trains Running*:

> A nigger with a gun is bad news. You can't even use the word "nigger" and "gun" in the same sentence. You say the word "gun" in the same sentence with the word "nigger" and you in trouble. The white man panic. Unless you say, "The policeman shot the nigger with his gun."

He particularly likes it when singers speak their names in song. "There's something wonderful about that," he says. "They're making a stand. They're saying, 'This is me. This is what I have to say.'" In the context of what Zora Neale Hurston called "the muteness of slavery," the notion of singing solo and making a personal statement is, for African-Americans, a comparatively new and extraordinarily potent thing, which Wilson dramatizes in his plays. In his theatrical vocabulary, "finding a song" is both the expression of spirit and the accomplishment of identity. Some of his characters have a song that they can't broadcast; others have given up singing; some have been brutalized into near-muteness; and others have turned the absence of a destiny into tall talk—the rhetoric of deferred dreams. But Wilson's most brilliant demonstration of "carrying other people's songs and not having one of my own"—as one character puts it—is in *Joe Turner's Come and Gone*, where a conjure man called Bynum, who has a song, discourses with Loomis, who has been separated from his. Bynum says:

> Now, I can look at you, Mr. Loomis, and see you a man who done forgot his song. Forgot how to sing it. A fellow forget that and he forget who he is. Forget how he's supposed to mark down life. . . . See, Mr. Loomis, when a man forgets his song he goes off in search of it . . . till he find out he's got it with him all the time.

Music, in Wilson's plays, is more than slick Broadway entertainment. A juba dance banged out on a table, a work song beaten out with chairs and glasses, a gutbucket blues demonstrate the African-American genius for making something out of nothing. They take an empty world, as Ma Rainey says, and "fill it up with something."

Blues people, Ralph Ellison once wrote, are "those who accepted and lived close to their folk experience." On the Hill, the blues cemented in Wilson's mind the notion that he was somehow "the conduit of ancestors." West's Funeral Home—which figures in *Two*

Trains Running—was just around the corner from Eddie's Restaurant, and Wilson, for some deep personal reason and not for art's sake, felt compelled routinely to pay his respects to whoever had died. "I didn't have to know them. I felt that this is a life that has gone before me," he explains. From Claude McKay's *Home to Harlem*, he learned of a hangout in his own neighborhood called Pat's Place—a cigar store with a pool hall in the back—where a lot of the community elders congregated. Pat's Place became Wilson's Oxford, and its garrulous denizens—"walking history books," Wilson calls them—his tutors. They called him Youngblood. "I was just like, 'Hey, man, how did you get to be so old, 'cause it's hard out here.' I really wanted to know how they survived. How do you get to be seventy years old in America?" Wilson recalls meeting one old man at Pat's Place who said to him, "I been watchin' you. You carryin' around a ten-gallon bucket. You carry that ten-gallon bucket through life, and you gon' always be disappointed. Get you a little cup. And, that way, if somebody put a little bit in it, why, you got sumpin'." Wilson adds, "I managed to cut it down to a gallon bucket, but I never did get that little cup."

"What I discovered is that writing was the only thing society would allow me to do," he said in 1991. "I couldn't have a job or be a lawyer because I didn't do all the things necessary. What I was allowed to do was write. If they saw me over in the corner scribbling on a piece of paper they would say, 'That is just a nigger over in the corner scribbling on a piece of paper.' Nobody said, 'Hey, you can't do that.' So I felt free." On the street, as a defensive maneuver, Wilson says he "learned to keep my mouth shut," but, according to Chawley Williams, "when August stood onstage and read his poetry, there was a difference in him that didn't exist at no other time. He stood tall and proud. He stood with that definiteness." He was supported in this pursuit by his friends in the neighborhood—Williams, Rob Penny, and Nicholas Flournoy, who were all aspiring poets. The group founded the Center Avenue Poets Theater Workshop, out of which came the journal *Connection* (Wilson was its poetry editor), then the Halfway Art Gallery, and, from 1968 to 1972, the Black Horizons Theater, which Wilson co-founded with Penny, who served as house playwright.

During this time, Wilson had a daughter, Sakina Ansari (to whom *Joe Turner's Come and Gone* is dedicated), in a marriage to Brenda Burton, which ended in 1973. "She moved out with the baby," Linda Jean says. "August came home to an empty house. The shock and pain were unbearable to him. In a nutshell, she thought his writing was a waste of time, he wouldn't amount to anything." Although Wilson himself always felt successful, he says, he still hadn't achieved what he calls, quoting the poet Robert Duncan, "surety—the line burned in the hand." He says, "I had been trying to get to that point. I didn't approach it lightly. I worked concertedly toward growth." Finally, in 1973, in a poem called "Morning Statement," Wilson found his poetic voice:

> *It is the middle of winter*
> *November 21 to be exact*
> *I got up, buckled my shoes,*
> *I caught a bus and went riding into town.*
> *I just thought I'd tell you.*

"The poem didn't pretend to be anything else," Wilson says. "It wasn't struggling to say eternal things. It was just claiming the ground as its own thing. For me, it was so liberating." But his liberation as a playwright didn't begin until March 5, 1978, when he moved away from the Hill, to St. Paul, Minnesota, where he married Judy Oliver, a white social worker. In doing so, he went from a neighborhood that had fifty-five thousand blacks to a state that had the same number. "There weren't many black folks around," he says.

"In that silence, I could hear the language for the first time." Until then, Wilson says, he hadn't "valued or respected the way that black folks talked. I'd always thought that in order to create art out of it you had to change that." Now he missed the street talk and wanted to preserve it. "I got lonely and missed those guys and sort of created them," he says. "I could hear the music."

III

By the time Wilson reached St. Paul, he'd directed a handful of ama- teur productions, and his friend the director Claude Purdy had staged a musical satire based on a series of Wilson's poems. But despite a paying gig at the Science Museum of Minnesota, where Wilson wrote children's plays on science-related subjects, he was, by anyone's standard, a theatrical tyro. As early as 1976, he'd begun work on a piece about Ma Rainey, but then, he says, "it never occurred to me to make the musicians characters in the play. I couldn't have written the characters." His dialogue had a kind of florid artiness. In one of his early dramatic experiments, which involved a conversation between an old man and a woman on a park bench, the woman said, "Terror hangs over the night like a hawk." Wilson had at least one play, *The Coldest Day of the Year*, produced in this stilted style. "It wasn't black American language," he says. It wasn't theater, either.

In the fall of 1977, Wilson came across the work of the painter Romare Bearden. As he thumbed through Bearden's series of col- lages *The Prevalence of Ritual*, he discovered his "artistic mentor." Bearden's paintings made simple what Wilson's writing had so far only groped to formulate: "Black life presented on its own terms, on a grand and epic scale, with all its richness and fullness, in a lan- guage that was vibrant and which, made attendant to everyday life, ennobled it, affirmed its value, and exalted its presence." He adds,

"My response was visceral. I was looking at myself in ways I hadn't thought of before and have never ceased to think of since." In later years, Wilson would stand outside Bearden's house on Canal Street, in New York, "in silent homage, daring myself to knock." He didn't knock, but, he has written, if Bearden "had answered . . . and if I were wearing a hat, I would have taken it off in tribute." (In the end, Wilson's true homage was his plays, two of which—*Mill Hand's Lunch Bucket*, which became *Joe Turner*, and *The Piano Lesson*— took their titles from Bearden paintings.)

Years before, Wilson, who then "couldn't write dialogue," had asked Rob Penny, "How do you make characters talk?" Penny answered, "You don't. You listen to them." Now, in 1979, when Wilson sat down to write *Jitney*, a play set at the taxi stand that had been one of Wilson's hangouts on the Hill, the penny, as it were, dropped. For the first time, he was able to listen to his characters and let them speak. "I found that exhilarating," he says. "It felt like this was what I'd been looking for, something that was mine, that would enable me to say anything." For Wilson, the revelation was that "language describes the idea of the one who speaks; so if I'm speaking the oppressor's language I'm in essence speaking his ideas, too. This is why I think blacks speak their own language, because they have to find another way." While writing *Jitney*, he proved to himself that he didn't have to reconstitute black life; he just had to capture it.

Wilson sat at Arthur Treacher's Fish & Chips, a restaurant up the street from his apartment in St. Paul, for ten days in a row until the play was finished. At Penny's suggestion, he submitted it to the O'Neill Playwrights Conference, a sprawling estate in Waterford, Connecticut, where each summer about a dozen playwrights are provided with a dramaturge, a director, and a cast to let them explore their flawed but promising plays. The O'Neill rejected *Jitney*; its incredulous author, assuming that no one had read it, submitted the play again. The O'Neill rejected it again. Wilson took serious stock of his newfound calling; his inner dialogue, he says, was " 'Maybe it's not as good as you think. You have to write a better play.' 'I've already written the best play I can write.' 'Why don't you write above your talent?' 'Oh, man, how can you do that?' 'Well, you can write beneath it, can't you?' 'Oh, yeah.' " Wilson turned back to the play on Ma Rainey and began to imagine it differently. "I opened up the door to the band room," he says. "Slow Drag and Cutler was talking about how Slow Drag got his name. Then this guy walked in— he had glasses, carrying the books—he became Toledo. I had discovered them and got them talking."

On August 1, 1982, the producer Ben Mordecai, who had recently become the managing director of the Yale Repertory Theatre, drove up to Waterford to see his boss, Lloyd Richards. Richards, who is of Jamaican descent, was the head of the Yale Drama School and, for more than thirty years, worked during the summer as the artistic director of the O'Neill. He is a man of few words, most of them carefully chosen. "Is there anyone here I should meet?" Mordecai asked Richards. "Meet him," Richards said, nodding toward the porch of the main building, where Wilson was sitting. When *Ma Rainey's Black Bottom* was accepted at the O'Neill, Wilson stumbled onto the right person at the right place at the right time. Other African-Americans, such as Ed Bullins, whose *Twentieth-Century Cycle* did for South Philadelphia in the sixties and seventies what Wilson would do for Pittsburgh, were not as lucky. With access to theaters and to grant-giving agencies, Richards, who had directed *A Raisin in the Sun* on Broadway, was well positioned to usher Wilson's talent directly into the mainstream. Richards became, Wilson wrote, "my guide, my mentor, and my provocateur," and all of Wilson's subsequent plays until *Seven Guitars* would follow the same golden path— from the O'Neill to Yale to Broadway.

When *Ma Rainey* went to Yale, in 1984, Richards took over. "We go into the room with the actors, we read the play," Wilson says, describing the first day of rehearsal. "An actor had a question about a character. I started to speak, and Lloyd answered the question. There was another question, and Lloyd answered it again. I remember there was a moment when I thought, The old fox knows what's going on. This is gonna be OK." "We had a pattern of work," Richards says of their partnership, which in time would become as influential as that of Tennessee Williams and Elia Kazan. "I would work on it, check it with him, so I included him, but I was the director." He adds, "August was very receptive in the early days. He had a lot to learn and knew it. He was a big sponge, absorbing everything." Richards sent him to the sound booth, to the paint shop, to the lighting designer. "As he learned structure—playwriting, really—he was also learning everything else," Richards says.

Richards is not a gregarious man, and his natural reticence complements his collaborative, indirect way of working: "I try to provoke the artist to find the answer *I* want him to find." When Wilson sent Richards a version of *The Piano Lesson*, he says, "Lloyd calls me up and says, 'I think you have one too many scenes there.' 'OK, Lloyd, I'll look at that.' End of conversation. I go to the play. I see this scene that looks like it's expendable. I pull it out. Talking to Lloyd about something else a couple of days later, I say, 'Oh, Lloyd, by the way, I took the scene out.' Lloyd says, 'Good.' To this day, I don't know if we were talking about the same scene." Richards says, "He cut the scene that needed to be cut." He adds, "August writes wonderful scenes. He must think they're wonderful, 'cause they go on and on and on. To the point where they advance the play much further than it needs to be advanced at that moment." Wilson's *Fences*, which was the second-most-produced play on American professional stages in 1989, was transformed by Richards, over several productions, from a four-and-a-half-hour first appearance at the O'Neill to its commercial length of less than three hours not just by cutting but by reorganizing. This began Wilson's practice of refining his plays in the regionals. *The Piano Lesson*—which involves a contest for ownership of a prized family piano between a sister, who wants to keep it as a symbol of her African-American heritage, and her brother, who wants to sell it to buy land on the plantation where their ancestors were slaves—had still not found a satisfactory ending after a year of touring. It finally got one when Richards suggested to Wilson that the battle between the brother and sister was missing a third party: the spirit of the white family who also had claims on the piano. "August wrote a wonderful speech describing how the piano came into the family and how they had stolen it from this white family," Richards says. "That brought the piece together."

When *The Piano Lesson* was made into a TV movie, in 1995, Wilson served as a producer, a shift in power that also augured a change in his relationship with Richards. At one meeting, a production designer, Patricia Van Ryker, who hadn't read the original play—which states that the piano's legs are "carved in the manner of African sculpture," to represent the characters' African heritage—laid out her plans to decorate the piano with images of plantation life that fit within the time frame of the play. Wilson exploded. "He was screaming," Van Ryker recalls. "'How dare you do this! You're insulting my relatives! My race!' It was like I'd thrown kerosene on him." Richards recalls the moment as "terrible," and says, "I don't function dictatorially. I don't give directives. I saw August in a position of power. I knew I couldn't work *for* him."

As Wilson grew in confidence, craft, and stature, it became increasingly difficult for him to play the protégé in the partnership. "The two of them artistically began drifting apart, which was, I think, a natural thing," Mordecai says. "The collaboration wasn't happening at the level it had in earlier years." As Wilson saw it, "Lloyd slowed down," but it's just as true to say that Wilson grew up. When a rewritten version of *Jitney* was up for production at the

Pittsburgh Public Theater, in 1996, Wilson chose as his director Marion McClinton, who had done inventive second productions of many of his earlier plays. Wilson may have lost a kind of father in the split with Richards, but in McClinton he gained a brother. Where Richards's productions were stately, McClinton's are fluid; where Richards's process was formal, McClinton's is relaxed. "The first conversation we had, August said to me, 'My style is I don't talk to the actors,'" McClinton recalls. "I said, 'I don't care if you talk to the actors. Whatever gets the information to them the clearest and cleanest, that's what I'm for.'"

"August is a soldier," McClinton says, and he's referring to more than Wilson's theatrical battles. Wilson, who cites the Black Power movement as "the kiln in which I was fired," describes himself as a "race man." And his very specific anthropological understanding of American history has led him to some hard, politically incorrect opinions. For instance, he believes that it was a mistake for African-Americans to leave the South. "The blood and bones of two hundred and fifty years of our ancestors are buried in the South, and we came North," he says. "I think if we'd stayed South and continued to empower ourselves, in terms of acquiring land—we already had acres of farmland that we owned—we'd have had ten black senators in the United States. We'd be represented. We'd be a more culturally secure and culturally self-sufficient people."

Wilson's insistence on preserving and sustaining an African-American identity led to a well-publicized argument with Robert Brustein, the artistic director of Boston's American Repertory Theater, that culminated in a formal debate at New York's Town Hall, in 1997. Among many contrarian points, Wilson argued against the current fashion for "color-blind casting"—a bias shared by McClinton, who refers to the practice as "Cyclops casting." "It's color-blind in one eye," he says. "You're quite aware of the fact that we're black—

that's why we're not asked to present that in our performance, where the white actors can bring whatever history and interior self-knowledge they have into a rehearsal process and into the making of character." In Wilson's view, to mount an all-black production of, say, *Death of a Salesman* is "to deny us the need to make our own investigations from the cultural ground on which we stand as black Americans." In his exchange with Brustein, Wilson pointed out the transparent inequity of having sixty-six regional theaters and only one that can be considered black. (He subsequently conceived and supported the African Grove Institute for the Arts, an organization that promotes African-American theater.) In America, "the subscription audience holds the seats of our theaters hostage to the mediocrity of its tastes, and serves to impede the further development of an audience for the work that we do," he said. "Intentional or not, it serves to keep blacks out of the theater, where they suffer no illusion of welcome anyway." This call for an African-American theater was immediately seized upon by the press as separatist, despite the fact that Wilson himself disputed the label. "We are not separatists, as Mr. Brustein asserts," he said. "We are Americans trying to fulfill our talents. We are not the servants at the party. We are not apprentices in the kitchens. . . . We are Africans. We are Americans." The aftermath of the debate—something of a tempest in a teapot—still lingers (and is still misconstrued). "He took that hit for a lot of other people," McClinton says. "That's what a champion does—a champion fights." When Wilson gave me a book of his first three plays, he inscribed it, "The struggle continues."

My first sighting of McClinton and Wilson at work was last November, in the rehearsal room of Chicago's new Goodman Theatre, where *King Hedley II* was the inaugural production. They sat shoulder to shoulder at the rehearsal table. McClinton, a heavy man, wore a baggy white T-shirt and a black fedora; he chugged at an economy-sized Dr Pepper. Wilson, in his trademark cap, sat bent slightly forward and absolutely still. His eyes were trained on the figure of Hedley, a former killer trying to make a go of it on the Hill, as he knelt in front of a flower patch demarked in rehearsal by a few stones on the concrete floor. His mother, Ruby, stood nearby, watching him. "You need some good dirt," she told him. "Them seeds ain't gonna grow in that dirt." Hedley responded, "This the only dirt I got. This is me right here." The words—the opening of the play—linked Wilson's newest protagonist to all the other desperate heroes of his cycle, and to himself: men attempting, in one way or another, to claim their inheritance. Wilson leaned across to whisper something to McClinton, who, keeping his eyes on the actors, nodded, took another hit of soda, and stopped the rehearsal to adjust the blocking. "King don't listen well," the actor playing Hedley said. "He's a king," McClinton replied. "Kings don't listen."

At the break, Wilson headed off to the theater's loading bay for a cigarette. There he brooded about Aunt Ester, the 366-year-old character whose death the play announces. "See, Aunt Ester is the tradition," he said. "If you don't value that, then you lose it. So, in 1985, these kids are out there killing one another. Aunt Ester dies of grief. People quit going up to her house. The weeds are all grown over. You can't even find the door no more. So she dies." He added, "If you had a connection to your grandparents and understood their struggle to survive, you wouldn't be out there in the street killing someone over fifteen dollars' worth of narcotics. You have to know your history. Then you'll have a purposeful presence in the world."

As he readied *Hedley* for New York, Wilson had been trying to make a start on his 1900s play, in which Aunt Ester is a central character. Like Romare Bearden, Wilson opens himself up to his subjects and communes with them until he finds a pattern: "I just invite some of the people I know to come into the room and give it an ambience." *Fences* began with the ending; Wilson says that he saw his hero, Troy Maxson, "standing out on this brilliant starry night with this baby in his arms, talking to this woman. I didn't know who the woman was." *Two Trains Running* began in a New Haven restaurant, where Wilson picked up a napkin and wrote, "When I left out of Jackson I said I was gonna buy me a big Ford. Was gonna drive by Mr. Henry Ford's house and honk the horn. If anybody come to the window, I was gonna wave. Then I was going out, and buy me a 30.06, come on back to Jackson and drive up to Mr. Stovall's house. Only this time I wasn't waving."

By contrast, Aunt Ester had been balky about making her presence known. "I said, 'OK, Aunt Ester, talk to me.' And she says, 'There's a lot of things I don't talk about.' And that threw me, because I didn't have anything to write then," Wilson says. A month later, he tried again. This time, he asked Aunt Ester, "OK, what *don't* you talk about?" "I don't talk about the trees. The trees didn't have spirits," she told Wilson. "What does that mean? What that means is that none of your world is present here. You're looking at this landscape that's totally foreign to you. So I started writing that," Wilson says. "Then she started talking about the water, and I find she's talking about the Atlantic Ocean. And she starts talking about a city, a half mile by a half mile, down in there. She has a map to the city," he adds. "I think the map is important, so I have to pick the right time to approach that idea about the map. If I do it this afternoon, I get something entirely different than if I do it next week. It's intuition. You have to keep your eyes and ears open for clues. There's no compass."

In *King Hedley II*, Hedley's sacrifice keeps a dying black tradition alive; in life, Wilson has also made a sacrifice to renew a connection to the past. He seems to know that the price he's paid for his enormous accomplishment is other people; and he has recently begun to take stock of his life and resolve "to do something different." He is making noises about retiring. Not long ago, when he returned to Seattle, Wilson, who had been away, by his own admission, "for the past two years," was dismayed to discover that Azula didn't know he lived there. "You live in all the places," she told him. "Boston, New York, Pittsburgh." "No, I live here," he said. He took Azula upstairs and showed her his clothes in the closet.

Wilson, who is an insomniac, shares a bed with both Azula and Constanza. At lights-out, Azula will say, "Don't let the bedbugs bite." Wilson will reply, "If they do, take a few," which leaves his daughter the final word: "'Cause I got them from you." When they wake up, Wilson says, "Good morning, Sunshine." Azula replies, "Good morning, Big Old Dad." But these moments of connection are only one side of the story. Wilson, who has created a universe of fully imagined characters, whose histories he knows in minute detail, is not as curious about the history of those close to him. "I've been married before," Constanza says. "He's never asked me a single question about that. I mean a lot to him, but what is it I mean to him if I'm not a complete person with history, with wants, with needs?" Constanza met Wilson at Yale fourteen years ago, when she designed costumes for *The Piano Lesson*, and she has a kind of clear-eyed fatalism about her life with this ambitious storyteller. "It's been hard," she says. "I don't get the love from him that all of me would like. I don't have a partner through the little things in life. He just doesn't reach that intimate part of everyday life." She continues, "In his mind, he's a great father, a great man, a great husband. One time, I was saying to Azula, when she was going to sleep, 'I'm going to teach you how to choose a really good husband for yourself.' And then August said, 'Just like your daddy.' And I was thinking to myself, No!"

"Be where you are"—a maxim Lloyd Richards drilled into Wilson—is a habit that Wilson is "still working at." When he is at home, Wilson is pretty much wrapped in his own solitude, "brewing," as his sister Freda calls it. "I call him the deepest pool I have ever seen in my life," Constanza says. "You can throw a rock inside this man and you'll never see it hit bottom. He's a mystery to me in many ways. He's reachable only in concise sentences." Wilson's plays are brilliantly furnished with characters and incident, but he hasn't yet managed to furnish his own home. "It's gone beyond eccentricity," Constanza says. "It's an outward symbol of our marriage being so out of the ordinary. We can't even furnish our own house. I mean, that's sad." Wilson's critical eye and Constanza's conviction that he would disapprove if she took the decoration into her own hands keeps them at a stalemate. "He's extremely critical," Constanza says. "The closer you are to him, the more critical he is. That's a pattern that his mother passed on to him."

Ordinarily, according to his wife, Wilson "has a hard time laughing at himself." But in the presence of his daughter the somber, self-absorbed Wilson drops away. "I've seen a different August with Azula," McClinton agrees. "She brings out such a playful side of him. He came to the first day of rehearsal in Seattle for *King Hedley II* wearing a bunny mask with the ears sticking up." Wilson has taught Azula some of the nonsense songs that he learned at the age of five from an uncle: together, they sing, "Jo and Mo had a candy store / Tellin' fortunes behind the door / The police ran in / Joe ran out / Hollerin' 'Run, Mo! / Policeman holdin' my hand!' " Recently, he wrote a story just for her that involved what he calls "telescoping"—a fusion of the spiritual and the diurnal "that I'm trying to do in the plays." The tale starts off in Seattle with a little girl who won't go to bed. "My aunt in Africa will grant you a wish if you will go to bed at the proper time," her babysitter says. "OK," the little girl says. "My wish is that it be daylight all the time so I never have to go to bed." The story then moves from reality into a fantastical world of sun gods and kings of darkness and chess games where the pieces come alive. "I think it's close to what would be an African-American world view—tree spirits and all those kinds of things," Wilson says.

"In this world, you can have a 366-year-old woman and you also gotta pay your bills. They exist side by side. They infuse life with a something that lifts it up, almost into another realm. Closer to God." Even Azula understands that her father's undertaking is somehow special and heroic and big in the world. At the Goodman Theatre, catching sight of him as he walked toward her in the lobby, she threw open her arms and said, "August Wilson!" Around that time, she also asked him, "Daddy, why you a writer?" "To tell the story," Wilson said. ▪

—*April 16, 2001*

Gem of the Ocean

"What one begs the American people to do, for all of us, is simply to accept our history," James Baldwin wrote in *The American Dream and the American Negro*. But that imaginative challenge, as August Wilson demonstrates in *Gem of the Ocean* (well directed by Kenny Leon, at the Walter Kerr), is as hard for blacks to achieve as for whites. *Gem*, which is set in the Hill District of Pittsburgh, in 1904, is the latest, and the introductory, installment to Wilson's magnificent ten-play cycle, in which each play dramatizes a decade of the roiling African-American experience of the twentieth century. At one point, Solly Two Kings (Anthony Chisholm), an old runaway slave and activist, asks Citizen Barlow (John Earl Jelks), a young man born into freedom and named for its promise, "You know about the Civil War?" He doesn't. History is lost on him; in fact, he is the first of many stunned characters who are "left over from history." The moment—a reminder of the depths of African-American impoverishment—is a sensational theatrical fillip; it is incidental to the plot but crucial to the spiritual dilemma the play addresses. Citizen Barlow has only just come North to find work and to fulfill the destiny of liberty; he stands before us in all his woe and wonder, already unmoored by the experience. He's freed from bondage but finds himself in economic slavery at the local mill. As payback for the mill's refusal to grant his wages, he steals a bucket of nails; another worker, who is blamed for the theft, drowns himself rather than be forced to admit guilt. Citizen has murder on his conscience. "I feel like I got a hole inside me," he explains. Wilson depicts Barlow as a by-product of the system of subjugation that stripped African-Americans of their language, their gods, their history, and their sense of reality. *Gem* bears witness to this historical mutilation, which leaves Citizen Barlow rudderless in a way that is particular to the African-American. As Baldwin writes, "It destroys the father's authority over him. His father can no longer tell him anything because his past has disappeared." Wilson's eloquent feat is to repossess African-American history and mythology and to make luminous the heroic African-American accomplishment of survival.

As the play opens, Citizen Barlow bursts into the high-ceilinged home of Aunt Ester Tyler (Phylicia Rashad), a 285-year-old conjure woman who is the repository of the race's historical memory, and who is rumored to "wash people's souls." Aunt Ester embodies African-American folklore, what Zora Neale Hurston calls "the boiled-down juice of human living." Ester's house, at 1839 Wylie Avenue—an address as iconic in dramatic literature as Grover's Corners—is a sanctuary in Wilson's *Two Trains Running* (1990), and in *King Hedley II* (2001), in which Aunt Ester dies of grief. However, at the beginning of the twentieth century she is in robust, cranky health, pestering her housekeeper and protégée, Black Mary (LisaGay Hamilton), with orders and speaking in parables full of wisdom from the journey she made in 1619 on the Middle Passage, the transatlantic route on which at least two million slaves lost their lives. "I'm on an adventure," she tells Citizen. She goes on, "I got a strong memory. I got a long memory. . . . I try to remember out loud. I keep my memories alive. I feed them. I got to feed them, otherwise they'd eat me up. I got memories that go way back. I'm carrying them for a lot of folk."

Aunt Ester's mission is Wilson's mission: to transmit into Citizen's soul a sense of his past. She, like him, does this by creating a piece of theater that throws Citizen back in time. In this case, she fashions a boat from her slave's bill of sale, which Citizen clutches in his hand, and, aided by Black Mary and her gatekeeper and friend, Eli (Eugene Lee), conjures up the slave ships and the City of Bones, an underwater world made from the bones of drowned slaves, which is first mentioned in Wilson's masterpiece, *Joe Turner's Come and Gone* (1986). The extravagant theatricality of Citizen's re-spiritualization is powerful stuff, even if it seems to be willed by the author rather than to flow organically from the situation. Nonetheless, Wilson superbly clinches Aunt Ester's ability to engineer identity when Black Mary finally rounds on her after being given one too many orders, and says, "I'm tired of it! Your way ain't always the best way. I got my own way, and that's the way I'm doing it. If I stay around here, I'm doing it my own way." Aunt Ester asks, "What took you so long?" and exits.

As Ester, Phylicia Rashad turns in an eerily inspired performance of old age. (She did the same thing last year on Broadway, in *A Raisin in the Sun.*) She has abdicated glamour and the desire to be adorable; as a result, detachment and coyness give way to daring and compassion. Dressed in Constanza Romero's beautifully designed, capacious purple knit dress, with a hem decorated in amulets that suggest majesty and magic, Aunt Ester speaks her own compelling metaphoric language. She tells Citizen, "You got to find a way to live in truth. If you live right you die right." It says a lot about the conviction of Rashad's big-hearted performance, and about Wilson's writing, that her authority is never in doubt.

"Freedom is heavy. You got to put your shoulder to freedom," a character says in Wilson's *Two Trains Running*, and the shock of freedom's strain is the real subject of *Gem of the Ocean*. Solly Two Kings, whose walking stick has sixty-two notches for the people he has led out of slavery, knows the price of freedom, and carries a link of his own ankle chain as a reminder. "The people think they in freedom. That's all my daddy talked about. He died and never did have it," Solly Two Kings tells Citizen. "I say I got it but what is it?" He adds, "You got to fight to make it mean something. All it mean is you got a long row to hoe and ain't got no plow. Ain't got no seed. Ain't got no mule. What good is freedom if you can't do nothing with it?"

Against this activist position—the sure knowledge that you have to bleed for freedom—Wilson pits a local constable, the well-named Caesar (Ruben Santiago-Hudson), who adopts the white man's momentum as completely as he absorbs his laws. It gives him direction and definition. In Santiago-Hudson's wonderful peacock swagger, Caesar is a man whose successful survival has been achieved at the expense of his own people and his own past. In him, the Bible has been replaced by the rule book. He is the hectoring, and incidentally hilarious, voice of reaction. "You know whose fault it is? I'll tell you whose fault it is," he says, storming into Aunt Ester's house with news of a riot over the stolen nails, which threatens to close the mill down. "It's Abraham Lincoln's fault. He ain't had no idea what he was doing. He didn't know like I know. Some of these niggers was better off in slavery. They don't know how to act otherwise." Santiago-Hudson, whose talk and look are sleek and urban, strides the stage with his badge and his gun, asserting the white man's authority. He catches every iota of irony in Caesar's messianic belief that he must keep his own race in line. By the finale, Caesar has lost his soul just as surely as Citizen has found his. "I'm a free man," Caesar says, spelling out the bright idea of property and the pragmatism that justifies it. "I'm starting out with nothing so I got to get a little something. A little place to start."

Gem of the Ocean is perhaps more discursive than Wilson's other plays; the characters seem to circle around themselves and their meanings, but that is appropriate for people who are literally assembling new identities and learning to pronounce them in a new world. Each character brings news of a brutalized life; each character is in search of a meaning but, in his incompleteness, is also, in Wilson's words, "fat with substance." Next year, *Radio Golf*, the final installment in Wilson's cycle, will be staged. Whether it succeeds or not, his herculean accomplishment, for the range and depth of its eloquence, is without peer in its time. Whatever its excesses and longueurs, Wilson's cycle is one of the high-water marks of American drama, transmuting historical tragedy into imaginative triumph. Wilson sees his storytelling as some kind of blues; *Gem of the Ocean*, like the rest of his oeuvre, blows loud and clear and beautiful—it's some kind of song that contains what Wilson calls "both a wail and a whelp of joy." ∎

—December 20, 2004

Joe Turner's Come and Gone

The late August Wilson thought of himself as a bluesman. His plays are chronicles of catastrophe, told lyrically; his theatrical mission was "to articulate the cultural response of black Americans to the world in which they found themselves," a world, he said, "that did not recognize their gods, their manners, their mores." Of the ten plays in Wilson's Century Cycle—which bear witness to the African-American experience in each decade of the twentieth century—*Joe Turner's Come and Gone* (revived, for the first time since its Broadway premiere, in 1988, at the Belasco, under the deft direction of Bartlett Sher) was his favorite and his masterpiece, the one in which the historical, the mythical, and the autobiographical reach their most ravishing equipoise. Wilson's brooding sense of dislocation and his decade-long struggle to discover his literary voice found a profound correlative in the floundering of the haunted, taciturn Herald Loomis (Chad L. Coleman), the hero of *Joe Turner's Come and Gone*. By the time Loomis wanders into a Pittsburgh boarding house, in 1911, at the start of the play, he has endured twin traumas: he was dragooned into slavery for seven years by a white plantation owner, Joe Turner, and he was abandoned by his wife, for whom he has been searching, with his now eleven-year-old daughter, Zonia (Amari Rose Leigh), for four lost years. A long gray overcoat and a hat pulled down low on his head give Loomis a defensive carapace. He is unknowable, both to others and to himself. Loomis is not only unmoored ("I been wandering a long time in somebody else's world"); he is a dismantled man "who done forgot his song," as the resident boardinghouse conjure man, Bynum Walker (the vivid Roger Robinson), tells him.

Loomis's challenge—the reclaiming of his moral personality—is foreshadowed by Michael Yeargan's set, which cleverly walks the same stylistic tightrope between the luminous and the mysterious as Wilson. Six legless brown chairs are silhouetted against the huge backdrop of a mackerel city sky. The surreal image of incompletion turns out to be a trompe l'oeil—the chairs do have legs, though they're masked from view—but the idea remains: the issue for Loomis is how to make himself whole, how to prop himself up in the world. "My legs won't stand up! My legs won't stand up!" he cries, at the end of act 1, as he is blown backward along the floor by a howling wind, which also plays as the internal tempest released by a vision of his ancestors, "the bones people," who were lost at sea in slave ships during the Middle Passage to the New World.

In this iconic boarding house, Wilson condenses the experiences of a floating population of African-Americans, who find themselves ill-equipped to survive their emancipation. "Niggers coming up here from the backwoods . . . carrying Bibles and guitars, looking for freedom," the proprietor, Seth Holly (the compelling Ernie Hudson), says. "They got a rude awakening." At a time just after *Plessy v. Ferguson*—according to which African-Americans were considered "separate but equal"—the separation, for the boarding-house residents, is spectacular: separation from history, from family, from education, from capital, from self. The twice-jilted Mattie Campbell (the poignant Marsha Stephanie Blake), who "ain't never found no place for me to fit," seeks in each romantic alliance "a starting place in the world." Seth Holly can't seem to make his mark on life, either; he has a sharp entrepreneurial mind and a talent for manufacturing pots, but he can't get a loan to expand his business. Bynum Walker seeks not money but a mission in the alienated landscape. Bynum's name suggests the kind of spell he casts, which is about creating community and binding people. "People walking away and leaving one another," he says. "Just like glue I sticks people together." Rutherford Selig (Arliss Howard), a white peddler and "people finder," on the other hand, exploits the chronic cultural restlessness for profit. "It's not an easy job keeping up with you Nigras the way you move about so," he says, taking a dollar from Loomis in exchange for the promise to keep an eye out for his wife.

Wilson wanted his dramatic world to be "fat with substance." To that end, he elevated his African-American roots—what he called "the blood's memory"—to "biblical status." When the residents decide to "Juba down"—to perform, around the kitchen table, a thrilling call-and-response dance "reminiscent of the Ring Shouts of the African slaves"—Wilson brilliantly demonstrates how slaves adapted the remnants of African rituals to their new Christian ones. Loomis walks in on the near-frenzy and is enraged by the sight and sound of the others chanting "Holy Ghost." "What's so holy about the Holy Ghost?" he shouts, before breaking down and speaking in tongues himself. The moment puts him in atavistic touch with his own ghosts, his lost ancestors, though it is a knowledge that he is unable to make use of until the end of the play.

At the finale, Loomis finally comes face to face with his missing wife, Martha Pentecost (Danai Gurira), in a powerful scene that turns out to be a farewell, rather than a reunion. "Now that I see your face I can say my good-bye and make my own world," Loomis tells her, handing over the bereft Zonia. The harrowing moment contains the woe of Wilson's own life. (Wilson's daughter Sakina Ansari, to whom *Joe Turner* is dedicated, was the price that he paid for the pursuit of his literary ambition; one day in 1973, he returned home to find that his first wife, Brenda Burton, who, according to his sister, thought that his writing was a waste of time, had left with their baby.) In the end, Loomis realizes that he has within him all that he needs in order to be reborn. "My legs stood up!" he says, just before he exits. "I'm standing now!" As he sets off, the air in this production is suddenly flecked with gold, a halo of sorts, meant to indicate Loomis's resurrection. I like to think of it, however, as the shine of Wilson's œuvre, "a wail and a whelp of joy" that was his hard-won and gorgeous song. ∎

—April 27, 2009

Seven Guitars

Somewhere in the middle of August Wilson's exciting *Seven Guitars*, which sends us stirring news of black life in the late forties, I found my mind wandering from the tribulations of his seven memorable characters to the blues. The show flashes back to the final days of a Pittsburgh blues singer named Floyd (Schoolboy) Barton. Before the play begins, Willie Dixon's "Little Red Rooster" and Arthur (Big Boy) Crudup's "That's All Right" rock the Walter Kerr Theatre, and when the lights come up, on Floyd's wake, a landlady named Louise (Michele Shay)—dwarfed by the production designer Scott Bradley's mammoth ghetto warrens of creosoted wood and brick and stone wedged between telephone poles and laundry lines—keeps the blues mojo working with a bawdy offer to the mournful assembly. "Anybody here wanna try my cabbage," she sings, "just step this way." What a pinched, desiccated, joyless century this would be without the blues' swaggering refusal to surrender. The seven guitars of the title are the seven characters whose straightforward story lines Wilson turns into beautiful, complex music—a funky, wailing, irresistible Chicago blues.

"I take the same approach as a bluesman, the same ideas and attitudes," Wilson recently told me. "For instance, lines that say, 'I'm leavin' in the mornin', I'm gonna start out walkin', And take a chance I may ride.' I simply go back and look through that. Contained in the expression is your whole world view." He added, "When the old folks sang, 'Everything's gonna be all right,' it *was* all right, simply because they sang. They made it all right by their singing. They just changed their attitudes. The blues emboldened their spirits and enabled them to survive whatever the circumstance was."

Here, in a Pittsburgh backyard in 1948, Wilson is bearing witness to a pivotal, ironic moment in black American history, when African-Americans were poised between their greatest hope and their greatest heartbreak. "We had just gone off and demonstrated our allegiance and willingness to fight and die for the country," Wilson said. "We actually believed that things would be different, and that we would be accorded first-class citizenship. We came back after the war, and that was not true." In the high times and dashed dreams of *Seven Guitars*, the seventh work in a ten-play cycle that will chronicle black experience in each decade of the twentieth century (his plays for the first decade of the century, the eighties, and the nineties still remain to be written), Wilson eloquently dramatizes this punishing contradiction.

Opportunity is what Floyd carries in his pocket when he is conjured up before us in all his high-stepping, smooth-talking glory. Floyd has discovered that there's a record deal waiting for him in

Chicago if he can just find the money to get his guitar out of hock and a ticket to ride. Keith David, as Floyd, gives the character a bravura air of confidence and cunning. Fresh from the workhouse, where he's done ninety days for vagrancy (the judge called his crime "worthlessness"), Floyd flaunts his prowess and his hope, trying to win back his shy, saturnine ex-girlfriend, Vera (Viola Davis), so he can take her to Chicago with him. He shows her a letter from Savoy Records. "Look at that. 'Mr. Floyd Barton,'" he says. "You get you a hit record and the white folks call you Mister." In one throwaway laugh line, Wilson catches a lifetime of second-class citizenship. But Floyd is ever hopeful. "It's different now," he tells Vera. "You get a hit record and you be surprised how everything change." What doesn't change for any of the black folk onstage, though, is their access to money. "You got to take the opportunity while it's there," Floyd says. Yet in order to seize his moment Floyd needs not only his own guitar but all his band's instruments, which are also at the pawnshop. The band has a hit record but nothing to play music with.

To finance his move, Floyd has to rely on his erstwhile manager, a white man called T. L. Hall. The plot point neatly incorporates Wilson's views on the failure of African-Americans to progress in American society. The playwright told me, "The thrust for integration and the lack of a relationship to banking capital meant that we could not continue to develop the economic base that we'd begun."

The waste of talent is implied here by the inventive energy the characters bring to the ordinary activities of their stalled days. Wilson is writing an oral, not an economic, history of his time, and it is all the more profound and persuasive because it teaches through joy, not through reason. In a catalogue of song, superstitions, stories, homilies, and food, the folkways of a lost time and place are gorgeously reimagined. For instance, Floyd's harmonica player and good friend, Canewell (the superb Ruben Santiago-Hudson, whose every syllable of tall talk is etched with tenderness), explains how to test the sweetness of watermelons. "You don't thump them," Canewell, who has eyes for Vera, says. "You treat a watermelon just like you do a woman—you squeeze them." The drummer, Red Carter (the droll Tommy Hollis), is a portly repository of black legend, especially his own. He tells how he juggled affairs with seven women at one time: "I tried to move my Friday woman over to Sunday, but she got mad. My Sunday woman quit me and my Monday woman wanted to see me on Saturday. I got so confused I say the best thing for me to do was quit my job."

For these characters, work is hardscrabble, but fun isn't. Wilson makes a point of showing off their high spirits and their talent when, after some artfully engineered badinage, the band members find themselves making wonderful music out of nothing. Canewell produces a spare harmonica and makes it "talk"; Floyd bangs his beat-up wooden guitar; Red produces drumsticks and beats out time on a card table and the backs of chairs. It's one of several showstopping moments that Wilson uses to make larger, powerful points about the personalities onstage. During another such scene, everyone sits outside on a sweltering night listening intently to a radio broadcast of the Joe Louis–Billy Conn championship fight. Boxing is the crudest of Darwinian metaphors; but, if the black man can't always survive in the real world, here, at least, he's victorious. (To underline the dramatic point, Wilson has moved the date of the Louis-Conn bout from 1946 to 1948.) The group erupts in a frenzied dance to celebrate the Brown Bomber's knockout—a victory that must stand for the characters' own frustrated battles against the white man. Red tries to teach Vera "the Joe Louis Victory Walk," telling her, "Now just let it roll. You ain't got to worry about rocking it—it'll rock by itself." Vera, who is slow to kindle, finally burns. It's a fabulous, ecstatic moment, and Vera's heat prompts Floyd to pull a gun on Red. (All the men are armed for the tough world they hustle in.) Later, in the second act, the dance is reprised by Vera and the others to celebrate the band's own victory at a local club called the Blue Goose. Life, briefly, looks as if it might come good.

Floyd's obsession is to get to Chicago and his record contract. "More people means more opportunity," he says. A lot of the play's talk focusses on whether or not to go to the Windy City. Pittsburgh is a kind of way station in the migration from the rural South to the urban North, and the implications of this migration are what Wilson is trying to trap in all the banter. A barnyard rooster that belongs to a next-door neighbor and announces itself in the play's second scene becomes the subject of much comic abuse, and a symbol of the spiritual dilemma of this shifting population. "You ain't gonna find no rooster living next to you making all that noise in Chicago," Floyd says. To Canewell, who has told us earlier that he owes his name to his grandfather's cutting cane in Louisiana ("Otherwise my name would be Cottonwell," he jokes), the rooster is a totem of the painful past. "The rooster didn't crow during slavery," he says. "If you think I'm lying go and find you somebody from back in slavery time and ask them if they ever heard the rooster crow." One character refuses to participate in the rooster jive: the demented wise man Hedley (Roger Robinson), who makes his living selling chicken sandwiches, and honors his black heritage with the sure knowledge that "the white man walk the earth on the black man's back." Hedley speaks in riddles, and he dreams that one day his dead father's inheritance will come to him from the cornet player Buddy Bolden, whom his father idolized. Sometimes Hedley's actions seem as capricious as his pronouncements. After all the grousing about the rooster, Hedley bolts from the backyard and returns with the offending piece of poultry in his hand. "God ain't making no more roosters," he declares. "It is a thing past. Soon you mark my words when God ain't making no more niggers. They, too, be a done thing." He continues, "You hear this rooster you know you alive." Then Hedley wrings its neck and slits its throat. The chilling moment works as both a curse and a prophecy. Wilson told me, "Hedley's whole warning is 'If the rooster has become useless, then what about you? Maybe you'll become useless, too.' If you don't connect to the past, then you don't know who you are in the present. You may prove to be unworthy of the past."

When Floyd's manager is jailed for an insurance scam, Floyd finds himself between a rock and a hard place. "Everything can't go wrong all the time," he says quietly. "I don't want to live my life without. Everybody I know live without. I don't want to do that. I want to live with. . . . Floyd Barton is gonna make his record. Floyd Barton is going to Chicago." He seizes his opportunity in the only way left to him: he robs for it. One of his friends is killed. Wilson allows Floyd a moment of glory at the Blue Goose before making him pay for his actions. Hedley discovers Floyd counting his stolen cash in the moonlight. In his dementia, Hedley mistakes Floyd, in his white city suit, for Buddy Bolden, and claims the cash as his. They quarrel, and Hedley kills Floyd.

"The odyssey of the African-American throughout the twentieth century has been one of loss and reclamation," Wilson told me. "It's about reclaiming those things which were lost during slavery." At Floyd's wake, Vera maintains that she saw him being taken up to Heaven, but his death is a necessary part of what Wilson sees as the African-American reclamation of "moral personality"—of taking responsibility for one's actions. "I always say that if the African who arrived chained and malnourished in the hold of a 350-foot slave ship is still, after four hundred years, chained and malnourished, then it can't be anybody's fault but his," Wilson told me.

When Wilson was growing up, in the Hill district of Pittsburgh in the late forties and fifties, his parents used to admonish him, "Don't go out there and show your color," but Wilson has dedicated his life and his art to doing just that: making a spectacle of blackness. No other theatrical testament to African-American life has been so popular or so poetic or so penetrating. In Wilson's long and successful partnership with the director Lloyd Richards, whose hand has guided this play through a protracted and difficult birth, he has won two Pulitzer Prizes, for *Fences* (1987) and *The Piano Lesson* (1990). If there were any justice in these things (there isn't), *Seven Guitars* would make it a hat trick. No one else—not even Eugene O'Neill, who set out in the mid-thirties to write a nine-play cycle and managed only two plays—has aimed so high and achieved so much. On Broadway, where shows are filled with bogus recipes for happiness, it's thrilling finally to hear a useful one. "You get you about three pounds of turnips and about three pounds of mustard," Canewell says, describing his method of making turnip greens. "I like to mix them together. . . . Put you in a little piece, about a quarter pound of salt pork in there with them. Turn the fire way down real low and let them cook up about six hours. Throw you some red pepper seeds in there first. Cook that up and call me when it get done." Me, too. ■

—*April 15, 1996*

3

TONY KUSHNER

On May 2, 2004, the humid Sunday that his musical *Caroline, or Change* was to transfer from the Public Theater, downtown, to the Eugene O'Neill Theatre, on Broadway, Tony Kushner left his apartment on the Upper West Side and ambled east through Central Park. He was seeking out Bethesda Fountain and the statue of an angel that graces it to ask for blessing. For luck, on opening nights, Kushner usually performs two rituals: before the curtain goes up he sings Cole Porter's "Begin the Beguine"—a song that, according to his will, must be played, along with Brahms's Fourth and Mahler's Resurrection Symphony, at his funeral ("I envision a lengthy service," he has written. "Bring lunch"); then, while the show is on, he slips away for a Chinese meal. On this occasion, however, Kushner found himself doubly in need of luck. Not only would the opening of *Caroline* mark his return to Broadway after more than a decade but a revised, nearly four-hour version of his play *Homebody/Kabul* was beginning a limited engagement at the Brooklyn Academy of Music.

Kushner had last been represented on Broadway in 1993, with *Perestroika*, the second part of his seven-hour epic, *Angels in America*. The first major play to put homosexual life at the center of its moral debate, *Angels* covered territory that ranged from Heaven to earth, from the AIDS epidemic to conservative politics, encapsulating, in its visionary sweep, the sense of confusion and longing that defined late-twentieth-century American life. "It gave a language to that generation," the director George C. Wolfe, who staged both

Angels in America and *Caroline, or Change* on Broadway, says. "It gave playwrights permission to think about theater in a whole new way. A play could be poetic, ridiculous, fragile, overtly political, sentimental, and brave all at the same time." *Angels* won Kushner two Tonys and a Pulitzer Prize. Last December, HBO aired Mike Nichols's sixty-million-dollar film version, for which Kushner adapted the play and which starred Al Pacino and Meryl Streep. (The film was nominated for twenty-one Emmys and won a record eleven.)

In Kushner's view, however, *Caroline, or Change*—a semi-autobiographical account of the relationship between a Southern Jewish boy, who has lost his mother, and his family's saturnine maid, Caroline—is his best-told story. Based on the "unexpected hidden life" of the Kushner family's maid, Maudie Lee Davis, the script is a radical departure from the standard forms of Broadway musical distraction. With its focus on race, class, and even economics, *Caroline* celebrates the ambivalent, instead of the upbeat. When it opened last year at the Public, it earned a strong critical response, not all of it positive. For some critics, the show's psychological subtlety was hidden beneath the folkloric, seemingly simplistic style of the production. ("*Caroline* might be regarded as the brooding person's *Hairspray*," Ben Brantley wrote in the *Times*.) Kushner felt, he says, "hugely disappointed" and only "cautiously, but definitely, endorsed."

Nevertheless, throughout the winter and into the spring, bolstered by the growing demand of the Public's audiences and by the success of the Nichols film, Kushner worked the phones and called in favors until a consortium of twenty Broadway producers put up five million dollars to move the musical to Broadway. No one was going to get rich, their mantra went, but Broadway would be the richer for it. The Broadway opening meant another round of reviews. "It would be lovely if suddenly there was sort of this Pauline conversion and people were coming and saying, 'I was wrong the first time; it's

great now,' " Kushner said. "But that isn't going to happen. Tomorrow there'll be some wonderful things and also maybe some not-so-
wonderful things. Then we have to take a deep breath and figure out
how we're going to give this a respectable run on Broadway." Kushner
admits that he is "preternaturally, even *prenatally*, thin-skinned."
He says, "I would like to care less about the things other people say
about me, but I can't imagine caring less. I think people pay heavy
prices for armor and callousness." Still, he adds, "it's very hard to
take criticism when it's inept, when it kills the chances of that show
being seen."

For a while, he sat on the low perimeter wall of the Bethesda plaza,
enjoying the scene. His gaze finally came to rest on the blousy bronze
angel in the center of the fountain, which plays an important role
in the finale of *Angels in America*. In the Biblical tale of Bethesda,
an angel appears on the surface of a pool and gives the water healing powers. The statue, Kushner explained, "commemorates the
naval dead of the Civil War. It's the first commissioned sculpture by
a woman in New York—Emma Stebbins, the sister of the parks board
president and a lesbian." He went on, "The other thing I love about it
is that it got terrible reviews when it was unveiled."

Kushner is a purveyor of what he calls "brave art"—"the best sense
we can make of our times." Several weeks before *Caroline* opened
on Broadway, in a debate sponsored by the Classic Stage Company, one of Kushner's great champions, the critic Harold Bloom,
spent the better part of two hours trying in vain to get Kushner to
admit that he was a theological writer. "I'm somebody who believes
in . . . a kind of relationship of complaint and struggle and pursuit
between the human and the divine," Kushner said finally. "And part
of that struggle involves politics. For me, drama without politics is
inconceivable."

He is fond of quoting Melville's heroic prayer from *Mardi and*

a Voyage Thither ("Better to sink in boundless deeps, than float
on vulgar shoals"), and takes an almost carnal glee in tackling
the most difficult subjects in contemporary history—among them,
AIDS and the conservative counter-revolution (*Angels in America*),
Afghanistan and the West (*Homebody/Kabul*), German Fascism
and Reaganism (*A Bright Room Called Day*), the rise of capitalism
(*Hydriotaphia, or the Death of Dr. Brown*), and racism and the civil-
rights movement in the South (*Caroline, or Change*). But his plays,
which are invariably political, are rarely polemical. Instead, Kushner rejects ideology in favor of what he calls "a dialectically shaped
truth," which must be "outrageously funny" and "absolutely agoniz-
ing," and must "move us forward." He gives voice to characters who
have been rendered powerless by the forces of circumstance—a drag
queen dying of AIDS, an uneducated Southern maid, contemporary
Afghans—and his attempt to see all sides of their predicament has
a sly subversiveness. He forces the audience to identify with the
marginalized—a humanizing act of imagination.

Kushner also has what he calls "a boundless appetite" for exploring the dramatic form. An early dance-theater piece, *La Fin de la
Baleine: An Opera for the Apocalypse*—about bad love, the blues, the
bomb, and bulimia—included a woman dancing on point with a tuba
and spouting water from her mouth. *Homebody/Kabul*, which began
with a first-person monologue, morphed into a third-person drama,
moving unexpectedly from closeup to long shot. With its visions and
poetic fulminations, *Angels in America* expanded the expressive
limits of naturalistic theater. Likewise, *Caroline, or Change* used
its visual, sonic, and linguistic vernacular to create a kind of American folk opera, in which the worlds of white privilege and African-
American impoverishment were woven together in a dreamlike
fable that bore the influence of Kushner's friend Maurice Sendak,
with whom he has written a children's book and an opera libretto.

Underneath Kushner's prodigious flow of language is a sense of incantation, which draws the spectator in and compels him to listen. His writing is defined by fluency and excess. He wrote the first draft of the opening monologue for *Homebody/Kabul* in forty-eight hours, *Caroline* in four and a half months, and he had just finished a 283-page draft of a screenplay for Steven Spielberg about the aftermath of the 1972 terrorist attack during the Olympic Games in Munich, which he wrote in three weeks. "I like big, splashy, juicy plays," Kushner says. "I like the audience to feel space to roam around in." (He refers to Samuel Beckett as "that matzoh of a playwright.") In his 1995 collection of essays, *Thinking about the Longstanding Problems of Virtue and Happiness*, Kushner writes, "A good play, like good lasagna, should be overstuffed. It has a pomposity, and an overreach. Its ambitions extend in the direction of not-missing-a-trick, it has a bursting omnipotence up its sleeve."

The swashbuckling quality of Kushner's intellectual aspirations is not borne out by his demeanor. At forty-eight, he is tall, courtly, unassuming, and flat-footed, with a tangle of wiry black curls—his "wackadoo hair," as his friend the director Michael Mayer calls it. He is by nature a "fummfler"—what Sendak calls "the Jewish fumbler who is in perfect control, who uses his comic character to somehow make everyone feel comfortable and loose." He talks extraordinarily fast, with a machine-gun-style delivery that reflects both his swiftness of mind and his nervousness. At the same time, his pace gives him a distinct comic advantage. When delivering the Class Day speech at Columbia University earlier this year, he reminded the students that he had been their fourth choice—after Warren Buffett, Supreme Court Justice Ruth Bader Ginsburg, and Jon Stewart. "I think I should begin by acknowledging your disappointment that I am not Jon Stewart," he said. "Your disappointment that I am not Jon Stewart will last one morning. I am disappointed at not being Jon Stewart every morning of my life." To graduates at Bard, where he was awarded an honorary degree, he observed, "I cherish my bile duct as much as any other organ. I take good care of it. I make sure it gets its daily vitamins and antioxidants and invigorating exposure to news of Antonin Scalia and everyone else working for the Bush family." At Cooper Union, receiving another degree, he began his speech by pronouncing President Bush's words of the previous day: "Thank you and good evening. I'm honored to visit the Army War College. Generations of officers have come here to study the strategies and history of warfare. I've come here tonight to report to all Americans, and to the Iraqi people, on the strategy our nation is pursuing in Iraq and the specific steps we're taking to achieve our goals." He paused, then added, "I just wanted to feel what it felt like to say that."

When Kushner speaks in public, his gambit is often to share with his audience a little secret, some complaint that downplays his own prestige: he's tired; he's nervous; he's unprepared; he's overworked; he doesn't know what to say. "He keeps dismantling himself, reminding himself of how weak he is and how many frailties he has," Nichols says. "He lets you see the vulnerability. It's part of a genius's self-protection."

"I don't look like Keanu Reeves," Kushner said in a 1994 interview. "So when people express an interest, which happens rarely but does . . . I sort of go, 'Well, why?'" Mayer says, "He's very disparaging about his chin, his nose, his weight. You don't imagine him lying on the beach in a bathing suit." Kushner is constantly at war with his body, alternately indulging and starving it. Between 1988 and 1993, when he was writing *Angels in America*, he gained about a hundred pounds. "I used to say, 'I'm pregnant. I'm eating for eight,'" he says. Then, just as dramatically, he shrank himself down.

In 1969, when Kushner was twelve, his mother, Sylvia, learned that she had breast cancer. (After a long remission, she died of inoperable lung cancer, on August 27, 1990.) At one point, when she was in a hospital in New York, he badgered his father, William, to buy him a pocket watch, then had it engraved with the words "Cogito, Ergo Sum" (a motto he'd acquired from Marvel comic books, not Descartes). "A thinker or nothing," he explains. "Because the body, clearly, betrays."

William Kushner, a Southern Jew from Lake Charles, Louisiana, who had studied at Juilliard, had been playing first clarinet with the New Orleans Symphony when he met Sylvia Deutscher, who, as first bassoonist, was one of the first American women to hold a chair in a major orchestra. She had been a professional musician since she was twenty-three. In addition to touring with Sadler's Wells and playing with the New York City Opera, she had recorded with Stravinsky and played at the first Pablo Casals Festival. Kushner says of his mother's music, "That nasal but open-throated, deep wooden vibrato sound echoed through my childhood. I think the idea of fluency made itself felt in me as something musical before it became something lingual. She had huge lung power. She could breathe into a candle flame and control the flicker of it with her breath." He also says, "She saved a good deal of her truthfulness, the things she couldn't say in the quotidian, for her music."

The youngest of four children from a first-generation socialist Jewish family in New York, Sylvia was noisy and emotional. Her father, an early member of the glazier's union, had been fierce and abusive. As a result, according to her sister, Martha Deutscher, Sylvia "was a needy person who was massively insecure about herself." Kushner's older sister, the artist Lesley Kushner, was born, in 1954, with severe hearing loss; she couldn't speak and couldn't easily comprehend what was said to her. Her frustration kept her in a more or less permanent tantrum. To spend more time with her and Tony, William and Sylvia, then in their early thirties and playing for the New York City Opera, decided to move back to Lake Charles, where William could earn a living in his father's lumber business. But Sylvia felt isolated in the South. "Leaving music professionally was very difficult for her," William says. "She hadn't succeeded as an artist," Kushner explains. "There was a sense of the world having not gotten her, and not appreciated her. She was furious about it."

When Kushner was born, in 1956, he entered a family dominated by an atmosphere of regret, disappointment, and, in the case of his older sister, murderous rage. "There was just no way to tell her, no way to make her understand," William recalls of Lesley's rancor over the sudden appearance of her brother. She had to be physically removed from Kushner's third-birthday party; when her father drove her away from the house, she tried to throw herself out of the car. The brutality of her behavior was, William says, "pretty devastating" to Tony—"it gave him a great sympathy with other people who were mistreated." Until Kushner reached high school, he and Lesley were at war. Adding to the tension, according to Kushner, was the fact that Sylvia had different notions of femininity than Lesley, who was a tomboy. "She took you and kind of rejected me," Lesley wrote in a recent e-mail to Tony. "Or as she put it, 'My father was an angry man and you were angry so I gave you to Daddy.'" A third child, Eric, who was born in 1961, absorbed his parents' professional ambitions. "They pushed Eric into music," Lesley says. "Every single week, they would drive him to New Orleans for horn lessons, four hours each way." (Eric is now first horn for the Vienna Symphony Orchestra.)

In 1969, Sylvia underwent a mastectomy, and nine years later William became the maestro of the Lake Charles Symphony—events that changed the family dynamic. While Lesley and Eric gravitated toward their father, Tony maintained the closest bond to Sylvia. From an early age, he'd been a fervent reader of comics—"I wanted to write books, to be an illustrator," he says. He made up his own stories for the comic characters and wrote their dialogue. "Momma read them and would delight in them," Lesley recalls. "She thought they were funny. Everything he said she just found delightful." Tony was equally enchanted by his mother, who had theatrical aspirations. At six, he watched her perform in Arthur Miller's *Death of a Salesman* at the local theater-in-the-round. "As Linda Loman, she changed from my beautiful young mother . . . to an old woman in the course of the evening," he wrote in 1997. "It was terrifying and wonderful. . . . I don't think I ever saw her the same way again." Over the years, he watched Sylvia play Anne Frank's mother, and Beatrice in *The Effect of Gamma Rays on Man-in-the-Moon Marigolds*. "I really think that it was seeing those plays and the special sort of power that her being in them gave to them that started me on a lifelong fascination with the theater," he has said.

Kushner has come to realize that William's love of writing—he and his family were great reciters of poetry and doggerel—was also an important influence on him. But, in his youth, what he got from his father was a sense of worry—the idea "that there was something wrong that he was trying to fix." As a boy, Kushner was not assertive or athletic. "I would become angry with Tony, frustrated with his helplessness," William says. "He wanted something from me that I wasn't giving him," Kushner recalls. William tried unsuccessfully to interest him in chess, ball games, bird-watching, sailing, and an Outward Bound course (they got as far as the orientation meeting). Around puberty, he began to give his son pep talks about sex. Kushner says, "As I got older, he figured it out. He finally said, 'I think you're a homosexual, and I want you not to be a homosexual. I want you to go to a therapist and fix it.' I was about sixteen."

Kushner had known that he was gay for almost a decade. He remembers rubbing the shoulders of his handsome Sunday-school teacher and thinking, Oh, this is fun, and also I shouldn't be doing this. Those impulses sent him through childhood with a sense of fraudulence. "You feel you are unacceptable to everyone, even to your parents, who love you but wouldn't if they knew," Kushner says. His persistent nightmare was of his classmates finding out "and killing me or burning the house down." His high-school friend Tom Tolin, an economist, says, "I remember him sitting in the bleachers and these guys around him giving him a hard time, calling him 'Kush-Kush.' He just sat there with his head buried in a book. It was painful." Kushner recalls, "I hated the kids that I was going to school with, the boys especially—aggressive, nasty, physically intimidating. I didn't know how to get protection, because I was too embarrassed."

For years, Kushner was, by his own admission, a terrible student. Then, to his astonishment, in high school he became a verbal athlete: a champion debater. "I may have been a sissy, but I was not without aggression," he says. "I became this incredibly mean arguer. I would not be defeated." He was also opinionated: in high school, he refused to stand for the Pledge of Allegiance; he leafletted Ku Klux Klan members for George McGovern; as early as junior high school, he alone on his debate team argued in favor of feminism. But his talent gave him, for the first time, a sense of his own power and a society to which he belonged. "I found the smart kids," he says.

As Kushner was finding his lung power, his mother was losing hers. In 1969, following her mastectomy, she was overradiated and developed osteomyelitis in her ribs, some of which had to be removed. "She was in a lot of pain, couldn't laugh, couldn't be hugged, and, of course, she couldn't play the bassoon," Kushner says. Her ambition settled instead on Tony, whose Promethean itch had its origins in her aspirations for him. "It was this huge thing to her if I succeeded," he says. "I don't recall her ever lavishing a huge amount of praise on me, but I remember the thrill in her voice when I told her I had won some debate tournament, or when I got an agent, or when I got a grant or a good review or any indication that what she expected— which was that I would be a successful artist—was going to come to pass. She would simply say, 'Go! Go! Go!' in a crescendo of pitch and volume, when I brought her good news." Speaking of the special connection between Sylvia and her children, Lesley says, "She kind of moved into your skin with you. You couldn't tell if it was what you

wanted for yourself or what she wanted for you. It was a sort of ven-
triloquist sensation." When Kushner was accepted to the graduate
program at New York University's Tisch School of the Arts, Sylvia came to see him a couple of times a year. "She visited with him
and nobody else," Martha Deutscher says. "It was always the two of
them." Once, when Sylvia, Kushner, and Deutscher were having coffee in the Village, Kushner and his aunt began to tease his mother
about some of her attitudes. "She turned to me and said, 'Don't you
turn my son against me!'" Deutscher recalls. "She was not joking.
She didn't want to share him."

When Kushner's play *A Bright Room Called Day* was staged in
London in 1988, Sylvia flew over for the opening. It was panned. "She
collapsed," Deutscher says. "When my mother died, I realized that a
certain degree of my ability to take pleasure in my own accomplishments was gone," Kushner says. "Without her to show it to, to do it
for—a circuit had been broken." Above his writing desk at his country house, in Manitou, New York, is a huge framed copy—signed by
the poet—of Robert Duncan's "My Mother Would Be a Falconress,"
which reads, in part:

> *My mother would be a falconress,*
> *and I her gerfalcon, raised at her will,*
> *from her wrist sent flying, as if I were her*
> > *own*
> *pride, as if her pride*
> *knew no limits, as if her mind*
> *sought in me flight beyond the horizon.*

Sexuality was one of the ways in which Kushner broke away from
his mother and, like the poem's falcon, flew "far, far beyond the
curb of her will." Kushner's parents had hoped that with therapy his
latent heterosexuality could be reinforced. When he was twenty-five,

he called home to tell Sylvia that he was gay. "She cried for a month," he says. "She was just heartbroken by it. I finally said, 'I'm not going to call you anymore until you stop, because it's getting creepy. I feel like I've died.'"

Although he now refers to his "desire-based identity" and an "endlessly raging libido," he had difficulty, at first, accepting his orientation. In his second week as an undergraduate at Columbia, in 1974, Kushner presented himself at the health center and asked to see a therapist. "I'm gay and I want to be straight," he said. He is, he says, "sexually flusterable." "The first time I ever saw two men kiss was when I was a freshman at Columbia and it completely freaked me out," he said in an interview last year. "It still took another three years before I began to come out of the closet." When Kushner did come out, according to the actor Stephen Spinella—who met Kushner in graduate school at New York University, and later starred in *Angels in America*—"he exploded. It was like a train. He was out, out, out."

A decade later, in 1995, Kushner and Michael Mayer, who had also met as students at NYU, found themselves, in the company of such celebrities as Roy Lichtenstein and Bob Hope, at the White House, during the first term of the Clinton administration. Kushner was seated at Al Gore's table. "I wore a triangle made out of pink rhinestones. Gore asked me what it was and I got to explain it to him," Kushner recalls. After dinner, there was a dance. "We were slow-dancing together next to Senator Alan Simpson and his wife, the Gores, everyone," Mayer recalls. "We may be the first men ever to dance together in the White House."

Kushner, in his senior year at Columbia, took Edward Tayler's famous course on Shakespeare. "Tayler taught Shakespeare in a profoundly dialectical way," Kushner says. To understand Shakespeare, Tayler told his students, "you only need to count to two." From him, Kushner learned that everything in Shakespeare was paradoxical and contradictory—and that this collision of opposites was the first principle of drama. He left Tayler's lecture on *Henry IV, Part 1* "shaking and in a fog." He recalls, "I was having trouble breathing. I felt like, Oh, I'm beginning to understand something about life, the idea that a thing can be both one thing and its opposite, that two opposites can exist simultaneously and not cancel each other out. Or they can transform one another through conflict into something new." Kushner had already gravitated toward the stage. He had attended theater and opera in New York, designed sets and props for university productions of *The Fantasticks* and *Marat/Sade*, served for a year and a half as the drama critic of the Columbia *Spectator*, and written his first dialogue in a playwriting class. By the time he graduated, he had also fallen under the spell of Brecht's *A Short Organum for the Theatre*, which set out the playwright's aesthetic for epic theater—his attempt to engage the audience in a play of contradiction that encouraged active critical thought and departed from the passive emotional catharsis encouraged by the Aristotelian principles of drama. "I wanted to *be* Bertolt Brecht," Kushner says. He applied to NYU, and, once there, studied under the German-born director Carl Weber, a Brecht specialist.

In his senior year at Columbia, while directing a university production of Ben Jonson's sprawling epic *Bartholomew Fair*, Kushner had become friends with Kimberly Flynn, a Barnard psychology major from New Orleans, who was working on the stage crew. "We fit together intellectually and, in some ways, emotionally, on a kind of molecular level," he says. Kushner and Flynn went everywhere together; they had no secrets. Flynn had, Kushner says, a "vast appetite for pedagogy—she loves explaining things to people" and was "a great synthesizer." Kushner, in turn, had a vast curiosity. "She led and I followed," he says. "She read Walter Benjamin and told me I should. And Marcuse, Adorno, Horkheimer. I had read some Freud and some Marx, but not nearly as widely." He continues, "As soon as I started writing, or constructing plays, she would read, comment, make suggestions. I would call her my dramaturge, but Kim was that to the power of twenty." Inevitably, though, there were struggles over ownership of ideas. In 1982, Kushner formed a theater company with several people, including Flynn and his first boyfriend, Mark Bronnenberg, to produce *La Fin de la Baleine*, among other plays. Flynn contributed the ideas; Kushner created the stage images, and got most of the credit for the show, which caused some bad feeling between the friends.

In 1984, Flynn was riding in a cab as it sped up the West Side Highway when the car went out of control and off the road, ramming into a tree in Riverside Park. During the next few days at the hospital, Flynn's garbled sentences, her repetitions, and her inability to distinguish left from right indicated to her, even before the doctors confirmed it, that she had suffered brain damage. Just as Kushner's theatrical career was taking off—he was appointed the assistant director of the St. Louis Repertory Theatre in 1985, and became the associate artistic director of the New York Theatre Workshop in 1987—Flynn was stymied, and she directed some of her enormous fury at Kushner. She told *The New Yorker*, "It was hard to deal with how angry I was, and with the idea that I was jealous and that I was in no position to be jealous—I was out of the game." Kushner agonized over moving to St. Louis. "I've had to make the hardest decisions of my life around Kim's illness," he has said. His guilt about her disaster and the difficulty of taking care of her is evident in *Millennium Approaches*, the first part of *Angels in America*. "She was everywhere in it," he says. (He gave Flynn 10 percent of the profits.)

Flynn eventually recovered sufficiently to become a full-time political activist, focussing on environmental issues. But in 1996, right before Kushner began work on *Homebody* and *Caroline*, he and Flynn decided to alter the nature of their friendship. "We tried very hard to figure out a way of staying close," he says. "We were just making each other, by the end, terribly, terribly unhappy." He continues, "It was an important turning point for me." In his cramped one-room office in Union Square, Kushner keeps a photograph of himself with Flynn at Bethesda Fountain.

Kushner's *A Bright Room Called Day*, which is dedicated, in part, to Flynn, crosscut the effect of the rise of Hitler on a group of friends in Berlin in the early thirties with a rant on American politics that linked Fascism with the Reagan revolution. It was meant, Kushner says, as "a warning signal, not a prediction." The play, which was workshopped in New York in 1985, drew little press attention, but the director Oskar Eustis saw one of the performances. "Tony's gift for language was completely apparent," he says. "He was deeply, specifically interested in politics, in political theory and how it related to political practice." He goes on, "*Bright Room* was about what all Tony's plays are about—people who feel themselves inadequate for the demands that history has put on them."

Eustis produced and directed *Bright Room* in 1987 at San Francisco's Eureka Theater, where it had a succès d'estime. But East Coast critics were less enthusiastic when they saw a reworked version in 1991 at the Public Theater in New York. "A fatuous new drama," Frank Rich called it in the *Times*. "An early front-runner for the most infuriating play of 1991." For all its intelligence and ambition, the play was dramatically inert. "I made an outline of twenty-four scenes," Kushner says. "I wrote twenty-four scenes. Each scene was exactly what I put down in the outline." Eustis says, "Tony understood everything else about theater, but he didn't understand about reversals, how that worked. The theater is about change, so change has to happen in the course of the play. In *Bright Room*, you'd have scene after scene of characters coming out, beautifully expressing how they feel, then leaving the stage without changing at all."

After the San Francisco run ended, Kushner began work on what he envisioned as a taut, one-set musical about AIDS. As he started to write for the first time about his own time and place—about homosexuality, AIDS, and right-wing American politics—the play quickly began to exceed his ambitions for it. "For the first-rate artist, there is a moment when he's really getting revved up, and the time just flows into him," Mike Nichols says. "It only happens once. It happens without his awareness at all. He planned nothing. He was just going ahead doing this next thing."

As Kushner was writing *Angels in America*, he gave himself to the characters, not to the outline; instead of imposing an ideology on them, he followed their lead. "I was two acts into *Millennium* and I didn't know what the fuck I was doing," he says. "So I thought, I'm gonna ask a character. Who's most like me? Louis. So I sat down, and I said, 'What is this play about?' I waited a few minutes and then 'Why has democracy succeeded in America?' popped into my head. Then Louis began to qualify himself, as he always did—the first of my big logorrheics. I wrote the line 'There are no angels in America.' Then I wrote on the side to myself, 'Louis is wrong.'" The story seemed to suggest itself from there. Still, the writing wasn't easy for Kushner. "I can't get these people to change fast enough," he complained to Eustis. "At first, I thought he was being self-indulgent," Eustis says. "What became clear is that the difficulty in these people changing *was* the subject of the play."

What eventually emerged was an epic discourse on American life that mixed social reality with theatrical fantasy, naturalism with Judaism and magical realism. It told its story in numerous dialects—camp, black, Jewish, Wasp, even Biblical tones. At the same time, it provided a detailed map of the nation's sense of loss. *Millennium Approaches* charts the heyday of the Reagan presidency through a series of characters who ruthlessly pursue their own sexual and public destinies: Prior Walter, an AIDS patient, is abandoned by his lover, Louis, at the time of his most profound need; Joe, an ambitious bisexual Mormon Republican chief clerk, leaves his lost, pill-popping wife, Harper, for a man; and Roy Cohn, the notorious right-wing lawyer and fixer, a closeted homosexual who is also dying of AIDS, rationalizes his own sensational rapacity. (Cohn, whom Kushner portrayed with Jacobean relish, personifies the barbarity of individualism.) In *Perestroika*, which ends four years after *Millennium*, in 1990, Kushner explores the possibility of progress and community, of redemption. Harper finally accepts the failure of her marriage and sets out on her own. Louis reconciles with Prior—in a scene that took Kushner years to write. "Failing in love isn't the same as not loving," Louis says. "It doesn't let you off the hook, it doesn't mean . . . you're free to not love."

Twenty-four characters, eight acts, fifty-nine scenes, and an epilogue: *Angels in America* turned the struggle of a minority into a metaphor for America's search for self-definition. "I hate this country," a gay black nurse called Belize says to Louis. "It's just big ideas, and stories, and people dying, and people like you. The white cracker who wrote the national anthem knew what he was doing. He set the word 'free' to a note so high nobody can reach it." Although *Angels* was not the first play to explore the AIDS pandemic—Larry Kramer's polemical *The Normal Heart* (1985) preceded it—it was the first to explore the particular claim of the disenfranchised to a romantic vision of America. "We will be citizens," Prior announces to the audience at the finale. "The time has come."

By the fall of 1988, it had become clear that the play would need two evenings to run its course, which meant that Eustis couldn't afford to produce it at the Eureka Theater. "A two-evening show about AIDS by a playwright nobody had heard of. I mean, it was just disastrous," Eustis says. In the end, he chose the play over his theater company. He left the Eureka for the Mark Taper Forum, in Los Angeles, where the artistic director, Gordon Davidson, had agreed to workshop *Millennium* and, eventually, to mount both halves of the play together under Eustis's directorship. The plan took a few years to complete. It wasn't until the spring of 1991, almost a year after

Kushner's mother had died, that he was able to wrench the three-hundred-page draft of *Perestroika* out of himself—in an eight-day writing spree in a cabin on the Russian River, in Northern California, where he holed up with a box full of junk food and cold cuts. "I would sleep two hours at a stretch, get up, write the next scene, and it just went on and on," he says. He finished the play on April 11. "It was maybe one of the happiest days of my entire life," he says.

Millennium had its first major production in Declan Donnellan's version at London's Royal National Theatre, in January of 1992. After a workshop of *Perestroika* at the Taper in May of that year, both parts of the play were performed together for the first time, over two nights, in November. By then, *Millennium* had won the *London Evening Standard*'s award for best play. When the Mark Taper box office opened for the complete production of *Angels*, the receipts broke the theater's record. At the Taper premiere, most of New York's theatrical establishment and its major critics were in the audience. Backstage, Kushner wrote a letter to the cast and pinned it on the bulletin board. "And how else should an angel land on earth but with the utmost difficulty?" it said. "If we are to be visited by angels we will have to call them down with sweat and strain, we will have to drag them out of the skies."

The plays, if not the Taper production, were triumphant. *Angels* was hailed as a turning point for theater, for gay life, and for American culture. Frank Rich, in the *Times*, spoke of *Angels* as "this vast, miraculous play," and *Variety* went even further: "*Angels in America* is a monumental achievement, the work of a defiantly theatrical imagination." In Charlotte, North Carolina—and in university towns in rural parts of Indiana and Texas—fundamentalists staged protests to stop subsequent local productions, a move that Kushner referred to in *The Nation* as "unconstitutional, undemocratic and deeply unwise." (A decade later, when the Nichols film aired on television, the climate of tolerance that *Angels* helped to create was used as a criticism of the play. When Kushner begins writing, he jokes about needing to banish his "inner John Simon," the voice of the acerbic theater critic of *New York*, whom he imagines saying, "You're completely terrible and everything you write is shit." But Simon's attacks—real or imagined—are nothing compared with the grapeshot vitriol of Lee Seigel in *The New Republic*. "*Angels in America* is a second-rate play written by a second-rate playwright who happens to be gay, and because he has written a play about being gay, and about AIDS, no one—and I mean no one—is going to call *Angels in America* the overwrought, coarse, posturing, formulaic mess that it is," Seigel wrote.)

After *Angels in America*, Kushner found it hard to start another play. Nonetheless, he wanted to be useful. He thought about training to be a teacher, a lawyer, a nurse. Instead, according to Eustis, "he reinvented himself as a public intellectual," becoming, among other things, one of America's most prominent gay-rights activists. His essays—some of which began as speeches delivered at gay-rights events—addressed sex, homosexual liberation, and socialism. He argued in defense of the activist and playwright Larry Kramer; of the controversial choreographer Bill T. Jones; and of Matthew Shepard, the Wyoming student who was murdered because of his sexuality. "Campaign for homosexual and all civil rights—campaign, not just passively support," Kushner exhorted the readers of his article on Shepard, which appeared in *The Nation* in 1998. "Matthew Shepard shouldn't have died. We should all burn with shame."

In 1995, Kushner was asked by President Clinton to submit some ideas for the forthcoming State of the Union address. In a letter, Kushner set out the tenets of his version of American democracy: "You need to be the full-blooded liberal Democrat I believe you want to be. You need to tell the American people that you stand for a strong Federal government, fully empowered to regulate industry, protect the jobs and lives of American workers, and protect our *extremely* endangered environment (and our health along with it). You have to declare war on the anti-tax, anti-government movement, calling it what it is: a scam perpetrated against the middle class, the working class and the poor in the interests of maximizing profits for multinational corporations and the very rich. . . . You have to have the courage you had in 1992 to declare that grown-up responsible citizens of a democracy *pay taxes*." He ended his eight-page letter with a plea for social justice: "You must support affirmative action, poverty, education, child care and jobs creation programs, and anti-discrimination legislation which *includes sexual orientation*." (Clinton read the letter, but nothing from it made it into the speech.)

These days, when Kushner visits college campuses, where he can command more than twelve thousand dollars a talk, he is the equivalent of a rock star. (Once when he spoke at Brown, loudspeakers had to be placed outside the hall for the overflow audience; last April, at Middlebury, in the school's auditorium, he spoke to a standing-room-only crowd.) Still, Kushner is a playwright who is an activist, not an activist who happens to write plays. One of the few serious playwrights who know how to write a joke, he is also one of the few political speakers who know how to deliver one. "When Republicans are upset, they fall over. Have you noticed this?" he asked Cooper Union's graduating class last June, before pointing out that Nixon had tripped at a New Orleans trade show, Gerald Ford often fell down stairs, Bush senior had fallen and then vomited on the Japanese prime minister ("And he was the Bush who was *good* at foreign relations!"), and Bush junior had collapsed while eating a pretzel. "What are they expressing, these falling people?" he asked. "A spiritual vertigo? The insupportable weight of all the power and ponderous wealth they have arrogated unto themselves, beneath which their legs eventually buckle? . . . Is it an unseemly yet uncontrollable desire to slither?"

The apotheosis of Kushner's kvetching persona was his appearance, in robe and slippers, at a fund-raising event for Friends in Deed, a charity that provides support for people with life-threatening diseases. Declaiming at a panic-stricken Gilbert-and-Sullivan clip, he read from his "diary":

Wednesday, August 28, 2002. Mike Nichols called today. He wants a favor: Could I write a funny ten-minute play for a benefit for some group he's on the board of, Friends of something-or-other. I love Mike. I would do anything for him. There's no one I admire or adore more in the whole industry, maybe in the whole world. He's really a great man, so busy and yet has the time to organize something like this. Wow! Me sharing the stage with six other incredibly intimidating playwrights of whom I am insanely jealous. Sounds like fun! I'm sure Mike doesn't love Robbie Baitz more than me.

"Two people alone on an empty stage for ten minutes." They can't mean a literally empty stage. Props and costumes, surely. And sets. Maybe five people. Would anyone complain if mine was fifteen minutes long? And does it have to be funny? Funny is hard. I wonder if we get paid for this. . . .

Friday, October 25, 2002. I have a cold. I think I'm gaining weight again. I wish Mike had never asked me. I can't write. . . . Why did Mike ask me? Maybe he was mad at me. Maybe he's resentful that he's been stuck filming my play since before the first Bush administration and he's doing this to humiliate me. I bet he wishes he could call Nora Ephron in for rewrites. . . . My God, my God, why have you abandoned me? STEVE MARTIN is writing one! I'm doomed! It's not a competition. It's not a competition. . . .

Tuesday, November 5, 2002. I couldn't write today, I had to go vote. I am optimistic, no matter what the polls say. Tomorrow,

WITHOUT FAIL, I will write this play. . . . I will be in a good mood after the election. It'll be easier to write then.

Wednesday, November 6, 2002. I wish I was dead. . . .

Wednesday, November 13, 2002. . . . Something will come. ANYTHING. Who cares? It's a benefit, for God's sake! They took my name off the goddam ad! . . .

Thursday, November 14, 2002. Mike just nixed my idea: a Nichols and May reunion. "Two people alone on an empty stage," that's what he said. And then he refuses to cooperate! He's ruined everything. Thanks a LOT, Mike. Schmuck! See if I ever do you a favor again!

If Kushner's laughter is combustible, so, in certain theatrical circumstances, is his temper. Eustis recalls, "One time, after seeing a run-through of *The Illusion*"—Kushner's 1989 adaptation of Corneille's comedy and his first commercial success—"he called me from his apartment after he'd destroyed every piece of furniture." He adds, "There was one particular moment where Tony told me that it was a mistake for me to ever have directed and I should give up the field. That was devastating. I can't tell you how many directors he's tried to get fired at crucial moments in the process." Although Eustis didn't finish the job on *Angels*, Kushner has worked hard to make sure that their relationship didn't end there and he now pays Eustis to dramaturge his plays. "I still consider Oskar one of my most important collaborators," Kushner says. "I spend hours with him weekly when I'm writing, talking about what I'm doing. I send him everything I write."

For Broadway, George Wolfe was brought in to energize the production of *Angels*. "Tony is nothing if not intrusive," Wolfe says. "He completely trusts me, but I think, ultimately, he'd prefer to do it himself." Wolfe admits to occasionally burning Kushner's extensive and fevered production notes, "because I get so hostile about some of the things he writes." As a play gets closer to previews, according to Wolfe, "his mind, not having a lot to do, starts to obsess about everybody else's work. He starts to spin his wheels. Now, the first time you encounter the spinning of the wheels you try to go inside and figure out every single spoke of the wheel. Then, over time, you go, 'Madness, madness, madness, madness, oh, really strong truth. Let me hold on to that.' You have to reach inside the hurricane and pull out that beautiful little baby." Kushner is quite aware that Wolfe thinks he's a few sandwiches short of a picnic. "He doesn't think I'm insane, just a very neurotic person," Kushner says. "We were at dinner somewhere, and he looked at a bouquet of beautiful flowers. 'This is what you're like,' he said, and snapped off one of the smallest flowers. 'Oh, now the whole thing is completely ruined.'"

Kushner's intrusiveness was so pervasive that, while *Caroline, or Change* was in rehearsals, Wolfe and the company made a legend of it. They were working in the large, high-ceilinged Martinson auditorium at the Public Theater—where a roof window looks down on the stage—when a pebble fell down onto the floor. Wolfe joked, "Tony's hiding up there. Jeanine"—Jeanine Tesori, who wrote the music for *Caroline*—"takes food up there so he can eat while watching us 'destroying' his piece."

Taking issue with Kushner is not easy. "It's like standing in front of a Mack truck," Tesori says. A few days before the show was to open on Broadway, she and Kushner still hadn't fine-tuned the epilogue. Wolfe insisted that he needed the scene the following night. Sitting at a table in her studio, Tesori said to Kushner, "It's too long."

"No, it's not," he replied. "Sometimes you need length. *Angels* is full of places that shouldn't work but do, and they're long."

"I don't care what worked in that," Tesori said. "That's not this. It's too long."

"Well, we're just gonna have to agree to disagree."

"Well, we're just gonna have to stare at each other till one of us does something," Tesori said.

For ten minutes or so, Kushner and Tesori stared at each other in silence.

"Finally, he conceded, 'Well, maybe we can move the first line?' " Tesori recalls. "I said, 'Maybe we could.' Then he started shifting."

In May, Kushner broke his usual pattern and agreed to attend the Broadway opening of *Caroline*, along with Mark Harris, his partner of six years, whom he married in a ceremony on April 27, 2003. (They were the first same-sex couple to have their wedding announced in the "Vows" column of the Sunday *Times*.) By the time the couple took their seats at the Eugene O'Neill—they were in row T of the orchestra, the seats farthest from the stage—they had already consumed their lucky sesame noodles and dumplings and Kushner had successfully sung "Begin the Beguine." The lights went down, and Kushner leaned forward, with his chin in his hands, to watch as the reimagined drab basement of his childhood home came into view and Caroline, played by Tonya Pinkins, entered with an armful of laundry to broadcast the mood of the brooding household:

Nothing ever happen underground
In Louisiana
'Cause they ain't no underground
In Louisiana
There is only
Underwater.

When the show was over, the audience, including Kushner, stood and cheered. Then he slipped into the aisle, where he, Tesori, and Wolfe, with their arms around each other and their heads touching, jumped up and down in a huddle. A few minutes later, for the first time on an opening night, Kushner took a bow from the stage.

He made a dismissive flourish to the crowd with his left hand, then disappeared into the back row of the cast. Afterward, when the rehearsal light was up and only a few people lingered in the orchestra, Kushner looked at the ropes and winches and out at the empty auditorium. "Western civilization can't have been so terrible if it made a machine like this," he said. "It really is a great gadget."

The joy of the opening dissipated in the following weeks under the pressure of the awards season, which was likely to decide the commercial future of the show. The prospect of competing in the musicals category rattled Kushner, who saw *Caroline* as "more like a play." In an e-mail, he wrote, "*Caroline* has as much in common with the shows it's up against, some of which I really like, as marquetry has to do with Olympic tobogganing. It makes me nuts." In the end, *Caroline* won only one Tony, losing the awards for best musical and for best book to *Avenue Q*, a jaunty show with puppets. But by the time *Caroline* got its closing notice, in mid-July—its final Broadway performance was on August 29—Kushner had fought his way through the gloom. "I'm devastated but fine," he said. "I can't join in with the general lamentation over the wretched state of Broadway, which has never really been in any other kind of state." (*Caroline*, at least, has had a second life at the Ahmanson Theatre, in Los Angeles, and will open this month in San Francisco.)

On a hazy afternoon in late June, Kushner and I drove to his country place in Manitou, in the Hudson Valley, a two-story house, with forest-green shingles and a red door, shaded on all sides by towering maples and oaks. Through the sloping trees, the river was visible. Amtrak's Hudson Line hugged the shore, and every twenty minutes or so a train hurtled by, blaring its presence. Kushner barely registered the sound. "I always write best here," he said. "It reminds me of Louisiana, in that it's so verdant." He went on, "Inside me, it's like a fist unclenching."

For Kushner, the house has other happy associations. When he

found it, six years ago, he had been ready to renounce New York altogether. "I thought, Fuck this," he says. "I'm just giving up on men. It
hasn't happened. It's not going to happen. I'll give up and move out
of the city." Kushner closed on the house in March of 1998; on April
16 of that year, at a party given by Michael Mayer, he met Harris,
a droll and intelligent man, seven years his junior, and an editor at
large at *Entertainment Weekly*. "Tony had this lovely combination
of brazen confidence, enthusiasm, and huge insecurity that I found
appealing," Harris recalls. A few days later, Kushner invited Harris to dinner at his place and prepared about five pounds of pasta.
"This was so Tony," Harris says. "It was like a cauldron the size of a
chemical-waste container on his stove. He bought a focaccia the size
of a tire. He'd made a salad that could comfortably feed ten. I was
completely terrified. 'This guy is gonna think I hate his food because
he's given me a week's worth.' "

Kushner stayed in the city, but Manitou is still his favorite retreat.
In his house, he has gathered pictures of Sylvia and her bassoon and
of William and his clarinet, as well as the last photograph taken of
his maternal great-grandparents in Vilnius before the Holocaust.
Even the light fixtures outside his front door carry a memory of
the past—they are from Temple Sinai, his childhood synagogue, in
Lake Charles. Above his desk, in a cabin at the bottom of the garden,
where he goes to write, hangs a photograph of Tennessee Williams,
smiling over a bottle of wine. Harold Bloom told Kushner recently
that Williams "is your most distinguished ancestor in the American
drama and one who I think you'll wind up rivalling." The two playwrights share, at least, a belief that struggle is the natural order of
things. "I'm deeply aware of what developmental psychologists call
'optimal frustration,' " Kushner says. "The way children learn is
that the task they have in front of them is always a little too difficult
and forces a degree of concentrated angry attention. It should be a
struggle. It's fun to struggle. We're born to it."

Just as he was leaving Manitou, Kushner got a call from a distraught Larry Kramer, whose play *The Normal Heart*, recently revived at the Public, had failed to find Broadway backing. Kramer was calling to say that the producers were closing the show that night. Kushner paced the driveway, commiserating, and they agreed to lament together over dinner. "We'll meet up and set ourselves on fire," he said.

A couple of weeks later, Kushner was back at work, mixing his activism with his art. For a MoveOn.org fund-raiser last summer, he went back to *Only We Who Guard the Mystery Shall Be Unhappy*, a play-in-progress that depicts Laura Bush attending an after-school reading program for dead Iraqi children. For the event, he added a second scene, in which the First Lady, an admirer of Dostoyevsky's writing, comes onstage to debate the play's literary merits with the playwright himself. Since the first scene was published in *The Nation*—the first play that the magazine has printed in its 139-year history—Patricia Clarkson, Marcia Gay Harden, and Vanessa Redgrave have all played the role of Laura Bush, who was invited to read the part herself. (Her office did not respond.)

Kushner likes to collect amusing tidbits about political figures. According to his research, Supreme Court Justice William Rehnquist has led judges and lawyers in sing-alongs of "Dixie"; Judge Jay S. Bybee, who wrote a controversial memo justifying torture, plays in an all-kazoo orchestra; and President Bush refers to the First Lady as "my lump in the bed." In the new scene of *Only We Who Guard*, Kushner, in full "fummfle," brings this up. "So I guess my point is that we're all like you," his character says to Laura Bush. "That we're all being fucked by your husband." The First Lady takes umbrage and gets up to leave. As a parting shot, she scolds Kushner. "Using the stage, the theater, ART! For, for tawdry propagandizing? You oughta be ashamed of yourself," she says.

"I always am," Kushner replies. ∎

—January 3, 2005

Angels in America

High on a hill in downtown Los Angeles, the thirty-six-year-old playwright Tony Kushner stood watching an usher urge the people outside the Mark Taper Forum to take their seats for the opening of *Angels in America*, his two-part "gay fantasia on national themes." It was the premiere of the play's long-awaited second segment, *Perestroika*, which was being performed, together with the first part, *Millennium Approaches*, in a seven-hour back-to-back marathon. "I never imagined that this was going to come out of sitting down in 1988 to write what was supposed to be a two-hour play about five gay men, one of whom was Mormon and another was Roy Cohn," Kushner said. "The level of attention that's being paid to the plays is completely terrifying." On the first day the Taper opened its box office for Kushner's twin bill, it took in $32,804, far exceeding the previous record in the theater's distinguished history; and just last week *Millennium Approaches*, which ran for a year at the Royal National Theatre in England, won the *London Evening Standard*'s award for best play. Driving to the Taper for his opening, Kushner said, he had thought, If I have a fiery car crash, the play will probably be really well received and no one will dare trash it, and it would be this legendary thing. Now Kushner was experiencing the actual rush of first-night terror: he couldn't feel the pavement under his feet. "I feel like I'm walking on some cushion, like dry sponge," he said. "Unsteady. Giddy."

Every playwright has a ritual for opening night. Some playwrights walk. Some drink. Some tough it out and watch from the back of the theater, silently coaxing the players over every production obstacle. Kushner takes himself away for a Chinese meal; in the case of this doubleheader, he'd need two meals. He had already taped his opening-night ticket into his journal. He'd fitted himself out with a lucky ceramic lion given him by his mother and with a medal of the Virgin Mary from Majagure, in what was formerly Yugoslavia. He had one more thing to do. "Once the curtain goes up, I sing 'Begin the Beguine'—it's the longest pop song without a chorus," he explained, shouldering a blue backpack. "I have to sing it *well* from start to finish. If I can get through the whole thing without fucking up the words, it's going to be OK." I left him to it.

Inside the 742-seat auditorium, the Taper's artistic director, Gordon Davidson, shmoozed with the first-nighters like a rabbi with his congregation. Over the twenty-five years of Davidson's stewardship, the Taper has generated a prodigious amount of theater work, some of which has invigorated Broadway and Off Broadway. Although the local press likes to bite the hand that feeds it, and periodically snaps at Davidson, no other American regional theater approaches the Taper's creative record. Recently, Davidson and his theater seem to have had a second lease on creative life, giving George C. Wolfe's innovative musical *Jelly's Last Jam* its first production and staging Robert Schenkkan's *The Kentucky Cycle*, which was the first play to win a Pulitzer Prize without being put on in New York. With *Angels in America*, which Davidson workshopped, and into which he has already sunk $1.3 million of the theater's budget, the Taper is poised for another scoop. Davidson worked the room, handing out butterscotch candies, as is his opening-night custom, and smiling the smile that has launched a few hundred shows but none more brazenly ambitious or better produced than Kushner's. The occasion felt more like a feeding frenzy than like a first night. Robert Altman was there, checking out the play as movie material. A good proportion of the New York theater's high rollers seemed to be there, too, eager to get a piece of Kushner's action: JoAnne Akalaitis, of the Public Theater, with whom Davidson will produce the cycle in New York in February; Rocco Landesman, of Jujamcyn; the Broadway producers Margo Lion and Heidi Landesman; and a host of critics, including

Frank Rich, of the *Times*, and Jack Kroll, of *Newsweek*. As the house-lights dimmed, Davidson found his seat and glanced at the copy of *Moby-Dick* that Kushner had given him as an opening-night pres-ent. "I felt it was appropriate for the occasion," Kushner's inscrip-tion read. "It's my favorite book, by my favorite writer, someone who spent years pursuing, as he put it in a letter to Hawthorne, 'a bigger fish.'"

Just how big a fish Kushner was trying to land was apparent as the lights came up on John Conklin's bold backdrop of the facade of a Federal-style building, leached of color and riven from floor to ceiling by enormous cracks. The monumental design announced the scope and elegant daring of the enterprise. It gave a particular sense of excitement to the evening, and bore out one of Kushner's pet the-ories. "The natural condition of theater veers toward calamity and absurdity. That's what makes it so powerful when it's powerful," he said before he decamped to Chinatown. "The greater the heights to which the artists involved aspire, the greater the threat of complete fiasco. There's a wonderfully vibrant tension between immense suc-cess and complete catastrophe that is one of the guarantors of the-atrical power." From its first beat, *Angels in America* exhibited a ravishing command of its characters and of the discourse it wanted to have through them with our society.

Kushner has not written a gay problem play, or agitprop Sturm und Schlong; nor is he pleading for tolerance. "I think that's a terri-ble thing to be looking for," he told me. Instead, with immense good humor and accessible characters, he honors the gay community by telling a story that sets its concerns in the larger historical context of American political life. "In America, there's a great attempt to divest private life of political meaning," he said. "We have to recog-nize that our lives are fraught with politics. The oppression and sup-pression of homosexuality is part of a larger political agenda. The struggle for a cure for AIDS and for governmental recognition of the seriousness of the epidemic connects directly to universal health care, which is connected to a larger issue, which is a social net." Set in 1985, at the height of the Reagan counter-revolution, *Millennium Approaches* maps the trickle-down effect of self-interest as Kushner's characters ruthlessly pursue their sexual and public destinies. Louis, unable to deal with illness, abandons his lover, Prior, who has AIDS; Joe, an ambitious, bisexual Mormon Republican legal clerk, abandons his dippy, pill-popping Mormon wife, Harper ("You, the one part of the real world I wasn't allergic to," she tells him later); and Roy Cohn, in his greed, is faithless to everybody. "There are no angels in America, no spiritual past, no racial past, there's only the political," Louis says, in one of the idealistic intellectual arabesques meant to disguise his own moral and emotional quandary, which Joe Mantello's droll characterization both teases and makes touching. Louis invokes Alexis de Tocqueville, and it's Tocqueville who put his finger on that force of American democracy whose momentum creates the spiritual vacuum Kushner's characters act out. "Thus not only does democracy make every man forget his ancestors, but it hides his descendants and separates his contemporaries from him," Tocqueville wrote. "It throws him back forever upon himself alone and threatens in the end to confine him entirely within the solitude of his own heart."

This isolation has its awesome apotheosis in the dead heart of Roy Cohn. "Hold," Cohn barks into the phone—his very first word. Turning to Joe (Jeffrey King), whom he's singled out as a potential "Royboy," he says, "I wish I was an octopus, a fucking octopus. Eight loving arms and all those suckers. Know what I mean?" This is a great part, which calls out of Ron Leibman a great performance. Roaring, cursing, bullying, jabbing at the air with his beaky tanned face and at the phone with his cruel fingers, he incarnates all that is raw, vigorous, and reckless in Cohn's manic pursuit of power. "Love; that's a trap. Responsibility; that's a trap, too," he tells Joe while trying to set him up as his man inside the Justice Department and spell out the deep pessimism behind his rapacity. "Life is full of horror; nobody escapes, nobody; save yourself." With his rasping, nasal voice swooping up and down the vocal register, Leibman makes Cohn's evil incandescent and almost majestic. ("If you want the smoke and puffery, you can listen to Kissinger and Shultz and those guys," he confides to Joe at one point. "But if you want to look at the heart of modern conservatism you look at me.") Cohn is the king of control and the queen of denial. He tells his doctor when he learns he has AIDS, "Homosexuals are men who in fifteen years of trying cannot get a pissant anti-discrimination bill through City Council. Homosexuals are men who know nobody and who nobody knows. Does this sound like me, Henry?"

But Cohn's hectoring gusto doesn't overwhelm the piquancy of the other stories. Kushner's humor gets the audience involved in the characters, and the play works like a kind of soap opera with sensibility, whose triumph is finally one of design rather than depth. Kushner doesn't impose personality on ideas but lets ideas emerge through careful observation of personality. He listens to his characters and, with his percolating imagination, blends the quirky logic of their voices with their hallucinatory visions. Prior (played by Stephen Spinella) dances with Louis in a dream. In her lovelorn grief, Harper (Cynthia Mace) fantasizes herself in the Antarctic, and later Joe comes hilariously alive, stepping out of a pioneer tableau, during Harper's vigil in the Diorama Room of the Mormon Visitors' Center in New York City. Ethel Rosenberg, who owed her execution to Cohn's single-handed, improper intervention with the presiding judge, appears at Cohn's bedside. These hauntings are sometimes dramatized as projections of parts of the self that have been murdered in order to survive. "Are you a ghost?" Prior asks Louis as he sways in the arms of his guilty lover to the tune of "Moon River." "No," Louis says. "Just spectral. Lost to myself." The final, ambiguous image of

Millennium Approaches, which brings the play to a halt, if not to a conclusive end, is the appearance of an angel to Prior while he languishes in his sickbed. "*Very* Steven Spielberg," Prior says as the set parts and the angel (Ellen McLaughlin) swings down on wires, to proclaim him Prophet and tell him tantalizingly that his great work is about to begin. With the help of jets of smoke, Pat Collins's evocative lighting, and the strong directorial hands of Oskar Eustis and Tony Taccone, the audience is brought bravoing to its feet. The production is far superior in every scenic and performing detail to the celebrated English version.

*P*erestroika is the messier but more interesting of the two plays, skillfully steering its characters from the sins of separation in the eighties to a new sense of community in the embattled nineties. Though *Perestroika* should begin where *Millennium Approaches* breaks off, it opens instead with an excellent but extraneous preamble by the oldest living Bolshevik, bemoaning this "sour little age" and demanding a new ideology: "Show me the words that will reorder the world, or else keep silent." Kushner can't keep silent; but, while his play refuses ideology, it dramatizes, as the title suggests, both the exhilaration and the terror of restructuring perception about gay life and about our national mission. The verbose Angel that appears to Prior now turns out in *Perestroika* to be the Angel of Death or, in this case, Stasis. She takes up a lot of time broadcasting a deadly simple, reactionary message of cosmic collapse. "You must stop moving," she tells Prior. "Hobble yourselves. Abjure the Horizontal, Seek the Vertical." But, once the characters get back on the narrative track of the plot, *Perestroika* finds its feet and its wisdom.

The real drama of *Perestroika* is the fulminating, sometimes funny battle the characters wage in trying to deal with catastrophic loss. Here, as in *Millennium Approaches*, Cohn, the fixer, is shrewdly placed at the center of the argument. Cohn will not accept loss, always stacking life's deck to maintain his fantasy of omnipotence. "I can get anyone to do anything I want," he tells his black male nurse, Belize (played with panache by K. Todd Freeman), before picking up the phone to blackmail an acquaintance for the drug AZT. "I'm no good at tests, Martin," he tells the acquaintance. "I'd rather cheat." And later, with his stash of AZT in a locked box in the foreground, he crows at his nurse like a big winner: "From now on, I supply my own pills. I already told 'em to push their jujubes to the losers down the hall." All change requires loss, and Cohn's power is a mighty defense against change. His emptiness is colossal. Significantly, Cohn dies mouthing the same words that introduced him in *Millennium Approaches*. Kushner shows his other characters growing through an acceptance of loss. "Lost is best," Harper says, refusing to take Joe back after his fling with Louis, and going with the flow of her aimlessness. "Get lost. Joe. Go exploring." Prior, too, has finally wrestled control of his life and what remains of his momentum from the Angel of Stasis. "Motion, progress, is life, it's—modernity," he says, unwilling to be stoical. "We're not rocks, we can't just wait. . . . And wait for what? God." His task is to make sense of death and, as he says, "to face loss, with grace."

Part of this grace is humor, the often heroic high-camp frivolity that both acknowledges suffering and refuses to suffer. When Cohn brags to his nurse, "Pain's . . . nothing, pain's life," Belize replies, sharpish, "Sing it, baby." Kushner uses laughter carefully, to deflate the maudlin and to build a complex tapestry of ironic emotion. He engineers a hilarious redemption for the politically correct Louis, who is forced by Belize to say Kaddish over Cohn's dead body in order to steal the remaining AZT to prolong Prior's life. Louis prays with Ethel Rosenberg's ghost over the body, and they end the Hebrew prayer with "You son of a bitch." And at another point in his emotional turmoil Prior turns to Louis and accuses him of having taken a Mormon lover. "Ask me how I knew," Prior says. Louis asks, "How?" Prior rounds on him: "Fuck you. I'm a prophet." Even Cohn gets off a cosmic joke, making a last-minute appearance from Purgatory as God's lawyer. "You're guilty as hell," he growls at the Deity. "You have nothing to plead, but not to worry, darling, I will make something up."

Perestroika ends by celebrating community, not individualism, auguring with eerie serendipity the spirit of the new Clinton era. Even the monstrous Cohn is acknowledged as a fallen victim by the brotherhood. "The question I'm trying to ask is how broad is a community's embrace," Kushner says. "How wide does it reach? Communities all over the world now are in tremendous crisis over the issue of how you let go of the past without forgetting the crimes that were committed." In the play's epilogue, which jumps to 1990, Kushner confronts the audience with the miraculous. Prior has lived four more years. He sits in Central Park in animated conversation with his friends. Then, turning the conversation up and down at his command (Kushner's homage to the ending of *The Glass Menagerie*), Prior steps out of the play world to talk directly to us. It's an extraordinarily powerful (if haphazardly staged) moment, in which the community of concern is extended by the author to the human family, not just the gay world. "Bye now," Prior says. "You are fabulous, each and every one, and I love you all. And I bless you. *More life.* And bless us all."

Backstage, Kushner stood dazed and rumpled among a crowd of well-wishers. "I've been working on this play for four and a half years," he said. "Tonight, a whole era in my life comes to an end. It's been an incredibly strange ride." His exhaustion and the happy fatigue of the cast members, who lingered in doorways, seemed to bear out part of Kushner's opening-night message, which was pinned to the stage-door bulletin board. "And how else should an angel land on earth but with the utmost difficulty?" it read. "If we are to be visited by angels we will have to call them down with sweat and strain, we will have to drag them out of the skies, and the efforts we expend to draw the heavens to an earthly place may well leave us too exhausted to appreciate the fruits of our labors: an angel, even with torn robes, and ruffled feathers, is in our midst."

Kushner and the excellent Taper ensemble had made a little piece of American theater history on that cloudless California night. *Angels in America* was now officially in the world, covered more or less in glory. It was a victory for Kushner, for theater, for the transforming power of the imagination to turn devastation into beauty. ∎

—November 23, 1992

Caroline, or Change

There are moments in the history of theater when stagecraft takes a new turn. I like to think that this happened for the American musical last week, when Tony Kushner's *Caroline, or Change* (at the Public), a collaboration with the composer Jeanine Tesori and the director George C. Wolfe, bushwhacked a path beyond the narrative dead end of the deconstructed, over-freighted musicals of the past thirty years. In place of the slick grab bag of boulevard distraction, *Caroline, or Change* offers the complexity of psychology and of history. Set in 1963, in a suburban enclave of Lake Charles, Louisiana, the musical concerns two stranded souls: eight-year-old Noah Gellman (Harrison Chad), who is suffering from the twin griefs of a recently deceased mother and a newly acquired stepmother, and his family's saturnine maid, Caroline Thibodeaux (Tonya Pinkins). Kushner's bittersweet autobiographical saga settles for no easy emotional solutions; it takes the musical back to storytelling, to a moral universe, to a dissection of American society, and to folklore—that is, the lore of the folk, both black and white, which Zora Neale Hurston called "the boiled-down juice of human living." Hurston, who had worked as a maid, argued as early as 1950 that, in order to rid themselves of the feelings of difference that inspire dislike and fear, people needed to bear witness not to the " 'exceptional' Negro" or to the "quaint" Negro but to "how the average behaves." The most extraordinary of this musical's many thrills is its ability—through an idiom in which the Washer, the Dryer, the Radio, and even the local Bus are incarnated and sing to Caroline—to plumb and to honor the ordinary.

The Gellmans' basement—an architectural oddity in the Gulf area, which is below sea level—is Caroline's humid purgatory. "They ain't no underground / in Louisiana / There is only / underwater," she sings in her drab warren. The terrain is a metaphor for Caroline's internal landscape: she is literally and figuratively swamped. "Doing laundry underground / for thirty dollars every week," she continues, as the Washer and the Dryer join in. "Thirty dollars every week / And I am mean and strong and tough but . . . / Thirty dollars ain't enough." A divorced and illiterate thirty-nine-year-old mother of three, Caroline moves through life under a terrible gravitational pull of woe and resignation. Rigor and righteousness are her defenses against envy. Unmoved and unmoving, she is as mean as a snake, striking out at the world around her. A coed acquaintance, Dotty (Chandra Wilson), gets her head bitten off for her collegiate style ("I don't like the way you do / You change"); Caroline's bright, outspoken daughter, Emmie (the perky Anika Noni Rose), is warned to mute her ambitions ("Don't give yourself options / Most folks lives without 'em"); Noah is rebuked for his curiosity about Caroline's life ("That ain't your bisness . . . / You a nosey child"). With a perpetual scowl and a voice that parses every innuendo of regret and rage, Pinkins never backs off from her character's sulfurous disappointment.

Noah is fascinated by the uncompromising Caroline in part because he, too, lives in a kind of suspended animation that he can't fathom. Superbly played by Chad—a pale pudding in a plaid shirt and black sneakers—he is a spectral presence in his own house. He moves unseen by his self-involved father, Stuart (David Costabile), who is as mournful as the clarinet he plays for a living; by his floundering, Northern stepmother, Rose (the expert Veanne Cox); and, of course, by his dead mother, who has vanished, according to his curt father, into the cosmic void. "Your mother is dead / and there is no God," Stuart tells his son. When Noah first pokes his curly head through the basement door and sees the sullen Caroline at work, he declares in a voice filled with wonder, "Caroline! / the President of the United States / Caroline who's always mad! / Caroline who runs everything! / Caroline who's stronger than my dad!" In Noah's collapsed world, Caroline's stony soul has a weight he can feel; it's a boundary he is certain of. She embodies the anger that he can't show to his family or to himself. Except for sharing a cigarette from time to time, though, Caroline wants nothing to do with Noah. "How come you like me?" she asks. "I ain't never nice to you." Noah tries to explain that her fierce will gives him courage:

> *My mama liked you!*
> *I do too!*
> *You're implacable,*
> *Indestructible, Mama said.*
> *I'm always sad.*
> *I like it that you're always mad*
> *And I can tell you like me too.*
> *At least I think you do.*

Kushner's lyrics are suggestive in their simplicity; if they don't always sit easily on Tesori's blues notes, their jaggedness makes the passion and the pain behind them all the more powerful.

The musical's title plays on the word "change." While the Kennedy assassination and the civil-rights struggle percolate at the edges of the story and inform it, the change on which the play immediately focusses is the quarters, nickels, and dimes that Noah is forever leaving in his pockets. This chump change ends up being Caroline's windfall. When she finds the money in his laundry, she is instructed by Rose to take it. What was intended as a parental lesson in financial responsibility is turned by Noah into a strategy of connection. "Caroline takes my money home! / Now I know what they talk about / at the Thibodeaux house, at suppertime," the boy sings. "Before it was a mystery. / Now they count my quarters and / they talk about me!" The coins become a paradigm of capitalism: instead of buying Caroline's labor, Noah stumbles onto a way of buying her attention. In Wolfe's excellent staging, Caroline's economic necessity is played off against Noah's emotional needs. Noah, the self-confessed "stoopnagle" who fantasizes about being "Noah Thibodeaux," hilariously tries to join in the hand-jiving playground palaver of Caroline's two sons, Jackie and Joe (the adorable Kevin Ricardo Tate and Marcus Carl Franklin). The boys sing about Wonder Woman: "Stronger than anyone, six times as pretty / An eagle brassiere with a wing on each titty!"

When Noah leaves a twenty-dollar Hanukkah dividend from his grandfather in his pants pocket and Caroline claims it, however, the master-servant relationship suddenly asserts itself. Noah demands his money back; in his panic, he blurts out a racist comment. Caroline gives him the money and a good-bye; in her humiliation, she walks off the job and stays away for five days. "That money reach in and spin me about / my hate rise up, rip my insides out," she sings in a sensational aria in which her pride fights a losing battle with her financial desperation. She can't afford to be out of work, but the price of survival is emotional death. In Pinkins's electrifying rendition, all the connotations of the word "change" come together: "Pocket change change me, / can't afford loose change, can't afford change." In order to lose her anger, she has to lose her sense of self; to cauterize herself against disappointment, she kills her heart. "What else God give me an arm for?" she sings, disappearing before our eyes.

"SLAM go the iron / SLAM go the iron. / FLAT! / FLAT! / FLAT! / FLAT!" The song is an act of psychic demolition. By the end of it, a deep detachment—"the muteness of slavery," Hurston called it—has fallen over Caroline like a permanent shadow.

Although the conclusion of the show somewhat haphazardly suggests that Emmie will carry the example of her mother's steely will into the new activism of her generation, there is no upbeat future for Caroline. She has put herself beyond dreams. To the end, she is wary and stolid and clear-eyed. "Will we be friends then?" Noah asks her when she comes back to work. "Weren't never friends," she says. Caroline, like the show, pulls no punches. On an intellectual level, Noah may not understand the import of what Caroline says to him; on an emotional level, however, they are bound together, wound to wound, as Caroline spells out:

> Someday we'll talk again
> But they's things we'll never say
> That sorrow deep inside you,
> It's inside me too,
> And it never go away.
> You be OK.

As Noah listens to Caroline's litany of losses, he asks wistfully, "Do you miss sharing a cigarette?" Caroline answers with heartbreaking directness: "You bet I do, Noah. / You bet, you bet." There are no hugs, no hands across the sea of cultural difference, no sentimental gestures of redress, just a stunning acknowledgment of the chasm between the two characters. Their worlds are negotiable, Kushner makes clear, but not bridgeable. *Caroline, or Change* gives the inconsolable a mature song, illuminating both worlds without condescending to either. ∎

—December 8, 2003

4

DAVID MAMET

When I met David Mamet this summer, he made me the gift of a Boy Scout knife. On one side of the knife was the Scout motto: "Be prepared." The words, which invoke both prowess and paranoia, seemed to sum up the twin themes of Mamet's work, and of his guarded life. We were sitting in the back room of his headquarters, on the second floor of a two-story yellow clapboard building on Eliot Street in Cambridge, Massachusetts, at a table with a large Second World War poster hanging over it which read, "Loose Talk Can Cost Lives! Keep It Under Your Stetson." There was no identifying name on the bell to the front door or on the office door. You had to feel your way along until you found Mamet hidden away, which is how it is with him. Mamet, who is masterly at communicating his meanings in public, is prickly in private. He is a small but powerfully built man; in the stillness of his presence and in the precision of his sentences, he exudes an imposing, specific gravity. "Fortress Mamet" is how Ed Koren, the cartoonist and Mamet's Vermont neighbor, refers to the emotional no-go area that Mamet creates around himself, and I was acutely aware of this hazardous moat as Mamet eased into a chair across the table from me, wearing his summer camouflage: a khaki baseball cap, khaki shorts, and a purple-and-brown Hawaiian shirt. Over the years, Mamet has adopted many fustian public disguises to counterpoint a personal style that Albert Takazauckas, the director of his first Off Broadway hit, *Sexual Perversity in Chi-*

cago, in 1976, characterizes as "blunt, blunt, blunt." He adds, "It's his lovely cover." As the star of Chicago's booming Off Loop theater scene in the early seventies, Mamet affected Che's guerrilla look: fatigues, combat boots, a beret, and, for good measure, a cape. After his Pulitzer Prize for *Glengarry Glen Ross* (1984), his play about salesmen in a cutthroat real-estate competition, Mamet assumed a Brechtian swagger: cigar, clear plastic eyeglass frames, and open collar, which consolidated in one iconic image the powerhouse and the proletarian. Now, in his mellow middle age, Mamet has forsworn the cigar and adopted the posture of rural gent: work boots, bluejeans, Pendleton shirt, and trimmed beard. In all these guises, the one constant is Mamet's crewcut, which dips like a tree line over the craggy promontory of his broad forehead and gives him an austere first appearance. "The crewcut . . . is an *honest* haircut," he has written. "It is the haircut of an honest, two-pair-of-jeans working man—a man from Chicago."

Mamet is certainly a workingman, even though, at $1.5 million a movie, he's far from a wage slave. He has written twenty-two plays, six collections of essays, two novels, and fourteen films, five of which he also directed. He belongs in the pantheon of this century's great dramatists; he has done for American theater at the end of the century what his hero, the iconoclastic sociologist Thorstein Veblen, did for American sociology at the beginning: provide a devastating, often hilarious new idiom to dissect the follies of American life. Mamet's muscular imagination strips dialogue of literary nicety and robs plot of that naturalistic decoration which has progressively tamed theater. His plays, though rooted in reality, are fables, whose uniqueness lies in their distinctive music—a terse, streamlined orchestration of thought, language, and character which draws viewers in and makes them work for meaning. No other American playwright, except perhaps Tennessee Williams, has ranged so widely. (Mamet is the only major American playwright ever to succeed as a screenwriter.) Three of his movies—*The Edge* (with Anthony Hopkins and

Alec Baldwin), *Wag the Dog* (with Robert De Niro and Dustin Hoffman), and *The Spanish Prisoner* (with Steve Martin), which he also
directed—are being released this year, which turns out, on November 30, to be his fiftieth.

Mamet claims he doesn't lose his temper, but anger still defines
him. "He's a coiled snake," his forty-six-year-old sister, the screenwriter Lynn Mamet, says. To those who have passed the test of loyalty, Mamet is an amusing, endearing, vigilant friend. "He was and
continues to be one of the funniest and silliest people I've ever met,"
says the comedian Jonathan Katz, who has been Mamet's best friend
since their days at Goddard College, in Vermont, and with whom
Mamet conceived the film *House of Games*. "He was a master of disguises. We would have this running gag. Whenever one of us was
meeting the other guy at the airport, we would be in disguise. One of
my favorite disguises was when he was sitting in the airport with a
paper bag on his head and smoke coming out of it. He was smoking a
cigar under the paper bag." In public conversation, however, Mamet
is courtly and wary; his style of discourse is not so much straight talk
as Indian wrestling. He wrong-foots the listener with a curious brew
of slang and erudition, mixing words like "ain't," "marvy," "jolly,"
"vouchsafe," "desuetude" in the same breath. There's a jaunty smile
in these sentences, but a smile with cold teeth. "Oh, goody gumdrops," he said when I told him I'd be able to join him in Cabot,
Vermont, where he owns a farmhouse and a hundred-acre parcel of
rolling land. "Goody gumdrops from the gumdrop tree."

As I attempted to ask him unwelcome questions about his childhood, the presence of the Boy Scout knife on the table reminded
me of the knife that the distraught ten-year-old boy John flashes
in Mamet's autobiographical masterpiece *The Cryptogram*—a play
about the betrayal of the boy by his parents. He is on the stairway
looking down at the living room, where his mother, abandoned
by his father and unable to meet his emotional needs, sits in the tortured last beat of the play. At whom, exactly, is the boy's murderous

energy aimed, himself or others? His gesture foreshadows the life
of the playwright, who learned to turn aggression into art: the knife
became a pen. Knives are tools of creation as well as of destruction,
and Mamet likes to whittle. His specialty is carving animal figures
for his three daughters—Willa (fourteen) and Zosia (nine), both
from his twelve-year marriage to the actress Lindsay Crouse, which
ended in 1991; and Clara (three), from his marriage, in the same
year, to the Scottish actress and singer Rebecca Pidgeon. The knife
as an ambiguous symbol of penetration is the central metaphor of
Three Uses of the Knife, a collection of Mamet's lectures about theater to be published later this year, in which he recounts an anec-
dote first told by the blues singer Huddie Ledbetter, better known
as Leadbelly, who once said, "You take a knife, you use it to cut the
bread, so you'll have strength to work; you use it to shave, so you'll
look nice for your lover; on discovering her with another, you use it to
cut out her lying heart." In its affecting irony, this progression illustrates for Mamet the essential elements of dramatic structure; it
also demonstrates, he writes, "the attempt of the orderly, affronted
mind to confront the awesome."

    If Mamet felt affronted now, it was by my request that he turn
back to the memory of his past. "My childhood, like many people's,
was not a bundle of laughs. So what?" he said. "I always skip that
part of the biography." After a while, he added, "This might help.
There's a movie I'm hoping to do in the fall about making a movie.
The female movie star is having a breakdown. She's crying. She says,
'I never had a childhood.' The director puts his arm around her. He
says, 'I had one. It's no big deal.'"

Despite his disclaimer, the dominating themes of Mamet's work—
the sense of not belonging, the imperative of speaking out, the
betrayal by authority—evolve directly out of his childhood. He was
the firstborn son of two handsome, highly intelligent, upwardly
mobile first-generation Americans, Leonore (Lee) and Bernie Mamet,

whose families were Ashkenazi Jews from Russia and Poland. "Are you an only child?" I asked Mamet when we first met, in 1983. "Yes," Mamet said, "except for my sister." "We lived in an emotional hurricane," says Lynn Mamet, the extrovert of the pair, who still speaks to her brother almost every day from her home on a scorched hillside canyon in Los Angeles. She adds, "We were safe for each other." Until their parents divorced bitterly, in 1958, when David was eleven and Lynn was eight, they lived on Euclid Avenue in Chicago's South Shore Highlands, in a capacious three-story red brick house that stood as a kind of totem to the Mamet family's self-invention. "My life was expunged of any tradition at all. Nothing old in the house. No color in the house," Mamet told me. "The virtues expounded were not creative but remedial: let's stop being Jewish, let's stop being poor." Lynn says, "There was a great deal of pressure for us to be the best Americans we could be. There was no room for us to make mistakes." She and her brother lived in fear of the ferocity of parental expectations—what Lynn calls "hoops of fire." "It was succeed or die," Mamet says.

Bernie Mamet, a tough labor lawyer who represented over three hundred unions, and once argued—and won—a case before the Supreme Court, preached an exacting semantic gospel of precision, nuance, and observation. "The map is not the territory" was one of Bernie's mantras, which voiced his bedrock belief that nothing was all black or all white. He hectored his children to listen "with the inner ear," and, according to his second wife, Judy Mamet, played games with them to build up their powers of observation and memory. " 'Stickler' is a soft word for my father's attachment to the absolute necessity of expressing yourself correctly," Lynn Mamet says. "It's just that what was correct changed on a daily basis." In the crossfire of family conversation, David grew quickly into an agile sparring partner for his parents, and also learned to listen defensively. "From the earliest age, one had to think, be careful about what one was going to say, and also how the other person was going to respond," says Mamet, whose celebrated "ear for dialogue" evolved out of listening for danger. "In my family," he once said, "in the days prior to television, we liked to while away the evenings by making ourselves miserable, solely based on our ability to speak the language viciously."

Indeed, Mamet's prolific output and his compulsion to master skills (writing, directing, piano playing, sharpshooting) are a daily reiteration of competence in adulthood which seeks to redress a childhood whose litany was "You are not living up to your potential." Lee, who Mamet says "kind of created this wonderful persona of elegance," also had a short fuse and a sharp tongue. "You just didn't know where it was coming from—she could blow at any minute," Lynn says. "When they harvested the bipolar patch, she ripened first." To Lynn, Lee said, "If only I could have had a pretty daughter"; and, to David, "I love you but I don't like you." Lee had elusive verbal ways of parrying her children's demands, and this mystification, where what was being said wasn't what was meant, brought with it a sense of helplessness and frustration. Mamet demonstrates the shifting sand of this dynamic in *The Cryptogram*, where John, the distressed young boy, can't make himself seen or heard by his self-involved mother, Donny. John is suicidal, and when he confesses his dark thoughts to her she seems to acknowledge them but then both literally and figuratively wanders away:

> JOHN: Do you ever wish you could die? (*Pause.*) It's not such
>   a bad feeling. Is it?
> DONNY: I know that you're frightened. I know you are. But at
>   some point, do you see . . . ? (*Pause. Exits.*) (*Offstage*)
>   John, everyone has a story. Do you know that? In their
>   lives. This is yours.

The boy's anxiety goes uncontained; throughout the play he is almost never touched or held. "They were not tactile," Lynn says of her parents. "If they were tactile, it was like being touched by a porcupine." Mamet is more forgiving: "They didn't have a clue," he says, explaining that Bernie and Lee had their children in their early twenties. Still, his portrayal of John's demoralized childhood and narcissistic mother connects to the notion of the "corrupt parent" that Mamet later outlined in one of his essays: "The corrupt parent says: 'If you wish to be protected you must withhold all judgment, powers of interpretation, and individual initiative. *I* will explain to you what things mean, and how to act in every situation.'" David himself was always in trouble for speaking up at home. "He would tilt at every fucking windmill," Lynn says. At such moments, his mother would say, "David, why must you *dramatize* everything?" "She said it to me as a *criticism*," Mamet told me. "I found out—it took me forty years to find out—that rhetorical questions are all accusations. They're very, very sneaky accusations."

Between his mother's mixed messages and his father's high standards, Mamet, who from an early age was a voracious reader but a wretched student, grew up believing he was stupid. "I was like the professor in *Oleanna*"—his controversial play about a university professor accused by his pupil of sexual harassment—"who all his life had been told he was an idiot, so he behaved like one," Mamet says. "I just always assumed people assumed I was gonna come to a bad end." In *Jolly*, an autobiographical one-act play that is part of three meditations on his past called *The Old Neighborhood*, which opens on Broadway this month, he addresses the psychological sleight of mind by which parents project their own inadequacy onto their children, as a grownup brother and sister sit talking about the sins of their parents:

BOB: . . . That's their way. That's their way. That's their swinish, selfish, *goddam* them. What *treachery* have they not done, in the name of . . .
JOLLY: . . . I know . . .

BOB: . . . of "honesty." God *damn* them. And always "telling" us we . . .

JOLLY: . . . yes

BOB: . . . we were the bad ones.

In Mamet's family, the helpless collusion of children with their
parents' sadism was acted out in good times as well as bad. In his
essay "The Rake" he recounts one such incident that took place after
the family went out to dinner. "My stepfather and mother would
walk to the car, telling us that they would pick us up," he writes. "We
children would stand by the restaurant entrance. They would drive
up in the car, open the passenger door, and wait until my sister and I
had started to get in. Then they would drive away. They would drive
ten or fifteen feet and open the door again, and we would walk up
again, and they would drive away again." He continues, "They sometimes would drive around the block. But they would always come
back, and by that time the four of us would be laughing in camaraderie and appreciation of what, I believe, was our only family joke."

In 1958, Lee married Bernie's law associate—a close family friend,
also named Bernie. She had moved out of the house with the kids,
and they ended up in Olympia Fields, on the outskirts of Chicago,
which Mamet called New South Hell. She didn't inform the children
of her wedding plans. "We'd been in Florida with my father," Lynn
says. "We came home. They said, 'How was your weekend?' We said,
'OK. How was yours?' They said, 'We got married.' David responded,
'So what else is new?' and went into the other room." He was profoundly distressed by his impulsive, fist-pounding stepfather, who
occasionally punched Lynn, and broke the glass top of the kitchen
table several times with his explosions of temper, "so the table was
associated in our minds with the notion of blood," Mamet writes in
"The Rake." His anxiety about this new "cobbled-together family"
is powerfully evoked in his description of one afternoon in Olympia

Fields, when, as his sister remembers it, she came out to call him in to dinner while he was raking leaves. He hit Lynn in the face with the rake. "He opened up the whole side of my face," Lynn, who still has a scar above her lip from her brother's outburst, says. "If you could pick a single incident in David's life which has constantly eviscerated him, it was possibly that act, which also explained a great deal to him internally. How he felt: his anger, his rage, his confusion, his life." But neither child—David out of guilt, Lynn "out of a desire to avert the terrible punishment she knew I would receive"—would fess up to Lee about what had happened. "My mother pressed us," Mamet writes. "She said that until one or the other answered, we would not go to the hospital; and so the family sat down to dinner, while my sister clutched a napkin to her face and the blood soaked the napkin and ran down onto her food, which she had to eat; and I also ate my food, and we cleared the table and went to the hospital." In a way, Mamet's iconoclasm as a writer is a means of understanding and of finding words for his fury. It also, he says, "stills two warring needs—the need to be accepted and the need to be revenged."

At the age of fifteen, after a series of blowups with his mother and stepfather, Mamet returned to Chicago to live with his father, on Lake Shore Drive. Although he was offered an airy, ample room, he chose to live in the maid's quarters near the back door, which made escape easy.

But Mamet could never escape his father. "Bernie Mamet was clearly the intense relationship of David's life, and there seems to be no aspect of the relationship of father to son that they did not explore to hell," says the director Gregory Mosher, who is Mamet's foremost interpreter and has collaborated with him on fifteen plays over the years. Mamet looked like his father; his skepticism and his savage view of entrepreneurial capitalism came from Bernie, who, according to Judy Mamet, regularly "railed against the inequities of commerce," and advised his son, "Don't trust an expert." Mamet remembers this theme being driven home in one of his father's early jokes: "A guy takes his son. He puts him on the mantelpiece, and to his son he says, 'Jump!' Kid says, 'Daddy, I'm frightened.' Father says, 'I'm your father. You kidding? Jump!' Kid jumps. Father steps back and the kid falls on the floor. Dad says, 'That's the first lesson. Don't trust anybody.' "

As a playwright and theorist, Mamet has adopted his father's advocate style of thinking against the system. "He was a winning lawyer. He believed in being smarter than the other guy and working harder than the other guy," says Mamet, who based the character of Jimmy Hoffa, in his 1991 film, on Bernie. "One of Dad's lines I put in the movie," Mamet says. "He said, 'Some people say that the client's gotta pay you to do your best. The client's not paying me to be best, the client's paying me to win.' "

Bernie, who had wanted to go on the stage himself as a young man, was deeply competitive even with his son. "He came to see *American Buffalo*," Mamet says. "He said, 'When are you going to chuck all this nonsense and go to law school?' " "He was a very hard man," says Sheila Welch, who observed them during the opening of *Edmond*, in 1982, and later became the producer of Mamet's Atlantic Theater Company. "He was very, very critical. I think he taunted Dave, almost like Mozart's father—you know, 'You have to be better'—but in a sense he secretly didn't want David to be better than him." For about four years in the eighties, the father and the son stopped talking to each other, but they made up after the birth of Mamet's second daughter, in time for Mamet to cast his father as a terrorist in his movie *Homicide*. The occasion is memorialized in a photo of them on the set, in which Bernie sits slumped at a table in the foreground, wearing a leather jacket, and above him, dominating the frame, David stands on a radiator giving orders. On July 5, 1991, Mamet stood over his father for the last time, at his funeral. (Bernie had died of cancer, at the age of sixty-eight.) He spoke at the service; afterward, as is the custom in Jewish ceremonies, the mourners filed forward one by one to shovel a spadeful of dirt onto the casket from a huge mound of earth beside the grave. Mamet had his turn. But when the gravedigger picked up the shovel to finish the job Mamet took the shovel back from him without a word and started to fill in the grave himself. It was a blistering summer day. After a while, he took off his jacket, and the wilted mourners watched for nearly forty minutes while he buried his father.

Mamet graduated from Goddard College, which he calls "sex camp," in 1969. By 1975, he was famous. His psychological makeup then, as now, was "essentially that of an unsure student who has finally discovered an idea in which he can believe, and who feels unless he clutches and dedicates himself to that idea, he will be lost." At sixteen, he had become a dogsbody and bit player at Bob Sickinger's innovative Hull House Theater, in Chicago. "It was the first time in my confused young life that I had learned that work is love," he wrote later. He was by then well read in the literature of avant-garde drama, especially the plays of Harold Pinter. "It was stuff you heard in the street," he says. "It was the stuff you overheard in the taxicab. It wasn't writerly." He adds, "Pinter was sui generis. He was starting out with his vision of the world, and he was going to write it." (Pinter would later champion Mamet. "He sent me, unforgettably, *Glengarry Glen Ross*, with a note saying 'There is something wrong with this play. What is it?' " Pinter recalls. "I wired him immediately. 'There is nothing wrong with this play. I'm giving it to the National.' ") Mamet began playwriting in his final year of college, after a summer vacation spent working as a busboy and odd-job man at Second City, Chicago's improvisational theater, and watching comic players like Peter Boyle, Robert Klein, and David Steinberg; the quick cuts and blackouts of their revue format became part of Mamet's early punchy minimalism. "For the next ten years," he said, "none of my scenes lasted more than eight minutes."

Mamet had also taken off his junior year to study acting in New

York with the renowned Sanford Meisner, at the Neighborhood Play-house. Meisner believed that "every play is based upon the reality of doing," that "good acting comes from the heart," and that "there's no mentality in it." He urged his students to "fuck polite"; he devised the Word Repetition Game, in which two actors play off each other, each repeating exactly the words the other has just said, in order to bring out real emotion and impulsive shifts in behavior. Mamet wasn't chosen by Meisner to go on to the next year of classes, but when he began writing plays his distinctive fractured cadences and overlapping dialogue gradually transferred the rigors of the Word Repetition Game from the stage to the page. "I think the rhythm of his dialogue actually comes from the repetition exercises," says Scott Zigler, who has been a member of the Atlantic Theater Company since its inception, in 1985, and is directing *The Old Neighborhood* on Broadway. "The rhythm is simply the rhythm of being in the moment." For instance, *Sexual Perversity in Chicago* begins:

> DANNY: So how'd you do last night?
> BERNIE: Are you kidding me?
> DANNY: Yeah?
> BERNIE: Are you fucking kidding me?
> DANNY: Yeah?
> BERNIE: Are you pulling my leg?
> DANNY: So?
> BERNIE: So tits out to here so.

But if it took Mamet a few years to absorb Meisner's teaching into his writing, it took him no time to incorporate Meisner's rogue ideas into what Mamet called his South Side Gypsy attitude. His senior-year project was his first completed play, *Camel*—a revue composed of thirty-four blackout bits based on "the more potent pieces in my journal." (It's a method that Mamet still uses, mining material from the daily ledgers he keeps.) He had never directed a play "in my whole sunlit lifetime," he wrote in the project notes. But, he went on, "I remembered that Acting is Doing. So I just started doing." Mamet had the chutzpah to charge fifty cents admission, a gesture that ruffled a lot of hippie feathers. "I wanted to communicate to the public at large that this was going to be no ordinary theatrical event," he wrote. Also, he added, "I felt like it." The last sentence of the project report served as Mamet's envoi to college life: "It's time for the actor to find another big rock to push up that long hill."

Everyone, including Mamet, conceded that he was not an actor. But in 1970, after undertaking various acting stints and odd jobs, Mamet found himself back in Vermont—this time teaching acting, first at Marlboro College and then, in 1971, at his progressive alma mater, which had no grades, no requirements, no tests. "So here comes Mamet dressed in tailored sailor pants, this tight shirt, with impeccably done hair. He walks like he's got a ramrod up his butt, and he just laid down the law," the actor William H. Macy, who is one of Mamet's closest friends, and who was nominated for an Academy Award last year for his performance in *Fargo*, says of Mamet's arrival in class. "The first thing he said was 'If you're late, don't come in. If you're not prepared, don't do the class. If you want to learn to act, I'm the guy who can teach you. If you're not here for that, leave.' The class just looked at each other, going, 'Who is this fucking guy?'" Macy continues, "But he won us over. He was not egotistical in any way. He just had this unshakable confidence." Mamet was in the habit of fining latecomers a dollar a minute and then burning their money. After about a year and a half of study, according to Macy, Mamet "walked in one day and said, 'I've written these plays.' It was *Sexual Perversity in Chicago*"—a comedy about the vagaries of dating which, a few years later, would become Mamet's first hit. "In that incarnation," Macy goes on, "it was a bunch of blackouts— about twelve of them. A role for everyone. Who knew he even wrote?"

———

Mamet himself seems never to have doubted his playwriting ability. "I was just sure," he says. "I mean, how are you sure you got a fastball?" He adds, "Writing was something I could do. I figured, Well, if you fuck this up, you deserve everything that's gonna happen to you." When Mamet was about twenty-two, a friend sent a draft of *Sexual Perversity in Chicago* to Mike Nichols, who had recently made *Carnal Knowledge*; he said he'd have turned it into a movie right away except that he'd just made one like it. "I thought, Oh my God, these guys actually believe in me," Mamet says. "I better start working right now. I better have another play and another play after that." In 1972, he formed the St. Nicholas Company, in Vermont, with Macy and another of his students, Steven Schachter; in 1973, they shifted their base to Chicago, where, Mamet writes, "the air feels new, and all things still seem possible."

Mamet, who worked in the Windy City only between 1973 and 1977, is either Chicago's most famous New York playwright or New York's most famous Chicago playwright. "Chicago is very, very different from New York," he says. "In Chicago, you lived with your theater company. The money that you made you shared. If you didn't work together, you starved. You weren't in it for an individual career." Chicago's earthiness extended to its pragmatic literary tradition, which carried with it "an intolerance for the purely ornamental." "Performance art—whatever the hell that may be—would have been completely foreign to Chicago, which is very meat and potatoes," Mamet says. "If it's a comedy it would be a good idea if it were funny." Mamet and his cohorts, who soon added the actress Patricia Cox to their founding group, lived by their wits. They helped fund their productions by giving acting classes. "We invented this myth of the Chicago theater scene," says Gregory Mosher, who considers having bumped into Mamet in 1975 "the central fact of my life." "What made the Chicago theater scene was that no one cared. The audience didn't care. They were profoundly indifferent to everything we did."

In those days, Mamet resided and wrote at the Lincoln Hotel. "His room was the size of a closet. He had no belongings. It was Spartan like you can't believe," Macy says. But "from the very first day I met him," a Chicago playwright, Alan Gross, recalled in the *Chicago Tribune* in 1982, "David told me he was an important American playwright. . . . He was completely self-encapsulated. He knew exactly what he wanted to do and what was expected of him; he had a great rap, a great act." According to the program note for the St. Nicholas's debut production, the company was named for the patron saint of "mountebanks, prostitutes, and the demimonde." And Mamet had a bit of the mountebank in him. "He was very, very fast on his feet," the company's first literary manager, Jonathan Abarbanel, says, referring to what he calls Mamet's "intellectual Barnumism." Abarbanel once told the magazine *Chicago*, "He would be talking—'As Aristotle said, blah blah.' Or, 'I was rereading Kierkegaard the other day.' I remember saying, 'Aristotle never said that! You weren't reading Kierkegaard!' And he'd go, 'Sshhh! Don't tell anyone.' "

While Mamet waited tables, drove taxis, and cleaned offices to support his theatrical habit, he turned Chicago into a kind of raffish playground. "He always had very good luck with the ladies," Macy says. "Oh, man, smooth as silk." (One of Mamet's best come-ons—"Is anyone taking up an inordinate amount of your time these days?"—is memorialized in *Sexual Perversity in Chicago*.) He explored the city's gritty corners, whose vernacular he savored and kept note of. Among his actor friends, Ed O'Neill had been a football star at Ohio University; Dennis Farina had been a policeman; and J. J. Johnston, a walking lexicon of underworld phrase and fable who was from the South Side, had been a bookie. Having been raised on high culture and hated it, Mamet was drawn to "people who don't institutionalize their thought."

"Dave got hit with the gangster bag early," Johnston, who recalls telling him about the old-time hoods, says. "These crooks, most of them, have pipe dreams. They can't do anything right. Like they say, these guys would fuck up a two-car funeral." Mamet, who has written a lot about criminals, including his screenplays for *The Untouchables*, *Things Change*, and an upcoming movie about Meyer Lansky, sometimes socialized with them and saw their pathos at first hand. "They're entrepreneurs," he says. "They speak their own language. Like many people engaged in violence, they're sentimental." He tried to talk his way into a daily North Side poker game of petty thieves, which was held in a junk shop owned by a fence called Kenny. "I came out several times, hung out, they didn't want to let me sit down," he says. "Then, one day, I wasn't there. They said, 'Where were you yesterday? We missed you.' I said I was teaching drama at Pontiac Correctional Center. It turned out later that many of them had done time at Pontiac. So they started calling me Teach, and they let me sit down on the game." It was out of this subterranean milieu that Mamet made his first masterpiece, *American Buffalo*—a tale of betrayal cloaked in the comedy of a botched heist, set in a Chicago junk shop. When he handed the script to Mosher, a stripling director just out of Juilliard who was in charge of the Chicago Goodman Theatre's Stage 2, Mosher told him he would read it over the weekend. "You don't need to read it," Mamet said. "Just do it." He paused, then added, "Tell you what. I'll put five grand in escrow, and if the play doesn't win the Pulitzer, keep the money."

Mamet didn't win that year's Pulitzer and never made good on the promise, but *American Buffalo* made his name. It was produced on Broadway in 1977, giving Mamet his first real payday; it was the beginning of his being able to make a living as a playwright. Though it was only his second full-length play, it was a great leap forward in his storytelling. As late as 1991, Mamet maintained that it was "the most structurally competent" of his plays. "It has the form of a classical tragedy," he said then. As he put it to me recently, "That's the only thing I ever really worked hard at in my life: plotting. Do it and do it, and do it again." He added, "I'm not looking for a feeling—I'm looking for an equation. Given the set of circumstances, what does it end up with? How is that inevitable? How is that surprising?"

What Mamet had excavated from the junk-shop poker games and captured in *American Buffalo* was the notion of a world and an idiom composed of waste. In the swagger of small talk he found a metaphor for the spiritual attrition of American capitalism. His small-fry characters hilariously emulate the badinage of big business. "You know what is free enterprise," says Teach, the punk who kisses himself in on a plan to rob the coin collection of a man who recently paid the junk-shop owner ninety dollars for a nickel. "The freedom of the *Individual* . . . to Embark on any Fucking Course that he sees fit . . . in order to secure his honest chance to make a profit. . . . The country's *founded* on this, Don. You know this."

Mamet's rhythm gave the words and the pauses an unusual emotional clout. "Dave's dialogue is a string of iambs, which can often be broken down into fives," Mosher says. "For example, 'But all I ever ask (and I would say this to her face) is only she remembers who is who and not to go around with *her* or Gracie either with this attitude: The Past is Past, and this is Now, and so Fuck You' is, I believe, twenty-seven iambs in a row." Joe Mantegna, one of Mamet's favorite actors, talks about seeing Mamet "tapping it out with his pen" while actors speak their lines. Sometimes Mamet could be even more insistent. "He sits in the back of the house going, 'Pick up, pick up, pick up!'" Mosher says.

In Mamet's plays, speech becomes the doing that reveals being; identity is dramatized as each character's struggle to speak his meaning. For instance, Teach, who is full of big plans, can't think clearly. When he makes his sensational entrance cursing "Fuckin'

Ruthie," who has insulted him for eating a piece of toast off her plate, we hear a syntax that reels backward like his fearful, scrambled mind:

> Only (and I tell you this, Don). Only, and I'm not, I don't think, casting anything on anyone: from the mouth of a Southern bulldyke asshole ingrate of a vicious nowhere cunt can this trash come.

Over the years, so many people have written Mamet to complain about the "language" in his plays that in the eighties he had a form letter printed which read, "Too bad, you big cry baby." Once, while talking on the phone in the kitchen to the producer Fred Zollo, Mamet reached into the refrigerator to help his daughter Willa get a Fudgsicle. "Oh, fuck," he said. "Daddy, don't use that language," Willa laughed. Mamet replied, "That language put that fuckin' Fudgsicle in your mouth." In his plays Mamet relishes slang for its impoverished poetry; it helps to create the sense of energy and of absence which his work dissects. In *Sexual Perversity* it's the absence of self-awareness (" 'Cunt' won't do it," Deb says to the inchoate Danny. " 'Fuck' won't do it. No more magic. . . . Tell me what you're *feeling.* Jerk"); in *American Buffalo* it's the absence of beauty and possibility ("There is nothing out there," Teach says after trashing the shop. "I fuck myself"); in *Glengarry Glen Ross* it's the absence of community and calm ("Fuck *you.* That's my message to you. Fuck you and kiss my ass," Shelly "the Machine" Levene crows at Williamson, the guy who gives out the property leads, after making what he fondly thinks is a sale). Out of the muck of ordinary speech—the curses, interruptions, asides, midsentence breaks, and sudden accelerations—Mamet carefully weaves a tapestry of motifs which he sees as "counterpoint." "The beauty of the fugue comes from the descant, from the counting," he says. "The melody line is pretty damn simple.

Anyone can write that." When he composes, Mamet says, he doesn't picture the characters onstage; he hears them. "The rhythms don't just unlock something in the character," he says. "They *are* what's happening."

Until Mamet emerged, American commercial theater was primarily a literary, naturalistic theater, where words were a libretto for the actor's emotions, and where the actor determined the rhythms. To be successful, the author had to become invisible. But Mamet brought the author's voice back onto the stage; his ideas about acting protect the author's voice at the expense of the actor's invention. "The words are set and unchanging. Any worth in them was put there by the author," he writes mischievously in *True and False*. "If you learn the words by rote, as if they were a phone book, and let them come out of your mouth without your interpretation, the audience will be well served." This is, to say the least, controversial. "It's completely nuts," says the director Karel Reisz, whose films include *Saturday Night and Sunday Morning* and *The French Lieutenant's Woman*. "In order to get what you want from the other actor, you have to invent, color, invest it with your own feelings. I think the notion of separating words from actions is very odd; words are part of the action. It's the reason why the shows he directs are so poor. The element of believability is not there; you have the sense of automata reciting the words."

Mamet, like Pinter or Beckett, is perhaps not the best interpreter of his own vision. (*The Cryptogram*, for example, was given an excellent English production by Mosher which Mamet did not see, and was directed by Mamet, first in Cambridge and then in New York, without the same impact.) But once he had defined his voice he was determined to defend it. He even traded punches with the actor F. Murray Abraham during the New York production of *Sexual Perversity in Chicago* when Abraham rejected Mamet's tempo in his line readings. "He was like a man on a mission," says Fred Zollo, who met Mamet in those early years and went on to produce most of his major plays as well as many of his films. "I just wanted to be so far ahead," Mamet says. "I didn't want to look back and find somebody gaining on me. If I couldn't write a play, I'd write a movie or I'd write a poem or I'd direct something or I'd teach a class or write a book. I didn't care." He continues, "I ain't gonna go home."

In 1976, Mamet moved to New York, married into show-biz aristocracy—Lindsay Crouse was the daughter of Russel Crouse, who, with his partner Howard Lindsay, wrote such Broadway smash hits as *Life with Father* and *The Sound of Music*—and got down to work. During this period, he began supplementing his playwriting with screenwriting. He got his first assignment through Crouse, who was on her way to audition for Bob Rafelson's 1981 remake of *The Postman Always Rings Twice*. He told her to tell Rafelson that "he was a fool if he didn't hire me to write the screenplay," he says. "I was kidding, but she did it." Rafelson called Mamet and asked why he should hire him. "I told him, 'Because I'll give you either a really good screenplay or a sincere apology.'" He also wrote *The Verdict*, and by 1982 he was at work on *Glengarry Glen Ross*, which had its debut at London's National Theatre and then went on to become a huge hit on Broadway. Crouse, who starred in such films as *Slap Shot* and *Places in the Heart*, for which she was nominated for an Oscar, "understood the joy and glamour of show biz," the playwright John Guare says, "and she had integrity." Guare remembers walking with her in Vermont: "She said to me, 'Just look at him. Do you realize that this man has made himself? He's been given no help.' I understood David's sense of will through her pride in it. She was so sublimely proud of him—until she wasn't." But in the years they were together Crouse was essential to him. "She saw herself as a creative partner, and in some ways she probably was," Sheila Welch says. She adds, "David wasn't very smooth socially. Lindsay had social graces.

David learned how to present himself in the theater world from her." Mamet was now properly seen as well as heard. "That's why I love the theater," a character says in *Edmond*. "Because what you must ask respect for is yourself." If he hadn't found the theater, Mamet has said, "it's very likely I would have become a criminal—another profession that subsumes the outsider, or, perhaps more to the point, accepts people with a not very well formed ego and rewards the ability to improvise."

"Injury has given David enormous energy," Sidney Lumet, who directed *The Verdict*, says. "I have no idea where it comes from, but there's a sense of 'I've been screwed.' A lot of the movies are very much about being had." In fact, all Mamet's movies, including the recent crop, and most of his major plays are about betrayal. Many of them revolve around con artists, those picaresque urban hunter-gatherers who scour the postindustrial wasteland in search of both surplus and leisure, and around con games, which give his sense of betrayal a dramatic form. Mamet himself has performed a mentalism act at county fairs, and when he was in college he shilled for his friend Jonathan Katz, then a nationally ranked Ping-Pong champion. "We would stage a game for money between him and me, and I would let him win," Katz says. "He wouldn't give me a rematch. I'd get 'upset,' but some other guy would give me a rematch, having just seen me beaten by David playing badly." The magician and master card manipulator Ricky Jay says of Mamet, "He has what a hustler has. He has 'grift sense.' It's what makes his plays work." In *House of Games* (1987), the first movie that Mamet both wrote and directed, the con illustrates the dilemma of trust. "I 'used' you. I did. I'm *sorry*," Mike, the con man, says to his mark Ford, who has caught him out. "And you learned some *things* about yourself that you'd rather not know." He continues, "You say I Acted Atrociously. Yes. I did. I do it for a living." Writers do the same in the service of their story, but with this difference: their lies are like truth. Mamet sees a parallel to the con game in writing for the theater. The con of performance is to rob the audience not of money but of its preconceived notions. "The trick is leaving out everything except the essential," Mamet explains. "As Bettelheim says in *The Uses of Enchantment*, the more you leave out, the more we see ourselves in the picture, the more we project our own thoughts onto it."

The con trick has a still more abiding pull on Mamet's imagination: it reverses the parental situation. In the con, the public is put in the role of the helpless child, while the con artist is the parent who knows the game and controls all the rules and the information. The whole enterprise is an assertion of omnipotence and a refusal to admit helplessness, which speaks to something deep in Mamet's nature. At the finale of *House of Games*, Mike is held at gunpoint by Ford, who has shot him twice. Ford says, "Beg me for your life." But Mike, a con man to the last, won't. He'd rather die than be infantilized and surrender his sense of autonomy. Ford shoots him again. "Thank you, sir, may I have another?" Mike says as Ford fires three more shots into him. In real life, Mamet also controls the rules of his game: he is the agent of all action, all answers, all interpretation. Even Mamet's instructions to actors, which demystify the notion of character ("There *is* no character. There are only lines upon a page"), are a way of insuring that the play's meaning and invention stay with him. "He controls the actors with an iron hand, in the rhythms and little quarter words and half words and stammers," Mike Nichols, who uses Mamet's work in his acting classes, says. "He says '*You vill do vhat I say!*' more than any writer that's ever written for the theater, with the possible exceptions of Lillian Hellman and Pinter. For the actor to force his life through this iron control leads to such exciting things." It can also sometimes flatten and dehumanize performances, as it did Lindsay Crouse's in *House of Games*. But as a film director Mamet has progressed from that static, unsure first effort, which one critic accurately observed was shot "like an Army training film," to the fluid, well-paced achievement of *The Spanish Prisoner*, in which a con trick played on a credulous company man becomes a moral lesson about how the getting of wisdom equals the getting of skepticism.

About every eighteen months, Mamet likes to direct a movie. "When I'm making a movie, I'm just about as happy as I can be," he says. "I'm playing doll house with my best friends in the world." He oversees these occasions with patriarchal good humor and consid eration. "He's an embarrassingly stand-up guy," the producer Art Linson says. "He expects nothing from people. So when somebody does something, the slightest gesture, he's truly moved." Every night after shooting, Mamet goes among the crew and thanks each member personally. His sets are exceptional for their congeniality. "I've had many happy movie experiences, but that one was right up there at the top," Steve Martin says about playing the heavy in *The Spanish Prisoner*. Mamet keeps a joke reel of each film, which is to say a partial record of his practical jokes. On the first day of *The Spanish Prisoner*, for instance, he laid out for the actress Felicity Huffman a Brünnhilde costume, complete with horned helmet. Once, during the shooting of *Oleanna*, he asked William Macy to learn a new full-page speech on the spur of the moment and he put it on cue cards for the take. "I start the speech," Macy recalls. "I do the first card. I get to the second card, and it reads, 'But what do I know? I'm just a dumb towheaded cracker from Georgia. You know, when Dave first picked me out of the gutter . . .'"

Of course, Mamet has less fun being a hired hand on other people's Hollywood projects. "Being a writer out there is like going into Hitler's Eagle's Nest with a great idea for a bar-mitzvah festival," he says. His streamlined screenplays, which have no embellishments or explanations, are not studio-executive-friendly. "They're dry sponges waiting for the water of performance," Sidney Lumet says. "And that's when they swell up to 5,000 percent." Mamet's script for *The Verdict* had been forgotten by the producers, who had spent more than a million dollars in development, but Lumet read Mamet's early version and said it was the one he wanted to shoot. Likewise, Paramount was indifferent to Linson's notion of going after Mamet to write *The Untouchables*. A cartoon of their first meeting, in 1984, is pinned on the wall of Mamet's cabin, with Linson giving his pitch: "Dave, don't you think that the best career move for someone who'd just won the Pulitzer Prize would be to adapt *The Untouchables* for a *shitload* of money?" Mamet's screenplay departed from the TV series, and, inevitably, the executives didn't like it. Nonetheless, when it was filmed by Brian De Palma it grossed over $200 million worldwide and gave Mamet considerable heat in the industry.

Actually, Mamet's minimalism and his notion of character suits screenwriting. He works up his story on file cards. "You know the movie's ready to be written when you can remember it," Mamet says. "When the progression of incidents is so clear that you no longer need the cards, then you're ready to write." He writes very fast. "He wrote the first draft of *The Untouchables* in what seemed like ten days or less," Linson recalls. "He has occasionally turned a script in to me and said, 'Could you please sit on it for a couple of weeks? I don't want them to think it's this easy.' Dead true. Once Dave gets something, it just kind of writes itself." Rewriting Mamet is very difficult. "It looks like somebody put a patch on a pair of Levi's," Linson says, and, though Mamet will accept notes and supply rewrites, "there'll come a time where the gate comes down and it's '*No más.*'"

Mamet's talent and his inflexibility have given him something of a bad-boy reputation in Hollywood, whose folly he memorialized in *Speed-the-Plow*. "I find that a smile and a hearty 'Fuck you' does the trick," he says of seeing off the intrusive suggestions of movie executives. Sometimes even his own producers get it in the neck. Mamet once handed Zollo a copy of *American Buffalo* to do as a movie. "Have you adapted it for the screen?" Zollo asked. "Adapted it?" said Mamet. "Have I fucking what? I'm going to adapt it right now for you." Mamet demanded the script back. "He crosses out 'A Play by David Mamet' and he writes 'A Screenplay by David Mamet,'" Zollo says. Mamet is fortified in his truculence by the lesson of his poker playing ("If you're smarter than the other guy, be smarter than the other guy") and by a favorite dictum of the English critic William Hazlitt, which he paraphrases as "Don't try to suck up or even be nice to your intellectual inferiors. They'll only hate you more for it." He adds, "Having read that makes my life a little bit easier." About two years ago, Bob Conte, of HBO, gave Zollo a few pages of notes to give to Mamet on his *Lansky* script, which is finally being produced this year. "Essentially, almost all of our notes concern the following issues: Chronology, Clarity, and Character (alliteration unintended)," Conte wrote. "Tell him to Suck My Dick," Mamet told Zollo. "Alliteration unintended."

Mamet's life as an uncompromising writer/director seems in direct contrast to—and is probably made possible by—the tranquillity of his surroundings. In Vermont, he lives in a converted farmhouse, originally built in 1805, that sits on the rise of a hill and looks down a sloping meadow onto a large beaver pond. There are deer, bear, and moose in the surrounding forests, where Mamet likes to walk and sometimes hunt—or, as he says, "take my gun for a walk." He never shoots anything. "My wife calls me the Deer Protection Association," he says. If he gets in his Land Rover, a gift from Linson for a week's rewrite, he can be at Goddard College in fifteen minutes; if he gets on his mountain bike, as he does with Rebecca several times a week to go into town for the mail, Cabot is less than four miles of hard pedalling away. Mamet's kingdom consists of the farmhouse, a red barn, and a cedar cabin whose shingled roof is tucked under the bough of a pine tree about 150 yards from the house.

Onto this rough-hewn masculine landscape Rebecca Pidgeon has put her graceful mark: red, white, and pink hollyhocks press up against the fence posts; under the kitchen window, she has planted an array of herbs among rows of rhubarb, spinach, and lettuce, which Mamet looks upon with the kind of wonder that Jack had for the beanstalk. "After roses, it's all broccoli to me," he says. Mamet's admiration for his wife's competence and for her attentiveness to the world around her is transparent and touching. "She's had a tremendous effect in anchoring him, in calming him down, in making him feel it's OK to be scared, it's OK to be upset, it's OK to fail," Lynn Mamet says. "There's nothing self-destructive about her. She's healthy. And I think it's allowed my brother to exhale for the first time in his life."

Mamet first laid eyes on Pidgeon, who is nineteen years younger than he is, at National Theatre rehearsals in London for a 1989 production of *Speed-the-Plow*, in which she was playing the tenacious, idealistic secretary who almost succeeds in making the producing goniff do good. "He came up to her and said, 'You know, I always wanted to meet a girl like that,'" the actor Colin Stinton, who played opposite Pidgeon, recalls. "She blushed and was sort of flattered by it, I think." Pidgeon, who had her own rock band in addition to her acting career, was resourceful, straightforward, and beautiful; and she didn't bore him. "You think she likes me?" Mamet badgered the painter Donald Sultan, with whom he had travelled to London. Sultan explains, "I said, 'Yeah, I think she likes you.' He said, 'What makes you think that?' I said, 'Well, every day for the last six months, every thought, every word, every action has been yours. How could she not like you?'" Pidgeon herself was surprised that she did. She says, "I had imagined him as this old, tall, very intellectual, cold, godlike kind of writer, and then I see this young, vibrant kind of street urchin. I thought, How could this be possible?" In the meantime, Mamet called his sister from London. "He said, 'I've found her,'" Lynn Mamet says. "He told me about her. I said, 'So, you'll marry her.' He went on for months, driving me crazy. 'She's in London, I'm here; she's got this career, I'm here; she's eleven, I'm here.'"

After a two-year long-distance courtship, they married; Mamet had found his bliss and a new mellowness. Zollo was surprised when Mamet agreed in 1994 to let him mount *The Cryptogram*, which he had kept in his trunk since the late seventies because of its intensely personal material. "He felt safe in his life," Zollo says, by way of explanation. Pidgeon says, "We're extremely compatible. There's no 'I'm going off to be a genius and be troublesome and mysterious and worried.' We have a very peaceful life." Contentment seems to have opened Mamet up even in literary ways. "I think his women's writing has improved since his marriage to Rebecca," Lynn says—a statement borne out by the complex rewrite of the mother's role in *The Cryptogram*, and by the corporate femme fatale in *The Spanish Prisoner*, a part well played by Pidgeon. Lynn goes on, "I don't think David has written a lot for women because I don't think he's been around that many women to whom he wishes to listen, and therefore replicate their voices."

Rebecca and Clara go down through the meadow to hunt for frogs at the beaver pond, and Mamet heads for the cabin. "I've never been anything other than happy here," he says as we approach the porch, whose left side is piled high with firewood. In the winter, when it can get to forty below and the snow is deep, Mamet makes the trek in snowshoes. When he arrives, his ink is frozen, so he improvises a trivet out of pie plates, putting pencils under the ink bottle and warming it up on the black Glenwood's parlor stove that dominates the front half of the room. There is an exhilarating sense of containment and comfort here, where Mamet's cherished objects are arranged carefully around him: a canoe paddle with a beautifully painted pike on its blade hangs on the beam separating the writing area from the reading area; there's a dartboard, a skeet thrower, a collection of campaign buttons, a .58 muzzle-loader, a nine-pound medicine ball, and bookcases full of outdoor reading like *The Parker Gun Shooter's Bible Treasury* and *Black Powder Gun Digest*. It's as if, instead of with the stove, Mamet were keeping himself warm with the things he loves. "Being a writer is all so ethereal that I think most of us tend to surround ourselves with tchotchkes so we can actually be sure we have a past," he says. "Or a life."

Mamet types with his back to the window on a blue Olympia manual typewriter, above which a kerosene lamp is suspended by a chain from a beam smudged black with smoke. The special calm of the place is in part the peace of having no electricity; it is also the peace of the activity that goes on there. Writing has always been Mamet's way of containing terror, or what he calls "mental vomit." "David's brain is a very busy place. It's very cluttered," Lynn Mamet says. "Writing's the only thing that stops the thinking, you know," Mamet says. "It stops all that terrible nonsense noise that's in there." In *The Edge*, where the billionaire bookworm thinks himself out of the backwoods, Mamet quite literally shows the triumph of thought over terror. It's something that he clearly works hard at in his own life. Across the room, on a table in front of the sofa, his serious reading is laid out: D. W. Winnicott's *Thinking about Children*; a special Hebrew prayer about "the good wife," whose twenty-two verses are traditionally read by the husband to his wife on holy days; and Seneca's *Letters from a Stoic*. Mamet has underlined only one passage in Seneca: "Each day . . . acquire something which will help you to face poverty, or death, and other ills as well."

When Mamet set out on his theatrical journey, the teachings of the Stoics emboldened him. "The stoical motto is 'What hinders you?'" he explains. "I'd like to be able to write clearer. 'What's stopping you?' I'd like to be able to figure a project out. 'What's stopping you?' I mean, let's say Sophocles took eighteen years to write *Oedipus Rex*. It's not under your control how quickly you complete *Oedipus Rex*, but it is under your control whether or not you give up." He adds, "It doesn't have to be calm and clear-eyed. You just have to not give up."

A heron lands on top of a sixty-foot tamarack tree that towers on the ridge above where Rebecca and Clara are starting back up the hill. Mamet studies it through the window, then walks over to his desk looking for his camera. Taped there is a blue file card with a snatch of dialogue on it, which I bend close to read. "Here, take it," Mamet says and hurries me into the bright day with his camera in hand. Clara and Rebecca are skipping up the path; Clara is clutching a heron's feather. Mamet darts around them trying to capture the scene. Clara drops her feather; Mamet stoops down to pick it up. Clara's hand touches the top of his bristly head. It's a fragile moment, whose mysterious joy sends him glancing up to see it reflected in his wife's eyes. In his high-school yearbook, to print beside his nerdy photograph, Mamet had chosen the quotation "And so make life and that vast forever one grand, sweet song." He seems somehow to have lived up to his early romantic plan, even if his song is a fierce, rueful, sometimes cruel one. Just how his talent and his life have come together so well seems, like all blessings, both miraculous and inexplicable. I glanced at the file card in my hand:

A) *Life*, maan . . .

B) . . . life.

A) It is so crazy—let me tell you: if you saw it in a movie, you would not believe it. You know why? BECAUSE IT HAS NO PLOT. ∎

—November 17, 1997

The Cryptogram

David Mamet, like the characters he puts onstage, tells us only so much about himself, and no more. We know, for instance, that he likes tricksters and magic. We know that he enjoys guys' things, like hunting and poker and cigars. We also know that he's divorced, and that, like any divorced parent, he has had to live with the grief of imposing on his children the bewildering pain of separation which he felt when his own parents divorced. In "The Rake," the first chapter of a 1992 memoir entitled *The Cabin: Reminiscence and Diversions*, Mamet has provided a rare and chilling snapshot of himself and his sister, Lynn, growing up with their new stepfather in a Chicago suburb. Mamet dredges up from the mystery of childhood a few images and scraps of half-understood conversation which have etched themselves on his imagination. He tells of his sister's hearing raised voices and following them down the corridor to the master bedroom, where she pushed open the door to see their mother coiled in a fetal position on the floor of the closet "moaning and crying and hugging herself," and their tyrannical stepfather gesturing toward the bed, on which the children's grandfather, their mother's father, was slumped. "Say the words," the stepfather was saying to the grandfather. "Say the words, Jack. Please. Just say you love her." Mamet writes, "And my grandfather said, 'I can't.'" Mamet's sister was hit in the face with a hairbrush for bearing witness to this humiliation. Such bleak and brutal terrain—full of cloaked threat and blighted feeling—is a large part of Mamet's emotional inheritance. He survived to dramatize its wary and perverse psychological climate—a ferocious, repressed atmosphere in which, out of fear and impotence and shame, people become willed strangers to themselves, and in which the cunning thrust and parry of language becomes a carapace that cuts them off from both the world and their own murky feelings.

The Cryptogram, Mamet's newest play, which recently had its world premiere at the Ambassadors Theatre, in London, is a difficult but important drama, in which Mamet works his way back to childhood—specifically, to that irrevocable, buried moment in a child's life when the safety net of the parental embrace collapses, and the world, once full of blessing, is suddenly full of danger. The play, which consists of three terse scenes, takes place in 1959 (Mamet was born in 1947), and Mamet's surrogate, John, is "about ten." Bob Crowley's beautifully painted set is dominated by a huge stairway, which winds its way up toward the flies, and a backcloth of behemoth zones of blue-green and charcoal gray separated by a band of pink. Like a Rothko painting (which the backcloth resembles), the play is about the resonance of contradictory and puzzling emotional intensities; and the staircase becomes an image of the almost unbridgeable space between the muffled grownup world downstairs and the child's insecure purdah upstairs.

Mamet foreshadows the play's moral debate in the opening beats. Here, in Gregory Mosher's vivid production, John's first words are "I couldn't find 'em." John (superbly played by the precocious Richard Claxton, who alternates in the role with the equally adroit Danny Worters) is apparently talking about a pair of slippers he has packed for a camping trip with his father, which is scheduled for the next day; but what John really can't find in the environment of subterfuge and coded speech which engulfs him is the reality of his parents and of his own emotional life. John can't sleep. This is a familiar enough childhood complaint, and the family friend Del (well played by the pudgy, weak-faced comedian Eddie Izzard) tries to jolly him out of it in a cozy late-night man-to-man.

"Where were we?" Del asks. John answers with a formal phrase obviously borrowed from earlier arguments with the adults. "Issues of sleep," he says. The phrase turns panic into a debating point, but we soon learn that John's sleeplessness is chronic. "*Every* night. *Every* night. There's some excuse. Some *reason*," says Donny, John's mother, played by the subtle Lindsay Duncan, whose pale elegance here disguises a steely detachment. Despite Del's special pleading and the excitement of the upcoming trip, Donny wants John upstairs and in bed. "Why aren't you asleep?" is her entrance line. John has picked up some anxiety that the household refuses to acknowledge.

"Why isn't Dad home?" he asks Del, who takes the conversation in another direction. Later in the scene, John tells his mother, "I want to wait till he comes home." His request is stonewalled by apparent reasonableness. "Well, yes, I'm sure you do," Donny says. "But you need your sleep. And if you don't get it, you're not . . ."

Sleeplessness, not John's fear, is what Del and Donny want to contain. No one deals with John's feelings or tries to alleviate them. The audience starts to feel a certain highly charged and unspoken frustration—a kind of emotional static. Mamet puts the audience where the child sits, taking the characters at face value, only to have its will to believe confounded by those characters' mixed messages. Psychological truth is never acknowledged. In fact, it is scrambled— like a cryptogram—so that everything means something else. The play's uncluttered living room, composed merely of two sofas covered with red blankets, becomes an impenetrable landscape of denial. Mamet announces the pattern brilliantly, with the offstage crash of Donny's teapot, which precedes her first entrance. "I'm alright!" Donny shouts from the wings. "I'm alright!" Clearly she's not all right, and Del uses the shattered teapot to draw an avuncular parallel between the anticipated camping trip and John's edginess:

> DEL: Well, there you go.
> JOHN: What?
> DEL: . . . a human *being* . . .
> JOHN: . . . yes?
> DEL: . . . cannot conceal himself.
> JOHN: that, that's, that's an example?
> DEL: Well, hell, look at it: anything, when it is *changed* . . .
>   *any*, um um, "upheaval," do you see? All of a sudden . . .

A broken teapot an "upheaval"? Del seems to be trying to ascribe John's sleeplessness to the prospect of a change of scenery, but his

stumbling and inappropriate choice of words is confusing. Something—everything—is being concealed. But what? Nothing is ever
directly stated. Even John's straightforward question about his
father—"Where is he?"—gets a confused and confusing answer
from Donny. "I don't know. Yes, I do, yes. He's at the Office. And
he'll be home soon." She seems to know, and yet not to know, that
something is awry. John's situation is never resolved; his anxieties
and his questions are never answered. When John is sent to tidy up
the attic, and reappears with a blanket—a totemic family object in
which he was wrapped as a baby—the blanket turns out to be torn.
John thinks he has torn it, but Donny knows he hasn't. Even this
projection of John's unspoken fear of having caused a rip in the fabric of the family is muddied by Del. "Because we *think* a thing is one
way does not mean that this is the way that this thing must be," Del
says. The evasions are confusing, and are meant to be. John's care-
takers interrupt him, and confound him with doubletalk. At the
end of the scene, John's worst fears are confirmed. A note somehow
materializes. "When did this get here?" Donny asks, and after she's
read it she sends John to bed. "Alright. I understand. I'm going," he
says, knowing, without quite knowing, that the worst has happened.
His father will not be going on the camping trip, or coming home.
The dialogue that ends the first scene has a flat, matter-of-fact tone,
but in the subsequent scenes it turns out to be part of a whole narrative of fraudulence:

> DEL: What is it?
> DONNY: It's a letter. (*Pause.*) Robert's leaving me.
> DEL: He's leaving you. (*Pause.*) Why would he want to do
>   that . . . ?

"I thought that maybe there was nothing there," John says to
Donny at the beginning of scene 2, explaining a kind of brainstorm

about the nature of reality. And, of course, he's right: what Mamet is about to unravel is the charade of human connection. John is starting to fragment before our eyes, and his night sweats—in this case, voices and specters that accompany his fear of abandonment and his sense of annihilation—are now coming out in his questions. "And how do we *know* the things we know?" he says. "And, and we don't know what's real. And all we do is *say* things." What Del says when he enters is that he has looked all over town for Robert and can't find him. He brings medicine for John. (The medicine that John really needs is love, but this is never offered.) John finally breaks down and buries his head in his mother's lap. "What's happening to me?" he says. Donny embraces him. "It's alright," she says. "Hush. You go to bed. It's alright. John. Shh. You've only got a fever. Shhh." It's a fierce and ironic moment: an act of violence couched in the language of love. Donny acts as if the truth would lull her son, but what's killing him is untruth.

The truth—a network of betrayals—is hard to admit or discover. Once John is safely upstairs, Del opens a bottle of whiskey, and he and Donny toast their friendship—a kind of strangulated toast, in which Del, who is gay but later confesses love for Donny, angles clumsily for some acknowledgment of deeper feeling from her:

DONNY: May We Always be as . . .

DEL: Yes.

DONNY: As . . .

DEL: Unified . . .

DONNY: Well, let's pick something more moving than that.

DEL: Alright . . . be. be. be. be. be-*nighted*? No, that's not
    the word I want to use . . . be-*trothed* . . . ? No.

DONNY: Close . . .

DEL: Yes.

DONNY: Close to each other.

DEL: As we happen to be right now.

Within a few minutes, though, Del is caught out in a lie about a knife he has used to open the whiskey. He claims that Robert gave it to him on a camping trip the previous week, but Donny has seen it more recently, in the attic. This leads to the revelation that Del lent Robert his apartment for a tryst and used the camping trip as a decoy—a collusion for which he was rewarded with the knife, Robert's cherished "war memento," which proves later to be as inauthentic as Del's shows of sincerity. Del, it turns out, is caught between an allegiance to the absent Robert and a yearning for Donny, who flirts with him but is finally uninterested. The audience hardly has time to tally up the extent of his fabrications. Del, who planted the "Dear Donny" letter, has known all along about Robert's adultery and abandonment of his family. Del's badinage with John, the story about looking for Robert, the toast to Donny and friendship—all are flimflam. "I'm sorry that it came out like this," he says to her. Then, having deliberately lied to Donny, he proceeds to lie to himself. "But we can't always choose the . . ." These revelations are interrupted by John's returning from upstairs to recount his own revelation: "I'm perfectly alone." And he is.

We see just how alone John is in the last, and best, scene, which takes place a month later, with Donny and John packing up to leave the house. Here, especially, Lindsay Duncan—one of England's finest actresses—brings Donny into bold, monstrous relief. John has suicide on his mind. "Do you ever wish that you could die?" he asks his mother, who replies ambivalently, "How can I help you, John?" She is, as Mamet shows, killing him slowly with kindness. "Things occur," she tells him. "And the meaning of them . . . the *meaning* of them . . . is not clear." But meaning, we see, is being consciously and unconsciously subverted. "If I could find one man," Donny bleats to Del, who has returned with the knife to "attune" for his sins. "In my life. Who would not betray me." Donny's rancor has a self-hypnotic power, but in fact Donny has betrayed John and Del, just as Del has betrayed Donny and John; and Robert, it turns out, has betrayed all three. When John appears on the stairway to interrupt her aria of victimization, Donny turns on her boy with unbridled fury. "Do you have no *feelings*?" she says. "I don't CARE. Go away. Leave me. Do you hear? You *lied*. You *lied* to me. I love you, but I can't like you. I'm sorry." Of course, it's Donny (and the other adults) who has lied to John; but John stands there, bewildered, trying vainly to make himself heard above Donny's double binds. All he wants is the blanket—his security blanket—but it has been packed. In a gesture typical of the adults' psychological obtuseness, Del gives John the knife to open the package. John, who has already broadcast suicidal thoughts, is called to attention on the stairway by Donny; she doesn't want to disarm him but, instead, to accuse him furiously of doing to *her* what she in fact is doing to him. "What are you *standing* there for?" she says. "Can't you see that I need *comfort*? Are you *blind*? Are you *blind*? That you treat me like an *animal*? What must I do?" It is a searing moment of emotional abuse. At the finale, John is looking down over the bannister at Donny and Del. He flicks the knife. The blade jolts into view with a startling *thwack*—a chilling sound that holds out the promise, as the lights fade, of murderous fury directed at John himself or at the world.

Mamet chose to attack the world, and *The Cryptogram* goes some way toward illuminating the source of the cruelty and faithlessness that his characters generally find in it. The shifting ground of the play makes it hard to engage with, but its aftershock is enormous. *The Cryptogram* may be short, but it is not miniature. The oblique, brilliant dialogue is not underwritten, nor are the characters unexplored. With remarkable concision and insight, Mamet has mapped out the dynamics of a soul murder. This daring, dark, complex play got respectful though mixed notices in London, but I suspect that in time it will take its place among Mamet's major works. ■

—August 1, 1994

Glengarry Glen Ross

If there's a better play about American business than David Mamet's majestic *Glengarry Glen Ross* (revived in a pitch-perfect production by Joe Mantello at the Royale), I don't know it. In a sort of three-card monte of verbal manipulation, a group of Chicago real-estate brokers fight to get the leads, get ahead of each other, close the sale, and get on the board. The world is a dogfight. It's survival at all costs, but with this difference—survival without the promise of blessing but only of barbarity. Language has lost its purchase on meaning; words are merely husks of feeling that decoy self-interest and connect the speakers to nothing but their own craven desire. Speech itself, powered by panic, becomes at once an identity and a destiny, a sort of awesome music that gets louder as the people who deploy it get emptier.

From the first beat of this production, the play swings; the virtuoso cast—Alan Alda, Liev Schreiber, Gordon Clapp, Jeffrey Tambor, Frederick Weller, Tom Wopat, Jordan Lage—sends it solid. Mamet's language plays like jazz: riffs of contrapuntal sound that create a force field of hilarity, sorrow, and fury. Take, for instance, Shelley (the Machine) Levene (Alan Alda, in an inspired performance), who, down on his luck, storms into the office having, he thinks, made a sale: "Get the *chalk*. Get the *chalk* . . . get the *chalk*! I closed 'em! I *closed* the cocksucker. Get the chalk and put me on the *board*. I'm going to Hawaii! Put me on the Cadillac board, Williamson! Pick up the fuckin' chalk. Eight units. Mountain View." Out of this competitive delirium, Mamet's hapless salesmen nonetheless become visionaries of a burned-out capitalist America. They dream of wanting, and everything they want is worthless. ∎

—May 9, 2005

5

SARAH RUHL

When the playwright Sarah Ruhl works at home, she sits at a desk in her young daughter Anna's bedroom, beside a window overlooking a paddle-tennis court amid a red brick apartment maze on the East Side of Manhattan. A white gate, like a picket fence, stretches across the width of the small room, dividing the toddler's play area from her mother's. Ruhl, who is thirty-four and has already won a half-million-dollar MacArthur Fellowship for her plays (which include *The Clean House*, a comedy that was a Pulitzer Prize finalist in 2005), writes in a poised, crystalline style about things that are irrational and invisible. Ruhl is a fabulist. Her plays celebrate what she calls "the pleasure of heightened things." In them, fish walk and caper (*Passion Play*), stones talk and weep (*Eurydice*), a dog is a witness to and the narrator of a family tragedy (*Dog Play*), a woman turns into an almond (*Melancholy Play*). Ruhl's characters occupy, she has said, "the real world and also a suspended state." Her new play, *Dead Man's Cell Phone*, now at Playwrights Horizons, is a meditation on death, love, and disconnection in the digital age; like her other works, it inhabits a dramatic netherworld between personal suspense and suspended time. "Cell phones, iPods, wireless computers will change people in ways we don't even understand," Ruhl told me. "We're less connected to the present. No one is where they are. There's absolutely no reason to talk to a stranger anymore— you connect to people you already know. But how well do you know them? Because you never see them—you just talk to them. I find that terrifying."

Looming over Ruhl's writing table is a poster of a photograph from Walker Evans's late-1930s series of New York City subway riders, a gift from her husband, Tony Charuvastra, a child psychiatrist. (They married in 2005, after a seven-year courtship.) The juxtaposition of photographer and playwright—both entrepreneurs of tone and atmosphere—is one of those unconscious visual provocations that Ruhl's plays relish. "I like to see people speaking ordinary words in strange places, or people speaking extraordinary words in ordinary places," Ruhl has said. Evans wanted to project, he wrote, the "delights of seeing"; Ruhl wants to project the delights of pretense, "the interplay between the actual and the magical." Evans once wrote about the "dream of making photographs like poems." Ruhl began her career as a poet—her first book, *Death in Another Country*, a collection of verse, was published when she was twenty— and she sees her plays as "three-dimensional poems." Evans's subway photos were taken at furtive angles, with his lens hidden in the buttonhole of his coat and an operating cable up his sleeve; Ruhl's narrative strategy is similarly oblique and cunning, and she aspires to a kind of reportorial anonymity. "If one is unseen, one has the liberty to observe and make things up," she told me. "It's very difficult to overhear a conversation if one is speaking loudly." One night, at the Lincoln Center production of *The Clean House*—a tale about an unhappy Brazilian maid looking for the perfect joke in the midst of her employer's family ructions—Ruhl sat unrecognized behind an elderly couple. "I didn't *not* like it," the woman said after the houselights came up. "I didn't *not* like it," her gentleman friend chimed in. "They turned to me," Ruhl recalled, and asked, " 'What did you think?' I said, 'I didn't *not* like it, either.' "

Ruhl, like her plays, is deceptively placid. She is petite and polite. Her voice is high-pitched, as if she had been hitting the helium bottle. She wears her auburn hair pinned back by a barrette, in demure schoolmarm fashion; in her choice of clothes, too, she favors an unprepossessing look—a carapace of ordinariness, forged out of her Illinois childhood and "the ability of Midwesterners to pulverize people who seem slightly precocious," she explained. ("In third grade, somebody sent me a poison-pen letter," Ruhl, who was bullied for being intelligent, said. "I corrected the punctuation and sent it back.") Nothing in her modest mien indicates her steeliness, her depth, or her piquant wit. Ruhl is reserved but not shy, alert but not aggressive. She feels big emotions; she just doesn't express them in a big way. "I had one boyfriend who really wished I would yell and scream at him," she said. Even her laugh is just three short, unobtrusive intakes of breath.

But if Ruhl's demeanor is unassuming, her plays are bold. Her nonlinear form of realism—full of astonishments, surprises, and mysteries—is low on exposition and psychology. "I try to interpret how people subjectively experience life," she has said. "Everyone has a great, horrible opera inside him. I feel that my plays, in a way, are very old-fashioned. They're pre-Freudian in the sense that the Greeks and Shakespeare worked with similar assumptions. Catharsis isn't a wound being excavated from childhood."

Lightness—the distillation of things into a quick, terse, almost innocent directness—is a value on which Ruhl puts much weight. "Italo Calvino has an essay that I think is profound," she told me, scouting a floor-length living-room bookshelf until she found Calvino's *Six Memos for the Next Millennium*, a series of posthumously published lectures on the imaginative qualities that the new millennium should call into play. Of his defining categories—among them quickness, exactitude, visibility, and multiplicity—lightness is foremost. "In the even more congested times that await us, literature must aim at the maximum concentration of poetry and of thought," he writes. Ruhl, in her plays, contends with the pressing existential issues; her stoical comic posture is a means of killing gravity, of taking the heaviness out of her words in order to better contend with life. "Lightness isn't stupidity," she said. "It's actually a philosophical and aesthetic viewpoint, deeply serious, and has a kind of wisdom—stepping back to be able to laugh at horrible things even as you're experiencing them." In *Melancholy Play* (2002), a farce about suffering, Ruhl dramatized the point. Among a group of sad sacks, who are gourmands of grief—they fight over "a vial of tears"—a bank teller named Tilly causes havoc when she pronounces herself happy. "I feel lighter and lighter," Tilly says. "I am trying to cultivate—a sensation of—gravity. But nothing helps."

Lightness, Ruhl said, was "probably a family style." She grew up in Wilmette, Illinois, where she had "a wonderful family. I'm not like a lot of artists in that way." Her father, Patrick, marketed toys for a number of years, a job that was a mismatch for his intellectual abilities. "He should have been a history professor," Ruhl said, though he loved puns, reading, language, and jazz. "I think Sarah's appreciation of music comes from him," her older sister, Kate Ruhl, a psychiatrist, told me. So, too, did her fascination with language. Each Saturday, from the time Ruhl was five, Patrick took his daughters to the Walker Bros. Original Pancake House for breakfast and taught them a new word, along with its etymology. (The language lesson and some of Patrick's words—"ostracize," "peripatetic," "defunct"— are memorialized in the 2003 *Eurydice*, a retelling of the Orpheus myth from his inamorata's point of view, in which the dead Father, reunited with his daughter, tries to re-teach her lost vocabulary.) Patrick died of cancer in 1994, when Ruhl was twenty. That year, because he was ill, the family had to forgo its usual summer trip to Cape Cod; instead, as Kate recalled, "we brought Cape Cod to our house. We pretended we were away—we would watch dumb summer movies, get the kid food we ate on the Cape. We were a really good foursome." Ruhl, recollecting her father's last days, said, "He'd be making jokes about having radioactive urine. We'd all be laughing. It was so gracious."

Ruhl's mother, Kathleen, who now holds a PhD in Language, Literacy, and Rhetoric, from the University of Illinois, added to the family's sense of caprice. For most of her children's growing up, Kathleen was a high-school English teacher who moonlighted as an actress and a director. She would come down to dinner—according to Ruhl, who calls her "vivid"—"doing the maid's speech from Ionesco's *Bald Soprano*." Ruhl said, "We were encouraged to play at home, so that art-making didn't seem like an escape from family or a retreat but very much a part of life." Even Kathleen's method of inculcating manners was a license to play. "We had Pig Night," Kathleen said. "One night a week, the girls could be as horrible as they wanted. The rest of the week, they had to make an effort." The Ruhl children knew all about performance. They were taken on summer pilgrimages to Stratford, Ontario, to see Shakespeare. Ruhl has memories of being bewildered and furious, watching *Julius Caesar* ("lots of white togas") and going backstage after *The Tempest* to look at the ship ("That was magical"). Kathleen would also tote them to her rehearsals. Even as a girl, Ruhl, who was considered an "old soul" by her family, had a keen analytic eye. "One of the most intense theatrical experiences for her was when I directed *Enter Laughing*," Kathleen said. "She got to know all the actors. By that point, people would ask her for her notes. She was six or seven."

"When other kids were outside playing, Sarah would be wrapped in a comforter drinking tea and reading," Kate said. "We used to joke that she had consumption." Ruhl told me, "There was always a little part of me that stood apart and observed and made things up. My mom says that, even before I could write, I would tell stories and she would type them up for me." Then as now, storytelling worked as an antidepressant for her. "If I'm sad in life, I'll tell someone something strange and funny that happened to me to make myself feel better," she said. The thrill of transformation is something she began learning at the age of ten, through improvisational games at the Piven Theatre, a seventy-seat venue in Evanston, Illinois, whose Young People's Company, to which Ruhl briefly belonged, can claim such accomplished graduates as John Cusack, Joan Cusack, Jeff Garlin, and Rosanna Arquette. Joyce Piven, the co-founder and artistic director, told me, "We acted stories, myths, fairy tales, folktales, then literary tales—Chekhov, Eudora Welty, Flannery O'Connor, Salinger." The theater, Ruhl said, "didn't use props, and didn't have sets. Language did everything. So, from an early age: no fourth wall, and things can transform in the moment." As an improviser, according to Piven, Ruhl "wasn't a standout—she's not basically a performer." (Ruhl concurs: "I don't like being watched.") But she began taking Piven's scene-study class, and ended up teaching the work. "She hears the play in all its dimensions," Piven said, adding, "She writes from a distance, so she can play. Even if you're writing about a very serious thing and invested up to your eyes, intensity can kill a lot for the actor and the writer."

Apart from a courtroom drama about a land-mass dispute between an isthmus and an island, which Ruhl wrote in fourth grade, and which her teacher declined to stage—"Perhaps that's why I'm writing plays now, to exorcise my psychic battle with Mr. Spangenberger," Ruhl says—she didn't start writing plays until her junior year at Brown University, in 1995. In *Dog Play*, her first piece, a ten-minute exercise assigned by her teacher, the playwright Paula Vogel, Ruhl synthesized Kabuki stage techniques with a suburban American environment to evoke her grief over her father's death. The Dog, whose baying "as though his heart is breaking" opens the show, says, "I dreamed last night that I could speak and everyone could understand. I was telling them that he is not dead, that I can see him. No one believed me." Vogel, who later cited Ruhl in her award-winning play *Baltimore Waltz* as one of the people "who had changed the way I looked at drama," told me, "I sat with this short play in my study and sobbed. She had an emotional maturity that no one else in the class had." Vogel added, "I said, 'I want to work with you,' and she answered, 'Well, I'm going to be a poet. I'm not gonna be doing playwriting.' My heart kind of sank, but I went, 'Well, OK. Good luck.'" But Vogel's appreciation of Ruhl's work prevailed. "I do think it's important having someone say, 'You could do this for life,'" Ruhl said. "Paula was that person."

Ruhl spent the next year at Pembroke College, Oxford, where she studied English literature, and when she returned, her sights were not on poetry but on playwriting. Her literary volte-face was due in part to her confusion about the confessional "I" of her poetic voice, which she felt had been exhausted in mourning her father. In "Dream," for instance, she wrote, "I wake this morning and gather a mouthful of dirt— / words—with a teaspoon, that you may speak to me again." "I didn't know what a poem should be anymore," she said. "Plays provided a way to open up content and have many voices. I felt that onstage one could speak lyrically and with emotion, and that the actor was longing for that kind of speech, whereas in poetic discourse emotion was in some circles becoming embarrassing."

The turning point for Ruhl came in 1997, at a production of *Passion Play*, her first full-length work, which Vogel had arranged at Trinity Repertory Company, in Providence, Rhode Island. Kathleen drove herself and Sarah to the event. They had an accident, and Sarah was briefly knocked unconscious. Nonetheless, she managed to see her play. "At a visceral level, watching the play, I thought, This is it," she said. "Some people stood. What whorish playwright wouldn't be excited about that? It was momentous and strange."

Ruhl's theater aspires to reclaim the audience's atrophied imagination. "Now, some people consume imagination, and some people do the imagining," she said. "I find it very worrisome. That should be one thing that people know they can do." Ruhl writes with space, sound, and image as well as words. Her stage directions often challenge her directors' scenic imagination as well. In *Eurydice*, the dead Father builds Eurydice a room of string in the underworld. The stage directions read, *"He makes four walls and a door out of string. / Time passes. / It takes time to build a room out of string."* Ruhl's goal is to make the audience live in the moment, to make the known world unfamiliar in order to reanimate it. Here the essential nature of the underworld—its sense of absence—is made visceral by the volumes of meticulously constructed empty space that the string defines.

"I'm interested in the things theater can do that other forms can't," Ruhl told me. "So theater as pure plumbing of self, in a psychological way, seems very readerly to me." Her plays are distinguished by a minimum of backstory; the audience is submerged in a series of unfolding dramatic moments. *Eurydice*, for instance, opens, wittily, with Eurydice and Orpheus at the beach. When Orpheus offers her the world, it's the real one. "All those birds. Thank you," Eurydice says. "And the sea! For me? When? Now? It's mine already? *(Orpheus nods.)* Wow." The dialogue and the situation have precise, ironic resonances, but the audience has to work for them. The play coaxes the spectators to swim in the magical, sometimes menacing flow of the unconscious. Ruhl prefers the revelations of the surreal moment to the narrated psychological one. In the prologue to *Passion Play*—a triptych that uses for its dissection of faith, politics, and political icons the organizing conceit of the staging of Christ's Passion in separate acts by the Elizabethans, Nazi-era Germans, and contemporary Americans—Ruhl announced her daring, playfully cajoling the public to focus on the moment and the mythic:

> We ask you, dear audience,
> To use your eyes, ears, your most inward sight.
> For here is day (A painted sun is raised)

And here is night (A painted moon is raised)
And now, the play.

As a storyteller, Ruhl marches to Ovid's drum rather than Aristotle's. "Aristotle has held sway for many centuries, but I feel our culture is hungry for Ovid's way of telling stories," she said, describing Ovid's narrative strategy as "one thing transforming into another." She went on, "His is not the neat Aristotelian arc but, instead, small transformations that are delightful and tragic." And she added, "The Aristotelian model—a person wants something, comes close to getting it but is smashed down, then finally gets it, or not, then learns something from the experience—I don't find helpful. It's a strange way to look at experience.

"I like plays that have revelations in the moment, where emotions transform almost inexplicably," Ruhl said. "The acting style isn't explicated, either. It's not psychological." In *The Clean House*, for instance, one stage direction reads, *"Lane cries. She laughs. She cries. She laughs. And this goes on for some time."* To Ruhl, this kind of emotionally labile performance is a "virtuosic" exhibition of behavior. "It feels true to me," she said. "Children are certainly that way. I'm interested in these kinds of state changes. 'I was happy, now I'm sad.'" She continued, "If you distill people's subjectivity and how they view the world emotionally, you don't get realism." The irrationality of emotion is one of the themes to which Ruhl's plays continually return. "I don't want to smooth out the emotions to the point where you could interpret them totally rationally, so that they have a clear reference point to the past," she said. "Psychological realism makes emotions so rational, so explained, that they don't feel like emotions to me."

In Ruhl's plays, turbulent feeling can erupt at any moment, for no apparent reason; actors are challenged to inhabit the emotional moment without motivation. Sometimes, during rehearsal, an anxious actor will approach Ruhl to try and pin down the role. She thinks to herself, "Oh, come on, just ride it." She told me, "I prefer an actor who says, 'My character doesn't have a backstory, so I won't concoct one. I will live as fully in every moment as I can. I will let the language move me, as opposed to a secret backstory of my own.' " She likes her actors to have "a sense of irony," and to be "touched with a little brush of the irrational."

One afternoon in January, in the fifth-floor rehearsal room of Playwrights Horizons, Ruhl took a seat beside the director Anne Bogart at the top of a horseshoe of white Formica tables. It was the second day of rehearsal for *Dead Man's Cell Phone*. Behind them was the maquette of the play's spare proscenium set—its backdrop of sky and its sliding side panels painted in the deep, sombre blues, grays, and browns of Edward Hopper's palette. The Hopper tones suggested the longing and the solitude that are the play's internal weather and that the cavernous, mostly furniture-free space magnified. As an epigram to her script, Ruhl appended an observation by Mark Strand about the people who wait in Hopper's paintings: "They are like characters whose parts have deserted them and now, trapped in the space of their waiting, must keep themselves company."

Dead Man's Cell Phone is a mad pilgrimage of an imagination as it is invaded and atomized by the phone, which transforms private as well as public space. At a café, when a man sitting next to the quirky Jean won't answer the intrusive ringing of his phone, she answers it herself, realizing only slowly that the man is dead. In the moment of recognition, staring into his transfigured face, which appears, the stage direction reads, "*as though he was just looking at something he found eminently beautiful,*" Jean falls in love. "I can be very medieval about love—like the notion that love is through the eyes and that it's very immediate, as opposed to modern and neurotic," Ruhl told me. Jean speaks to the corpse; the stage direction reads, *"She holds his hand. She keeps hold of it."* In the image, Ruhl's main thematic tragicomic preoccupations of being both disembodied and disconnected coalesce. To keep alive the reality of her new-found love object, Jean answers his calls and fabricates stories about his dying thoughts to lovers, business partners, and family, all of whom she eventually meets. (The Dead Man's name, it turns out, is Gordon, and he sold body parts for a living.)

Of the many ghostly figures in this bright play—Jean, who declares, "I like to disappear"; Gordon's termagant mother, who sees it as her job "to mourn him until the day I die"; Dwight, an unnoticed second son—the Dead Man is the only bona-fide ghost. This being a Ruhl play, he is, naturally, heard from.

"Have a seat," Bogart said to Bill Camp, the actor who was then playing the Dead Man. "Take your time. And see if we might help you, or not." The Dead Man has a soliloquy at the opening of act 2, and Bogart was planting the seed of using the audience as an acting partner in the scene. Ruhl is a fan of direct address. In *Melancholy Play*, her production notes admonish theatricals: "The audience knows the difference between being talked to and being talked at. Talk to them, please." Ruhl told me, "We're in the theater and people are speaking to us. You could say it's more real." She said to Camp, "There is charm in the monologue—the slow, easy charm of talking to an airplane partner in first class. Don't be afraid of it."

"I love that image of being in first class," Bogart said. Then Camp got to work. "I woke up that morning—the day I died—thinking I'd like a lobster bisque," he began. Ruhl cast out her sentences straight and true like a fly line, their rhythms setting ideas down crisply and carefully for her listeners to catch. Sometimes she did it with a fillip of observation ("I got onto the subway. A tomb for people's eyes"); sometimes with a flick of humor ("It doesn't really make your mouth water, does it, lentil soup?" Gordon asks. "Something watery—something brown—and hot carrots. Like death"); sometimes with the surprise of information ("Ate my sushi," Gordon says, in a detour about a restaurant run by a former Chinese surgeon who did organ extractions. "You can tell with tuna whether they slice it from the belly or from the tail end. He always gave me the belly. It's the good part"). By the point in the soliloquy where Gordon arrives at the café, where he learns that the last bowl of lobster bisque has just been sold, the rhythm and command of Ruhl's language have slyly let out a lot of the story line. "I'm thinking, That bitch over there ate all the lobster bisque, this is all her fault," Gordon says as he begins to have a heart attack. "And I look over at her, and she looks like an angel— not like a bitch at all—and I think—good—good—I'm glad she had the last bite—I'm glad. Then I die."

Afterward, parsing the soliloquy with Camp, Ruhl returned to the sushi-eating story. In the text, she said, it seems that the character is "talking about something important, like organs, when actually it isn't that important in his moral structure. But sushi is the important part of what he's talking about. There was something thrilling in the way you were talking about the 'belly is the best part of the tuna.' That was the place where you slowed down, even though it was parenthetical. That seemed really right to me." She added, "This is a man who is used to talking at length and to having people listen. There's a kind of confidence. He's allowed to improvise and to surprise himself with language the way most people aren't, because people stop listening."

Ruhl takes the same pleasure in language. On the way to a preview, eight weeks later, she worried about the calibration of the words in a rewrite of her ending. "I hope I'm not overarticulating," she said, striding through the chill night air in bluejeans, backpack on her shoulders. In the lobby, the director Mark Wing-Davey, who will stage *Passion Play* at the Yale Repertory Theatre later this year, swept Ruhl up against his massive body like a grizzly bear hugging a salmon. "She's a playwright with a voice that thrums," Wing-Davey told me as we took our seats. He went on, "You hear that voice and you think, That doesn't come around that often." Ruhl's theatrical authority bred trust in the audience. In the game of hide-and-seek she played with it, there was always something to be found. It gave them permission to play. No matter how wild the zigzags of logic or the lampoon of conventional storytelling—what she called her "anti-money shots"—the audience was right with Ruhl's flights of goofy fancy: a cell-phone ballet set to the chattering gab of the spheres, a rendezvous with Gordon on his rung of Hell, a redemptive finale. "I intend the ending to be an actual hymn to love," she told me. Out of the atomized half lives of the characters, Ruhl's tale, true to comedy's mission, stage-managed wholeness: Jean says to Dwight, Gordon's brother, "Let's start loving each other right now, Dwight— not a mediocre love, but the strongest love in the world, absolutely requited."

In the lobby after the preview, I talked to Wing-Davey about the oddness of the play's ironic detachment and its unabashed optimism. "Why shouldn't it be?" he said, adding, "Right now Sarah's life is great—a young child, newly married, the darling of the American theater scene, her plays are done." Nonetheless, for good luck at each opening night, Ruhl comes armed with an amulet, a small pink Ganesh-type elephant. If her sister or her husband is beside her in the theater, as the lights come down, Ruhl's ritual is to whisper the words of a young, excited, theatergoing Minnesota girl from her favorite childhood series, the Betsy-Tacy stories, words that to Ruhl signal "the experience of opening and of forgetting." "The curtain goes up! The curtain goes up!" she says. ∎

—March 17, 2008

Eurydice

At the theater these days, we are rarely asked to play. Producers, who live or die on the accuracy of their reading of the public mood, have registered the current climate of fear and exploited our need for succor. The glut of movies-into-musicals and refurbished revivals is a kind of "Pimp My Mind" of theater. Audiences are happy to pay top dollar to see what they already know; it's the unknown that petrifies them. Sarah Ruhl's *Eurydice* (at the Second Stage, under the direction of Les Waters), a luminous retelling of the Orpheus myth from his beloved wife's point of view, is exhilarating because it frees the stage from the habitual. Watching it, we enter a singular, surreal world, as lush and limpid as a dream—an anxiety dream of love and loss—where both author and audience swim in the magical, sometimes menacing, and always thrilling flow of the unconscious.

Scott Bradley's set powerfully conjures up Hades: a cavernous shower room, where the echo of dripping water and shimmers of glinting light bounce off hand-lettered aquamarine tiles that cover the walls. Over time, the tiles take on meaning: they are the petitions of the dead to the living—undelivered letters to the bright, silent world above. This deceptively simple and gorgeous stylization mirrors Ruhl's literary attack: an exercise in imaginative freedom, in which riddle and reality coexist, as light as a game and as grave as a decision. Ruhl's theatrical voice is reticent and daring, accurate and outlandish—"the voice that comes from *there*, a *there* that is always *here*," as Octavio Paz wrote of Elizabeth Bishop.

Ruhl shows her whimsical hand in the play's first beat. The lovers sit on a beach—Orpheus (Joseph Parks) in Bermuda shorts, Eurydice (Maria Dizzia) in a cotton sundress. With a flourish, Orpheus gestures to the sky. "All those birds? For me? Thank you," Eurydice says, adding, "And—the sea! Now? It's mine already? Wow." When

Orpheus throws in the sky and the stars, Eurydice suggests that he's being "perhaps too generous." The droll lines play on the gush of romantic idealization; Eurydice is a girl who really *has* found her god. Both inhabiting a myth and commenting on it, Ruhl walks a tightrope between the mythic and the mundane. In her retelling, Eurydice is perky and pragmatic. When Orpheus ties a string around her fourth finger to memorialize their love, she prompts, "Maybe you could also get me another ring—a gold one—to put over the string one." Orpheus, for his part, is a slightly goofy-looking artist, always in his own head, hearing the melodies that make him the greatest musician in the universe. Eurydice can't carry a tune; she is, however, a reader, with an appetite for argument, which grates on Orpheus's notion of originality. When Orpheus confides that he has just written a song for her, he adds, tartly, "It's not *interesting* or *not-interesting*. It just is." For him—and, one suspects, for Ruhl—expression is an end in itself.

As lovers do, the young couple swear their allegiance; they marry; they dance and sing to "Don't Sit Under the Apple Tree." Then Eurydice, enticed by a Nasty and Interesting Man (Mark Zeisler), who claims to have a letter from her deceased father, wanders off. Her disappearance turns out to be from life itself. "I was not lonely," she says later, in a brilliant speech describing her death, "only alone with myself, begging myself not to leave my own body, but I was leaving." Ruhl concentrates on Eurydice's experience, not Orpheus's: there is no demented wandering, no boy's own subjugation of the guards, no ghoulish dismemberment by Thracian maenads. Eurydice's descent into the underworld is ingeniously indicated by illuminated tiles, which chart her arrival like that of an elevator. When a door in the upstage wall opens, Eurydice is revealed in a downpour, carrying a suitcase and an umbrella, water sluicing onto the tiled floor and over the lip of the stage. The stunning image establishes both the geography of the place and the state of her consciousness, which is being

leached of the past. (In Ruhl's underworld, each lost memory is signalled by a ping.) At first, Eurydice is bemused by her forgetfulness;
she can't recall Orpheus's name. "I know his name starts with my
mouth shaped like a ball of twine," she says. "Oar—oar. I forget."
The moment is as punishing as it is poetic. Identity is memory; when
memory disappears, the self dissolves and love with it.

Here this nothingness is foreshadowed by a chorus called the
Stones (Gian-Murray Gianino, Carla Harting, and Ramiz Monsef)—
a trio who speak and move in unison, a sort of vaudeville of vacancy.
They can't feel; they can't cry; they can't think. "'Father' is not
a word that dead people understand," they tell Eurydice's father
(Charles Shaw Robinson), when his daughter fails, at first, to recognize him. *Eurydice* speaks in perfectly pitched images as well as
words. It's as if we were gazing at the shadows of a grief beyond language. When Eurydice first arrives in Hades, she insists on finding
a place to sleep, not realizing that no one sleeps in the underworld;
her father tries to contain her distress by building her a room out of
string—a sensational piece of theatrical magic that suggests both a
room and the emptiness that fills it.

Although she knows that Orpheus is coming for her, Eurydice
confides some ambivalence to her father. "This is what it is to love
an artist," she says. "He is always going away from you. Inside his
head there is always something more beautiful." Nonetheless, when
Orpheus arrives, she follows him. In Bray Poor's evocative soundscape, as Orpheus leads his wife up to the surface, the sound of water
dripping gives way to the honking of car horns. Then, as the myth
foretells, Orpheus turns at the last minute to look at Eurydice; suddenly, they begin to recede from each other.

"There is never any third act in a nightmare," the critic Max
Beerbohm said. "They bring you to a climax of terror and then leave
you there. They are the work of poor dramatists." Not in this case.
Somehow, this subtle production works the trick of imagining the

unimaginable. When, at the finale, Orpheus is in the underworld and can no longer hear the music of the spheres, that small moment of silence is spectacular, full of both woe and wonder. ∎

—July 2, 2007

Stage Kiss

Sarah Ruhl is, at thirty-seven, one of America's most frequently produced playwrights. In the past year alone, 244 individual productions of her plays were performed around the country, and there are currently plans for eighteen foreign productions, in twelve languages. Ruhl's droll, limpid, surreal works explore the interplay between the actual and the magical. She likes to call them "anti-money shots"; her newest comedy, however, the smart, rollicking *Stage Kiss* (which was commissioned by the Goodman, in Chicago, and is premiering there), is a bonanza. While some earlier Ruhl plays are perhaps too arcane for a mass audience, *Stage Kiss* (crisply directed by Jessica Thebus) gets down to the carnal, where everyone lives. At once a knowing sendup of the hazy half-truths of stage naturalism and a goofy meditation on the nature of desire and sexual fantasy, the play manages to be both wholly original and instantly recognizable to the audience. And, as a satire of theater and theatricals, *Stage Kiss*, with its combination of hilarity and trenchancy, is right up there with George Kelly's *The Torch-Bearers* and Neil Simon's *The Sunshine Boys*.

Here two former lovers, He (Mark L. Montgomery) and She (Jenny Bacon), actors who parted bitterly about fifteen years earlier, find themselves, on the first day of rehearsal for a revival of a 1930s boulevard melodrama—a lemon called "The Last Kiss"—cast opposite each other, as former lovers. They rehearse scenes of arch palaver ("I want to kiss you all day," her character tells his. "And I you," he replies), and, in between, relive the humiliating moments of their own turbulent past. She cheated on him; He called her names and threw things. He was "baffled for years"; She admits, "I was afraid of you." She is married to Harry (Scott Jaeck) and has a teen-age daughter. He's shacked up with Laurie (Erica Elan), a Pollyanna schoolteacher, and is an overgrown adolescent, "a seventeen-year-old in man pants." Nonetheless, She, haunted by their lost love, has seen all his stage performances; He has watched every one of her *Law & Order* episodes. In a sense, *Stage Kiss* is a ghost play in which both the play-within-the-play and the rebarbative lovers keep the past present. Is life imitating art? Or is art imitating life? Ruhl, in her gleeful counterpoint, gets to have it both ways.

Although *Stage Kiss* owes its inspiration to a plethora of lame Broadway entertainments of the thirties, its comic setup is a reworking of Noël Coward's 1930 play *Private Lives*, in which a quarrelling former husband and wife meet on adjacent hotel balconies while on their respective honeymoons with lackluster new partners, only to rekindle their passion and bolt to Paris for a romantic idyll. Likewise, in *Stage Kiss*, the quarrelling lovers, as they rehearse a saga of sexual paradise regained, fall once again under the spell of romance. They jilt their new partners—who are thrown together by their heartbreak—to live for a while in a cocoon of lust. ("It was like giving bacon to a hungry vegetarian," Harry, the dutiful, abandoned husband, later concedes.)

Private Lives is a comedy of bad manners; *Stage Kiss* is a comedy of bad writing. Coward revels in camp mischief and revenge, Ruhl in memory and harmony. Where Coward is subversive and outrageous ("Certain women should be struck regularly, like gongs"), Ruhl is contemplative and wry. ("Pass me the hot-and-sour soup," She says, while lolling with her lover in a rumpled foldout bed. "It's cold now," He replies. "It's cold-and-sour soup.") But, for all their emotional differences, Coward and Ruhl share three crucial dramatic gifts: for structure, for immediacy, and for frivolity. "Lightness isn't stupidity," Ruhl told me. "It's actually a philosophical and aesthetic viewpoint, deeply serious, and has a kind of wisdom—stepping back to be able to laugh at the horrible things even as you're experiencing them."

In *Stage Kiss*, passion and fidelity engage in a kind of elegant pas de deux over the issue of the stage kiss. According to Harry's calulations, She, as the dying Ada Wilcox, who suffers from the incurable "Johnson's disease," snogs her ex—He plays a sculptor named Johnny Lowell, who rushes to her bedside from his home in Sweden—a grand total of 288 times during the run of the play. "That's not love. That's oxytocin," Harry says, catching the pair in *flagrante* and urging his wife to come home. A kiss is a kind of invasion, an invitation to transgress. The gesture is loaded with complicated feeling, which Ruhl parses to brilliant effect. In her comedy, contrary to the song, a kiss is not just a kiss—it's a battleground fraught with danger as well as delight. But before He and She get down to sharing a real kiss—an event that is delightfully postponed until the end of act 1—they prolong the anticipation by discoursing about tongue hockey, which He maintains the public doesn't like to watch. "They don't enjoy it. They tolerate it," He says. "It signifies resolution . . . but they don't really like to see the act of kissing onstage, only the idea of kissing onstage. That's why actors have to be good-looking, because it's about an idea, an idea of beauty completing itself. You don't like to see people do more than kiss onstage, it's repulsive."

Ruhl gets a lot of mileage out of the repulsion for "swapping spit." When the two actors first start to rehearse together, She bobs and weaves away from him like a glass-chinned bantamweight; and when they finally embrace She says squeamishly, "Did you brush your teeth?" But love changes everything, and the stage kissing rekindles intimacy, so when He breaks his ankle just before opening night, and the gay understudy, Kevin (Jeffrey Carlson), has to stand in, Ruhl turns the moment into a wonderful spectacle of disgust, first by contriving for the poor boy to have crumbs around his mouth and then by lampooning his moves. "He makes this face—this weird face—like he's going to eat me—like a placoderm—you know, one of those jawless prehistoric fish—with teeth," She bleats to the Director (the excellent Ross Lehman), who tries to show her how to fake an embrace, shaking her so hard that he throws out her back.

"I'm interested in poking holes in naturalism," Ruhl said in a pre-show talk. With a deft, withering touch, she exposes the gears of dramatic exposition. For instance, when He has to perform on crutches, Johnny offers up a narrative alibi: "I must be the only sculptor to have had a marble head fall on my foot," he says. Later in the same scene, Johnny and Ada sing and dance: "No one says farewell these days / They hire a car or fly. . . . Farewells are for the birds." At the word "birds," Johnny raises his crutches, giving himself the ludicrous wingspan of a condor. There are verbal pratfalls, too. "Don't speak of death now that we are out of his crutches—clutches," Ada's husband says. In *Stage Kiss*, back walls wobble, and actors trip over thresholds and struggle with costumes and cumbersome props, like a divan. "Divan? Divan? Divan," He says, going briefly off script in the middle of a seduction to get his mouth around the strange word. And Ruhl has great fun mocking the preposterous deluxe milieus of thirties comedies. Ada's house is equipped with a solarium, a library, a billiards room, and a butler called Jenkins. ("I'm playing, you know, Jenkins and the Doctor," Kevin, the understudy, says to the Director, of his two bit roles. "I'm wondering how to do the emotional-journey part? I don't really have a back story?")

Coward's feuding lovers tiptoe away from chaos in the last beats of *Private Lives*; Ruhl's divided couples, on the other hand, repair their madness and achieve a kind of order. "Marriage is about repetition," Harry says to his wife at the finale. "Every night the sun goes down and the moon comes up and you have another chance to be good. Romance is not about repetition." If She has learned a lesson about reality, Harry has learned one about fantasy: he asks to be taught about acting. "Once a week, I can be whoever you want me to be, and you can be whoever I want you to be," he says. "Kiss me in a place with no history and no furniture." The ending is a fairy-tale picture of blessing and balance. Fantasy *and* convention, Ruhl seems to be saying, are part of life's meaning and its joy.

On its journey to New York, *Stage Kiss* will, I suspect, acquire higher-definition players and a director with a surer command of the dynamics of comedy. This admirable premiere, however, has brought a bright and buoyant thing into the world. So, like Ruhl herself, let's quietly kick up our heels and be glad. ■

—*May 30, 2011*

6
CLIFFORD ODETS

On April 17, to mark the centennial of the birth of the playwright Clifford Odets, Lincoln Center Theater will open a new production of *Awake and Sing!*, Odets's first full-length play and the one that made him a literary superstar in 1935, at the age of twenty-eight. In the years that followed, this magazine dubbed Odets "Revolution's No. 1 Boy"; *Time* put his face on its cover; Cole Porter rhymed his name in song (twice); and Walter Winchell coined the word "Bravodets!" "Of all people, *you* Clifford Odets are the nearest to understand or *feel* this American reality," his friend the director Harold Clurman wrote in 1938, urging him "to write, write, write—because we need it so much." "You are the *Man*," Clurman told him.

Odets died, of colon cancer, on August 14, 1963, a month after his fifty-seventh birthday. Nine weeks later, in a high-ceilinged hall above a kosher restaurant, Elia Kazan, the artistic director of the newly minted Lincoln Center Repertory, convened the first rehearsal of the company's first play, Arthur Miller's *After the Fall*. As Kazan rose to address the gathered theatricals—among them Miller himself, who had been influenced by Odets's "unashamed word joy"—Odets was much on his mind. Throughout the early thirties, Kazan and Odets, as members of the Group Theatre, had been sidekicks and disgruntled warriors in the same artistic battles. Kazan had shared Odets's dreams of greatness and of change; they had also shared a railroad flat on West Fifty-Seventh Street—the apartment, "saturated with disappointment," Kazan later said, where Odets wrote *Awake and Sing!*, in a room so small that his typewriter, which he nicknamed Ambition Corona, had to rest on his lap. Kazan had been among the players who shouted, "Strike, strike, strike!" at the finale of *Waiting for Lefty*, Odets's one-act agitprop salvo heard around the world in 1935. He had appeared in Odets's first Broadway hit, *Golden Boy*, and in his last play for the Group Theatre, *Night Music*. He had also been a regular visitor in Hollywood, where Odets spent the last two decades of his life writing screenplays that he referred to as "fudge" and "candy pie," and, in films such as *Sweet Smell of Success* (1957) and plays, later made into movies, such as *The Big Knife* (1949) and *The Country Girl* (1950), mining the legend of his own collapse.

"The tragedy of our times in the theater is the tragedy of Clifford Odets," Kazan began, before defending his late friend against the accusations of failure that had appeared in his obituaries. "His plan, he said, was to . . . come back to New York and get [some new] plays on. They'd be, he assured me, the best plays of his life. . . . Cliff wasn't 'shot.' . . . The mind and talent were alive in the man." On his deathbed, at the Cedars of Lebanon Hospital, according to Kazan, Odets had "raised his fist for the last time in his characteristic, self-dramatizing way and said, 'Clifford Odets, you have so much still to do!' "

Odets had not always resisted the notion of death. By the time he was twenty-five, he had tried to kill himself three times. He was a man of intemperate romantic emotion, haunted by a sense of doom and of transcendence. "I am homeless wherever I go, always lonely," he wrote at the height of his early fame, in his fascinating 1940 journal, published under the title *The Time Is Ripe*.

The first child of three, he was born in 1906, in Philadelphia, to ill-matched first-generation immigrant parents. Pearl Geisinger had emigrated from Romania when she was eight. At sixteen, she was married off to Lou Odets, a pathological powerhouse from Russia, whose cocksureness was contradicted by the modesty of his achievement. Sixteen months later, Pearl gave birth to Clifford. Her life was a history of abdication and lamentation. Trapped, voiceless, and chronically exhausted by her children—her second child, Genevieve, was crippled by polio—Pearl salted away pennies from her family allowance for an "escape fund," which she kept in her sewing basket. (By the time she died, in 1935, she had amassed the considerable sum of three thousand dollars.) "Make a break or spend the rest of your life in a coffin," a character in *Awake and Sing!* pleads to his unhappily married lover. In the play, the woman leaves her family to claim her desires; Pearl never did. Instead, she incarcerated herself at home, cleaning obsessively (she was nicknamed Sanitary Pearl) and enduring her husband's mockery and philandering, punishing him sometimes with days of silence.

According to Margaret Brenman-Gibson, in the superb biography *Clifford Odets, American Playwright*, the family atmosphere was so deadly that the children "dreaded bringing friends home." After Genevieve's illness, when Odets was four, "no one could recall seeing Pearl kiss him." "She wanted to be consoled," Odets later wrote. "So did I. She was lonely, distressed and aggrieved; so was I. As a child, I expected to be petted, brought in (not cast out), consoled, and comforted; and she begrudgingly would do none of these things for me; she was, after all, a child herself." He added, "Any autumn will come, and dusk, and when I am 101, my heart will hurt that when the streets were cold and dark that, entering the house, my mother did not take me in her arms."

Lou, "the business hound," as Odets called him, was no more biddable. Eradicating all hints of the Old World from his speech and his story, the go-getting Lou insisted that he was "born American." He changed his name from Gorodetsky—"city man," in Russian—and added a middle initial, inviting people to address him as L.J., which he felt was a more commanding, all-American moniker. L.J. began his career as a feeder in a print shop and soon rose to own a series of small businesses in Philadelphia and New York; he was also the author of a book called *How to Smooth the Selling Path*. A disciple of "the theology of making a fast buck," as Odets put it in *Sweet Smell of Success*, L.J. never felt the need to apologize for his rapacity. He wanted to be, he said, "a big man—number one." To his son, he was "a two-bit czar," a blowhard with "the insane belief that he must pass on (approve or modify) everything the other person is doing." "I had to fight him every inch of the way not to be swamped and engulfed, to stay alive," Odets wrote.

Even when Odets was an adult, L.J. continued to belittle him as "big boy." "My father [is] driving nails into my head," Odets wrote to a friend. Although he offered L.J. substantial financial assistance— between 1935 and 1950, he gave him more than a hundred thousand dollars—the harangues continued. Trying to persuade Odets to employ him as his manager in 1935, L.J. wrote, "Tell me young man, where have you gotten *all* the experience in the world, you think you have? I have seen men that was raised higher than you, and then seen them drop lower than that. . . . Yes, you are still the 'White Hope' but you are dropping." When, in 1937, L.J. learned that Odets had separated from Luise Rainer, the two-time Academy Award– winning actress, with whom he had a tempestuous three-year mar- riage, he sounded off in all his brutishness: *"I'm ashamed of you. You are the dummist chunk of humanity I have ever come in contact with. . . . Your all ass backwards and sitting on your brains."* Odets internalized this constant excoriation, berating himself in his jour- nal as a "pig," a "pissant," an "idiot," a "loafer," and "twice an ass." He wrote, "It is the father you have *incorporated*, his characteristics and hated elements—*that* is the father to be afraid of!" L.J.'s toxic voice also found its way into some of Odets's most seductive stage villains—the gangsters Eddie Fuseli (*Golden Boy*), Kewpie (*Paradise Lost*), and Moe Axelrod (*Awake and Sing!*), the womanizer Mr. Prince (*Rocket to the Moon*), and the Hollywood mogul Marcus Hoff (*The Big Knife*). As a child, Odets sought refuge from his humiliation in dreams of public heroism. "All my boyhood and youth I thought of the word *nobility* and what it meant," he wrote. An autodidact who read twelve books a week, Odets was especially moved by Victor Hugo, whom he called "the mother of my literary heart." Hugo "inspired me, made me aspire," he noted. "I . . . longed to do heroic deeds with my bare hands, thirsted to be kind to people, particularly the weak and humble and oppressed. From Hugo I had my first feeling of social consciousness." Initially, and perhaps inevitably, as the child of histrionic parents, Odets gravitated to performing. He was, he recollected, "wild . . . to get my name in front of the public," "to get into people's love." Among his first jobs after school was to spin records on New York's WBNY, offering "custom-made commentary" and using the exposure to finagle the free theater tickets that made him the city's "youngest critic," according to Winchell. At seventeen, Odets got his first professional acting job.

When Odets joined the Group Theatre, eight years later, in 1931, he saw it as a creative rebirth—"from the ashes the phoenix," he wrote. He had spent the intervening years as a journeyman actor in an American theater that was still in its teething stages—poor scripts, poor training, poor conditions. "I live low . . . low low low, deep in the stink and slime," he wrote in *910 Eden Street* (1931), an early, autobiographical stab at playwriting. There were times when he existed, he said, on ten cents a day; he holed up in squalid, bug-infested hotels, surviving for months on a diet of shredded wheat and cans of herring. For the most part, his artistic ambitions far exceeded his opportunities. "It is a very horrible thing, having energies and no wagon to hitch them to," he wrote to a friend.

The Group was that wagon. Founded by three theatrical idealists—Clurman, the director Lee Strasberg, and the producer Cheryl Crawford—the company was an attempt to redefine the nature of American theater and to restore dignity to the acting profession. With its emphasis on Stanislavsky's Method and on the notion of a performing collective, it answered Odets's artistic desire to merge with something larger than himself. ("I have begun to eat the flesh and blood of the Group," he wrote in the daybook of the Group's first summer program. "I am passionate about this thing!!!") The Group's embrace of Odets, however, was tentative. "No one thought much of him as an actor except Clifford himself," Kazan wrote in his memoir, *Elia Kazan: A Life*. Certainly, Clurman and Strasberg were not overwhelmed. But, finally, Clurman played his hunch. "Let's have him," he said. "Something is cooking with that man. I don't know if it's potato pancakes or what, but what's cooking has a rich odor."

Odets was hired at thirty-five dollars a week, but, much to his increasing resentment, he never got a good part: in his first four years with the Group, he played a tenant farmer with one line and a bum on a park bench with his back to the audience, and was an understudy. Though he was initially thrilled at the prospect of being directed by Lee Strasberg, he soon discovered that "those actors who had the good parts got the real and best benefits of Strasberg's training, and the others did not." "You felt like a little kid with its nose pressed against the window saying, 'I wish I could get in so I could get some more of those "geegaws" off the Christmas tree,' " he told the theater professor Arthur Wagner. (Out of that resentment came Odets's subsequent practice of writing for an ensemble; in all his early plays, instead of one or two starring roles, there are seven or eight characters of equal importance.)

By his own admission, however, without the Group Theatre Odets would not have become a playwright. His work as an actor encouraged a confidence in his own internal resources. "The so-called

'Method' forced you to face yourself and really function out of the kind of person you are," he said. It also taught him fearlessness and emotional honesty. In 1931, he began to experiment with plays. He wrote a piece about life in Philadelphia and another about a musical genius of the Beethoven variety. He asked for feedback from others in the Group, especially Clurman, who was then Odets's "favorite character outside of fiction." Clurman wrote of the music play, "It showed no trace of talent. I suggested instead that he write about the people he had met and observed the past few years." The suggestion took. "I am sure of it now, know the definite feeling of what to do and how," Odets wrote, at the age of twenty-six, as he began work on the play that would become *Awake and Sing!* "I am filled with materials."

On January 5, 1935, within two minutes of the lights going up on *Waiting for Lefty*, at the Civic Repertory Theatre, on Fourteenth Street, the audience began to clap. "Line after line brought applause, whistles, bravos, and heartfelt shouts of kinship," Clurman wrote. Odets and Kazan, who were part of the cast, were sitting together as plants in the audience. "You saw for the first time theater as a cultural force," Odets recalled. "There was such an at-oneness with audience and actors that the actors didn't know whether they were acting and the audience didn't know whether they were sitting and watching it, or had changed positions." He continued, "I found myself up on my feet shouting 'Bravo!' . . . I forgot I wrote the play, forgot I was in the play. . . . The proscenium arch disappeared." Kazan—who later directed the premieres of *A Streetcar Named Desire* and *Death of a Salesman*—said, "It was the most overwhelming reception I've ever heard in the theater."

Waiting for Lefty, which Odets wrote in three days, crosscut a union meeting with scenes of the aftermath of the Depression, which had left more than one in four workers unemployed. Odets saw life through a Marxist lens, but his play wasn't ideological. With its notes of hurt and hope, *Lefty* depicted effectively onstage, for the first time, the brokenhearted world that Odets knew so well, where, as he said, "there is only shame and regret, resignation and anxiety." Agate, one of the union organizers, tells the workers:

> Well, maybe I don't know a thing; maybe I fell outa the cradle when I was a kid and ain't been right since. . . . Maybe I got a glass eye, but it come from working in a factory at the age of eleven. They hooked it out because they didn't have a shield on the works. But I wear it like a medal 'cause it tells the world where I belong— deep down in the working class! . . . This is your life and mine! It's skull and bones every incha the road! Christ, we're dyin' by inches! For what? For the debutant-ees to have their sweet comin' out parties in the Ritz! Poppa's got a daughter she's gotta get her picture in the papers. Christ, they make 'em with our blood. . . . Slow death or fight. It's war!

Waiting for Lefty became, as Odets said later, "a kind of light machine gun that you wheeled in to use whenever there was any kind of strike trouble." At the end of the premiere, there were twenty-eight curtain calls, and for twenty minutes afterward the dazed audience did not leave the theater; some climbed onto the stage, waiting for the actors to come back out. It was "the birth cry of the thirties," Clurman said. "Our youth had found its voice." Kazan wrote, "None of us was ever to be the same again, and I suppose we all knew it. But we had no idea how far and how fast this change would go. Cliff was to become a god."

"When I mention the word 'American,' it is myself I mean," Odets said, echoing Walt Whitman, after whom he named his son. Like Whitman, Odets, according to Clurman, felt a "blood-tie with the average guy in the street," but, whereas Whitman sang the body electric, Odets sang the body politic. His internal landscape—"the homeless thing"—exactly paralleled the nation's sense of dispossession. And, in his dissection of the American disease, he brought onto the stage a whole range of hitherto undramatized souls. *Waiting for Lefty* made literary material of union goons. *Awake and Sing!* was one of the first sightings on the Broadway stage of the Jewish-American family. "How interesting we all were, how vivid and strong on the beat of that style," Alfred Kazin wrote of the play. "The words, always real but never flat, brilliantly authentic like no other theater speech on Broadway, aroused the audience to such delight that one could feel it bounding back and uniting itself with the mind of the writer."

Idiomatic speech was the key to the tempo of Odets's plays, which expanded the boundaries of stage naturalism. As an understudy to the lead in John Howard Lawson's *Success Story*, Odets had learned the poetic power of the colloquial. "It showed me the poetry that was inherent in the chaff of the street," he told Wagner. "There was something quite elevated . . . in the way people spoke." Odets believed that "new art work should shoot bullets." His wisecracks reached across the footlights with a wallop that no previous American writing for the stage had achieved: "I'm in you like a tapeworm"; "I'm versus you! Completely versus!"; "Diphtheria gets more respect than me!"; "Cut your throat, sweetheart. Save time." At once comic and trenchant, his big-city idiom exposed the brutal adaptations of personality to brutal times; epigrammatic tough talk rippled through the plays and created an unsettling lyrical undertow. "Here without a dollar you don't look the world in the eye," the matriarch Bessie says in *Awake and Sing!* "Talk from now to next year—this is life in America."

Odets thought of his plays as songs. "Perhaps I am the only one . . . who realizes how closely my talent is related to that of songwriters," he said in his 1940 diary. "We start together from a core of lyric. Each of my plays . . . I could call a song cycle on a given theme." Odets brought his passion for music to the construction of dialogue as well; his instinct, according to the film director Alexander Mackendrick, with whom he collaborated on *Sweet Smell of Success*, seemed to be "always to devise patterns of three, four, or five interacting characters." In the swiftness of the ricocheting lines, Odets created a thematic and harmonic density. The first few notes of distinctive complaint in *Awake and Sing!*, for instance, conjure up the stalled life of the Berger household:

> RALPH: Where's advancement down the place? Work like
>   crazy! Think they see it? You'd drop dead first.
> MYRON: Never mind, son, merit never goes unrewarded.
>   Teddy Roosevelt used to say—
> HENNIE: It rewarded you—thirty years a haberdashery
>   clerk!
> *(Jacob laughs)*
> RALPH: All I want's a chance to get to first base.
> HENNIE: That's all?

"All I wanted was two clean rooms to live in, a phonograph, some records," Odets said. In fact, he got a lot more than he bargained for. His meteoric emergence from the lower ranks marked a shift of power within the struggling Group Theatre. In 1934, Odets and the other actors began to take control of the Group's artistic management. Odets and Strasberg were, Odets recalled, "always on the outs." Strasberg had privately dismissed *Waiting for Lefty*, which had been rehearsed without him; discussing *Awake and Sing!* in front of the company, he had humiliated Odets. ("You don't seem to understand, Clifford. We don't *like* your play," he said.) Odets's rise signalled Strasberg's decline. "We decided that Lee inhibited the actors and we should be wary of his influence," Kazan recalled. "I think it cost him his creative life," Odets said. "Because he never recovered." Within a year, Odets had four plays on Broadway.

"An Odets play was awaited like news hot off the presses, as though through him we would know what to think of ourselves," Arthur Miller wrote in his memoir *Timebends*. "In Marxism was magic, and Odets had the wand." Odets himself felt the magic. "Now not only was I a man with a ten-million-dollar arm but I could really direct the ball now just where it wanted to go," he said. He was both inspired and lumbered by this new responsibility. He was the Group's cash cow, and, it seemed to him, he had to provide a calf every season. "I dropped this calf and some people would rush up and grab it, wipe it off and take it away and I would be left there bellowing," he said. "I would let them do it but with a great deal of resentment. They had to have those veal chops on the table."

Walking into the show-biz hangout Lindy's one day, in 1940, Odets was stopped by the actor Lionel Stander. "You are a first-class man," Stander said. "What are you doing with these nitwits?" It was a question that haunted Odets, who by then had grabbed fame's live wire and couldn't let go. He travelled back and forth between New York and Hollywood; he was a habitué of café society; he was living in a Village penthouse; he had a Cadillac and was building a treasure trove of modern art. At the same time, he needed calm and isolation in order to write. "I was not the same young man I used to be but trying to hold on to him," he said. The monk and the winking courtier were perpetually at war inside him. Odets saw his voluptuary itch as a legacy from his mother. "When the child needs consolation . . . and the mother will not give it," he wrote, "the child will later . . . move towards a series of consolations. . . . Sex, self-sex, distractions, arts, gourmandizing, . . . rich clothes, etc." And it was his need both to win his father's approval and to triumph over him that kept Odets forever in thrall to Hollywood's big bucks—money being

L.J.'s only measure of achievement. "I want to be a poor poet and a powerful businessman, a sensational young man and a modest artist with a secret life," Odets wrote in 1940. "There are contradictory pulls—one to live with tightened discipline, sharp, hard and cold; the other to go hotly and passionately to hell as fast and as fully as possible."

His plays charted his struggle for equilibrium, "the aching balance," as he called it. The heroes of *Golden Boy* and *The Big Knife* are both torn between commercial success and artistic fulfillment, driven crazy by their decision to live against their natures; both murder themselves out of nostalgia for their lost integrity. Unlike his characters, however, Odets killed himself not sensationally but by degrees. "I see so plainly what you are trying to do!" he wrote to himself with weird prescience in his 1940 journal. "You will never conquer the MORAL MAN within you! You are trying to kill him, but he will not permit it; he will murder you with regret and anguish first." Still, in his unflinching struggle between heart and appetite, Odets saw honor and perhaps some kind of redemption. "Inner contradictions are not solved by throwing out half of the personality, but by keeping both sides tearing and pulling . . . until an AMALGAM ON A HIGH LEVEL OF LIFE AND EXPERIENCE IS ACHIEVED," he wrote. "Wrestle, Bernie . . . you may win a blessing," the heroine of *The Country Girl* advises the would-be lover she rejects, in the play's last lines. "But stay unregenerate. Life knocks the sauciness out of us soon enough."

Hollywood and the House Un-American Activities Committee were a one-two punch to Odets's reputation. In the thirties, he used much of the proceeds of his lucrative screenplay work to support the Group Theatre. When, after the dissolution of the Group, in 1941, he continued to devote himself primarily to screenplays—among them *Humoresque*, the first draft of *It's a Wonderful Life*, and *None but the Lonely Heart*, which he also directed—Odets was perceived as a sellout to the high art of the theater. "But to what theater was he supposed to remain faithful?" Miller asked. "There was nothing to return to, no theater or theater culture, only show business and some theatrical real estate."

In 1947, the committee listed Odets as one of seventy-nine members of the film community affiliated with the Communist Party. By the time he appeared before HUAC as a "friendly witness," in May 1952, he had married and divorced his second wife, the actress Bette Grayson, and was the father of two children, Nora and Walt. According to Walt Odets, who is now a clinical psychologist in Berkeley, Nora had "serious developmental disabilities. She was going to psychologists, neurologists, endocrinologists her whole childhood. . . . My father was supporting all that." In other words, Odets could not afford to lose his Hollywood income. (In 1954, when Grayson died suddenly, of pneumonia, Odets became a single parent and those paydays became even more important.) According to Victor Navasky, who wrote a history of the era, Odets both "read the Committee the riot act and, in the vocabulary of the day, 'named names.'" His testimony cost him friends and, according to some, his talent. "He was never the same after he testified," Kazan wrote. "He was no longer the hero-rebel, the fearless prophet of a new world. It choked off the voice he'd had."

This point, however, is debatable: Odets wrote both *Sweet Smell of Success* and *The Flowering Peach* after his testimony; the former is one of the era's classic films, and the latter, produced on Broadway in 1954, was originally selected by the judges of the Pulitzer Prize, only to be overruled by the Pulitzer committee, which instead gave the award to *Cat on a Hot Tin Roof*. Odets didn't lose his talent; he lost the attention of his audience. His "ringing tone" was pitch-perfect for the floundering nation in the mid-thirties, but as early as *Night Music*, which was written in 1939, when the country was mobilizing for war, his bursts of passion had begun to sound forced, even to him. "Your fight is here, not across the water," a police detective says to an aspiring soldier in the play. "You love this girl? And you mean it? Then fight for love! You want a home? Do you?—then fight for homes!"

Different times required a different way of speaking. The postwar boom brought abundance to the Republic, and a shift in the cultural ethos, from self-sacrifice to self-aggrandizement. The nation had calmed down and turned inward; so had Odets's idiom, which turned from sociology to psychology. Sometimes judged "dated," because of their schematic construction, Odets's later plays, with their study of bad faith, bear witness to a certain kind of American emptiness that is evergreen. "Half-idealism is the peritonitis of the soul," he wrote in *The Big Knife*; it was an epitaph both for his own self-deception and for what he called "the strange dry country" around him, which had fought a war for freedom abroad only to begin a witch hunt at home.

After the commercial failure of *The Flowering Peach*—he netted only four thousand dollars for two years of work—Odets settled his motherless ménage in Beverly Hills, where he remained until his death, in a series of cluttered rented dwellings. In these chaotic accommodations, according to his son, Odets could usually be found lying on the sofa "in a terry-cloth bathrobe, listening to Beethoven and smoking cigarettes." He was an affectionate but erratic father. "He was like a furious machine," Walt told me. "He lived in a kind of intensity that was constant and relentless." Nora continued to absorb much of Odets's time and energy. As a rebellious teenager, Walt asked to be sent away to boarding school, but Odets refused, saying, "I can't let you go away and leave me alone with Nora." "*That* I couldn't forgive him for," Walt said.

In the five years before he decamped for California, Odets wrote seven plays; in the twenty-two years he lived after the demise of the Group Theatre, he wrote three. "I am seething and swollen, lumpy, disordered and baffled, as if I were a woman fifteen months pregnant and unable to sleep or turn, crying aloud, 'Oh, God, out, out, out!' " he wrote to Brenman-Gibson in the early sixties, by which time even the film work was drying up. To make ends meet, he had to sell some of the paintings off his walls. Odets, who had always been adrift, now was just swamped. "Hapless and helpless," he wrote. "The Jewish prophet is being eaten alive by the Jewish father in me, and if somewhere it doesn't stop soon, I shall be indeed dead."

On the cheap maple kitchen table where he wrote, Odets, at the time of his death, had placed two *Time* articles, both with photographs showing him at his typewriter: one was a 1938 story with the renegade battle cry "Down with the general Fraud!" as a caption; the other was a 1962 clipping headlined "Credo of a Wrong-Living Man," snidely reporting the news of Odets's appointment as a script supervisor and writer for the NBC TV series *The Richard Boone Show*. "I may well be not only the foremost playwright manqué of our time but of all time," Odets wrote in 1961. "I do not believe a dozen playwrights in history had my natural endowment."

It's possible that Odets's narrative of decline is what has kept him from claiming the privileged place in the theatrical discussion that he deserves. Odets's plays showed a way for the next generation of playwrights to combine linear movement with psychological complexity and depth. He brought a new demotic music to stage speech. His subject was always the struggle of the heartbroken American soul under capitalism. "I will reveal America to itself by revealing myself to myself," Odets wrote. His plays and his life, full of unique lament and liveliness, eloquently fulfill his prophecy. ▪

—April 17, 2006

Golden Boy

"With me it is simple: what I am I can write," Clifford Odets said. When the thirty-one-year-old playwright sat down, in 1937, to write a new play to bankroll the foundering Group Theatre—where he had made his name, two years earlier, with *Waiting for Lefty* and *Awake and Sing!*—he felt as if he were being pulled painfully in opposite directions: "one to live with tightened discipline . . . the other to go hotly and passionately to hell as fast and as fully as possible." On the East Coast, where he had a reputation as the Great White Hope of theater—"Bravodets," Walter Winchell had nicknamed him—the Group was hounding him for a hit. On the West, where he was living, he was newly married to the two-time Academy Award–winning actress Luise Rainer and had just completed his first Hollywood screenplay for what seemed like crazy money. ("It was like putting steak before a starving man," the film's director, Lewis Milestone, said of Odets's ten-thousand-dollar fee.) Odets was struggling to hold himself together, and *Golden Boy* (now majestically revived by Lincoln Center Theater, at the Belasco, under the direction of Bartlett Sher), with its emphasis on the struggle between art and commerce, between authenticity and celebrity, was evidence of the tumult of his divided heart. It was also just what the Group Theatre needed. The play, which ran for two seasons on Broadway, was the Group's most successful show; it was turned into a film, in 1939, and a musical, in 1964, which played nearly six hundred performances.

In twelve muscular, psychologically complex scenes, whose economy and structural nuance incidentally reveal how much his theatrical storytelling had benefitted from his Hollywood experience, Odets found a form that, best of all his plays, captured his own internal conflict between, as he characterized it, "the monk and the lewd winking courtier." The hero of *Golden Boy*, the thin-skinned, twenty-one-year-old "cock-eyed wonder" Joe Bonaparte (the excellent Seth Numrich), who gives up the violin for the boxing ring and "who could build a city with his ambition to be somebody," is a simulacrum of Odets as a young whippersnapper, "wild to get my name in front of the public." Joe, like his creator, embraces fame as a form of revenge against the humiliations of his impoverished immigrant childhood; he also finds himself living on the momentum of celebrity and its fantasy of invulnerability. "Speed, speed, everything is speed—nobody gets me!" Joe says. (IIis "speed machine" of choice is a deluxe Duesenberg, which he buys with his first winnings.) Odets's thrilling tale, in which Joe literally and figuratively "makes a killing" in the ring, is a duel between the contending forces of success and integrity. (In early drafts, the play was subtitled "a modern allegory.") Joe's willful self-destruction—he meets his death in Babylon—was a literary intimation of what Odets feared most in life: his own spiritual atrophy.

In *Golden Boy*, for the first time in his oeuvre, Odets put aside speechifying and let dramatic action convey his view of the nation's "purblind sterile life." He was not so much talking to America as listening to it. In Sher's impeccable production, what we hear first is Franklin Delano Roosevelt's offstage voice announcing the formation of the Works Progress Administration. We are deep in the Depression; a sense of desperation has drifted like soot into every corner of American existence, including the tatty Broadway office of the well-named boxing manager Tom Moody (Danny Mastrogiorgio), who "hasn't had a break in years" and whose current palooka has just been scratched from the boxing card due to injury. "It's the Twentieth Century, Tom . . . no more miracles," Lorna Moon (Yvonne Strahovski), Moody's hardboiled mistress, tells him.

No one has written better than Odets about society's bottom-feeders. In one of the best displays of American ensemble acting I've seen, his robust gallery of criminals, cabdrivers, immigrants, union organizers, boxers, and kibitzers is celebrated in all its vivid bustle and vernacular bravado. The stage is filled with memorable characterizations, none more exciting than Strahovski's, in her Broadway debut. As Lorna's name implies, she is "forlorn"; it's hard to find a modern actress who can embody her particular defensive quality—a refusal to hope. Willowy and wan, Strahovski is a beauty who seems wrapped in solitude and sorrow, as if she'd stepped straight out of an Edward Hopper painting in her sturdy two-tone brogues. "I've been underwater a long time," Lorna says, and you believe her. When she is sent by Moody to babysit the wayward Joe, she recognizes in him her own sense of worthlessness. "The thing I like best about you," she says, "you still feel like a flop." When Joe makes a pass at her, he says, "You won't let me wake you up! I feel it all the time—you're half dead, and you don't know it!" "Maybe I do," Lorna replies, half smiling. It's a ravishing line. Strahovski's performance humanizes Numrich's Joe, makes him more than just a mug with a slug. And it's great to see the whole rich shambles of love so well dramatized. "Go to hell!" Lorna tells Moody, as they argue in the opening scene. "But come back tonight."

If Lorna offers Joe the promise of romantic salvation, Joe's loving father (the subtle Tony Shalhoub) offers a path to wisdom. He disagrees with his son's decision to give up the violin, but he won't intervene. "What ever you got ina your nature to do isa not foolish," he says. The lines don't come off the page with the heartbreaking restraint and dignity with which Shalhoub invests them. His Mr. Bonaparte exerts a quiet but commanding gravitational pull on his son and on the story. To Joe, his father is the voice of the Old World and the old values. "I'm out for fame and fortune, not to be different or artistic! I don't intend to be ashamed of my life," Joe tells his father in the dressing room before a crucial bout. "Now I know . . . is'a too late for music," Mr. Bonaparte replies. "The men musta be free an' happy for music . . . not like-a you. Now I see whatta you are . . . I sorry for you." Between father and son, this moment of grief and regret is huge and unbridgeable. It culminates with Joe sobbing into the chest of his understanding trainer, Tokio (the expert Danny Burstein). After his knockout win, however, he exults. His hands have been broken. "Hallelujah!" he shouts. "It's the beginning of the world!" In this terrific moment of vindictive triumph, Joe has lost his guilt, his ability to play the violin, and his soul.

The deep satisfaction of *Golden Boy* lies not just in its prescient critique of American individualism but in the swagger of its slangy idiom, which is always pushing the envelope of realism. Odets can make words dance; they hop, dip, and surprise, like a knuckleball. "You can't insult me. I'm too ignorant," Siggie (Michael Aronov), Joe's brother-in-law, says to Mr. Bonaparte, when he refuses to give him the money to buy a taxi. And when the well-dressed and lethal gangster Eddie Fuseli (the persuasive Anthony Crivello) slinks into the gym, Lorna looks him over and says, "What exhaust pipe did he crawl out of?" For decades, Odets has languished in the discussion of American theater, perhaps the most underrated of America's great playwrights. In this distinguished, almost symphonic production, Sher and Lincoln Center have done a great thing: they have put Odets finally and forever in the pantheon, where he belongs. ▪

—December 17, 2012

DAVID RABE

On the wall of David Rabe's television room, at his home in Connecticut, is a photograph of him as a football player at Loras Academy, the Catholic high school in Dubuque, Iowa, where he was a hard-driving running back and linebacker; in the image, he is being tackled, pushed into the dirt by three opponents. Rabe, now a large, white-haired sixty-eight-year-old with an athlete's body and a writer's stoop, writes the way he used to run: at full tilt, instinctively feeling for an opening, then plunging forward into the unknown. "I get a sentence, an idea, an image, and I start," he said. "I don't know anything beyond it. I follow it." Rabe's theatrical universe is at once vivid and mysterious, a pageant and a puzzle, where his bemused characters glimpse only the barest outline of what one of them calls "the unrelenting havoc" in which they flounder. "Often my characters don't know what the issues of the play are," Rabe told *Bomb* magazine in 2005. "They think they're doing one thing but something else is actually orchestrating their lives." Even Rabe can take some time to fathom what's going on between his characters. Of his four plays set during the Vietnam War, *Streamers* (currently in revival, in a Roundabout Theatre Company production) was begun first—soon after he was discharged, in 1967, from the Army's Sixty-Eighth Medical Group—and was finished last, in 1975. "My way seems to be to work, move on, and then go back," he said in the *Bomb* interview. "*Streamers* . . . came out in three periods of writing consisting of four or five hours at each sitting, but these sittings were spread out over seven years."

In his writing, Rabe—who has produced a wide-ranging body of distinguished drama (four of his twelve plays have been nominated for Tony Awards, and *Sticks and Bones* won one, in 1972), four finely wrought film adaptations (*Casualties of War, Streamers, Hurlyburly, I'm Dancing as Fast as I Can*), and three works of fiction—plays a primal game; his goal, he has said, is to show how "the past hangs on to you and shows up in spooky ways." He is obsessed with the things that haunt us. "People carry those things like physical realities almost," he told me. "They have a definite weight to them." Rabe's daringly stylized dramas hover in the realms between the natural and the metaphorical: angels mediate for the dead; a blinded Vietnam vet comes home to his TV-sitcom parents, Ozzie and Harriet; a gangland caper is played out in "an apartment in the underworld." Rabe's work is a challenge to what he calls the "clockwork universe, clockwork play," in which "certain motions delivered certain consequences in a predictable proportionate way." "What I was after is more like nuclear fission in which the explosion of something minuscule unlooses catastrophic, ungovernable devastation," he wrote in a 1992 afterword to some of his plays.

Rabe's explorations of the psyche mine *rasa*, a concept found in Sanskrit literature, which he defines as "the life thing"—the startling, underground anarchy of the unknown. Soldiers and psychopaths, gods and gangsters, icons and executives parade through his dramas—all, in their unique, vernacular way, eloquent in their unknowing. "Whatsa matter with me?" says Chrissy, a go-go girl in *In the Boom Boom Room* (1972), whose search for her authentic self strands her at a strip club, a masked, topless receptacle for other people's projections. "What'd I do that for?" Phil, a psychopathic ex-con turned actor, asks another palooka, in *Those the River Keeps*, the 1991 prequel to *Hurlyburly*. Just out of prison, Phil has punched and killed a dog that urinated on his hand while he was sleeping. After he hits it, the dog "gets this look . . . like he has been asked a question the likes of which he has never heard of it before and he ain't got a chance in hell of gettin' it right," Phil says. In the face of life's blows, Rabe's characters register a similar traumatized incredulity. His America is a dim and brutalizing landscape of the lost, not so much a "moronic inferno" as "an epic fucking fog," to quote Eddie, the master of *Hurlyburly*'s toxic ceremonies.

For Rabe, the drama between the surface and the subterranean began in Dubuque, in a blue-collar district near the Mississippi River. In the cramped quarters that he shared with his parents and, later, his younger sister, Marsha, there was, according to Marsha, "a tremendous lack of emotional, physical, psychological privacy." She added, "We had to have a lot of inner life, 'cause there wasn't much room for outer life." Rabe's father, William, slept on a pull-out sofa in the living room; his other accommodation to necessity was to give up a poorly paid job at Loras Academy, where he taught history and coached freshman football, for more lucrative work at the local slaughterhouse, a decision that "knocked him for an awful loop," Marsha said. William had been educated at the University of Illinois. "He'd walked out of college and into the Depression, and had had a rough time ever since," Rabe said. At one point, William had played farm-team baseball in Texas; he had also written a couple of unpublished novels. The combination of financial frustration and deferred dreams gave the household an unsettling undercurrent of disappointment. In these strained circumstances, speech and emotion had to be repressed. "The lid was on," Marsha said. Rabe grew up with a certain wariness, which passed as shyness. He became a keen listener and observer, taking up residence in his imagination. When he was a teenager, he directed several eight-millimeter action movies. "Beatings, fist-fights, prison breaks," Rabe said. "We had no money, so I was really frugal about how much I shot."

James Dean—and Dean's death, in 1955, when Rabe was fifteen—had a seismic effect on him. "It was as much his sensitivity as his rebelliousness," Rabe said. "It was the idea that you could take that and turn it into something—art. I didn't know what I was gonna do with it." Rabe became obsessed. He bought a tape recorder and, after each Dean movie, he'd recite the large sections of dialogue he remembered into it. "We would listen to the dialogue and rehearse the scenes," Marsha recalled. "I got to be Natalie Wood, Carroll Baker." Of these experiments, Rabe said, "It was, like, 'Can I act? Can I do this?'" He was tall, good-looking, and, he said, "emotionally truthful and willing to tap into it." Once the idea of becoming an actor had claimed him, he pursued it with fervor, scrutinizing Dean's trajectory from the Actors Studio to the Method and, finally, to Stanislavski's *An Actor Prepares*. "It was like a psychosis," he said of the demands he put on himself. "I thought I was high-level Method acting. I studied, studied, studied."

In his undergraduate years at Loras College, Rabe submerged himself in creative writing and in theater and became a proficient actor. "In the right thing, I was pretty good," he said. To his pragmatic parents, the idea of acting was "appalling, too flamboyant, too outgoing," but Rabe followed his desires. He enrolled in graduate studies in theater at Villanova University, in Pennsylvania, and began to write plays in earnest. But, after two years, feeling "suffocated and needing to knock around"—"I felt I didn't know enough about anything to write," he said—Rabe dropped out and supported himself with a variety of odd jobs, including parking valet and bellhop. Then, in 1965, at the age of twenty-five, he was drafted.

Rabe was stationed in Vietnam in early 1966, before the height of American involvement in the war. His tour was spent doing clerical work and guard duty and building hospitals in an area that soon became the military hub Long Binh. His company was not under daily threat; he was not exposed, he said, "to the horrors of risk." In fact, things were so safe that Rabe felt "secondhand guilt about not being in a combat unit." His big discovery in Vietnam was not the enemy but the emotional anarchy. He has referred to Vietnam as a "carnival." "Barriers were down; restrictions were down; behavior outside the norms," he said. "There was this giddy thing. You could go around one corner and see something horrible, around another and see something thrilling. It was a little like the Wild West." He added, "Had I been there in Tet, it would have been a different story."

Rabe returned from duty in January 1967, so changed by what he had witnessed that he decided he never wanted to act again. "The range of human response was so much more vast and varied than I had imagined," he said, adding, "My writing was liberated once I abandoned acting." While he sorted out his thoughts and the appropriate way to express them, he finished his master's degree, married, and put in two years as a journalist at the *New Haven Register*. During this period, he became "very, very angry" about Vietnam. "I started to feel that nobody over here had anything at stake," he said. "There was just nothing in jeopardy. Everything was so abundant." He added, "Suddenly I had a subject."

Rabe's first professionally produced play, *The Basic Training of Pavlo Hummel*, addressed his own basic training; the clueless, bereft, almost slapstick Hummel—a liar, a thief, and an attempted suicide—looks for himself in the military and finds only abuse, barbarity, and, eventually, death at the hands of a cohort. Hummel has no way to understand his own inchoate feelings. "Real insight never comes," Rabe wrote of this character. "Toughness and cynicism replace open eagerness, but he will learn only that he is lost; not how, why, or even where. His talent is for leaping into the fire." What radiance Hummel does register is seen through closed eyes. "You black on the inside," Ardell, a black guardian angel visible only to Hummel, says. "In there where you live, you that awful hurtin' black so you can't see yourself no way. Not up or down or in or out."

Joseph Papp, the founder of the Public Theater, discovered the script of *Pavlo Hummel* in a pile on his desk in 1971. Before it opened, later that year, Papp told Rabe that he'd produce anything he wrote; he mounted five more of Rabe's plays in the course of the next decade, calling his work "the most important thing I did at the Public." In an e-mail, Rabe wrote, "I have come to believe that without him none of those first plays would have been done. After all, they'd been turned down everywhere, and, without them, probably nothing else would have found its way to the light of day."

In Rabe's second play, *Sticks and Bones*, which delivers a mordant contrast between actual and psychological blindness, David, a blinded vet, tries to open his blinkered family to "a poetic sense of themselves," as Rabe calls it. "I have so much to tell you, to show you," David tells his parents, who don't want to see it. "If I have to lie to live, I will," Ozzie says. David speaks from the soul, where words are evocative, metaphoric, full of feeling and thought; Ozzie and Harriet and their other son, Rick, speak from the defended heart, where language is sterile, uninflected, and doctrinaire. David is deranged, tormented by the apparition of his lost Vietnamese love, Zung. With linguistic pieties and domestic punctilio, Ozzie and Harriet try to spackle over his despair. Rabe writes, in an introduction to the play, "David says of the girl he loved, 'She was a girl to weigh no more than dust.' Ozzie says, 'You pronged a yellow fucking whore.' The simple, real event is hidden by each character in the language he uses." As the play reaches its visionary conclusion, Zung materializes before the family. "Touch her, embrace her," David says. Ozzie strangles her. Ozzie, Harriet, and Rick then help David slit his wrists. Harriet bustles in with pans to catch the blood and towels to cover his lap. "You'll look so grand," she tells him. "No more funny talk." The curtain falls to the upbeat sound of Rick's guitar, which has, according to the stage directions, "a drive of happiness that is contagious":

HARRIET: He's happier.

OZZIE: We're all happier.

RICK: Too bad he's gonna die.

OZZIE: No, no; he's not gonna die, Rick. He's only gonna
      nearly die. Only nearly.

RICK: Ohhhhhhhhhh.

HARRIET: Mmmmmmmmmmmm.

With its allegorical collision between trauma and retreat, *Sticks and Bones* marked better than any other play of its era the bitter spiritual divide between American generations.

To Rabe, Vietnam was a kind of X-ray of the American collective unconscious, "an obscene illumination against whose eloquence we closed our eyes." *Streamers*, the last and best of his Vietnam plays, was the first to truly capture the lethal drift of the culture around him, the unacknowledged desperation, savagery, and selfishness that, in time, turned American streets into a slaughterhouse. Rabe's soldiers, unmoored by an absurd sense of death, shared with American society what he calls "a dizzying impression of being sent on a compassless march."

When the curtain rises on the Virginia-barracks setting of *Streamers* (at the Laura Pels, under the muscular direction of Scott Ellis), it rises on fear. A recruit is pacing, saying, "I just can't stand it." His wrist has been bandaged after a suicide attempt. "We've got to make up a story," Richie (Hale Appleman), a gay soldier, says. He's talking about the recruit, but Rabe is talking about the military itself, and the fiction that it imposes order on chaos. Within the hubbub of his story line, Rabe captures the particularly toxic chemistry of boredom and dread. At the well-scrubbed and meticulous barracks (even the mop hangs from a clip at a right angle to the floor), the recruits work to keep their spirits and their space "looking good," while awaiting their assignment. In the mounting anxiety over where they'll be sent—it's 1965, and the men are being dispatched to Vietnam, or "Disneyland," as they call it—the barracks are a kind of safe house, the bonds of friendship the only fortification that the soldiers can build between themselves and terror. Two drunk sergeants, Cokes and Rooney (Larry Clarke and John Sharian), stagger into the barracks and tell of a daredevil paratrooper who released his parachute from his backpack, intending to grab the lines with his hands (a "streamer" is a parachute that fails to open). They pantomime his fall to earth. "He went right by me," Cokes says. "We met eyes, sort of. He was lookin' real puzzled." Then, to the tune of "Beautiful Dreamer," they mock his hapless descent and his death itself. The bravado of the men brilliantly serves to magnify the panic that it is meant to mask. Everybody onstage here is in free fall.

Caprice arrives in the hulking shape of Carlyle (Ato Essandoh), a transgressive black soldier full of rage and riffs, who comes wanting to befriend Roger (J. D. Williams), another black recruit. "Do you know they still got me in that goddamn P Company?" Carlyle says. "That goddamn transient company. It like they think I ain't got no notion what a home is. No nose for no home—like I ain't never had no home. I had a home. IT LIKE THEY THINK THERE AIN'T NO PLACE FOR ME IN THIS MOTHER ARMY BUT KP." Eaten up by envy, at once funny and fulminating, Carlyle is one of Rabe's most thrilling inventions. Rabe, who writes black characters better than any of his white peers, made his first black friends in the Army. He lets Carlyle express the "looser, noisier, easier" black sense of self he was drawn to. "That the black man's problem altogether," Carlyle tells a white boy in the barracks. "You ever consider that? Too much feelin'. He too close to everything. He is, man; too close to his blood, to his body. It ain't that he don't have no good mind, but he BELIEVE in his body."

As Essandoh superbly plays him, Carlyle is all danger and desperation. At one point, making machine-gun sounds, he slithers drunkenly into the barracks, bringing with him all the primal fears that the homey little cadre room is pitched against. "Practicin' my duties, my new abilities," he says, adding, "Oh, sure, you guys don't care. I know it. You got it made. . . . You got a little home here, got friends, people to talk to. I got nothin'. You got jobs, they probably ain't ever gonna ship you out, you got so important jobs. I got no job. They don't even wanna give me a job. I know it. They are gonna kill me. They are gonna send me over there to get me killed, goddamnit."

Rabe is expert at building the awful pressure of impending woe. The competent cast of this production hits the notes but not always the music of his writing. Nonetheless, his vision is vivid and devastating. When violence comes to *Streamers*, it comes quietly at first. Richie suggests that his two bunkmates leave for a while so that he and Carlyle can have sex. One of them, Billy (Brad Fleischer), is outraged, and throws a shoe at Carlyle. That shoe becomes for Carlyle a symbol of everything the white world has thrown at him. He turns on Billy with a switchblade, cutting his hand. In a fury, Billy denounces Richie as a "gay little piece of a shit cake" and Carlyle as "Sambo." He seems to move past Carlyle, only to fall back and collapse from a mortal wound. "Fuck it, fuck it, I stuck him. I turned it," Carlyle says, his eyes bulging in panic. "This mother army break my heart. I can't be out there where it pretty, don't wanna live!" Rooney accidentally walks into the mayhem. Breaking his beer bottle to defend himself against Carlyle, he cuts his hand. Carlyle bolts out the door. The moment is terrible and hilarious. Rooney bawls, "I hurt myself. I cut myself." Then, as proof that, as Rabe has said, "violence, once it is let loose, has its own mind," Carlyle races back into the room in full psychotic mania and stabs Rooney to death. Even as he is arrested and hauled off, his mad voice proclaims his loneliness. "This is my place, not your place," he shouts from offstage.

———

Rabe sees war, and its sanctioned murder, as part of "the eternal human pageant"—the search for identity. "The poison was not so much that we did what we did as the way we denied that we were doing what we could see ourselves doing on television," he has written. His Vietnam plays bear witness to the fog of war; his later plays are testimony to the postwar psychological blowback—a fog of denial, in which the characters are lost to themselves. ("I was in that fog, among the compassless," he said.) In the early eighties, Rabe began listening to tapes about Eastern philosophy by the spiritual leader Ram Dass and puzzling over the freedom of Shakespeare. "I'd started to see that Shakespearean language was free largely because it was creating the reality surrounding the character—the reality of the character's psyche—not so much expressing what already existed," Rabe wrote in an e-mail. He discovered a similar verbal freedom in gangster lingo, which allowed him, he said, "to struggle with certain complexities and make those complexities fresh, though they might never make it fully into light."

Goose and Tomtom (1982) was Rabe's first full-fledged experiment with mobster patois, and also with the notion that "words create reality rather than reflecting it." The play's title characters, two fearful, loutish, deracinated thugs—the Vladimir and Estragon of petty theft—have abducted the sister of a gangster whom they wrongly suspect of robbing them. Thought, for these two, is notional; they seem to have almost no reflective capacity. Although they exhibit a cornucopia of presenting symptoms—paranoia, guilt, psychotic rage, projective identification—they have no psychological or symbolic imagination. This absence of penetration makes for its own kind of poetry. "I ain't in the expressions on my face and I ain't in my eyes. I don't know where I am," Goose says. Goose and Tomtom spin the wheels of rationality and get nowhere. Out of their manic strategies of self-defense—their surreal fear and loathing, their slapstick violence, their Dadaist banter—a palpable sense of doom emerges, "a doom they can't specify, a doom they persist in seeking to find and to define in order to strike before it arrives," according to Rabe. Unable to deflect their aggression onto other things, they turn it on each other. "I feel like you're gonna—like you're gonna knock me down on the floor and kneel on my shoulders and punch me inna face," Goose says to Tomtom, who categorically denies the intention. "I got it in my head you wanna," Goose says. "Who's puttin' it in my head you do if you don't? I don't know. You don't know. It's confusin'. You promise you ain't." Tomtom promises, then picks up a chair and hits Goose over the head. "Goddamn chair, committin' suicide," Goose says.

"*Goose and Tomtom* sort of opened the door for me," Rabe said. "I didn't know what they were going to say next, and it wasn't going to be rational, necessarily. They were going to imitate each other; they were going to say whatever they wanted. The language was creating the next moment, not their wills, not their thoughts, not their plans."

Goose and Tomtom foreshadowed the literary freedom and the existential misery of Rabe's masterpiece, *Hurlyburly* (1984). In this extraordinary examination of Hollywood's aimless delirium ("My brain has been invaded with glop," one character says), Rabe's characters struggle more consciously than in earlier plays to express the psychic undertow that seems to drag them away from their best interests, but find themselves still unable to describe it: "There's a name for this—it happens—there's a word for it—everybody knows it," Phil, the ex-con turned actor, says. A sort of cosmic fog settles over everyone—a fog, Rabe said, "of half truths, half memories, ideas spun to serve a purpose and so not ideas at all but subterfuges, or spells." Phil conjures it up as he makes his first entrance into the Hollywood Hills home of Eddie, a casting director:

> You know this fog, and I was in it and it was talking to me with
> her face on it. Right in front of me was like this cloud with her

face on it, but it wasn't just her, but this cloud saying all these mean things about my ideas and everything about me, so I was like shit and this cloud knew it.

"To me the unconscious is a sort of fun house," Rabe said. "It has this power of expanding something. Everything gets distorted—it gets bigger than the proportions of the play might justify." *Hurly-burly* is a dark, hilarious, and eloquent testament to this proliferating explosiveness. Phil is one of Rabe's major tragicomic messengers, "the chaotic deliverer of unconscious information that ultimately kills him," Rabe said. A self-confessed "totally out-of-control prick," in the course of the play Phil head-butts a girl, pushes a blind date out of a car, cold-cocks a guy in a bar whose overheard conversation offends him for reasons that he can't recall, and, eventually, kidnaps his baby from his wife, who is in the process of divorcing him. "How come everything turns to shit?" he asks in the middle of his manic mayhem. Phil knows that he's inhabited by some force that works against him. Rather like a meteorologist, he reports on its path as it sweeps across the kingdom of his disoriented self: "We get those dark thoughts . . . you don't think you're thinkin' 'em, so we can't even nail that down, how we going to get beyond it? They are the results of your unnoticed inner goings-on." In the end, embracing suicide as a kind of destiny, he drives at high speed off a canyon road.

Coked to the eyeballs, bingeing on TV and women, Phil's counterpart, the hyperbolic Eddie, is the fulcrum of the play, a scintillating confection of poetry and paralysis. Phil's volatility is, for Eddie, a sensational distraction from his own desperation. "No matter how far you manage to fall, Phil will be lower," Mickey, Eddie's aloof business partner and housemate, tells him. Eddie's ability to answer Phil's constant stream of questions is what gives him confidence. Verbal command is his defense against his own lostness. Plumes of thought sprout from Eddie's monologues, gorgeous arias full of meaning and meaninglessness, whose exhilarating prolixity gives listeners a sense of Hollywood as a vacuum calling attention to itself:

> I mean, the aborigine had a lot of problems—nobody is going to say he didn't—tigers in the trees, dogs after his food; and in the Middle Ages, there was goblins and witches in the woods. But this neutron bomb has come along and this sonofabitch has got this ATTITUDE . . . about what is worthwhile in the world and what is worth preserving. And do you know what this fastidious prick has at the top of its hierarchy—what sits at the pinnacle? THINGS! . . . It annihilates people and saves THINGS. It loves things. It is a thing that loves things. And whether we know it or not, we KNOW it—that's eating at us. And where other, older, earlier people—the Ancients might have had some consolation from a view of the heavens as inhabited by this thoughtful, you know, meditative, maybe a trifle unpredictable and wrathful, but nevertheless UP THERE—this divine onlooker—we have bureaucrats. . . . The air's bad, the ozone's fucked, the water's poison, and into whose eyes do we find ourselves staring when we look for providence? We have emptied out the heavens and put oblivion in the hands of a bunch of aging insurance salesmen whose jobs are insecure.

Mike Nichols, who directed the brilliant first production of *Streamers* (the play is dedicated to him), also directed the Broadway premiere of *Hurlyburly*. The play, the *Times* said, "offers some of Mr. Rabe's most inventive and disturbing writing, in a production of any playwright's dreams." But, unfortunately, not the dreams of Rabe himself, who broke with Nichols over it. "I was desperate for him to cut," Nichols told me, when I interviewed him for a profile in 2000. "I kept saying, 'I won't do this to the audience.'" Rabe admitted that the original script he gave Nichols was "massive" and "needed more work." He added, "I was willing to cut, but I didn't feel I could do it prematurely. We just hit a wall about one scene." In the scene in question, Phil talks about his fear of having a child. Rabe agreed to cut it temporarily, with the proviso that it would be rehearsed later. The scene, however, didn't make it into the production. "Without it, Eddie's caring about Phil doesn't have any resonance," Rabe said. He refused to make any further cuts and went mute in protest. "He couldn't reach me," he said of Nichols. "I wasn't listening." Nichols saw the 2005 New York revival, which staged *Hurlyburly* with the scene restored, and, according to Rabe, said to two of its stars, "Tell David he was right." "We were both right," Rabe says now. "But under the pressures of production and personality, a genuine, equitable solution wasn't possible." Nichols gave Rabe a hit show, but it cost them their relationship.

Rabe had already lost his first creative mentor, Joseph Papp. "I've never known anyone as contradictory," Rabe has said of Papp. "He had a powerful artistic human side that was in unresolved conflict with a tremendous ambition and desire for control. I've met people who were as generous and helpful and creative as Joe, and I've met people who were as dangerous as Joe, but I've never encountered these things in any other single person." Papp admired Rabe's mastery, but he was frustrated by his metabolism. Papp's rhythm was restless and swift; Rabe was reflective and slow. " 'For David to change course, to change his mind, it's like an aircraft carrier turning around,'" Rabe recalled Papp saying. " 'It takes a long time.'" Increasingly, Rabe found himself caught between Papp's need for product and his own process of discovery. In this conflict, institution trumped artist. *The Orphan* (1973), a play that didn't find wide critical or popular success, failed, according to Rabe, because it was mounted before being fully explored. The final break between Rabe and Papp occurred over the latter's botched 1982 production of *Goose and Tomtom*, a difficult play, which Papp had scheduled and cancelled once before. Papp wanted to make certain changes in the play. "I said, 'You can make those changes, Joe, as long as you don't open it to the press,'" Rabe said. "Then one day I picked up the paper and saw that it was opening to the press. I tried to send telegrams to the various critics saying I didn't approve. Anyway, it opened. I felt I couldn't trust him to work with."

"I've done far less than I thought I would when my first play was performed professionally," Rabe wrote, in the clear-eyed afterword to his second volume of Vietnam plays. "I never found a professional environment that made the production of plays efficient. Teamwork is demanded, but there are very few teams." Although in recent years Rabe has found allies in the New Group and the Roundabout Theatre Company, to a certain extent he has withdrawn from the playing field. In 1994, he moved to a sixteen-acre estate in the northwest corner of Connecticut, with his second wife, the actress Jill Clayburgh. "I feel a little strange about the theater," he told me when I visited him there. "I feel the longer I'm out of it, the less likely I'll be let back in it. Moving up here has truncated my relationship with the theater."

His focus, he said, had shifted. "The change was more a turning toward something than a turning away from anything," he wrote in an e-mail. "I have a sort of reclusive side to my nature that was coming to the foreground. I was older. Time could be seen to be running out." These days, Rabe works in a converted two-story garage, a few yards from his back door. When there is no one at home (Clayburgh is gone for months at a time, shooting the TV series *Dirty Sexy Money*, and their two children have moved away), Rabe often sleeps in a bed in the corner of the ground floor—a small clearing in a forest of files and papers. Upstairs, past a water cooler, a James Dean poster, and photographs of his dogs, the five-hundred-square-foot space is a sea of books—books in bookcases, books in piles, books stashed, according to subject matter, in dozens of black bags that litter the floor. Three writing desks, two computers, and chairs loom like islands in a literary deluge. "There's no demand for a body of work, though writers will be criticized for not having produced one," Rabe noted about playwriting, in 1992. In recent years, he has spent more of his time writing fiction than plays. He has several novels under way. "I hope to finish a lot of these things, but who knows," he said. Writing his latest novel, *Dinosaurs on the Roof,* "was a deeply satisfying time." "I just felt I was really on something alive, which is all you can ask for, frankly," he said. ▪

—November 24, 2008

Hurlyburly

David Rabe's *Hurlyburly,* written in 1984 and well revived by the New Group's deft, high-octane cast (at the Acorn, on Theatre Row), is some kind of great play—a wild, daring, mysterious brainstorm that channels the horror and hilarity of the chaotic household of two debauched TV casting directors in the Hollywood Hills. As the assembled wastrels stumble, snort, and screw through their days, explosions of paranoia and rage, of sexual and moral carelessness flare across the stage in wonderful, frenzied riffs of inspired vernacular. "I mean, basically we all know the MO out here is they take an interesting story, right?" the coked-up casting director Eddie (Ethan Hawke) explains to his sidekick, Phil (Bobby Cannavale), an ex-con and an aspiring actor. "So like every other whore in this town, myself included, you have to learn to lend your little dab of whatever truth you can scrounge up in yourself to this total, this systematic sham—so that the fucking viewer will be exonerated from ever having to confront directly the fact that he is spending his life face to face with total shit."

In a consumer society, the American sociologist Ivan Illich observed, "there are two kinds of slaves: the prisoners of addiction and the prisoners of envy." *Hurlyburly* brings together both constituencies. All the characters are conspicuously wasted. They have sunk to the bottom of their own emotional sea. Terminally distracted, unable to think, and, finally, even to find words for their feelings—"Rapateta, rapateta. Blah blah blah" is the play's mantra—they are lost not only to the world but to themselves. Their minds may be racing, but their souls are stuck in a hell of their own making. This spectacle of faithlessness, which is directed by Scott Elliott, is at once awful and beautiful. ■

—February 14, 2005

8
HAROLD PINTER

On a grisly London evening last October, as the Victorian street lamps of Holland Park were flickering in the twilight, I arrived too early for an appointment at Harold Pinter's handsome town house. Pinter, who is seventy-seven, and who, for the past five years, has battled esophageal cancer and a rare skin disease that has twice brought him near death, had insisted that I come by, even though he'd been ill earlier in the week. "Better strike while the iron is hot," he'd said. I could see him through the high, arched window of his living room, parked in an armchair by the fire, almost sculptural. A walker was strategically positioned behind him. For decades a dynamo—the author of some thirty plays and two-dozen screenplays, the director of more than twenty productions, and an influence on such dramatists as Heathcote Williams, Joe Orton, David Hare, and David Mamet—Pinter was winding down.

Over the years, Pinter's work has inspired a journal (*The Pinter Review*), added words to the English language (*The Oxford English Dictionary* lists "Pinteresque," "Pinterism," "Pinterian," and "Pinterishness" as acceptable terms), won dozens of awards, including the Nobel Prize in Literature, in 2005, and made him an object of perpetual public fascination in Britain. (His recent performance in Samuel Beckett's *Krapp's Last Tape*, at the Royal Court—he began his career as an actor—sold out its entire run in sixteen minutes.) No other British playwright since Noël Coward has so dominated and defined the theatrical landscape of his time. Even Coward, who hated the New Wave that put him out of fashion, considered Pinter an exception. "Your writing absolutely fascinates me," he wrote to Pinter in 1965 after seeing his third full-length play, *The Homecoming*. "You cheerfully break every rule of the theater that I was brought up to believe in, except the cardinal one of never boring for a split-second. I love your choice of words, your resolute refusal to *explain* anything and the arrogant, but triumphant demands you make on the audience's imagination. I can well see why some clots hate it, but I belong to the opposite camp—if you will forgive the expression."

I leaned against a wall rereading *The Homecoming*, which was what I'd come to discuss with Pinter and which was about to celebrate the fortieth anniversary of its debut on Broadway with a new production at the Cort Theatre (directed by Daniel Sullivan). The paperback copy of the play that I held in my hands had been purchased during the Broadway debut, at the Music Box, under the sensational direction of Peter Hall, in 1967. I'd seen the show on a Tuesday, bought the play at intermission, and returned to the Wednesday matinee to notate the blocking.

The Homecoming changed my life. Before the play, I thought words were just vessels of meaning; after it, I saw them as weapons of defense. Before, I thought theater was about the spoken; after, I understood the eloquence of the unspoken. The position of a chair, the length of a pause, the choice of a gesture, I realized, could convey volumes. In 1967, I didn't know quite what I'd seen; I knew only that the play's spectacular combination of mystery and rigor had taught me something new about life, about language, about the nature of dramatic storytelling. Pinter had taken the narration out of theater: *The Homecoming* offered no explanations, no theory, no truths, no through line, no certainties of any kind. I was drawn to the charisma of the work in the same way that Pinter—I later learned—had been compelled by Shakespeare. "You are called upon to grapple with a perspective in which the horizon alternately collapses and re-forms behind you, in which the mind is subject to an intense diversity of atmospheric," he wrote in "A Note on Shakespeare," in 1950, six years before he started to do a similar thing with his own plays.

I was teaching night school when I first saw *The Homecoming*, and I wanted to use the play in my class. I wrote to Pinter in care of the theater. To my amazement, he replied. We met at Sam's, near the Music Box, on Forty-Fifth Street. I was twenty-six. I had never met a playwright before. I couldn't have known then how frequently our paths would intersect over the decades: *The Homecoming* was the subject of my first book; for a few years in the early eighties, Pinter's son, Daniel Brand, from whom he is now estranged, was a tenant in my house; and my friend and downstairs neighbor in London, the director Karel Reisz, was probably the best interpreter of Pinter's later plays and the director of one of Pinter's best screen adaptations, *The French Lieutenant's Woman* (1981). While Reisz and Pinter were working on their screenplay, Pinter's silver Mercedes convertible was often parked outside our house. Once, just before a work session, my wife and our four-year-old son, Chris, sat at Reisz's kitchen table with Pinter as he held forth in his commanding manner. When Pinter left the room, Chris turned to us and asked, "Is he a policeman?" "No," his mother said. "He's a very good writer." "Can he make a 'W'?" Chris asked. (Pinter alluded to that incident in his introduction to volume 4 of his *Plays*; "One of the most interesting— and indeed acute—critical questions I've ever heard," he wrote.)

The Homecoming is the last and best play of Pinter's fecund early period (1957–65). It is a culmination of the poetic ambiguities, the minimalism, and the linguistic tropes of his earlier major plays: *The Birthday Party* (1958), whose first production lasted only a week in London, though the play was seen by eleven million people when it was broadcast on TV in 1960, and *The Caretaker* (1960), an immediate international hit. *The Homecoming* is both a family romance and a turf war. A professor of philosophy, Teddy, returns to London after six years in America to introduce his wife, Ruth, to his father, a butcher named Max, to his uncle Sam, a chauffeur, and to his brothers, Lenny, a pimp, and Joey, an aspiring boxer, all of whom haunt Max's cavernous living room, a sort of cave for the barbarians within.

By contrast, Pinter's living room is capacious and elegant, overflowing with books, family photographs, paintings, and flowers. The first time I met Pinter to talk about *The Homecoming*, he was dressed in a black leather jacket, a black turtleneck, and black pants; forty years later, he was still in black, except for a raffish pair of pink wool socks that he wore, he explained, for circulation reasons. Pinter has always been as vigilant about his look as about his prose. He is not a dandy; he is an actor in the habit of watching himself go by. The beloved only son of a Jewish East End tailor, he was, even as a young man, what might then have been called "natty." Black, his favored color, set him apart and generated an aura of authority about him; it also worked as a kind of spotlight, focussing the viewer's eye on the sharp features of his large head. Like his plays, the young Pinter combined an external formality with an internal ferocity.

Even now, recuperating from illness, he had an exactness, a scrupulousness of mental focus, that generated a palpable tension. In his negotiations with the world, Pinter always seems braced. "There is a sense of danger about him all the time," Peter Hall, who has directed seven of Pinter's plays, including *Betrayal* (1978), the best drama of his middle period, told me. "Although he's the most good-hearted and generous man, people are frightened of him. He has this stentorian voice and a very rich vocabulary. He also has a kind of physical presence. You can quite see him hitting somebody." When I leaned forward to pour the wine that had been set out for us, Pinter took the bottle away from me. "I can still pour a glass of wine," he said.

"The author's position is an odd one," Pinter said in his Nobel Prize acceptance speech. "The characters resist him; they are not easy to live with; they are impossible to define. You certainly can't dictate to them. To a certain extent, you play a never-ending game with them, cat and mouse, blind-man's bluff, hide-and-seek." In *The Homecoming*, Pinter's game of hide-and-seek begins with the play's ironic title. Whose homecoming is it? At first glance, it seems to be Teddy's. Or is it Ruth's? As we discover, she was born nearby. Ruth knows the lay of this desiccated land, with its reservoirs of furious disappointment. Her comfort in this milieu is what makes credible her eventual outrageous decision to leave Teddy and her three children and stay in Max's female-starved household. In this neglected environment, Ruth, at last, feels needed. In one way or another, she is the object of each man's hidden desires: the aging Max wants to feel potent; Sam wants company; Joey wants to be nurtured; and Lenny wants a trick to put on the game. Sensual, elegant, and private, Ruth hides her anger behind a facade of self-control—which Pinter makes clear, in a scene in which she encounters Lenny on the night of her arrival. Ruth knows Lenny's argot; she reads the vulnerability behind his brazen aggression. Later, when Lenny tries to take a glass of water from her hand, Ruth calls his bluff. She holds her glass toward him:

RUTH: Have a sip. Go on. Have a sip from my glass.
He is still.
    Sit on my lap. Take a long cool sip.
She pats her lap. Pause.
She stands, moves to him with the glass.
    Put your head back and open your mouth.

LENNY: Take that glass away from me.

RUTH: Lie on the floor. Go on. I'll pour it down your throat.

LENNY: What are you doing, making me some kind of
    proposal?

She laughs shortly, drains the glass.

The Homecoming's territorial free-for-all is waged with a rhetorical panache that is almost Jacobean in its richness and its ferocity. Its vulgar verbal impasto created a stage sound that was entirely
new. Pinter, according to David Hare, "cleaned the gutters of the
English language." "He kicked the whole thing down," David Mamet
said. Nowhere in the decorous restraint of postwar British theater
could you hear, for instance, anything approaching the brio of Max's
roaring tirades at his "wet wick" brother: "One lot after the other.
One mess after the other. . . . Look what I'm lumbered with. One
cast-iron bunch of crap after another. One flow of stinking pus after
another." Until Pinter, contemporary British playwrights had purveyed a series of well-made forms of exposition. Terence Rattigan
admonished society in neatly resolved problem plays; John Osborne
hectored Britain and took its temperature; Noël Coward made
charm his solution; Arnold Wesker sent a Socialist message through
his characters, and T. S. Eliot a Christian one. "The attitude behind
this sort of thing might be summed up in one phrase: '*I'm* telling
you,' " Pinter said in 1962.

Pinter's plays, on the other hand, offered no exhortations, no
admonitions, no solutions, no common ground among people. "I
think there's a shared common ground all right, but that it's more
like a quicksand," he wrote. "We are faced with the immense difficulty, if not the impossibility, of verifying the past. I don't mean
merely years ago, but yesterday, this morning. What took place,
what was the nature of what took place, what happened?" Pinter's
plays reenact this difficulty of knowing. "Meaning which is resolved,

parceled, labelled and ready for export is dead . . . and meaning-less," he wrote in a letter to the first director of *The Birthday Party*, in which he refused to explain his characters. In another letter, to a British theater magazine, in 1958, Pinter wrote, "To supply an explicit moral tag to an evolving and compulsive dramatic image seems to me facile, impertinent, and dishonest. Where this takes place it is not theater but a crossword puzzle. The audience holds the paper. The play fills in the blanks. Everyone's happy. There has been no conflict between audience and play, no participation, nothing has been exposed. We walk out as we went in."

At the brilliant finale of *The Homecoming*, as Ruth is enthroned in Max's chair, with the new order established and the men grouped around her, Max falls to the floor and sobs; he crawls toward Ruth, who is stroking Joey's hair like a lap cat. "I'm not an old man," Max says. "Do you hear me? Kiss me." As the curtain falls, it is clear that the distribution of power among the people onstage is poised to change. But neither the characters nor the audience knows what that rearrangement will be. Earlier in the play, Lenny tells a tall tale about having beaten a woman who was "falling apart with the pox." Ruth punctures his story with a practical question: "How did you know she was diseased?" "How did I know?" Lenny says. "I decided she was." The truth, in other words, is anybody's guess. Meaning is what you make it. (Pinter's refusal to draw conclusions in his plays means that some productions capitulate to the anxiety of the unknown. When the curtain came up on a Bulgarian staging of *The Homecoming*, he thought he was in the wrong theater. "A large man and a small woman were running around the stage, looking into a lighted house," he said. "They kept coming back, these two, in various guises and modes." These additions turned out to be two frequently invoked but always offstage characters—MacGregor, Max's legendary mate, and Jessie, Max's faithless wife.)

The territorial battle being waged in *The Homecoming* is ulti-

mately not about the house or the woman but about whose perception of reality will prevail. Teddy, a professional maker of meanings,
insists, "I'm the one who can see. That's why I can write my critical works." Ruth, however, has a physicality that overrides Teddy's
epistemology. "Look at me," she says. "I . . . move my leg. That's all
it is. But I wear . . . underwear . . . which moves with me . . . it . . .
captures your attention. . . . The action is simple. It's a leg . . .
moving. My lips move. Why don't you restrict . . . your observations
to that? Perhaps the fact that they move is more significant . . .
than the words which come through them." The thrill of the play is
its realization of Pinter's aesthetic: a precarious balance between
ambiguity and actuality. "There are no hard distinctions between
what is real and what is unreal, nor between what is true and what
is false," Pinter said in his Nobel speech. "A thing is not necessarily either true or false; it can be both true and false." This paradoxical approach forces both the actors and the audience to play harder.
Both are drawn into a highly charged dramatic metaphor in which,
as Pinter said, "everything to do with the play is in the play."

The characters' parries, challenges, and volte-faces are violently
emotional improvisations, whose drama is only underscored and
heightened by Pinter's signature pauses. "The speech we hear is an
indication of that which we don't hear," he once wrote. "It is a necessary avoidance, a violent, sly, anguished or mocking smoke screen
which keeps the other in its place." "When we were rehearsing *The
Homecoming*," Peter Hall told me, "I remember Paul Rogers saying
to me, very early on, 'What's all this about the pauses? We decide
where the pauses are.' And I said, 'No, you don't. Not anymore. The
author has decreed where the pauses are. It's our job to find out why
they're there.'"

"One pause is quite unlike another pause," Pinter said suddenly
as we were talking, then stopped. "There, I just paused. That didn't
take me very long. A pause can be a breath. What it has to do with

is thought: what has just been said and how to respond to what has been said. Pauses are not musical devices. They should be natural." Pinter's wife, the historian and biographer Lady Antonia Fraser, describes pauses as "the curse of Pinter." Pinter has sometimes cursed them as well. He attended a rehearsal for one all-star production of *The Homecoming* (with Pierre Brasseur, Emmanuelle Riva, and Claude Rich, at the Théâtre de Paris) that he thought ran an hour too long. "They took my word 'pause' literally," he said. "It was an extremely tedious enterprise."

*T*he Homecoming is a summation of the iconoclasm and the truculence that brought Pinter to the peak of his writing career. When he was a young man, anger defined him. "I'd never met anyone like this before," Dilys Hamlett, an early girlfriend of Pinter's, told his biographer Michael Billington. "I always have an image of Harold striding down the street in his navy-blue coat with a rage against the world. But it was also a rage for life, a rage to do something, a rage to achieve something." By the time he was twenty, Pinter had renounced Jewish orthodoxy, military service (he was a conscientious objector), and the Royal Academy of Dramatic Art; by the time he was thirty, he had abdicated the principles of contemporary dramaturgy.

He wrote *The Homecoming* in six weeks in 1964. "It kind of wrote itself," he said. He remembers being surprised by the process and laughing a lot at the toxic, belligerent family that was emerging from him. By then, Pinter had got together enough money to move, with his first wife, the actress Vivien Merchant, and their infant son, from a cramped flat in Chiswick to a bow-fronted Regency house in Worthing, on the Sussex coast. The magnificent barrenness of the play's North London setting was imagined as he sat at his writing desk overlooking gardens, within earshot of the sea.

When Pinter finished the play, he gave it to Joe Brearley, the inspirational teacher who had first introduced him to drama when he was still a student at Hackney Downs Grammar School, in the mid-forties. (Brearley had also cast Pinter as Macbeth in a school production in which he got national attention—"Master Harold Pinter made a more eloquent, more obviously nerve-racked Macbeth than one or two professional grown-ups I have seen in the part of late years," Alan Dent wrote in the *News Chronicle*.) Brearley had been adopted as an honorary paternal member of Pinter's close-knit gang of friends, whose competitive camaraderie played a crucial part in his coming-of-age, and he happened to be visiting Pinter in Sussex. "I gave him the play to read," Pinter recalled. "I waited in another room. About two hours later, I heard the front door slam. I thought, Well, here we are. He doesn't like it. About an hour later, the doorbell rang. I answered it. He said, 'I had to get some air.' He said, 'It is your best.'"

Pinter, on some level, agrees. "I think it's the most muscular thing I've written," he told me. "I delight and relish in language. I certainly did with *The Homecoming* to an extent that I probably haven't done in any other play." Pinter, who wrote poetry long before he attempted a play, creates drama like a poem, working entirely out of the unconscious. He starts with an image or a phrase; he teases it out, listening and rearranging until the words suggest a character and the character suggests an action. In an early note for *The Homecoming*, he scrawled the word "jealousy." Beside it, like a sort of rhyme scheme, he wrote:

A of B and C
C of B and A
B of A and C

When the characters finally arrive on the page, Pinter knows no more than what they tell him. As he told a group of drama students in 1962, "You and I, the characters which grow on a page, most of the time we're inexpressive, giving little away, unreliable, elusive, evasive, obstructive, unwilling. But it's out of these attributes that a language arises. A language, I repeat, where under what is said, another thing is being said." In this sense, Pinter took the actor's understanding of subtext and turned it into a metaphysic. This discovery allowed him to distill and reconfigure the inspiration of Samuel Beckett—he was reading Beckett from 1950 on—into his own distinctive rhythmical, alliterative idiom, which made a drama of utterance, not explanation, and where the appearance of reality was an uncompromising dissection of the unknown. Mamet, speaking of Pinter and Beckett, said, "They did what few dramatists have done in modern times: they construed the drama not as the interplay of ideas but as the interplay of *sounds*. That is, they understood the drama as a poem, which had the capacity to move, as does a real poem, musically—to affect on a pre-rational level."

"Over the previous ten years, there'd been quite a lot of talk about the regeneration of theater in poetic terms—Eliot, Fry, Auden," Hall told me. "Harold seemed to me to encompass all that and more. He should be seen as a poetic dramatist. It's the use of words in an extremely disciplined, contained way. It uses, in fact, all the time-honored devices of rhetoric, but it doesn't parade them. Harold didn't want something that made a statement, because a statement was lacking in ambiguity." After years of performing thrillers and melodramas in repertory, Pinter also wanted, he said, "nothing from the bargain basement" of boulevard entertainment.

For *The Homecoming*, he began with a sentence, the play's opening words: "What have you done with the scissors?" "I didn't know who was saying it," he said. "I didn't know who he was talking to. Now, the fellow he was talking to—if he had said, 'Oh, I've got them right here, Dad,' there would have been no play. But instead he says, 'Why don't you shut up, you daft prat?' Once that's said, there's a spring of drama, which develops and follows its own course. I had no idea what the course was going to be. I hadn't planned anything. In the back of my mind, I think I knew there was another brother going to come back. I think I saw them quite early in a big house, with the doors being taken down, leading to a stairway. I saw them moving in that space."

"An old house in North London": *The Homecoming*'s first stage direction situates the play both in an internal landscape and in the atmosphere and the idiom of Pinter's Hackney youth. "It's all to do with me in some way or another," he said in a television interview in 1965. "You're not consciously looking back to Hackney, to the life, the values, the threats. Not at all. . . . But it's a world related to you, otherwise you wouldn't write it." The play's dialogue, a kind of constant face-off between characters, is lifted from the Cockney lingua franca with which Pinter and his mates used to tease each other, as well as the local fascists who bullied them. "We'd go into one of their cafés and say, 'Cup of tea and a sort-out, please,'" Pinter's longstanding friend the actor Henry Woolf told me. "We had a few encounters. I've seen Harold hold off a whole mob of them."

Even then, among his friends, Pinter was a pathfinder. "He was extremely adventurous," Woolf said. "I must give him credit for that. We were just beginning to trot, and he was galloping. Socially, sexually, he was precocious. He was sniffing around London." In *The Homecoming*, the characters also bowl around London—the docks, the West End, Eaton Square, Wormwood Scrubs. Like the claustrophobic dereliction of Max's house, Hackney was, for Pinter, "a kind of prison." In time, that oppressiveness fuelled a group exodus. One of Pinter's closest friends, Morris (Moishe) Wernick, having secretly married, immigrated to Canada, where he taught high-school history; eight years later, in 1964—just before *The Homecoming* was written—Wernick returned for the first time to introduce his wife and his children to his father. That situation was Pinter's springboard. Max was also fabricated partly from Pinter's Wernick-family memories. "The image of Moishe's father in cap and plimsolls was one I carried with me," he told Michael Billington. "I knew him to be a pretty authoritarian figure. A really tough old bugger." When Woolf saw the play, he called the resemblance "otherworldly." "Harold had captured the tone of the voice and the environment," he said. "There was just the same sniff in the kitchens of the two houses."

The success of *The Homecoming* catapulted Pinter into an unmooring few years. In 1964, he moved Merchant and their son into an imposing six-story town house on Hanover Terrace, overlooking Regent's Park. "Nobody just rings the door and comes in," he said. Antonia Fraser told Billington, "It was the grandest house I've ever been in. . . . Every room was immaculate with this terrible silence." As Pinter's circumstances changed, so did his plays. They became smaller in scale, more internal, more mannered and abstract. (Only in his late masterpiece *Moonlight*, of 1993, did Pinter provide a metaphor as searing and complete as in *The Homecoming*.) Increasingly cut off by his celebrity from the roiling world that had made him, Pinter soon hit an impasse. "I am writing nothing and can write nothing," he said, while accepting the Shakespeare Prize, in 1970. "I don't know why. It's a very bad feeling, I know that, but I must say I want more than anything else to fill up a blank page again, and to feel that strange thing happen, birth through fingertips." He added, "When you can't write, you feel you've been banished from yourself."

Pinter waited out his unconscious by hiring himself out as a director and screenwriter between plays. The screenplays—including *The Quiller Memorandum*, *The Go-Between*, *Accident*, and *Langrishe, Go Down*—allowed him to practice his craft and bide his time until his own characters returned.

In the forty years since the debut of *The Homecoming* on Broadway (it received a lukewarm critical reception before becoming a cause célèbre), the play has gone from controversy to classic. As one of drama's preeminent stylists, Pinter has had the good fortune to live long enough to instruct other theatricals about his idiom and to have enjoyed a number of first-rate productions of his work. In the beginning, *The Homecoming* was a vexing avant-garde conundrum; now it's essential reading on every modern-theater syllabus. Time has made the audience and the actors more aware of Pinter's game; this relaxation allows for a greater appreciation of the gusto of his humor, as well as of his intellectual daring. Among the many pleasures of the current Broadway revival—a fine ensemble, adroit playing, limpid interpretation—the most piquant is the revelation that the play is profoundly funny.

Laughter can excuse many things; here, it triumphs over Eugene Lee's misjudged set, which sits like a lean-to in the middle of the Cort's wide stage, flanked on either side by flats designed to look like shiny black brick walls—which have neither the whiff of authenticity nor the appropriate atmosphere of collapse. This incongruity is not as bothersome, however, as the set's lack of containment— there are no sidewalls—which allows the psychic pressure of the jousting to dissipate somewhat. "What do you think of the room? Big, isn't it?" Teddy (the excellent James Frain) says, when he introduces Ruth (Eve Best) to the place. The line is startling not because the room is vast but because it isn't. From the tattered hallway wallpaper and the exposed beams above the living room's threshold, it's clear that Max's house is dilapidated; however, it is still, to my eyes at least, overdecorated, with a colored pitcher and glasses, a mirror, Joey's dumbbells visible under a record player. The set does little to enhance the play's minimalist resonances, but at least it doesn't impede the nuance of Pinter's language, which like all great poetry yields up more insight with each viewing.

There are many tasty interpretations here—the punishing punctilio of Michael McKean's Sam, the lapdog loneliness of Gareth Saxe's

Joey—but Eve Best's Ruth is the most revelatory. The original Ruth—
Pinter's first wife, Vivien Merchant—was memorable but arch. Best
is soft and accessible, which makes Ruth's battened-down alienation
all the more exciting. At one point in act 2, Ruth, perched on the arm
of a chair, looking into the middle distance, and holding a cup of coffee, begins to tell Max about her past. "I was . . . different . . . when
I met Teddy . . . first." "No, you weren't," Teddy says. "You were the
same." Teddy refuses to see Ruth as she is. Best turns her head away;
her cup chinks against the saucer. The sound, like that of a stone
dropped into a well, registers the depth of the distance between them.

Best's articulate energy raises Frain's game. His Teddy unearths
from the script's buried treasures something new to me: he makes
us see the ruthlessness of Teddy's indifference. Teddy doesn't give a
damn about Ruth. ("You can help me with my lectures when we get
back," he says, by way of trying to lure her home to their American
life.) Just as Teddy comes downstairs with their bags packed, Lenny
(Raúl Esparza) asks Ruth for a dance. They sway together to a moody
tune, then they kiss. As Best pulls out of the embrace, her head tilts
back as if she were gulping water after a long thirst. The moment is
terrific. Ruth's desire is finally both acknowledged and answered.
Because Best is able to chart this emotional desert with such depth
and precision, Ruth's final line to Teddy as he leaves—"Don't become
a stranger"—illuminates the enormity of her perverse revenge, at
once devastating and tormenting.

Ian McShane, as Max, knows the Pinter terrain well; he gets all
the music he can out of Max's scatological rants. Max's vituperative
gas, as McShane deftly demonstrates, is a coverup for his sexual
inadequacy. McShane's biggest acting challenge—he's a handsome,
virile sixty-five—is to make the audience believe in both Max's age
and his impotence. McShane pulls it off, but some padding in his
costume and some cumbersome weight on the cane that he bran-
dishes with a majorette's aplomb wouldn't go amiss.

———

"I've stopped writing plays," Pinter told me, as our conversation was drawing to a close. "I'm weary." The previous week, he'd gone to the hospital for a brain scan. "You know what you'll find in there," he had told the lab technician. "A lot of unwritten plays." I asked him if writing required a ferocity that he no longer had. Pinter smiled wanly. "I still have quite a bit of ferocity knocking around," he said. "It's how to embody it."

Pinter's literary strength—his easy access to his own turbulent internal climate—has also been his public weakness. The press, which has consistently berated him for what it portrays as his vainglorious diatribes, has never quite understood that his arrogance is the flip side of his brilliance; you couldn't have the big artist without the big mouth. "I'm well aware that I have been described in some quarters as being 'enigmatic, taciturn, terse, prickly, explosive and forbidding,'" Pinter said in 1995. "Well, I do have my moods, like anyone else." To call Pinter's outbursts "moods" is like calling a tsunami a wave. Pinter, like his characters, is porous; bellicosity is the firewall that he has built against threats to his interior, whether from people or ideas. On the page, his volatility has made art; in life, all too frequently, it makes headlines. It can be argued that Pinter's dramas, with their undermining of authority and their dissection of the power plays in group dynamics, are essentially political. (The 1984 play *One for the Road* and 1988's *Mountain Language*, among others, are specifically political plays.) In the last twenty years, as the gaps between plays have grown longer, Pinter has channelled some of his anger onto the world stage. Nothing if not unpredictable—he voted for Margaret Thatcher in 1979 ("the most shameful act of my life," he later said)—he has lent the muscle of his voice to a variety of causes, among them the Sandinistas, the freedom of Slobodan Milosevic, the end of the Iraq war, and the trial of Tony Blair as a war criminal. But his preeminent target is American foreign policy. "The crimes of the United States have been systematic, constant, vicious, remorseless, but very few people have actually talked about them," Pinter said in his Nobel speech. In the rhetorical fulminations of his political poetry, he has aspired to smash through America's self-portrayal "as a force for universal good." *American Football*, a salvo against the 1991 Gulf War, ends almost as *The Homecoming* does:

> We blew their balls into shards of dust,
> Into shards of fucking dust.
>
> We did it.
>
> Now I want you to come over here and
> kiss me on the mouth.

For such outcries, Pinter has found himself both lambasted and lampooned. But, since the conferring of the Nobel, and since the fiasco of the current Iraq war has borne out some of Pinter's dire warnings, the tabloid teasing has diminished, though not Pinter's attitude toward it. "Fuck the press," he told me, leaning slowly forward. "That is exactly what I felt then, even more so what I feel now." He paused. "They can just go fuck themselves," he said. ∎

—December 24, 2007

Moonlight

Harold Pinter is the pathfinder of postwar English drama. No modern British playwright has been more controversial, more imitated, more influential, or more published. Since Pinter's London debut, in 1958, with his first full-length play, *The Birthday Party*, he has written at last count twenty-six volumes, including plays, screenplays, and poems, and has also directed and occasionally acted for the stage. He has been a mentor to such highly original and varied dramatists as Heathcote Williams, Joe Orton, and David Mamet. Besides his own body of work, he has generated a mountain of critical studies and doctorates filtering his ambiguous images through any number of ideological lenses. Such is the vastness of this academic enterprise that there is even a journal devoted exclusively to Pinter studies. This year alone, Pinter has performed in the successful West End revival of his *No Man's Land*; directed David Mamet's *Oleanna*, which is soon to transfer to the West End after a sold-out run at the Royal Court; and had his film version of Kafka's *The Trial* released. And last week, at the resourceful Almeida Theatre, in Islington, he opened his first full-length play in fifteen years, *Moonlight*.

"I have no aim in writing other than exploring the images that come into my mind," Pinter said in 1988. "I find some of those images really shocking, so they shock me into life and into the act of writing." In public, Pinter is sometimes intemperate and hectoring, but in his writing he remains a poet, open and unjudgmental of the images served up by his unconscious, and courageously waiting for their mysterious arrival. This is not a happy situation, and he has had to learn to live with uncertainty. When a play finally does materialize, the anxiety of the unknown is inevitably part of the drama and the structure. "My characters tell me so much and no more," he said in his earliest and clearest account of his method, in the Sunday *Times* in 1962. This murky imaginative territory of unresolved and probably unresolvable feeling yielded an extraordinarily fecund early period. There was *The Birthday Party*, *The Caretaker* in 1960, and *The Homecoming* in 1965, followed by an impasse that was announced in *No Man's Land*, of 1975—a place, as one character says, "which never moves, which never changes, which never grows older, but which remains forever icy and silent"—and that was finally broken, in 1978, by the more direct narrative of *Betrayal*. After that,

Pinter, styling himself as an activist, managed a series of increasingly slighter, less convincing polemical finger exercises (*Mountain Language, Party Time, The New World Order*). And then, in
the playwright's sixty-third year, *Moonlight* suddenly happened—a
gift that bears out W. B. Yeats's dictum "We make out of the quarrel
with others, rhetoric; but out of the quarrel with ourselves, poetry."
Grief-stricken and furious, *Moonlight* lays an ambush of language
and imagery to catch the unspoken and unspeakable sorrow that
surrounds a dying man's sad little wish to be loved. *Moonlight* is a
big, brave play, as dramatically compact and as emotionally searing
as anything Pinter has written.

Moonlight is the apt shadowy, mercurial ambience for Pinter's
characters, who exist in an unstable state of half-openness, moving perpetually between the seen and the unseen, sleep and wake-
fulness, outer and inner life. Pinter resists interpretation, and so
does David Leveaux's expert production. "The play works as a direct
appeal to the unconscious," Leveaux says. "One must try one's best
to remove the anxiety of interpretation or intellectual obfuscation
for an audience. Otherwise, the air is too noisy for an audience
collectively to receive things at the level at which they need to be
received. What Pinter is trying to show is the most intensified form
of reality, as opposed to a kind of metaphorical reality." Accordingly,
Leveaux's stage pictures have a limpid, supra-real quality. Even
Pinter's stage directions hint at magic realism: "Fred in bed. Jake
in to him." "Enter" would suggest that the characters were coming
from somewhere. The surreal is also implied elegantly in Bob Crowley's minimal set, which offers the audience a world that is literally
divided—by a painted piece of white gauze that extends from the
large gray upper chamber of the stage, where the sixteen-year-old
Bridget (Claire Skinner) first addresses the audience ("I can't sleep,"
she says, a sleepwalker announcing the restlessness of the play's
other uneasy souls), to the floor below, separating the bunk bed of

a son's sleeping quarters from the more substantial brass bed of his dying father.

Moonlight is a haunted play that begins and ends with a haunting. Bridget, in bare feet and a white cotton nightgown, stands before us in the half-light, willing herself to be quiet for her parents' sake. She sounds a new note in the usual furious hubbub of Pinter's plays: an innocent, who speaks without guile. "They need to sleep in peace and wake up rested. I must see that this happens," she says. "It is my task. Because I know that when they look at me they see that I am all they have left of their life." Although Bridget talks of her parents, they hardly ever mention her name, and the lilies placed downstage in a vase hint at a far greater loss, which the audience only gradually understands. She is the manifestation of a catastrophe of which her dying father, Andy, and his wife, Bel, can hardly speak. She is dead. ("I want to put my cards on the table about one thing," Pinter told David Leveaux. "There are many things I don't know about the play, but I have a strong feeling Bridget is dead.") Just how or why she died we never know. But she brings glimpses of the shadow world that grows closer for Andy with each beat of the play. Bridget, as her family says, is the one who understands. In one gorgeous monologue, she talks of journeying through "fierce landscapes" into a sheltering jungle. "I can hide. I am hidden," she says, in a speech that suggests the father's fantasy of solace. "The flowers surround me but they don't imprison me. I am free. Hidden but free. I'm a captive no longer. I'm lost no longer. No-one can find me or see me. I can be seen only by eyes of the jungle, eyes in the leaves. But they don't want to harm me."

Shame, which has its root in a word for "cover," is what sends the dying Andy (and all Pinter's characters) scurrying into nervy defensive maneuvers, those famous and still potent Pinter evasions, put-ons, and put-downs, with which they attempt to face off the prying eyes of the world. "Where are the boys? Have you found them?" are Andy's first, punishing words. Played with rueful, bullying brilliance by Ian Holm (returning to the stage after fourteen years), Andy is shamed both by the memory of loss and by the fact that his sons will not come to his deathbed. He is unwanted as a parent, and unreachable as a husband. Andy's impotence is overwhelming. He says later, fumbling in the moonlight for a nightcap: "No fags, no fucks. Bollocks to the lot of them." Pinter's dialogue marvellously subverts each clinched emotional moment, moving by turns from pain to mockery and on to corrosive rage as Andy tries to manufacture a sense of potency from the dross of his humiliation. "Where are they?" he says. "Two sons. Absent. Indifferent. Their father dying." Bel (played superbly by Anna Massey, with sad-eyed sangfroid) reminds him that they were good boys, who helped her do the dishes. "The clearing of the table, the washing-up, the drying. Do you remember?" The question allows Holm, who played Lenny in the original production of *The Homecoming*, and who knows how to drive a Pinter line hard to its lethal payoff, to swoop down on her like a bird of prey:

> You mean in the twilight? The soft light falling through the kitchen window? The bell ringing for Evensong in the pub round the corner? [*Pause*] They were bastards. Both of them. Always.

The invective at once admits and conceals hurt not just about the children but about the absence of intimacy between Bel and himself. Mockery is their oxygen and their substitute for passion. Pinter invokes the word "mockery" in the first five minutes of the play and, in the next hour and a quarter, proceeds to demonstrate all its penetrating guises: sometimes killing grief ("You're not a bad man," Bel says to Andy. "You're just what we used to call a loudmouth") and sometimes causing it ("Think of the wonder of it," Andy says. "I betrayed you with your own girlfriend, she betrayed you with your husband and she betrayed her own husband—and me—with you! She broke every record in sight! She was a genius and a great fuck"). Andy's onslaughts are beaten back by Bel, who gives as good a low blow as she gets. "She's probably forgotten you're dying," she says to Andy when he complains that the girlfriend isn't there to console him. "If she ever remembered."

But words can't reach Andy's sons, the bedridden and perhaps dying Fred (Michael Sheen) and the caustic Jake (Douglas Hodge). They won't talk to him, or even mention his name except to viciously belittle his memory. "Oh, your father? Was he the one who was sleeping with your mother?" Fred says to Jake. In their suffocating and unrelenting sendups, Pinter magnifies Andy's spiritual isolation. No claim of the father is allowed to stand unmocked. The public admiration of Andy as a civil servant is a source of his sons' private ridicule. They call him The Incumbent. Andy's value as a provider, and even his paternity, are turned upside down. The terror behind this manic subterfuge reflects Andy's volatile temperament. "In all your personal and social attachments the language you employed was mainly coarse, crude, vacuous, puerile, obscene and brutal to a degree," Bel says at one point. "Most people were ready to vomit after no more than ten minutes in your company." Andy's sons are victims turned victimizers. They show no remorse and offer no reconciliation. In the play's penultimate moment, Bel finally makes the call to her boys. Jake picks up the phone and says, "Chinese laundry." "Your father is very ill," Bel says softly, her eyes brimming with tears. Jake hands the phone to his brother. "Chinese laundry," he says. The silence that follows is noisy with a lifetime's unspoken regret and fury. Family is refused a place in the boys' reality, and the only way to reach them is to live within their fiction. "Do you do dry cleaning?" Bel says, finally. The harrowing and brilliant scene ends with Jake, having hung up, bending over the phone and shouting, "Of course we do dry cleaning! Of course we do dry cleaning! What kind of fucking laundry are you if you don't do dry cleaning?"

The play's sense of grief is all the more immense for being unspoken. There are no words for the kind of loss Pinter is talking about—only intimations. At one point, late in the play, under the cover of darkness, Andy inhabits the shadowy space usually occupied by Bridget, who materializes briefly in his empty bedroom, and talks to himself. "Ah darling," he says, filling the silence with heartbreaking remorse. "Ah my darling." In this brief and eloquent moment, we feel a hurt beyond repair. Bel appears in the moonlight. They look at each other and turn away: a dumb show of the unbreachable and infuriating separation from others which the play's final moments incarnate. As Bridget tells one last story, all the characters are set out in a tableau of disconnected angles. Bridget confides a dream in which she is invited by, perhaps, her parents to come to a party but is told to come when the moon is down:

> When I got to the house it was bathed in moonlight. The house, the glade, the lane, were all bathed in moonlight. But the inside of the house was dark and all the windows were dark. There was no sound. [*Pause*] I stood there in the moonlight and waited for the moon to go down.

When the moon finally does vanish, Andy will be dead. Meanwhile, Pinter leaves us with a final image of abandonment and total disconnection. The sense of separation is cavernous.

Moonlight is Pinter's most satisfying play since *The Homecoming*, and ranks among his major works. It will bring Pinter yet greater glory. But what is so cunning and so courageous about the play is that it's a testament not only to the audacity of his terrific talent but to the frightful price he has paid for it. Many interpretations of the play will follow. For me, it's a magnificent map of individualism's dead heart; and, for those who know how to read it, *Moonlight* shows where the bodies are buried. ■

—September 20, 1993

The Room and *Celebration*

"The world is full of fictional characters looking for their stories," the photographer Diane Arbus wrote. Her words came back to me as I watched the drama of identity taking shape in a fascinating Harold Pinter double bill (well directed by Neil Pepe, at the Atlantic Theater Company), which brings together his first play, *The Room* (1957), and *Celebration* (1999). The winner of this year's Nobel Prize in Literature, Pinter, as a playwright, a screenwriter, a director, and a mentor, has had an enormous influence on the theatrical landscape of his time. He began his career as an actor, and, even at the outset, with comparatively crude command, he turned his actor's understanding of subtext into a metaphysic. "The speech we hear is an indication of that which we don't hear," he said. "It is a necessary avoidance, a violent, sly, anguished or mocking smoke screen which keeps the other in its place." He added, "One way of looking at speech is to say it is a constant stratagem to cover nakedness."

Pinter claims to know only so much about his characters, who arrive as images from his unconscious; his ignorance of their history is matched by the characters' own vagueness about themselves. *The Room*, for instance, opens with a woman called Rose (Mary Beth Peil) padding around a bed-sitter, serving tea to a resolutely unresponsive man named Bert (Thomas Jay Ryan). "It's very cold out, I can tell you," Rose announces. "It's murder." Later, she adds, "This is a good room. You've got a chance in a place like this. I look after you, don't I, Bert?" Bert doesn't answer. Who are these people? Where do they come from? What do they really want? Is what they say true? Every person who subsequently crosses the threshold calls into question Rose's domestic daydreams about the room and about herself. In this surreal nightmare, things feel real and turn out to be otherwise. When a blind black man, Riley (the excellent Earle Hyman), arrives unexpectedly, we discover that Rose also answers to the name Sal, though whether or not she and Riley have had a relationship remains unclear. At the finale, Bert kicks Riley senseless. "Can't see," Rose says, clutching her eyes. "I can't see." Her blindness plays both as a response to the weight of the unknown and as a refusal to know. In this jejune and portentous one-act, Pinter stumbled on a psychological truth that he continued to explore brilliantly for half a century: mankind's passion for ignorance.

Blindness, as Pinter has dramatized it over the years, is something internal. The habit of not seeing is for his characters a sort of narrative device, an evasion of self-awareness that allows them to sustain their stories of themselves; the very syntax of their speech carries them ever farther from a real understanding of their own emotions. *Celebration*, which takes place at two adjacent banquettes of an elegant restaurant, makes the point with hilarious panache. Here language is the main character, used in deft counterpoint to the unmooring silence at the heart of each speaker. With mockery, weasel words, tall tales, the syncopation of repetition, and, of course, a carapace of pauses, the characters perform a sensational exercise in denial.

At one table, a smarmy banker, Russell (the droll Brennan Brown), and Suki (Kate Blumberg), his eager but long-in-the-tooth companion, buttress their emptiness with the slap and tickle of seductive swagger:

> RUSSELL: All right. Tell me. Do you think I have a nice
>   character? . . .
> SUKI: Yes, the thing is you haven't really got any character
>   at all, have you? As such. Au fond. But I wouldn't worry
>   about it. . . . I don't have any character either. I'm just a
>   reed. I'm just a reed in the wind. Aren't I? You know I
>   am. I'm just a reed in the wind.

RUSSELL: You're a whore.

SUKI: A whore in the wind.

At the other table, an East End wide boy, Lambert (the superb Patrick Breen), and his wife, Julie (Betsy Aidem), are loudly celebrating their toxic marriage, with Julie's sister, Prue (Carolyn McCormick), and her husband, Matt (Thomas Jay Ryan), who is Lambert's brother. Pinter has great fun playing the unwitting testimony of his characters' inner turbulence—the rawness of their aggression and their longing—against the cool chic of the surroundings. When the talk gets around to kids, Matt's bitterness seeps into his bravado. "Children," he says. "They have no memory. They remember nothing. They don't remember who their father was or who their mother was. It's all a hole in the wall for them." He is interrupted by the maîtresse d', Sonia (Christa Scott-Reed), who comes to the table. "Everything all right?" she asks. "Perfect," Julie says. The slinky Sonia seems to have more on her mind than working the room, as she brags to the table about the restaurant's international clientele. "I've often said, 'You don't have to speak English to enjoy good food,'" she says. "Or even understand English." She goes on, "It's like sex isn't it? . . . You don't have to speak English to enjoy sex. Lots of people enjoy sex without being English."

All the put-ons and put-downs here form an undertow of profound defensiveness, which is personified by the stately waiter (David Pittu), who politely but authoritatively interjects himself into the conversation at each table, in order to explain his delusional pedigree. "I thought you'd be interested to know that my grandfather knew T. S. Eliot quite well," he tells one group. "He was James Joyce's godmother." To the other table, he claims a connection to "the old Hollywood film stars"; his grandfather, he says, "was one of the very few native-born Englishmen to have had it off with Hedy Lamarr." The waiter is an inspired creation, a transparently false self. His litany of connection makes us feel the humiliation of his disconnection: cut off from history, from purpose, from even an iota of authenticity. "My grandfather introduced me to the mystery of life and I'm still in the middle of it," he tells us, as he stands alone in the restaurant after the guests have left. "I can't find the door to get out. My grandfather got out of it. He got right out of it. . . . He got that absolutely right." As the lights fade, he adds, "And I'd like to make one further interjection." But he says nothing. The silence—the force that compels all of Pinter's manic motormouths—is huge, terrifying, and, in Pinter's masterly hands, visionary. ▪

—December 19, 2005

9
WALLACE SHAWN

The playwright and actor Wallace Shawn was eating soup not long ago in a coffee shop on the Upper East Side, with his friend and early champion the novelist Renata Adler, when a group of young women surrounded the table. "They spied us through the window, obviously riveted by Wally. Then they came inside," Adler recalls. "'Aren't you—Oh, my God! Weren't you in *The Princess Bride*?' 'And *Clueless*?' another one said. 'I loved *Clueless*. Wait till I tell my sister!'" Shawn admits that he finds such attention "very, very strange—even weird and disturbing." When I interviewed him recently, he told me, "People sometimes literally define me, and even embrace me, for something, in a certain way, that I don't think of as being the main thing I do. They say, 'Hey! You're the guy who was in *The Princess Bride*!' And quite frequently I might be walking down the street thinking, Who the hell am I?"

Shawn made his film debut in 1979 as a sight gag in Woody Allen's *Manhattan*, where he was cast as the partly bald homunculus who is catnip to Diane Keaton, and since then he has appeared as a character actor in forty-one movies, co-written one cult film, *My Dinner with André*, and starred as the eponymous hero in another, *Vanya on 42nd Street*. But all this—and Shawn's charming, clownish public persona—has obscured his larger talent as one of American theater's finest prose stylists and most subversive playwrights. Even *The International Who's Who 1995–96* lists Shawn's "stage appearances"—*Aunt Dan and Lemon, Marie and Bruce*, and *The Fever*—without noting that Shawn in fact *wrote* those excellent plays. Although Shawn's work has recently been the subject of a critical study, *Writing Wrongs*, by W. D. King, and his plays have been staged at the most distinguished theaters in England and throughout Europe, he admits, "My plays are not actually performed in my own land." He adds, "It's very, very hard for your arrow to hit the target here. I'm not that discussed. That's why I'm going to England."

Shawn's newest play, *The Designated Mourner*, debuts in London at the Royal National Theatre on April 24. It is directed by David Hare and stars, among others, Mike Nichols, who has been lured back to the stage, where he first made his name, by what he calls the "strange combination of glamour and horror" with which Shawn writes about the present.

The Designated Mourner is a kind of ghost story. The narrator, Jack (played by Nichols), who once married into an elite literary coterie within which he was merely a hanger-on, survives an authoritarian clampdown after an uprising of the underprivileged. He finds that he is the only remaining witness to the otherwise extinct highbrow community. His famous writer father-in-law, Howard (David de Keyser), and his ex-wife, Judy (Miranda Richardson), are conjured up, along with the pleasures and the problems that follow when a "very special little world has died." In a series of exquisite crosscut monologues, there emerges a vivid picture of patrician sensibility and snobbery, and of the reprisals that Jack blithely refers to as "the disembowelling of the overbowelled." Jack asks the audience, "I mean, are you with me here? Am I going too fast?" and then describes the underclass: "We're talking about people who have no resources—none at all—no *money*, you could say. . . . They just don't like us. They *don't like* us." Jack and his listeners share that chilling moment in the evolution of mankind when "everyone on earth who could read John Donne was now dead," and Shawn charts Jack's downward trajectory from erstwhile highbrow to militant lowbrow. He has survived by the willed failure of his imagination: he consigns Donne to the trash heap and embraces his attackers' disdain for any kind of individual excellence. It's not just the past that's dead; it's Jack's soul. His search for comfort and for escape from the anger that envy inspires brings him and us, almost without realizing it, face to face with the death of culture.

In Shawn's work, the stage is stripped of most of its comforting dramaturgical devices—no plot, no set, no action—so the audience has nothing but the actor, the words, and its own moral compass to steer by. "My plays are really about the audience," he says. "The main character is you." His plays are a trap for consciousness and conscience. "I'm just too ambitious, really, to feel that it's enough to provide a little distraction for the few people who see my plays," says Shawn, who left college with "every intention of becoming a diplomat" who would "make some difference in the world." Shawn, himself the son of great privilege—his father was the late William Shawn, the renowned editor of this magazine from 1952 to 1987—is hard on his privileged audience. "I mean, the American upper class doesn't primarily need to be soothed and comforted," he explains, "although, like everybody else in the world, that's what they would like. That's not what I provide for them because I feel that they're too soothed and comforted already."

"There's nothing more fun than scaring the shit out of an audience," Mike Nichols says. "And I think *The Designated Mourner* really scares the shit out of an audience." The event has already generated a lot of excitement, and has all the markings of a theatrical breakthrough. "I decidedly lose my underdog status with this production," Shawn says. "It's being done in a way that anyone in the world would envy."

Being both an underdog and an object of envy is a contradiction that Shawn embodies in his person. "A human being happens to be

an unprotected little wriggling creature," he writes in his one-man
show, *The Fever*. "A lime raw creature without a shell or a hide or even
any fur, just thrown out onto the earth like an eye that's been pulled
from its socket, like a shucked oyster that's trying to crawl along the
ground. We need to build our own shells." Shawn's whimsical public
shell is rock solid. Although he claims not to understand stage sets,
his droopy, comic silhouette provides a distracting backdrop for
his own contradictory nature. He is at once arrogant and modest,
inept and cunning, dithering and bold, selfless and ambitious, well
mannered and radical, materialistic and spiritual. In his dark tur-
tlenecks, his woodsy jackets, and his sensible rubber-soled shoes,
Shawn is a kind of rumpled, walking Lands' End catalogue. He is
small, about five feet four. He is bald, with distinctive patches of side
hair, which in the early seventies gave him the air of a mad professor.
He has a lisp, which slightly deflates his seriousness, and when he's
intellectually treading water he punctuates a conversation with dec-
larations ("Well, uh," "Gee," "That's . . . just . . . incredible") that
in his mouth, onscreen and off, become a fetching comic decoy for
his acid thoughts, like the trout fly that hides the fishhook. Shawn's
often-parodied voice is halting and high-pitched, conveying a reflective tentativeness. "The difficulty with saying 'I love you,'" he once
said to the director André Gregory, "is that it presupposes that you
know who 'I' is and that you know who 'you' is." (Even his answering
machine won't promise a quick reply: "Unfortunately, your message
may be answered only after a long interval.") But Shawn's round,
pug-nosed, sweet face, which screws itself into various noncom-
mittal moods of bafflement, is the final, risible touch. Shawn presents himself as the opposite of predatory. He disguises himself as a
fumbling, somewhat timid schlub: not someone streamlined for the
brightness of day but, rather, an almost invisible night creature, like
a slow loris, which survives in the jungle by playing dead.

Metabolism is style, so it's inevitable that Shawn's prose, like his
persona, hides its seriousness behind a kind of semantic shuffling

that disarms and attacks at the same time. "My style as a human being is to indulge people who need to escape," he has said. "Yet I insist on confronting them as a playwright. It's quite embarrassing, it's quite unpleasant, it's quite awkward." Shawn has learned that in order to make people swallow the barb of insight, he and his characters have to play the worm. In *The Fever* Shawn compares himself to a water bug ("It's waiting, squatting, deciding which way to move"), and in *My Dinner with André* the Wally character recalls his life as a dog. "I was just treated, uh, in the nicest sense of the word, like a dog," he says of feeling invisible when he was starting out in New York, in the late sixties, as a Latin teacher at the Day School. "I mean, I literally lived like a dog. I mean, you know, I would be at a party where there would be all these great personalities, and the idea that I could participate in things in any way except to sort of pad through on all fours and sort of lick people's trousers was just inconceivable."

In real life, however, Shawn has had access to almost everyone. He could get the script of *My Dinner with André* to Louis Malle within days of its completion and have Malle accept it immediately; he could invoke Henry Kissinger in *Aunt Dan and Lemon* and then lunch with him at the Four Seasons to discuss it; he could imagine Mike Nichols's inflections while writing *The Designated Mourner* and then call up Nichols when it was completed and get him to read the play—at Richard Avedon's apartment, where Shawn and Gregory had sometimes gone to write their movie. Shawn has been plugged into this network of attainment throughout his life: his Kirkland House group at Harvard included the sons of the presidents of the American Bar Association and the Federal Reserve Bank; his sidekick at Oxford was the film director Terrence Malick; and his longtime companion is the distinguished short-story writer Deborah Eisenberg. This is not to undervalue Shawn's talent or his accomplishments but to put his work in the context of the spiritual contradictions it addresses—the battle he sees in the world between privilege and neglect. Shawn's plays are critiques of American individualism as observed from its airless empyrean.

Although Shawn claims to feel sometimes like "an aristocrat in the seventeenth century," he lives more like a peasant. He has no television. He has no computer. He has no fax machine or microwave. One of his frequent retreats is at an undisclosed address above a laundry somewhere outside the chic boundaries of Manhattan. "I don't believe in habits or routines. I try not to have them," he says, and what he does for most of his day is also his secret. "You can say," Shawn told me, "that even the people who know him best honestly don't know what the fuck he does all day long." This seems to be true. André Gregory, who has directed three of Shawn's plays and considers him "one of my closest friends in the world," isn't quite sure where Shawn works. "I think he has an office down in the Village somewhere," Gregory says. (Some of the actors from his *Vanya* company once followed Shawn in the subway to try to see where he worked.) "The truth is I move around a lot," Shawn, who is almost always lugging a large satchel, says. "There's a kind of wandering-minstrel thing going on." Shawn won't discuss his writing routine ("I think it's bad luck"), and characterizes much of his day-to-day activity as sort of molelike, "doing little things." He also spends as much time as possible travelling in poor countries, which he sees as a form of corrective behavior. "In the face of enormous suffering," he told me, "humorous detachment is too grotesque even for me." He spent his first year out of college in India, and has subsequently "hung out" in Mexico, Guatemala, Nicaragua, and El Salvador, and in Poland and Czechoslovakia, before and after their revolutions.

Shawn lives the way he does for a reason: nothing about him betrays the privilege of his education, the almost occult power of his family's literary connections, or the tenacity of his ambition, all of which might call down upon him hostile, envious attack. "A lot of his behavior is display that precludes attack," Renata Adler says. In fact, Shawn, who admits he's actually "a very arrogant and vain person," preempts envy by constantly spoiling any picture of his own distinction. "Wally had this persona when he arrived at Harvard, at seventeen," says Jacob Brackman, a college friend who wrote for *The New Yorker* before becoming a screenwriter; his film *The King of Marvin Gardens* used Shawn as the model for its hero, Jason Stabler (Jack Nicholson), whom Brackman describes as "this little underground man who sort of saw everything and had it all nailed down but was keeping you at arm's length all the time." Brackman adds, "In many ways, Wally was like a little Mr. Shawn, who was the biggest fumbler in the world. Wally's fumbling was completely from his dad. He was very polite and very stylized: he was telling you that he's just a miserable little worm." In Shawn's career as a character actor, no single performance has been more enduring than his presentation of himself, a cunning role-reversal of fortune. "He looks like a born victim—a not very well-dressed victim," the *Guardian* wrote in 1982, referring to Shawn's sartorial eccentricity of wrapping himself up in his black-and-white Magdalen College scarf in May.

Shawn was wearing that signature scarf when I first met him, in the early seventies. He appeared at my doorstep in Manhattan (sent at the suggestion of André Gregory), and was bearing six of his plays, entitled, unceremoniously, one through six. "I want you to read these," Shawn said. "But I don't want to know what you think." The gambit was typical of how Shawn wrong-foots life: a combination of frankness and imperiousness, dished up with po'-faced innocence. I recognized instantly that his modesty was the cover for an adamantine will; I sensed the familiar combination of power and panic which is the birthmark of a famous pedigree. We were both sons of cultural royalty: his father was a king of high culture, mine of low culture. We'd both lived on Manhattan's Upper East Side, attended

Ivy League colleges, done postgraduate work at Oxford, gone into theater. (The karma continued into adulthood when, in 1987, Wally played a jokey version of me in the film of my biography of Joe Orton, *Prick Up Your Ears*.) The world we grew up in was a wonderful but worrying place, because there seemed to be no loss in it. We were equipped for pleasure but not for life. In *The Fever* Shawn describes our kind of cosseted childhood: "My friends and I were the delicate, precious, breakable children, and we always knew it. We knew it because of the way we were wrapped—because of the soft underwear laid out on our beds, soft socks to protect our feet." Part of this atmosphere was what Shawn calls "the unique element to what each of our fathers did," which increased the sense of separation from others and lent an undiscussable yet unswerving conviction that went well beyond the word "entitlement."

"I grew up expecting great things of myself," Shawn says, and the awed eyes of the world reflected his manifest destiny back to him. "From day one, the teachers at school expected great accomplishment and were interested." The fact that he was William Shawn's son was "a little bit of glamour in their day—it attracted them." He adds, "I didn't realize why they were grovelling at my feet, and it made me a very self-confident person until the age of forty, when I sort of figured it out—when I had a bit of a crisis of confidence." Shawn refers to the blessings of his life as "the voluptuous field that was given to me." He and his younger brother, the composer Allen Shawn, performed musical puppet shows and sketches, as many kids do for family friends, but in his family the shows were about Horace, the dynastic decline of China, *Paradise Lost*, and Wittgenstein, and the friends were people like Naomi Bliven, Philip Hamburger, Whitney Balliett, and Janet Flanner. (These and other assorted literati would turn up at the family's occasional buffet suppers.) He went to the Dalton School, where in fifth grade he wrote and performed in a play about the death of Socrates. He played Socrates. ("It was a philosophical play, not that different from the plays I have written subsequently," Shawn says.) At school, he vied with Chevy Chase for the title of class clown. Chase was then, as he is now, a noisy entrepreneur of slapstick, while Shawn, who was reading *Ulysses* at fifteen in order to discuss James Joyce with the writer Joseph Mitchell, radiated a kind of lèse majesté. He expounded on the uselessness of literature and tried to coax his classmates into not doing their Latin homework. In his own adolescent eyes, he had already become a kind of dandy of detachment.

"*The New Yorker* was not really like Eustace Tilley looking at the butterfly through a monocle," Shawn says. "But in some ways the son of *The New Yorker* is like that." He continues, "I have a certain coolness, which maybe someone who didn't like me would call coldness. A certain detachment. I'm not always totally in the moment. There's usually a certain amount of observing going on on my part. It's a habit I formed early. A teacher in high school said to me, 'You know, Wally, people were not actually put on the earth just to amuse you.' " Shawn, who bears a physical resemblance to his father, also acquired his father's byzantine quality of containment, and, from the beginning, theater offered release from his self-consciousness. "When I was twelve, I saw *The Iceman Cometh*," says Shawn, who by thirteen had read the Random House collection of nine O'Neill plays. "My parents would have died rather than see *The Iceman Cometh*, but Bruce and Naomi Bliven took me to see it. It had an overwhelming influence on me." The next year, he saw *Long Day's Journey into Night* twice. "I remember the intensity of watching and doing plays, the intense seriousness contrasted to the shallow life of being a twelve-year-old with somewhat silly preoccupations," he says. "My life was placid on the surface. Somehow, when I encountered Eugene O'Neill I immediately thought, Yes, this man is really telling the truth. I had that double identity that I still have today. Some people think of me as a clown, but my natural bent is to deal with heavier issues of life and death, torment and tragedy."

The dissimulation in Shawn's persona and his interest in thinking against his privilege are ways of shouldering the weight of his regal birthright. "Well, I mean, it is defensive, but what can we do?" he said to me. "I can't wipe the stain of all that off me. I was treated like a little prince. I mean, that goes very deep. I was raised with the absolute understanding that I was a very special little being. A little king." Shawn mythologized the contradiction neatly in the opening speech of *My Dinner with André*, where the down-at-heels version of Wally "trudges" uptown to eat with André, the glamorous experimental stage director. "When I was ten years old, I was rich," Wally's voice-over says. "I was an aristocrat, riding around in taxis, surrounded by comfort, and all I thought about was art and music. Now I'm thirty-six, and all I think about is money."

The joke is typical of the game of three-card monte that Shawn plays with his background. It's true that life as a playwright proved a far greater struggle for Shawn than he had first imagined. "My expectation was always that I would be immediately received and immediately respected," he says. But Shawn was reinventing the theater to suit his own idiosyncratic attitudes and abilities. During his time at Oxford, he entered a playwriting competition. He didn't win, but he was hooked. In New York, a number of his Harvard classmates—Brackman, Hendrik Hertzberg, Tony Hiss, George Trow, and Jonathan Schell—were being brought onto *The New Yorker* as staff writers. Schell, in fact (in what must have been a complicated Oedipal drama for Wally, since Schell had been his roommate at both Putney and Harvard), was being groomed by Mr. Shawn as his successor. But while Wally's friends were becoming hot literary items in the big shopwindow of the magazine, he was supporting his playwriting habit with a series of improbable jobs: shipping clerk, Xerox-machine operator, garment-district porter. "I thought that was cruel," Philip Hamburger says of Mr. Shawn's nonemployment of his son. "It didn't strike me as displaying the sublime sensitivity that Shawn was supposed to possess." Now the younger Shawn makes a show of sweet reasonableness about his exclusion from the halls of literary power. "If you want to be a writer, it's dangerous to have a job," he says. "My own father was an example. He wanted to be a writer. He ended up getting a job, and his life followed the direction of the job." Back then, Wally was forced to follow his own quirky, unconventional path. He told me he'd "sold stock in himself"—his way of rationalizing a $2,500 loan he took from a consortium of friends in the sixties, in order to go off and write his plays. (To this day, the investors receive a small yearly check.)

He spent months watching rehearsals of the Manhattan Project in order to write a modern version of *Peer Gynt* (which he ended up abandoning), and then delivered a cauterizing satire about a seventies cocktail party, called *Our Late Night* (1972). This was his professional debut—a wild, foulmouthed foreshadowing of the yuppie free-for-all of the eighties, in which the actors explore, in graphic terms, the sexual facts of their inner lives. It was produced at the Public Theater in 1975, and even Joseph Papp, never fulsome about his employees, noted, "Wally is a very rare species. He is a dangerous writer." Gregory, who directed the play, recalls, "The dance critic John Gruen came to a preview and said it was the most dangerous night in the theater since the opening of Nijinsky's *L'Après-Midi d'un Faune*. Somebody tried to hit an actor. People would scream 'Shut up!' and 'Stop it!' It was very scary in the audience. I think what they were offended by was their own shadow—that Wally was seeing something under the surface of Americans."

Shawn certainly didn't foresee the row that erupted in the House of Lords when *A Thought in Three Parts* (1975)—three short plays that focussed on aspects of sexuality, including masturbation—was produced in London, by Max Stafford-Clark and the Joint Stock Company. Lord Nugent of Guilford, quoting from a *Daily Telegraph* review that called the play "as likely to give offence as anything I have ever seen in the theater," called on the government to "protect the public against this sort of pollution"; the attorney general considered prosecution for obscenity; the charity commissioners threatened an investigation of Joint Stock's grant; tabloids were inundated with mail from the left and the right; and for a tense forty-eight hours Shawn actually feared deportation. In 1985, at the Royal Court in London, the debut production of *Aunt Dan and Lemon*, which explores Shawn's contention that "a perfectly decent person can turn into a monster perfectly easily" and, incidentally, foresaw the resurgence of anti-Semitism in the nineties, was booed and heckled by some members of the opening-night audience, who mistook the false logic of Lemon's proto-Nazi conclusions for Shawn's own.

"My characters are much wilder than me," Shawn told the *Times* in 1980. "I'm really a buttoned-up little creep." He explained to me, "I don't know a hell of a lot about real life, to put it mildly. That isn't my strong suit, a knowledge of life. Obviously, my weak point in school was sports. I was brought up in that Jewish tradition where the man is a reader of books and does nothing physical. B. H. Barry will never have a job choreographing a fight in one of my plays. If I think, What do I actually understand, appreciate, and know how to deal with?, it would probably be sitting in a chair and talking. I do have some grasp of that."

Shawn expressed this reflective side of himself—and courted a new kind of attack—in his last production, *The Fever*, which he has described as "some kind of human exhortation which is meant to arouse thought and action, not appreciation or enjoyment." (It was his father's favorite of his plays.) In 1990, he performed the show in the homes of friends, turning himself into a kind of Marxist Ancient Mariner, and putting his cultural guilt and his despairing sense of self literally under the audience's nose. "There was a certain point in my life—in my early forties—where an awareness of my own position in the world created a kind of permanent unease and pain," Shawn told me. In the monologue, the Wally character describes shivering and vomiting in a tropical hotel bathroom as he meditates on the contradictions of the killing fields outside his window and his own deluxe life, and on the sin of separation, which insures the poor's perpetual enslavement. *The Fever*, Shawn says, was a way, in the form of a play, of "trying to speak to people and to say something I genuinely believed about myself, them, and the world that we actually live in." Shawn's home delivery was a way of "taking it off the cultural menu of entertainment" and of keeping the play from being turned into an art object. (I saw an exhilarating performance of it in his London hotel room.) When Shawn finally did put the play on the stage, at various New York venues, in late 1990 and 1991, he dispensed with the paraphernalia of commercial theater in his most minimalist setup to date: no program, no dressing room, no costume, no curtain call. In Europe, *The Fever* was respectfully received; in New York, it was mugged. "A musty radical chic stunt destined to be parodied," Frank Rich wrote in the *Times*, and, without discussing the issues raised in Shawn's spiritual quandary, he swatted it away with such ferocity that the play—and the chance of Shawn's ideas' having wider debate—was stopped dead. In Germany he received more than twenty-five productions; in America there was just a handful. "I was absolutely sort of destroyed by his review," Shawn told me, in his bob-and-weave manner.

Now, five years later, Shawn's vision of the havoc of injustice has been reimagined in a more ambiguous, more oblique story. "And the poor, don't forget," he wrote in *The Fever*. "They live on their rage. They eat rage. They want to rise up and finish us, wipe us off the earth as soon as they can." In *The Designated Mourner*, a repressive state has arisen to prevent them from doing just that. The play brings together in one metaphor the fear of envious attack and the appeasing defensive maneuvers around which Shawn's whole social persona is organized: it is Shawn's *A Modest Proposal*. Through

Jack, he is demonstrating the systematic devaluation of the self in modern life as an adaptation to envy, which finally leads to the dumbing of society.

Jack is a projection of Shawn's fears—what he has no wish to be but what he sees our distracted society becoming. "As long as I preserve my loyalty to my childhood training, I will never know what it is to be truly comfortable," Shawn has written of growing up in the moral climate of a liberal household. "I feel a fantastic need to tear that training out of my heart once and for all so that I can finally begin to enjoy the life that is spread out before me like a feast." Shawn can't, which is his struggle and his peculiar genius. He lives with the contradiction of his continuous unease. "What is my role on the planet?" he says. "Is it just to consume and be a parasite and a happy hedonist?" At one point in *The Fever*, he contemplates divesting himself of everything and resolving the dilemma of what he calls "being an overdog from the point of view of class analysis." He writes, "I could perfectly well put an end to the whole elaborate performance. If people are starving, give them food. If I have more than others, share what I have until I have no more than they do. Live simply. Give up everything. Become poor myself."

The flip side of Shawn's impulse toward abdication is Jack's self-abnegation. Instead of becoming poor, Jack impoverishes his own nature. Shawn wants to shrink the separation between himself and others—that distance which American individualism makes glorious. Jack just wants to shrink. Referring to John Donne at the finale, Jack says, "The rememberers were gone, and I was forgetting: forgetting his name, forgetting him, and forgetting all the ones who remembered him."

Shawn is alone among American playwrights in challenging the prestige of individualism. "A good deal of what Jack says about the self I agree with," Shawn says, and adds that he finds the obsession with "the character called 'I' completely ludicrous." Certainly Jack has good sport with the notion of "I"—"this strange little thing that everyone has, this odd, tiny organ which the surgeons can't touch"—and with his own inner dialogue, his "idiotic arpeggios of self-approbation." Shawn steers the character not toward selfless-ness but toward emptiness, which brings a new, barbarous sense of power. In his so-called "Experiments in Privacy," Jack records episodes of shitting on books and pissing on poetry; he binges on television, tabloids, and pornography, and practices mindlessness. "Perhaps I could learn how to pass more easily from one moment to the next, the way the monkey, our ancestor, shifts so easily along from branch to branch as he follows the high road through the forest at night," Jack says, willing himself *down* the evolutionary ladder. "Let me learn how to repose in the quiet shade of a nice square of chocolate, a nice slice of cake."

In Shawn's unblinking prophecy, civilization dies not with a bang or a whimper but with a sneer and a sigh of pleasure. Shawn has sur-vived his parents and his pedigree but not his guilt at upper-class comfort. "We need solace, we need consolation, we need nice food, we need nice things to wear, we need beautiful paintings, movies, plays, drives in the country, bottles of wine," he writes in *The Fever*. "There's never enough solace, never enough consolation." His is a battle of conscience and contradiction in which there is no truce. "I know what I'm taking out of the world," Shawn told me. "What am I putting back? Am I putting something back in that is of value? I wouldn't be the one who knows." ▪

—April 15, 1996

The Designated Mourner

Wallace Shawn's *The Designated Mourner* had its sold-out world premiere in 1996, at the Royal National Theatre, in London. I was there. The cast of three, directed by David Hare, sat on a dais in front of a gold backdrop and fired Shawn's extraordinary words at the audience in a kind of glorified staged reading. Aided by an auto-cue for what must surely be the longest spoken part in contemporary theater, Mike Nichols came out of theatrical retirement to give a bravura performance as Jack, the *soi-disant* mourner of a vanished world of literary sophistication and social privilege, of which he claims to be the last standing member. The production was imme-diately filmed, and Shawn was placed in the weird position of hav-ing his play released in America as a movie before it could be seen as a play.

Now, after a sporadic rehearsal period of about nine months over the past two years, Shawn has teamed up with his friend and cohort the director André Gregory to produce a radically different Ameri-can stage version, in which he himself takes on the main character. Shawn began his acting career in the early seventies, in Gregory's controversial production of *Endgame* (he played a blind violinist), and whenever these two dreamy theatricals emerge from the cocoon of their process, it's good news for the American theater. Their dis-tinguished collaboration has created many fine stage productions and two defining films directed by Louis Malle, *My Dinner with André* and *Vanya on 42nd Street*. But *The Designated Mourner* is surely the high-water mark.

The play, which is a short history of abdications in the form of intercut monologues, manages to dramatize a profound cultural and spiritual shift in the land—what Philip Roth recently referred to in these pages as "the narrowing of consciousness." Escape, not exploration, is the culture's new momentum; and in Shawn's apoc-alyptic tale an uprising of the underclass and a clampdown by the new authoritarian regime depose Jack's elite and, in the process, turn him from an uncomfortable highbrow into a militant lowbrow. (Shawn makes this rebellion sound like Latin-American terrorism, but, after the LA riots and the flight of the rich from Beverly Hills, it's not so difficult to imagine it on our own doorstep.) The play begins, it turns out, at the moment when our intellectual history is about to be forgotten, and elegantly flashes back to recount the world that has been lost and the one that has been found.

Ambivalence is Shawn's ozone. In life and onstage, he wrong-foots the world with a cherubic mask of impudence and innocence. He is a daredevil disguised as a schlub, and, from the first beats of this play, he is up to his old dissimulating tricks. As Jack prepares to introduce his father-in-law, Howard, a literary lion he mourns with an almost gleeful hate, he looks us in the eye and says, "I'm serious—honestly—let's forget me and let's talk about someone who actually *is interesting*—let's talk about someone we can all *revere!*" What follows is the longest study of self-absorption since *Hamlet*. Irony allows Shawn at once to mock and to mourn, to produce the negative and the positive in virtually the same breath. You never know quite where you are, and this tension is part of the show's captivating charge. Without the comfort of conventional plot or set, the audience is forced back to the words and to its own moral compass. You have to work to understand the play; in fact, you have to work just to *get* to the play.

The cunning rigor of Shawn's text is matched by an equally suggestive and supple theatrical environment. You can't just roll up to this show. It's a kind of treasure hunt—a geographical adventure that turns into an intellectual one. You take the No. 2 or 3 train to Wall Street and head south until you come to an incongruous mock-Tudor walkup—a former men's club—wedged between hulking skyscrapers on South William Street. You follow yellow construction lights up the stairs, pausing on the third floor, where Bruce Odland's strange, sepulchral sounds echo through a dank, chandeliered dining room; then it's a quick ascent up winding marble steps to the fifth floor. There, in a corner amid peeling gray-and-white walls,

Eugene Lee and N. Joseph DeTullio have carved out a performance space. The audience sits not on makeshift benches but on solidly comfortable chairs—there are only thirty of them—for which Shawn and Gregory have, at their own expense, provided blankets. It is a chill, dilapidated, crepuscular place, a perfect atmosphere for the moral *froideur* of Shawn's ghost story. Canvas coverings on the bed, chairs, and oak furniture of the set—later pulled off by the actors— lend a haunted feel to the room, and as Shawn paces around it in full view, before the show begins, even he seems a little cold; he sports a rather flamboyant black-and-gold scarf over his turtleneck sweater.

The liberal intellectual empyrean that Jack celebrates and scorns—"the old unbearables," he calls Howard's prestigious crowd— is reminiscent of the world of almost occult power whose smug pedigree Shawn inherited, as the son of William Shawn, the distinguished editor, from 1952 to 1987, of this magazine. Here the playwright is aided by his longtime partner and one of America's finest short-story writers, Deborah Eisenberg, who brings to the evening a special sense of inbred refinement and arrogance. As Judith, Jack's wife, from whom he eventually becomes estranged, Eisenberg is superb; her chic—the long neck, the tapered fingers, the dark hair with gray highlights, the aquiline nose that sniffs at every vulgarity—evokes a stylish, elite world even before Shawn's words nail it. Judith dotes on her delicate and judicious poet father, who, she tells us, is on a first-name basis with the president. Larry Pine plays Howard with just the right droll note of noblesse oblige. "You know, he *was* lazy," he confides to us about Jack, who, he says, "wasn't actually a bad fellow." "He was so lazy that his favorite foods—I'm not making this up, because I observed it quite carefully—were soup, risotto, mashed potatoes, and ice cream. I'm not exaggerating!"

Jack, of course, is the play's set piece, a tour de force for Shawn, who enjoys surviving in the jungle by playing dead. Within the first few moments of the play, Jack has referred to himself as an "asshole," an "idiot," "boring," "a former student of literature who—who—who went downhill from there." The stammering, the guffaws, the lisping hesitation are all part of Shawn's special music, the endearing jack-o'-lantern grin that hides an ambitious and withering intellect. Jack's vulnerability is so winning that it can make the snidest remark feel almost like a compliment. "It was remarkable simply to make the *choices* he made," he says of Howard. "To dress in blues and greens and not reds or grays; to know about the Sumerians but not about the Assyrians." Shawn's game is subtle and unsettling. The audience needs to sympathize with a character, if only to evade thought, to pigeonhole personality as good or bad, but Shawn won't allow that. Here, as he did in *Aunt Dan and Lemon* (1985), he shows that "a perfectly decent person can turn into a monster perfectly easily." He manipulates his paying customers into liking Jack, only to suck them into the whirlwind of his spiritual free fall. *The Designated Mourner* turns out to be a tale *really* told by an idiot.

When the underclass wreaks its revenge on privilege, in an attack that Jack gleefully refers to as "the disembowelling of the over-bowelled," Jack's reaction is not what one would expect. He takes a certain lip-smacking pleasure in the spoiling. In one powerful scene, he spins a globe. "Wretched," "miserable," "unfortunate," "desperate," "powerless," "poor," he says, pointing his stubby finger over all the hemispheres. "God bless them, they're people who simply don't have any resources of any kind at all. And these particular people— and, you know, God knows why—well, they just don't like us." A lowbrow in training, Jack has been eaten alive by his envy of the intellectual elite and by the sense of inadequacy they have instilled in him. "I was clever enough to know that John Donne was offering something that was awfully enjoyable—I just wasn't clever enough to actually enjoy it," he says. He continues, "I was kept out of it all, kept away. Howard, on the other hand, was let right in. Come in, they said. Here we are. Come talk, come be with us." Extraordinary gifts

require extraordinary vigilance; and Jack, who really is lazy, seeks
release from the oppression of scruple and excellence—the disci-
plines of heart and mind that are the gifts of surplus. Confronted
with violent upheaval—the disappearances, the murders, the long
jail sentences—Jack succumbs to his own incipient barbarity. "How
much longer could I keep on pretending to be hurt and shocked by
unspeakable acts?" he asks at the end of act 1. Jack is not just numb;
he is morally bankrupt.

At the beginning of act 2, Gregory leads the audience into the
neon glare of a squash court on the floor below. Shawn and Eisenberg are already there, although only the tops of their heads are visible, until we walk around the sofa they occupy and take our seats.
Here, in the aftermath of the uprising, we witness the full trajectory of Jack's decline. "What *was* the self," Jack wonders out loud.
"I understood that my self was just a pile of bric-a-brac—just everything my life had quite by chance piled up—everything I'd seen or
heard or experienced—meticulously, pointlessly piled up and saved,
a heap of nothing." Shawn and David Mamet are the only contemporary American playwrights who debate the nature of individualism and its "I"—"this strange little thing that everyone has, this
odd, tiny organ which the surgeons can't touch." In his version of the
hilarious sophistry of Swift's "A Modest Proposal," Jack finds happiness by surrendering to the senses. "Let me learn how to repose
in the quiet shade of a nice square of chocolate, a nice slice of cake,"
he says. He wills himself back to the primitive, and, in the process,
he abdicates love, loyalty, knowledge, excellence, meaning. In the
privacy of his bathtub, in an experiment he deems a success, Jack
pisses on poetry, takes a shit on books. "Things were shrinking for
me—everything was shrinking," he says. "Sometimes even trying
to read the paper, you know, was sort of like spooning food into the
mouth of someone who you happen to notice has suddenly died. So
actually the thing that became most real, most visible, for me was

this little collection of, actually, sex magazines." When Jack finds his bliss, it's the amnesia of ignorance. "I was forgetting," he says, imagining John Donne crying at not being remembered by future generations. "Forgetting his name, forgetting him, and forgetting all the ones who remembered him."

At the end of the play, the actors file out, followed by Gregory, and we are left to applaud the palpable, punishing vacancy that is the production's most awesome accomplishment. *The Designated Mourner* is, I think, among our generation's few great plays, one of the most memorable evenings of theatergoing in my life. It traps, with irony, the grief and fury behind our culture's delirium of distraction. "The actors will be on the third floor if you want to join them," a production assistant told the audience as it filed out. So I did. Over the course of three hours, Gregory and Shawn had managed to break almost every rule of the theater, so why not this last one? ■

—May 15, 2000

Grasses of a Thousand Colors

London's Royal Court Theatre has made this spring a Wallace Shawn season. In addition to showing Shawn's cult movies *My Dinner with André* (1981) and *Vanya on 42nd Street* (1994), the theater has staged his 1990 one-man show, *The Fever* (with the estimable Clare Higgins taking on Shawn's role), his 1985 play *Aunt Dan and Lemon*, and Shawn's first new play in more than a decade, *Grasses of a Thousand Colors*, in which the pug-nosed provocateur himself performs the central part. This is a big deal. The Royal Court, one of the most influential theaters in Europe, is doing for Shawn what the Beatles did for Little Richard: rediscovering for a new generation a singular American talent who had been marginalized in his own country. In the United States, Shawn, as a playwright, is a relatively unknown quantity without an artistic home; in England, his works, which prey on both consciousness and conscience, are published under the rubric of "contemporary classics."

"What do you think a human being is?" Shawn asks in *The Fever*. "A human being happens to be an unprotected little wriggling creature . . . without a shell or a hide or even any fur, just thrown out onto the earth like an eye that's been pulled from its socket, like a shucked oyster that's trying to crawl along the ground. We need to build our own shells." In life and onstage, Shawn's carapace of congeniality is rock solid. An aesthete and an intellect, he dissimulates the rigor of his fierce brain and the clout of his princely pedigree—his father was for thirty-five years the editor of this magazine—behind a droll mask of tentative comic collapse: he's a wolf in schlub's clothing.

At the beginning of the three-hour *Grasses of a Thousand Colors* (superbly directed by André Gregory), Shawn is at it again: he stands before us as Ben, a scientist and a memoirist, in a black dressing gown, black monogrammed slippers, and black cravat, and plays his familiar wrong-footing game of self-deprecation. He is dressed as an agent of darkness, but he is bright with good will. "Well. Hello, everybody. Hello! Hello there!" he says, in his lisping, halting, high-pitched voice. He goes on, "When you're all so nicely sitting there and listening to me, I'm deriving a great deal of pleasure from each and every one of you, as if you were chocolates I was eating." In this futuristic dream play, eating and being eaten are important leitmotifs. Ben, we learn, is one of the barbarians who have devoured the planet, and, beneath his charm, he is as unrepentant as a hedge-fund manager. *Loaves, with Fishes, for Dinner* is the title of the memoir from which he reads to us, and which hints at his majestic self-infatuation.

Ben is perhaps the most unreliable of Shawn's many unreliable narrators. His smugness—"I was born lucky"—is rivalled only by the imperialism of his convictions. "We're fixers, improvers," he says of his optimistic generation. The thing that he has fixed, it turns out, is the "problem of food." As he pompously puts it, "There was, on the one hand, an enormous crowd of entities—ourselves and others— roaming the planet, trying to sustain themselves, or, in other words, looking for something to eat; and on the other hand there was a tiny, inadequate crowd of entities available on the planet to *be eaten*." The appliance of Ben's science allows the animal kingdom—frogs, cows, his own dog, Rufus, and, by implication, *Homo sapiens*—to feed on its own kind, as well as on the corpses of other animals. The discovery has made him rich; it has also destroyed the food chain. Things have gone disastrously wrong: animals are dying, and people are vomiting and keeling over.

Unnerving memory flashes of his first wife, Cerise (Miranda Richardson)—brilliantly designed by Bill Morrison to resemble surrealist Rayographs, which are projected onto the entire back wall of the stage—haunt Ben with news of the sickening world. Cerise reminisces nostalgically about the time when "people ate and digested the same foods for their whole lives." Blond hair piled on top of her head, her legs and face lightly brushed with glitter, she then enters magically through the back wall and slithers over the back of the sofa and onto Ben's lap. As Richardson piquantly plays her, Cerise is at once lithe and lethal, as cool, mercurial, and flirty as a cat; in fact, in Shawn's fairy tale she is half cat, half human. "Cats *like* to tease mice. They like to play with them a little. Are you with me so far?" she asks when she enters, adding, "And, of course, everyone knows that cats *punish* mice."

With her talk of the "good old days" of shrimp and asparagus, Cerise certainly punishes Ben; he throws his memoir into the trash and, in the following two acts, escapes from the toxic environment he has helped engineer into an unrivalled, often hilarious saga of priapic pleasure. Not since Barry Humphries's well-hung Sir Les

Patterson, with his mythic "frequently felt tip," has the male organ received such eloquent and sidesplitting objectification. Ben's tale is an epic account of the battles of his penis, a sort of Iliad of onanism. "My erect penis is monstrous, actually—it looks violent, extreme, almost out of control," he says. "And yet, particularly when it's in repose and completely relaxed, I do think my friend has a wonderful face. It's so simple—no eyes, no nose, just a simple mouth—a face that looks out at the world with just a sad, hopeful smile."

Traditional fairy tales are exercises in sublimation; in Shawn's retelling of parts of "The White Cat," a seventeenth-century French folktale, the impulse is turned upside down, and the id runs riot. Between his sexual bouts with Cerise and other women—the zaftig, smoky-voiced Robin (the excellent Jennifer Tilly) and the vulnerable Rose (the compelling Emily McDonnell), for whom he seems to have feelings—Ben is compelled to sneak away into the woods, where he is introduced to cat society and where he finds Dionysian ecstasy with Blanche, a long-haired white. "My God—finally. Finally, to be known, I thought, as hot sperm flowed out of me, flowing over her paw as if it would never stop," he says. Over the course of the tale, Robin decapitates Blanche, only to have the cat's head begin to grow back as she lugs the eviscerated carcass home. In this protean landscape, Blanche becomes a woman, and Cerise appears to become Blanche. (The gorgeous intercut projections of Richardson as a cat with green eyes, a red collar, and whiskers make this metamorphosis all the more surreal.)

Like all dreams, *Grasses of a Thousand Colors* resists interpretation, even as it blurs the distinction between the natural and the civilized. In its imaginative dissonance, the play seems to me a model of the grotesque as Edgar Allan Poe once described it: "much of the beautiful, much of the wanton, much of the *bizarre*, something of the terrible and not a little of that which might have excited disgust." In Shawn's 1996 masterpiece, *The Designated Mourner*—which

predicted the terrorism and the philistinism of the past decade—
the narrator will do anything to survive. In 2009, Shawn's narrator, sitting at the edge of a barbarous and convulsed world with his
own death partially in view, shows some small signs of humanity.
By the end of the play, Ben can at least acknowledge the folly of his
intellectual arrogance. "As I approached the age of sixty, I could feel
the ghosts of all the things I'd never get to do, crowding around me,
suffocating me," he says. "I'd been wrong about people, about why
things had happened, even about facts that had seemed completely
indisputable."

"I've decided to take a bet on my subconscious," Shawn told the
Guardian recently. In *Grasses of a Thousand Colors*, that bet is
hedged by his collaboration with a number of expert theatrical talents. Gregory's subtle, suggestive staging adds a witty counterpoint
to the torrent of Shawn's articulate but prolix text (which would be
even stronger with some muscular editing). Eugene Lee's cunning
minimal set—well lit in warm hues by Howard Harrison—is primarily a large white sofa and a back wall that is a field of high, waving grass, through which the characters vanish. The grass plays as
a coda of hope. If we leave nature alone, Shawn seems to be saying,
regeneration and beauty may still be possible. In the meantime, his
visionary satire of decadence powerfully dramatizes our country at
a spiritual tipping point. ∎

—June 1, 2009

10
NEIL LABUTE

Once upon a time in the early nineties, in the irony-free zone of Off-Off Broadway, the writer and director Neil LaBute sat onstage doing triple duty as an actor in his barroom play, *Filthy Talk for Troubled Times: Scenes of Intolerance*. One of the barflies was in the middle of a riff about AIDS and about her fear of infection—"I say, put them all in a fucking pot and boil them . . . just as a precaution"—when a member of the audience sitting right up front shouted, "Kill the playwright!" LaBute, who is thirty-eight and whose wiry black hair and pug nose give him the look of a large, amiable hedgehog, says his first thought was "to get to the exit, to lead the crowd out to safety"; another part of him was thrilled, because "people were listening enough to go out of their way to make a response." The angry patron stayed for the rest of the play, which is a testament to LaBute's good writing and to his canny view of theater and film as "a contact sport," which "should be the most of whatever it is—the most joy, the most terror."

LaBute, whose first play-turned-film, *In the Company of Men* (1997), made his name and also earned him the sobriquet "the angriest white male," courts provocation not for the sake of shock but to make an audience think against its own received opinions. His production company is mischievously called Contemptible Entertainment; his work is cruel, dark, and often very funny. *In the Company of Men* is about two corporate eager beavers—the venomous Chad and his sidekick, Howard—who conspire to find a vulnerable woman, woo her, and then hurt her. "It's a simple story," LaBute wrote in the introduction to the published screenplay. "Boys meet girl, boys crush girl, boys giggle." *Your Friends and Neighbors* (1998), adapted from his play *Lepers*, is a sexual merry-go-round among friends. Together, the two films are a kind of *Rake's Progress*, and LaBute's model for them is Restoration comedy, which, as he explained to me when we met in Hollywood this spring, "gets down to the dirt of the way we live with each other and treat each other." He pays homage to his source in *Your Friends and Neighbors* when, during a rehearsal of Wycherley's *The Country Wife*, the drama professor and sleazy sexual predator, Jerry (Ben Stiller), sitting in the auditorium in periwig and frock coat, explains to his cuckolded best friend, Barry (Aaron Eckhart), why he bedded his wife:

> JERRY: . . . I just feel . . . Fuck, I don't know how to put this,
>   I just feel . . .
> BARRY: "Bad"?
> JERRY: "Bad." Exactly! Bad.
> BARRY: I mean, my wife . . .
> JERRY: I'm sorry.
> BARRY: The same hotel room even.
> JERRY: I am sorry.
> BARRY: Yeah . . .
> JERRY: But I . . . I mean, I still feel . . .
> BARRY: . . . "Bad."
> JERRY: Right. "Bad."

The moral and emotional nonchalance of LaBute's characters echoes the amorality and privilege of the Restoration fops, who, LaBute has said, are "well-to-do people with time on their hands who go around hurting each other, doing things that are pretty

unpleasant, just because the opportunity presents itself." The original court entertainments emphasized the notion of appearance versus authenticity. "Behind that great sense of costume—the wigs and
makeup—there was a sense that all was well, even while bugs were
crawling in the wigs and the physical self was falling apart," LaBute
said. "There was still the sense that it was better to look good than
to feel good." LaBute's contemporary fops have no authentic self to
hide: they are all facade. He links this to the nineties obsession with
style and with the insistence on appearance as reality. "There's a
huge sense in the nineties of 'I can become anything I want as long
as I present it tenaciously enough.' Clinton would be a fair example."

LaBute, who calls himself "a part-time moralist," is a practicing
Mormon; he converted to the faith in the early eighties, before he
married Lisa Gore, a psychotherapist who is deeply involved with
the Church of the Latter-Day Saints. The Mormon obsession with
moral improvement and with "pretending nothing bad happens," as
he says, accounts in large part for LaBute's relish of transgression.
The absence of surface detail in his films—*In the Company of Men*
takes place in a nameless city and at a nameless corporation where
nameless executive tasks are performed—allows the viewer to focus
on the psychological aspects of the piece: the casual cruelties we
commit, the ways in which we displace our anger. "Neil always wants
you to personalize his work," says the actor Aaron Eckhart, who
starred in both *In the Company of Men* and *Your Friends and Neighbors*, and has a part in the forthcoming *Nurse Betty*, LaBute's first
mainstream Hollywood movie and the only one of his films that he
has not written. "He wants you to say, 'I'm that person' or 'I have
done that.' "

For the same reasons, in his stage work LaBute favors the black
box—the unadorned proscenium—and the confines of the monologue. His versatility in this form is shown to brilliant and unsettling effect in a trio of short pieces collectively called *Bash*, which

opened last week at the Douglas Fairbanks Theatre, starring Calista Flockhart, Ron Eldard, and Paul Rudd. Here, in one of the pieces—a tandem monologue entitled "A Gaggle of Saints: A Remembrance of Hatred and Longing"—a soon-to-be-married college couple recount a road trip to New York City with a few Mormon college friends for a party at the Plaza. During the day's long trajectory of good times, the guys find themselves attacking a homosexual in a Central Park latrine:

> Tim leans into him one more time, takes a little run at it, smashing his foot against the bridge of this man's nose and I see it give way. Just pick up and move to the other side of his face. Wow. And then it's silence. Not a sound. And for the first time, we look over at Dave. . . . What's he thinking? And right then, as if to answer us through revelation . . . he grabs up the nearest trash can, big wire mesh thing, raises it above his head as he whispers, "Fag." I'll never forget that . . . "fag." That's all. And brings that can down right on the spine of the guy, who just sort of shudders a bit, expelling air.

Clearly, LaBute does not follow the Mormon line about the showing of good. On the contrary, his work is built on the belief that great good can come from showing the bad.

I visited LaBute on the set of *Nurse Betty*, which he describes as "a feel-good hit that includes scalping, love, a cross-country car chase, shoot-outs, comedy"—in other words, an entertainment, and perhaps a holiday from his usual despair. LaBute, dressed in a blue-and-black plaid shirt, jeans, sneakers, and a slicker with a packet of raisins tucked into the cuff, spent much of the first morning skulking around a crowded Pasadena bungalow, inspecting every cranny of a room where one of the film's heavies, played by Chris Rock, goes looking for Betty, the title character (Renée Zellweger). The film is essentially a chase movie, in which Betty, a waitress, sees her ne'er-do-well husband murdered for the cache of drugs he has hidden in her car; traumatized and deluded, she sets off for Los Angeles to marry her "fiancé," the doctor on her favorite soap opera. On the set, LaBute engages his cast as he does the world—with an almost presidential bonhomie, at once solicitous and standoffish. He speaks with the low-key collegial composure of someone who knows who he is—the boss. "Love that Tide!" he called to the set decorator, who was positioning the soap-powder box so that the camera would catch it in the corner of the frame. "Love that box of Tide!" The scene called for the actress Kathleen Wilhoite to hold a baby as she answered the front door; on this bright morning, the professional toddler, a hefty lump called Robert, was bawling himself red in the face. LaBute swooped up the child and cradled him in his thick arms, as adept at handling kids as adults. (He has an eleven-year-old daughter, Lily, and a seven-year-old son, Spencer.) "You'll have the baby in your arms. That'll give you an acting challenge," he said to Wilhoite. "It'll steal the scene," she said. LaBute shot her a grin as he walked away. "They often do," he said.

On the bungalow's front lawn, amid a scrum of technicians and prop hands, LaBute, an almost constant nosher, munched a few raisins. "My mom is very happy, because I'm doing more than she hoped for," he told me. "But she'd rather I was doing comedies. I told her, 'I just did, so wait till I do a drama.'"

Chris Rock ambled over, dressed like a Bible salesman, in a loose-fitting black suit. "He's great with scenery," Rock said. "He's the best hair director that ever lived." LaBute gave him an owlish look, greeted him as "Mr. Rock," and said they were nearly ready to shoot. "I don't smile in this movie. I brood," Rock said as he walked away. "Cheating America of the bullshit that is Chris Rock."

It is typical of LaBute that he would find a way to exploit Rock's edgy, darker essence rather than his show-biz surface, even in a commercial film. *Nurse Betty*, written by John C. Richards and James Flamberg, is the first of a two-picture deal that LaBute cut with Propaganda Films (the company that joint-produced the four-million-dollar *Your Friends and Neighbors* last year). After he'd signed the contract, he had second thoughts and wanted to bolt; now he seemed to be contentedly and firmly at the helm. "There are a lot of firsts for me here," he said as the other children in the scene were being rounded up and given their orders. "First crane. First squib shot. First in all the things that you may not have dealt with—like anyone pulling a gun, let alone using it." To that list of firsts could be added: first big production (thirty million dollars), first seven-figure payday, first star-studded cast (Rock, Zellweger, Morgan Freeman), first happy ending, first film without his own narrative voice.

Even so, the Hollywood machine hasn't completely expunged LaBute's instinct for mischief, which became apparent a few hours later, when he was slumped in front of a monitor with two producers at his back worrying about the lack of coverage for an interracial sex scene. On the small screen, Rock was kneeling on a bed behind a white girl, pumping her for information while rogering her doggy style, as Jerry memorably does to Terri in *Your Friends and Neighbors*. "This is why I wanted to do the script," LaBute joked. In fact, he said, he shot the scene without coverage on purpose, so it could not be edited, in the hope of finessing his case against the inbred conservatism of the studio. "We talked about the sex," he explained. "Frontal would have been too intimate—he's getting information from the girl. It seemed less personal from behind. They have the same amount of clothes on—in fact, more than they had on in *Your Friends and Neighbors*. I think it comes down to the race thing. I really do."

After about ten minutes of calm discussion with the producers, LaBute accepted the postcoital option. "Just them in bed," he said.

"Her sitting smoking. He's lying next to her, and they're talking." He shoved his fingers into a bag of Cheetos. "Let's do it!" he shouted to his assistant. "Light the bed. Let's look right down on them. And off we'll go. She'll blow a little smoke in his face."

The next day, the production caravan moved to a low-rent side street of downtown Los Angeles. "This is your 'I found the coke' scene. Your daddy will be proud of you," LaBute said to Rock. Rock started over toward his screen father, Morgan Freeman, who was sucking on a toothpick and looking like a Marlboro man, in cowboy boots and pressed jeans. By the time LaBute got the shot he was talking about, it was midday and a tent had been erected to protect the monitors from the glare of the sun. LaBute and his director of photography, Jean Yves Escoffier, watched the screens as Freeman and Rock, for about the tenth time, sauntered toward a parked LeSabre and pried its trunk open. "I shoulda been a film director when I was a kid," LaBute said, happy with the take. "Time would have gone by much quicker. Waiting for Christmas? Go make a movie."

LaBute, who has an encyclopedic knowledge of pop culture and can as easily imitate Don Knotts ("My body is a weapon") as discourse on Werner Herzog's *Stroszek*, is a curious amalgam of theatrical influences. "What the fuck's her name? I mean, tits like that must have a name, correct?" has the vernacular wallop of a David Mamet line; actually, it is the self-incriminating telephone talk of Cary in *Your Friends and Neighbors*. LaBute writes with the same linguistic cunning as Mamet and characterizes his admiration for the playwright as "beyond fan—stalker perhaps. Psychological stalker." He even managed to mount an expurgated version of Mamet's *Sexual Perversity in Chicago* during his undergraduate days, at Brigham Young University: "My posters were so rococo that the passerby couldn't read what they said."

Where Mamet hears violence and evasion under conversational

speech, LaBute hears a kind of moral and emotional entropy—what he calls "the chill factor"—under his characters' jabbering. "I tend to hear a false sense of warmth in the way we lead people in sentences," LaBute says. " 'You know,' 'I mean,' 'Listen.' People are constantly trying to embellish what they say with this false sense of camaraderie—'I'm with you,' 'I'm with you on this.' A phrase that suddenly started coming up more and more and that I incorporated in *Your Friends and Neighbors* was 'Is it me?' These men were constantly asking, without any sense of wanting to know the answer, 'Who's doing this?' "

In *Filthy Talk for Troubled Times* LaBute developed this idea by orchestrating a counterpoint of monologues in which people talk about wanting to connect while the form of the play insures that they aren't listening to each other. "Women. Fucking broads! . . . You can't fucking trust them," one drinker says to another. "Well . . . personally, I could never trust anything that bleeds for a week and doesn't die." The complete absence of empathy expressed by this vicious joke also finds a powerful metaphor at the end of *In the Company of Men*, when the contrite Howard (Matt Malloy) goes in search of the female victim, Christine (Stacy Edwards), and finds her working in a bank. She wants no part of him or his apology; she leaves the bad feeling with him. "Listen," he says to her, then starts to shout when she doesn't acknowledge him. "Listen! Listen!! Listen!!! Listen!!!!" "It's so selfish," LaBute says of Howard's desire to have his impulse toward goodness acknowledged. "I think a lot of the characters I write, and certainly a lot of the male characters, are selfish. They just indulge themselves in taking care of their needs."

This sense of entitlement is the presenting symptom of most of LaBute's characters, and is part of what makes his work so distinctly contemporary. In addition to Mamet, he admires Wallace Shawn, whom he calls "the great chronicler of the ease with which we slowly tumble." "The difference between a perfectly decent person and a monster is just a few thoughts," Shawn writes in the appendix to his play *Aunt Dan and Lemon*, which LaBute cites as an influence on his own modest proposals. Charles Metten, who taught directing at Brigham Young, calls LaBute "a young Ibsen," which is perhaps pitching it a bit high. But LaBute is an original voice, and the best new playwright to emerge in the past decade. He brings to his observations about human nature something that other contemporary American writers have not articulated with quite such single-minded authority: a sense of sin.

"The 'should's and 'have to's of Mormonism make Neil struggle with the sinful life," Metten says. "The Latter-Day Saints standards are so high. The humanness of Neil sends him in the other direction. He gets even in his writing." LaBute's plays, which percolate with corrosive skepticism, are, in fact, by-products of the righteous life. "The interesting thing about sin is that we've gotten a bit away from it," LaBute says. "There's a right and a wrong that goes beyond the daily practice of living, and I think we have gotten away from that idea, yet it sort of hangs over all of us." His stories show a sense of goodness being leached out of the lives of his characters and, more hilariously, out of their vocabulary. In *Your Friends and Neighbors*, the subject comes up over a meal:

BARRY: Do you think you're good?

CARY: What, a good fuck?

BARRY: No, "good." I'm asking you, do you think you're good?

CARY: "Good," what do you mean, "good"? What kinda question is that?

BARRY: I'm asking . . . I'm saying are you, you know, like, a "good person"?

CARY: Hey, I'm eating lunch . . .

Later, when the thorny issue of salvation comes up—the question of whether they'll ultimately have to "pay" for their behavior,
in Barry's weasel words—Cary says, "I mean, if there ends up being
a God or something like that whole eternity thing out there, like,
then, yeah, probably so. I dunno. We'll see. But until then, we're on
my time, OK? The interim is mine." LaBute's characters are so lost
to themselves, so separated from their souls, that they can't feel anything; they hurt people in *order* to feel something. The murderous
mothers and fathers, the violent college boys, the conniving friends
and rampant seducers in his work continually dramatize sin as the
inability to imagine the suffering of others.

As a boy, LaBute often went to church and participated in Bible
study, even though his parents didn't. He grew up with intimations
of a faithless world—what he calls "a vague foreboding that something was not quite right." He explains, "I'm sure a lot of my love
of stories—of watching film or theater, imagining myself in some
other context—came from the unsettling environment at home."
When LaBute's producing partner, Stephen Pevner, called him at
the Seattle Film Festival, after the initial success of *In the Company
of Men*, in 1997, Pevner remembers getting LaBute's soft-spoken
mother, Marian, on the phone. "I said, 'It's taken so long. It must feel
so good. He did it, he really did it!' She goes, 'I know. He captured his
father perfectly.' I said, 'Well, I actually meant he did it. He pulled it
off.' And she goes, 'I know what you meant.'"

"There's a great deal of my father in a lot of the characters that
people find somewhat unseemly," LaBute says. Richard LaBute, who
was ten years older than his wife, had wanted to be an airline pilot
but ended up a truck driver; he specialized in long-distance hauling
during Neil's childhood, which was spent mostly in Liberty Lake,
Washington, outside Spokane. "As a kid, you get a sense of betrayal
you can't put specifics to—a sense of women down the line is what

one can make a leap to," LaBute says of his handsome father's long
absences. (Richard and Marian were divorced about five years ago,
after thirty-five years of marriage.) "My mother never talked about
it. When I was old enough to talk about it, I really wasn't interested
to find out the truth." He continues, "There must be something
there that I don't necessarily want the answer to, because it helps
fuel the writing."

Neil, the second child (his brother Richard Jr. is a linguist and
digital-processing executive in Minneapolis), was a bookish, sensitive, goofy-looking kid. Aaron Eckhart describes Neil's father as "a
hard-ass" who was "always chipping at him." The family pattern,
LaBute says, was to "spackle over problems" and "keep everything
hidden—any kind of strife that would make my father angry. I
can remember when he came home, a great sense of anticipation,
because of not knowing what mood he'd come back in." His father's
temper gave LaBute a sense of casual brutality and of "how much
damage could be done with language." He goes on, "I can remember
working with my father on a car. He'd gone inside. The only thing that
really sets me off is inanimate objects, because there's no reasoning
with them. I let out a tirade that would have made someone proud. I
didn't realize he'd come back into the garage. He looked at me, and I
got the sense of 'So this is part of the legacy I've left behind.'"

When LaBute gets angry, according to Eckhart, "he crawls inside
himself." Pevner says, "If you're good to him, he's extremely good to
you. If you're bad to him, forget it. What's worse than the wrath of
God? You won't get anything. You will get nothing." LaBute doesn't
like to be touched; he resists intimacy. "He doesn't want people
to know too much," the actress Hilary Russell says. "He's the only
friend of mine that I feel very close to but I don't know absolutely
everything about. There's a lot of dark stuff, and he's trying to figure it all out." LaBute's cordiality and his mystery are confounding.
It is as if, like his plays, the warmth of his surface disguises colder

depths. "He's very hard to read," says Pevner, who has worked with LaBute for a decade and still doesn't know the exact address of his home, in a northern suburb of Chicago. "He likes ambiguity. He will end up doing something he doesn't want to do, simply not to have a confrontation. He articulates through his writing, and that's it."

LaBute's mother, a fervid Anglophile, encouraged her son's love of drama and film, but his father did not; from the age of ten, Neil waged a perpetual losing battle against his father about his being what he calls "an indentured servant" on a farm that his father operated as a sideline. To LaBute's knowledge, his father, whom he hears from infrequently, has never seen one of his plays or films. Charles Metten recalls sitting in his office at Brigham Young with LaBute, who was planning to write a play about fathers and sons for Metten to direct. "I asked, 'Will it be another *All My Sons*?' He said, 'No, it's gonna be better.' Then, for the first time in our friendship, he started to talk about his father. Tears welled up. He got very, very emotional. In fact, he left and went to the rest room."

Though LaBute was the president of his high-school class, he refused to attend Friday-night football games, because they coincided with the weekly changing of the feature at the local cinema. His yearbook is filled with pictures of him: in *You're a Good Man, Charlie Brown* (he played Snoopy), *Arsenic and Old Lace*, and *Don't Drink the Water*. At Brigham Young, which he attended on a scholarship, LaBute continued to act, but he preferred the detachment of writing. He began providing monologues and scenes for friends going into the Irene Ryan Acting Competition, one of whom got to the finals. "I had a quick ability to write short, kind of pungent sketches and monologues," he says. "I had the hardest time writing anything of length, because I hated the idea of stopping. I loved to sit down and finish something. I was always writing short pieces. It was the opposite of writer's block." LaBute earned a BA in 1985; he married Gore, whom he had met at Brigham Young, and they moved to

New York, hoping that he could parlay his sketch-writing skills into a berth on *Late Night with David Letterman* or *Saturday Night Live*.

In his first, frustrating taste of the New York scene, LaBute's confidence was severely tested. A friend gave him the home telephone number of Lorne Michaels, *SNL*'s executive producer, and LaBute cold-called him. " 'How did you get my number?' " LaBute remembers Michaels saying. " 'Please don't call me here again. Send it in to the show.' That was the extent of my sketch-writing career. From then on, I started to say, 'Well, then, I'll just make it happen for myself as much as I can.' "

LaBute's early plays were the subject of scandal and concern at Brigham Young, where he worked toward a PhD in the early nineties. "The faculty revered Neil, but they were also afraid of him," recalls Eckhart, who first performed LaBute's work as an undergraduate. "This material was absolutely subversive. They thought it was going to tear down the theater department." The Mormon atmosphere "forced Neil to be more creative, because of the restrictions, the no-nos," Metten says. "Neil was in constant battle." For instance, in order to prevent the staging of *Lepers*, which LaBute had rehearsed for three months, the administration locked up the theater and even the lightboard; LaBute, who was able to get into the theater only to give a final exam, cut short the exam and did his play. "There was a glee in him," says Tim Slover, who taught playwriting and in whose postgraduate course LaBute wrote *In the Company of Men*. "He knew he was doing important work. But the glee was over the fact that this important moral work had surface features that appalled people."

In the larger world, LaBute's uncompromising scripts—which he typed all in lower case, so as not to impede the flow of his thought, and with no stage directions—were hard to sell. "There was a long period of writing plays and putting them away," says LaBute, who supported himself by teaching, and by working in a series of psychiatric hospitals and correctional institutions, where he was able to write late at night. Except for the productions he generated, mostly in university settings, his plays were not getting done. He was, he says, "torn by the hunger to get the work out there and have people see it."

"He wanted to be the greatest living playwright in America," Metten says of his student, whom he characterizes as "a pain in the butt because he was a genius." He adds, "When he would do his work, he knew it was darn good and that he would be ostracized from the regular community." LaBute's plays brought him into conflict not just with the community but with forces closer to home. At Brigham Young, his wife was conspicuously absent from his productions. "I came right out and asked 'Doesn't it hurt your feelings?'" Hilary Russell says. "He's like, 'You know, it did at first.' He just kind of hardens himself. She must know his work, and she's just avoiding it—she's going against every single Mormon standard in not supporting her husband." Although Lisa Gore is listed as a creative consultant on *In the Company of Men*, there seems to have been serious disagreement on *Your Friends and Neighbors* up to the first day of filming. "There was a major issue of Lisa's being afraid he'd be excommunicated—I mean, in the Mormon church you're not supposed to even think impure thoughts," says Russell, who was on the set the first day, when LaBute got his wife's phone call. "She said, 'You can't make it. How can you make this film?' I knew something was wrong just by his eyes."

LaBute's exploration of self-aggrandizement is also, by inference, about self-sacrifice: it reflects in theatrical terms his own internal battle to be at once great and good. "There's the Church telling you, 'You can't make these films or you'll go to Hell,'" Eckhart says of LaBute. "And there are other ramifications. Neil's wife holds a position in the Church. You got the whole social thing. It's very acute. I think everything in his life, on a certain level, is telling him in some way to forsake his true love—his work."

Before he got the financing for *In the Company of Men*, Eckhart remembers LaBute's saying, "I don't know if I can make a film. Who's going to trust me?" He was an unknown director, with an unknown script, unknown performers, and an unhappy ending. His father-in-law, an importer of industrial silks, declined to invest, but two of LaBute's former students stumped up their insurance payouts from a car accident. The actors got themselves to Fort Wayne, Indiana, where, in the mid-nineties, LaBute was teaching at St. Francis College; his next-door neighbor put them up. "We had a wonderful DP and sound guy, but, as far as everyone else, they were all volunteers from Fort Wayne—I mean, postal workers, college students, housewives," Stacy Edwards, who played the woman, says. "Neil was doing everything that normally would take at least six people to take care of."

LaBute shot *In the Company of Men* in eleven days, on twenty-five thousand dollars. Later, Sony added a quarter-million dollars in postproduction money to the film, and it grossed over five million dollars. "We knew through the entire shoot we really only had two takes per scene," Edwards says. "So you had to get it right." Eckhart recalls, "Stacy and I were sitting at that restaurant. It was six o'clock at night. We didn't close the restaurant down, because he had no money. Those customers are real, and they're kicking us out. So Neil comes up to me and says, 'Aaron, we've done it once, and it isn't right.' It was on my closeup and the last shot of the day. He says, 'Aaron, we've got one hundred feet of film left. We're getting kicked out of the restaurant.' He goes, 'Don't feel any pressure, but you have to get this one.' How many times did I hear that?"

There was no video playback, there were no dailies, and there was almost no movie when the lab gave LaBute three days to pay his bill or lose the film. But the end of the struggle came with a standing ovation at the Sundance Festival, where *In the Company of Men* won the 1997 Filmmakers Trophy. "In the middle of the screening, I turned to Matt Malloy and said, 'This thing is hot,'" Eckhart says. "I knew

Neil felt that way. When we came out, it was right there on his face—
'All right! This is going somewhere. I'm vindicated. Everything that
I knew about myself has just happened.' He didn't say it. I saw it."

I last saw LaBute in Projection Room 7 of a squat building off Santa
Monica Boulevard, where he was hunkered down in the far-right-
hand corner of the first row of a screening room, watching seven
hours of dailies. For this marathon, the members of his team were
spread out behind him over five rows: they came and went, snoozed
and talked as clapper board after clapper board announced a new
take of shots 87 A through D. I sat directly behind LaBute, hoping he
might talk to me during the process. He didn't. Instead, he worked
away at a large bag of Doritos and a Pepsi as he watched a well-shot
sequence that included a white Mercedes tearing up the ramp of
a hospital emergency entrance and ramming an ambulance; an
exchange of gunfire; flying bodies; breaking glass; and Nurse Betty,
in her hospital disguise, pressed into real medical service by some
gun-waving gangbangers who mistake her for the genuine article.

In the film, Nurse Betty is spellbound; and it struck me over the
next hour that perhaps the purpose of this exercise for LaBute was to
live, however briefly, in the exhilarating spell of the Hollywood system that had captivated him as an adolescent on those Friday nights.
LaBute had accomplished the hardest thing: he had found both a
style and an audience for his point of view. Now, for the moment at
least, he was giving up the personal for the impersonal, the subversive for something that conformed more or less to the commercial
formulas that his other movies shunned. *Nurse Betty*, a will-she-or-
won't-she saga, plays against LaBute's great strength, which is to
force the audience to take a position rather than to abdicate thought
for the sake of fun. I tried to see it through his eyes. Pevner had told
me, "I think he wanted to acquire power—you know, psychological
power, emotional power, financial power. To overcome his obstacles.
I think he's truly a romantic figure."

In a way, a full-blown Hollywood movie could be seen as LaBute's victory lap—a little moment of vindictive triumph, to show the panjandrums of commerce who'd rejected his early work that he could succeed in this part of the business, too. In the past, he had access to nobody; now he was on the Rolodex of everyone in town. He was an artist with money chores to be done, and sometimes it was wise to give the piper a dance. There were historical precedents: Scorsese's *Cape Fear*, Hitchcock's *Dial M for Murder*, Huston's *Annie*. Then again perhaps this dance was not for the piper at all but for the Mormon brethren, and maybe even for his wife, who wanted him to delight the world rather than disenchant it.

When LaBute and I talked again, a couple of weeks ago, he was making plans to come East for rehearsals of *Bash*. He declared himself pleased with *Nurse Betty* and with the new bag of tricks he'd mastered. "It's sort of freeing," he said. I asked him if the film was LaButian, and, with typical LaButian ambivalence, he answered, "Yes—and no." He did see some thematic connections with his plays and his tougher work. "There is a series of mediocre-to-bad men and a woman scrambling to save themselves," he said. With LaBute, one way or another, salvation remains the issue. ▪

—*July 5, 1999*

The Mercy Seat

There is no playwright on the planet these days who is writing better than Neil LaBute, whose magnificent new play, *The Mercy Seat* (at the MCC Theater, at the Acorn), only goes to prove that it's always darkest before it's totally black. For a hundred minutes, the audience seems to hold its breath as Sigourney Weaver and Liev Schreiber, giving performances of a depth and concentration that haven't been seen in New York for many seasons, take us through the torment of two lovers the day after September 11, 2001—the day, it turns out, that they are faced with the decision of whether to slip away from New York and start a new life together.

LaBute, who also directs, is a subtle storyteller, and his furtive heart reveals itself through cunning, powerful indirection. Here, he lets the accumulation of detail—a loft apartment, its high windows white with dust; a man's long, pensive silence as he ignores a ringing cell phone on the sofa beside him; the faint sound of fire engines—lure the imagination into a numbed terrain of unspoken desperation. At first, the man—Ben—appears to be a dazed survivor of the catastrophe (which he missed, we learn later, because he happened to have stopped off at the apartment of his boss and mistress of three years, Abby, who was giving him a blow job at the time the planes hit the Twin Towers). Thirty-something, married with two daughters, sexually confident but emotionally bewildered, Ben has all the backbone of a chocolate éclair. He is a slippery character, so used to covering his tracks that he is no longer able to find himself. The moral maze he inhabits is accompanied by a linguistic one, a confounding smoke screen of unfinished sentences—a sort of syntactical stuttering—in which the word "whatever" suffices to stonewall any attempt he makes to think himself out of it.

He is like one of those jungle animals that survive an attack by playing dead. Abby, by contrast, has a vocabulary; she is a kind of conscience, albeit a steely, sarcastic one. More than a decade older than Ben, she fulfills the motherly function of reflecting him back to himself. As she enters the apartment, after a foray to the market, Ben's ringing phone prompts her to ask if he has made "the call." She is speaking of a call to his family to say that he is alive. "I'm . . . I was, ahh . . . I was going to, maybe," Ben says, gazing straight ahead. "I keep trying to. . . . Yeah, but . . . but I'm . . . " The words trail off into entropy. Late in the play, Abby asks Ben if he loves her. "Abby . . . of course. You know that, I . . . yeah," he says. "That's really not the same as just saying it," she replies. Her sharp jabs pick away at Ben's guardedness ("I'm not sure anyone could ever *know* Ben Harcourt"), his philistinism ("You're just, like, a complete cultural moron"), his plan to seize what he calls "the opportunity" to reinvent himself as a new man with a clean slate by running away ("your, you know, *Lazarus* thing"), and his childishness ("You're like a twelve-year-old").

It is not hyperbolic to say that in *The Mercy Seat* Schreiber does for emotional ambivalence what Brando did for sexuality in *A Streetcar Named Desire*—his is the uncanny, defining performance of a remote soul, paralyzed by guilt and grief. Schreiber has a strapping muscular body and a chubby-cheeked baby face; he shuffles and flops his way around the stage with his shirttail out, obsessively knotting his fingers and playing with his tie. He is, in other words, an adolescent trapped in a man's body. And, like all adolescents, he wants everything all the time. He wants Abby; he wants his kids; he wants to be perceived as heroic; he wants redemption and absolution without having to work for them. His plan—which he calls his "meal ticket"—would allow him to avoid guilt, ignominy, even himself. Pushed by Abby to articulate why he wants to bolt rather than admit he's alive and divorce his wife, he says, "She would have buried me on a divorce, you know that." Ben, as he acknowledges, repeatedly takes the path of least resistance. "This *is* me," he says to Abby. "I always take the easy route, do it faster, simpler, you know, whatever it takes to get it done, be liked, get by. That's me. Cheated in school, screwed over my friends, took whatever I could get from whomever I could take it from."

But, if they are going to have a life together, Abby argues, it must be an honorable one. "You, umm, you want me to . . . what, make the call that I was gonna make yesterday, right?" he says. "That's what I want. Yes . . . I need you to do it for me," Abby replies. "*You* have to choose," she tells him. But to make a choice you must have the confidence that you can survive the consequences. Ben doesn't want to choose, because he doesn't want to lose; he seems doomed to immaturity. And, by the time he finally admits to Abby that he is "a little lost right now," she is no longer willing to help him find his way. "I'm not gonna give you any cash or maps, or, you know, *waterproof matches*," she says. "I'm not Harriet Tubman." As the curtain falls, LaBute's hero is, both literally and symbolically, in the same place where he began: staring into space alone, as the phone rings.

A song by the Smiths, the defiant "How Soon Is Now?" ("You shut your mouth / How can you say / I go about things the wrong way"), played the curtain up; now the band's hymn to suicide, "Asleep" ("Sing me to sleep / Sing me to sleep / and then leave me alone"), brings the curtain down. This sense of exhaustion—of being fed up with lacerating internal arguments—is a new note in LaBute's lugubrious music. In the preface to *The Mercy Seat*, LaBute says, "I have no idea why I wrote this play. Really, I don't." I think he does. Political terrorism sometimes calls out other kinds of terrorism, one form of which LaBute calls "the painful, simplistic warfare we often wage on the hearts of those we profess to love." Here, with extraordinary daring and elegance, he faces the division in every heart, including his own. History will decide if *The Mercy Seat* is a great play; certainly, for me, it is the work of a master. ▪

—January 6, 2003

11

SAM SHEPARD

"I just dropped out of nowhere," Sam Shepard said of his arrival in New York, at nineteen, in the fall of 1963. "It was absolute luck that I happened to be there when the whole Off-Off Broadway movement was starting." Shepard, a refugee from his father's farm in California, had spent eight months as an actor travelling the country by bus with a Christian theater troupe, the Bishop's Company Repertory Players. Acting had been his ticket to ride; he'd been so scared at his Bishop's Company audition that he'd recited the stage directions. "I think they hired everybody," he said. Once he'd taken up residence in Manhattan—"It was wide open," Shepard said. "You were like a kid in a fun park"—he proceeded to knock around the city, "trying to be an actor, writer, musician, whatever happened." He had no connections, no money (he sold his blood to buy a cheeseburger), and nothing to fall back on but his lanky, taciturn Western charisma. He did, however, have renegade credentials and a store of arcane knowledge: he had been a 4-H Club member, a sheepshearer, a racecourse hot walker, a herdsman, an orange picker, and a junior-college student.

Shepard was homespun and handsome, with a strong jaw and a dimpled chin. He exuded the mystery and swagger of a movie star, which he would eventually become. (In addition to writing four dozen or so plays—the latest of which, *Ages of the Moon*, opened last week, at the Atlantic Theater Company—Shepard, who is now sixty-six, has appeared in some forty films; he was nominated for an Oscar for his performance as the test pilot Chuck Yeager, in *The Right Stuff*.) But even as a new arrival in the city he seemed instinctively to understand the importance of image. "Use yer eyes like a weapon. Not defensive. Offensive," a character in his play *The Tooth of Crime* (1972) says, adding, "You can paralyze a mark with a good set of eyes." Shepard had such a pair. His almond-shaped blue eyes looked out at the world with wry detachment; they imposed on his passionate nature a mask of cool. His smile was tight-lipped—half knowing, half strategic (it hid a mouthful of craggy teeth). Years of living with invasive family aggression—"The male influences around me were primarily alcoholics and extremely violent," he said—had taught Shepard to play things close to his chest: to look and to listen. "I listened like an animal. My listening was afraid," Wesley, the son in Shepard's 1978 play *Curse of the Starving Class*, says, describing his method for coping with his drunken father. Shepard was a man of few words, many of them mumbled. Compelling to look at but hard to read—at once intellectually savvy and emotionally guarded—he exuded the solitude and the vagueness of the American West.

Though Shepard lacked East Coast sophistication—he was poorly read in those days—he brought news of what he called "the whacked out corridors of broken-off America": its blue highways, its wilderness, its wasteland, its animal kingdom, its haunted lost souls, its violence. "People want a street angel. They want a saint with a cowboy mouth," a prescient character in one of Shepard's early one-acts said. Shepard, it turned out, was the answer to those prayers. He got a job busing tables at the Village Gate, and began to write in earnest. "I had a sense that a voice existed that needed expression, that there was a voice that wasn't being *voiced*," he said. "There were so many voices that I didn't know where to start. I felt kind of like a weird stenographer. . . . There were definitely things there, and I was just putting them down. I was fascinated by how they structured themselves." Ralph Cook, the Village Gate's headwaiter, who was a former

bit-part actor in Hollywood Westerns and a fellow-Californian, provided him an entry into the downtown scene through a new space he
was starting on the Bowery—Theatre Genesis—where Shepard made
his playwriting debut, in 1964. By the following year, the twenty-
two-year-old Samuel Shepard Rogers VII, who was known as Steve
to his family and friends, had reinvented himself as Sam Shepard,
whom the *Times* described as "the generally acknowledged 'genius' "
of the Off-Off Broadway circuit.

Shepard's early plays, written between 1964 and 1971, were full of
surprises and assaults on the senses—people spoke from bathtubs or
painted one another, colored Ping-Pong balls dropped from the ceiling, a chicken was sacrificed onstage. The plays express what Shepard called the "despair *and* hope" of the sixties; they act out both
the spiritual dislocation and the protean survival instinct of trau-
matic times. Better than anyone else writing in that fractious hubbub, Shepard defined the fault lines between youth culture and the
mainstream. "You were so close to the people who were going to the
plays, there was really no difference between you and them," he said,
pinpointing both his work's value and its limitation. The mockery,
the role-playing, the apocalyptic fears, the hunger for new mythologies, and the physical transformations in his work gave shape to the
spiritual strangulation of the decade—which, in Shepard's words,
"sucked dogs." "For me, there was nothing fun about the sixties," he
said. "Terrible suffering. . . . Things coming apart at the seams."

In their verbal and visual daring, Shepard's early plays aspired
to match the anarchic wallop of rock and roll. He had been playing
drums since the age of twelve, when his father, a semi-professional
Dixieland drummer, bought him a secondhand set and taught him
how to play. (He continued drumming into his adulthood, with such
bands as the Holy Modal Rounders and T Bone Burnett's Void.) In
his writing, he gravitated toward rock's maverick energy; he listed
Little Richard among his literary influences, along with Jackson

Pollock and Cajun fiddles. (Later, he befriended Keith Richard, lived briefly with Patti Smith—"He was a renegade with nasty habits / he was a screech owl / he was a man playing cowboys," she wrote of him—chronicled Bob Dylan's Rolling Thunder Revue, and co-wrote, with Dylan, the eleven-minute song "Brownsville Girl.") In plays as varied as *The Tooth of Crime*, *Forensic & the Navigators* (1967), and *Operation Sidewinder* (1970), music and song are a crucial part of Shepard's dramatic attack. Of these plays, *The Tooth of Crime*, which involves a style war between an old rock king, Hoss, and his upstart challenger, Crow, is the most visionary work. Here Shepard carried the language of drugs, rock, and political struggle from the street to the stage:

> CROW: So ya' wanna be a rocker. Study the moves. Jerry Lee Lewis. Buy some blue suede shoes. Move yer head like Rod Stewart. Put yer ass in a grind. Talkin' sock it to it, get the image in line. Get the image in line boy. The fantasy rhyme. It's all over the streets and you can't buy the time. You can't buy the bebop. You can't buy the slide. Got the fantasy blues and no place to hide.

Rhythm led Shepard to character. "When you write a play, you work out like a musician on a piece of music," he wrote. "You find all the rhythms and the melody and the harmonies and take them as they come." His early plays, which he refers to now as "cavorting," were riffs, written at speed—wild, energized, and slipshod—following the rhythmic strategy of his drumming. "Break it all down in pairs. Make the pairs work together, with each other. Then make 'em work against each other, independent," he wrote in his 1969 play *The Holy Ghostly*. His pieces were abstract flights of illuminated feeling, like the work of the jazz greats—Thelonious Monk, Dizzy Gillespie, Gerry Mulligan, Nina Simone—he heard at the Village

Gate, more vectors of energy than maps of psychology. "I preferred a character that was constantly unidentifiable," Shepard said. As he explained in his note to the actors in *Angel City* (1976), instead of embodying a "whole character" the actor should consider his performance "a fractured whole with bits and pieces of character flying off the central theme," and aim "to make a kind of music or painting in space without having to feel the need to completely answer intellectually for the character's behavior." In those years, by his own admission, Shepard was "dead set against revisions because I couldn't stand rewriting." For him and for his downtown audience, the plays were exercises in spontaneity and emotional discovery. "They were chants, they were incantations, they were spells," he said in *Stalking Himself*, a 1998 PBS documentary. "You get on them and you go."

Shepard's talent soon attracted a wide range of interest; he found himself collaborating on movies with Robert Frank and Michelangelo Antonioni, and on theater pieces with Joseph Chaikin's experimental Open Theater. Despite his disdain for the uptown theater scene, his increasingly ambitious plays required larger casts, bigger budgets, better production values, and greater narrative finesse than his downtown habitat encouraged. "As far as I'm concerned, Broadway just does not exist," Shepard told *Playboy* in 1970. Nonetheless, the same year, in a move that in Off-Off Broadway circles was the equivalent of Dylan going electric, Shepard transitioned above Fourteenth Street to Lincoln Center, with *Operation Sidewinder*, a picaresque apocalyptic fable about political oppression, told in a cool pop style, which required, among other things, a seven-foot snake, the performance of a Hopi ritual, a '57 Chevy, and a rock band. "I am whipped, I am chained. I am prisoner to all your oppression. I am depressed, deranged, decapitated, dehumanized, defoliated, demented and damned! I can't get out," the play's hero says, using the snake as a tourniquet to shoot up. (Shepard himself was no stranger to heroin in those years.)

As the literary manager of Lincoln Center at the time, I was responsible for bringing Shepard uptown. The year before, he had married O-Lan Johnson, an actress who had appeared in *Forensics & the Navigators*. When the two of them came to Lincoln Center for the first preview, the bartender tried to shoo us all out of the lobby because we looked too scruffy. As I noted in my diary, communication between cultures soon turned into a collision:

> The show goes well for the first act. At the intermission Sam is nervous, obviously disgruntled. "Don't you think it's too smooth?" Talking about the audience he says, "I'm not worried about the old people, I'm worried about the young ones." . . .
>
> At the theater—Sam looking gloomy before the show, goes to the bar and sneaks a beer in under his shirt. The audience is tough. They laugh at the Hopi dance scene. . . . On the way out, one girl said, "Do you think he's serious?"

Afterward, I was shown responses from the bewildered Lincoln Center subscription audience: "Terrible, terrible, terrible," "The artistic director and anyone connected should be fired." The play was better received by the critics, who dubbed it "possibly significant" (the *Times*) and "the wildest and most ambitious show yet at Lincoln Center" (NBC). But, not long afterward, to get off the Village streets and off drugs, Shepard moved to London with his wife and their young son, Jesse Mojo. From leafy Hampstead, he raced greyhounds, wrote plays, and took stock of the homeland from which he felt alienated. "I wanted to get out of the insanity," he told Matthew Roudané, in his interview "Shepard on Shepard." "Of course I was also running away from myself!"

After returning to the United States, in 1974, however, Shepard made facing himself and his emotional inheritance the central project of his adulthood. The quartet of major plays that he produced between 1978 and 1985—*Curse of the Starving Class*, the Pulitzer Prize–winning *Buried Child* (1978), *True West* (1980), and *A Lie of the Mind* (1985)—are not traditional psychological dramas. "Plays have to go beyond just 'working out problems,'" he said. They are quasi-naturalistic meditations, in keeping with his plan to move "from colloquial territory" to "poetic country." But they drew on the deepest recesses of Shepard's emotional memory.

Seven Plays, the collection in which three of the four plays appear, is dedicated "For my father, Sam," to whom Shepard owed a large part of his identity, his damage, and his subject matter. "Sometimes in someone's gestures you can notice how a parent is somehow inhabiting that person without there being any awareness of that," Shepard told *Rolling Stone*. "Sometimes you can look at your hand and see your father." Shepard could see Sam Rogers in his own fierce eyes, his infatuation with solitude, his bouts of alcoholism, his ornery single-mindedness, his short fuse, and, especially, his reckless Western machismo. "I've been involved in many dangerous foolish things," Shepard said in *Stalking Himself.* "I've been upside down under falling horses at a full gallop. I've been fired upon by a 12-gauge Ithaca Over-and-Under. I've rolled in a 1949 Plymouth coupe." Shepard sees himself as a "victim" of his father's tough-guy persona. "My old man tried to force on me a notion of what it was to be a 'man,'" he said. "And it destroyed my dad."

As a child, amid the violence of his family, Shepard, who has spoken of "tremendous morning despair," was something of a sleepwalker. He grew up feeling as if he were living "on Mars"; "I feel like I've never had a home," he said. "Sometimes I just stand outside and watch my family moving around inside the house," he wrote in his 1982 memoir, *Motel Chronicles*. "I stand there a long time sometimes. They don't know that I watch them." Playwriting called those indigestible family experiences out of him. Shepard's dramatic world is peopled with derelict, disappointed somnambulists: Tilden, the "burned out and displaced" son in *Buried Child*, who returns to his family after a twenty-year exile in Mexico; Weston, the quixotic drunken father in *Curse of the Starving Class*; Lee, the feral thief, who wanders out of the desert in *True West*. Taken together, these unmoored souls form a kind of tribe of the living dead, deracinated men trying to escape a sense of shame that they only vaguely understand. They recede from family, from society, and, through drink, from themselves. All these figures are fragments of Shepard's father, a Second World War bomber pilot and high-school teacher, who moved the family (Shepard has two younger sisters, Roxanne, an actress, and Sandy, a singer-songwriter, who composed the songs for Robert Altman's film version of Shepard's 1983 play *Fool for Love*) from Illinois, where Shepard was born, to an avocado ranch in Duarte, California, and who spent his last years alone in the desert because he didn't "fit with people."

"My dad had a lot of bad luck," Shepard said in Don Shewey's 1985 biography *Sam Shepard*. "You could see his suffering, his terrible suffering, living a life that was disappointing and looking for another one." Sam Rogers's family history is retold in detail by Pop, the main character in *The Holy Ghostly*. "Me, I never got no real breaks," Pop begins. "My old man was a dairy farmer. Started hittin' the bottle and lost the whole farm. Things started goin' down hill from that point on." Shepard attributes part of his father's downfall to postwar trauma. "My dad came from an extremely rural farm community . . . and the next thing he knows he's flying B-24s over the South Pacific, over Romania, dropping bombs and killing people he couldn't even see," he said. "These men returned from this heroic victory . . . and were devastated in some basic way . . . that's mysterious still. . . . The medicine was booze." The booze often led to abuse. "Those Midwestern women of the forties suffered an incredible psychological assault," Shepard recalled. "While growing up, I saw that assault over and over again, and not only in my own family." In 1984, Rogers was hit by a car, after a drunken quarrel with a girlfriend in a New Mexico bar. "You either die like a dog or you die like a man. And if you die like a dog you just go back to dust," Shepard, who had his father cremated, said later. After the ceremony, Shepard picked up the leather container holding the ashes. "It was so heavy," he said. "You wouldn't think the ashes of a man would be so heavy."

"Let's leave the old man out of it," Austin, the successful screenwriter in *True West*, says to his brother, Lee, of their father, who lives in abject isolation in the desert. But, for Shepard and for his characters, there is no escaping the father. "He put stuff into me that'll never go away," a character complains of her father in *A Lie of the Mind*. (A New Group production of this play, directed by Ethan Hawke, will open in February.) Likewise, Wesley, in *Starving Class*, describes his father's psychic imperialism: "Part of him was growing on me. I could feel him taking over me. I could feel myself retreating." Shepard's legion of feral male characters keeps alive aspects of the toxic Sam Rogers. "He was a . . . maniac, but in a quiet way," Shepard said.

Shepard's early success made him an object of envy to his floundering father; it also made his father an object of guilt to him. In *The Holy Ghostly*, Pop's childish demands for allegiance from his son (who has changed his name to Ice) come with a jealous attack on his achievements. "Don't go givin' me none a' yer high falootin' esoteric gobbledy gook, Buster Brown," Pop says. "Just 'cause ya' struck off fer the big city on yer own and made a big splash . . . don't mean ya' can humiliate an old man." From the stage, Shepard broadcast his fierce refusal to regret his decisions. "For eighteen years I was your slave," Ice says. "I worked for you hand and foot. Shearing the sheep, irrigating the trees, listening to your bullshit about 'improve your mind, you'll never get ahead, learn how to lose, hard work and guts and never say die,' and now I suppose you want me to bring you back to life. You pathetic creep. Hire yourself a professional mourner, Jim. I'm splitting." In the third act of *The Late Henry Moss* (2000), a dead father comes back from the grave to berate his son, Earl, for not having saved him from a squalid exile and from his self-destructiveness:

> HENRY: You coulda stopped me but you didn't.
> EARL: I couldn't. I—I—I—was scared. I was—just—too—scared.
> HENRY: You were scared! A what? A me? You were scared of a dead man?

Shepard's quartet of family plays is an act of both reunion and resolution. "I'm not doing this in order to vent demons," he said. "I want to shake hands with them." The subject called out of him an unprecedented degree of urgency and eloquence. A wife brain-damaged by her husband's jealous violence (*A Lie of the Mind*); the corpse of a murdered child exhumed (*Buried Child*); a mother's home trashed by her sons (*True West*); warring parents trying to sell the family home out from under each other (*Starving Class*)—the plays are allegories of mutilated love, bearing superb witness to Shepard's violent memories. Told in a more textured, complex narrative style than his early work—Shepard's association with Joseph Chaikin had taught him the virtues of rewriting—the plays resound with bewilderment at the absence of familial normality: "What's happened to this family?" (*Buried Child*), "What kind of family is this?" (*Starving Class*). The refrigerator in *Starving Class*—it's either empty or stuffed with inappropriate food by the boozy Weston—becomes a symbol of the fiasco of nurture. "You couldn't be all that starving!" Weston bellows. "We're not that bad off, goddamnit!"

The impoverishment is psychological, the crime pathological carelessness. In *True West*, the mother returns home to find her sons strangling each other and her house torn apart. Coolly surveying the mess, she says to one son, "You're not killing him, are you?" before decamping to a motel. In *Starving Class*, Weston breaks down the kitchen door; his wife, Ella, boils the chicken that her daughter has painstakingly raised for a 4-H demonstration; and the son, Wesley, urinates on his sister's presentation. Love is unavailable; hatred is the only form of intimacy. The perversity of family combat is brought together in a brilliant final image, as mother and son try to recall Weston's story of an eagle that carried off a cat in its talons:

> ELLA: That cat's tearing his chest out, and the eagle's trying
>   to drop him, but the cat won't let go because he know if
>   he falls he'll die.
> WESLEY: And the eagle's being torn apart in midair. . . .
> ELLA: And they come crashing down to the earth. Both of
>   them come crashing down. Like one whole thing.

Like planets in their own orbits, Shepard's family members revolve around one another without ever intersecting. In *Starving Class*, Weston remarks on the circle of solitude that his father inhabited. "He lived apart," he says. "Right in the midst of things and he lived apart." In *Buried Child*, the atmosphere of disconnection is remarked upon by a young visitor, who has "the feeling that nobody lives here but me. . . . You're here but it doesn't seem like you're supposed to be." ("What a bunch of bullshit this is!" Sam Rogers said, drunk and disorderly at the Greer Garson Theatre in New Mexico, where he saw the play. "The ushers tried to throw him out," Shepard told *The Paris Review*. "He resisted, and in the end they allowed him to stay because he was the father of the playwright.")

Shepard's characters are not so much warped as unborn; clueless and rudderless, they can't find their way. In *Starving Class*, Weston explains to his son that he is unable to navigate his own life:

"I couldn't figure out the jumps. From being born, to growing up, to droppin' bombs, to having kids, to hittin' bars, to this. It all turned on me somehow." Like so many of Shepard's derailed men, Weston has killed off his empathetic, female side. In the finale of *True West*, the brothers, sensitive writer and reckless thief, square off against each other, the two sides of Shepard's own divided personality. "You know in yourself that the female part of oneself as a man is, for the most part, battered and beaten up and kicked to shit just like some women in relationships," Shepard said. In *A Lie of the Mind*, Jake, who has beaten his wife so badly that he thinks he's killed her, says that it's "like my whole life is lost from losing her. Gone. That I'll die like this. Lost." When he does finally make contact with his brain-damaged wife, he kisses her, then surrenders her to the affections of his gentler other self—his brother, Frankie.

Taken together, these four plays constitute a sort of empire of the damned, whose inhabitants are caught in desperate but impossible retreat from their legacy of self-destruction. "It always comes. Repeats itself. . . . Even when you try to change it," Ella says, in *Starving Class*. "It goes back and back to tiny little cells and genes. . . . We inherit it and pass it down, and then pass it down again." "Character is something that can't be helped," Shepard said. "It's like destiny. . . . It can be covered up, it can be messed with, it can be screwed around with, but it can't be ultimately changed. It's like the structure of our bones, and the blood that runs through our veins." His characters are doomed by their unconscious, which they can't or won't examine. In fact, they'll do anything for an unexamined life.

"Theater is a place to bring stuff from your life experience," Shepard said in the PBS documentary. "You send this telegram, and then you get out." Since his career as a screen actor took off, in the eighties, he has written fewer plays, and the results have been uneven. "I've never been able to write a play while I've been acting in a film," he told *Rolling Stone*. "You get enraptured for a long time . . . and it's difficult to do that in an actor's trailer." The message inside the bright comic envelope of Shepard's new play, *Ages of the Moon*, is one of heartbreak.

In recent years, Shepard has had some rocky moments with the actress Jessica Lange, his partner since 1983 (they met while co-starring in the 1982 movie *Frances*), with whom he has two children. In *Fool for Love*, Shepard examined the turmoil of his exit from his fifteen-year marriage to Johnson. In his last play, *Kicking a Dead Horse* (2007), a Beckett-influenced monologue, the narrator, Hobart Struther, standing in the desert beside his dead horse, delivers a litany of his losses: his horse, his youth, his authenticity, and, perhaps imminently, his wife:

> She was amazing to me. She was.
> Was?
> Is. Still. But then—
> In the past?
> Yes. In the past. She was beyond belief. I thought I'd died and gone to heaven.

In *Ages of the Moon*, that loss has been accomplished. Ernest Tubb's "Have You Ever Been Lonely" plays as the show begins; after the lines "How can I go on living / Now that we're apart," the lights come up on two codgers drinking on the porch of a Kentucky-style brick country house. "Here's the really sour part of the whole deal," Ames (the expert Stephen Rea), who cuts a comic figure in suspenders, short khaki work pants, and black-and-white wingtips with no socks, says in the play's first line. "She discovers this note—this note from this girl, which to this day I cannot for the life of me remember. . . . I swear, some girl I would never in a million years have ever returned to for even a minor blow-job." Byron (Sean

McGinley), his old friend, who has come to console Ames for the breakup of his marriage, replies, "Minor?"

Under the direction of Jimmy Fay, *Ages of the Moon* has the loose banter and percussive rhythms of Shepard's early plays—it even has an eleven-o'clock "aria"—but the evening has more splash than sizzle; nonetheless, since Shepard is a cunning craftsman, the play's charm is insinuating. Ames and Byron are intended as clowns of inconsolability, a kind of country-and-Western Vladimir and Estragon. They drink; they argue; they fight; they pass the time from midday to midnight waiting for an eclipse of the moon. Twice during the evening, Byron calls Ames "hopeless"; the word evokes his marriage. "I can't ever go back now," Ames says. "I know. I can see it. The writing's on the wall."

The play is slight; the weight of its sorrow is not. Shepard leaves his characters gazing poignantly into the gloaming. "Sliver of moonlight fades to black," the stage direction reads. As Ernest Tubb's bright voice sings them into shadow—"When you look at me with those stars in your eyes / I could waltz across Texas with you"—the men sit, drinks in hand, staring into space. The falling darkness plays as the declivity of Shepard's life and love. "I hate endings," he once said. "Just detest them. Beginnings are definitely the most exciting, middles are perplexing, and endings are a disaster." ■

—February 8, 2010

True West

When Walt Whitman surveyed the American republic, in his 1871 essay *Democratic Vistas*, he described it as a vast, well-endowed body "with little or no soul." Emptiness had already become as defining a by-product of American abundance as the good life, and Whitman's poems were intended to be an antidote to the malaise

of materialism, a "tremendous force-infusion" of spirit. Unfortunately, Whitman's strong medicine couldn't remedy capitalism's
fever, which, in his eyes, turned democracy's great experiment
into a great debacle—"cankered, crude, superstitious and rotten,"
in which the "depravity of the business classes . . . is not less than
has been supposed, but infinitely greater." The pioneer Americans
had been made barbarous by the lawless frontier; now, as Whitman
saw, modern Americans were being made barbarous by the laws of
the free market. These twin wildernesses are brought hilariously
together in Sam Shepard's *True West* (written in 1980 and now given
a thrilling revival by the director Matthew Warchus at the Circle in
the Square).

In the daring long pause that begins the play, the sounds of the
Los Angeles night, its crickets and coyotes, compete with a sulfurous silence between two brothers, Lee and Austin, who face off in
their mother's tidy modern kitchen. With his jeans, crude tattoos,
and cowboy boots, Lee (the craggy, brilliant John C. Reilly), who has
rolled up on his mother's doorstep after some months in the desert,
is an intrusive, beer-swilling outlaw whose only expertise seems to
be in breaking and entering. The nervy Austin (played by the incomparable interpreter of introverted fury Philip Seymour Hoffman)
is a put-upon Ivy League screenwriter with a Hollywood movie to
pitch and the responsibility of house-sitting his mother's plants
while she vacations in Alaska. Out of this clash of personalities and
life chances, Shepard spins a droll tall tale of sibling rivalry. In the
brothers' rootless isolation, the play traps a deeper spiritual atrophy
in the land and, incidentally, also acts out Shepard's own fierce division between the claims of success and rebellion.

True West avoids the tangle of pretension and obfuscation that
mars so much of Shepard's work; it's an appealingly modest play,
which skillfully translates psychology into behavior—in this case,
the murderous, spoiling work of envy. "I mean you never had any

more on the ball than I did," Lee tells his brother, early in the play. "But here you are gettin' invited into prominent people's houses. Sittin' around talkin' like you know somethin'." Jealousy is eating Lee alive, but Austin won't bite. "Well, you invite yourself," he says. Later, when Lee ponders the local suburban homes he's cased, his coruscating sense of inferiority surfaces again. "Kinda' place that sorta' kills ya' inside," Lee says, of the affluent furnishings. "Kinda' place you wish you sorta' grew up in, ya' know."

Reilly's roaring and Hoffman's repressed hostility make for a wonderful contrast and a satisfyingly equal battle of wills. (For half the run, the actors switch roles; then Hoffman's derelict eyes, slurred sea-dog voice, and preternatural comic skills make the contest entertaining but lopsided.) But all of this is only Shepard's shrewdly engineered preamble. Before the end of the first act, Lee's envy will have achieved its violent mission. At first, Lee goes after, and gets, Austin's car; next, he befriends Austin's producer (the clever Robert Lupone, in a robin's-egg-blue suit and white loafers); then he's writing his own screen treatment, and, before you can say, "It's a wrap," Lee's terrible movie idea has superseded Austin's in the producer's dead heart. Austin's deal, his livelihood, ultimately even his billing, are appropriated by Lee.

By the second act, the brothers' roles have completely reversed: Austin is the drunk slumped in the kitchen, singing "Red Sails in the Sunset" and lobbing bitter zingers at his brother, who pecks away at the typewriter. "I don't want my name on that piece of shit," Austin says. "I want something of value. . . . You got any tidbits from the desert?" The thought crosses Austin's befuddled mind that if Lee can do his job, then he can do Lee's. "You couldn't steal a toaster without losin' yer lunch," Lee brays, pulling ribbon out of the typewriter as if it were fishing line.

When the lights come up on the two brothers in the next scene, Austin is burnishing one of a dozen newly acquired toasters ("There's

gonna' be a general lack of toast in the neighborhood this morning,"
he says); meanwhile, in the foreground, Lee is taking out his writer's block on the typewriter, smashing it to smithereens with a nine
iron. Here, Shepard is at his best: loose, intuitive, his dialogue rip-
pling with subtle shifts of mood and ideas. In this impeccably staged
piece of slapstick, while Reilly tears up the dining alcove looking for
a pencil, Hoffman pads behind him, priming his toasters with white
bread and talking about going back to the desert with Lee. "There's
nothing real down here, Lee! Least of all me!" he says. The frenzy
builds to a sidesplitting, infantile epiphany. Lee knocks the toast out
of Austin's hand, then, as Austin drops to his hands and knees to
pick it up, grinds each slice into the floor.

The brothers' mayhem is topped only by the detachment of their
mother (the excellent Celia Weston, in an appropriately misjudged
turquoise suit), who doesn't bat an eyelash at the havoc in her house
when she returns early from her trip. She surveys the devastation,
then crosses to the refrigerator, where she realigns the fruit mag-
nets on the door as Austin rolls at her feet, strangling Lee. "You're
not killing him, are you?" she asks, before deciding to decamp to a
motel. "Stay here, Mom," Austin pleads, hunkered over Lee's body.
"This is where you live." She looks around the stage and offers a judgment that plays like a familiar Shepard jeremiad about America. "I
don't recognize it at all," she says. At the finale, Lee appears to be
dead, but, as Austin makes a move to leave, he jumps to his feet. The
play ends with the haunting final image of a murderous standoff
between blessing and barbarity. ■

—March 27, 2000

12

WILLIAM SHAKESPEARE

John Barton

One day this spring, John Barton, the director, playwright, and Shakespeare swami, looked up from his notes to discover that the actors in his workshop had assembled in their seats in an attic rehearsal room at the Brooklyn Academy of Music. Barton, who has a princely knowledge of literature but is hardly "the glass of fashion and the mould of form," went over to greet the actor Tony Randall, who sat natty as a jaybird in a blue blazer and pink shirt in the second row. Barton, with his unbuttoned shirt cuffs drooping down off his wrists, towered above Randall like a scarecrow. "We're going to put you through your paces today," he said. Randall rumbled in reply, apologizing for his "morning voice." Barton, a reticent man, cranked up a big smile of uneven teeth. "Creeping like snail unwillingly to school," he teased, quoting Jaques's soliloquy from *As You Like It*, which was Randall's homework assignment for the day. Randall was one of twenty-two selected actors with a Shakespeare pedigree—including Kevin Kline, Helen Hunt, Sam Waterston, Ruben Santiago-Hudson, Kate Burton, and Stephen Spinella—who had rousted themselves from their beds in the untheatrical early hours of the morning and trudged to Flatbush Avenue, where, over three three-day weekends of eight-hour sessions, Barton was giving a workshop in what might be called Shakespeare's word chemistry.

Barton, who is sixty-nine and who was enlisted by Peter Hall when he founded the Royal Shakespeare Company in 1960, doesn't exactly lecture, and he doesn't exactly teach acting, and he doesn't exactly interpret the text. What he does is offer the actors a practical method for understanding the acting clues that are buried within the text—a kind of Shakespearean map-reading technique. His message to the group seated in a semicircle around him on the first day is more or less the same as Hamlet's directions to the players in the sketch he stages at court. "Speak the speech, I pray you, as I pronounc'd it to you, trippingly on the tongue," Hamlet tells them, delivering one of Shakespeare's few public pronouncements on stagecraft. "Suit the action to the word, the word to the action." As Barton explains to the actors assembled, "The Elizabethan way is to put it all into the words and the words only." Shakespeare, who had a vocabulary of twenty-five thousand words (our core vocabulary is only fifteen thousand), was writing for a primarily verbal culture. A company of Elizabethan actors—who, records show, performed as many as forty plays a season—must have been able "to tune in much more quickly and easily to a text than people today," Barton says. "They must have picked up and seen acting clues in the text." By scrutinizing a text—its syntax, its verse forms, even its minimal punctuation—he shows the actor how to recognize those clues and how to exploit them, bringing vividness and variety to a role.

"The character is the text," he says, quoting the RSC's current artistic director, Adrian Noble. Barton mischievously reminds the actors that to the Elizabethans the word "character" meant only a letter in the alphabet. The modern concepts of "character," "relationship," and "intention" didn't evolve until centuries after Shakespeare wrote the plays. "Digging into 'character relationships' would have been alien to the Elizabethan actor," he tells them, adding that "you can go a long way without talking about character at all." He explains, "The 'character's journey' suggests a through line that makes sense. But Shakespeare sets up expectations that he continually contradicts. So when an actor looks for a 'character's journey,'

I know he'll get lost." His modest proposal to actors is that if they learn to properly mine what's in the words and speak them, the character will emerge of itself.

When he's on the prowl for swallowed end lines, dodged rhymes, the wash of lyricism, or the false fluency he so dislikes, Barton pads about in his socks; his shoes, in any case, have been so worn down at the back that they're essentially leather slippers. He usually lurks on the periphery of the room, poised and tilted forward like a bird dog on the scent. The effect of his frequent interruptions is a kind of dramatic brass rubbing, where the definition of the performance is heightened with each pass. Barton leaped up after Kevin Kline's first attempt at the Prologue to *Henry V*, which sets the scene of battle between the English and the French, to call attention to Shakespeare's comments on dramaturgy:

> *And let us, ciphers to this great accompt,*
> *On your imaginary forces work.*

"He invites the audience to work," Barton said.

"In today's entertainment we're rarely asked to work," Kline said, then went into comic mode. " 'You're going to have to *use* your imagination.' " He paused and reflected: "The speech is about war. It's pretty ugly. I suddenly heard 'famine,' 'sword,' 'fire.' They're usually not exciting."

"Spot on," Barton told him. "Let's look at it again. Let's look at the contradictions." Early in the sessions, Barton introduces the term "antithesis" to describe Shakespeare's dynamic, ever-changing play with contradictions in language and in his characters' minds. Out of these contradictions, a play's argument emerges. "It's vital to look for the argument," Barton told the group. "If you don't think, communicate, play with the antitheses, a great deal of Shakespeare becomes difficult to follow. If you do go with it, he's much easier to follow and enjoy. The trap is that if you look for the emotional truth you may not find the argument, but if you find the argument you may find the character." Shakespeare's dramaturgy, Barton says, is built on "jagged contradiction and the confounding of surprise." Much of his workshop is spent analyzing the progression of the contradictions in the characters' speeches and emphasizing the "gear changes" that move them forward to their resolution. In approaching passages like the Prologue, Barton advises the actors, "Look out for the antitheses and play them." Or, as Shakespeare writes in *Richard II*, "Set the word itself / Against the word."

Barton reminded Kline of this as they continued to discuss the text. "Set the word against the word," he said, venturing a few lines: "Can this cockpit hold / The vasty fields of France? Or may we cram / Within this wooden O the very casques / That did affright the air at Agincourt?" His emphases spurred Kline, on his next pass, to stress the graphic contradiction between the cramped theater and the vast fields, so that each phrase, as Kline hit the key words, made a vivid picture. He seemed to find the instructions in the words themselves, with the lines "Think, when we *talk* of horses, that you *see* them / Printing their proud hoofs i' th' receiving earth."

"Am I making too much of a meal of it?" Kline asked afterward. Barton didn't think so. "If it's done genuinely. Where it's coined in the moment, you can't make too much of the moment." He paused. "Something which was descriptive on your first try became active and dynamic. It's the difference between a snapshot and a moving picture."

Later, as we rode back into the city, Kline told me, "I don't think I knew until John pointed it out how important antitheses were, not only as a rhetorical device you can't ignore but how you can harness it. American actors will generalize. They don't understand that they have to know why they are saying every word. They will kind of read a passage and go, 'He seems to be angry about something here.' Yeah, but why does he choose that word, what does that antithesis mean? They don't *use* the language. The language is something they have to get through so they can get to the acting part."

Barton is himself an exemplar of the Elizabethan ideal he admires, a rare mixture of vigorous thought and action. He sometimes totters a bit on his right leg because of an injury sustained long ago in a staged sword fight, and for three years in the fifties he was the lay dean of King's College, Cambridge. While he says that the label of scholar "always deeply embarrasses me and infuriates my wife, who *is* a scholar" (Anne Barton is a professor of English at Trinity College, Cambridge), he has by his count adapted about twenty plays for the RSC over the decades. He wrote the linking blank verse that turned Shakespeare's Henry VI plays into one saga, *The Wars of the Roses*, which he co-directed and which became the defining production of the RSC in the sixties—an examination of kingship in the age of Kennedy. *The Hollow Crown*, his study of the changes in the English monarchy and in the English language over the centuries, which he adapted for the stage, directed, and performed in, proved a huge RSC success in the sixties and seventies. Over the past decade, he has completed nine of ten plays collectively called *Tantalus*, a retelling of the story of Troy, which Peter Hall is keen to direct and which Barton undertook "as an attempt to break through a thirty-five-year block as a writer." Although some fifteen years have passed since Barton last directed a Shakespeare production in England, he has been dispensing his practical understanding of Shakespeare in workshops around the world for nearly two decades; in 1983, Britain's Channel 4 produced *Playing Shakespeare*, a fascinating nine-part series of Barton wrestling the "textual juices" out of a handful of famous English actors. He has directed many of Britain's outstanding talents (Dame Judi Dench, Helen Mirren, Sir

Ian McKellen, Alan Rickman, Ian Holm, Peter O'Toole, the late Sir Michael Hordern) and is much loved by them for both his unjudgmental astuteness and what the producer Michael Kustow calls "his slapstick element." "He was giving a company notes onstage while smoking and leaning back on his chair," recalls Kustow, who worked at the RSC in Barton's heyday and is producing his *Tantalus* plays. "He tipped backwards into the front stalls. They couldn't see him anywhere, but the voice was still coming up from the stalls. The notes went on."

In an age when most directors take a broad, high-concept approach to Shakespeare, Barton is going in the opposite direction by forcing modern actors to engage more deeply with the text. The BAM workshop, co-funded by the National Actors Theatre, is a kind of Shakespeare summer camp, where actors can play without pressure. "It's like messing around in boats," Sam Waterston says. "It's messing around in Shakespeare." Kline, who has done a number of Shakespeare productions, including a memorable *Henry V* in the Park, and has attended many of Barton's workshops, comments, "What I find sad is that there are not more directors here. The directors should be in this workshop. Most directors of Shakespeare in this country don't know about the text. In fact, they don't direct off the text. They think visually." Barton observes that Shakespeare these days is often purveyed by the "would-be conceptual director who thinks he has a mighty concept and doesn't actually do the play." He explains, "He does an adaptation or paraphrase and puts himself in the hands of a designer, who puts sets on top of actors, so the actors are subdued and distorted by set and costume. The actor doesn't care a fuck about Shakespeare. The director doesn't care a fuck about Shakespeare. He never really encounters Shakespeare." Barton's workshops are a kind of rearguard action meant to bring about that missing encounter between the player and the playwright. Elizabethan actors had no director; they also had very little rehearsal time. And Barton, whose process is to marry the Elizabethan and the modern traditions, wants to place the storytelling responsibility where the Elizabethans placed it—with the actors.

"Taste it, feel it, smell it, get comfortable in it," Barton continually exhorted the group about the rich impasto of Shakespeare's English. "The Elizabethans would have delighted in this, which is difficult for us today. There's a tendency in our acting tradition to run away from verbal relish. It's that gap in particular I'm trying to fill." To illustrate the power of Shakespeare's language to stimulate the imagination, Barton chose the moment in *King Lear* when Edgar pretends to his blind father that they are on a cliff peering down at the sea. Here one character, who is "acting" for another character, creates the verbal magic that Shakespearean actors must work on the audience itself. Barton made the actors shut their eyes. "I want you to listen and not watch," he said, as the soft-spoken Stephen Spinella tried out Edgar's speech:

> *The fishermen that walk upon the beach*
> *Appear like mice; and yond tall anchoring bark,*
> *Diminish'd to her cock; her cock, a buoy*
> *Almost too small for sight. The murmuring surge,*
> *That on th' unnumb'red idle pebble chafes,*
> *Cannot be heard so high. I'll look no more,*
> *Lest my brain turn, and the deficient sight*
> *Topple down headlong.*

"Did you feel you could picture it?" Barton asked the others; they couldn't. Spinella attempted the passage again, with only partial success. "You're seeing something a long way away," Barton said. "You've got to create a sense of space." He was equally incisive when Peter Francis James began Claudio's meditation on death in *Mea-*

sure for Measure: "Ay, but to die, and go we know not where." Barton stopped him and took him through the progression of Claudio's images: frozen in ice, blown by the winds. He added, "He says 'we know not where.' Everybody tends to play the scene as if they know exactly where they're going."

Barton asks the actor to be vigilant both about the content of the words and the style they're couched in: "When Shakespeare shifts from a naturalistic to a poetic line, I believe something very important is happening. The actor has to ask himself why." For instance, in *Twelfth Night* the haughty Olivia falls for Viola, disguised as a man—at which point she abandons prose for verse ("Your lord does know my mind, I cannot love him, / Yet I suppose him virtuous, know him noble"). "When she falls in love, then she starts to go with it," Barton told Helen Hunt, who was working on the part. Frequently, he asks the actors to ask themselves why their characters use so many words and why the punctuation falls as it does. He and Ruben Santiago-Hudson discussed Brutus's assassination soliloquy from *Julius Caesar*, which begins:

It must be by his death; and for my part,
I know no personal cause to spurn at him,
But for the general. He would be crown'd:
How that might change his nature, there's the question.
It is the bright day that brings forth the adder,
And that craves wary walking. Crown him that,
And then I grant we put a sting in him
That at his will he may do danger with.

"The sentences keep starting in the middle of the verse—it's a big acting clue," Barton said. "It's quick thought. His mind is buzzing. A choice is posed about character." Here Barton paused also to dispute the punctuation of a line. "The verse and the grammatical full stops don't go together. 'Crown him that' I think should be a question," he said. "A question involves us and makes it necessary to go on." One of Barton's most often repeated maxims is "With Shakespeare, always play the question." The question "passes the ball to the audience." For instance, in Henry's meditation on kingship in *Henry V*:

> *And what have kings, that privates have not too,*
> *Save ceremony, save general ceremony?*
> *And what art thou, thou idol Ceremony?*

Barton detects Shakespeare's theatrical intentions even from short verse lines. He demonstrated the point in a terse scene from *King John*, where the King speaks to his accomplice Hubert about the killing of the boy Arthur:

KING: Death.

HUBERT: My lord?

KING: A grave.

HUBERT: He shall not live.

KING: Enough.

"A short verse line suggests a pause, and this kind of shared verse line says, 'Pick up the cue,' " he explains.

In all of these examples, Barton was clarifying a distinction between what's poetic on the page and poetic on the stage. He dislikes using the word "poetry" in the rehearsal process "because it's a generalized word." He also dislikes the term "iambic pentameter"—a "horrible phrase," which was alien to the Elizabethan actor—as a description of the alternation of light and strong stresses in the blank verse. Shakespeare's blank verse serves as an actor's help; it gives him both phrasing and momentum. But poetry, as Barton points out, "doesn't necessarily have anything to do with verse." Barton's intent is to help the actors achieve a balance in their

playing between naturalistic and heightened language, to free performance from both the deadliness of the vaguely poetic and the
naturalistic extreme personified in what he calls "the Al Pacino
Fallacy," where, as he puts it, "you get the juices *between* the words
rather than *in* the words." In Pacino's *Richard III*, according to Barton, there are as many as five pauses to the line. "You actually can't
get the machine off the ground," he says. "Pacino breaks up every
line, so you lose your way—you lose wit, you lose the thought. It's like
a gramophone playing at half speed."

In examining the proper balance between heightened and naturalistic language, Barton continually reminds the actors of a paradox: "The most moving tends to be the simplest and monosyllabic."
Among the many instances of Shakespeare's monosyllabic power
that Barton cited was King Lear's reunion with Cordelia. "This was
my first dim memory of Shakespeare," he said. "I remember reading
this line and first getting interested in Shakespeare." In the scene,
Cordelia asks, "Sir, do you know me?" and a few lines later Lear asks,
"Where have I been? Where am I? Fair daylight?" "It's like Tambur-
laine waking up in a Beckett world," Barton muses, cautioning the
actor not to milk it or try too hard. Later in the scene, Lear says, "I
know you do not love me, for your sisters / Have (as I do remember)
done me wrong: / You have some cause, they have not." To which Cordelia replies, "No cause, no cause."

"The monosyllables compress human feeling and meaning," Barton says. "Cordelia speaks so simply, but somehow 'no cause, no
cause' is more moving than something very metaphorical and poly-
syllabic. It's moving because of its reticence." He adds, "Isn't that a
poetic scene without being a 'poetic' scene in the normal currency
we tend to use?"

One day while the group was rehearsing the banishment scene in
Richard II, Barton dropped a startling tidbit of information. "One
of the few facts we're pretty sure of is that Shakespeare's stage

was forty-three feet wide," he said, "which is enormous." Nearly as large, in other words, as a Broadway stage. The space had its effect on the staging of relationships and language, which Barton was trying to point out to the banished royals, Kline and Kate Burton, and the political emissary Northumberland, played by Waterston, who comes with the bad news that the King will be jailed in Pomfret Castle, not in the comparative comfort of the Tower. The momentousness of the separation and the Queen's impassioned monologue prior to Richard's arrival ("This way the King will come, this is the way / To Julius Caesar's ill-erected tower, / To whose flint bosom my condemned lord / Is doom'd a prisoner by proud Bolingbroke") immediately forced the actors together; and Northumberland, too, came into their circle of intimacy to deliver his bad news. "It goes off the boil when it all gets close and too tied up," Barton interrupted. "If you have heightened language and you get on top of each other it can't work. You're in a traffic jam. The instinct to move closer is a modern one and doesn't work." He added, "You have to open up and share the language."

"If you're far enough away, you have to engage the language," Kline said after the next try, with the actors at a greater distance apart, proved a considerable improvement. "If you blow too softly into a sax, you can't hear the notes."

"Heightened language and argument need space," Barton said.

"Also, the public nature of the speaking," Waterston said. "This is for history."

"Very good," Barton said.

Space is also related to what Barton calls "the need to speak." This need, Barton suggests, is what Shakespeare alludes to in Hamlet's acting instruction: "to show . . . the very age and body of the time his form and pressure." "Unless there is a pressure," Barton says, "there isn't a need to speak." During the workshop, Barton quickly tried to wean the actors off their scripts and "share the text" with the audience. The exercise is a way to get the actor to define for himself to whom he is speaking. "I personally believe that it's right ninety-nine times out of a hundred to share a soliloquy with the audience," Barton has written. "I'm convinced it's a grave distortion of Shakespeare's intention to do it to oneself. If the actor shares the speech it will work. If he doesn't it'll be dissipated, and the audience won't listen properly."

All the issues Barton had discussed came together in Othello's monologue, where the Moor decides to kill Desdemona. The first two lines were bedevilling Peter Francis James: "It is the cause, it is the cause, my soul; / Let me not name it to you, you chaste stars, / It is the cause." "I think these two lines are difficult because you're talking to yourself," Barton told him. "Why don't you try using the first two lines to come on with, and then you can face the audience." He paused and continued, "In Elizabethan theater, they had to bring it on with them. The fact that we don't know quite what you mean makes it dramatic. If someone comes on stage and then contacts us, it's a different chemistry than somebody just talking to himself." James was doing well as he built to the conclusion of the speech:

So sweet was ne'er so fatal. I must weep,
But they are cruel tears. This sorrow's heavenly,
It strikes where it doth love.

"Oh God!" James broke off, stunned at the simple revelation that Othello's tear has dropped on Desdemona's sleeping body. " 'This sorrow's heavenly.' It's on her!"

"What did you get from that?" Barton asked him.

"A lot of opportunities," James said.

"If you are aware of the audience, they can do things to you," Barton explained. "When I said, 'Come on,' Peter made the decision to come on quickly. We tend nowadays to be discovered in scenes. The

Elizabethans had to come on stage. To potter in, medium tempo, usually doesn't work." Afterward, standing in the late-day sunlight outside, James expanded on the revelations of his lesson: "After speaking to someone in the audience, which actually forced me to cry, because they were in a place that fed me, I looked down at her. I realized that the next line in the text was something I'd never quite understood. It's not about the act he's going to perform ('I'm going to kill her later'). He's simply talking about watching his tears fall and strike his wife. It is literally a stage direction, which is so kind to the actor. He's saying you don't have to act—just talk about what it looks like to have your tear go splat on your wife's face." James concluded, "The hardest thing is to remind yourself of the basics. The heavy-weight boxer loses because he drops his left. Ted Williams loses his swing because he steps in the bucket. The answer is we all step in the bucket. And John goes, 'Don't step in the bucket.' What's so great about him is that you get back to the simple principles. He's coming there from a long route of study."

Barton's last session, an open lecture attended by the participants as well as by ticket buyers, turned out to be as much an act of drama as an act of exposition. He chose to conclude not with a piece of mas-terly Shakespearean eloquence but with the strange eloquence of the immigrant Italian anarchist Bartolomeo Vanzetti speaking to the court on behalf of Nicola Sacco and himself just before they were sen-tenced to death in 1927 for a crime of which the judge who convicted them knew they were innocent. The speech, read by Peter Francis James with a slight Italian inflection, seemed a compendium of many of the strategies Barton's principles had teased out of Shake-speare: the contradictory argument, the need to speak, the passion and coolness of words newly minted in the moment, the power of monosyllables, even the galvanizing sense of whom the speaker is speaking to. But the choice was also a reserved man's signal about his own mysterious and fervent heart. As a coda to the courtroom speech, Barton had added some text from a conversation Vanzetti had with a reporter in his cell a few days after the sentencing. The audience and James's fellow-actors grew silent under the spell of Vanzetti's simple words as the passage reached its peroration:

> If it had not been for this thing, I might have lived out my life talking at street corners to scorning men. I might have died unmarked, unknown, a failure. Now we are not a failure. This is our career and our triumph. Never in our full life could we hope to do such work for tolerance, for justice, for man's understanding of man, as now we do by accident. . . . Our words—our lives—our pains—nothing! The taking of our lives—lives of a good shoemaker and a poor fish peddler—all! That last moment belongs to us—that agony is our triumph.

Barton, who had been leaning against the wall to listen, tottered forward for one last word. His eyes seemed full. "Something poetic happens in him," he said, before dismissing the company. "It's natural in human beings." ▪

—September 7, 1998

Hamlet

Hamlet is a play that tests the best actors of each generation, and also each generation's sense of itself. Over the last thirty years, in England, no fewer than three *Hamlet*s have served as such cultural bellwethers. In 1965, during the Vietnam War, David Warner gave us an untidy undergraduate Hamlet who was frustrated by Denmark's military-industrial complex. In 1980, as Britain's economy went into a weird free fall, Jonathan Pryce's Hamlet was possessed by the ghost of his father, who spoke through him in a frightening supernatural flirtation with madness. And now, in the neutral, post-Thatcher nineties, Ralph Fiennes has pitched his drop-dead matinee-idol profile and the modesty of his sensitive soul into a postmodern *Hamlet* whose refusal to risk interpretation reflects Britain's current bland and winded times.

Fiennes, an intelligent, reticent player, seems almost as unwilling to enter the vortex of Hamlet's torment as Hamlet himself is to take action. Fiennes radiates an elegance of spirit that rivets the audience with its sense of unspoken mystery. His performance is a stylish event, much more the "mould of form" than the "glass of fashion." He has a mellow, reedy voice that filters Shakespeare's gorgeous complexity and gives the language an accessible colloquial ring. Fiennes is not one for grand histrionic gestures. His personality doesn't take up a lot of space. He compels attention by his decency, not by his declaiming. Fiennes, who has limpid green eyes and tousled chestnut hair, and who is a laid-back, brooding, romantic star, is catnip to the public and oxygen at the box office. (The Almeida Theatre Company's production, which began its much ballyhooed life at the Hackney Empire, the wonderful old music-hall venue in London's East End, has arrived at the Belasco for a fourteen-week Broadway engagement.) This *Hamlet* has been designed to be a people's *Hamlet*, which is to say a *Hamlet* in which the plot, not the psychology, is complicated, and in which the cast works the room instead of working for meaning. Inevitably, therefore, Fiennes's Hamlet is not a navel-gazing scholar or an alienated adolescent or a demented psychological case study. His Hamlet turns out to be the guy Horatio always said he was: a "sweet prince," a sort of rogue and *pleasant* slave.

The director, Jonathan Kent, who last year transferred the Almeida's *Medea*, with Diana Rigg, to Broadway with great success, has set the play in Edwardian England and has lopped an hour off the playing time. The speed favors breadth over depth; the streamlining suits the cut of Fiennes's jib, and he wears James Acheson's period clothes well. What we have here is a ripping Shakespearean yarn that shows off the thrills and chills of the story's melodramatic elements: the ghost of a murdered king, a mother's hasty marriage to her husband's murderer, a prince driven to near-madness and revenge, a lovelorn suicide, a lot of ghoulish high jinks around graves, a terrific sword fight, and a quadruple poisoning. The result is lucid without being moving: a kind of aerobic *Hamlet*, which works hard to keep up the pace while going nowhere.

The lights come up on a bare, raked stage, and the sound of crashing waves fills the auditorium. In the background, the environs of Elsinore are suggested by faint, blurred beams of light projected through a murky scrim on which the outlines of rocks are just visible. A sentinel climbs up through a trapdoor—more for effect than for sense, it seems, like many things in this production. "Who's there?" he calls. That's the play, the whole existential ball of wax. Hamlet's entire dramatic journey is foreshadowed in these first words. He, too, must penetrate the surrounding darkness and tease out the reality of his parents, of the corrupt court, and of himself. By finally taking action—which means accepting loss, including the loss of his own life—Hamlet sees clearly into the heart of things and achieves his adulthood. In this sense, *Hamlet* is both a detective story and a metaphysical investigation. The practical and the philosophical aspects of the tale need time to build properly; as the saying goes, "No delay, no play." But here, with the proceedings speeded up, the text is not so much examined as *done*. It's significant that Fiennes attacks the "To be, or not to be" soliloquy, which sets out Hamlet's spiritual quandary, by coming toward us in manic stutter steps and turning the famous meditation into yapping thought. He skirts the issue of interpretation by turning talk into behavior. The image is novel; but little nuance comes across the footlights. In this ranting mode, dissembling a madness that is really giddy grief, the barefoot Fiennes grabs Ophelia's crotch and insolently shoves Claudius's shoulder. But Fiennes can't really get up a convincingly antic head of steam. He is slow to kindle and never really burns. He's not so much tormented as pissed off.

Fiennes has his best moment with the Gravedigger (the excellent, grizzled Terence Rigby, who also plays Hamlet's father's ghost and the Player King). Listening to the Gravedigger expound matter-of-factly on how a body decomposes, and learning that a skull he has unearthed belonged to Yorick, the former King's jester, Hamlet gently takes this relic of his old acquaintance from the Gravedigger. "This?" Fiennes says, uttering the word with a huge sense of recognition, wonder, and sadness. His sensitivity and the mournfulness of the moment coalesce. "Where be your gibes now? your gambols? your songs? your flashes of merriment, that were wont to set the table on a roar?" Fiennes says, with a delicacy that delivers Shakespeare's observations about mortality like a punch to the heart.

The production's obsession with surface has its most effective expression in Peter J. Davison's sets. He creates a dark, lugubrious officialdom of behemoth ceilings, heavy brown-stained doors, and large shuttered windows that turn the actors into scuttling Lilliputians. Hamlet is first seen framed by one of these gigantic windows, standing upstage with his back turned away from the bustle of power, whose aggrandizement is reflected in the monumentality that surrounds it. Still, Davison, too, succumbs to the production's impulse to startle rather than compel. The ghost is conjured up on a high platform behind the scrim. There, lit from above by the white glare of a halogen lamp and announced by a jolt of electronic sound, Hamlet's dead father appears twice, in his carapace of armor: a *Star Wars* effect that is a projection of commercial instincts more than of Hamlet's unconscious. Similarly, Jonathan Kent's eye for business is sometimes shrewder than his eye for detail. When Laertes and Hamlet take turns leaping into Ophelia's grave and embracing her body, each trying to outdo the remorse of the other, the poor dead girl bobs up and down like a hand puppet. And at the finale, when Fortinbras (Rupert Penry-Jones, who is also Fiennes's understudy) arrives to take over the kingdom that Hamlet has died to save, his Aryan good looks and the gray capes of his lieutenants make it seem as if the Luftwaffe had invaded Denmark.

In American theatrical circles, the definition of a genius is anybody from England. But the prestige of this production can't hide the unevenness of its seasoned supporting cast, who prove the adage that British actors are either tours de force or forced to tour. Besides Terence Rigby, only the lanky, bearded Peter Eyre, as Polonius, breathes distinctive life into his role. Eyre plays the meddling bureaucrat as a long drink of cold water: cleaning his pince-nez as he counsels his hotheaded son to "neither a borrower, nor a lender be," and withholding his hand from Laertes when he goes, Eyre misses no opportunity to have fun with the old blowhard's pedantry. Polonius rushes to the Queen with a letter that Hamlet has sent his daughter, and reads it to her as a presenting symptom of Hamlet's lunacy. Reciting " 'To the celestial and my soul's idol, the most beautified Ophelia,' " Eyre's Polonius bristles with dopey patrician disdain. "That's an ill phrase, a vile phrase, 'beautified' is a vile phrase," he says, and gets one of the evening's best laughs.

Others are not so much at home in Shakespeare's climate of delirium. Tara Fitzgerald, a talented young actress with a bright future, flounders as Ophelia. There is nothing fractured or vulnerable about her, and when Ophelia goes mad Fitzgerald won't let her rip. Fitzgerald's behavior—the compulsive walking back and forth, the sexual taunts directed at Claudius—feels tame and glib: a trick of the mind, not a journey of the heart. Often, when English actors are nowhere near the center of their parts they rely on the power of their articulate voices; James Laurenson's Claudius falls into the trap of such posturing. Claudius is John Gotti with a pedigree—carnal, vicious, power-hungry, ruthless—but Laurenson gives us chicanery on the half shell. He does a lot of Urgent Shakespeare Acting. A few wheeling turns upstage, some nips at the top of his hand, a little booming oratory, and—presto!—you have a villain. This stock rep stuff is also dished up by the beautiful Francesca Annis, as a Gertrude who can't manage much grief at the sight of Ophelia's dementia but does manage a long, lingering kiss with Hamlet. It's a bit of business that has become the theatrical baggage of the role in this century, but the incestuous overtone seems inappropriate, especially in such an unanalytic production.

A word about Hamlet's duel. Jonathan Kent and the fight director, William Hobbs, have built up this face-off between idealism and treachery into a scintillating contest that takes excellent advantage of the story's melodrama. A cream-colored tarp is rolled downstage for the match, and the court sits watching upstage right, in gray upholstered chairs. Hamlet fights with graceful, playful enthusiasm, unaware that he's up against the double whammy of Laertes's poisoned sword and Claudius's poisoned chalice. Hamlet gets the first couple of touches; then Laertes's temper flares, and he cuts Hamlet. They scuffle, and in the hurly-burly their swords get mixed up. Hamlet chases Laertes around the rooms, sending chairs flying and courtiers scurrying for safety. It's exciting and well-staged hokum, in which Laertes ends up hoist with his own petard. At that point, the Queen, who has drunk from the chalice, collapses; then the Grand Guignol of Shakespeare's ending quickly plays itself out. At the finale, Fortinbras's men lift Hamlet's corpse on their shoulders and, swaying, carry him slowly upstage and toward the light beyond. Fiennes's head falls back, giving the audience one last glimpse of the star. Even backward, upside down, and dead, Fiennes exits looking good. ▪

—May 15, 1995

The Winter's Tale

In Ingmar Bergman's majestic production of Shakespeare's *The Winter's Tale* at the Royal Dramatic Theatre in Stockholm, the play begins with the program. In it Bergman pretends to be the translator of a letter (actually, it's by Bergman himself) written in 1925 by a German professor who was returning a nineteenth-century theater poster to the Royal Library of Stockholm. The poster is reproduced on the opposite page. It announces *The Winter's Tale* as part of Miss Ulrika Sofias's nineteenth-birthday celebration, over Christmas, in the Grand Hall of Hugo Löwenstierna's hunting castle. The professor has underlined one of the cast, the writer Jonas Love Almqvist, who has a bit part, and, in passing, mentions that another professor considered him "as good as Strindberg." On that throwaway, faux-naïf sentence the full weight of Bergman's knowing, gorgeous production rests; his *Winter's Tale* is presented as part of Löwenstierna's Christmas festivities. (The production comes to the Brooklyn Academy of Music next May, along with Bergman's *Madame de Sade* and, possibly, *The Misanthrope*.)

Almqvist (1793–1866) is one of Sweden's great literary figures; his poetry, novels, songs, and progressive educational ideas made him one of the most controversial figures of his day. Almqvist was an early champion of Shakespeare in Sweden, so his presence at this Christmas production has some historical rationale. Bergman uses Almqvist's music, which delicately mixes Romantic melancholy with Christian idealism, to frame in a kind of lyric embrace Shakespeare's perplexing tale of murderous jealousy and improbable redemption. Almqvist songs begin and end each of the play's two acts, and intensify the realms of regret and spiritual longing that Bergman meticulously explores. And Almqvist's own story hovers around this haunted play like yet another ghost. Almqvist, like Leontes, seems to have perpetrated an act of absurd violence: he was accused of killing a moneylender in 1851 and fled to America, where he lived until 1865. He died an outcast, protesting his innocence, in Bremen, Germany, in 1866, and his body was not returned to Sweden until 1901. The conceit of a Christmas celebration gives Bergman a brilliant scenic framework with which to keep the play's polarities of tragedy and joy, loss and rebirth always dynamically visible, and the stunning complexity of his structure perfectly suits the arabesque quality of Shakespeare's writing in the late plays.

When the audience takes its seats, the pre-play festivities are already in progress, and the Grand Hall of the hunting castle turns out to be a subtle replica of the Marble Hall of the Royal Dramatic Theatre. The theater's Art Nouveau windows, its gold Egyptian light fittings, its gilt columns, and even part of Carl Larsson's ceiling fresco, *The Birth of Drama*, are reproduced in Lennart Mörk's elegant set. The world of the play and the world of the theater are one. In a swirl of song, dance, and party hubbub the guests foreshadow aspects of their Shakespearean personae. The shambolic man struggling with his lines will become Autolycus (Reine Brynolfsson). The no-nonsense lady calling for the songs to begin and leading a young boy across the stage will be the tenacious Paulina (Bibi Andersson), who faces up to Leontes. A youngster, who will play Mamillius, looks over his shoulder for his parents in the same way that Mamillius will watch the disintegration of his parents' relationship in the play. The pure, compelling voice of Irene Lindh serenades the assembled with Almqvist's "The Heart's Flower," a song that sets the play's ambiguous spiritual stakes of suffering and mercy with the lines "The heart asks God why did you give this rose to me / God's heavenly answer, the blood from your heart has given the color to the rose." And then, in one of the many magnificent transitions that Bergman engineers, the bittersweet mood is reversed when the children at the party start ringing bells and calling for the play to start.

As the Shakespearean exposition begins in the foreground, the children, now wearing white-faced masks of comedy and tragedy, pull a platform bearing the host and hostess and a friend of theirs down toward the action. When the platform reaches the front of the stage, these three have become the blue-robed Leontes (the superb Börje Ahlstedt), the green-robed Polixenes (Krister Henriksson), and the charming Hermione (Pernilla August, who played the lame servant girl in Bergman's *Fanny and Alexander* and Bergman's mother in *The Best Intentions*, and who here, draped in a vibrant-red Empire gown, radiates serenity and an irresistible generosity of spirit).

Why does Leontes, who begins the play by asking Hermione to use her charms to make his beloved brother stay at court, suddenly go berserk when she succeeds? As a tragic character, Leontes poses a theatrical problem for any director. Unlike Othello or Lear, he doesn't smolder with inner turmoil. He simply crashes and burns in a blaze of jealousy. He acts out passion's awful agitation, which Shakespeare himself records in Sonnet No. 147: "Past cure I am, now reason is past care, / And frantic mad with evermore unrest." (The sonnets were published in 1609; and *The Winter's Tale*, the thirty-fifth of Shakespeare's thirty-six plays, was first produced in 1610–11.) Bergman's Leontes suffers from the dementia of the perception of a love triangle similar to the one in which Shakespeare was caught—between the third Earl of Southampton (Henry Wriothesley), who was his patron, and the Dark Lady. Here the sexual charge of Hermione is unmistakable. Pernilla August gives Hermione a sense of ripeness and openness. She continually touches her husband's body, and he playfully drapes her red shawl around his neck; but when she turns to Polixenes the intimacy between them is also palpable. She's so comfortable with both men that if you can't understand Swedish it's not clear at first just who is husband and who is brother-in-law. The power of her connection with Polixenes hits Leontes like a brainstorm, and he suddenly begins to demonize his wife. His braying hatred is the flip side of idealized passion—the vindictive volte-face that Shakespeare makes in Sonnet No. 147:

> *For I have sworn thee fair, and thought thee bright,*
> *Who art as black as hell, as dark as night.*

As Leontes begins his litany of accusation, the red shawl of passion, which once connected them, now lies between them like a river of blood. Leontes plots to murder his brother and settles on exiling him from his kingdom; nearly stomps his newborn daughter, Perdita, to death in her cot before sending her into uncertain exile; generates the grief that his son, Mamillius, dies from; and imprisons Hermione and then calls her before his kangaroo court, which, so it seems, kills her. Bergman handles the melodrama of this fury in brilliant collaboration with the choreographer Donya Feuer. When Leontes glimpses Hermione and Polixenes circled in a dance—a stunning image of exclusion, which evokes the furious isolation in Edvard Munch's *The Dance of Life*—a rush of stabbing anguish overcomes him; he's grabbed the live wire of possessiveness and can't let go. Leontes breaks into the circle, casting Polixenes out and embracing Hermione. He holds her at arm's length while she nestles his hand gently against her cheek. Suddenly, Leontes whispers something obscene to her, and Hermione breaks away. Leontes grabs a nearby female member of the court and begins to rape her. It's a beautifully staged and awful moment. What compounds Leontes's passion and his violence, Bergman seems to be saying, is the middle-aged king's unconscious terror of impotence. In its opening moments, the play hints at the brothers' sexual prowess when Polixenes talks to Hermione about the vigor and innocence of their idyllic youth. "You have tripp'd since," Hermione coyly jokes, and Polixenes adds, "Temptations have since then been born to 's." But Bergman makes Hermione much younger than her husband, and eliminates from the first scene any visible sign that she is nine months pregnant. Later in act 1, when Leontes overrules the Delphic oracle, which has proclaimed Hermione innocent, he flails the behemoth Sword of Justice—a gesture that broadcasts both tyranny and sexuality. Leontes's hectoring and violence are self-hypnotic gestures, magically reinforcing his sense of potency.

In his productions, Bergman always maps out a thirteen-by-twenty-foot playing area that he calls "the optical and acoustic center." Here, having cut the text to the logistical minimum and concentrated the drama on the business of living and dying, he has turned over to Feuer twice the space—twenty-six feet by forty—in which to choreograph the subtext. It's a bold collaboration, which physicalizes the multiplicity of messages and mysteries in Shakespeare's new minting of the English language. "There is movement in his text—real physical movement, which you experience in speaking it, hearing it, even working with it," Feuer says. "His language was a carrier all the time of other meanings and other messages. This is part of Shakespeare's choreographic spirit." Together, Feuer and Bergman deliver unforgettable stage pictures. When Leontes decides to put Hermione on trial, the *figuranter* (chorus members) reappear out of a bleak snowy landscape as passersby off the street: an organ grinder, a thief: a cripple, a chimney sweep—ghostly figures whose ragged gray presence mirrors Leontes's fragmented, unreceptive self-involvement. His baby daughter's tempest-tossed journey into exile is dramatized by a billowing gray cloth hurtling around the stage, with a clipper ship held aloft on sticks, while veiled women in ribbed gray skirts writhe like waves to the sound of a wind machine as it's cranked before our eyes. In the final act, Hermione is traditionally revealed to Leontes as a statue—an unreachable, idealized object, who turns into flesh and blood when she's perceived as a person, and literally comes off her pedestal. Here Hermione is carried in from the wings on a catafalque by four *figuranter*, who march at a funereal gait. The moment, like so many of Bergman's solutions, is simple and daring.

"It is a bawdy planet," Leontes says in act 1, and Bergman never lets the audience forget that in the midst of death there is life. He breaks off the gloom and apprehension of act 1 with a call to dinner. The bear that has chased Antigonus as per Shakespeare's famous stage direction "Exit pursued by a bear" reappears happily for supper carrying his costume head in his hand and a little girl on his shoulder. This is, after all, a feast; and even in the last part of the play, which begins sixteen years later in a monastery, with Leontes abasing himself in front of a living statue of the Virgin Mary, a laurel wreath from the Midsummer Festival is hung unobtrusively on the corner of a screen. The Madonna to whom Leontes prostrates himself is the Bleeding Maria, with a sword plunged in her heart, and her body held up in a posture of crucifixion. Bergman subtly carries the symbols of Christian rebirth through the production: the evergreen Christmas tree in the Grand Hall of act 1; the Midsummer Festival tree—a cross decorated with ivy and a Swedish flag—in act 2; and, in the finale, the Crucifixion itself. In the intervening years, Leontes has tortured himself with remorse. When he rises to meet the banished Perdita, now to be married to his brother's son, Florizel, his flagellated back and stomach have bled through his shirt. Hermione, who, unbeknownst to him, has been in purdah awaiting the oracle's promise of her daughter's return, comes to life before his eyes. Leontes and Perdita fall to their knees in shock, and Leontes is held up by his brother. "Present your hand," says Paulina, who orchestrates this stage-managed resurrection. The moment is also theatrical revelation. Leontes is beyond forgiveness, and he knows it. He has accepted grief as his destiny and his due. He sits down beside Hermione and slowly, tentatively, stretches his hand over hers. Perdita does the same. "O, she's warm," Leontes says. Perdita lays her head in her mother's lap. Hermione's head brushes against Leontes's shoulder. It's an intense gesture, a miracle of the heart, which Bergman stages like a Pietà. Hermione speaks almost inaudibly to her daughter: "Where hast thou been preserv'd? where liv'd? how found / Thy father's court?" Perdita and Leontes raise Hermione up, and Perdita places her parents' hands together. They exit hand in hand to continue the conversation offstage. At that moment of salvation, snacks are announced. Life's banquet goes on.

"A sad tale's best for winter," Shakespeare says in the play. The mayhem of *The Winter's Tale*, like a horror movie's submersion in death, is meant to renew the living's sense of life. Here, in the liquid northern moonlight, Bergman calls up the spirits of Almqvist and Shakespeare and himself in one final song, the prayer "The Listening Mother of God":

O my God, how beautiful it is,
To hear the sound of a holy angel's voice,
O God, how wonderful it is,
To die to music and to song. . . .
Quietly sink, O my holy spirit, in
The arms of God, the Living, the Good.

On that note of grace, Time (Kristina Adolphson) rises from the front row of the orchestra section and, having opened act 2, now ends the play. She is a regal, white-haired lady in a formal black dress with a red train. She holds a cheap brass alarm clock and now sets it on the lip of the stage. As she moves upstage to leave, she looks back over her shoulder at us, and a smile plays briefly across her face. The clock's hands are at five minutes to twelve. For Shakespeare in *The Winter's Tale*, for the seventy-six-year-old Bergman, and for us in the theater, Time is almost up. In this eloquent production, imbued with the calm authority of genius, Bergman leaves us with the ticking of the clock and the urgency of forgiveness and blessing. ∎

—October 3, 1994

Othello

At the end of *Othello*, as Desdemona lies smothered on the conjugal bed, the warrior Moor turns to his assembled officers with the full knowledge that the deeds of valor which won him fame as a general for the Venetian state will forever be overshadowed by his mad gesture of jealousy. "I pray you, in your letters, / When you shall these unlucky deeds relate, / Speak of me as I am," he says. "Nothing extenuate, / Nor set down aught in malice." He invokes his love for Desdemona, insisting that his psyche was "perplexed in the extreme" by Iago's wily manipulations, and then he tells one final story, from his time in Aleppo, when he came upon "a malignant and a turbaned Turk" who was beating up a Venetian. "I took by th' throat the circumcised dog," he says. "And smote him—thus." On the word "thus," to illustrate both his heroism and his odium, Othello stabs himself. He is killing, his story makes clear, both the foreign emotion of jealousy ("the sun where he was born / Drew all such humors from him," Desdemona says earlier) and the foreigner in himself, his sense, as a black man in a white world, of being perpetually other. Still, Othello's tragedy lies not so much in the obvious externals of racial difference as in an overwhelming sense of his own unworthiness, which lies hidden beneath his heroics. "Rude am I in my speech," he says at one point, in the presence of Iago, offering both Iago and us a window into the self-doubt that will be his undoing. For all his accomplishments, Othello cannot believe that he is truly lovable to a white woman.

Among recent memorable Othellos, Laurence Fishburne, the first black man to play the role on film, was fierce and smoldering, and Sir Laurence Olivier—black-faced and eye-rolling—almost camp ("Desdemon *day-ud*"). In Michael Grandage's thrilling new production (at the Donmar Warehouse, in London, until February 23),

Chiwetel Ejiofor, a British-born actor of Nigerian descent who made his name as a screen actor—in Stephen Frears's 2002 *Dirty Pretty Things* and Ridley Scott's *American Gangster* (2007), among other films—brings to the character a natural nobility and a decency that are a kind of poetic revelation. (Tickets to the highly praised production, which sold out, have gone for as much as fifteen hundred dollars.) Although the script insists on the difference in age between Othello and his beautiful young bride, Ejiofor is only thirty-three; yet he has a gravitas that gives him a sense of seniority, and an ease with himself that is almost aristocratic. When he says, "I fetch my life and being / From men of royal siege," you believe him. He parses the Shakespearean verse with an African lilt, which, while it retains the familiarity of the music, continually reminds the audience that a foreigner is speaking. His brilliant attack on the role lacks the usual histrionics and hand-wringing; as a person, his Othello is centered, keenly intelligent, charming, and calm. "I saw Othello's visage in his mind," Desdemona (Kelly Reilly) tells her father, Brabantio. When Ejiofor's Othello is reunited with Desdemona in Cyprus, he sweeps her up in his arms with an excited flourish. "O my soul's joy," he says, and we feel all of it—the excitement, the appetite, the solace of connection.

Ejiofor gives as eloquent a shape to heartbreak as to love. When Othello asks for "ocular proof" of Desdemona's transgression, Iago (Ewan McGregor) describes the finagled handkerchief on which Cassio, he claims, has mopped his beard. "O monstrous! monstrous!" Ejiofor says, shaking his head, in a quiet voice that has had the life knocked out of it. He expresses the exclamation points in the text not with his voice but with his body, which is suddenly still, the image of a stunned psyche overcome by trauma. Faced with the intolerable, Ejiofor's Othello falls into a fit. Because he is so sympathetic and poetic, the madness of his jealousy seems all the more tragic. Othello emerges from the fit enraged; his annihilating anger, however, can never quite wipe out the memory of his love. Even as he bends to murder Desdemona—a scene that Dr. Johnson said was "not to be endured"—he is compelled to kiss her. "One more, and that's the last," he says. "So sweet was ne'er so fatal." When, minutes after her death, Othello learns the truth from Iago's wife, Emilia (Michelle Fairley)—"Moor, she was chaste. She loved thee, cruel Moor"— Ejiofor's instinct is, again, not to rant but to freeze. It's an electrifying moment: Othello is struck dumb with a grief beyond words.

As Desdemona, Reilly has a luminous, almost ethereal charisma. Her delicate alabaster profile plays potently against that of the sturdy bearded Ejiofor. At once tender and knowing, Reilly acts with a genuine light in her eye and kindness in her heart. She has backbone and her own brand of modest bravado. When Cassio (the compelling Tom Hiddleston), Othello's beloved lieutenant, is manipulated into a drunken brawl by Iago, he begs Desdemona to intercede on his behalf with her husband, who has demoted him. "My lord shall never rest," Desdemona tells Cassio. "I'll watch him tame, and talk him out of patience." And so she does. "Excellent wretch!" Othello says, conceding affectionately to her wish, adding, "When I love thee not, / Chaos is come again." When chaos does, of course, come, Reilly is able, in the muted and moving lament of the Willow Song, to make Desdemona's stoicism and her goodness shine through her bewilderment at Othello's abuse. Desdemona remains loyal to her last breath. When Emilia asks, "Who hath done this deed?" Desdemona cannot bring herself to name her husband as her killer. "Nobody," she says. "I myself. Farewell."

Whereas Othello and Desdemona are, both in their own way, models of the genuine, Iago, with his machinations, makes a myth of disingenuousness. Why does he do it? Within seven lines of the start of the play, Iago is reminded of his frequent avowals of animosity for Othello. "Thou told'st me thou didst hold him in thy hate," Roderigo says. Iago has been passed over for promotion in favor of Cassio. But there is more than that to his desire for revenge. "I am not what I am," he tells Roderigo. Iago relishes the art of deceit. Malice—what Coleridge referred to as Iago's "motiveless malignity"—may, in this case, be an end in itself. At one point, although it seems highly improbable, given Othello's dignified mien, Iago claims that the Moor has bedded Emilia. "I hate the Moor, / And it is thought abroad that 'twixt my sheets / He's done my office," he says, adding significantly, "I know not if't be true, / But I, for mere suspicion in that kind, / Will do as if for surety." In other words, a lie will do as well as the truth: what matters to Iago is that he feel something, anything. Anger is a great antidepressant. In Iago's existential emptiness, machinations take the place of meaning; destruction becomes a destiny.

Although McGregor doesn't quite nail Iago's pathological glee, he gets the character's cold-blooded personality across. At the finale, Iago, in the face of his wife's full-throttled outrage at his actions— "Let heaven and men and devils, let them all, / All, all cry shame against me, yet I'll speak," Emilia raves—finally kills her to shut her up. (Fairley is astounding in this scene.) Iago's herculean capacity to spoil seems a barometer of the intensity of his negativity—he feels envy not only of youth, power, love, and glory but of life itself. "Will you, I pray, demand that demi-devil / Why he hath thus ensnared my soul and body?" Othello asks. Iago's last lines embody vindictiveness. "What you know, you know," he tells Othello. "From this time forth I never will speak word."

At the Donmar, this dark murderous narrative plays out against a gorgeous mottled gray-brown wall, designed by Christopher Oram, which is as vivid and subtle as the rest of the production. As the play opens, rain drips down the wall, sluicing into a sewer at its base; the slate floor is dark with water. The stains, the shadows, the rumble of the rain as it drains underground all suggest the murk of the unconscious, from which the action emerges and to which it remains a wonderful and terrible testament. ∎

—January 21, 2008

Macbeth

Among the many contemporary things that Shakespeare's *Macbeth* exploited in its day—the accession to the throne of the first Scottish king of the British Isles; the King's fascination with witchcraft; the climate of terror that followed the Gunpowder Plot to blow up Parliament—the most significant for us is the Elizabethan public's newly acquired appetite for hair-raising eloquence. "It was addicted, one might say, to the fortissimo eloquence of inner lives magnificently tortured," Ted Hughes writes, in his introduction to *The Essential Shakespeare.* To the verbalization of tragic frenzy, Rupert Goold's inspired modern-dress Stalinist version of *Macbeth* (starring Patrick Stewart, at BAM's Harvey Theater) adds a scenic and sonic frenzy that is symphonic in its orchestration and its penetration. Goold's brilliant production team—with Adam Cork's soundscape; Lorna Heavey's smash-cut video and projections; Howard Harrison's moody lighting design; Anthony Ward's brutalist set—unsettles the senses and sets the stage for the deracinated and the uncanny. It infuses Macbeth's crepuscular world with the kind of fear that makes your tongue taste of brass.

At a thrilling first stroke, with the clatter and cries of a wounded soldier being wheeled in on a stretcher, the play bursts the somnolence of a dingy field ward—linoleum, white tiles, an iron-gated upstage elevator, a washbasin whose spigots will in time run red with blood. We are thrust into the heart-stopping hurly-burly that Shakespeare's prologue merely prophesies. The walls flicker with projections of a flatlining soldier's electrocardiogram printout. The Nursing Sisters hover. With sanitary face masks over their mouths and noses and starched wimples on their heads, which make them look like bustling predatory birds—one of them even holds a hacksaw—they swoop around the traumatized soldier as he babbles news of battle and of Macbeth's military bravery.

The audience is shocked to discover that the Nursing Sisters are Shakespeare's witchy Weird Sisters, who greet Macbeth in the ward with a prophecy of his rise to power, and who are all the more terrifying because they successfully masquerade as part of the ordinary world. "All hail, Macbeth!" they incant three times, promoting him in each prediction from "Thane of Glamis" to "Thane of Cawdor" and, finally, "That shalt be King hereafter." The words stop Macbeth in his tracks. "Good Sir, why do you start, and seem to fear Things that do sound so fair?" his cohort Banquo asks. In the witches' "imperial theme," Macbeth instantly recognizes his own murderous subterranean ambition: his self-destructive course is set. Traditionally, the Weird Sisters are staged as the Fates, and their scenes verge on Halloween voodoo. Goold stages the Sisters as their psychologically astute author intuited them to be—as incarnations of Macbeth's unconscious. In this production, the Sisters, spectres of the subversive, are rewoven into the entire fabric of Macbeth's saga; they ratchet up the atmosphere of menace, shadowing action with the unsaid and the uncontrolled.

Goold turns the Sisters into auguries of anxiety; they reflect and manufacture a disease. They give off a whiff of the malign. Appearing in the kitchen as scullery maids (sometimes they wield real knives to cut meat; at others, they clutch imaginary ones), waiting table at Macbeth's feasts, they haunt Macbeth silently, as our unconscious haunts us. Even at the finale, when Macduff bundles "the butcher" into an elevator to kill him, the Sisters walk defiantly downstage and face the audience. They rule, and they know it.

As Macbeth, Patrick Stewart is masterly; he makes the character's journey from tentativeness to tyranny with unhistrionic aplomb. As a promoted war hero nearing the end of his career, Stewart cuts a trim, staunch, but older figure. He's easy in his body, he's sexual, and he's playful, which makes his outbursts all the more terrifying. But the age difference between him and Lady Macbeth (the fine, fierce Kate Fleetwood) raises the vexing issue of masculinity, and that works well for the complexity of Macbeth's balky bloodlust. When he first refuses to kill the king, Duncan ("I have no spur to prick the sides of my intent, but only vaulting ambition"), Lady Macbeth, all bony shoulders and barbarity, rounds on him. "When you durst do it, then you were a man," she says. "And, to be more than what you were, you would be so much more the man." As a killer, Macbeth has a lot to learn; at first, he forgets to plant the daggers on Duncan's guards, whom he's also killed, in order to frame them. But, over time, the arithmetic of his atrocity adds up to a scorched-earth policy.

The murderous couple learn the rigor of masquerading their dead hearts. "False face must hide what the false heart doth know," Macbeth says. The impulse to dissimulate their deeds, to force all feeling underground, ultimately leads to madness. The unmoored Lady Macbeth sleepwalks with flashlight in hand. "She has light by her continually," an attendant says—a brilliant line suggesting a soul so lost that it fears not being found. Macbeth also has a psychotic break. Here, to emphasize both the external and the internal horror of his collapse, Goold plays Banquo's ghost scene twice. At the end of the first part, he appears as a gory nightmare vision, striding the length of the long dining tabletop to confront the agent of his doom, who falls off his chair in shock. At the opening of the second part, the scene is replayed as a dumb show without the ghost, a clever demonstration of Macbeth's splitting off of his guilt-ridden panic. But nothing suggests the dimension of the horror, "where violent sorrow seems a modern ecstasy," more powerfully than the daring silence of Macduff (the excellent Michael Feast). Upon learning that Macbeth has murdered his wife and three children, Macduff struggles to fathom a grief beyond words. After almost a minute of silence, he speaks. "My children, too," he says quietly. ∎

—March 3, 2008

King Lear

The director Michael Grandage has a deft Shakespearean touch: his productions—and his *King Lear* (at London's Donmar Warehouse) is the best to date—are swift, limpid, and forensic in their dissection of the text. Here, the hurly-burly of family betrayal is played out in a box of wooden planks, painted in turbulent swirls of white and gray, which lend the space a sense of tempest-tossed motion and abstraction. In Christopher Oram's rough-hewn arena, there is nothing for the eye to settle on except the actors and their actions.

As Lear, the seventy-two-year-old Derek Jacobi gives one of the finest performances of his distinguished career. Pink-skinned and white-bearded, he exudes an air of royal indulgence and hauteur. After decades of working the audience, Jacobi seems to have become all face: his head is a sort of large, flat professional mask that well suits the King, whose last great show of authority is the ceremonial handing over of his land, his cares of state, and his best-loved, youngest daughter, Cordelia (Pippa Bennett-Warner), in marriage. Jacobi winkles out the vainglory in Lear's vaunted prospect of a retirement in which "we unburdened crawl toward death." As his command that his daughters compete in avowals of affection demonstrates, Lear is all about the display of power. Cordelia's refusal to play her father's game threatens more than his magnanimity. By reminding him that half of her love and her allegiance belongs to her future husband, Cordelia unwittingly attacks Lear's potency, releasing the first primal flash of his "hideous rashness." He disowns her.

Rage is not only the consequence of events in *King Lear* but part of the play's dramatic substance. In this production, which will play at BAM in the spring, Lear's inclement internal weather is visible; the audience can see the squall of fury well up in him long before it swamps him. In Jacobi's subtle interpretation, Lear comes to understand his rage, correctly, as madness, not hate, which would fall within the realm of reason. Provoked beyond endurance by the exquisite cruelty of Goneril and Regan—"I gave you all," he tells Regan, who replies, "And in good time you gave it"—he fights a heartbreaking battle for his sanity. "O, let me not be mad, not mad, sweet heaven! / Keep me in temper, I would not be mad!" he says to his Fool (the excellent Ron Cook), laying his frazzled white head on the Fool's diminutive shoulder.

When Lear does go mad, he's all the more powerful for not being a roaring loony. Instead of ranting into the storm, Jacobi whispers his words—an affecting demonstration of the mind splitting off and burrowing inward. Lear emerges exhausted from his "wheel of fire," but, for both the character and the actor, it's a heroic emotional journey. Jacobi finds just the right tone of enervation and enlightenment. "Pray do not mock me: / I am a very foolish, fond old man," Lear says in his moving reunion with Cordelia. He has gone from being royal to being real, from wanting a performance of devotion to wanting a connection. "Come, let's away to prison: / We two alone will sing like birds i' th' cage," he tells Cordelia as they're led off. In this well-cast and exciting production, Grandage adds his own grace note to Shakespeare's: with Cordelia and Lear both dead, he brings the lights up briefly to the sound of birdsong, and then the stage goes black. ▪

—January 3, 2011

PART II
PRODUCTIONS

For a couple of years in the early seventies, I was the literary manager of the Lincoln Center Repertory Theater in New York. I was also reviewing regularly for the *Village Voice*, which put me in the comical position of being both an Indian and a cowboy: I'd watch my first-night colleagues from the wings when they came to write about Lincoln Center shows. My catbird seat, however, proved instructive. As a group, critics were considered by management to be a "dead audience"; the prevailing wisdom was to seat them strategically around the auditorium so that their habitual unresponsiveness—an absence of energy, which was palpable from the stage—would not affect the players or the paying customers.

From the wings, I could see why critics were a bad audience: they weren't seeing all of the play. The notepads on which they scribbled functioned as a wall between them and the experience. With heads frequently bowed, they divided their focus between the page and the stage. The critic's job, it seemed to me, should be to be present. "To pay attention, this is our endless and proper work," the poet Mary Oliver said of her craft. But that kind of special alertness requires training. To learn to surrender to the event, I had to wean myself off the tyranny of notation. Having a printed script on hand for reference did away (almost) with the necessity for pen-pushing. What I needed to know, I would remember; what the play meant, I would feel. Inevitably, the adventure of finding the play's meaning was also bound up with the adventure of finding myself.

Contrary to received opinion and conventional newspaper review-ing, the plot is not the play; the plot gives a framework to the playwright's ideas and observations. In the theater's game of show-and-tell, the critic's job is to paint a picture both of the play's events and of the meaning beneath the narrative hubbub. The play-wright always speaks with more than words; the critic must some-how learn how to read the other elements that convey the author's intention: lighting, set, space, costumes, groupings. The play and the actors are making a metaphor; the critic must interpret that metaphor for the audience members, who don't always understand what they've seen, and for the actors, who don't always know what they've made.

Theater is a transient game: great performances cannot be pre-served; great plays close. All that is left is the memory of exhila-ration and illumination. So, it seems to me, the responsibility of drama criticism is to provide a historical record. It requires a special eloquence to describe the moment and preserve the past, to provide a context for the play, as well as a judgment of it. In the end, critics are in the preservation business, keeping alive both the story of the theater and the memory of their pleasure. My own passage through time is punctuated by theatrical moments: seeing my father's anguish, as Estragon in *Waiting for Godot*; watching Pearl Bailey sass the audience in *Hello, Dolly!*; discovering Al Pacino's menac-ing swagger in *Indian Wants the Bronx*; watching Dame Edna rise up on a cherry picker to sing to "the paupers" in the balcony, and, a decade later, acknowledge me on Broadway ("Spin doctors have spun me / Dominic's done me / I'm even a book by John Lahr," the Dame sang to my everlasting delight); and, of course, listening as Elaine Stritch, in a white silk shirt and black leggings, came downstage, at the finale of her one-woman show, to ask the audience in her sourest rhetorical growl: "So what's this all been about, then? This existen-tial problem in tights." The huge laugh this got was all the more rav-ishing because I wrote the line.

In addition to the poetry of star turns, there is the prophesy of defining productions. When I was teaching night school at Hunter College in the late sixties, Harold Pinter's *The Homecoming* changed how I understood language; long before fame—and the psychic imperialism of the famous—had become such a toxic ingredient of contemporary life, Heathcote Williams's *AC/DC* made me understand its oppression; long before 9/11, Wallace Shawn's *The Designated Mourner* prophesied terrorist attack and the implosion of democracy; David Mamet's *American Buffalo* incarnated the brutalizing envy behind America's competitive sweepstakes. "You know what is free enterprise?" Mamet's Teach, a petty criminal, asks. "The freedom . . . of the Individual . . . to Embark on Any Fucking Course that he sees fit . . . in order to secure his honest chance to make a profit." These productions rocked my world. We go to the theater not just to lose ourselves but to find ourselves. Human behavior confounds us, words fail us, and pain defies description, but certain plays can crystallize the shifting moods of the culture or clarify the conundrums of life. Discussed here are some of the productions that led me to an exhilarating new place in myself and in my thinking about art.

Arcadia

In Tom Stoppard's 1966 novel, *Lord Malquist and Mr. Moon*, Malquist remarks, "Since we cannot hope for order, let us withdraw with style from the chaos." This notion has made Stoppard a very rich man. He says that his favorite line in modern English drama is from Christopher Hampton's *The Philanthropist*: "I'm a man of no convictions—at least, I *think* I am." Over the years, in twenty-one plays, Stoppard has turned his spectacular neutrality into a high-wire act of doubt. "I write plays because dialogue is the most respectable way of contradicting myself," he once explained. The three-ring circus of Stoppard's mind pulls them in at the box office, where news of the intellect, as opposed to the emotions, is a rarity. Marvel at his marriage of Beckett and Shakespeare in the death-defying clown act of *Rosencrantz and Guildenstern Are Dead* (1967). Watch him play with logical positivism and the meaning of God in *Jumpers* (1972). See him juggle Oscar Wilde, James Joyce, and Lenin in *Travesties* (1974). Stoppard's mental acrobatics flatter an audience's intelligence and camouflage the avowed limits of his plotting and his heart.

In *Arcadia*, at the Vivian Beaumont—to my mind, his best play so far—Stoppard is serving up another intellectual stew (the recipe includes "a seasoning of chaos and a pinch of thermodynamics following a dash of quantum mechanics," he says), but with a difference. Stoppard, whose stock-in-trade is parody, which is skepticism in cap and bells, has found a metaphor that takes him beyond parody to vision. Here, despite some casting glitches, Trevor Nunn's elegant production pits the heart against the head in a subtle theatrical equation, which factors out into a moving ambiguity.

The play begins and ends with an image of Eden before the Fall. In this lush, tranquil landscape painted onto a curtain, lit from behind, that wraps around the thrust stage like a kind of illuminated lampshade, no animals and no fear intrude on perfect pastoral harmony as Eve holds out to Adam the Apple of Knowledge. Only scudding gray clouds in the background suggest the confusion about to beset mankind once Adam takes a bite. The consequence of curiosity, once the curtain goes up, is a vaudeville of consciousness in a fallen world. "Septimus, what is carnal embrace?" the thirteen-year-old math brain truster Thomasina Coverly (the pert Jennifer Dundas) asks her handsome tutor, Septimus Hodge, in the play's first line. The question mirrors the image of Paradise about to be lost, and Stoppard's play goes on to answer her question. To embrace the flesh is also to embrace all the sins that the flesh is heir to—the sins to which Stoppard's labyrinthine plot, whose ingenious twists and turns involve greed, rapacity, vainglory, skulduggery, cruelty, delusion, confusion, and genius, bears ample witness.

The brilliance of *Arcadia* is not so much in the wordplay as it is in the construction. Stoppard has built his story along two time lines: life at Sidley Park, the Coverlys' country house in Derbyshire, in 1809, and life at present in the same house, where a couple of academics are picking over the bric-a-brac of Coverly family history. The action is set in a high-ceilinged room of grand Georgian design, which is dominated by a large oblong table cluttered with books, implements of learning, and a dozy pet turtle. A fissure in the cupola of Mark Thompson's shrewdly designed interior is the only physical hint of the skewing of world views that takes place around the table as the play shuttles back and forth in a nanosecond between centuries. (Actors in one time frame exit as actors from the other enter.) By cross-cutting the Coverly family story and the story of the contemporaries trying to reconstruct it, Stoppard utilizes the ironies of history—the symmetries and accidents that lead, nonetheless, to a kind of order—as a way of demonstrating the outcome of chaos theory; that is, as the program note explains to us scientific simpletons, how reality "can be both deterministic and unpredictable." This is an enormous theatrical feat—a kind of intellectual mystery story—in which Stoppard provides the audience with the exhilarating illusion of omniscience. We become cosmic detectives, outside time, solving the riddle of history from the clues and connections that we see but the characters, who are caught in time, do not. For instance, the equation that Thomasina works out to explain the asymmetry of a leaf: her "New Geometry of Irregular Forms" later turns out, with the help of computers, to undo the assumptions of Newtonian physics. She is to classical mathematics what Picasso is to art history. The spirited youngster, who shouts "Phooey to Death!" in the first scene, works out a formula that, by the last scene, prophesies the ultimate doom of the universe, which is collapsing like a chocolate soufflé from the slow loss of heat. Even Thomasina's offhand doodle on the landscape architect's plans for a Gothic vista at Sidley Park—she sketches a hermit to inhabit the planned Romantic hermitage—turns out to have been a prophecy of Septimus Hodge's destiny. The caprices of history, like the accidents that become inevitabilities in a plot, are the charms of chance that Stoppard and the audience stand in awe of.

Life's terrifying randomness is a mystery that compels mankind to impose order. Chaos is psychologically intolerable; man's need for coherence is greater than his need for truth. Landscape, like ritual, is consoling because it holds the magical promise of permanence. "English landscape was invented by gardeners imitating foreign painters who were evoking classical authors," says Hannah Jarvis (Blair Brown), a modern who is writing a book about the Sidley Park hermitage and the garden. The imaginative ideal is made into a reality; and Stoppard contrives to dramatize a moment in the life of the estate when the old illusion of reality is being adapted to fit a new one. At Sidley Park, Nature was originally tamed according to a neoclassical symmetry. The projected Romantic version, for which Stoppard supplies fascinating visual aids, is a triumph of the picturesque over the well proportioned. The planned irregularity and "naturalness" of the reimagined landscape capture the nineteenth-century drift toward Romantic individualism: from formality to spontaneity, from aristocratic public space to middle-class privacy, from the balance that reflects the Enlightenment's God of Reason to the brooding Romantic freedom that makes a god of the self. "The decline from thinking to feeling, you see," Hannah says. No wonder Septimus (Billy Crudup, making a persuasive Broadway debut) refers to the landscape architect who engineers the loss of this particular version of Paradise as the Devil. "In the scheme of the garden he is as the serpent," Septimus says. The wildness of the picturesque style is an attempt to contain chaos by building the unpredictable into the landscape, just as Thomasina, in her algebraic equation, is unwittingly introducing chaos into the physical laws of life.

Meanwhile, the lives and loves of these citizens take their apparently ordinary lustful course. The philandering Septimus cunningly evades a duel with the cuckolded poet Ezra Chater (Paul Giamatti), who enters in fury and exits in flattery, inscribing Hodge's copy of his poem "The Couch of Eros," after the tutor, lying, promises to review it favorably. "Did Mrs. Chater know of this before she— before you—" Chater sputters, seeing his wife's infidelity not as a leg over for her but as a leg up the literary ladder for him. Septimus encourages this delusion, and Chater is triumphant. "There is nothing that woman would not do for me," he crows, thereby illustrating Stoppard's larger theme—that people will rationalize anything to avoid chaos.

The compulsion for coherence has its comic apotheosis in the biographical sleuthing of Bernard Nightingale, a don from Sussex University who is a whirlwind of spurious intellectual connections. Nightingale (played with swaggering and hilarious arrogance by Victor Garber) has stumbled on the copy of Chater's "The Couch of Eros" that contains both the poet's inscription and an unnamed challenge to a duel, and he has traced the volume to Byron's library. A literary climber of the first order, Nightingale sniffs a mother lode of lit-crit kudos in making the connection between Byron and Chater. No one is better at this kind of academic flimflammery than Stoppard, and he has a good time teasing the literary second-guessing that too often passes for biography. Within minutes of insinuating himself into Sidley Park, and Hannah's orbit, Nightingale is spinning his academic wheels and turning what we know to be Septimus's facesaving deceit into a sensational case of adultery, literary infighting, and the death of Chater in a duel with Byron after the latter poet's devastating review of Chater's work appears in *Piccadilly Recreation*. "Without question, Ezra Chater issued a challenge to *somebody*," Nightingale says, reading from his completed paper in the tour-de-force opening of act 2. "Without question, Lord Byron, in the very season of his emergence as a literary figure, quit the country in a cloud of panic and mystery, and stayed abroad for two years at a time when Continental travel was unusual and dangerous. If we seek his reason—*do we need to look far*?" Hellbent on literary glory, Nightingale rushes past the truth—"Is it likely that the man Chater calls his friend Septimus Hodge is the same man who screwed his wife and kicked the shit out of his last book?" The paper is proof positive of the cynic's adage that "history is something that never happened written by someone who was never there."

Arcadia uses intellectual argument as a kind of riptide to pull the audience under the playful surface of romance with which the characters in both time frames fill their days and nights. In *Arcadia*'s comic conceit, seismic intellectual shifts are treated as superficial, while superficial changes of the heart are treated as monumental. For the evening to work, the audience must feel the pull of sexuality as well as the play of knowledge. In London, with Felicity Kendal, Emma Fielding, and Harriet Walter in the major female roles, the erotic amperage was high; here, though, the American actresses can articulate the words but not the sexy twinkle beneath them. As Hannah, Blair Brown shows a sharp intelligence, but she can't give Stoppard's lines that nervy bluestocking spin which flirts with learning and turns the alarming into the charming. "Oh, shut up," she tells Nightingale, when he is upbraiding her after discovering she has written a letter to the *London Times* giving the facts of Chater's death. (He was killed by a monkey bite in Martinique after discovering the dwarf dahlia.) "It'll be very short, very dry, absolutely gloat-free," she says of her letter. "Would you rather it were one of your friends?" The strut of Stoppard's epigrams is also missed by Lisa Banes as Lady Croom, who delivers some of the most delightful *mots* without the louche aristocratic aura of entitlement that makes them properly pay off. "Do not dabble in paradox," she says to Captain Brice (David Manis). "It puts you in danger of fortuitous wit." Even the pint-size Jennifer Dundas, who has the smarts to make Thomasina a credible, if cloying, prodigy, hasn't the stature to make her a compelling object of desire. The cumulative effect is not to undermine the production but to dim it.

Still, the brilliance of Stoppard's metaphor shines through. In the final scene, Thomasina is horsing around with her brother when Septimus enters with her latest diagrams under his arm. "Order, order!"

Septimus shouts to his rambunctious pupil, now nearly seventeen years old, who would rather waltz than work. By the end of the scene, when Septimus comprehends her latest equation, he sees that order—the Enlightenment notion of it—has entirely collapsed. Now the time frames merge, with the characters in the present overlapping with and commenting on the issues raised by characters in the past. "It's a diagram of heat exchange," says Valentine Coverly, a graduate student of mathematics (played expertly by Robert Sean Leonard), looking at the same diagrams that Septimus is studying. Septimus looks up. "So, we are all doomed," he says. "Yes," Thomasina answers cheerfully, not knowing that she is soon to become another integer in her equation of chaos. (She will perish the same night in a fire; and Septimus will become the hermit of Sidley Park, speaking to no one except his pet turtle.) But for the moment, with the geometry of the universe's doom in his hand, Septimus says, "When we have found all the mysteries and lost all the meaning, we will be alone, on an empty shore."

At the prospect of such an awesome, godless void, Thomasina suggests that they dance, and finally gets Septimus to his feet. The audience knows the outcome but the dancers don't: they live in the comedy of the moment, not in the tragedy of history. Hannah waltzes with Gus Coverly (John Griffin), a smitten teenager who has given her the final piece of the puzzle of Septimus's story. Together, the couples whirl around the old table covered with the inventory of centuries of learning. The ravishing image moves the play, in its last beats, from story to statement. The dance becomes the dance of time: one awkward, one graceful; one in celebration, one in resignation. The waltz, an act of grace in the face of gloom, is a perfect embodiment of Stoppard's spiritual standoff. Playwriting, like the dancing, is a way of giving off heat in a cooling universe: an assertion and an abdication at the same time. It's the dance of a stoic, and, from where I sit, it is brave and very beautiful. ■

—April 17, 1995

The Pajama Game

I went to see *The Pajama Game* in 1954, at the invitation of my god-father, Eddie Foy Jr., who played Hines, the perennially jealous, stopwatch-toting time-study man at the Sleep Tite pajama factory in Cedar Rapids, Iowa, where the musical's drama of labor and sexual relations is acted out. In the area of sexual relations, Uncle Eddie's legend preceded him: when his wife threatened to leave him, he reportedly nailed all her clothes to the floor. He certainly nailed the part. The show was a smash. With its crafty, unpretentious buoyancy, *The Pajama Game* was a first on Broadway in a number of important ways: it was the first Hal Prince production, and the first show to be choreographed by Bob Fosse; it had the first hit score by Richard Adler and Jerry Ross, and the first significant performance by the dancer Carol Haney (who was later replaced by her under-study, Shirley MacLaine); and it was the first musical I ever learned by heart. Still, it seems to me that the Roundabout's revival (deftly directed and choreographed by Kathleen Marshall, at the American Airlines) outshines the original in both its production values and its male lead, Harry Connick Jr. This is also some kind of first.

Here, the curtain rises on the gorgeous hubbub of Derek McLane's set. Huge pink and orange buttons decorate the proscenium arch. Like a comic simulacrum of Jean Tinguely's absurdist *Rotozaza*, revolving wheels send a steady stream of red-and-white striped pajama tops through the air above the stage. The factory girls below, wittily costumed by Martin Pakledinaz, lean over their sewing machines, pushing plaid and polka-dot fabrics past humming needles while singing their mantra of mildly alienated labor: "Hurry up, hurry up / Can't waste time, can't waste time / When you're racing with the clock . . . /And the second hand doesn't understand / That your back may break and your fingers ache."

The Pajama Game is set in the mid-fifties, a time when Americans were enjoying a postwar boom in productivity and one of the greatest per-capita rises in wealth in the history of Western civilization. The opening number, nonetheless, establishes the workers' plaint: they want a seven-and-a-half-cent raise, and they may have to strike in order to get it. In the original Broadway production (and in the movie), John Raitt played Sid Sorokin, the factory's ambitious new supervisor, who takes on the head of the Grievance Committee, Babe Williams. Raitt was the quintessential Broadway leading man of the period; he had a barrel chest and a bowwow baritone. Onstage, he was foursquare and as clean as a whistle, and he struck a slightly humorless heroic pose. By contrast, there's something louche and loosey-goosey about Harry Connick Jr., who is making his Broadway debut in the role. He's gangly and a little furtive; his almond eyes seem to be hiding something, which only adds to his mischievous appeal. Connick is not what Broadway deems conventionally handsome. He has no beefcake swagger; he doesn't force himself on the audience. He has, instead, the confidence of talent—and the sex appeal that comes with it. Here, when boy meets girl there is credible chemistry.

Connick's real prowess, of course, is as a musician and song stylist—he has sold more than twenty million records since his first album was released, in 1987. His voice is particularly well suited to Adler and Ross's clever score, which boasts at least a half-dozen bona-fide hits. (In the mid-fifties, Broadway was still the purveyor of many of America's most memorable popular songs.) Raitt's voice came from operetta; Connick's is all jazz—slangy, smooth, and playful—which fits the colloquial verve of the lyrics. His best acting is done in song. "Hey There," for instance, begins with Sorokin dictating a memo to himself about his attraction to Babe (the excellent Kelli O'Hara), then, as he plays back and responds to his own recorded voice, the song turns from a bittersweet soliloquy to a tortured duet:

MACHINE: Better forget her

SID: Forget her

MACHINE: Her with her nose in the air

SID: Her with her nose in the air

MACHINE: She has you dancin' on a string

SID: A puppet on a string

MACHINE: Break it and she won't care

SID: She won't care for me

Whatever their industrial disputes, there's no disputing that Babe cares for Sorokin. In "There Once Was a Man," a sort of Frankie Laine Western pastiche, Connick and O'Hara, who has an ingenue's sweet face and a svelte body that tells a different story, make sparks fly off the lusty paean to love ("It rocks muh whole solar plexus. It's bigger than Texas"). In another scene, Sorokin puts his charisma to work on the boss's bookkeeper, a gargoyle named Gladys (Megan Lawrence), in order to get a look at the accounts. Pinning the drunken and susceptible Gladys against an orange baby grand, Sorokin expresses his desires by hitting a few deep chords, which she answers faintly at the other end of the keyboard. At one point, Gladys finds herself on her knees behind Sorokin and thrusts her hands between his legs to continue the duet. It's a terrific gag, which the production then brilliantly tops. Connick—a virtuoso at the keyboard—launches into a thrilling stride-piano version of "Hernando's Hideaway," in what is one of the few genuinely showstopping musical moments in recent years.

The show's fizz and flow never falter; the book has been efficiently souped up by Peter Ackerman, who has put into bold relief the cunning placement of the songs. I would have appreciated a little less mugging from Lawrence and a little more tartness from the charming Michael McKean, as Hines. Nonetheless, even in its last beat *The Pajama Game* manages to be breathtaking. When Babe and Sorokin come downstage—"Married life is lots of fun / Two can sleep as cheap as one," they sing—she's wearing only a pajama top decorated with red hearts, and he's bare-chested, in matching pajama bottoms. At the sight of Connick's bronzed pecs, my sophisticated date blurted out, "Oh . . . my . . . *God!*" She was not alone. ▪

—March 6, 2006

The Retreat from Moscow

Once upon a time, when my only son was eleven, I leaned over his bed and heard myself say, "Your mother and I are separating." He was silent for a while; then he said, "I don't want your unhappiness." As I left the room, I naively thought, How did he know we were unhappy? This memory, in all its bright grief, came rushing back to me in the middle of *The Retreat from Moscow* (at the Booth), William Nicholson's subtle and powerful evocation of the half-life of a dying marriage.

Resignation—a sort of emotional fog—has settled over the thirty-three-year marriage of an English couple, Edward (John Lithgow), a high-school history teacher, and Alice (Eileen Atkins), an editor; their reserved thirty-two-year-old son, Jamie (Ben Chaplin), is strategically positioned between them—at once a beacon and a buffer. The curtain comes up on Edward reading aloud from a text about Napoleon's disastrous Russian campaign; this historical event, it soon becomes clear, is a metaphor for Edward's own emotional exhaustion, his longing for escape, and the deep regret he feels over the tactical blunders he has made in life. As Lithgow superbly plays him—a big, passive man with a small, dithering voice—Edward refuses to engage; he hides behind his books, his silences, and his vagueness. He is a present absence, a sort of ghost of himself. "It's like somehow you've sneaked away while I wasn't looking," Alice, who animates the family life and always tries to provoke conversation, says. "It's as if you've taken the easy way out." She adds, "I want a real marriage." Edward's refusal to fight and to assert his needs signals his nihilism; he doesn't care enough to argue. He will do anything to have an easy life, even disappear.

Alice, on the other hand, does all she can to stay in view. "When a woman reaches middle age she becomes invisible," she says. "I don't quite know how to cope with it, except by getting angry, which I do more or less all the time these days." People, especially her husband, don't seem to take her in. Her perpetual note of sprightly grievance—the drizzle of discontent that is the hysteric's trademark—is coupled with another trope of hysterical behavior: she repeatedly tries to force her inner life into the consciousness of others. Cunningly shaded by Eileen Atkins's keen intelligence and sense of humor, Alice is a scintillating characterization, an appealingly batty woman who is also a kind of emotional terrorist. This element of her personality is foreshadowed in an entertaining yarn she spins for Jamie, at the beginning of the play, about how a faulty printer has prevented her from finishing the poetry anthology she's working on. A snide computer salesman, she says, told her that the problem was not with her printer but with her. "I was so angry I wanted to hit him," she tells Jamie. "I said to him, 'You're the kind of man who doesn't love anybody and nobody loves you. You've got no friends and your wife hates you, and your children never talk to you.' He looked quite surprised for a moment or two. Then he said, 'Do you know me from somewhere?'" The story tells the audience a lot about Alice. She's clever; she's intuitive; she's well defended; she gets inside people; and she unsettles them, often by making a spectacle of her own state of mind—knocking over tables, threatening suicide, pursuing her husband into the school staff room to berate him, which, as the badgered Edward tells us, sends him out onto the playing field, where she strips off her skirt and her bra, saying, "There, I've made you look at me at last." (Even Eddie, a dog that Alice acquires for companionship after she and Edward separate, is made to enact her murderous wishes. "Show Uncle Jamie your new trick," she says to the dog. "Sit! Watch this, Jamie. Die, Edward! Die!")

Alice, of course, wants to talk but she doesn't listen; she wants to be seen but she doesn't see. "It's not at all like me," Jamie says, after she recites a poem about "his beautiful face." "Yes, it is," she counters. "Mother knows best." Her faith in the force of will and of struggle engages the head but evades the heart. She wants Edward to get real, but she herself has taken up residence in a private reality, in which spiritual and poetic thrills replace carnal excitement. When Jamie suggests to her that you don't have to have a family to have a love life, she replies, "Oh, that's just sex. You'll grow out of that."

Jamie, it turns out, is Nicholson's spokesman, the character from whose point of view the story is told. Striking an elegiac note at the close of the play, he tells his parents, "I had hoped to be able to help you, but in the end all I can do is honor you." The play dramatizes that filial love but also shows its reverse: Edward and Alice don't honor their son by keeping their argument—the confessions, the threats, the entreaties, the silences—away from him. Unwittingly, they appropriate him for their own needs, weighing him down with their unconscious baggage. Alternately witness, interlocutor, bulwark, spokesman, emissary, and judge, Jamie is required by his parents to be everything but his own man. "Forgive me for being your child," he says in the play's last line, accepting the burden of guilt that should belong to them, and thereby reinforcing their pattern of denial. Inevitably—and this is the psychological brilliance of the play, which is teased out by Daniel Sullivan's adroit direction—the couple's climate of retreat seeps into Jamie, who is handsome, educated, and capable, but solitary and unable to sustain intimate relationships. He hasn't so much left home as reconstructed the arid but familiar familial solitude in his London flat. The parents are stalled,

and, without any model of a nurturing sexual and emotional relationship, so is their son.

Edward's awkwardness with his son is explained toward the middle of the play, after he has finally left Alice, for the mother of one of
his students. "My father was a reserved man," he tells Jamie. "I don't
remember him ever embracing me." He recalls a day, soon after his
father died, when for a moment he thought he'd caught sight of him,
alive, on a railway platform. Afterward, he sat on the train in tears.
When he told the woman sitting across from him in the train com-
partment why he was crying, she said, "You must want to see him
again very much." To a man as emotionally impoverished as Edward,
this intuition of his feelings struck him as a profound revelation. "I
was astounded," he says. "I felt as if I had stepped through a door-
way into another world, where the inhabitants could read my heart."
He continues, "It was your mother, of course. It was Alice. . . . I made
a mistake about Alice, right at the beginning, and she made a mistake about me. We thought we were like each other, and we weren't.
I didn't know it." From a moment's caprice, the seeds of a lifetime's
sorrow are sown.

What makes this riveting, toxic landscape hard to fathom at
first, for both Jamie and the audience, is the fundamental decency
of the characters involved, the good manners with which provincial
British life is lived. They mean well; they just don't *do* particularly
well. Their doom is civilized and quiet, measured out in cups of tea
and crossword puzzles and Sunday Mass. John Lee Beatty's abstract
set—an elegant filigree of intertwined branches surrounding transparent walls—turns the stage, at any emotional moment, into a
tangled web, a cave, a morass. Nicholson's prose, however, is not as
didactic as the set. The author of *Shadowlands* and the co-author of
Gladiator, he trusts in the first principle of cinematic dramaturgy:
character is action. The seductiveness of what his characters say is
often belied by the irony of what they do.

At the finale, which plays, I think, as an expression of deep love and deep disturbance, Jamie moves between the figures of his mother and father, whose backs are now turned to us, as if they were figments of his imagination—as, indeed, they are. (Edward has moved away with his new family; Alice has moved forward, too. "I suppose I'll go on," she tells Jamie.) "My beloved explorers," he addresses them. "As you suffer, so I shall suffer. As you endure, so I shall endure. Forgive me for worshipping you." The speech is at once moving and chilling: idealization is what a child starts out with, not what an adult ends up with. A paean to symbiosis, Jamie's monologue is an attempt to preserve his bond with his parents and to forestall the project of adulthood, which is to separate from them. In the marvellous emotional complexity of *The Retreat from Moscow*, this scene is the final shock. We are told that Napoleon took 450,000 men into Russia and that only 20,000 survived; Jamie, it seems, may not be one of the survivors in the family battle. The play's last retreat belongs to him—a retreat from maturity. ∎

—November 3, 2003

Private Lives

On Noël Coward's bookplates was a caricature of him winking—a gesture that announced both his raffish insouciance and his high-camp refusal to suffer. Coward was his own unrepentant invention, and he made a myth of his separation from others. "I am related to no one except myself," he said. He was an egotist; he was a gay man who passed for a heterosexual matinee idol; and he had the public's number. His wink was the visual equivalent of a raspberry blown at convention. Coward gives that impulse a voice in the most gossamer of his good plays, *Private Lives*, when his spokesman Elyot Chase says, "Let's be superficial and pity the poor philosophers. Let's blow trumpets and squeakers, and enjoy the party, as much as we can, like very small, quite idiotic school children." Coward's trumpets and squeakers blow full force in the acclaimed London production directed by Howard Davies (which has been imported to the Richard Rodgers, along with its two theatrical grandees, Alan Rickman and Lindsay Duncan). "You mustn't be serious, my dear one; it's just what they want," Elyot tells his former wife, Amanda, after they've rediscovered each other, on adjacent patios in Deauville, while both on their second honeymoons with new mates. He goes on, "All the futile moralists who try to make life unbearable. Laugh at them. . . . Laugh at everything, all their sacred shibboleths. Flippancy brings out the acid in their damned sweetness and light."

Private Lives is a comedy of bad manners, whose emotional and structural minimalism turns all the cumbersome proprieties of English drawing-room drama upside down. The play was first staged in 1930, as the decorum of the turn of the century was giving way to a post–First World War sense of dissolution, in which romance was a put-on, honor a masquerade, and communication a kind of false trail of language that led only back to solitude:

> AMANDA: China must be very interesting.
> ELYOT: Very big, China.
> AMANDA: And Japan—
> ELYOT: Very small.

In the play's brilliantly constructed first scene, Amanda and Elyot don't meet cute; they meet in high dudgeon. Elyot smokes a cigarette, and Amanda crosses over to his balcony. "Give me one, for God's sake," she says. They are furious with each other and with their new marriages of inconvenience. They stand looking out at the sea, and at the Duke of Westminster's yacht. Amanda says, "I wish I were on it." Elyot replies, "I wish you were too." Thus begins the rebarbative banter, the vinegar in which Britain's sophisticated twenties and thirties were pickled.

Elyot and Amanda—two dandies of detachment who jilt their spouses and run away together to a Parisian love nest—do no real work and have no faith, no principles, and no commitment to anything but their own pleasure. "Within a few years," one dyspeptic early critic wrote, "the student of drama will be sitting in complete bewilderment before the text of *Private Lives*, wondering what on earth these fellows in 1930 saw in so flimsy a trifle." On the contrary, Elyot and Amanda are among the first enduring sightings on the British stage of what might be called "the modern." Coward—who wrote, in the song "Twentieth Century Blues," "What is there to strive for / Love or keep alive for?"—managed to translate his metaphysical stalemate into comic action. English life had lost its sense of continuity, and Elyot and Amanda are, like the plot, aimless. Their capriciousness is at once galling and, when viewed from Coward's slyly renegade perspective, gallant. His totemic wink surfaces dramatically at the play's finale, during a humiliating showdown between Elyot and Amanda and their outraged mates, Sybil and Victor, who hunt them down and are hellbent on castigating them. The castoffs start to bicker—"I fail to see what humor there is in incessant trivial flippancy," Victor says, when Sybil defends her feckless husband—and, just then, Elyot slips the wink to Amanda. The plot hinges on this moment: it acknowledges the defiant bond of caprice and engineers peace between the exes. As the curtain falls, Sybil and Victor are pummelling each other; Elyot and Amanda tiptoe away from the chaos and out the door. For Coward, who never fully revealed himself in public, this image of evasion is iconic—he repeats it at the end of *Hay Fever* and of *Present Laughter*—and it works as a sort of mission statement for all of his comedy.

In an attempt to disarm critics as well as the public, Coward wrote a series of acute assessments of his plays, which serve as introductions to them. "*Private Lives*, from the playwright's point of view, may or may not be considered interesting," he wrote, "but, at any rate, from the point of view of technical acting, it is very interesting indeed." As usual, the Master was right; as Elyot and Amanda, Rickman and Duncan have a field day with Coward's nuanced silences, with all the verbal tics and physical revelations of repressed feeling. They understand and convey the essential spiritual conundrum of their characters, who are at once overexcited and underinvolved. I have heard it said that Rickman is a selfish actor—an opinion I heartily decry. He has a sensationally droll presence, underscored by his oboe-like voice, which is bored at the edges and content to make its own mellow ironic music. Words—especially consonants—hold their fire, then spill out with hilarious precision. "Mr. and Mrs. Victor *Prynne*," he says to Amanda, rolling her new name on his tongue with teasing condescension. In mockery, Rickman can be lethal. He also knows the value of being still; his underplaying draws the audience in. In the face of his jejune, pert new bride (the excellent Emma Fielding), Rickman uses his heavy-lidded eyes to parse every aspect of ennui—resignation, sorrow, fatigue, scorn. Standing on Tim Hatley's witty hotel balcony, with the other white balconies above him cantilevered backward like a tilting wedding cake, he strikes something more than the usual clipped, pukka Coward stereotype. Like Coward, he exudes an adamant faith in his own intelligence.

This confidence positively combusts when it meets up with Duncan's quick-witted combination of sex and steel. Duncan is, for me, the finest and most versatile English actress of her generation. In the first scene, she strides onstage in a sleek black-and-white dressing gown, and before she even opens her mouth you know, from her particular aura of containment, that a wild heart is trapped within the cage of her politesse. Duncan has the look of an angel and the mischievous eyes of a devil. When she confesses to her lanky, jug-eared husband (the expert Adam Godley) that her young heart "was jagged with sophistication," she reveals both a sharp mind and a wicked tongue. With her bravado, Duncan hints at shadow but never shows it.

"Manners are especially the need of the plain," Evelyn Waugh joked. "The pretty can get away with anything." *Private Lives* proves the point. Act 2 finds the giddy goats ensconced in Amanda's garret, a large crimson split-level pad, overflowing with pillows and couches. Elyot and Amanda, who are "beautiful people," are now working hard to behave beautifully with each other. Rickman and Duncan have a great time walking on these emotional eggshells. They foxtrot around the parquet floor; they sing; they make a playful spectacle of their mental agility; they even staunchly refuse to fight.

> AMANDA: It's nice, isn't it?
> ELYOT: Strangely peaceful. It's an awfully bad reflection on our characters. We ought to be absolutely tortured with conscience.
> AMANDA: We are, every now and then. . . .
> ELYOT: You're even more ruthless than I am.

Coward understands that manners are about reciprocity, which is well beyond these two. All avowals to the contrary, Amanda and Elyot can't get beyond themselves—a tragedy in life, but a gold mine in comedy. Their outrageousness works a kind of psychic jujitsu that dethrones the serious and neutralizes moral indignation. Thrown off guard by the characters' irresistible high jinks, the audience finds itself accepting the unacceptable; "bad" becomes "good." This is Coward's deft and exhilarating game.

Howard Davies's radical notion is to play Elyot and Amanda's physical passion for real, rather than opting for the standard notional sexual allure. This allows him to capitalize on the wonderful chemistry between Rickman and Duncan, and gives them some memorable moments of "big romantic stuff" while snuggled up on sofas, but it also throws the comedy weirdly off kilter. Coward knew that this particular fun machine was jerry-built—"As a complete play, it leaves a lot to be desired," he wrote—and that speed was essential to make its jokes and its artificiality pay off. Here act 2, which is the play's set piece, goes on too long. When the tormenting couple shout out their code word for silence ("Sollocks") and call for a two-minute cool-down period, the actors amble wordlessly around their garret for two real minutes. When Elyot sits at the piano to sing "Some Day I'll Find You," the song turns into a medley, in which he is joined by Amanda. The famous battle royal that ends the second act is transformed by Davies from a spontaneous free-for-all into a self-conscious production number. Although well executed, it mutes the hilarity of Sybil and Victor's shock when they walk in on their spouses, only to find them rolling on the floor, going at each other hammer and tongs. Still, if the pacing sometimes falters, the stars' bad behavior does not. Rickman and Duncan give the best comic performances that have been seen on Broadway in a very long time. ∎

—May 6, 2002

Company

When Stephen Sondheim's *Company* debuted, in 1970, it was immediately acknowledged as a kind of musical watershed: no characters, no linear story, no happy ending. In the late fifties, Sondheim had written about everything coming up roses; now his fleurs were more or less *mal*. Full of lucid doubt, songs such as "The Little Things You Do Together," "Marry Me a Little," and "Sorry-Grateful" opened up a whole Pandora's box of ambivalence. The show, Sondheim's first collaboration with the director Harold Prince, which revolved around Bobby, a commitment-averse thirty-five-year-old bachelor,

and his married friends, portrayed marriage as a particularly per-
ilous adventure: "The concerts you enjoy together/Neighbors you
annoy together/Children you destroy together/That keep marriage intact."

"What happened to the good-time musical?" Ethan Mordden
asked rhetorically in his book *Broadway Babies*. Vietnam is what
happened. The culture had lost faith in both its goodness and its
gladness. Sondheim's revolution was one not just of style but of soul.
With this brilliantly innovative show, he replaced the American
musical's gleeful sense of life with a gleeful sense of death. Behind
the restless pursuit of pleasure and of distraction in *Company* was
the sure knowledge that, as Sondheim observed in the song "The
Ladies Who Lunch," "everybody dies." Resonating with the spiritual
fallout of the war, *Company* expressed not America's big heart but
its numbed one; it brought the musical up to the minute.

John Doyle's slick revival (at the Barrymore) allows a new generation of theatergoers to experience some of the show's original chilling wallop. The combination of fear and entropy that marked the
Vietnam years has, if anything, been compounded by recent political events, and the shellac of Sondheim's cynicism doesn't seem
dated. Here the back wall of the theater is painted black—an effect
that emphasizes the sound, not the Manhattan locale, and makes
the musical feel more abstract. A Steinway is positioned at stage
right; a vase of white calla lilies on top of it echoes the huge white
Doric column that rises from the center of the stage like a phallic
assertion of the music's potency. But the real landscape of the show
is the instruments, which the actors play as they sing, and which are
perched, at the opening, on revolving chairs and glass boxes.

Doyle used the same musician-performer trope last year in his
thrilling revival of *Sweeney Todd*. There it brought out the strength
of the musical's libretto; here, despite the superb staging, it only
underscores the weakness of George Furth's book. Doyle's produc-

tion provides no semblance of a naturalistic environment, and the actors have little plot and no place to give them dimension. As a result, novelty stands in for personality, and *Company* is exposed as the song cycle that it really is—albeit a spectacular one. The songs themselves, which are built like mini-plays, become the scenes, which has the benefit of allowing the audience to appreciate the dramatic sinew of their structure. In "Barcelona," for instance, Sondheim conjures in terse strokes the melancholy vacancy of Bobby's sexual games. After bedding a dim stewardess named April (Elizabeth Stanley), Bobby (the excellent Raúl Esparza) feigns irritation at her having to leave for the airport; he insists that she "stay a minute," telling her, "You're a very special girl, not just overnight." Bobby's palaver is meant to convince both him and her of his decency. So, when the worm turns, it's a moment that is at once hilarious and heartbreaking:

> APRIL: That's not to say
>   That if I had my way . . .
>   Oh well, I guess OK.
> BOBBY: What?
> APRIL: I'll stay.
> BOBBY: But . . . Oh, God.

Sondheim's tour de force of reversal and revelation is "Getting Married Today," in which Bobby, the best man at a wedding, looks on while the bride-to-be, Amy (Heather Laws), has an astonishing, perfectly pitched hysterical meltdown. "Go, can't you go? / Look, you know / I adore you all, / But why watch me die / Like Eliza on the ice," she sings. Her emotional collapse is topped by Bobby's moral one. At one point, after she has sent her fiancé away, Bobby asks Amy to marry him instead; his desperate, craven gesture is what finally gets Amy to the altar. The song works as a sort of three-act play, which, like the musical itself, is an extraordinary show of prowess and of misery.

Doyle's theatrical conceit works best at the stately opening, during which Bobby is propped nonchalantly against the piano while the other performers, wielding instruments, troop around him, like fragments from a dream, calling his name and besieging him with concern. But, for the most part, although the songs get across, the performances lack the exhilarating clout they should have. In "You Could Drive a Person Crazy," for instance, the doo-wah fun of the Andrews Sisters pastiche ("You could drive a person crazy, / You could drive a person mad. / Doo-doo doo-doo doo") is ceded to three saxophones, whose riffs are weak tea compared with the song's original bebop daftness. For "The Ladies Who Lunch," a great number that will always be owned by Elaine Stritch, and is sung well enough here by Barbara Walsh, Doyle avoids both invidious comparison and showstopping expectation by strategically running the song directly into the ensuing dialogue, thus refusing the audience a chance to respond.

At the finale of *Company*, Bobby is asked to blow out the candles on his birthday cake and make a wish. "Want something, Robert," one of his friends says. "Want *something!*" But Bobby doesn't know what he wants or how to get it. "Make me alive" is his final plea—the cry of a victim, not a hero. ■

—December 11, 2006

Sweeney Todd:
The Demon Barber of Fleet Street

After the sensational first production of *Sweeney Todd: The Demon Barber of Fleet Street*, in 1979, Stephen Sondheim underwent media canonization as the patron saint of the American musical. "Is Ste-

phen Sondheim God?" one magazine headline asked. Since then, as
Sondheim's musical experiments have repeatedly disappointed as
narratives, *Sweeney Todd*—the brooding, gleeful story of a vengeful
barber who dispatches his clientele with a razor and then has them
served up in meat pies—has loomed ever larger as the composer's
enduring masterpiece. From the poisoned wells of Victorian oppression, Sondheim drew his purest water; and it is in *Sweeney*'s toxic
nihilism that his own heartbroken detachment found its strongest
voice. But reverence, like habit, can be a great deadener, and, on the
face of it, the imported British revival of *Sweeney* (at the Eugene
O'Neill), which shrinks the cast of thirty to ten, with actors dou-
bling as musicians, looks like yet another exercise in high-art zeal-
otry. In fact, under the bold direction and design of John Doyle, this
minimalist reimagining is almost unbearably exciting. Its thrilling
transparency liberates the show from the operatic exquisiteness that
too often infects Sondheim productions, filling it instead with the
vulgar, raffish immediacy of showmanship. The result, it seems to
me, is luminous and a sort of landmark.

There are no painted vistas of derelict London, no barber's chair,
no chute to send the corpses plummeting into Mrs. Lovett's basement, no jolly proles gobbling pies made from human flesh, no
glowing oven into which Mrs. Lovett is finally herself dispatched.
Eschewing many of the musical's traditional visual delights, Doyle's
production relies on one delight that is rarely called upon by the
Broadway musical these days: the imagination. With eight chairs,
a coffin, and a ladder, Doyle conjures up a universe of woe and wonder; the actors are not just characters and musicians—they are also
the scenery. The blood here is of the Brechtian, not the Grand Guignol, variety, and the real spectacle is the dynamism between song
and story, which, for once, turns a spotlight on the brilliance of the
show's librettist, Hugh Wheeler.

"As is often the case in Sondheim's musicals, we don't care about characters," Frank Rich wrote in a *Times* review of *Sunday in the Park with George* (1984). This is the problem. Most of Sondheim's scores—*Pacific Overtures, Assassins, Sunday in the Park*—favor abstraction over narrative, which is why Wheeler's contribution is so important. Incorporating the class consciousness of the British playwright Christopher Bond's adaptation into his own edgy story, Wheeler grounds Sondheim's genius both in a moral universe and in the elegant architecture of event, which shrewdly defines character and builds tension. Sweeney, who was transported to Australia for fifteen years on a trumped-up charge by a judge who lusted after his wife, returns to London in disguise to find his wife apparently dead and his beloved daughter the ward of the very judge who sent him away. Revenge is his oxygen. Of the libretto's many felicities of reversal and surprise, the delay of Sweeney's rough justice on the judge is a particularly piquant construction. Wheeler's cunning economy distills each dramatic moment to its essence.

The stage at the Eugene O'Neill is dominated by a black wood coffin, a reminder that death is at the heart of every lyric moment. Tipped up, the coffin becomes the bench over which the judge presides; tipped down, it is the alcove where Sweeney's daughter and her lover sing of escape. The coffin is also the place from which Sweeney (Michael Cerveris) emerges in all his dark majesty. His head shaved, his body cloaked in black leather, Cerveris is a terrifying Sweeney, a model of sulfurous restraint. A sense of rage and regret percolates through every syllable he speaks, never more eloquently than in his first song upon returning to England: "There's a hole in the world / Like a great black pit / And the vermin of the world inhabit it / And its morals aren't worth / What a pig could spit / And it goes by the name of London."

Patti LuPone is Sweeney's pragmatic and pathological helpmate, Mrs. Lovett. A gargoyle of toughness, with an angular haircut, red lips and nails, a short skirt, and fishnet knee socks, LuPone looks positively Weimar. If Doyle's version deprives Mrs. Lovett of some of her shtick, at least it equips her with a tuba, which gives the term "big entrance" a meaning all its own. LuPone is never better than when Mrs. Lovett hits on the idea of disposing of one of Sweeney's victims by getting others to swallow the evidence. "Think of it as thrift / As a gift / If you get my drift," she sings. The new business partners' giddiness at the brainstorm is matched by Sondheim's pyrotechnical verbal display, as Sweeney and Mrs. Lovett imagine serving up a whole spectrum of English society in their new line of mean cuisine. "What is that?" Sweeney sings. Mrs. Lovett replies, "It's fop / Finest in the shop. / Or we have some shepherd's pie peppered / With actual shepherd on top."

In this production, which sheds the eggy trappings of naturalism, even the star-crossed young lovers, Anthony (Benjamin Magnuson) and Johanna (Lauren Molina), who usually come across as ninnies, take on a refreshing, compelling sweetness. Every emotional gesture they make finds a parallel in the music they play. For instance, when Sweeney learns that the judge has consigned Johanna to a madhouse for "safe-keeping," Johanna, on the other side of the stage, draws her bow across her cello in a single tremulous punishing note that suggests the howling inmates.

With its beautiful choral elements stripped back and the Victorian extravaganza all but eliminated, the musical is both darker and more vital. As life and theater have taught us, there is no escape from the power of the perverse. "There he is, it's Sweeney! / Sweeney! Sweeney!" the company sings at the finale, pointing out into the audience. At the curtain call, on the night I saw the show, from the orchestra to the farthest reaches of the mezzanine, the audience was on its feet. ∎

—November 14, 2005

Me, Myself & I

For more than fifty years, Edward Albee has been telling us stories about his interior. A wary, sharp-eyed customer, Albee is expert at putting a bright smile on his bleak vision—a vision that began with his birth, in 1928. In a questionnaire, Albee tersely characterized his family as "adoptive—we never got along." At eighteen days old, and at a cost of $133.30, he was taken into the Larchmont, New York, home of Reed and Frances Albee. (His adoptive father was a scion of the Keith-Albee vaudeville-theater chain.) "I was not what they bargained for, what they thought they had bought," Albee said. In his arid family, there were "no touchies, no feelies." At play on the grounds of his parents' estate, Albee was soon a veteran of privilege and neglect. He repaid the indifference with insolence. A smart lad and a recalcitrant student, he ricocheted among a series of expensive boarding schools: Lawrenceville, Valley Forge Military Academy, Choate. "I was not happy being away at school. I was not happy being at home. Obviously, I wasn't happy anywhere," he told his biographer, Mel Gussow, in *Edward Albee: A Singular Journey*. Dr. Allan Heely, the headmaster of Lawrenceville, recognized the parental problem and tried to intervene on Albee's behalf when he applied to Choate. "Very confidentially, he dislikes his mother with a cordial and eloquent dislike which I consider entirely justifiable," Heely wrote, adding, "I can think of no other boy who, I believe, has been so fully the victim of an unsympathetic home background or who has exhibited so fully the psychological effect of feeling that he is not wanted." In 1949, at the age of twenty-one, having been expelled from Trinity College after less than two years, Albee set out on his own.

Seventeen years later, after his fame had brought renewed glory to the Albee name, he reconnected with his imperious mother, but when she died, in 1989, he discovered that she had revised her will, removing him as her primary heir and eliminating him as a trustee of her estate. Going through her papers, Albee came across his adoption certificate, which contained the startling news that his birth name, which he had never known, was Edward Harvey. Only then, Albee said, did he start to wonder, "How did I get this way? Where did I develop this peculiar mind?" Given the similarity of the two names, it's easy to see how Albee, with his playful and ironic bent, could be drawn into the notion of Edward Harvey as his doppel-gänger, a kind of imagined twin. Albee's 2008 play, *Me, Myself & I* (crisply directed by Emily Mann, at Playwrights Horizons), is, as its title suggests, about the landscape of the self and the drama of claiming an identity.

Me, Myself & I focusses on a pair of identical twins and on the role of the maternal embrace—or the frustrating lack of it—in shaping a sturdy personality. It is at once a lament and a lampoon, its characters revolving around one another like planets in an alien galaxy. The set is a minimal white box, which suggests both the realm of the interior and a kind of cage. Perched center stage on a double bed, with her lump of a partner, the Dr. (the droll Brian Murray, in a pin-striped suit and a red tie), beside her, the Mother (Elizabeth Ashley) is literally and figuratively unable to tell her two sons, now in their twenties, apart. "Who *are* you? Which one *are* you?" she says in almost her first words to her son OTTO (Zachary Booth), adding, "Are you the one who loves me?" With her auburn hair teased up into a kind of Medusa do and her throaty Southern drawl simultaneously cooing and killing, Ashley makes a hilarious monster of nurture: her mind is as sharp as her tongue; she's both seductive and speedy, which works perfectly in this role. Mother, as Ashley plays her, is an infuriating, tantalizing, and destructive object of desire, flouncing around on the bed in an orange-and-bronze negligée with a precipitous décolletage, pouting, kicking, and working herself up into an eye-rolling comic tizzy:

MOTHER: (to OTTO) . . . I've seen you every day of your life, over and over, twenty times a day for all the years, but I don't know who you are.

DR.: (to Mother) You're speaking metaphorically here.

MOTHER: No, you asshole! I don't know who he *is*. Maybe I did . . . once.

OTTO: All right; (*pressing*) When?!

MOTHER: . . . When I looked down and saw each of you on a nipple. *Raising* you, raising the two of you, all the years. . . .

In Albee's shrewdly pitched dialogue, the *idea* of motherhood—not actual mothering—is what captures Mother's imagination. She wants to be looked at but not looked into. The result is emotional chaos, which Mother, with her sensational shallowness, has compounded by giving her identical twins identical names. "I named the twin at my right breast OTTO, after his father's grandfather's whatever, and the other, at my other one, otto," she explains. "One loud; one soft. Perfect boys; perfect breasts; perfect names." She goes on: "They would nestle there and enfold and . . . become one—be one. They were . . . Otto. My Ottos were Otto." The name, with its palindromic symmetry, acknowledges the identical external reality of the twins but outrageously denies them their individual interiors. It's soul murder given an absurdist spin. "I don't think existence determines much of anything," Mother says, levelling her big almond eyes at the audience. "Do *you*?" Identity, as the play cleverly dramatizes, is a collaboration of the self with the other. *Are we making sense? Are we communicating? Are we loved?* If the eyes that we fix on at birth don't reflect us back, the effect is deracinating. We're lost to ourselves.

"Do you like my mother?" OTTO asks the audience at one point in act 2, after declaring that his brother no longer exists for him. "Otto and I . . . *used* to find her perplexing, exhausting, maddening, deeply loving, terribly destructive. . . . But now, of course, I can't say, since my twin and I . . . no matter." From the play's first beat, the rebellious OTTO tells us that he wants to stir things up and get clear of his family; he announces to his family that he's going to China to become Chinese. Only later in the play does he tell otto (Preston Sadleir) that he wants him to disappear, too. "My brother *did* exist, but now I need him *not* to. Clear?" OTTO confides to us.

The psychic terror of invisibility, the need to have your life somehow witnessed, is played out primarily through the character of otto, who represents the biddable, vulnerable, insecure side of Albee's divided self, the son who wants to love his mother and his girlfriend, Maureen (Natalia Payne), but who is sent into an existential meltdown by OTTO's declaration of independence. "You *see* me. You see *me*," otto beseeches the bewildered Maureen. "You *feel* me! . . . You *see* me. You *feel* me." The lethal OTTO does his best to humiliate and debase his tender twin, to kill off the soft part of his heart—going so far as to impersonate otto and bed Maureen. "I'm not nice, am I!! Never have been; good dissembler though," OTTO says. In the end, he negotiates a kind of truce with otto. "My twin, perhaps, but not my brother," he says.

Who, then, is OTTO's brother? The play's answer is OTTO's own reflection in the mirror. "This was the *real* me. This was me— identically," he says. The name of this interloper is *Otto*—in italics. "He's real. He *does* exist," OTTO insists to his twin. "I guess we'll just have to think of ourselves as triplets." The joke brings the warring selves into some kind of harmony. OTTO and otto embrace. "I think the play's over," OTTO says. "Let's go join the curtain call." The twins pivot away from us and stand with the other actors to take their bows—a moment that plays as both a termination and a liberation.

Albee once said of his double parental abandonment, "I used to care about it, but then I discovered that I was a writer. . . . I found out who I was through my plays." In *Me, Myself & I*, he makes a spectacle of that discovery, of the strength to be found through self-expression. Along its jaunty way, the play nods to the Greeks (with a deus-ex-machina happy ending), to Samuel Beckett (Hamm's dark glasses, Vladimir and Estragon's bowler hats and exasperated banter), and, for me, anyway, to musical comedy. In Frank Loesser's *How to Succeed in Business without Really Trying*, the ambitious hero peps himself up by singing a love song to his reflection in the bathroom mirror: "And when my faith in my fellow man / All but falls apart, / I've but to feel your hand grasping mine / And I take heart, I take heart." ∎

—September 27, 2010

Oklahoma!

In 1959, when Richard Rodgers and Oscar Hammerstein II were beginning work on *The Sound of Music*—the story goes—their co-producer Richard Halliday, who was also the husband and manager of the show's star, Mary Martin, came to them with a great idea for her first entrance: she would be discovered in a tree and, as she climbed down, catch her bloomers on a branch. Rodgers and Hammerstein rejected the idea out of hand. Halliday was incensed. "You know what's wrong with you guys?" he said, stalking out. "All *you* care about is the *show*!"

In that joke lies the essence of Rodgers and Hammerstein's revolution in musical storytelling, which began in 1943, with *Oklahoma!* In its out-of-town tryouts, the show, then titled *Away We Go!*, was billed as a "musical comedy"; by the time it arrived in New York, with its now indelible brand name, it had become a "musical play." With that semantic mutation, the musical's job description changed, virtually overnight. Anarchic, freewheeling frivolity that

traded in joy—in other words, in the comedian's resourcefulness—
was renounced for an artful marriage of music and lyrics that traded
in narrative. Seriousness replaced sass. Big names were no longer
needed to carry the show; the show itself was the star. In show-biz
terms, Rodgers and Hammerstein had hit the mother lode. They
had engineered the musical equivalent of the interchangeable part,
which insured a sort of quality control. Improvisation was no longer
an element, and the musical was now, in principle, anyway, infinitely
repeatable. Rodgers and Hammerstein were not just a sensation—
they were a corporation.

Because of *Oklahoma!*'s enormous subsequent influence, its nov-
elties—no opening ensemble number, chorus girls in long dresses,
dancers who don't appear until late in the first act, the integrated
score—have lost some of their original luster. In the Royal National
Theatre's three-hour revival (now at the Gershwin), directed by
Trevor Nunn, the show's heady mixture of wonder and ambition is
best captured in its production values. Anthony Ward's picturesque
set immediately submerges us in a gorgeous world of folk innocence.
As the scrim of blue sky flies up, Aunt Eller Murphy's spread—the
farmhouse billowing gray smoke from its chimney, the windmill,
the smokehouse—is revealed in miniature. In the next beat, the set
revolves from long shot to closeup; corn as high as an elephant's eye
looms into view, as two white birds wheel above it. By the time Curly
McLain (the big-voiced and charming Patrick Wilson) ambles somewhat theatrically onstage to celebrate the joys of the radiant morning, the charm of the pristine landscape and of the homesteading
values that go with it has been clinched.

In the making of musicals, Nunn, who has directed *Cats*, *Les
Misérables*, and *Sunset Boulevard*, among others, is a four-star
general. His stage pictures spill over with meticulous, articulate
energy. But technique, which can make the show work, is not enough
to make it wonderful. Here, I think, the issue of cultural chemistry

comes into play. To the English—and I've lived in London for thirty years—Americans are a sort of mutant breed, whose optimism is a sure sign of emotional aberration. The English are constitutionally unable to fathom it, and for good reason. American optimism has its root in abundance and in the vastness of the land that *Oklahoma!* celebrates. Britain, on the other hand, is an island the size of Utah. Its culture is one of scarcity; its preferred idiom is irony—a language of limits. In the retranslation of an award-winning English version of an American classic to its natural Broadway habitat, an emotional lopsidedness has become evident, particularly in the casting.

The linchpins of the show are Aunt Eller, played by the gritty, droll comedienne Andrea Martin, who is American and nails it, and the feisty, lovelorn Laurey, played by the fine-voiced, demure Josefina Gabrielle, who is English and doesn't. It's not talent that's at issue here—Gabrielle is the first Laurey to dance her own Dream Ballet—but national character. The show is about Western women, and Gabrielle's Laurey lacks that very American sense of gumption, a combination of buoyancy and backbone. The problem is even more egregious in the casting of Jessica Boevers. Ado Annie is the girl who can't say no; Boevers is the girl who can't bring any genuine humor to the role. Without a whiff of the sexual ripeness that should brighten the part, she plays Ado Annie as a squealing airhead. Her terrific songs, of course, still get laughs. With lines like "I cain't resist a Romeo / In a sombrero and chaps. / Soon as I sit on their laps / Somethin' inside of me snaps," how can you miss? Ado Annie's "Persian" paramour is Ali Hakim (the Willie Howard look-alike Aasif Mandvi), an itinerant peddler turned into an interminable running gag that is really about the chiselling Jew. English audiences may be comfortable with the racist stereotype, but Broadway audiences quickly weary of it, and of him.

There are stupendous pleasures in the show nonetheless. Many of them are due to the high-spirited, humorous choreography of

Susan Stroman. In the Dream Ballet, which becomes a nightmare—Laurey imagines marrying Curly and then being raped by his rival for her affection, the beefy ranch hand Jud Fry (the excellent Shuler Hensley)—there's a magical moment when the dancers first appear through quivering corn stalks. Stroman also gives some thrilling moves to Justin Bohon, who plays Will Parker, the lariat-throwing, back-flipping dervish who returns from Kansas City determined to take Ado Annie as his bride. In the rousing production number "The Farmer and the Cowman," which opens act 2, all the scenic and literary excellences of the script come together. In one singing, dancing swoop, the show manages to raise a roof, make a sociological point about class division on the range, have a hoedown and a punch-up, and move the plot along: Laurey loves Curly, and wants him to bid on her food basket at the Box Social; Jud pines for her, but loses the bidding war. Trouble is brewing in the prairie paradise.

In many ways, the character of Jud Fry is both *Oklahoma!*'s inspiration and its dramaturgical sack of rocks. Overweight and ugly, Fry is a compendium of society's darkest forces. He's a loner. He has no social skills. His hovel is papered with pornography, and, to put the icing on the devil's-food cake, he admits to being capable of murder. Of *Oklahoma!*'s many innovations, certainly its most enduring one lies symbolically here. With Fry, Rodgers and Hammerstein made a place for darkness within the bright world of the American musical. By emotionally embracing all of life, they coaxed the musical out of its long adolescence and forced it to grow up. They also made another useful narrative discovery: to show brilliance, you need shadow.

Yet, in *Oklahoma!*, their first outing as a writing team, Fry feels like a forced fit. As far as I can tell from the libretto, Curly, after learning that Laurey may be driven to the social by Jud, moseys down to Jud's house to check out the competition. He walks in the door, scopes out the pornographic pictures while Jud cleans his gun, and then "cheerfully" suggests that Jud hang himself from the rafters. In the song "Pore Jud Is Daid," Curly paints a picture of Jud's death and burial. Jud "becomes then, for a while, not just wicked, but a comic figure flattered by the attentions he might receive if he were dead," Hammerstein wrote. "He becomes also a pathetic figure, pathetically lonely for attentions he has never received while alive. The audience begins to feel some sympathy for him, some under-standing of him as a man." I believe Hammerstein. What I don't believe is the way the song is set up—that Curly would walk into the lair of a subnormal lout, especially one with a gun in his hand, and in less than a minute brightly suggest that he kill himself.

In the second act, Jud puts a clumsy move on Laurey and she kicks him off the farm, only to have him come back three weeks later to haunt her wedding to Curly, like the Ancient Mariner at the feast. In Jud's menacing intrusion, his brawling, and his demise (he falls on his own knife and dies), there is no doubt, and therefore no drama. There is also, really, no necessity. Having just lustily sung the famous title song at the wedding banquet, the cast is in high festival mood, a fitting climax to the romance. The evening feels over. Jud's sud-den reappearance adds nothing to the plot and, after 150 minutes, is about as welcome as a returning kamikaze pilot. Although it's her-esy to say it, the production could lose the last fifteen minutes—Jud's revenge, his death, and Curly's subsequent trial, in a sort of kanga-roo court that excuses him to continue his marriage—and only the purists would mind. *We* know that Curly is innocent, damn it; and the whole brouhaha has as much clout as a popgun.

In his memoir, *Musical Stages*, Rodgers averred that the show's opening scene—a cowboy strolling onto the stage where a single woman is churning butter—announced to the audience, "Watch out! This is a different kind of musical." He went on to say, "Every-thing in the production was made to conform to the simple open-air spirit of the story; this was essential, and certainly a rarity in the musical theater." Trevor Nunn's version of *Oklahoma!* preserves the crowd-pleasing commercial zest of the original; but on the evening I saw the show only a handful of audience members stood to applaud the hardworking cast, confirming my suspicion that the open-air spirit of the evening had been slowly leached away. *Oklahoma!* is still a beautiful piece of craftsmanship, ravishing in its music and lyrics, stunning in its design. But the fun machine needs some souping up. Understandably, the owners are loath to lay a hand on the engine. I counsel tough love. As Aunt Eller herself says, "You cain't deserve the sweet and tender in life less'n you're tough." ■

—April 1, 2002

The Light in the Piazza

Once upon a time in the early sixties, the composer Mary Rodgers suggested to her gloomy father, the composer Richard Rodgers, that he adapt for Broadway Elizabeth Spencer's novella *The Light in the Piazza* (which occupied almost an entire issue of this magazine in 1960); the great man demurred. Four decades later, however, Mary Rodgers's son, the gifted composer and lyricist Adam Guettel, took up the challenge. Among the many delightful surprises in the resulting show, which opened last week at Chicago's Goodman Theatre, is its overture. Has any other American musical in the past twenty years had enough memorable melody to warrant such a thing? Guettel's tunes are richly textured and warmly atmospheric; like the Tuscan light of Spencer's story, they create "the sense that everything is clear and visible, that nothing is withheld."

Using violin, piano, and harp, Guettel's overture evokes the sun-dappled summer of Florence in the mid-fifties, where Margaret Johnson (Victoria Clark), a Southern lady of means and manners, has brought her jejune twenty-six-year-old daughter, Clara (Celia Keenan-Bolger), to see the sights. The production's central metaphor is a red-ribboned straw hat—in its design, somewhere between schoolgirl and Schiaparelli. At the beginning of Bartlett Sher's poised production, the hat drops from above into Margaret's hands before ending up on Clara's pert blond head. Soon it is blown back up and into the eager clutches of a twenty-year-old Italian charmer named Fabrizio (Wayne Wilcox). Clara's and Fabrizio's eyes meet, and—well, you know the rest. Or you think you do. The hat is an emblem of something lost and found, a symbol of hope that foreshadows the tempestuous trajectory of the story to come.

In a full skirt and white gloves, Clara seems a picture postcard of fifties normality, punch-pressed from a book marked "Ingénue." Her looks and her attitude—buoyant, dutiful, sweet, naive—conform to the bright banality of the time, giving her an air of coherence, and this is part of the play's drama and Clara's tragedy. Because, by degrees, and with little euphemistic clues from Margaret—"She isn't regular," she's "not quite as she seems"—Clara's strangeness emerges, like a shadow growing longer at the end of the day. There's the girlish, round-shouldered way she runs with her head down, the sudden emotional squalls, her charming forthrightness. "Look, a scar!" she says to Fabrizio, lifting her ponytail to show him something behind her ear. Her profound scars are, of course, invisible and not as easy to define. Her "dreary secret," as the story calls it, is revealed only late in the show; as a young girl, Clara was kicked in the head by a Shetland pony. She has a mental age of twelve.

But in this whirlwind romance—where neither lover comprehends the other's language or culture—otherness is the climate of connection. "I don't understand a word they're saying," Clara sings in "The Beauty Is." "I'm as different here as different can be / And the beauty is I still meet people like me." In fact, on an unconscious level, Fabrizio's acceptance of Clara's oddness is what draws her to him. He sees her in no context other than her own. This sentiment is conveyed brilliantly in "Love to Me," in which he reimagines the moment when he first caught sight of Clara. "Ohhhhh, you're not alone," he sings. "This is how I know / This is what I see / This is love to me." Fabrizio's fractured English doesn't prevent him from making himself known to Clara. "Now is I am happiness with you," he sings in "Passeggiata." In both deficiency and desire, Clara and Fabrizio are equals, and that is what makes intimacy between them possible. In a gorgeous duet, "Say It Somehow," Guettel has his handicapped lovers sing, "Say it somehow anyway you can / You know me . . . / I know the sound of touch me. / I think I heard the sound of wrap your arms around me." Their inadequacies force them beyond reason and competence to pure feeling.

Instead of the anodyne commercial musical formula, which promises distraction, *The Light in the Piazza* offers a complex contemplation of the well-defended emptiness in every man and woman. "Something is very wrong," Clara tells Fabrizio toward the end of the show, as she attempts to break off their relationship. "I would fix it if I could, knew how. I can't." She goes on, "Everyone has been disappointed in me. . . . I'm the one that's not good enough. You just don't see it now." Confronted with Clara's quandary, we are audibly silent—not manipulated into frenzied Broadway-style forgetfulness but roused to reflect on our own unexplainable wounds. What are the mysterious things that hold *us* back from embracing life or allowing it to embrace us? Can our own forms of suffering be redeemed? To this last question, Guettel's answer is an absolute maybe.

"Things are often hard," Margaret drawls at one point. Her understatement, borrowed from Spencer's story, is indicative of the good face she puts on her doomed life. In light of the truth about Clara, Margaret's comic attempts to keep her woman-child safe from predatory Italians assume an altogether different dimension. Her cosseting turns out to be a kind of courage. When Margaret finally realizes that love, family, even happiness may be possible for Clara, her longing and her long-suffering are unleashed in a powerful reprise of "The Beauty Is." "So much wanting something," she sings. "So much reaching for it / So much wishing just to have one moment back / So much being patient / So much blind acceptance." Superbly played by Clark, Margaret is a potent amalgam of charm, civility, and cunning. "Women like Margaret Johnson do not surrender; they simply take up another line of campaign," Spencer writes. Clark gets Margaret's backbone and blind spots just right. Her desire to treat her daughter as if she were normal prevents her from ever coming clean with Fabrizio's family about the nature of Clara's affliction; and it compels her to gamble on a marriage for her daughter that she knows will be intolerable to her buttoned-down businessman husband, in whose eyes, she sings, she "can see the winter." As Margaret recognizes the magic of love that transforms her daughter, she also recognizes the atrophy of feeling in her own marriage. Craig Lucas, who wrote the book for the show, is responsible for this narrative undercurrent, which also lends a whiff of flirtatiousness to Margaret's relationship with Clara's suave prospective father-in-law (the first-rate Mark Harelik). It's a substantial improvement on Spencer's otherwise excellent story line, which includes two hand-wringing reversals on the way to the altar. In "Fable," a heartrendingly beautiful song that ends the show and works as both epiphany and envoi, Margaret turns to the audience as her nervous daughter sets off down the aisle and sings of love as a leap of faith:

If you find in the world
In the wide wide world
That someone sees you
That someone knows you
Love! . . .
Love, if you can, oh my Clara,
Love, if you can and be loved
May it last forever . . .
The light in the piazza

Guettel's music and lyrics take nothing from the razzle-dazzle bargain basement of feeling; they represent, instead, a genuine expense of spirit. Rather than selling a cheap-and-cheerful redemption, the show offers only the prospect of repair. *The Light in the Piazza* doesn't want to make theatergoers feel good; it wants to make them feel deeply. This it does, and that is why, despite the show's quality, I suspect that the swamis of the rialto will pass on bringing it to Broadway. Still, Guettel's kind of talent cannot be denied. He shouldn't change for Broadway; Broadway, if it is to survive as a creative theatrical force, should change for him. ■

—February 2, 2004

The Light in the Piazza *was produced by the Lincoln Center Repertory Theater in 2005 and ran for 540 performances.*

Orpheus Descending

"The irresponsible days of my youth are over," Tennessee Williams wrote of the life-changing moment in 1940, when in Mexico he received a telegram from the Theatre Guild urging him to return to New York for his first Broadway production. The play was *Battle of Angels*. By then, Williams had won literary acknowledgment from the Group Theatre, been taken up by the prestigious Liebling-Wood agency in New York, and, having survived a painful childhood and three Depression years of soul-destroying work in the shoe company at which his bullying father was an executive, set himself on the single-minded pursuit of his artistic destiny. "Out of the sheer surfeit of being beaten down, I gathered out of my father's fierce blood the power to rise somehow," he wrote to a friend. "And how could the rise be gentle." Tom Williams had been reborn Tennessee Williams, the self-proclaimed "Homo Emancipatus—the Completely Free Man," and *Battle of Angels* was the first full-scale assertion of his remodelled romantic self.

Williams had given his surrogate hero both his own age (twenty-nine) and a surname, Xavier, that was phonetically linked to Sevier, a distinguished name in his own family tree. It also sounded like "Saviour"—and that is how the jejune Williams saw his calling, which he described in another play of the same period as "the high reach of the spirit." In the fictional Southern backwater of Two River County, the empathetic Val Xavier, who answers to the nickname Snakeskin (he wears a snakeskin jacket), is a catalyst for transformation. Like another Williams spokesman, Tom Wingfield, in *The Glass Menagerie*, he has "tricks up his sleeve." In fact, Val is surrounded by magic: summoned up, seemingly from nowhere, by the Choctaw chant of a local conjure man, he works his spell, within the play's "nonrealistic" story, with the guitar he carries. Newly arrived in town, he wanders into a drygoods store looking for work. Soon he has called life out of the store's joyless proprietress, Lady Torrance, and the other local womenfolk who project their longing onto him; the threatened men, on the other hand, project their hate, and they succeed in driving Val's free spirit away and finally destroying it. Xavier is an irresistible and mysterious amalgam of Williams's sexual and spiritual ideal, one of his many solitary, dispossessed, fugitive minds who hanker for both passion and purity. "I lived in corruption, but I'm not corrupted," the unpredatory Val says. In a brilliant speech, which incidentally explains the salvation Williams found in writing, Val calls his guitar "my life's companion": "It washes me clean like water when anything unclean has touched me."

In *Battle of Angels*, Williams contrived to set the savage forces of life and death against each other in order to demonstrate his own battle between the pressures of philistine society and of his truth-seeking bohemian soul. "We of the artistic world are the little gray foxes and all the rest are the hounds," he said around the time he wrote the play, which dramatizes the traditional hunt. "It is a fight to the death."

———

Whatever the strengths of Williams's romantic vision of self-aggrandizement, the beginning of the Second World War was no time to preach it. *Battle of Angels* closed in Boston before it reached Broadway. Seventeen years later, when the conformity and violence of the fifties had turned America into a version of what Williams called "beanstalk country," he substantially rewrote the play as *Orpheus Descending* and sent it out into the world as an "emotional record" of his youth, in which the public could "find the trail of my sleeve-worn heart." Despite Sidney Lumet's fascinating screen version, *The Fugitive Kind* (with memorable performances from Marlon Brando and Anna Magnani), the revision didn't fare much better, and its failure sent Williams briefly into psychoanalysis. The most recent Broadway production, mounted in 1988, with Vanessa Redgrave doing a pidgin-Italian imitation of Magnani, didn't help matters.

But Nicholas Hytner's lucid revival (at London's Donmar Warehouse) restores both luster and honor to Williams's subtle spiritual autobiography, allowing the audience to see beyond the play's showy exterior to its compelling internal drama. The set plays the same game as the story, manufacturing a stunning world of light and shadow, which, as Val says, "*do* get—*mixed.*" Bob Crowley's gray and derelict latticed roof, with its suggestive cobwebs, fans out above the drygoods store like an ominous bird's wing; an upstage staircase—well lit by Hugh Vanstone—leads to the unseen living quarters above the store where the dying malevolent Jabe Torrance (the chilling Richard Durden) and his captive wife, Lady (Helen Mirren), cohabit in hatred-hard separation, and throws long shadows up the gray brick back wall which suggest a cage. But the real source of light here is Val. Hytner has struck lucky with Stuart Townsend, who is thin and delicate-featured but strong and centered in himself. If Townsend's Val doesn't generate the same sense of animal magnetism and mischief as Brando (who could?), he still generates heat: a palpable combination of sweetness and sexuality. He is, I suspect, the Next Big English Thing. Almost as soon as Townsend makes his entrance, he accompanies himself with some prowess on the guitar, performing a song that shows him off as both sex symbol and searcher:

Then my feet come down to walk on earth,
And my mother cried when she gave me birth.
Now my feet walk far and my feet walk fast,
But they still got an itch for heavenly grass
They still got an itch for heavenly grass.

Townsend is a good match for Helen Mirren's very specific and riveting gravity, and both actors play well against Williams's melodrama, which can veer toward the operatic unless carefully watched. To Williams, who was raised in an Episcopal rectory and whose plays are Christ-haunted, the enemy of the liberating romantic notion of self is the suffocating Christian notion of self-sacrifice. Here, Lady is Jabe's dutiful chattel. Unlucky in more than love (she aborted a baby after her lover jilted her for a society marriage), she was orphaned as a girl when her Italian-immigrant father died fighting a blaze in his vineyard—set by racists because he sold wine to blacks. "He bought her, when she was a girl of eighteen!" one of the gossiping town biddies says of Jabe. "He bought her and he bought her cheap because she'd been thrown over and had her heart broken." Lady, whose domination is signalled by the constant pounding of Jabe's cane from the floor above, is always dressed in black and always at Jabe's call. In Mirren's superbly controlled performance, she is a force field of willpower, an embodiment of the living death of resignation—until the seed of freedom is planted in her imagination by Val's famous speech about legless birds that never touch the earth. "They live their whole lives on the wing, and they sleep on the wind," Val explains to Lady, who tells him that she'd like to be one of them. "So'd I like to be one of those birds," Val continues. "They's lots of people would like to be one of those birds and never be corrupted!" As a character, Lady belongs to a line of remarkable, long-suffering Williams heroines—Alma Winemiller, Blanche du Bois, Rose della Rose—who, cut off from life and from their feelings, have been warped by their devotion to others. Lady has killed her heart; Val resuscitates it. Her victory—the play's romantic apotheosis—is the unlearning of repression and the seizing of bliss, albeit short-lived.

In Hytner's production, the brooding forces that compel Val to leave town—the murderous ignorance, fear, and violence of rural life—coalesce in the huge and menacing form of Sheriff Talbott (the terrifying William Hootkins). Talbott and his henchman virtually tree Val, who leaps on the store counter as knives swipe at his legs. Before she can leave with him, Lady is gunned down by Jabe, whom the stage directions describe as "death's self." All that remains of Val in the community is his snakeskin jacket. "Wild things leave skins behind them, they leave clean skins and teeth and white bones behind them," says another Delta free spirit and outsider, Carol Cutrere (Saskia Reeves), as she cradles the coat in her arms. "And these are tokens passed from one to another, so that the fugitive kind can follow their kind."

Williams, whose nickname was Bird, managed to live, like his legless birds, more or less on the move. He understood his peripatetic destiny early. "Oh God . . . there is so much hurt in the world," he wrote to a friend, soon after the failure of *Battle of Angels*. "You have to evade and evade." And his oeuvre serves the same poetic function for his century as Val's snakeskin jacket: his characters and symbols—like stones on a bushwhacked trail—are a kind of map of the soul's struggle to be both great and good; they mark one man's dangerous ascent to the furthest reaches of individualism, where ultimately even he lost his way. By 1957, the year *Orpheus Descend-*

ing was first staged, Williams had admitted, "I can't be the best part of myself anymore." But the longing—the heavenly itch Val sings about and embodies—never left his life or his luminous work. ∎

—July 17, 2000

The Rose Tattoo

On December 30, 1947, the thirty-six-year-old Tennessee Williams boarded a ship bound for France, sailing away from America and from the tumultuous success on Broadway, only a few weeks earlier, of *A Streetcar Named Desire*. Almost immediately, he hit creative still water, finding it "frightfully hard to discover a new vein of material." When, in late 1948, his play *Summer and Smoke* failed on Broadway, Williams's confidence dipped still further; he felt, he said, like a "discredited old conjurer." To his champion Brooks Atkinson, the drama critic of the *Times*, he wrote in June 1949, "The trouble is that you can't make any real philosophical progress in a couple of years. The scope of understanding enlarges quite slowly, if it enlarges at all, and the scope of interest seems to wait upon understanding. . . . All artists who work from the inside out, have all the same problem: they cannot make sudden, arbitrary changes of matter and treatment until the inner man is ripe for it."

During this stalled period, Williams was falling in love with Frank Merlo, a high-spirited twenty-five-year-old Sicilian-American, who was to be his companion and factotum for the next fourteen years. Merlo's steadfastness stabilized Williams and brought him unexpected happiness. "He was so close to life," he said. "He tied me down to earth." Williams's theatrical testament to this romance is the 1950 comedy *The Rose Tattoo*, which is generally considered the runt of his major plays. The current expert revival now at London's Royal National (under the robust direction of Nicholas Hytner and the late Steven Pimlott), however, adds new luster to the text—and reinforces the role that the National has played over the past decade in resuscitating Williams's international reputation.

Williams dedicated *The Rose Tattoo* to Merlo, whose rambunctiousness and decency, along with his olive skin and sculpted physique, are incarnated here in the clownish Alvaro Mangiacavallo ("My name . . . means 'Eat-a-horse,'" he explains), who brings the inconsolable self-dramatizing seamstress Serafina della Rose back to life. Beneath the hubbub of the play's setting, in a Sicilian neighborhood of an American Gulf Coast town, Williams finally discovers a new thematic note: the joy of deliverance from creative and emotional impasse.

At the National, even before the play begins, the battle of opposing spiritual forces—life vs. death is a constant motif in Williams—is signalled by two dressmaking dummies that stand behind Serafina's sewing machine: one wears a white wedding dress, the other black widow's weeds. They are intended, according to the stage directions, to "face each other in violent attitudes, as though having a shrill argument." If Mark Thompson's shrewd stage design doesn't quite follow Williams's symbolic directions, it is eloquent in its ability to capture the deeper implications of Serafina's hysteria. Her bungalow is positioned in front of a scrim of mackerel sky and revolves, like a sort of clapboard Rubik's Cube, to reveal a gaudy, cluttered interior. When we first see her, Serafina (the superb Zoë Wanamaker) is poised on the sofa, eagerly awaiting the return of her husband, Rosario, a truck driver. Her appearance—she "looks like a plump little Italian opera singer in the role of Madame Butterfly," Williams says—hints at her comically grandiose and romantic core.

Almost immediately, Williams introduces two messengers of disenchantment: a local healer who tries to sell Serafina a powder to decrease male goatishness, and a light-fingered female customer who steals a framed photograph of Rosario while urgently requiring a shirt made from rose-colored silk for a man who is "wild like a Gypsy." The audience may twig to Rosario's misbehavior at this point, but Serafina remains staunchly under her own romantic spell. She idealizes Rosario's pedigree and his passion; and, in the process, of course, she inflates herself. (She claims that her drug-smuggling husband is of noble lineage; the Baronessa is the community's tongue-in-cheek nickname for her.) "For love I make characters in plays," Williams famously wrote; likewise, Serafina constructs a sustaining fiction. From Rosario's absence, she invents a permanent presence. "The memory of the rose in my heart is perfect!" she says. Such is their union, she claims, that a rose-shaped tattoo similar to the one on Rosario's chest appeared on her breast—a sort of stigmata—at the moment of conception of their second child, with whom she is pregnant. Serafina hymns Rosario's hair, his chest, his lovemaking; she counts the exact number of nights—4,380—that they have spent together in their twelve-year marriage. "Each time is the first time with him," she says. "Time doesn't pass."

When Rosario is killed and Serafina, in her grief, loses the baby, her melancholy becomes morbid. She can't part with Rosario's body; against the wishes of the Church, she keeps his purified ashes in an urn on the mantelpiece. For the next three years, she locks herself away, alone with her uncontested memories. To keep her vision of the marriage bright, she represses any shadow of doubt. "To me the big bed was beautiful like a religion," she tells the local priest. "Now I lie on it with dreams, with memories only! But it is still beautiful to me and I don't believe that the man in my heart gave me horns!" Serafina's abiding emotion turns out to be a passion for ignorance; she's "a female ostrich," one neighbor rightly observes.

Nonetheless, suspicion breaks through in fragments of remembered dialogue. "He was—wild like a—Gypsy," she says. " 'Wild—like a—Gypsy'? Who said that?—I hate to start to remember, and then not remember." In fact, her performance of grief is an act of disremembering, a defensive strategy of radical innocence. This extends to her teenage daughter, Rosa (the fetching Susannah Fielding), whom she tries to prevent from taking her final exams and from seeing a young sailor she has fallen for. Rosa, at her graduation, is awarded, in addition to her diploma, "The Digest of Knowledge"; for Williams, sex always marks the beginning of knowledge, and carnality arrives here in the shape of Mangiacavallo (the excellent Darrell D'Silva), another truck driver.

The uncouth Mangiacavallo—another of Williams's primitives— seeks refuge in Serafina's house in order to have a cry after losing a fistfight. "I always cry after a fight," he tells her. "But I don't want people to see me. It's not like a man." He is humiliated, vulnerable, down to earth, honest; he has no pedigree (he is "the grandson of the village idiot," he says) or property ("Love and affection is what I got to offer"). He is, psychologically speaking, everything that Serafina is not. Inevitably, as Williams's stage directions instruct, there is a "profound unconscious response" between them. Mangiacavallo's pragmatism punctures Serafina's grandiosity. When she learns the name of Rosario's mistress, a blackjack dealer at a local casino, and sets off to stab her with a kitchen knife, Mangiacavallo literally and figuratively disarms her. He calls the woman and confirms Rosario's infidelity. Wanamaker, who has a fine, fierce sense of comedy, makes this moment of disillusionment sensational. As in all fairy tales, it is not the enchanted but the disenchanted who are free. Rosario's ashes are scattered; Serafina's desire returns. Tears give way to laughter, and time—in the form of a Bulova watch that Serafina buys for her daughter—resumes. Williams's heroine is no longer out of time but in the moment.

At the finale, the shirtless Mangiacavallo hides on the embankment above the house; in order to coax him back down, Serafina throws the disputed rose-colored silk shirt to the town folk, who rush it up the embankment, "like a streak of flame shooting up a dry hill," the stage directions read. It's a gorgeous, beautifully managed image of desire. The shirt, once a totem of humiliation, is transformed into a semaphore of hope. As Serafina, too, heads up the embankment, she is finally in motion, moving forward. Although the scene has its own poetic theatrical integrity, for those who know Williams's story it also marks a poignant, pivotal moment when life held out a brief reprieve from what he called the "little cave of consciousness." ∎

—May 28, 2007

Carousel

On the English stage, Americans are forever depicted as the clowns of capitalism—predatory, credulous, barbarous, and loud. If there has been a positive portrait of an American by a major English playwright in the last twenty-five years, I'm not aware of it. But when it comes to American musicals, the English can't get enough. Currently, there are five American musicals on London's West End; two more are scheduled for the spring. What's endearing about this fascination is how ineptly most of the musicals are performed. The fundamental problem is spiritual. The British don't believe that everything's coming up roses, and that something's coming—something good—if you can wait. American optimism, which is built on abundance, is not fathomable by the British imagination, because England is a culture of scarcity, and its favored idiom is irony, which insists on limits to expectation. As a result, American musicals in England frequently lose a part of their energy and their resonance in translation. They also lose a lot of their production values, because the English will not—and usually cannot—spend enough to get the shows to work properly. So it's a strange and wonderful twist of theatrical fate that the Royal National Theatre's daring, elegant production of Rodgers and Hammerstein's *Carousel* should blast away the aspic in which the show has been preserved and reinvent this classic "musical play" along darker, more ironic lines, making it compelling for the American nineties.

The nine musicals of Richard Rodgers and Oscar Hammerstein II engineered a revolution in American entertainment. Hammerstein was forty-seven when he joined forces with the forty-year-old Rodgers, in 1942. He'd been a co-author of some of the biggest hits of the twenties (*Rose-Marie*, *The Desert Song*, *Show Boat*), but his fascination with operetta ran aground in the theatrically conservative, and he had a decade of failures. On the other hand, since 1935 Rodgers, partnered with Lorenz Hart, had produced a string of eight sassy hits, including *Pal Joey* and *By Jupiter*. The new Rodgers and Hammerstein partnership smashed the old Broadway formula of "no girls, no gags, no chance." Before Rodgers and Hammerstein, there was "musical comedy," in which smart songs and capering star turns elevated frivolity into an art form. After *Oklahoma!* (1943) and *Carousel* (1945), America had musical theater. Rodgers and Hammerstein's discovery did for the precision of musical production what the interchangeable part did for mass production—insured quality control. The musical became "actor proof," a fun machine in which the makers, not the stars, controlled the product, and in which song, star, and choreography served a finely tuned story. "Song is the servant of the play," Hammerstein said. "It is wrong to write first what you think and then try to wedge it into a story. . . . A rhyme should be unassertive, never standing out too noticeably. . . . If a listener is made rhyme-conscious, his interest may be distracted from the story."

And in *Carousel* it's the story, Hammerstein's faithful, cunningly filigreed adaptation of Ferenc Molnár's *Liliom* (1909), that elevates the show's main characters—the wife-beating carnival barker, Billy Bigelow, and his masochistic jailbait, Julie Jordan—into dramatic literature. Currently, our musicals are full of moralizing but are unconnected to the moral universe of narrative. Character, context, and plot have been replaced too often by idiosyncrasy and abstraction. What memorable characters have emerged from our recent musical theater? Tevye in *Fiddler on the Roof.* Mrs. Dolly Levi in *Hello, Dolly!* Sweeney Todd in Stephen Sondheim's masterpiece of the same name. That takes musical theater to 1979. Since then, owing largely to the experiments of Sondheim, who was Hammerstein's protégé, the musical has gone down a postmodernist road, which only Sondheim can travel with any sense of occasion. "The form Rodgers and Hammerstein developed tells a story through character and song," Sondheim said in 1978, after he'd begun "to explore the reduction of human character in a situation of its most succinct form," and he added, "It expands the characters, and the characters therefore cause things to happen in the story, and it goes song-scene, song-scene, song-scene." While acknowledging Hammerstein's importance to his own work ("Oscar taught me how to construct a song like a one-act play"), Sondheim deconstructed the Rodgers and Hammerstein musical and gloated over its demise. "Their work appeals mostly to those over fifty, which doesn't bode well for posterity," he said.

But the concept musical that has evolved from the musical play is too often merely a song cycle. Audiences seem to get smaller as the songs get smarter. A smart lyric in the mouth of a stick figure is a theatrical nothing. This mutation has robbed the musical of an essential playfulness and penetration. Atrophy has been declared art, and instead of being a game of show-and-tell the musical has become a song-heavy game of tell-and-tell. Recently, the arrival of George C. Wolfe's *Jelly's Last Jam* opened the musical up to new mythologies and new aesthetics, showing Broadway how to be at once pertinent and populist, kinetic and not camp. And now the success of the reinterpreted *Carousel*, which may arrive on Broadway as early as next fall, has thrown down another challenge to the aridity of current musical storytelling techniques. "I don't think anybody in the nineties could recapture the optimism of the forties," says the director, Nicholas Hytner, whose previous musical megahit was *Miss Saigon*. "But I would hope that this production might give those people writing musicals faith to approach material again in the way Rodgers and Hammerstein did."

Hytner, who has a fine partnership with the designer Bob Crowley, had three years to prepare for the show. Every inch of the National's Lyttelton Theatre is filled with the painstaking boldness of their imaginative collaboration, and it gives the play a hard scenic and intellectual edge. "*Carousel* is one of those shows that have outgrown the theatrical conventions of their first performance," Hytner told me just before the show went into rehearsals, last October. "I think it's the best of the great romantic musicals. I was surprised at how tough and real it was when I read it: Julie Jordan *picks up* Billy Bigelow—you could never do that on the stage in 1945. There's a very interesting tension between the sweetness of the music and the powerful sexual undercurrents of the play. In this *Carousel* the dark, subterranean sexuality, which has traditionally been kept in the background of productions, explodes into the foreground."

The sense of heat is evoked first by the set: a vast Shaker-blue box fronted by a scrim displaying an abstract blue circle with a wispy corona of red, like an eclipsed sun. It's a powerful, authoritative mark, which foreshadows the sense of smoldering passion Hytner manufactures in the first beat of the musical. Instead of opening the show with the famous dance prelude at the fairground, Hytner brings the curtain up on the claustrophobic, shadowy New England textile mill where Julie and her friend Carrie Pipperidge work. The sumptuous sweetness of Rodgers's "Carousel Waltz" plays underneath that image and underscores the frustrated liberty of these wage slaves. The circular emblem on the scrim transmogrifies into the luminous face of a clock: the natural order of the heavens giving way to the unnatural order of the workplace. So when the clock strikes six and the girls are released into the twilight of the New England spring, the thrill of the fairground hubbub and the exhilaration of their momentary freedom gorgeously coalesce with Richard Rodgers's sweeping melody. It's an extraordinary theatrical moment. Suddenly, the empty blue box—a blue that demarcates the sea and sky of this nineteenth-century coastal community—is swarming with carnival life. Bearded tattooed ladies, Uncle Sam on stilts, a house of horrors spin in and out of sight as the carousel is put together before our eyes. And when Billy Bigelow brazenly scoops Julie up and onto an orange wooden horse, with the merry-go-round's neon canopy fanning out above them like the petals of a flower, the stage is brilliantly set for passion.

Traditionally, Billy Bigelow is cast as a macho beefcake baritone who carries his balls in a wheelbarrow (John Raitt, Howard Keel, Gordon MacRae). But Bigelow, like Liliom, is a lethal combination of pugnacity and panic—he's wild rather than bad. His easy sexual charm and braggadocio hide an anger that he can't explain but that he exhibits in sudden, unaccountable abusive outbursts. "I was looking for James Dean with a voice," Hytner says about discovering Michael Hayden, who was just out of Juilliard when he was given the role. "After we'd had two years of auditioning the 'Soliloquy,' maybe two hundred times, Hayden was the only one who made us listen. Until him, only Chippendales with voices were coming in."

From the moment Hayden throws his leg over the rearing head of the carousel horse to face Julie Jordan on her ride, his sexual brazenness is never in doubt. He is a strong, if not a seasoned, performer: a fascinating amalgam of the vulnerable and the volatile. He has the pint-size muscularity of Gene Kelly, for whom the part was conceived, and is a restless, lupine presence. This quality is magnified in the ingenious staging of the terrific duet "If I Loved You." Here

Billy and Julie are positioned on a rolling hill bounded by a picket fence that climbs sharply upward to a Colonial church in the background. Billy can't sit still. The set, like the delicate music underneath the lovers' stage-managed skepticism, pitches them toward each other despite their efforts to stay apart. Hayden doesn't have a pure, crisp, effortless singing voice, like that of Joanna Riding, who plays Julie, and this takes some of the shine off his dazzling attack. In the seven-minute "Soliloquy," at the end of act 1, in which Billy first imagines himself as a father and concludes prophetically by imagining stealing to provide, Hayden acts the song well, but he is sometimes flat in the upper registers, and this keeps "Soliloquy" from clinching its overwhelming emotional moment. "The more he plays the part, the more his voice will open out," Hytner says. Even now, though, the success of *Carousel* is rooted in Hayden's clever connection of violence to self-hatred, which makes Bigelow compelling and redeemable.

By another stroke of good casting karma, Hytner chose Clive Rowe as Mr. Snow, the subject of Carrie Pipperidge's delightful "When I Marry Mr. Snow." Snow, who rises from fisherman to fishing-fleet owner, is everything Billy is not: dutiful, homeloving, hardworking, bursting with bourgeois dreams of glory. In her song Carrie (Janie Dee) confides everything about him to Julie—or *almost* everything. In this production, Mr. Snow is black. When he pops up in the middle of Carrie's reprise about their imminent wedding, singing, "Then I'll kiss her so she'll know," the pause that ensues announces the surprise of both the characters and the audience. On the first day of rehearsal, according to Hytner, Rowe introduced himself to the cast saying, "I'm Clive Rowe. I play Mr. Snow, and that's the first and last time you'll laugh at that gag." Fortunately, the audience laughs with delighted surprise every night, and this bold piece of nontraditional casting adds a considerable dimension of poignance and charm to the show's embodiment of American pluck and luck. "There aren't many black people in Maine now, and there probably weren't then," says Hytner, who chose Rowe for his ringing tenor voice, with a heroic top A, and his warm, roly-poly stage presence. "But they didn't dance classical ballet as a regular form of discourse, either." The casting is shrewdly in keeping with the provocative racial overtones of *Liliom*, where the subplot love interest was a Jew who becomes a successful restaurateur. And the importance of community, which was one of Hammerstein's abiding liberal themes, has its apotheosis in the image of Mr. Snow and his nine variously hued children melding happily into this closely knit New England town at the high-school-graduation finale. "I don't see how you could end a show with 'You'll Never Walk Alone' and be staring at thirty-nine white faces," Hytner says.

Among the many astonishments of this *Carousel* is seeing the National Theatre, which is notorious for over-designing contemporary plays whose action cannot otherwise fill the enormous stage, function at its full technical and scenic capacity in a show that actually demands large, eloquent space. Hytner and Crowley use the stage revolve poetically, fading in and out of scenes with wonderful images, among them sand dunes, sun-blanched clapboard docks, a party of rowboats, and a spectacular streamlined Heaven, complete with a phantasmagoric tapered Shaker box that holds the stars and rises high into the ozone. The spectacle doesn't push the customers back in their seats—it draws them forward in participation. They have to work to make all the show's articulate emotional connections.

Sir Kenneth MacMillan's restaging of Agnes de Mille's pioneering choreography also makes scintillating links with the story. "I actually saw the original London production in 1950, and it's a very serious thing I've been asked to do—to try to equal what Agnes de Mille achieved," Sir Kenneth said to me last fall, before rehearsals. "Nowadays, dance has disappeared from the musical. Jazz dancing features a lot in musicals like *Cats*. You can get away with an awful lot, but there's been nothing to really challenge dancers in a way that would stretch their technique. Perhaps this show will restore the balance." Sir Kenneth, who died a few weeks later, in the middle of rehearsals, certainly created exciting challenges for the accomplished dancers in the prelude and in Louise's ballet (beautifully danced by Bonnie Moore and Stanislav Tchassov). But the choreography of "June Is Bustin' Out All Over" and "Blow High, Blow Low" is more athletic than inspired, and it leaves at least one old pro, Patricia Routledge, who plays Nettie Fowler, seeming not too pleased to have her heft shifted about so vigorously onstage.

Rodgers thought that *Carousel* was his finest score, and when the patina of forties bonhomie is scraped away from the stage pictures, Hammerstein's adaptation and lyrics also look to be among his best. The scenes, which follow Molnár's traffic plan and use great chunks of his dialogue, are complex and well constructed. And the issues of abuse bring the show right up to the minute. Molnár, who in Budapest café society was rumored to be a wife-beater, tried to face the combination of omnipotence, emptiness, and denial in Liliom, who will admit to neither love nor shame. "Who's ashamed?" he says of his abused wife's weeping to the Heavenly Magistrate (Hammerstein changed this to the more benign Heavenly Friend), whom he meets in the next world, after his suicide, and he goes on:

> But I couldn't bear to see her—and that's why I was bad to her. . . . We argued with each other—she said this and I said that—and because she was right I couldn't answer her—and I got mad—and the anger rose up in me—until it reached here [*points to his throat*] and then I beat her.

In Hammerstein's version, Billy Bigelow admits perhaps more shame and forgiveness but no more clarity about the perverse hun-

gers of the human heart. Billy is as fierce in his mistreatment of
Julie as she is accepting of his abuse. She embodies the romantic
ideal of suffering with reward. As she sings in "What's the Use of
Wond'rin'":

> *So, when he wants your kisses*
> *You will give them to the lad,*
> *And anywhere he leads you you will walk.*
> *And any time he needs you,*
> *You'll go runnin' there like mad.*
> *You're his girl and he's your feller—*
> *And all the rest is talk.*

The show, like the song, allows good and bad, joy and pain, to
coexist onstage, as they do in life. "It's possible, dear, fer someone
to hit you—hit you hard—and not hurt at all," Julie says to her teenage daughter, Louise, who is slapped by Billy when he comes down
from Heaven a generation later to set things to rights. Both Molnár
and Hammerstein wimp out on the slap, which is to Louise's hand
when it should be to her face. ("We may gain courage with that later
on," Hytner says.) Hytner prefers to think that Julie's controversial
line about hurt, like all the stories about Billy that Julie tells Louise, is false. But this doesn't answer the questions of balance and of
healing, which Hammerstein's finale tries to stage. "I see plays and
read books that emphasize the seamy side of life, and the frenetic
side, and the tragic side," Hammerstein said. "I don't deny the existence of the tragic and the frenetic. But I say that somebody has to
keep saying that isn't all there is to life. . . . We're very likely to get
thrown off our balance if we have such a preponderance of artists
expressing the 'waste land' philosophy."

From the distance of half a century, the finale seems a far more
mature and resonant ending than the saccharine pieties of the film,

which is what the general public remembers of *Carousel*. Hytner reduces the religiosity by cutting "The Highest Judge of All" and by paying scrupulous attention to psychological detail. With Billy whispering to Julie, as her face lightens, "I love you, Julie. Know that I loved you!" and the Doctor telling Louise and the rest of her graduating class, "Don't be held back by [your parents'] failures. Makes no difference what they did or didn't do," the finale reads as metaphor both for the acceptance of loss and for the need to achieve gratitude for what remains of life after the losses. The moment speaks as powerfully now, in the midst of a pulverizing recession, as it did in 1945, after a world war. As the song says, "Walk on, walk on, with hope in your heart . . ."

The reinterpretation of *Carousel* is a vivid antidote to the boulevard nihilism that has so soured the American musical, which once made legends of hope and now makes legends of collapse. What's important about Hytner's revival is that it doesn't deny the darkness but shows how to fit that darkness into some larger picture, which includes sun, stars, and earth. "I believe in wind and willow trees," Hammerstein once told Sondheim, who didn't. And perhaps, before the musical can evolve beyond Sondheim's blasted joys and lucid doubts, which are now the state of the attenuated art, musical theater has to return somehow to its big-hearted origins. This is why Hytner's approach to *Carousel* is important to ponder. In it, the murderous and the miraculous share the stage. Ambiguity replaces both optimism and anxiety as the prevailing credo, and in the show's updated modernity both nostalgia and deconstruction are kissed good-bye. *Carousel* is not "through-sung." It submits the audience to the differing pleasures of song and prose. Song is an enchantment (in fact, the word "enchantment" has its root in the Latin for "to sing") that is palpable and long-standing. A song makes an audience feel, but prose makes it discriminate. Those are fighting words to the Young Turks in musical theater, but *Carousel* belies the so-called advances of the new musicals. Its well-balanced narrative approaches some deeper sense of life, which is theatrically more satisfying for embracing both misery and mystery. As St. Teresa said, "All the way to heaven is heaven." ▪

—January 18, 1993

PART III
DIRECTORS

"I give a director one week," my father used to say. "After that, I'm on my own." He was a clown, after all, reared in the free-for-all of American burlesque and vaudeville; taking direction was not a regular part of his job description. Long before I knew exactly what a director did, the profession was associated, for me, with danger. In our house, besides "fuck" and "goddamnit," the only two words that could *never* be spoken were "Alan Schneider," the name of the director who oversaw the first, botched out-of-town tryout of the production of Samuel Beckett's *Waiting for Godot* that Dad ultimately premiered on Broadway.

The idea of a stage director—a person exclusively in control of the spectacle and the performance—is a relatively recent one in the history of theater, and it wasn't much welcomed by the actors who mounted plays more or less by themselves until the end of the nineteenth century. In the United States, a director's credit was first listed above the title of a play in 1947, when the phrase "An Elia Kazan Production of" appeared before "A Streetcar Named Desire" on the marquee and the program. Kazan's star billing announced, for the first time in commercial theater, the artistic control of the director, or "overlord," to use Kazan's word.

Much of what is considered great in modern theater is due to the visionary and psychological prowess of these protean intermediaries. Kazan's ability to turn psychology into behavior transformed stage naturalism. "Kazan, Kazan / The miracle man / Call him in / As soon as you can" went a jingle on Broadway. Ironically, the avant-garde directors who conspired to liberate theater from naturalism and to turn the theatrical experience into something kinetic, poetic, and anarchic took much of their inspiration from the knockabout early-twentieth-century low comedy of which my father was one of the supremos. What, for instance, was the model for Antonin Artaud's so-called Theatre of Cruelty? The Marx Brothers. Who did Vsevolod Meyerhold, in his rebellion against Stanislavski and stage naturalism, have in mind when he named the fairground juggler the acting model for a new theater, in which words were "only embellishments on the design of movement"? Charlie Chaplin.

Many of the great productions of the last fifty years have emerged out of the visionary playbooks of these directors. If I shut my eyes, I see again the singular astonishment of the gigantic hippogriffs and dragons in Luca Ronconi's ravishing operatic epic *Orlando Furioso* (1974), swooping above me as I tried to dodge the knights errant and damsels in distress who were being pulled around on carts in Bryant Park, in a space the size of a football field, bounded at each end by proscenium curtains. As the audience groped its way through the labyrinth of language and event, dodging twenty-foot horses and their riders, who were bearing down on them in battle, its members, like the characters in Ariosto's picaresque tale, became a thrilled community of seekers. I had the same exhilarating sense of being awake in a dream during André Gregory's singular *Alice in Wonderland* (1970), for which the audience entered, one at a time, into a claustrophobic room, in which a parachute billowed like a tent, turning the playing area into a circus arena, and where the characters burst through a back wall made of newspaper, emerging literally out of print into a new clownish world of play. Peter Brook's *A Midsummer Night's Dream*, for which the fairies were embodied by luminous insects cast with fishing rods over the heads of the aston-

ished audience, was a minimalist experiment in theatrical presti-
digitation, in which acting and acrobatics conjured up the magic of
Shakespeare's fable.

The weird alchemy of directing is hard to pin down and sometimes even hard for the actors to understand. Talking about Mike
Nichols, Al Pacino told me, "He's the greatest director I've ever
worked with. He simply is. He doesn't say anything, and yet he does.
When I asked him about something, he just sort of body languaged
me." A director is a combination of psychologist, critic, *pater famil-
ias*, and con man. Part of the required skill set is the ability to create
an atmosphere of trust and confidence in the players. The director
has to be strategic. Kazan achieved consensus by stimulation, not
command. "He would send one actor to listen to a particular piece
of jazz, another to read a certain novel, another to see a psychiatrist,
and another he would simply kiss," Arthur Miller recalled. During
rehearsals, Miller added, Kazan "grinned a lot but said as little as
possible. Instinctively, when he had something to tell an actor, he
would huddle with him privately, rather than instruct before the
others, sensing that anything that really penetrates is always to
some degree an embarrassment. . . . A mystery grew up around what
he might be thinking, and this threw the actor back upon himself."
Kazan's trick was to make his ideas seem like the actors' discoveries.
"He let the actors talk themselves into a performance," Miller said.
"He allowed the actors to excite themselves with their own discoveries, which they would carry back to him like children offering some
found object back to a parent."

Ingmar Bergman, another arch manipulator, told me, "To force
an actor to do something is silly. You can convince him, you can
talk to him. Then we have the opening, and he makes what you want
him to make. Then, five days after the opening, he starts to change
a little of what I've said to him. Then suddenly there are ten actors
who start to change a little of what the director has told them. There

is no rhythm anymore. There is no performance anymore. . . . So it's a good idea to have the actor feel good about the blocking, the thinking, the rhythm. Then we will make a common creation."

Casting—that intuitive ability to decode an actor's core, in the service of a role—is a crucial, often unremarked part of the director's legerdemain. Of all the contemporary directors, Nichols and Kazan stand out in their forensic talent for objectifying the personalities of their actors. Nichols famously held out for Dustin Hoffman as the lead in *The Graduate*; Kazan put Marlon Brando up for Stanley Kowalski in *A Streetcar Named Desire*. The actor's "life experience is the director's material," Kazan said. "They can have all the training, all the techniques their teachers have taught them—private moments, improvisations, substitutions, associative memories— but if the precious material is not in them, the director cannot get it out. That is why it's so important for the director to have an intimate acquaintance with the people."

One way or another, the multi-faceted, theater-savvy directors included in *Joy Ride* are all in the business of being sensational. Their authority rests on their sure, deft hands. Nicholas Hytner, the most distinguished artistic director of London's Royal National Theatre in its long, celebrated life, is that rarest of theater leaders: a man who can produce as expertly as he directs. Bergman, until his death in 2007, was the artistic director of Sweden's Royal Dramatic Theatre, in Stockholm, as well as one of the century's great film directors; Susan Stroman, who is one of only about a dozen directors in the world capable of mounting a professional musical, and one of only a few women ever to do so on Broadway, was a dancer and a musical choreographer before she became a director. Nichols, whose full and illustrious career, included being half of the comedy team Nichols and May, lived his first theatrical career in front of an audience. From the outset, with his erudition, eloquence, and piquant wit, he was a purveyor of aplomb. Nichols, who died in 2014, exuded onstage and off an air of startling, irresistible command. When he first made the transition from performing to directing, he debuted with Neil Simon's *Barefoot in the Park* (1963). Robert Redford came to him to complain about being upstaged by Elizabeth Ashley, who was raising her leg when they kissed. " 'I feel like I've been used. I'm embarrassed,' Redford said. And I said, 'Why don't you do it, too?' So he did and it got a huge laugh." "And she stopped?" I asked. Nichols looked down his long nose. "Of course," he said.

13

NICHOLAS HYTNER

If you stand on London's Waterloo Bridge, overlooking the Thames as it carries the dust of the ages toward the sea, you will find yourself in one of the most strategic spots in Great Britain. To the east, behind the refulgent dome of St. Paul's Cathedral, is the City, one of the banking capitals of Europe; to the west are the Houses of Parliament; to the south, at the apex of this triangle of British power, is the Royal National Theatre, where the worlds of spirit, money, and politics come together in play. These days, the Church is embattled, the City is in disrepute, and Parliament is floundering, but the National, under the canny stewardship of Nicholas Hytner, is on a roll unmatched in its nearly fifty-year history.

In his twenty-three-year association with the National, the past nine of them as artistic director, Hytner has been responsible for staging some of the theater's most popular and memorable shows: Rodgers and Hammerstein's *Carousel*; the two-part adaptation of Philip Pullman's *His Dark Materials*; Martin McDonagh's *The Cripple of Inishmaan*; Alan Bennett's *The Madness of George the Third* and *The History Boys*; and, most recently, *One Man, Two Guvnors*, Richard Bean's adaptation of Carlo Goldoni's 1743 commedia dell'arte classic *The Servant of Two Masters* (which opens at New York's Music Box on April 18 and is running concurrently in London's West End). *War Horse*, the international blockbuster, which began at the National, was also developed on Hytner's watch.

His directorial talent has brought renewed luster to the National; his skills as an impresario have also generated a robust balance sheet. (Last year, the theater, which is open for business fifty-two weeks a year, took in an income of more than seventy million pounds, almost half of which came from box-office receipts.) Once upon a time, the National, which is spread over five acres, with three stages—the Olivier, the Lyttelton, and the Cottesloe—was considered "the home counties' theater"; now, thanks in part to National Theatre Live—a program that Hytner developed in 2009 to broadcast the National's performances via satellite to cinemas around the world—the joke no longer applies. In 2011, the National's productions were seen by more than a million and a half people in twenty-two countries and broadcast in venues as far-flung as Bulgaria and Tasmania. Helen Mirren, who starred in Hytner's 2009 staging of Racine's *Phèdre*, which was NT Live's debut, told me, "He will be remembered as overseeing an incredible golden era in British theater."

In Britain, the theater has traditionally been where the public goes to think about its past and debate its future. The formation of the National Theatre, at the Old Vic, near the South Bank, in 1963, institutionalized the symbolic importance of drama by giving it both a building and state funding. (The National's subsidy this year is more than seventeen million pounds.) Laurence Olivier, a statue of whom faces the current buildings, which were designed by Denys Lasdun and Peter Softley and opened for business in the mid-seventies, was the first artistic director. Hytner is the fifth. (The others were Peter Hall, Richard Eyre, and Trevor Nunn.) Presiding over a vast range of writing, performing, designing, musical, and directorial talent, Hytner is a kind of commander in chief of British culture. "The job is about projecting confidence about the British theater," he told me.

Hytner was recruited for the National by Richard Eyre, whose attention he'd caught with productions at Manchester's Royal

Exchange, the English National Opera, and the Royal Shakespeare Company. "He has a face like a mime—Barrault from *Les Enfants du Paradis*—oval face, arching eyebrows, animated, almost over-animated," Eyre wrote in his diary in 1987, after the two first met for lunch. "Flights of ideas and gossip, riffs of enthusiasm, indignation, then repose; latent violence, subverted by a childlike smile. He's prodigiously talented, has a great facility for staging and a great appetite for work." Two years later, Eyre brought Hytner into the fold as an associate director. When Eyre retired, in 1997, Hytner knew the workings of the organization well, but he resisted Eyre's pressure to apply for the job. "I wasn't ready for it," Hytner told me last February, when we met in his small fourth-floor office at the National, overlooking a string of barges moored in the murky Thames. "I really didn't see how to do it differently from the way Richard had done it."

Hytner had earned his fortune directing *Miss Saigon*—Claude-Michel Schönberg and Alain Boublil's loose retelling of *Madame Butterfly*, in which a US marine deserts a Vietnamese woman and their son during the fall of Saigon. (The show ran for a decade on both sides of the Atlantic.) And he was able to indulge in the free-lance director's "life of glorious promiscuity," as Eyre called it. He made Hollywood movies, including *The Crucible* (1996) and *The Object of My Affection* (1998), though he now claims to be proud only of his film adaptation of Alan Bennett's *The Madness of George the Third* (1994). "I don't instinctively think through the camera," Hytner said. He flirted with opera, but, despite some success, he felt that his work became too "timid" and was an "aesthetic mistake." He told me, "My premises were wrong. I tried to find the kind of circumstances where I could achieve in the rehearsal room an illusion of spontaneity—a form of spontaneity which is not useful and not expressive to opera singers trying to get on with the business of delivering an opera." By the time the National job came up again, in 2001, Hytner had "been around the block," as Eyre put it, and the artistic directorship of the National offered him a unique opportunity to become his own producer: if he wanted to stage a show, he had only himself to ask.

Hytner's big idea from the outset was to democratize the National. At his first press conference, he made, by his own admission, a rookie mistake. "I am not against older folk coming here and having a good time," he said, "but the age of the audience will come down when we reflect something other than the homogeneous concerns of a white, middle-aged, middle-class audience." Hytner told me, "It was very callow . . . a ridiculous thing to say. I've learned that there are scores of audiences." Nonetheless, in his first season, determined "to charge less for a more demanding repertoire," Hytner jump-started the slumping box office at the Olivier Theatre—the National's largest stage—by selling two-thirds of the seats at ten pounds and the rest at twenty-five. (Travelex agreed to underwrite the scheme.) At a stroke, the National opened its doors to a whole new public.

Eyre had capitalized on American talent, mounting an early production of Tony Kushner's *Angels in America* and the premiere of Wallace Shawn's *The Designated Mourner*, as well as important revivals of Tennessee Williams's great plays. Hytner made a counterintuitive shift away from the classic (and profitable) Broadway musicals, which he felt "had all been done" and were "in danger of defining this place." (*Guys and Dolls*, *A Little Night Music*, *South Pacific*, and his own staging of *Carousel* had been huge hits.) Instead, he debuted Richard Thomas and Stewart Lee's campy and controversial 2003 musical *Jerry Springer: The Opera*, and threw the stage doors open to a new, "scrappy, pugnacious, energetic, and ambitious" generation of British playwrights, directors, and performance groups. Since Hytner took over, more than thirty new writers (Lee Hall, Mike Bartlett, Lucy Prebble, Conor McPherson, and Enda Walsh among them) have seen their works performed at the National. In his first season, he premiered Kwame Kwei-Armah's *Elmina's Kitchen*, a play about drugs and crime in London's West

Indian community, which won its author the Evening Standard Award for Most Promising Playwright. Hytner was "slightly sticking his fingers up to the demographic that actually comes to the National," Kwei-Armah, who has now had three plays produced at the National, told me.

On a bright morning in February, Hytner sat down with Simon Russell Beale, one of the nation's great Shakespearean actors, and the designer Tim Hatley to discuss the 2013 season and how he planned to approach *Timon of Athens*—the story of a wealthy Athenian who gives away all his money and is then refused help by his former "friends." Retreating to the wilderness, Timon discovers hidden treasure, but instead of returning to Athens to rebuild his life there he hangs himself.

Lean, soft-spoken, and unassuming, Hytner has the crisp mien of a banker. He rose to greet his colleagues as they entered, then settled back in his chair. A neatly printed copy of his *Timon* adaptation was in his lap. The play, one of the least popular of Shakespeare's dramas, was, he said, a fable, "in tone and structure unlike anything else by Shakespeare." He explained, "The objective of doing the play is to find a context where there's genuine emotional life in Timon," who is usually thought to be cold and cynical. "It's a savage play, but I think we can get everybody with him, despite the fact that he's plainly a fool in that first half. There is an emotional void there, which he can fill only by buying people's friendships. I think it's good to start from there, rather than from something more venal or corrupt. You can empathize with a fool who can only imagine human relations in terms of what he is able materially to give. And he's involved in a world which is completely, bizarrely, startlingly like the world we live in."

"The bonus-driven culture," Russell Beale, slumped on the sofa, said.

"The culture where nobody is worth anything, except in terms of what they are able to display," Hytner said. "The unforgiving world of the super-rich. I think the big point is that you can get an audience to follow him through, if, when he turns against that world, he is expressing on our behalf a kind of existential dismay at the world we know we're part of."

"I'm sure there's a part of Timon that knows he can't buy love," Russell Beale said. "So that when they finally say, 'No, we're not gonna help you out,' it's an of-course moment. All the cynics in Shakespeare do that. They all have a high expectation of what the world should be like. A Romantic expectation, which is then broken."

"Well, that's Hamlet, isn't it?" Hytner said. "It's 'Timon of *Athens*.' Of course, it's Athens. But in some way it's an abstraction of the super-rich corner of every city. It plays upon all the contemporary intimations of apocalypse. There is some sense that the whole thing can be brought crashing down."

Hytner handed Russell Beale and Hatley his revised script of the play. In order to up the emotional ante, Timon's loyal servant, Flavius, had been turned into a woman, Flavia. Otherwise, Hytner explained, "my strategy has been to take stuff away, rather than add. This character Alcibiades—who is, they reckon, written almost entirely by Middleton—has a long scene in the first half, a completely incomprehensible scene. It makes no dramatic sense whatsoever. So that went. I've added probably a total of twelve lines in three places, three insertions of about four lines each, where the rich people and the senators all worry about—this is all from *Coriolanus*—what's going on in the streets. What I'm wanting to do is create from the very beginning the sense that the place is a tinderbox; the street is full of people who are on the point of eruption."

Turning to ideas about the set, Russell Beale said of the wilderness, "I imagined a sort of endless expanse of something. I wasn't sure whether it was water. It felt very sort of flat and barren and stark. That's what came into my head. Exposed. Naked, almost."

"I love this idea of cleansing," Hatley noted.

Speaking of the city scenes, Hytner said, "I think it should be like London, Athens, or New York, where it's breathtaking but around the corner, one block away, there's people on the streets. I'd love to do that." He added, of the play, "It doesn't vibrate in its text. It starts to vibrate only when Timon gets angry, in the second half. That's when you hear Shakespeare. So I think one of the things we've got to do is give it some visual music."

Perhaps the best of many examples of Hytner's visual music was his majestic, radical staging of *Carousel*, which premiered at the National in 1992 and, in 1994, transferred to New York, where it won five Tony Awards. The production, which Eyre remembers as "pure bravura," examined the dark, subterranean sexuality that is traditionally kept in the background of American versions. Instead of opening the show with the famous dance prelude at the fairground, Hytner brought the curtain up on the claustrophobic, shadowy New England textile mill where Julie Jordan and her friend Carrie Pipperidge work. The sumptuous sweetness of Richard Rodgers's "Carousel Waltz," playing softly, underscored the frustration and constriction of the factory girls. A luminous clock face appeared on the scrim, and when the clock struck six and the girls were released into the spring twilight the exhilaration of their temporary freedom coalesced gorgeously with Rodgers's sweeping melody. It was an extraordinary theatrical moment, which Hytner then topped by having the carousel materialize gradually, while carnival life swarmed around a revolving stage. As the set designer, Bob Crowley, recalled, "Bit by bit, one by one, these little horses are being wheeled in on their own plinths, going up and down, then suddenly all the horses are there. This umbrella hit the ground and opened up." By the time Billy Bigelow brazenly scooped Julie up onto a wooden horse, with the carousel's neon canopy fanning out above them like the petals of a flower, Hytner had set the stage for passion.

"Nick's wonderfully objective about sexual attraction," the playwright Richard Bean told me. "He's interested in it whether it's man-woman, man-man, woman-woman. He just understands it." (Hytner's 2000 production of Tennessee Williams's *Orpheus Descending*, with Helen Mirren and Stuart Townsend, remains one of the best and steamiest examinations of desire I've ever seen.) Hytner appreciates the poetry of slapstick, as well as sensuality. A scene in *One Man, Two Guvnors*, in which an octogenarian waiter teeters at the top of a staircase and then plummets down it, got the longest sustained laugh I've heard in forty years of theatergoing.

As flamboyant as Hytner's stagings often are, the man himself can be so self-effacing that he almost disappears. "He's not a person who drives into a room and takes over," Mirren said. "At his own parties, it's quite hard to find him." His friends and colleagues all speak of his unnerving habit of lapsing into silence, "of not returning the ball," as Eyre described this "conversational tic." His small talk is "not reliable," according to Nick Starr, the National's executive director. Once, Starr said, Hytner was sitting in his office, "and we lapsed into silence for probably quite some time. The playwright David Edgar walked past, then came back and put his head in the door: 'What's happened?' 'Nothing.' 'The two of you were just sitting there in complete silence. It looked as if something awful had happened.'"

Before Hytner assumed command at the National, in 2003, he was introduced to the company by its departing sachem, Trevor Nunn. Frances de la Tour, one of the repertory's stars, raised her hand. "As an actress in the company, I just want to welcome Nicholas Hytner. I'm sorry I don't know who you are, but welcome," she said, thus beginning an enduring friendship. Hytner, who is gay and single, now refers to de la Tour as his wife. (When he was knighted, in 2010, de la Tour told him, "I refuse to be called Lady Hytner." He said, "No, no, you will always have the honor of being Mrs. Hytner.")

Hytner's tendency to disappear has its origins in his childhood, when he spent much of his time alone in his third-floor bedroom, in Didsbury, a suburban enclave of Manchester, hiding from the "domestic psychodrama" of his parents' marriage. His father, Benet, was a bookish, Cambridge-educated barrister; his mother, Joyce, who was awarded an OBE for her fund-raising services to the arts in 2004, was eighteen when she married, twenty when Hytner was born, and "restless and frustrated, understandably." To young Hytner, the turmoil of his parents' marriage "made no sense," he said. He added, "Not because it was particularly out of the ordinary— cast of three, ran almost as long as *Cats*—but because it was barely acknowledged. On the contrary, we were a model of contentment and stability." (His parents divorced in 1980, and remarried in 2003.)

Hytner retreated from what he calls "the unpredictable, uncontrollable world" of his home life to a realm of his own invention. He covered the walls of his room with images of Shakespearean characters, ordered through the *Times*, and, in a toy theater, ran a rotating repertory, in which Victorian pantomime alternated with a miniature version of Olivier's *Hamlet*, performed by tiny cutouts of Olivier, Jean Simmons, and Stanley Holloway. "I remember very vividly fantasizing about having a troupe of flesh-and-blood Lilliputian actors," he said. "So I probably stumbled onto the idea of directing plays, even running a theater, earlier than I like to think. It occurs to me that forty-odd years ago I was pushing Olivier around a toy theater on a wire, and now I have his job."

Hytner is the eldest of four children. "It took me into adulthood to connect properly with my siblings," he told me. "I'd withdrawn that much." But his love of classical music began when he was eight, and, on Sunday evenings, he joined his parents at the Hallé Orchestra subscription series. For his birthday every year, he was taken to Stratford-upon-Avon, where he saw three plays in a weekend. He played the flute and sang in the Manchester Grammar School Boys

Choir, and found a way, through the arts, "to plunge in, to understand what was really going on in the world," though he "tiptoed
around the small domestic stuff." (To this day, Hytner does not like
to stage plays about family situations; he has never directed Pinter
or Chekhov and has mostly stayed away from twentieth-century naturalism. "I don't respond to, and certainly would not like to direct,
plays which involve an interior journey only," he told me.)

Hytner had early dreams of becoming an actor, but, after his first
term at Cambridge, he had more or less figured out that directing
would be his path into theater. He learned his craft "on the hoof,"
through apprenticeships at the English National Opera and at Manchester's Royal Exchange. "If you can't act, and you can't write, it's
the next best thing," he said. "It gives you the impression of first-
degree creativity." It also gave Hytner an opportunity to explore and
to control the dynamics that he had avoided as a child. "What I do
now, in part," he told me, "is to help create (if only temporarily) sta-
ble families, which can play happily with the most outlandish forms
of emotional anarchy, all the too-hot-to-handle stuff. In the rehearsal
room and in the theater, there is nothing but relish for every kind of
craziness, every grief, every danger, every cruelty, every joy." In this
context, he is unafraid of failure. "I barely ever feel defeated in the
theater," he said. "There is no disaster that doesn't seem survivable.
I have almost total faith in the capacity of the group to find a way
through."

At the National, Hytner's most conspicuous influence has been,
perhaps, on the playwright Alan Bennett, with whom he has collaborated on six plays. In the course of their partnership, Bennett has
evolved from a successful sketch writer and performer to one of the
country's most popular theatrical storytellers. "Just write it, and
I'll make it work," Hytner told Bennett when they began working
together, in 1990, on an adaptation of *The Wind in the Willows*. And

so it has proved. "He's got a magic that can transform things," Bennett told me. "And, if that's not art, I don't know what is."

According to Hytner, the early drafts of a Bennett play have "a huge amount of material looking for a nudge." Bennett has always written piquant dialogue, but he struggles with structure and spectacle. "The plays all require the exercise of stagecraft, which Alan very happily turns over to me, because he claims he has no capacity for it," Hytner said. His nudging has pushed Bennett toward stronger story lines, greater depth, and more scenic surprise to shore up his wry, bittersweet voice. "I feel entirely at home with Alan's sensibility and sense of humor," Hytner said. "A lot of the time, he's writing about people who have, if you like, shut themselves in a room. It's how you open the door. He makes theater out of that effort."

Bennett describes his relationship with Hytner as "schoolmasterly"—"in the sense that I want to please him." He added, "It's not that I want the play approved. I just want *him* to approve." Bennett usually slips a first draft through Hytner's letter box—he lives a few leafy streets away from Bennett, in Primrose Hill. Hytner returns the script with notes scribbled in the margins, then follows up with more forensic suggestions. "I don't fight," Hytner said of his method. "There's no point getting Alan to do what he doesn't want to or can't do. I've always found a good idea is to speak a little and then beat a retreat. I think a director can completely ruin a new play by pushing too hard for it to be something it's not."

In the case of *One Man, Two Guvnors*, however, Hytner made a hit play by imposing his desires. While looking for a vehicle for the low-comic spark of James Corden, who had acted in *The History Boys* and co-created the popular British TV series *Gavin and Stacey*, Hytner thought of Goldoni's *The Servant of Two Masters*, in which he had once performed in a school production. Hytner considers re-creations of commedia dell'arte "precious." But, with Corden, he saw a chance to turn Goldoni's freewheeling style into something contemporary and wild, a comic counterbalance to some of the National's more weighty offerings. "It's what our theater has always done," he said. "King Lear rubbed shoulders with the clowns here on the South Bank four hundred years ago." To adapt the play, he approached Richard Bean, a former standup comic whose irreverent take on immigration, *England People Very Nice*, Hytner had directed in 2009. In Bean's makeover, which the *Guardian* called "one of the funniest productions in the National's history," eighteenth-century Venice became Brighton in 1963, and the set pieces of commedia dell'arte—*lazzi*—became pantomime shtick. The show, which has played to nearly 100 percent capacity since it opened, in 2011, exudes the noisy vulgarity of a Brighton-pier entertainment.

In early March, I went with Hytner to a rehearsal of *One Man, Two Guvnors*, which was about to begin its second run in the West End. On the way, Hytner moved as he thinks—at speed—breezing out of his office, past his administrative staff at their desks, through a warren of poster-lined hallways, down in an elevator, and into Rehearsal Room 1, where the cast was waiting for him. With his blue jeans and boxy blue checked shirt, Hytner could have been mistaken for a stagehand until he called the actors onto the floor. Then he entered a whole new zone of concentration. First, he set to work fine-tuning the comic delivery of the actor Owain Arthur, a sweet-faced Welshman, who plays a failed skiffle player named Francis. In act 2, Francis sits at a pub, enjoying a cigarette and confiding his feelings to the audience:

> So I've eaten. Now, after a lovely big meal there's a couple of things I just can't resist doing. One is having a little smoke— *drags on cigarette. Then he lifts a buttock and farts*—And that's the other. Beautiful. Now, some of you out there, who understand your commedia dell'arte, you hummus eaters, might now be asking yourselves, "If the Harlequin"—that's me—"has now eaten

what will be his motivation in the second act?" Has anyone here said that? No. Good. Nice to know we don't have any dicks in tonight.

"You know a little too much at this moment," Hytner cut in. "You've got to play that straighter. I think the relationship you've got to have with the audience all the way through is—they're all like you, all chancers. They're your mates, not your audience."

Arthur made the adjustment, and Hytner stepped away from his chair against the back wall to watch Jodi Prenger, as the cheeky, high-heeled Dolly, encounter Francis and his lecherous glances. "At your service, gorgeous," Francis says to her. Dolly, too, takes the audience into her confidence:

> Calling a woman "gorgeous" is patronizing, and Chauvinist, obviously, but since I fancy him rotten, and I haven't had a proper sorting out for a while, I'll forgive him. (*To Francis*) You've got honest eyes.

"Could you make that mean something much more obscene?" Hytner said. Prenger repeated her lines, and his scrutiny was almost palpable. Arms across his chest, he was speaking Dolly's lines to himself. Prenger addressed the audience again:

> I've done worse. We've all done worse, haven't we, girls? We've all woken up "the morning after the night before," taken one sorry look at the state of the bloke lying next to us, and we've all leapt out of bed, sat down and written to our MPs demanding that tequila should be a controlled drug.

Hytner interrupted Prenger, then fell silent for about twenty seconds as the actors waited on his words. He seemed to be fast-forwarding, in his mind's eye, to see how Prenger's choices would play later in the scene. "I'll buy that," he said, finally. "You've got to think right through to the end of it. Don't pause as much as you are after 'state of the bloke lying next to us.' Don't speed it up—just know that where you are heading is right through to the MPs." He added, "You did that beautifully."

Later, Francis turns to the audience and asks for suggestions of a good place to take a girl on a first date, a trope that leads to audience participation, which, since it's improvised, can eat up a lot of stage time, an important issue in any Hytner production. "He's a man who gets bored incredibly quickly," Bean told me. When skating on thin ice, Hytner's impulse is always for speed. If the audience's answers were ordinary, he told Arthur, "my hunch is you should cut your losses. One in four times you get lucky, otherwise just play on. Don't feel under pressure to milk this one. You can be confident about moving on, confident by being really definite in your response. 'I've got a play to do here.' "

After an hour, Hytner gave a little bow to the cast. "Thank you, everyone," he said. "I'll see you all next week. I'm not gonna have much to do." Then, as quickly and quietly as he'd entered, he was gone.

Back at his office, Hytner reflected on the highlights of his career. Of all his moments in the theater, the one that still speaks most powerfully to him is the finale of his 2007 staging of *Much Ado about Nothing*, which starred Simon Russell Beale and Zoë Wanamaker as the quarrelling Benedick and Beatrice. "They dance, as required," Hytner said. "I pulled Beatrice and Benedick out of the dance. As the show is ending, everybody else is partying, and they've found a quiet corner. Once they find each other, they've got so much to talk about. That's all they're going to do for the rest of their lives: talk *to* each other, not *at* each other. The world is there for them. They can leave it and join it at will. Contentment is in being in quiet retreat."

Hytner paused, and gazed across the river toward the clock on the Savoy Hotel. "It's what I want," he said.

In 2010, at Hytner's initiative, the National launched the National Theatre Future Project, a seventy-million-pound plan to transform and refurbish the buildings. Below Hytner's balcony, work on the expansion was noisily under way. The project is expected to be completed in 2014; and then, Hytner told me, he planned to move on. "I'd like to have one more chance at a life," he said.

Meanwhile, he was running late. On his desk, the schedule for the rest of his day was laid out in front of him: a script meeting; a performance of a play for primary-school children; a meeting with a technical director about problems with the Olivier's lighting grid; a model showing for the newest production in the Cottesloe; an interview with the Spanish newspaper *El Pais*; a briefing on a fund-raiser later in the week; a preview of the new show at the Lyttelton. It was a schedule, I suggested, that could rival the Queen's.

As it turned out, the Queen, who not long ago went to see *War Horse* at the New London Theatre, where it transferred after its sold-out National run, had been in touch with Hytner's office to make Joey, the brilliant three-man puppet horse and star of the show, an offer he couldn't refuse. The Queen had first made Joey's acquaintance last summer, when he put in a surprise appearance at Queen Victoria's stables at Windsor Palace, where she was inspecting the guns of the King's Troop Royal Horse Artillery. The Queen was thrilled. She insisted on looking at Joey's hooves, and asked for one of the King's Troop to ride him. So Joey trotted around the stables with a soldier on his back. Now Her Majesty was requesting Joey's company for a private screening of Steven Spielberg's film version of *War Horse* at Windsor Palace this spring. The invitation was later rescinded when the event was changed, but the offer itself was news, a victory for the power of the dramatic imagination. The idea of Joey and the Queen watching the movie together gave the old question about the relation between life and art new meaning. Hytner's blue eyes fairly sparkled at the prospect. "It's delicious," he said. "She's taken a real shine to him." ∎

—April 23, 2012

The History Boys

"How do I define history?" asks one of the grammar-school high-fliers cramming for their Oxbridge exams in Alan Bennett's *The History Boys* (London's National Theatre production, now at the Broadhurst, under the superb direction of Nicholas Hytner). "It's just one fucking thing after another." The joke is typical of Bennett's mischievous wit. Bennett began his adult life as a medieval historian at Oxford; by the age of twenty-seven, he was making his own history. As one of the quartet of Merry-Andrews whose revue *Beyond the Fringe* (1961) changed the shape of postwar British comedy— and remains one of the few comic imports to survive the transplant to Broadway—Bennett was an owlish bundle of neurotic tics, hiding his wicked tongue behind a show of tentativeness. Nowadays, the clown in Bennett contends with the codger, and *The History Boys* brings him back to Broadway in the fullness of his talent and his command. At seventy-one, he is not only one of Britain's most popular storytellers onstage and onscreen; he is the iconic voice of its comic disenchantment, charting the spiritual attrition of the country's concessions to the marketplace and to modernism. Bennett, a butcher's son from Leeds, is a kind of laureate of loss and littleness. "It's a little life," his mother used to say, a line that is echoed in *The History Boys* by the rambunctious general-studies teacher Hector (Richard Griffiths, in a performance as huge as his girth), whose love of knowledge for its own sake is forced to take a back seat to the glib methods of another teacher, Irwin (Stephen Campbell Moore), who is hired to get exam results. At one point, Hector, after watching his workhorses being put through their paces for the Oxbridge interviews, invokes the poet Frances Cornford's words to describe them. "Magnificently unprepared / For the long littleness of life," he says.

In Bob Crowley's suggestively minimal classroom, with posters for *Casablanca*, *Citizen Kane*, and *La Dolce Vita* pinned up on the walls, these gleeful grinds who have done well on their A-levels—"those longed-for emblems of your conformity," as Hector calls them—are in search of a passport to the good life; Hector, with his erudite badinage, entices them instead to a life of the mind. His classroom is a sort of ravishing intellectual revue: the students are called upon to recite poetry, to improvise scenes using the subjunctive and conditional forms of French verbs, to act out classic movie scenes, even to sing popular songs. At least three times during the evening, Scripps (Jamie Parker) sits at the piano and accompanies Posner (the compelling Samuel Barnett), as he sings, among other things, a fetching rendition of "Bewitched, Bothered, and Bewildered."

Posner, who has unrequited feelings for the cocky class Lothario, Dakin (Dominic Cooper), gives the Lorenz Hart lyrics an incidentally appropriate reading, as he intones, "I'll sing to him / Each spring to him / And worship the trousers that cling to him." Posner is Bennett's surrogate. ("Watching Sam Barnett playing the part, I wince to hear my own voice at sixteen," he writes in his introduction to the play.) Posner's sexual confusion is also a simulacrum of Bennett's adolescent emotional life. "There can be few of us, after all, who don't feel that we were to some extent behind the door when sex was handed out," Bennett writes in his new prose collection, *Untold Stories*. Bennett negotiates the choppy waters of sexual solitude with masterly elegance. As Hector lectures Posner about compound adjectives in the poetry of Thomas Hardy—the trope of adding "un" to a noun or a verb—the explanation goes beyond the poetic to a poignant immanence of the personal. "Un-kissed. Un-rejoicing. Un-confessed. Un-embraced," Hector offers. Hector's fondling of his students, who take turns riding pillion on his motorcycle, is depicted in the same spirit of comic tolerance with which Bennett famously parried an inquiry into his own sexuality: "To enquire if I was homosexual was like asking someone who had just crawled across the Sahara Desert whether they preferred Malvern or Perrier water," he said.

Into the mix, Bennett adds the blustering vainglorious Headmaster (the expert Clive Merrison) and the no-nonsense Mrs. Lintott (Frances de la Tour), Hector's history-teaching cohort. With her hangdog look and her laconic sourness, de la Tour transforms a small part into a droll star turn. Midway through the play, after most of the other characters have confided their private thoughts to the audience, she turns to us and says, "I have not hitherto been allotted an inner voice, my role a patient and not unamused sufferance of the predilections and preoccupations of men. They kick their particular stone along the street and I watch."

In addition to these well-told stories of the schoolroom, Bennett provides a larger and more subversive critique of the nature of British public discourse—or, more specifically, of the expertise in bluffing that he sees, correctly, as a legacy of an Oxbridge education. In Bennett's eyes, the Oxbridge system emphasizes presentation, rather than penetration, the "free-floating state of cleverness," as one British journalist put it. The Socratic dialogue is replaced with the technique of paradox, and eloquence trumps relevance. Irwin's strategy is about winning, not learning—and he succeeds all too well. "Paradox works well and mists up the windows," he says. We are in the realm of "truthiness" here; or, as a student called Rudge bluntly puts it, "They keep telling us you have to lie." In the elegiac last moment of the play, Hector reminds the class that his inspired brand of teaching was really just the old party trick of Pass the Parcel. "Take it, feel it, and pass it on," he says. "Pass it on, boys. That's the game I wanted you to learn. Pass it on." *The History Boys* does just that: it sensationally passes on Bennett's sly civility. ◾

—May 1, 2006

14

INGMAR BERGMAN

In *The Hour of the Wolf*, a film that is probably the darkest of Ingmar Bergman's journeys into his shadowy interior, the protagonist, an artist beset by night sweats, is fishing off a craggy promontory on an island where he has come to live. A pesky young boy materializes and by degrees invades the artist's tranquillity. They grapple; the boy scrambles onto the artist's back, tearing at his neck and trying to devour him. The artist smashes the boy against the cliff, then beats his head in with a rock, and finally, with a curious gentleness, lowers the vanquished demon of childhood into the sea. The scene, in its choreographed ferocity, is an allegory for Bergman's lifelong struggle to fend off the ghosts of his past, which he is determined to defeat, but with reverence.

The flat, windswept island in *The Hour of the Wolf* (1968) recalls Fårö, in the Baltic Sea, where Bergman, now eighty, spends most of his time. His single-story gray-brown house, which he built in 1966 for himself and Liv Ullmann, who was then his partner, sits unobtrusively on the island's isolated southeastern edge, hidden by a forest of scrub pines and overlooking shale beaches and the empty sea. The island—a two-hour hop by plane and ferry from Stockholm, where Bergman now ventures only in order to work—also provides the brooding setting for *The Passion of Anna* (1969), and its extremes match Bergman's roiling temperament. "I have such difficulty calming down—my stomach, my head, reality, everything. That is the reason I live in Fårö," he said this March, in Stockholm. "I have a feeling of complete balance. The sea, the house, the loneliness, the light. Everything is clearer. Much more precise. I have the feeling that I am living on a limit, and I'm crossing that limit sometimes." We were sitting in his small, soundproofed office at the Royal Dramatic Theatre, known as the Dramaten, where he was re-rehearsing Per Olov Enquist's *The Image Makers* for its American debut. The play, which will appear at the Brooklyn Academy of Music next week, is a fictional account of the first screening of Victor Sjöström's silent film *The Phantom Carriage*, for the Nobel Prize–winning Swedish novelist Selma Lagerlöf; her book about her alcoholic but idealized father was the basis for Sjöström's screenplay.

Bergman, who watches *The Phantom Carriage* once a year on Fårö, and who cast Sjöström memorably as the aging professor in *Wild Strawberries* (1957), also revisits his family in his work, but his method is the opposite of Lagerlöf's idealization. His films, which amount to a singular courageous act of emotional autobiography, explore ancient humiliations; his gift lies in his access to dark feelings and in his ability to call them out into the open, where they can be seen and acknowledged and finally understood. And though most of the Western world knows Bergman only as a filmmaker, his work in the theater—from Shakespeare to Mishima—is of similar stature. With Enquist's play about Sjöström and Lagerlöf he dramatizes the struggle of all artists to impose their particular spirit on their material: in the act of reimagining their lives they somehow preserve and redeem both the inadequate parent and the memory of pain. This aesthetic transformation—the play calls it "resurrection"—is a game in which Bergman is without peer. While most people spend a lifetime building up defenses against the hurts of childhood, Bergman's defense is to embrace them. "I have always had the ability to attach my demons to my chariot," he writes in his 1990 book, *Images: My Life in Film*. "And they have been forced to make themselves useful. At the same time they have still managed to keep on tormenting and embarrassing me in my private life."

———

When Bergman and I had last met, in 1996, during the opening in Stockholm of *The Bacchae*, Bergman compared his theater work to carpentry, and said he was eager to lay down his tools. He thought the play would be his farewell to the theater. (He had bid adieu to filmmaking more than ten years earlier, after his Academy Award–winning *Fanny and Alexander*.) He was looking forward to Fårö's solitude. He does not like noise—"Quiet" signs are posted around the Dramaten when he's at work. He does not like lateness: he positions himself outside the rehearsal hall at 10:00 each morning in case the cast wants to fraternize, and rehearsals begin promptly at 10:30; lunch is at 12:45; work finishes at 3:30. He does not like meeting new people or people in large groups. He does not like surprises of any kind. "When I'm in Stockholm, I'm longing every day for that island—for the sea, for nature," he told me. "To listen to music. To write. To write without deadlines. When he was my age, my father—he was a clergyman—relearned Hebrew with a friend. They read Hebrew and wrote to each other in Hebrew. There are so many books I want to read. Difficult books. That's what I intend to do and what I'm longing for."

Bergman's retirement didn't last. "If I don't create, I don't exist," he told the Swedish press in 1976, when charges of tax fraud (from which he was completely exonerated in 1979) sent him into voluntary exile in Germany, where he stayed for several years. Since he was young, Bergman says, he has "created reality around me the way I wanted." He began as a boy, with puppets and magic-lantern shows, and has since contrived to be in rehearsal almost all his life. "Through my playing, I want to master my anxiety, relieve tension, and triumph over my deterioration," he writes in *Images*. "I want to depict, finally, the joy that I carry within me in spite of everything, and which I so seldom and so feebly have given attention to in my work."

Indeed, when we think of Bergman's films, joy is not the first word that comes to mind: for most viewers, they call up an atmosphere of agitation, a tense balance between scrutiny and unknowing, a sense of the silence that rustles underneath personality. Yet through this mist of unhappiness another kind of joy is discernible—in the audacity of Bergman's camera, in the vigor of his argument against evasions of all kinds, and in the ruthless (and sometimes humorous) penetration into the contradictory drives of human nature. Before Bergman, film was mostly about what could be seen and depicted in the external world. Very little of important cinema was psychological: it was wars, chases, situation comedy. Bergman was the first filmmaker to build a whole oeuvre through the exploration of the internal world—to make visible the invisible drama of the self. For future generations of filmmakers, he was a kind of bushwhacker, who found a way of embracing the Freudian legacy in cinematic terms and cut a path deep into the psyche—"the soul's battlefield," as Woody Allen calls Bergman's cinematic terrain.

In a career of nearly sixty years, Bergman has written some sixty films, most of which he directed; by the end of this year, he will have added another, *Faithless*—an account of his involvement in a love triangle, which Liv Ullmann is to direct. He has also mounted more than seventy plays; next February he will stage a new production of August Strindberg's *Ghost Sonata* at the Dramaten. When Bergman is in Stockholm, he lives in an apartment built on the spot where Strindberg lived, and the connection is more than spiritual: as Sweden's most expert storyteller, Bergman is Strindberg's heir. And anyone wishing to map the geography of Bergman's genius will find clues in the streets of Stockholm, where he grew up.

The Hedveg Eleanora Church is a high-domed ocher building on the fashionable east side of the city, where Bergman's father, Erik, served as minister for two decades, beginning in the mid-thirties, when Bergman was a teenager. The church stands just two blocks north of the Dramaten, where Bergman would eventually set up a kind of alternative ministry—first as the artistic director, for a few years in the mid-sixties, and later as a staff director and resident genius. It's startling that the church of Bergman's youth and the theater of his adulthood should be so close together: a metaphor for the twinned inconsolability and solace with which his rebellious work always contends. Hedveg Eleanora is austere, monumental, and calm in the watery northern daylight; the Dramaten is an Art Nouveau promise of sumptuous pleasure: warm, noisy, bustling, bright.

But it was in Hedveg Eleanora that Bergman got his first extended lesson in masquerade. In the canopied gilt Baroque pulpit, which is thirty feet high and looms above the teal pews, Pastor Bergman, who was tall and handsome, cut an imposing figure; the young Bergman "never dared go to sleep when my father was preaching." "It was some sort of theater," he recalls. "Fascinating and boring. The room had a magic, you know. It was always sold out. My father was a marvellous actor." Erik's performance of a righteous, receptive minister in public was entirely at odds with what the young Bergman saw at home—a "lamentable terrified wretch" full of "compressed hatred." The contradiction was the basis of Bergman's confounding sense of insecurity. "Offstage he was nervous, irritable, and depressive," Bergman writes of his father in his autobiography, *The Magic Lantern*. "He worried about being inadequate, he agonized over his public appearances, kept writing and rewriting his sermons." Bergman adds, "He was always fretting and given to violent outbursts."

In the limestone solemnity of the church, Bergman senior spoke of good and evil and the promise of eternal life; his son was fascinated by something else. "Death was always present, because under the floor in the church there were graves," Bergman says. "I thought of the skeletons and the dead. Always in contact with the dead." It was not just the actual dead but the emotionally dead parts of his parents which Bergman was obsessed with. "You can't escape me," the ghost of the humorless, punitive Bishop says to his stepson Alexander, tripping the boy on his face at the end of *Fanny and Alexander* (1982). And Bergman never could escape. At nineteen, he had a sensational falling-out with his father. "The mountain of aggressions between us was so heavy and so terrible, I had to go my own way," he says. "I said to my father, 'If you hit me, I'll hit you.' He did, and I did it. I can still remember his face." The estrangement lasted some thirty years. "I look at him and think I ought to forget, but I don't forget," Bergman writes of his father in the autobiographical novel *Sunday's Children*. "No, in fact, that's not true. I *wish* I could forget him." After Bergman's mother, Karin, died, in 1966, Bergman, then forty-eight, began visiting his eighty-three-year-old father every Saturday at four o'clock. "It was good to sit there with him," Bergman says. "We didn't talk about complicated things or the past. I think it was some sort of therapy for us both. When he died, we were friends."

Ingmar Bergman was interested not in saving souls but in baring them. Pastor Bergman invoked the Holy Spirit; his son made a spectacle of spirit and of his own version of the mysteries—what he called "the administration of the unspeakable." In his films and stage productions, Bergman always leaves room for the unknown, the intuitive, the invisible; he may have lost his faith in God but not his sense of the miraculous. He likes to recall a time when he and his father went to church, and the pastor, who was sick that day, told his parishioners that there would be no Communion. Erik Bergman went back to the sacristy, reemerged in vestments, and assisted the pastor by offering Communion. Bergman used the moment as the ending of *Winter Light* (1963); it also provided him with, as he writes, "the codification of a rule I have always followed and was to follow from then on: *irrespective of everything, you will hold your communion*." The theater's communion is an altogether different kind; there are no sacraments, but in Bergman's profound dissection of character and feeling there is a sense of the sacramental.

The Dramaten is probably the best repertory theater in the world. It currently employs 306 people, including fifty actors, and this year, for the cost of about three Broadway musicals ($25 million), it mounted thirty-two productions, eighteen of which were new shows. Bergman saw his first play there in 1928, when he was ten. From the outset, it was a stimulating holiday from the deadly silence, evasions, and disciplined repressions of his family. "For me, the stage was a free zone, where everything was allowed," Bergman told me one afternoon as he took me to seat 675, in the second row of the upper circle, which is where he sat that first day, and where he still occasionally comes to sit and think about things after rehearsals or before an appointment. Dressed in his usual rehearsal mufti (a cardigan sweater, brown corduroy slacks, cashmere socks, white Reebok sneakers with a piece of black masking tape over the left toe), he eased his rangy, slightly stooped frame into the seat as stagehands loaded his production of Witold Gombrowicz's *Princess Ivona* onto the main stage.

"Oh my God, I love this house," he said, and immediately flashed back to his first visit. "I was alone. It was a matinee. A Sunday in March. My God, I'll never forget it. I was so excited I got a fever. So I had the enormous advantage of being ill on Monday, when there was some sort of math test at school. My mother had been a hospital nurse. You could never bluff her. I had a real fever, so I could stay at home. I was in bed the whole day. Not talking to anybody. Lying under the covers. Thinking of what I'd seen the day before."

Early in the film version of *Sunday's Children* (1992), Bergman's towheaded proxy, Pu, sits with his playmates in the upstairs room of the blacksmith's house, where the blacksmith's bovine wife suckles a boy of five as well as her own infant. "Can I taste?" the dour Pu asks. The other children laugh. The woman says, "I don't mind, Pu, but you'll have to ask your grandmama or mum first." The easy access to emotion, attentiveness, embrace—all the coherence and pleasure that the breast symbolizes for a child—was never certain for Bergman.

"I was quite sure I had been an unwanted child, growing up out of a cold womb," Bergman writes. When Karin's account of her more than fifty-year marriage was found in a safe after her death, it left her husband devastated and Bergman vindicated in his childhood hunch about his mother's ambivalence toward him. Bergman ends his autobiography with an entry from his mother's diary written shortly after his birth, in 1918. She'd been married five years.

> Our son was born on Sunday morning on 14 July. He immediately contracted a high temperature and severe diarrhea. He looks like a tiny skeleton with a big fiery red nose. He stubbornly refuses to open his eyes. I had no milk after a few days because of my illness. Then he was baptized in an emergency here at the hospital. He is called Ernst Ingmar. Ma has taken him to Våroms, where she found a wet nurse. Ma is bitter about Erik's inability to solve our practical problems. Erik resents Ma's interference in our private life. I lie here helpless and miserable. Sometimes when I am alone, I cry. If the boy dies, Ma says she will look after Dag, and I am to take up my profession again. She wants Erik and me to separate as soon as possible. . . . I don't think I have the right to leave Erik. . . . I pray to God with no confidence. One will probably have to manage alone as best one can.

Ingmar was sandwiched between his bullying older brother, Dag, whose bed he once tried to set on fire, and his sister Margareta. Besides the children, Karin was saddled with her agitated husband and a full parish workload: she didn't have the emotional reserves to satisfy Ingmar's hectoring neediness. "Her reactions to me were incomprehensible," Bergman says. "She could be very warm and tender to me and very standoffish and cold."

Ingmar was frequently punished. When he wet his bed, which he did chronically, he was forced to wear a red skirt for the entire day; minor infractions of family rules meant that the child was temporarily "frozen out," meaning that "no one spoke or replied to you"; serious misdemeanors were met with thrashings, which were carried out with a carpetbeater in his father's study. "When the punishment quota had been established, a hard green cushion was fetched, trousers and underpants taken down, you prostrated yourself over the cushion, someone held firmly onto your neck and the strokes were administered," Bergman writes. "After the strokes had been administered, you had to kiss Father's hand, at which forgiveness was declared and the burden of sin fell away, deliverance and grace ensued."

Inevitably, in an environment ruled by caprice and control, Bergman became a showoff and a wily fabulist. "I was a talented liar," Bergman says. In *Fanny and Alexander* he repeats the true story of telling his school class that his mother had sold him to the circus. For the young Bergman, the unmooring anxiety was that he couldn't seem to hold his parents' attention—a distance emphasized by the fact that he was never allowed to address them with the intimate *du*. The excruciating frustration of not quite being able to reach a parent is a powerful mood in many of his films. In *The Silence* (1963) a boy languishes outside a hotel room where his mother has gone to bed with a stranger; in *Fanny and Alexander* brother and sister are locked away from the warmth of their mother in a drab room of the Bishop's house. These are chilling traces of Karin's iciness, which burned and numbed him at the same time.

"Already as a little boy, I had to figure out how to get my mother warm," Bergman recalls. "When I was five, I started to train myself to read my mother, her way of thinking and reacting. Then it went from my mother to the people surrounding me." This childhood maneuver became his greatest directorial asset. "He's a camera," the grande dame of the Swedish theater, Anita Björk, says. "He looks at you and sees everything." Bergman's uncanny, prolonged cinematic scrutiny of the face—"No one draws so close to it as Bergman does," François Truffaut said—originates in a desire to get under Karin's skin.

From an early age, Bergman re-created in himself a kind of alternative mother—giving himself, in his fantasy-obsessed play, his own form of undivided attention. Bergman's puppets, toy theaters, and magic-lantern shows were worlds that he totally controlled and that were all-embracing reflections of him. In his films the consoling embrace is an iconic motif: in *Cries and Whispers* (1973), in which two sisters and a maid circle each other in a deathwatch over a third sister, the maid bares her breast and holds the dying Agnes to her; in *Sunday's Children*, as Pu and his father find shelter from a rainstorm during a bicycle trip, the father wraps his jacket around his son's shivering shoulders.

These images resonate with Bergman's defining longing for what he calls "contact in the belly." "I wanted to touch," he says. "I had a very strong longing to touch other human beings. Still do." Bergman's hectic emotional life (he has had five wives, nine children, and mistresses in almost epic numbers) has been dominated by this ancient, unslakable emptiness and avidity. "He sought the mother," Liv Ullmann, who had a daughter with Bergman, writes about their five-year relationship in her own memoir, *Changing*. "Arms that would open to him, warm and without complications."

Only Bergman's upper-class maternal grandmother, Anna Åkerblom, who had been a teacher, offered him unconditional acceptance. "To her I was not a child, I was a human being," Bergman says, recalling summers at her house in the country. "Every evening we'd sit down together on the same green sofa, perhaps for half an hour. We'd sit holding hands and we'd discuss things. Or she'd read something to me." Together, they went to the movies, they invented ghost stories, and, as he writes in *The Magic Lantern*, they created their own crude cinematic scenarios: "One of us started by drawing a picture, then the other continued with the next picture, and thus the action developed. We drew 'actions' for several days. They could amount to forty or fifty pictures, and in between the pictures we wrote explanatory texts."

Bergman was the beneficiary of a focus that his grandmother had not been able to lavish on Karin, and that Karin, in turn, could not provide for her son. "Were we given masks instead of faces?" Bergman asks his mother in *The Magic Lantern*. He answers his own question in *Persona* (1966), whose title has its root in the Latin for "mask." He separates the dead and the caring parts of his mother into two warring characters, who in the course of the drama merge, in a weird symbiosis, into one face. In the dreamlike prologue a bookish boy tries to touch the large fading image of a woman who looms and recedes at the same time; this turns out to be Alma (Bibi Andersson), who is a nurse, as Karin was—the bright, duty-bound, positive side of the mother. In the course of the film, Alma is infiltrated by the negativity of her patient, an actress called Elisabeth Vogler (Liv Ullmann), who rejects both speech and motherhood, and even goes as far as to rip up a picture of her son. "It's amusing to study her," Elisabeth writes in a letter about Alma, who has opened up to her over time, and who intercepts the letter. She feels betrayed, and her humiliation becomes an articulate, almost visionary energy, which she projects into the mute Elisabeth, conjuring her voice and speaking her story, which echoes the story of Karin and Ingmar:

> The child was sick. It cried unceasingly, day and night, I hated it, I was afraid, I had a bad conscience. . . . The little body had an incredible, violent love for his mother. I protect myself, defend myself desperately, because I know I cannot repay it. . . . And so I

try and try. But it leads only to clumsy, cruel encounters between me and the boy. I can't, I can't, I'm cold and indifferent, and he looks at me and loves me and is so soft I want to hit him, because he won't leave me alone.

Persona puts the audience where the child in Bergman sits: full of contradictory feelings and images that are imminences of the betrayal of love and its even graver consequence, the loss of meaning. "The picture grows white, grey, the face is wiped out. Is transformed into Alma's face, starts to move, assumes strange contours," read the stage directions for the end of the film, which was originally called *Cinematography*. "The words become meaningless, running and jumping, finally vanishing altogether. The projector stops, the arc lamp is extinguished."

From the moment when the ten-year-old Bergman cranked his first projector and ran his first three-meter film loop through a magic lantern—lit by a paraffin lamp and throwing a trembly brown image on the whitewashed wall of his nursery wardrobe—the shadows on the wall, he says, "wanted to tell me something." He goes on, "It was a girl, a beautiful girl. She woke up. Stretched her arms out. Danced just one circle and went out. How I concentrated on this girl! Then I could move it the other way, so she came back!" The apparatus of film could retrieve or reverse the past; it could make the inert come to life; it could penetrate the senses and speak soul to soul with or without words. It was—and remains—a miraculous hedge against loss. Bergman says, "I still have the same feeling of fascination. It hasn't changed."

"Almost from the beginning, Ingmar knew exactly what he wanted," says Bergman's best friend, Erland Josephson, who starred in *Scenes from a Marriage* (1973), among many other Bergman projects. His performing partnership with the director dates from his student days, when the twenty-one-year-old Bergman cast him as Antonio in a university production of *The Merchant of Venice*. "He was very strict and honest with the text, and very practical," Josephson says, adding, "He always knew that this is a profession for experienced people, and that he had to get experience as fast as possible." The Swedish painter Ann Romyn, who knew Bergman in his early professional years and found his energy "menacing," says, "He was a sort of sorcerer. He had powers, I would say. Imaginative powers. He could influence people."

In 1941, at the age of twenty-three, Bergman undertook for the first time to write uninterruptedly. The result in that first year was twelve stage plays and a libretto. One of the plays, *Kasper's Death*, got him a job in the script department of Svensk Filmindustri, and there, from nine to five every day, he joined a "half-dozen slaves" trying to make screenplays from novels, stories, and scripts in need of doctoring. Soon the company was producing one of Bergman's original screenplays, *Torment* (1944)—an anguished Expressionist tale about a student who falls in love with a woman and finds out that he shares her with his sadistic, crypto-Nazi Latin instructor. The film's director was Alf Sjöberg, a grandee of the Dramaten, whose reputation for excellence would be surpassed in his lifetime only by Bergman's own; he adopted the young author as a kind of protégé. When Sjöberg was otherwise engaged, Bergman even got to shoot the film's final exteriors, which represent his first professional footage. "I was more excited than I can describe," he wrote later. "The small film crew threatened to walk off the set and go home. I screamed and swore so loudly that people woke up and looked out their windows. It was four o'clock in the morning."

Over the next few years, Bergman made *Crisis* (1946), *It Rains on Our Love* (1946), *Port of Call* (1948), *Music in Darkness* (1948), *Prison* (1949), and *Thirst* (1949), all of which telegraphed in their titles a rebellious pessimism that shocked the Swedes. Except for

Music in Darkness, a story about a pianist blinded in military service, which was a box-office success, the films were generally not well received. "Bergman was treated like a subversive, blasphemous, and irritating schoolboy," Truffaut wrote in *Cahiers du Cinéma* in 1958. Nevertheless, Bergman was gathering support from the Swedish film industry. The producer Carl Anders Dymling allowed him to start from scratch on *Crisis* after three weeks of disastrous dailies. Victor Sjöström, then the artistic director of Svensk Filmindustri, taught him "about the power of the naked face and to be simple, direct, and tell a story," Bergman says. Sjöström also offered advice about the politics of persuasion both onscreen and off. "Don't keep having rows with everyone," he told Bergman. "They simply get angry and do a less good job. Don't turn everything into primary issues. The audience just groans." The film editor Oscar Rosander revealed "a fundamental truth—that editing occurs during filming itself, the rhythm created in the script." Several of Bergman's early scripts were co-authored, but increasingly he relied on his own narrative skills; he often writes his scripts in novel form before breaking them down into screenplays. "Ingmar had to do his own scripts simply because there were no novelists or playwrights who were any good in Sweden," Michael Meyer, the British translator and biographer of Strindberg and Ibsen, says. "They didn't have a Graham Greene."

At the same time that Bergman was directing films, he headed up a series of civic theater companies—first at the Helsingborg City Theatre, where his appointment as artistic director, at twenty-six, made him the youngest in the nation's history. He continued this double duty throughout his career, and many of his early masterpieces (*Wild Strawberries, The Seventh Seal, Smiles of a Summer Night*) were engineered in part to keep his theater company together and working. By the early fifties, he had assimilated his influences (Cocteau, Anouilh, Hitchcock, classical theater), and his films took an introspective turn: they moved from posing social problems to analyzing personal ones. When Bergman tried to dramatize the happiness of Swedish youth—in *Summer Interlude* (1951), *Summer with Monika* (1953), and, even tangentially, in the masterly *Wild Strawberries*—the films were strained, and Bergman understood why. "I myself never felt young, only immature," he wrote in *Images*. "As a child, I never associated with other young people. I isolated myself from my peers and became a loner. When I had to formulate dialogue for my young characters, I reached for literary clichés and adopted a coquettish silliness."

Bergman was better at dramatizing his demons—what he calls the "heavy inheritance of universal terror" which permeated everything in his life. Liv Ullmann remembers a trip they took to Rome together, when he was "nervous of the plane and of everything." They stopped off in Copenhagen, and he needed to wash his hands, which meant leaving her, "the safe person," and taking the elevator down to the men's room. "After about ten minutes, I saw him come out of the lift. He had a proud little smile. He had done it!" She adds, "I still think of that little smile, which seemed to say 'Do you know what I've done all by myself?' He'd mastered his fear—and his fears are so everyday."

By his mid-thirties, Bergman had fresh anguish to add to his childhood material. His philandering was legendary: one revue song of the period went "I don't mind being wild and free / As long as Ingmar Bergman fancies me." Bibi Andersson, who took up with Bergman in the mid-fifties for a few years, says, "He was considered a rebel and a genius and brave and a little dangerous. He walked around with this beard and beret and boots. Too thin, too energetic, but wild. I thought he was the sexiest thing the world had created." She adds, "When he asked me to be with him, I thought to myself, I don't give a shit if I'm in love or not. I just want to be around this mind. I want to hear things. I want to learn things. My mother kicked me out." Andersson, who remains a close friend of Bergman's, sees him as "a very hysterical personality."

But Bergman was beginning to make something of his hysteria—

something that, unlike his artless childhood outbursts, forced thoughtfulness from his audience about his mortified inner life. It was with *Sawdust and Tinsel* (1953) that he took his initial step into murky autobiographical terrain, and his soul-searching and his cinematic language brilliantly coalesced for the first time. In the character of Albert Johansson—a circus owner caught between his longing for a settled existence with the wife he has abandoned and his vagabond life with a circus bareback rider—Bergman created "a walking chaos of conflicting emotions" who was a simulacrum of his own erotic confusions. He had found his cinematic vein.

"*Sawdust and Tinsel* was my first true picture," Bergman says. "You know, my lying went on for a long time. Suddenly I understood that I had to stop. I saw that the lies were some sort of filth on my pictures. . . . I had the conscious feeling 'Now, Ingmar, you must tell the truth every minute.' Then, in 1955, before *Smiles of a Summer Night*, I was together with a girl. We were very much in love. I had to tell her the truth, and I did. 'I'm not going to marry you. I don't love you that way. I want to fuck you.' That was the beginning. Poor girl." Bergman's art now squarely acted out his anxiety, which he calls "my life's most faithful companion, inherited from both my parents, placed in the very center of my identity—my demon and my friend spurring me on." Erland Josephson says, "He is inconsolable, and he wants to be that—to be close to his own hurt parts." Out of this brokenness, Bergman generated a plethora of unsettling images: the clock with no hands (*Wild Strawberries*), the spectral dance of death (*The Seventh Seal*), the cuckolded clown bearing his naked wife over a rocky shore (*Sawdust and Tinsel*), and always the mysterious, protean illuminations of the human face.

Bergman's God-haunted stories gave an uncompromising form to the existentialist angst that was the intellectual vogue of 1950s Europe, sounding the rumble of loss under everything: love, sex, faith, identity. The films created a seismic disturbance when they were first shown, and nowhere more than in America, which embraced Bergman with an enthusiasm that Sweden never matched, perhaps in reaction to the insipidity of American entertainment in the post-war boom. Bergman was the antidote to the fluffy world of Doris Day, George Axelrod, and William Inge. "*The Seventh Seal* and *Wild Strawberries* came to New York," Woody Allen recalls. "I was stupefied. I was on the edge of my seat. They could've burned down the theater, I wouldn't have known." Allen continues, "He's a great entertainer. This is what finally makes him great. It's not homework to go to his movies."

Not homework, perhaps, but sometimes hard work: *The Rite* (1969), about a trio of players being investigated by a judge, is, to all intents and purposes, incomprehensible. Occasionally, Bergman's stories collapse under the weight of their ambition to be at once in the avant-garde of cinema and of suffering. The suggestion of incest between sisters in *The Silence* seems arid; the schizophrenia in *Through a Glass Darkly* (1961) feels pat; the pessimism in *The Serpent's Egg* (1977), Bergman's study of 1920s Berlin, verges on self-parody.

And Bergman, as the éminence grise of the art house, whose images are iconic and at times pretentious, is an easy target for parody. In *The Seventh Seal*, for instance, Death arrives, in all his medieval regalia (white face, hooded cloak, scythe), and plays chess with the Knight. Woody Allen adored the scene, and sent up the figure in both film (*Love and Death*) and fiction: in a piece called *Death Knocks*, the Grim Reaper reappears for a game of gin rummy with a schlepper. Bergman himself is not above laughing at the solemnity of his cinematic idiom. For example, in *The Magician* (1958), when the ghost of an actor returns to haunt the mute impresario of a travelling magic show, he says, "I'm a ghost already. Actually better as such. I have become convincing, which I never was as an actor." Then there's the subversive joy of Bergman's Uncle Carl, his mother's soft-headed inventor brother, who turns up as a character in *Fanny and Alexander* and astonishes the kids by blowing out candles with his farts.

Although his movies are complex, Bergman usually manages to make his ideas clear and exciting for an audience. His startling dramatic fillips reveal a story's pulse—as, for instance, in *Cries and Whispers*, where Agnes dies twice, to allow Bergman to expose her sisters' cold hearts. "If you find the rhythm, the heartbeat of the play, or if you can make it in the film, it is much easier for an audience to live with the story and accept it," he says. "The wonderful thing about Ibsen or Strindberg or Shakespeare or Euripides is there is a drive, a rhythm. You feel, My God, I can listen to this. It's a fantastic feeling. It's breathing."

The oxygen of Bergman's own seductive intelligence is most apparent in his work with actors. He is very selective about whom he collaborates with, and careful about choosing roles that will exploit an actor's particular qualities. "Without that actor, he's not interested," says the choreographer Donya Feuer, who has worked with Bergman since 1964. Bergman's explosive intensity and his acute attentiveness put actors in a powerful creative force field. "It's very much in the way he looks at you," Feuer says. "There's something so naked, so exposed, so vulnerable, so available to him all the time, no matter what he's doing, and that availability, I think, is part of his talent. . . . He really listens. He's not listening to what he wants to hear. He's listening to what he's hearing, and understanding it, not criticizing it."

Bergman, who is deaf in his left ear but claims that with his right ear he can "hear like a three-year-old child," explains, "If I listen to them, they not only listen to themselves, they also listen to each other. And, if I do speak, it's important to say the precise word and not to start a discussion. That is the worst thing you can do as a director. Don't discuss. Just say the right word at the right moment. If it's planned, it will be unspontaneous and make the actors suspicious. That was a great difficulty when I worked in Germany for six years. I had to translate. My intuition told me the right thing in Swedish, but in the time it took to translate the word the moment had passed."

When Bergman walks into a rehearsal, he is meticulously prepared. "I read and reread and reread the play," he says. "The writing and the blocking take me four pages a day, every day except Sundays." On the rehearsal floor, Bergman works very close to his actors. "He's sitting on your shoulder all the time," Elin Klinga, one of Bergman's recent acting discoveries, says. He can be seen consistently right up under his actors' chins in a television documentary about the making of *In the Presence of a Clown*, Bergman's superb TV play, in which Uncle Carl leaves a sanitarium to take his newest brainstorm—a "living talking picture" about the last days of Schubert—on the road. At one point, Bergman smooths Erland Josephson's furrowed brow. "Don't wrinkle so much," he says. In the theater, Bergman doesn't sit and watch from the auditorium until it's time for technical rehearsals. According to his son Mats, an actor at the Dramaten (he was a memorably lubricious fop in Bergman's version of *The Misanthrope*), when his father is displeased with what he's watching "he looks at you but not very long, a very short glimpse, and then he looks at something else." It's easier to tell when he's pleased. "He's shouting, screaming, laughing 'Good!' Like a cheerleader."

Sometimes, in the hubbub of blocking and in order to cut through conversation, Bergman will grab actors and walk them through a particular movement to show what he has in mind. "When he grabs your arm to lead you around, it's very frustrating," Bibi Andersson says. "You feel how he trembles. If you feel your arm resist in any way, he feels that. It's like taking your pulse. He takes you literally by the wrist." She continues, "I bridled at that until I realized that he doesn't do it to be in charge of me—he does it to sense if I'm with him."

"When I work, it's not important what I'm saying, it's the contact," Bergman says, and he recalls that the talented, taciturn Ingrid Thulin once said, "Ingmar, when you talk to me I never understand what you say. But when you don't talk to me I understand completely what you mean." Bergman goes on, "A good actor is very physical. I can talk to his body, and I know before he knows if his body-mind accepts or doesn't accept what I want. I feel it in my body." He adds, "To force an actor to do something is silly. You can convince him, you can talk to him. Then we have the opening, and he makes what you want him to make. Then, five days after the opening, he starts to change a little of what I've said to him. Then suddenly there are ten actors who start to change a little of what the director has told them. There is no rhythm anymore. There is no performance anymore. . . . So it's a good idea to have the actor feel good about the blocking, the thinking, the rhythm. Then we will make a common creation."

Bergman has a special empathy for his actresses, from whom he's been able to coax, in Truffaut's words, "dormant genius": Maj-Britt Nilsson, Harriet Andersson, Eva Dahlbeck, Gunnel Lindblom, Ingrid Thulin, Bibi Andersson, Liv Ullmann. (To this film list should be added Bergman's stage collaborations with Lena Endre, Marie Richardson, Pernilla August, and Elin Klinga.) Bibi Andersson compares him to Strindberg, who "needed women to feed him. When they couldn't inspire him, it was over. That's similar to Bergman. In his younger years, he had women. Now he has actresses. He still loves to create around an actress." And the actresses all have to grapple with Bergman's desire to decipher and to possess them. "He wants to be the only one for you," Klinga says. "He told Anita Björk and me when we were working with another director, 'I'm very jealous.' And he was. We hugged him and said, 'We're yours.' That's like a twelve-year-old boy again." As Bibi Andersson puts it, "He really wants to get under your skin." She adds, "He also feels penetrated." In this exchange of energy, there is a significant erotic charge. The reciprocated gaze—the thing that so bedevilled Bergman as a child—is what gives him his power as a director. "You feel absolutely recognized," Ullmann says. "I have the feeling of finally being seen, and because I'm being seen I blush more. I come out with words in a way I never knew I would. I dare to laugh, which I always thought was very difficult. I dare to cry."

For Bergman, rehearsals impose an exacting discipline, not only on the actors but on his own explosive emotions. It's a situation in which, as Erland Josephson has written, Bergman is "overpoweringly self-assured in his efforts to overpower insecurity; full of empathy in order to keep his impatience under control; full of impatience in order to keep his empathy under control." Bergman says, "If I'm in the rehearsal in my own private turmoil—either fury or love—then I can't hear the actors, I can only hear myself. When I go into the rehearsal room or into the film studio, I must switch. I am the director."

As much as possible, Bergman leaves nothing to chance. "Everything must be predictable and predicted," Josephson says. "The only thing allowed to surprise Bergman and others is Bergman himself." He hates "tumult, aggression, or emotional outbursts," but he has been prone to all three. "No one could be as angry as Ingmar," Ullmann writes in *Changing*. Once, on Fårö, she remembers questioning something he did. Bergman flew into a rage. "He ran after me. I knew I was going to die," Ullmann says. "I went into the bathroom. I locked myself in. Then suddenly he kicked right through the door. His slippers landed on me. He started to laugh. I came out because he thought it was so comical. We made it up immediately." She adds, "If you disagree, he feels he's not loved. I think he feels that to be

loved he must be loved unconditionally." In his early days as a director, Bergman threw chairs as easily as tantrums; even now he still
believes in the occasional well-planned "pedagogic outburst."

"Sometimes when he's at his most angry and controlling—he can
be really tough to work with, because he wants everything his way—
deep down you can be very moved," Ullmann says. "He is protecting
that one place where he feels safe: his creativity. The director. The
writer. The master of it all." When Bergman's control is challenged,
onstage or off, life can get complicated. In 1995, Bergman cancelled
what was to be his farewell production in America, the New York
engagement of his glorious version of *The Misanthrope*. The Stockholm production, which ranks among my top-ten productions in a
lifetime of theatergoing, was the best Molière I've ever seen—a court
world turned into a den of gorgeous and predatory animals. It ran for
a hundred performances, and caused an unholy row within the Dramaten and in the Swedish press. "He came, he saw, he cut them to
bits," declared the *Expressen* when Bergman came in from Fårö to
see the production again before rehearsing it for the New York trip
and found certain "deviations" from the interpretation he'd initially
agreed on with the cast. "If I think I am being betrayed, I am quick
to betray," Bergman writes in *The Magic Lantern*. "If I feel cut off,
I cut off." Bergman felt he couldn't trust even a re-rehearsed production to be performed without more surprises. So he withdrew
his imprimatur and prevented his beautiful production from travelling. Lars Löfgren, then the head of the Dramaten, tried to reason
with Bergman. "I said, 'You're a staff director. You're supposed to
be here to work,' " Löfgren recalls. " 'If the production is not good
at the moment, it has been good, and it must be rehearsed, because
we're going to New York with it. I want you back with me.' He said,
'You don't respect my artistic work.' I said, 'Of course I do. That's
why I want you back.' He didn't come."

Though Bergman characterized the incident as "a sneeze in eternity," it ended his long friendship with Löfgren. Bergman regards such shows of aggression as occasionally necessary, even if he feels repentant about them afterward. "I discovered early into our rehearsals that to be understanding and to offer a sympathetic ear did not work," he writes of directing Ingrid Bergman in *Autumn Sonata*. The actress, in the role of a concert pianist who gave everything to her art and nothing to her children, had worked out her intonations and gestures before she arrived at the read-through; in the manner of an American film star, she also objected to some of Bergman's lines. "When it was over and we were alone, Ingmar said, 'I can't go through with this,'" says Ullmann, who co-starred in the film, and who had rarely seen the director "really, really down." "She'd stop every other sentence and say, 'Is she going to say something like this? I can't say something like this.'" Ullmann continues, "You know, none of us had ever criticized anything Ingmar wrote." Ingrid Bergman bridled at the dialogue for a scene in which Ullmann, who plays the daughter, delivers a tearful, corrosive diatribe against her. "Help me!" are the words that the script called for the mother to come back with. As Ullmann recalls, "She said, 'I'm not saying that. I want to slap her face.' Ingmar got so shocked. They walked out of the studio, and we heard them shouting out in the corridor. Terrible. We looked at each other and thought, This is the end." Finally, the actress spoke the words, but on the screen her eyes tell a different, indignant story. Out of the tension between her and Bergman she'd made something that even he was amazed by.

"We have to have direct contact with the childish," Bergman says. "Actors who don't have direct contact with their childhood are not good actors. They are boring intellectual actors." But the very childishness that is the wellspring of Bergman's genius is also the source of his occasional capricious cruelty. After Josephson went to Paris for a weekend while in rehearsal for a Bergman show, he and Bergman stopped talking for about a year. "Ingmar didn't like it,"

Josephson explains. "I didn't miss any rehearsals, but he was angry because I took the risk. I was out of his control for a weekend. He started talking about my face, my chins. It was terribly aggressive. He has a talent for knowing where to put the knife."

Humiliation may be Bergman's theme, but it can also be his practice, as Sir Laurence Olivier discovered when Bergman directed a 1970 National Theatre production of Michael Meyer's version of *Hedda Gabler*, with Maggie Smith. Olivier—whom Bergman always referred to in private as "Lord Olivier"—was then the National's artistic director. Meyer recalls sitting with Olivier and watching Bergman work with the actors: "Suddenly Larry said, 'Oh, Ingmar?' So Ingmar, who hasn't been interrupted, I think, in about forty years, turned around and said, 'Yes, Larry.' Larry said, 'I'm only suggesting this and you may think this is absolute rubbish . . . ' And then there was a ghastly hush at this really sort of very melodramatic suggestion. Ingmar said with a pause—no one knows the value of a pause better than Ingmar Bergman—'Perhaps, we'll see,' and went on directing." Meyer continues, "In the afternoon, Larry made some equally fatuous suggestions. This time, Ingmar didn't even turn around. He just paused for I should think a full minute with his back to Larry and then said, 'Yes,' and went on directing." The next day, Olivier was absent from rehearsals. Some weeks later, after a ponderous dress rehearsal, Bergman asked everyone up to Maggie Smith's dressing room "to thank us all personally." Meyer continues, "We all trooped up there. And when Larry naturally enough came up, Ingmar publicly and very rudely excluded him from the meeting. This was the unforgivable thing, to humiliate him in that way."

When Bergman left Sweden in 1976 to live in Germany, he wrote a long letter to his countrymen, published in the *Expressen*, which concluded on a supercilious note: "I quote Strindberg, when he went mad, 'Watch out, you bastards, I'll see you in my next play.' " But the

Bergman who returned to Sweden in the early eighties was not the same man. "It was like night and day. There was an enormous humility," Donya Feuer says. "I think he suddenly felt he had nothing to protect. He was open to what was going on with other people. He was more considerate of everyone." Part of this transformation was the influence of his fourth wife, Ingrid von Rosen, whom he married in 1971 and with whom he lived happily until her death, from cancer, in 1995. "I had contact with reality through Ingrid," Bergman says. Feuer explains, "She managed everything—telephone calls, letters. She was the only one who could read his handwriting and type out the scripts. . . . She was very upper class, very well educated, and very refined. She never competed with his professional work. She was responsible for bringing all the children together."

For Bergman's sixtieth birthday, in 1978, all nine of his children gathered at Fårö for the first time. From that moment, Bergman, who is referred to jokingly within the family as the Big Gorilla, became an unlikely but beloved patriarch. "He was nonexistent as a father—except now, when the children are grown," Liv Ullmann says. "They idolize him. I think he's been very lucky with the mothers, because I, at least, have never bad-mouthed him. I must say there were years when Linn didn't see him." When Linn, their daughter, was about seven and was keeping her mother company in the dressing room, Ullmann remembers Bergman's encountering her for the first time in four years. " 'Oh, Linn,' he said, and swung her around in his arms for half a minute. Then he said, 'You know, Linn, Daddy has work, too. He has other things to do.' And then he left the room. That was it."

Bergman now has more contact with his children, some of whom are in the arts. Linn is a novelist; Eva runs the Backa Theatre, in Göteborg; Daniel directed *Sunday's Children*. But, even though Bergman has renovated a few buildings on his Fårö property as a summer enclave for his children, it's not easy to get near him. "They have dinner once, maybe, if at all," Ullmann says. "Then they fight to sit at his side. Sometimes he comes by for coffee. They never know when, and it's an honor. Then he has his cinema. He invites some to the cinema in the afternoon, others in the evening."

When Ullmann shuts her eyes and thinks of Bergman, she sees, she says, "this man who sits in a chair with this smile—a kind of half smile—and very, very lonely, feeling he is a stranger." She adds, "He is connected to his creativity, but not necessarily to the world." The isolation that defines Bergman is part of what animates the uncanny atmosphere in his work and activates his unconscious. He claims that there are two ghosts—a judge and a cobbler—who occupy his Fårö outbuildings, and who appear only at night. "I have heard voices," he says. "Once I saw my mother. I was sitting looking out at the sea. Then suddenly I felt that somebody was standing behind me. I looked, and she was there. Very beautiful and very young."

For more than half a century now, Bergman has traded in the mysteries with the sure knowledge "that there are a lot of realities in our reality." He says, "We don't know anything about those realities. The musicians and the prophets and the saints have given us some messages—have given us intimations of the ineffable." Bergman can hear it at the end of Beethoven's Ninth Symphony. "The chorus is going higher and higher, and suddenly is silent," he says. "Then you hear four or five bars, and you have a feeling that reality has opened up. Beethoven, who was deaf, had heard something that never had been written before." Part of Bergman's gift to his century has been to make visible the mystery he sees around him—to glimpse the eternal in the stage-managed transcendence of play. "Anything can happen, anything is possible and likely," the Grandmother says to Alexander, reading from Strindberg's *A Dream Play*, in the last beat of *Fanny and Alexander*. "Against a faint background of reality, imagination spins and weaves new patterns."

"Ingmar got the life he wanted," Erland Josephson says. "He is the protagonist of his own life. It's a drama. He's creating that drama all the time. Now we have to discuss how to end the drama—some philosophy for leaving the stage." Josephson continues, "We've promised if we get senile to say to each other, 'No, that's enough.' " For the moment, it's not. Bergman's strategy seems close to Edmund Wilson's stoic dictum: "Keep going; never stoop; sit tight; / Read something luminous at night."

"I'm my own god, I supply my own angels and demons," a Bergman character says in *The Rite*; Bergman is also his own clown. A few months ago, he walked into the office of one of the Dramaten's dramaturges, Ulla Åberg, and pinned on her bulletin board a color photograph of himself with a clown's red nose. The image is apt. Bergman, like Uncle Carl in *In the Presence of a Clown*, is capering with the absurd: defying death in his art and watching oblivion loom ever closer in his life. But mortality is the one thing Bergman can't redeem through imagination. "I couldn't manipulate being born," he says. "When Ingrid came home and told me she had cancer, I knew the whole time that it was hopeless, but Ingrid didn't know. That was the second time I saw reality. It was impossible to manipulate that." Bergman is curious about the third time he'll come up against that intractable reality. "I'm an old man. I am close to the great mystery," he says. "I am not afraid of it. I am fascinated, not afraid."

A few years ago, when Lars Löfgren was still head of the Dramaten, he and Bergman walked past the greenroom, a spacious place full of oil paintings of the theater's old luminaries and big pieces of well-upholstered furniture, which give it the cozy feel of a gentlemen's club. The greenroom door was open, so Bergman walked in. Nobody was there. Löfgren recalls, " 'Listen!' Bergman said. I couldn't hear a thing. 'What is it?' I said. Bergman said, 'They're all here.' 'What do you mean?' 'The actors,' Bergman said. 'They're not finished with the theater.' " Löfgren continues, "He looked around the room and turned to me and very lovingly said, 'One day, we will be with them.' " ∎

—May 31, 1999

Madame de Sade

On November 25, 1970, the novelist Yukio Mishima orchestrated his famous suicide, committing hara-kiri and then having his head cut off. At a stroke, the mind-body split he wrote about was finally resolved. Mishima's death, at forty-five, was, like his life, an act of fanatical will and aesthetic principle. He had written forty novels, twenty volumes of short stories, and eighteen plays, among the last of which was *Madame de Sade* (1965), a meditation on the metaphysics of desire. De Sade, who, like Mishima, was a voluptuary of the perverse, never appears in the play, but the memory and the import of his libertinism dominate six women who wait and worry about him through his long incarceration. Mishima projected onto de Sade his own quest, in which perversion became an act not of debasement but of discovery. In a late poem, "Icarus," Mishima wrote:

> *Why, still, should the lust for ascension*
> *Seem, in itself, so close to madness?*
> *Nothing is that can satisfy me;*
> *Earthly novelty is too soon dulled.*
> *I am drawn higher and higher, more unstable.*

Both Mishima and de Sade were romantic individualists who embraced pain as a way of defeating boredom and extending the limits of consciousness. In this romance of the self, both were quintessentially modern: destroying themselves for meaning. De Sade had a prodigious genius for perversion, and Mishima seems to have instinctively understood the sense of blessing implicit in the monstrous. His play makes a case for the necessity of evil. Recounting de Sade's being beaten with a broom 859 times, Comtesse de Saint-Fond, the play's female libertine and de Sade's disciple, says,

"If you increase numbers until they are no longer believable, evil itself becomes a miracle." She argues that de Sade, whose miracles "have nothing in common with the miracles lazy people merely wait for," works for his spiritual enlightenment.

So does the director Ingmar Bergman, who understands the deeply religious nature of Mishima's inquiring into the profane. Bergman's formidable gifts of penetration and design turn *Madame de Sade*, which on the page is apparently all talk, into a magnificent exhibition both of Mishima's subtle moral debate and of his own incomparable stagecraft. It is one of the most noble evenings I've ever spent in the theater. The show is part of a Bergman doubleheader (along with *Peer Gynt*) and will play for three days at the Brooklyn Academy of Music, starting on May 20; for four years, it has been in repertory intermittently at Stockholm's state-subsidized and exquisite art-deco Kungliga Dramatiska Teatern (where I saw it three weeks ago). In it Bergman sets himself the challenge of containing the play's turbulent passions within the formal spirit in Japanese drama. He does away with all period decor. He streamlines Mishima's baroque text (herein quoted from Donald Keene's translation). He allows his actors no excessive gestures. The play speaks through the dramatic interplay of groupings, costume, color, words, and subtext. Every acting moment is filled, every inch of stage space is dynamic. It's a thrilling and educational encounter, which makes American theater and most European theater, by comparison, look like minor-league stuff.

"What I like about Ingmar is that he very rarely speaks about what he means," says Donya Feuer, the American-born choreographer who worked with Bergman on his film of *The Magic Flute* and his opera version of *The Bacchae* and has perfectly realized the "choreographic spirit" behind Bergman's reading of *Madame de Sade*. "By what he does, you understand what he means. Everything Ingmar does is emotion. To give a place for this emotional response, he has to get the actors in the same place he is—to touch them in the most secret part of their imagination. In *Madame de Sade* we didn't want to do anything that was Japanese in itself. But the exactness of Mishima's language demanded an exactness in the actors' movements and in their attack. The way they looked and didn't look. The way they listened onstage, and waited, and exited. Since it's an open space and very exposed, all the tension and the boundaries had to be created by the women themselves in relationship to each other. We began to work with that. There isn't a moment in this performance which doesn't fit Ingmar's plan. In every scene Ingmar searches for a space—a kind of rectangle, which varies several inches one way or another—that he calls 'the acoustic and optical center' of the stage. From this glowing place everything comes. Every single moment has a form."

From the play's first beat, when the housekeeper, Charlotte (Helena Brodin), scurries onstage in Japanese fashion but dressed as a period French servant, Bergman announces the game of contrasts he is about to play. Charlotte, previously the housekeeper of Comtesse de Saint-Fond, is a bridge between the worlds of liberty and respectability. Bergman uses her like a kind of silent chorus, alternately astonished and appalled as she eavesdrops from behind the background arches. The boundaries of the debate are established at once when the "saint," Baronesse de Simiane (Margaretha Byström), whose piety will put her in a nunnery by the finale, comes face to face with the "sinner," Comtesse de Saint-Fond. Bergman uses Charles Koroly's magnificent costumes to make palpable the implications of this battle between denial and freedom. Simiane, soon to be joined by her counterpart in containment—the hostess, Madame de Montreuil—is decked out in the periwigged and corsetted formality of eighteenth-century high fashion. A wall of fabric and wire barricades both women off from the world. By contrast, Comtesse de Saint-Fond (the brilliant and brazen Agneta Ekmanner) enters in streamlined riding gear, her breasts clearly visible through a pale-marigold tunic. The effect is as teasing and shocking as her personality. She is neither powdered nor periwigged. The red of her lipstick and the small ruby pendant she wears hint at blood.

"It's a very dangerous part," Ekmanner told me. "I feel very exposed onstage. But it's no time to lie. You can't offend the public in doing this extremely difficult part—full of sorrow and longing— without doing it as honestly as possible." Ekmanner lays herself recklessly open to the audience, just as Saint-Fond does to the women on whom she has come to call, and who dismiss her as decadent. Montreuil wants Saint-Fond to trade sexual favors with the High Court officials in exchange for their lifting de Sade's death sentence. Saint-Fond recounts the offenses that have brought de Sade to this pretty pass: a menu of infamy that includes orgies with whores, the use of Spanish fly, sodomy, and flagellation. This news sends a *frisson* of fear through Baronesse de Simiane, who in the script protects herself from contamination by making continual signs of the cross, and in Bergman's version does so by hiding half her face behind her fan.

When Madame de Montreuil enters, the minuet of vanity and outrage steps up a pace. Montreuil (played with regal detachment by Anita Björk) is as chilly as her pale-blue dress, and as imposing. She is baffled by de Sade's capers but admits that "the one thing I *could* understand was honor." She wants de Sade's freedom for the sake of her distraught daughter, Renée, who is de Sade's long-suffering wife and whom she dubs "the bride of the King of Hell," and for the honor of the family name. Saint-Fond reads Montreuil's snobbery correctly, and continues to tweak the vanity of Montreuil's righteousness with her unrepentant knowledge of the flesh. "The most striking characteristic of the marquis' illness is how pleasant it is," she tells her. "Immorality has always been for me a perfectly appointed, completely self-sufficient preserve. It has its shepherds' cottages and its windmills, its brooks and lakes."

In Stina Ekblad's delicate and sharply defined interpretation,

Renée puts her intelligence and her longing for meaning into the myth of her fanatic devotion, and allows de Sade to carry both the darkness and the passion that she won't own in herself. "Bergman gave me inspiring word pictures for the role," Ekblad told me. "For instance, of Anne, my sister in the play, he said, 'She's building a cathedral around her in which she is worshipping herself.' Of my character, Renée, he said, 'She's a hymn echoing in this cathedral.' Renée is more of a tune—changing, echoing. She's like a bell." In act 1, Renée gives lip service to conventional behavior. She presents herself in the role of dutiful and heroic victim. Saint-Fond brings this hypocrisy into focus with a mischievous question. "How does he treat you?" she asks Renée. The impropriety sends Montreuil and Simiane plunging behind their upturned fans. Decadence and duty square off. "If you were to see our marital bed," Renée says, saving face for the moment, "there would be nothing I should ask you to keep a secret."

Renée is wedded as much to the idea of marriage as she is to de Sade. In her transparent goodness, she lives up to her mother's idea of repute. Madame de Montreuil exhausts herself restoring the family name, and Renée is no less tireless both in living a blameless life and in whiting out the dark parts of her life. She rationalizes de Sade's yearning for blood—she says it's related to "the glory of his distant ancestors who served in the crusades"—and she refuses to listen to her mother's pleas to leave him. But what on the surface seems devotion is also a rigid defensiveness. In this, she is definitely her mother's child. But she is also a weird, refracted image of her husband. Both de Sade and Renée are in the avant-garde of suffering. Both are strangely inconsolable. De Sade acts out his anger on others; Renée murders parts of herself. He fiercely admits himself; and she, just as fiercely, hides herself away. The play skillfully brings this ambiguity to a head at the end of the first act, when Madame de Montreuil's other daughter, Anne, returns from Italy. The stunning and capricious Anne, superbly played by Marie Richardson as a languorous Fragonard seductress whose eyes sparkle with self-regard, announces that her companion in Italy was none other than de Sade, escaped from prison and in hiding. Montreuil begs her not to tell Renée. "She knows we went to Italy," Anne tells her flabbergasted mother, who has only just finished hearing Renée's entreaties to save her husband from prison. "And where Alphonse is hiding." Both Renée's devotion to de Sade and Montreuil's devotion to getting him released are at a stroke called into question. The carapace of convention—what Mishima calls "the unoriginal concepts of duty"—has cracked from the dangerous pressures it's meant to contain: the temptation of the imagination.

Life seems to have changed for the de Sade household at the beginning of act 2, as the curtain comes up on Renée reading Anne the court order announcing de Sade's pardon and his release from prison. In the intervening six years, which take us to the fall of 1778, de Sade has been internalized differently by each character. His genius for suffering has somehow deepened them and—on the surface, at least—made them mellower. To capture the change in the quality of their suffering and their passion, Bergman first changes his palette. At the opening of the act, a flamelike tree is projected against a red cyclorama, foreshadowing the fierce passion to follow. Time has left its mark on the sisters; and Koroly's dresses, in resonating shades of dark red and terra-cotta, convey an earthier, weathered sense of life. Renée's denial now takes the form of claiming kinship with de Sade. "My unhappiness has at last reached the level of Alphonse's sins," she says. A tone of resignation and skepticism has come into her voice. She understands that claims of happiness are a tapestry of denial, in which the woman "painstakingly weaves in, eye by eye, solitude, boredom, anxiety, loneliness, terrible nights, frightening sunrises." And when Anne bitchily suggests that de Sade never loved anyone, including Renée, she can hear the idea, while deflecting its hurt. "Everyone is free to have fantasies," she says. "Alphonse taught me the power of fantasy." The intoxication with suffering is most clearly dramatized by Saint-Fond, who, announcing her boredom with licentiousness, describes being stripped naked and used as the altar for a black mass. In this speech, full of grief and strange glory, Saint-Fond recounts the rebirth of feeling at an orgy where the blood of a sacrificial lamb coursed over her naked body and candles dripped hot wax on her outspread palms. She holds up her arms and points to scars like stigmata. She has been crucified and redeemed in the flesh, not in the afterlife. "Alphonse was myself," she says. They are bound together by a sense of absence which perversion turns into a kind of heroism.

Bergman savors every twist of plot and passion, then makes it pay. Saint-Fond tips the decorum of Madame de Montreuil's house toward delirium when she informs Renée that the pardon was merely a trap set by her mother to rearrest de Sade, and that he is now in jail again. The stage is then left to the play's most extraordinary passage—a furious, stylized battle between Montreuil and Renée. Mother and daughter at first circle one another, with Renée begging her mother to free de Sade, and Montreuil asking what happiness his freedom would bring her. "The happiness of poverty. The happiness of shame," Renée says, in a hymn to her masochistic devotion. "That is the happiness with which I shall be rewarded for setting Alphonse free." The words outrage Montreuil, and in a sudden and stunning outburst she throws her fan across the floor: "You're lying, lying." She paints a lacerating word picture of an orgy at which her informant witnessed the conduct of Renée and de Sade, during another of his brief escapes from prison. Montreuil stands above her daughter, with her arms crossed in imitation of Renée's bound hands as her whipped nude body hung from a chandelier. "You dangled half unconscious in pain," she says. "With his tongue, he cleansed your body. It wasn't only blood he cleansed." She tears at the bodice of

Renée's dress to expose her scars. Bergman sends mother and daughter reeling in fury to opposite ends of the proscenium, and then launches them toward each other in a flurry of accusations. As they descend on one another, their bodies lower to the ground like snarling animals in a standoff. "You never attempted, even in your wildest dreams, to imagine what it would be like to unlock the strange door that opens on a sky full of stars," Renée taunts, defending de Sade for opening her up to extremes of experience where "holiness and shame imperceptibly switch appearances." Hunkered down in front of her daughter, Montreuil counters, "That's right. We never tried to open the gates of Hell." De Sade has called out of Renée a demonic force. In this coruscating stage picture, Bergman demonstrates that Renée has been infected not only by de Sade's ideas but by his manic metabolism. On the last beat of the act, Renée, too, is saying, "Alphonse is myself."

Projected clouds and the rumble of wind forecast the threatening wild card that history deals the de Sade menage at the opening of act 3. Twelve more years have passed, and we are at the beginning of the French Revolution. The change in public mood is prefigured by Charlotte, the housekeeper, who now wears her hair loose on her shoulders. In her transparent insolence and her assertive walk, she registers the bumptious new democratic spirit. The violent search for new answers and new freedoms has made the dead Comtesse de Saint-Fond an icon of liberation, and even de Sade will become one of the Revolution's spokesmen. He is soon to be released from prison, and Madame de Montreuil, always with an eye to survival, now looks forward to his return. "Alphonse's vices may serve as a bill of acquittal not only for himself but for our whole family," she says, rationalizing de Sade's evil as a source of potential good. Renée's actual goodness has not been rewarded; in fact, she has been debased by de Sade in his novel *Justine*, which cannibalizes her years of devotion to make a myth of vice. "Justine is myself," she says. Unexplained scars on Renée's wrists recall Saint-Fond's "stigmata" but not her redemption. Renée's public humiliation persuades her to take holy orders. And there is a still greater paradox about de Sade to be faced. "His fascination with destruction ended in creation," Renée says. In pursuing the light, she has learned through de Sade that it can come from improbable dark sources. The play neatly brings the audience to the spiritual impasse of modern life: one person dedicating the self to God and the other making a god of the self.

At the finale, de Sade arrives at the house and knocks on the door. "Tell me how the marquis looks," Renée says twice, a heartbreaking repetition. Charlotte describes an old, fat man with sallow skin and nervous eyes. "Please ask him to leave," Renée says. "And tell him this: 'The marquise will never see him again.'" With that, Renée exits, leaving Charlotte to pick up the discarded volume of *Justine*. She starts to step on it, then reconsiders, and instead of destroying it she takes the book and walks off with it under her arm. Renée's history with de Sade may be over, but de Sade's life with the public imagination and the complex notion of individual freedom is about to begin. On that grace note, Bergman ends this flawless production, in which his genius is entirely in the service of the play's meaning. Next year, Bergman will be doing two plays at the Kungliga Dramatiska Teatern. Believe me, I will be there. ∎

—May 10, 1993

The Misanthrope

Alceste, the central figure of Molière's comedy *The Misanthrope* (1666), is probably the greatest refusenik in dramatic literature. He makes the dour Ancient Mariner look like a party animal. He is in the grip of a terrible fury at the sinfulness of the world, a man drawn both to the life of the court and to the flesh but unable to abide the fallibility of either. He will accept life only on his own terms of impossible purity. "I wish no place in a dishonest heart," he proclaims. Among literature's heroes of absurd negativity—Kafka's Hunger Artist, Melville's Bartleby the scrivener—Alceste, with his clownish outbursts, is surely the funniest. He's adolescent hell on a short fuse; he rails against the vanity of the corrupt and acts out the vanity of the righteous. But how honest is Alceste? This is the question that Ingmar Bergman explores in his third attempt at the play (he directed earlier productions in 1957 and 1973), on the main stage of the Royal Dramatic Theatre of Sweden, in Stockholm. In Bergman's reinterpretation, Alceste's idealism is a mask for his sexual jealousy, and Alceste himself is as much a victim of appearances as the world he hectors. What Bergman engineers in masterly style is both a wonderful comedy of manners and a subtle dissection of the nature of manners themselves. *The Misanthrope* is the third in a trio of monumental Bergman productions. The previous two— Shakespeare's *The Winter's Tale* and Yukio Mishima's *Madame de Sade*—will be presented in late May and early June at the Brooklyn Academy of Music, as part of a city-wide Bergman festival; *The Misanthrope* will come to BAM in the spring of 1996. Taken together, these are the finest displays of stagecraft I have ever seen.

The curtain comes up on a painted scrim of Watteau's *La Partie Quarrée*: three seated figures and a standing Pierrot figure, whose back is to us, are shown conversing against a background of Arcadian tranquillity. But comedy, in general, and *The Misanthrope*, in particular, are anything but tranquil. The scrim makes a spectacle of pastoral containment—an approach that Bergman immediately begins to test in the realm of manners. Another Pierrot figure, this one in the flesh and facing us, watches from the side of the stage as the scrim starts to play tricks on our comforting sense of coherence. A peephole opens in the gold skirt of one of the Watteau maidens, and an actor peers through it, then waves. Behind the curtain, there are sounds of laughing and then screaming, then a sudden silence, then the clatter of pails, and then the scrim itself starts to wobble, as if shaken by a poltergeist. The contradiction between the serene surface and the rowdiness behind it becomes, as we soon discover, the theme of the play.

When the scrim rises, we see the entire cast, in all its fustian regalia, about to begin a game of blindman's bluff. Alceste's beloved Célimène (the gorgeous Lena Endre) has been blindfolded and is being spun around in the middle of a circle by Pierrot, who is the spirit of comedy and Bergman's alter ego. The dance—the ritualized dance of manners, which Veblen called "a symbolic pantomime of mastery on the one hand and of subservience on the other"—begins around her. Célimène's groping is a metaphor of the play's inquiry. At issue here is not just whom Célimène will favor as her lover but how to find and hold on to status, how to search out who and what are real. Alceste (the handsome Thorsten Flinck, wearing an austere black frock coat) breaks out of the dancing circle in disgust, stopping the game just as Célimène finds herself on her knees, fondling the crotch of one of her foppish suitors, Oronte (played with superb swagger by Jarl Kulle). As the moment has been choreographed, by Donya Feuer, it captures in one unforgettable image the polarities of libertine court life: a hypocritical world of social constraint and sexual concupiscence, veering, as it were, between snow jobs and blow jobs.

The game of blindman's bluff leads swiftly into a procession, with the actors walking upstage through large green doors, beyond which an array of delicacies, on a sumptuous candlelit banquet table, is briefly glimpsed. No sooner have the doors closed behind the court revellers than they open again and Alceste is flung out. He sprawls downstage in front of us, his knees bleeding and his dander up. The scrim, the dance, the banquet, and the expulsion are all part of Bergman's brilliant preamble to Molière. The play proper begins with Philinte (Thomas Hanzon) asking his friend Alceste, "Now, what's got into you?" (The play is performed in Swedish; I'm using Richard Wilbur's English translation.) The answer, it turns out, is nothing. Alceste can't partake of life's banquet. He is a kind of moral anorexic, who won't take in the world except in his own irrational and controlling way. Alceste spoils things for the world while claiming that the artificiality of court life is spoiling him. He lectures Philinte:

> *Ah, no! we should condemn with all our force*
> *Such false and artificial intercourse.*
> *Let men behave like men; let them display*
> *Their inmost hearts in everything they say;*
> *Let the heart speak, and let our sentiments*
> *Not mask themselves in silly compliments.*

In the abstract, Alceste's indictment rings true, but in reality what Alceste is proposing is a form of social suicide. Philinte politely suggests to him:

> *Wouldn't the social fabric come undone*
> *If we were wholly frank with everyone?*

Alceste won't gild any lily. What he misses—and what Molière and Bergman understand—is the essential theatricality at the core of personality, "personality" being a word whose Latin root means "mask." Manners are the ritual care that human beings—little deities of a self-created universe—require as worship: the ceremony that insures for the participants a sense of public congruence with their idealized selves. To maintain "social face," some form of dissimulation is necessary: seeming prevails over being. *The Misanthrope* is all about the protecting, the hiding, and the refusing of "face." In this production, Alceste frequently stands turned away from others. He wants to remove his face from public view, to avoid the inevitable collusion that manners require:

Sometimes, I swear, I'm moved to flee and find,
Some desert land unfouled by human kind.

When, in act 1, Oronte flounces in, his speech piled as high with rhetorical flourishes as his periwig is with blond curls, Alceste won't make a symbolic show of friendship. It's a hilarious battle of the vanities. Oronte fishes for compliments from Alceste for the banal sonnet he has penned. But Alceste refuses to reflect even a smidgen of Oronte's grandiosity back to him.

ORONTE: Others have praised my sonnet to the skies.
ALCESTE: I lack their art of telling pleasant lies.

Oronte, with his good manners, tries to disarm Alceste, but his subsequent humiliation leads him first to pull his sword on Alceste and then to pull a fast one by supporting another man's suit against Alceste for slander. "Social face," the sociologist Erving Goffman wrote, "is only on loan . . . from society; it will be withdrawn unless [the individual] conducts himself in a way that is worthy of it." Manners, inevitably, put mankind under wraps.

The twin predicaments of manners—self-inflation and self-imprisonment—are translated with spectacular success in the exaggerated silhouettes of Charles Koroly's magnificent costumes; they go beyond the baroque to the rococo. "It's screwed-up rococo," Koroly told me. "This rococo does not exist, it's so completely artificial. It's as if we had created a world of beautiful and poisonous insects." Koroly, who spent ten months designing the costumes, most of which weigh about twenty pounds apiece, added, "Rococo is not coming close to other people or being close to your own feelings. It's being encapsulated in a mannerism and a form of manners." In a sense, Koroly's costumes are the real set of the play; Bergman has kept his stage almost bare, so the actors can give full meaning to the bulky carapaces of fabric which house them. From the second week of Bergman's eight-week rehearsal schedule, the cast was wearing the show's coats, shoes, crinolines, and corsets, not just to eliminate obstacles in wearing them but to let the costumes inform the artificiality of the characters. In such outfits, you can't sit, stand, walk, or breathe in a natural way, and the architecture of unnaturalness brings its own inevitable mutation of character.

Alceste is besotted by Célimène, who is his exact emotional opposite: warm, witty, politic, mature, calm. The alluring Célimène is given the most seemingly natural of silhouettes. Bergman stages Célimène's second appearance boldly: she is lolling over breakfast with Alceste in her pale-green canopied bed. As Célimène, Lena Endre is potent stuff: a radiant intelligence. Her loose-fitting white linen negligee and her mane of auburn hair signal spontaneity and naturalness. The illusion engendered by someone as physically exquisite and fresh as Célimène is that she must also be morally exquisite. "All your speeches are enraged and rude," she tells Alceste, dabbing jam on his impertinent nose. "I've never been so furiously wooed." Endre could send the salmon upstream in the flintiest of male hearts; and the appearance of two courtly dandies at her levee—the smug Acaste (clever Mats Bergman), who lubriciously dangles a cameo from its fob into the open mouth of a kneeling servant girl, and the epicene Clitandre (the leggy and ludicrous Claes Månsson), who flashes a long red nail on his little finger—fuels Alceste's jealousy. To Célimène, Alceste's passion only confirms the power of her sexual appeal and its novelty value in the ritualized tedium of court philandering.

Alceste, who is an expert at lying to himself, claims to be incapable of dissimulation; but the flirtatious Célimène is a master of it.

She faces down the puritanical Mme. Arsinoé (the superb Agneta Ekmanner), who fancies Alceste herself, and who scuttles around the stage, in a layered purple-black dress, like an Egyptian scarab; clutching a prayer book, she delivers salvos of spite in a pinched voice full of piety. "One must avoid the outward show of vice," Arsinoé warns Célimène, who for most of this sensational war of words has her back turned to Arsinoé or glides around her, so that her face never loses its marvellous composure under the older woman's onslaught of malice. Ekmanner, who radiates a regal inner fire, has a field day in the role. Her austere elegance and the frozen angularity of her neck and hands reinforce her starchy propriety as Célimène herself goes on the attack. Célimène says, "When all one's charms are gone, it is, I'm sure / Good strategy to be devout and pure." Arsinoé takes revenge on her by showing Alceste a compromising letter from Célimène to Oronte. (She later provides him with letters from *all* of Célimène's suitors.) When Alceste confronts Célimène with the letter, she is calmly arranging roses in a vase whose dragon design is the only predatory clue; she brushes her face occasionally with a bloom as she gives him a disarming answer. "Pretend, pretend, that you are just and true," Alceste begs, dropping to his knees and holding her hand to his cheek. "And I shall make myself believe in you." Significantly, at this moment of crisis Alceste has more faith in his powers of denial than in the power of love. Célimène touches his face, and in that gesture—electric with feeling and with irony—she brazens it out: "Just why should I *pretend*?"

By act 5, Alceste, scandalized by the victory against him in the courts for slander, is almost levitating with rage. He fumes to Philinte:

This age is vile, and I've made up my mind
To have no further commerce with mankind.

Here the intemperate Alceste suddenly walks through an upstage wall. The spectacle is hilarious, and Alceste's notorious virtue takes another pratfall when Oronte forces Célimène to choose between him and Alceste. This turns into a kind of jamboree of humiliation, during which all Célimène's lovers and the hated Arsinoé (now dressed in a harsh black-and-red gown and emitting little squeals of vindictive triumph from behind her fan) congregate across the width of the proscenium to witness Célimène being confronted with her own bitchy private thoughts about her lovers as Acaste reads them aloud. Célimène is turned toward the audience with chagrin on her face and nowhere to hide. Faced with true feeling, society collapses around her. One by one, the betrayed men exit, pouring scorn on Célimène's beautiful turned head, which she struggles to hold high. Acaste is the last to leave. He approaches Célimène in her humiliation and holds out a fan—the instrument for saving face and "composing herself"—and then, in a huge theatrical moment, drops the fan at her feet as he exits. It's a chilling revenge.

Alceste offers to marry the ostracized Célimène, but on the condition that they go "To that wild, trackless, solitary place / In which I shall forget the human race." Célimène protests that she is only twenty and would be bored. She starts to make another proposal, but Alceste cuts her off in a rage. She will accept life on his terms or not at all. He rejects her out of hand. Alceste cannot take anything in but himself; he is incapable, finally, of any mutuality. Quite naturally, in this production, Célimène runs screaming from him. Alceste then makes a breathtaking volte-face and, in the next beat, is talking about proposing marriage to Célimène's cousin, the idealistic Eliante (Nadja Weiss). When she confesses her love for Philinte, Alceste bids them, and us, a self-pitying farewell:

Meanwhile, betrayed and wronged in everything
I'll flee this bitter world where vice is king,

And seek some spot unpeopled and apart
Where I'll be free to have an honest heart.

Alceste's flight from court life is also a flight from his own problematic inner life. His legendary negativity is shown in Bergman's majestic production to be a defense against any emotional surrender.

On opening night, the burghers of Stockholm began clapping politely at the end of the play, as if surprised that Molière's comedy should come to such an abrupt and unsettling conclusion. But by the third curtain call, quite unexpectedly, the applause turned to stomping. After a while, the audience seemed to rise en masse from the plush blue seats and kept up the huzzahs for about ten minutes, until both they and the actors were exhausted. The Swedes know greatness when they see it. ■

—May 8, 1995

15

SUSAN STROMAN

By 9:30 in the morning on Martin Luther King Day, a blustery Arctic wind had emptied West Forty-Second Street of most pedestrians, but on the neon-lit fourth floor of the New 42nd Street Studios the mood was the opposite of frigid. It was the first day of work on a musical adaptation of Woody Allen's 1994 movie *Bullets over Broadway*, a high-spirited story of gangsters, showgirls, and theater, set in Manhattan in 1929, just before the crash. (The show opens at the St. James, on West Forty-Fourth Street, on April 10.) Susan Stroman, the show's director and choreographer (Allen wrote the book), had arrived early for a ten-o'clock call and was inspecting a miniature model of the set, designed by Santo Loquasto. Two weeks before, she had taken two dance assistants to a rehearsal studio and, using them more or less the way a sculptor would use clay, had danced all the characters and "worked out the landscape of movement and all the set changes." "So I absolutely know how the show moves," she said. Nonetheless, she was feeling a kind of parental anxiety. "When it's just me and my assistants dancing and singing in a room, there's no nervousness. It's just art pouring out of you. But now you have the responsibility of passing that on to the actors and also protecting them and being there for them. So there's an extra energy."

A stickler for research, Stroman had prepared a twelve-page information packet for the dancers who had been called for day 1. In the packet was a glossary of terms, including "Greenwich Village," "bohemian," "Prohibition," "gangster," and "flappers," along with citations for the show's visual influences. To give the cast a taste of the playground of New York in the twenties, Stroman had inserted a couple of pages from the May 23, 1929, issue of *The New Yorker*: "A Conscientious Calendar of Events Worth While." Because *Bullets over Broadway* is also set in Woody Allen's world, there were thumbnail explanations of references to Kant, Rousseau, Spinoza, Schopenhauer, and Aristotle. The handouts sat on a Formica table at the entrance to the rehearsal hall, beside a set of black script binders, fanned out flamboyantly like a royal straight flush. Chairs had been arranged in two semicircular rows around the director's table, and Stroman's show Bible—a folder, fatter than a quarterback's playbook, that held her script, her notes, her scene-by-scene breakdown of the cast's exits and entrances, the traffic plan of each musical number, and her e-mail exchanges with Allen—stood on a music stand, in front of the empty seats: the Book of Broadway, from which Stroman would soon begin to preach the gospel of good times.

Stroman, who is fifty-nine, has blond hair, a round open face, high cheekbones, and a ring-a-ding smile. "She puts joy on the stage because it's in her nature," Hal Prince, who hired Stroman to choreograph his brilliant 1993 revival of *Show Boat*, said. "She is a shiny person." Being sensational is Stroman's business. The credo attributed to her childhood idol, Fred Astaire—"Do it big, do it right, and do it with style"—is hers, too. She has choreographed such long-running hits as *Crazy for You*, a musical featuring the work of George and Ira Gershwin (1992; four years, 1,622 performances, and the first of five Tony Awards), and Mel Brooks's *The Producers* (2001; six years, 2,502 performances). From 1994 to 2003, she choreographed Alan Menken and Lynn Ahrens's *A Christmas Carol* spectacular, which packed the Paramount Theater at Madison Square Garden every year. She was also the first woman to choreograph and direct a full-length performance at New York City Ballet. An homage to silent films, *Double Feature* (2004), two fifty-minute dances set to the music of Irving Berlin and Walter Donaldson, remains among the most popular programs in the repertory.

Stroman's appearance on the scene, in the nineties, revitalized Broadway storytelling after a dismal decade dominated by dance-challenged British musicals. Where Jerome Robbins's dances had brought athleticism and line to Broadway, and Bob Fosse's had brought iconoclasm and style, Stroman's choreography offered wit and raise-the-roof rambunctiousness. The secret to her musical game is transitions—how people enter and exit, how the characters interact with the set, how the story is told through the swift shifting of spatial and emotional gears. For the song "Slap That Bass," in *Crazy for You*, for instance, the chorines became bass fiddles, and in the show's sensational first-act finale the miners of Deadwood, Nevada, learned rhythm from Broadway showgirls, who pulverized their prospecting pans and were swung around on mining picks. For "Springtime for Hitler," in *The Producers*, Stroman invented pigeons with swastikas on their wings, and in "Along Came Bialy," in the same show, a crowd of lusty old coots danced through Little Old Lady Land with their walkers. Even in last year's *Big Fish*, an adaptation of the Tim Burton movie, which failed to please the critics, Stroman, who directed and choreographed, managed a couple of unforgettable moments, including a circus fantasy, during which three behemoth elephants shook their backsides and tap-danced. "There's a part of her, a secret well of joy, that she doesn't let the world touch," Mel Brooks said. "It's there in her work."

At the New 42nd Street Studios, Stroman was dressed in her director's uniform: black shoes, black pants, black tunic. Her clothes, like everything else in her life, are designed to make her more effective at her job; she strategically plays down her looks and plays up the "worker bee," as she describes her style. "You can't think about yourself when you get dressed. You can only think about what you're working on here," she said. Even her nickname, Stro, by which she is almost universally known on the Rialto, conjures up a kind of hail-fellow, defeminized image, which for years she encouraged by wearing a baseball cap and a ponytail.

Pondering the stage picture that ends the first act of *Bullets*, Stroman reached into the model set, pulled out a plastic cup full of characters, and fished out a figurine of Olive, a showgirl who longs to be a Broadway actress and gets her gangster sugar daddy to buy her a starring role in a lame Broadway play. Then Stroman picked up a toy-size crimson-and-gold railroad car and put it on the set. "Over here is the end of act 1," she said. "A big train comes on and we see the principals in each window. At the end, of course, girls are tapping on the very top of the train. Then there's a girl hanging off the back in an Art Deco pose. Just wonderful."

Toting water bottles and scripts, the ensemble began to clatter into the room. Stroman excused herself. "I've got to go hug everybody here," she said. When the cast were settled in their seats, she stood to rally the troops. "Happy New Year! What's better than starting it with a Broadway show?" she said. One at a time, the performers gave their name and the number of Stroman shows they'd done. Before they were sent off to sing through the score, Stroman instructed them on the inspirations for the dance movements they'd be perfecting over the next three months. "You know, when I say to you to make this more turned in, this way, more like a stick figure— that's based on John Held's photos and cartoons of that time," she said, holding up a John Held Jr. cartoon of two knock-kneed Charleston dancers from her information packet. She continued, "On page 4, there are a lot of Erté images. I know we always say to the ladies, 'You're hitting an Erté pose.' So that's what you're hitting when you see that. Also the Vargas girls, the famous Vargas girls from the twenties. You know, in 'Tiger Rag,' when you're sitting on the floor, there are a lot of poses there that are based on the Vargas girls. The

whole show is immersed in that time period, choreographically."
Then it was time for the ensemble and the musical director to go to
work. Stroman left them to it.

Room 7-B, on the seventh floor of the New 42nd Street Studios, is
dedicated to Stroman's late husband, Mike Ockrent, a British director, who died of leukemia in 1999, at the age of fifty-three. His motto,
"Rehearsal is the best part," is emblazoned, along with his name, on
a plaque beside the door. When Stroman works on the seventh floor,
before the start of every day she runs her fingers across the deeply
indented letters of his name. "It feels like a sculpture in your hands,"
she said.

The two met in 1991 and collaborated on *Crazy for You*, which
Ockrent directed. "When Mike left to go back to London, I swear I
didn't feel anything or know anything," Stroman said, as the *Bullets*
chorus, down the hall, belted out "I'm Sitting on Top of the World."
"He was my director at that time. He went to London—" She broke
off. "I'm going to cry," she said. She wiped her eyes, then continued,
"He called a couple of weeks after we'd opened and said he had to
come back. I said, 'Why is that?' In my mind, I was thinking there
was a problem with the understudies, or why else was he coming
back? He said, 'I have to come back because I've fallen in love with
you.' I thought, Well, let's start dating. We've been through a tech
together, so now I know everything about this man."

Intimacy requires equality; Stroman and Ockrent teamed up
when both were in their artistic prime, and each had expertise to
offer the other. The curly-haired Ockrent, who had studied physics at the University of Edinburgh, was well spoken, well read, and
well informed; his sophistication and encouragement pitched Stroman's professional ambitions higher. "He was her Henry Higgins,"
said David Thompson, who wrote the book for five of Stroman's
musicals, including *The Scottsboro Boys* (2010), her bold, minimal-

ist experiment with social comment. "Mike got Stro to start look-ing at what the theater could be from a different perspective, to look at herself as a bigger artist." For her part, Stroman made Ockrent laugh. Throughout their time together, he left mash notes for her around the house. "I know I made him happy," Stroman said. "I was an American girl who was kind of curious, a little bit loud, in his mind, funny and optimistic."

The pair were married in 1996, and Stroman, who had lived in a dark basement apartment on the Upper West Side, found herself in a penthouse on Fifty-Seventh Street, configured around a cozy farmhouse-style kitchen to cater to Ockrent's culinary inclinations. (To this day, Stroman rarely applies heat to food. "I order in well," she said.) One day, Mel Brooks knocked on the door, launched full voice into a rendition of "That Face"—"That face/that face/that fabulous face!"—danced down their long corridor, jumped on the sofa, and said, "Hello, I'm Mel Brooks." By the end of the meeting, he had hired Stroman to choreograph and Ockrent to direct *The Producers*. In the middle of their planning, however, Ockrent fell ill. "He was very determined—it was not like the kind of thing where he knew that he was on a fast track out," Thompson said, recalling how he and Stroman had smuggled a cake into Sloan Kettering for Ock-rent's birthday. "And then he died. I think the surprise of it upended Stro's world." After that, Stroman said, "I didn't feel like working, and Mel came over, kind of stormed in. And he said, 'Look, I really want you to direct and choreograph this.' And he said, 'You'll cry in the morning, and you'll cry at night. But when you're with me during the day you will laugh. And that will save you.' It did." After Ock-rent's death, Stroman bought a bench in Central Park, on Literary Walk, near the statue of Robert Burns, whose birthday they had cel-ebrated every year. In commemoration of their New Year's wedding, the bench's plaque refers to Burns's most famous song: "Dear Mike, 'We'll tak' a cup o' kindness yet, for Auld Lang Syne.' Love, Stro."

In 2005, Stroman directed and choreographed a movie version of *The Producers*, working with the seasoned Hollywood editor Steven Weisberg, who had edited such films as *Men in Black II* and *Harry Potter and the Prisoner of Azkaban*. Three years later, Weisberg came to New York for a job and asked her out to dinner. "After the third time, I thought, I wonder why he's asking me out for these meals," Stroman said. "I'm not going to make another movie. I'm only involved in the theater. And then he walked me home and planted a big kiss on me. And he said, 'You're not the boss of me anymore. So now we can have a real relationship.' "

Weisberg was tall and handsome, with a lively interest in literature and jazz. Two years later, he moved into Stroman's penthouse. Stroman playfully referred to him as "an old hippie." "He was laid back and not precise," she said. "Very different from me, and very different, of course, from Mike." Weisberg would occasionally overlook Stroman's birthday or turn up late for dinner—forgivable lapses—but after he almost drove her into oncoming traffic and lost important footage in an Avid editing suite, she took him to see a neurologist. Tests revealed that tragedy had found her again: at fifty-five, Weisberg had early-onset Alzheimer's. "Once he was diagnosed, we got closer," she said. "I think because I realized that all those times that he would forget Christmas, or New Year's, or my birthday, it had nothing to do with his not loving me."

Over the next couple of years, various film friends stayed at Stroman's apartment to help her take care of Weisberg. "I know that those last years with me were wonderful years for him. I made them wonderful. But it was clear he needed something more," she said. Last September, during the vexed production of *Big Fish*, Stroman moved Weisberg back to Los Angeles, into an assisted-living accommodation, with twenty-four-hour care, where he could be supported by his Hollywood network. "It was devastating to say good-bye," Stroman said, looking down at her hands. "As of about last week, he doesn't remember me."

In many of Stroman's musicals—*Crazy for You*, *Contact* (1999), the 2000 revival of *The Music Man*, and even the film *Center Stage* (2000)—song and dance are dramatized as redemptive: they resuscitate dead communities and resurrect the downcast. What was petrified now flows. Contriving a schedule that allows her to stay as much as possible in "the ecstatic moment," as she calls it, Stroman has turned to the musical as her own Rx for heartbreak. Her dance card for the next year includes *Little Dancer*, a Lynn Ahrens and Stephen Flaherty musical (at the Kennedy Center, in October); *Take Five, More or Less*, a ballet set to the music of Dave Brubeck (at the Joyce, also in October); and *The Merry Widow*, at the Metropolitan Opera (starring Renée Fleming, opening New Year's Eve). "I'm really happy when I'm immersed in the art of it all—immersed in the music, the dance, the visual. Tapping into joy—it saves you," Stroman said.

Stroman has been tapping into joy since the age of five, when every night, for at least an hour before dinner, her father, Charles—an appliance salesman during the week and a pianist at local watering holes on weekends—sat at the upright in the den of the family's modest house, on the outskirts of Wilmington, Delaware, and worked his way through the American songbook, while Stroman danced on the linoleum floor. Sometimes her soft-spoken Irish-Catholic mother, Frances, would come out of the kitchen to sing along. Musical talent ran in the family. Charles's mother, Ella, was also a fine pianist, who for years accompanied the silent films at the Loews Theater in Wilmington. And Stroman's brother, Corky, who was eleven years older and the self-proclaimed "black sheep" of the family, was already touring with his own trio when Stroman was a girl; he ran a nightclub in Puerto Rico for years.

As a salesman, Charles traded on his ability to instill confidence. "The only thing you really need to make it is a bottle of Listerine and a thesaurus," he told Stroman. He burnished his life story with tall tales, in which he was the hero of every improbable escapade. "Everything was a sale. Everything was big and grand and outrageous," Debbie Bouma-Moore, Stroman's best friend since her teenage years, recalled. "If he told me a story, I would have to assume that it was false." A child of the Depression, Charles took pride in being self-made. "He had talent, but he never had the dream of becoming a professional musician," Stroman said. "He wanted to have a home, to send a daughter to college." (Stroman majored in English at the University of Delaware, graduating in 1976.) Still, he encouraged her to take chances. "What's the worst that can happen?" was his mantra. (He was less supportive of Stroman's younger sister, Debbie, who wasn't as musical. "He doted more on Susan, almost as if he knew she was going to be successful," Debbie said. "He actually pushed me around a bit and called me some foul names.")

From an early age, Stroman visualized music. "I imagined it filled with a cast of people and costumes and lights," she said. "I would dance and make up songs and stories and play characters. I was that kid. If I hadn't become a choreographer and a director, I would have just gone crazy with the visions." Although she was taking dance classes by the age of six, her focus was on creating, not performing. When Fred Astaire and Ginger Rogers movies came on television, the family would sit mesmerized on the sofa, Stroman recalled, "as if we were watching gold pour out of the television set." Even then, she recognized that music supported choreography. "I knew that when Fred Astaire turned or jumped in the air, so did the orchestra," Stroman said. She also understood "how he would structure his dance steps almost like a story, with a beginning, a middle, and an end."

At John Dickinson High School, Stroman donned the blue-and-white school colors as a baton twirler, adept at toss turns, double and triple turns, around-the-world, and choreographed her crew for half-time shows. "I think that's why I'm so good with props," she said. "I can catch the baton behind my back and everything." At home, she cocooned herself in dreams of movement, covering her bedroom wall with a decoupage of phrases and photographs, so firmly affixed that the entire wall had to be removed when the family sold the house, in the eighties. Between images of Fred and Ginger dancing "Pick Yourself Up," Rita Hayworth on a giant piano keyboard, Degas's *Blue Dancers*, and dancing ducks, Stroman pasted up such quotations as "Life is a cabaret," "I have a place where dreams are born, and time is never planned," "Feeling groovy," and, from Martha Graham, "All that is important is this one moment in movement. Make the moment important, vital and worth living. Do not let it slip away unnoticed and unused."

The summer before their senior year of college, Stroman and Debbie Bouma-Moore took a trip to San Francisco, where they were going to house-sit. They arrived in style, in a black Cadillac Eldorado convertible that a local car company needed delivered to the Bay Area, but soon ran out of money. "All we had left in the house was bread and jello that we put on the bread," Bouma-Moore said. Walking along Fisherman's Wharf, Stroman noticed the many buskers working the busy sidewalks: a trumpet player; a man in a refrigerator box, billing himself as "the Human Jukebox," who'd sing a song if you put a quarter in a slot. "I thought, OK, we could do this," she said. "We went from musician to musician. Nobody wanted us," Bouma-Moore recalled. Finally, they came upon a man playing a guitar with a drum on his back, cymbals on his knees, and a harmonica in his mouth. "How would you like two blondes dancing in front of you?" Stroman asked him. The girls went back to the house, put on their tap shoes, and worked up five routines "that could go with any song he could possibly play," Stroman said. Performing under the sobriquets Lindsey and Sunny—Bouma-Moore's nickname for Stroman—they earned around eighty dollars a day. Their act became so popular with tourists that the police were frequently called to clear the sidewalk, and local entrepreneurs made buttons featuring their beaming faces. At the end of the summer, they were spotted by scouts for the *Tonight Show*, who flew them to LA and planted them in the audience for a talent segment. Tap-dancing in the aisle to the tune of "Little Brown Jug," Stroman won a steak dinner and her first national attention.

In March 1977, at twenty-two, Stroman drove from Wilmington to New York for her first professional audition: she was one of three hundred dancers competing for three places in a revival of Vincent Youmans's 1927 musical *Hit the Deck*, which was being produced by Goodspeed Musicals, in East Haddam, Connecticut. By then, Stroman was choreographing at community theaters in Wilmington and teaching at a local dance studio. "It wasn't enough. I was itching for something more, and it wasn't coming to me," she said. Stroman, who had been to New York only once before, found Times Square frightening. "I was a goon magnet walking down the street," she said. "I remember being amazed at the number of dancers in the rehearsal space." That night, she saw *Pippin*, her first Broadway show. She returned home, not expecting anything to come of the audition. The next week, she got the job. She sold her red Opel GT and, that June, set off to start her life in show business, at a hundred dollars a week.

Stroman's departure was "a huge struggle," according to Corky. "My parents were afraid that 'real' show business might hurt me," Stroman said. "They saw that music did not help my brother. When he left town, he strayed down the wrong path." But, she added, "when you dance off the stage you are always leaping into darkness. I needed to take this leap into darkness for real." After Goodspeed, Stroman made a beeline for Manhattan, rented a one-bedroom ground-floor apartment on West Eighty-First Street for $235 a month, and then went home to pick up her things. The last item she loaded into her U-Haul was her father's small red piano.

Within six months, Stroman was touring as a dancer with the

national company of Kander and Ebb's *Chicago*, directed by Bob Fosse, and starring Gwen Verdon, Chita Rivera, and Jerry Orbach. For interested cast members, Orbach held a weekly acting class, where he preached the gospel of stage focus, which became Stroman's credo, too. "You have to remain in character when you're singing and dancing and acting, throughout the whole piece," she said. Perhaps the best example of her fierce concentration is *Trading Places* (1983), a showcase at the Equity Library Theatre, which Stroman devised with Jeff Veazey, her lanky dance partner of four years. In the heart-lifting piece, Stroman and Veazey play two film-obsessed fans who re-create the work of famous dance teams—Astaire and Rogers, Danny Kaye and Vera Ellen, and others—in synch with projections of the originals. "Jeff and I would work at Jeff's studio apartment," Stroman said. "We danced on a piece of plywood that he kept under his bed. We would work out all the dance steps in a very small space. When we were able to understand the steps, we would rent a studio and dance through it."

Stroman keeps on her laptop a three-minute clip of their rendition of "Begin the Beguine," dancing in exuberant tandem with Astaire and Eleanor Powell. Projected onto two screens against a starry backdrop, Astaire and Powell tap nonchalantly into view. After thirty seconds, Stroman and Veazey skitter onto the stage and fall into breezy lockstep with the dancers above them. With the full skirt of her bias-cut dress billowing, Stroman is every bit Powell's poetic equal, living both the joy of the dance and an almost platonic ideal of movement. Eventually, the music falls away, and the dancers dare each other in rhythm. With taps, claps, and dynamic changes of volume, the syncopation builds to a pinwheeling finale, whose thrilling commotion concludes with Stroman and Veazey on the same beat and in the same silhouette as Astaire and Powell. An extraordinary exhibition of concentration and control, *Trading Places* got Stroman and Veazey booked to demonstrate teamwork at many industrial shows. (Stroman had already begun to earn about eight hundred dollars a week choreographing shows for Ford, MetLife, and IBM, among others.) From Veazey, Stroman said, she learned about partnering. "There's a push and pull when you partner, almost like a rubber band," she said. "You become one, really, when you dance together." But in 1988 Veazey died of AIDS, at the age of thirty-three. "Jeff's death hit me hard," Stroman said. She gave up performing: "I did not want to dance with anyone else. It was time to get on the other side of the table."

Stroman had already begun the transition by choreographing, in 1987, an Off Broadway revival of Kander and Ebb's 1965 musical *Flora the Red Menace*, for her friend the director Scott Ellis. (David Thompson rewrote the book.) Ellis and Stroman had first met as performers in *Musical Chairs*, a 1980 Broadway flop. "It was springtime, and we would sit on the stoop of the stage door of the Rialto and lament about how much we wanted to make the move to create for the theater," Stroman said. A few years later, at Ellis's instigation, they plucked up the courage to approach Kander and Ebb and got permission to downsize *Flora* by staging the Communist love story as an amateur production at a WPA Federal Theater in the 1930s. The staging won *Flora* a new following. "We became this little family," John Kander recalled. "And then they had an idea of doing a revue of our songs." The revue, titled *And the World Goes 'Round*, which opened Off Broadway in 1991, ran for more than four hundred performances. *Flora* had brought Stroman to the attention of Hal Prince, who then hired her to choreograph *Don Giovanni* at New York City Opera. Liza Minnelli saw *And the World Goes 'Round*, and put Stroman in charge of the choreography for her show *Stepping Out at Radio City*, which was directed by Fred Ebb. In Radio City Music Hall's plush lobby Stroman met Mike Ockrent for the first time. "It was a combination of the comedy in *And the World Goes 'Round* and the show-biz extravaganza of Liza's show that made him think I would be right for *Crazy for You*," Stroman recalled. "He asked me right then and there if I would choreograph his show."

Before the opening-night party for *Crazy for You*, on February 19, 1992, Thompson and Ellis went over to the *Times* office to see if they could get an early copy of the review. "We went to the party, and I knew I had this thing in my hand that was going to change Stro forever," Thompson said. "I handed her this paper and just stepped back as she read." The show was reviewed by Frank Rich, who began this way:

> When future historians try to find the exact moment at which Broadway finally rose up to grab the musical back from the British they just may conclude that the revolution began last night. The shot was fired at the Shubert Theater, where a riotously entertaining show called *Crazy for You* uncorked the American musical's blend of music, laughter, dancing, sentiment and showmanship with a freshness and confidence rarely seen during the *Cats* decade. . . . The miracle that has been worked here—most ingeniously . . . by an extraordinary choreographer named Susan Stroman and the playwright Ken Ludwig—is to take some of the greatest songs ever written for Broadway and Hollywood and reawaken the impulse that first inspired them. . . . Ms. Stroman's dances do not comment on such apparent influences as Fred Astaire, Hermes Pan and Busby Berkeley so much as reinvent them. Rather than piling on exhausting tap routines to steamroll the audience into enjoying itself, the choreographer uses the old forms in human proportion, to bring out specific feelings in the music and lyrics. . . . Short of George Balanchine's *Who Cares?* at the New York City Ballet, I have not seen a more imaginative choreographic response to the Gershwins onstage.

"It burned through the party," Thompson recalled. "It just burned through the night."

Stroman's particular directorial gift—her ability to fill an empty space not just with people but with story—was there in embryo in *Crazy for You*. Her transition to director-choreographer, however, came seven years later, after a meeting with Lincoln Center Theater's artistic director, André Bishop. Bishop had seen all of Stroman's work in the nineties and had been impressed. "The dances that she did had a narrative, and the dancers had characters," Bishop said. "There was depth to them. There was an attention to detail in those dances that I had rarely seen in Broadway choreography." He offered Stroman a commission.

Months earlier, Stroman and Ockrent had found themselves in a dive in the meatpacking district that was a pool hall by day and a swing-dance club by night. At one in the morning, the place was a scrum of black-clad dancers. "Into this sea of dark fashion stepped a girl in a yellow dress," Stroman recalled. "You couldn't help but notice her: it was a very bold color to wear at night—lemon yellow— the same color you find on a traffic light. When she wanted to dance, she would step away from the bar and some man would ask her to dance." Stroman continued, "I was obsessed with watching her. I knew she would change some man's life that night." From that single image, Stroman developed "Contact." The dance was too short for an evening, so she added "Swinging," a sexy capriccio based on Fragonard's "The Swing," and "Did You Move?," about a woman rebelling against the control of her abusive husband. The triptych, titled *Contact*, which the *Times* called "an endorphin rush," became Lincoln Center Theater's longest-running production at the time. Neither a ballet nor a musical, *Contact* was sui generis, a novelty that was first billed as a "dance play." Although it had about five minutes of dialogue, its stories were told almost entirely in movement to recorded music. (The American Theatre Wing invented a "Special Theatrical Event" category after *Contact* won four Tonys.) "When the show was a hit, I went back downtown to find the club,"

Stroman said. "It had been demolished. So the girl and the club had disappeared—like Brigadoon." Stroman, however, was now uniquely visible as a female director-choreographer on Broadway.

Stroman had never met Woody Allen when the producers called her, in April 2012, to see if she would be responsive to his material. "People who knew her told me she was a pleasure to work with, very creative, and had a wonderful sense of humor," Allen said. "She had worked very well with Mel." Allen had scuppered all previous proposals to turn *Bullets over Broadway* into a musical. "He hates the new music for shows, the new composers," his sister, Letty Aronson, one of the lead co-producers for *Bullets*, explained. "So I said, 'Look, we can use the existing music of the time.'" Then, according to Allen, "a light bulb went off." Allen and Stroman worked together on the fifth floor of his Upper East Side town house. "We would take the stairs, because he won't go in the elevator," Stroman recalled. "We worked in the children's playroom. We sat on children's chairs at a low children's table." Stroman's knowledge of the American songbook and her expertise at juggling music and dialogue made Allen a believer. "I would be rattling off songs that I thought only I would know, but she knew them all, and knew songs that I didn't know," he said. "She was ultra-meticulous about wanting to make sure that every song advanced the plot." The musical of *Bullets* has a straighter story line than the film and, because of the song and dance, is also more dynamic. "My wife prefers this to the movie," Allen told me.

On the morning of January 23, the nine principals made their first appearance in the *Bullets* rehearsal room for the meet and greet, a ritual of Broadway that is a cross between a kaffeeklatsch, a pep rally, and a shareholders' meeting. ("I'll see you at the meet and greet, but I hope I don't have to meet or greet anybody," Allen had e-mailed Stroman beforehand.) Well-dressed investors picked their way through the rows of wooden chairs toward a lavish smorgasbord

of breakfast foods. Producers hobnobbed with actors. Theater owners chatted with leggy chorines in full makeup, with high heels and
bright smiles. Zach Braff—who plays the aspiring playwright forced
to cast a gangster's tootsie in order to finance his play, only to discover that her minder, a galoot called Cheech (Nick Cordero), is the
one with the genuine literary gift—wandered the room with practiced nonchalance, in a Detroit Tigers baseball cap. Stroman min-
gled and beamed and posed for a photographer. Success was in the
air: the musical's story was tight and tested, the songs were classics,
cleverly massaged, and Stroman, the doyenne of Broadway dazzle,
was at the helm. "When it works, it's like the oil business," the producer Roy Furman said to the nabobs from the Jujamcyn Theaters,
which owns the St. James. The word "gusher" was heard.

When Allen arrived, looking as if he'd walked out of an Orvis
catalogue—brown pants, olive work shirt, tan all-weather brogans—
Stroman ushered him toward the model of the set and talked him
through her box of scenic tricks. Allen listened intently with head
bowed and hands clasped behind his back. "She knows the field
much more than I know it," he'd told me earlier. "I could do it in the
movies, but she's the one on the stage. It's really Susan's show, 95
percent." He bent to scrutinize the set as Stroman explained how
it would transform from one scene to the next: the sprung furniture that would allow would-be lovers to bounce Chagall-like across
the stage for "Let's Misbehave"; the Erté proscenium, with niches
for "living sculpture"; the revolving stage, which would be used to
re-create the gangsters' rampage through the theater at the finale.
"That never would have occurred to me," Allen said. Then, after a
few minutes of being passed around to various high rollers like nuts
at Christmas, he politely took his leave. Stroman stayed behind to
address the crowd.

"I couldn't be more excited about the design," she said, as Santo
Loquasto and the costume designer William Ivey Long flanked

her. "We're going to just show you some things in tandem—I'll do interjections—but I'm going to pass it off. Hit it, Santo!" Stroman's openness turned the occasion from a business chore into an entertaining instrument of consensus. After Loquasto and Ivey Long had done their part, she turned the spotlight on the chorus. When she got on the subject of gangsters, she pointed to a strapping young dance-ensemble member in the third row—Casey Garvin, whose grandfather's uncle was Michael (Trigger Mike) Coppola, of the Genovese family. "I looked him up. He was Lucky Luciano's hit man," Stroman said. Casey smiled, swivelled in his seat, and nodded to the applauding audience. "He's got a very secure job," Stroman said. Then she sent the producers and investors back to their bagels and badinage, and she went back to work.

An hour later, the food and formalities finished, the chorus girls, now in tap shoes and clutching prop daisies, stepped toward the director's table, where Stroman sat. "I'm Mary!" "Annie!" "Jeannie!" "Rose!" "Betty!" "Daisy!" "Olive!" they called out, and began to sing:

> We'll be glad when you're dead, you rascal you.
> We'll be glad when you're dead, you rascal you.
> When you're dead in your grave
> No more women will you crave.
> We'll be glad when you're dead, you rascal you.

As the dancers belted out the number and worked their routine, Stroman scrutinized the line, seeming to listen as much with her body as with her ears. Her shoulders moved to the rhythm; her hands kept up their own semaphore. Stroman is a taskmaster—"She's in my pantheon of fanatics, guaranteed," Ivey Long, who has collaborated with her on twenty-eight shows, said—but she is exacting without being persecuting. At one point, she moved into a corner of the room with her arms crossed, shuffling her feet as she imagined a new step. At the end of the number ("We'll be gay and merry / At your obituary"), the chorines were meant to exit blowing kisses. Stroman, back in her seat, leaned forward. "Kiss with the middle finger," she said. For a few minutes, the dancers tried to perfect their mordant farewell. Stroman stopped them again. "Blow it off your hand," she said, standing up to demonstrate. "No, not here—get it way out here. Five, six, make a kiss. Flat, yeah, so the kiss flies right out of your hand." Next, she attended to the chorus's wagging fingers as they scolded the rascal with "You know you done us wrong, you rascal you." "Some of you have just gone down and then gone down, down, down," she said, letting her pointed finger droop. "Don't just go down. My finger goes up, up. Take your whole arm with it. My hand's going to move a little bit, but my focus is on my finger." Then, getting in front of the mirror with her dancers, Stroman said, "We're looking down this way, so out, out, step, hit it!" The dancers reran the moment. "Looking good," she said. "Better, better!"

"You Rascal You" is a nightclub routine performed at Nick's Place, which is owned by Nick Valenti, the palooka whose girl wants to be a star. Valenti is played by the hulking Vincent Pastore, better known to the universe as Big Pussy, in *The Sopranos*. Pastore, who carries with him his own saturnine atmosphere, was leaning against a wall, watching the rehearsal and rolling an unlit cigar between his thick fingers. He seemed bemused at the hubbub of Stroman's blocking. She waved him over as two thugs practiced rushing across the room with a fedora-clad dummy lying face down on a gurney under a bloodstained sheet. "You are the set change," Stroman explained to Pastore, whose face was a mask of puzzlement. "As soon as the music stops, I say the line?" he asked. "Yes," she said, putting her arm through his and steering him toward the piano. "It's a musical. Wait for the music," she said. The pianist played the scene in: the corpse was rushed across the room, and Pastore waited for the music to stop, and then, in his deep, sludgy voice, announced, "He tripped!" The room exploded with laughter. "Love it!" Pastore beamed. "All right!"

On February 1, a week after the meet and greet, the production was temporarily thrown off balance by what the producers began to refer to as "the Situation." Allen's estranged daughter, Dylan Farrow, published an open letter on the *Times* website, repeating allegations of sexual abuse by Allen that had first been raised at the time of a 1992 custody suit. The piece came out on a Saturday, and that Monday morning Stroman convened the cast. "We never go into the personal lives of those around us," she recalls saying. "We don't know anything about personal lives—we only know about talent. We're here to put on a show, and we're here to talk only about the show." Stroman never broached the subject with Allen. "We have no small talk. He's never asked me anything about my personal life, and I wouldn't ask him anything about his," she said. "For us, this collaboration has always been about the work. This is my work. This is William Ivey Long's work and Santo Loquasto's work. This is the work of the actors. This is the work of an entire team of people who love what we do." Nevertheless, Farrow's letter set off a wave of media scurrility that cast a long shadow over the prospects of Allen's latest movie, *Blue Jasmine*, at the Academy Awards, as well as over the Broadway opening of *Bullets*. Ultimately, Cate Blanchett's performance in *Blue Jasmine* won her the Best Actress Oscar, and the *Bullets* box office was also unaffected. On February 7, Allen published a rebuttal in the *Times*, which Stroman said calmed "any kind of fear that anyone might have had." In the early days of the brouhaha, she asked the producers about advance ticket sales. "I was told they were steady and growing," she said. "After that, I stepped on the gas."

At the St. James Theatre five weeks later, Stroman sat on a blue padded bench stretched across the armrests of several seats in row H; this allowed her to see over the large slanted director's table in front of her, where yellow Post-it notes were lined up like rows of corn. "Tonight we're running act 2 with music," she said, pulling her hair high above her head with both hands.

The theater was only two city blocks from the rehearsal room, but it had taken five laborious tech weeks to get the fun machine of *Bullets over Broadway* up and running there. Stroman, who keeps a hawkeye on every production detail, had even kept watch over me, issuing periodic e-mail bulletins:

> Woody . . . loved the new numbers. He even left smiling. I had to laugh at one scene—when I asked him about changing a line— he started to cough—I asked him if he wanted some water (which was sitting in front of him) and he said in his Woodyish way, "No, let me struggle. I like to struggle."
>
> Can you tell I've been up since 5:30? Just excited about the tech. Can't wait to get there. As each set unfolds, it's like . . . a big present rolling towards you downstage.
>
> I am heading to the sitzprobe now. That is the first time the cast hears the orchestrations and meets the band. . . . I talked Woody into coming. . . . I bought some Snickers bars. He always loves to have a Snickers bar when he visits.
>
> The sitzprobe was amazing. I was going to try to find another word, but I can't. . . . I am sure I am the first and only person to tear up at "Tiger Rag"! When those opening chords were played, the past two years of meetings and ideas and collaboration came flooding into my brain. Now there was a musical where there never was a musical before. Woody was very happy. He would spontaneously applaud, but quietly under the table.

As the designers fiddled at their computers, Stroman studied the show curtain, which bore an image of high-stepping chorines, their tilted bodies jousting with slide trombones. "When the curtain comes up, I have the girls in the same pose," she said. "I was inspired by Santo." She drifted down to the lip of the stage to consult with her musical supervisor, Glen Kelly, and with Marin Mazzie, who plays Helen Sinclair, a diva who is trying to manipulate the playwright, David Shayne (Braff), into beefing up her role. Sinclair's seduction of Shayne is performed to the Bessie Smith belter "I Ain't Gonna Play No Second Fiddle"; to give the vamp more drive and drama, Stroman upped the tempo and adjusted Mazzie's delivery, instructing her to give a lusty sigh at Braff's touch. Where Mazzie had sung " 'Cause Mama don't sing/And Mama don't swing/For a man who won't let her play lead," she was now down and dirty: " 'Cause Mama don't *Uumph*/And Mama don't *Unnh*/For a man who won't let her play lead." There were whoops of approval from out front.

Stroman, according to Kelly, "rules by niceness." She also rules by being extraordinarily organized. Her office, which is on the tenth floor of her apartment building, is decorated entirely in black and white, a startling tabula rasa, with a white Formica desk, stacked with legal pads and pencils, at its center. "I wanted the room to have no show posters or anything in it that would take my mind off the particular project I was doing," she said. Everything is arranged so that she has to think only about dance: "Having things organized— water bottles lined up, surfaces clear and clean—is about keeping distractions to a minimum so I can stay focussed. I feel like I lose time and energy if I have to rummage for a pencil or a cup of tea." Likewise, when she gives notes the emphasis is on eye contact, on making her ideas felt without the impediments of paper and pen. As she speaks, the associate director, Jeff Whiting, stands just behind her with a wedge of index cards, like a quiz-show host. When Stroman has covered a point, Whiting fields the note and hands her the next card. After the session, he copies her notes in a legible hand and slips them under the actors' doors. On a hard day, an actor may get as many as ten cards under the door.

The day of the first preview—March 10—was uncharacteristically warm, the kind of sudden release after a long winter freeze that is always good for comedy. "It's an omen," Allen recalled thinking as he left his house that morning. For the pre-show tune-up that afternoon, he sat to Stroman's left at the director's table. Stroman, who looked tired, set out two Snickers bars for him, as if to say that it was going to be one of those days. The previous night's dress rehearsal, in front of an invited audience, had been a disaster: because of a faulty stage elevator, the show had had to stop for twenty minutes. "It was ragged," she said. "We lost what little audience we had." Worse, the company had missed its chance to calibrate the show to the audience's reactions. For the actors and the crew, the preview that night would be their first real test.

Slumped in his seat, Allen watched as Stroman adjusted the lighting on the bullet-riddled corpse as it was wheeled through Nick's Place. Over the mike to the lighting designer, Donald Holder, Stroman requested "a low glow, as if we're heading somewhere but we don't know where yet." She added, "I want the club later." The fix worked: now, as the corpse was wheeled offstage, the nightclub loomed into view, a surprise for the audience. "The fluidity with which she makes things go from scene to scene is amazing," Allen said. "I would be so lost. For me, it would be like a day at the Strategic Air Command." When Allen had a query, he leaned over to Stroman with the tact of a butler. "I'm not suggesting this, but did anyone feel that the first act is too long?" he said. "Yes," Stroman replied with no hint of defensiveness. "Is there anything that can be done about it?" Allen asked. "I'm doing it now," she said, showing him some nips and tucks in the script. "You go in and carve," she said. "Cuts are always good," Allen said later. "Good riddance!" With only an hour left to tweak before the cast had to get ready for the evening's performance, Allen's main concern was the balance of story and song. "I want to try to bring the book a little more forward," he said. "The music is a little loud, and so the audience misses some of the lines."

At 7 p.m., the weather was so mild that the Naked Cowgirl was posing for photos in a black bikini at Forty-Fourth and Broadway. A line had already formed under the marquee of the St. James. Onstage, the actors were gathered in a circle around the two lead producers, Aronson and Julian Schlossberg, who told them to "win one for the Gipper." Stroman worked her way up the aisle to her catbird seat in the back row. After the fiasco of the dress rehearsal, she was nervous for the actors. "I want them to be able to tell the story without worrying about anything else," she said. Allen had also arrived early, accompanied by a towering young female Italian assistant—a sort of sequoia of solicitude. "*Voodee*, the doors are opening," the assistant said. For a moment, Allen panicked, uncertain whether to take his aisle seat or to bolt to a private room up in the mezzanine. "*Aaah!*" he dithered, then hightailed it up the stairs, returning to join Stroman at curtain time.

The cheering began with the show's first beat, as a spray of machine-gun bullets spelled out the show's title in white lights, and it never really stopped. Mazzie belted, Braff squirmed, Cordero menaced, Pastore was dopey and deadly, and even Trixie the Pomeranian got her laughs on cue. The sight gags, which had been miniature notions a month earlier, were now huge comic realities: the dancing hot dogs in "I Want a Hot Dog for My Roll," the sprung chairs that lent surreal hilarity to "Let's Misbehave." Stroman's signature piece of showmanship was "Runnin' Wild"—the rollicking finale to act 1, in which all the ricocheting characters and their desires came together, as the chorus girls skittered around the stage in black hot pants and red conductor caps and tap-danced on top of the railroad car.

During the performance, Stroman occasionally leaned over and put her head in her hands, as if embarrassed. But it was shock that she was feeling. "I couldn't believe the roar of the audience," she said later. "I think we did our job." At the finale, the cast launched into "Yes! We Have No Bananas," a goofy anthem for the evening's caprice and a song that rejects the negative: instead of admitting defeat at the lack of bananas, the number celebrates all that *does* exist—scallions, onions, tomatoes, potatoes, and, this being Broadway, blintzes, knishes, and chopped liver, too. As the actors congaed around the stage, the gleeful song played both as a refusal to suffer over loss and as gratitude for all that remains. At the curtain call, Allen rushed up the stairs toward his private room, but paused at the top. There, alone in the low amber light, he bent over the balustrade to gaze at the crowd standing to applaud. For a full minute, he studied the jubilation, then finally slipped away.

At midnight, Stroman was still there in the quiet auditorium, deconstructing the performance, figuring out cuts and light changes for the next day's rehearsal. There was a month to go before *Bullets over Broadway* had its official opening: time to find even more momentum, more laughter, more delight. Stroman, who has "shaken the hand of grief," as Ivey Long put it, long ago dedicated herself to banishing gravity from the stage. For the audience and for herself, *Bullets* was a joy ride. "I try to choose joy," she said. "It's not easy. But even if we have no bananas we all have to keep going." ▪

—March 31, 2014

The Producers

Mel Brooks, who is seventy-four and a tummler of note, once said, "I went into show business to make a noise, to *pronounce myself.* I want to go on making the loudest noise to the most people." The reckless abandon of his manic shtick is preserved on records—he is the incomparable Two-Thousand-Year-Old Man (Joan of Arc: "Know her? I went with her!")—and in films (*Young Frankenstein* and *Blazing Saddles* among them). But *The Producers* (at the St. James), the new Broadway version of the 1968 movie that Brooks wrote and directed, tops his lifetime of tumult. After opening night, in the spirit of the craven avidity that characterizes Brooks's fictional producers, Max Bialystock and Leo Bloom, the show's real producers hiked the ticket price to an all-time Broadway high of a hundred dollars, added two computers to the theater's lobby, and commandeered two more box offices at the Shubert theaters across from the St. James to accommodate overflow business. The Tele-charge lines were jammed; and, among Broadway swamis, all of this was a sure sign that a gusher— so rare in recent years—had been struck. On the day after it opened, *The Producers* sold 33,598 tickets, taking in a total of $3,029,197 (it will recoup its eleven-million-dollar investment—almost twelve times the cost of the movie—in thirty-six weeks); these are the biggest numbers ever in the history of Broadway. (One person, who tried to beg a ticket for a friend dying of cancer, was told by the producer, Rocco Landesman, "That's not good enough.") At a stroke, the diminutive Brooks—"the little maestro," Kenneth Tynan called him—has turned into the Ponce de León of commercial theater. He has found the secret that Broadway feared it would never find again: not money (there are plenty of spondulicks around) but joy.

Brooks is a licensed zany. The paying customers know that he has the comic goods, and they giggle excitedly as the curtain goes up— even before there is anything remotely funny onstage—like virgins about to be bedded by a rampant old pro. What's first-rate about this particular seduction is not the lyrics or the music or the choreography but Brooks's antic imagination and the atmosphere of audacious liberty with which he whips up both the audience and his collaborators. In *The Producers*, Nazi pigeons "*Sieg heil!*," dirty old ladies dance with their walkers, and, with the song "Springtime for Hitler," Brooks offers the goofiest production number since Jewish refugees danced over barbed wire in the musical version of *Exodus*—they really did! Here, Brooks turns atrocity into travesty, with a fabulous high-kicking chorus in swastika formation singing to "ev'ry hotsy-totsy Nazi" and with parading showgirls doing their Ziegfeld strut while balancing behemoth beer steins, pretzels, and bratwursts on their heads. In this high-camp heaven, expertly staged by Susan Stroman, Brooks somehow also manages to satirize the shallowness and moral exhaustion of a world that he can't help loving in all its clapped-out vulgarity. In the process, and for the first time in about forty years, Brooks has, however inadvertently, asserted the authority of the comedian as the engine behind the Broadway musical. This is good news for a vivacious theatrical form, which for a generation has been hijacked by the forces of high art and lumbered with more heavy intellectual furniture than it can carry.

After *Oklahoma!* (1943) raised the hegemony of the musical's score and book over the idiosyncratic high jinks of its comedians, the genre became increasingly sophisticated and artistically ambitious; "musical comedy" became "the musical." Humor, if there was any, was relegated to the subplot or to an eleven-o'clock number. By the late sixties, when Brooks wrote *The Producers*, the comedians who had made the musical the great noisy, democratic, popular art form it had been into the mid-fifties were either dead or more or less out to pasture. Vietnam had put paid to the musical's thematic stock-in-trade: optimism, innocence, and abundance. Broadway was left with nothing to sing about and no way to incorporate the culture's sense of collapse. *The Producers*—in which two scoundrels try to bilk their investors by staging a surefire failure, entitled "Springtime for Hitler," which turns out to be so bad that it becomes a hit and thereby scuppers their larcenous dreams—was Brooks's effort to marry the enchantment of the old form with society's newfound mood of mockery and disenchantment. Stephen Sondheim's *Company* was still two years away. Now, more than thirty years later,

Sondheim's deconstructed musicals are the state of the art, and Brooks has brought back to Broadway, in a well-written libretto, that old formula of "no girls, no gags, no chance." Both as a narrative and as a spectacle, the stage version of *The Producers* is far superior to the movie—which, in itself, is another Broadway first.

With the help of his deft and witty co-author, Thomas Meehan, a playwright and a former *New Yorker* humorist, who hit his first mother lode as the author of *Annie*, Brooks reins in his compulsion to tell four jokes where one will do, and the jokes he does tell almost always hit their mark. Brooks and Meehan give the story a proper ending, which it didn't have in the movie, and also provide Leo Bloom (the excellent Matthew Broderick), the hapless accountant who accidentally hits upon Bialystock's scam, with both a love interest and a compelling reason for joining forces with the con man—he has always dreamed of being in theater. Or, as Brooks, who wrote both the music and the lyrics, so piquantly has Bloom sing, "I just gotta be a producer / Drink champagne until I puke." In general, Brooks's lyrics are formulaic; but when they abandon any attempt at articulacy and revel in Yiddish folderol they are sublime. For instance, when the helmeted Nazi author of "Springtime," Franz Liebkind (well played by Brad Oscar), interrupts a fey audition rendition of "Haben Sie Gehört das Deutsche Band?" to show the assembled how the macho Führer really sang, he breaks into a Jolson hard sell, all elbows and wonderful, dopey sound: "Mit a bang / Mit a boom / Mit a bing-bang bing-bang boom! / . . . Mit a zetz, mit a zap, mit a zing." Brooks, who pays sidesplitting homage to Judy Garland when the play's director-turned-Hitler (Gary Beach, having a field day) sits on the edge of the stage mouthing "I love you," also pays homage to himself: in the middle of "Springtime," a storm trooper lip-synchs to Brooks's smoky Brooklyn voice, saying, "Don't be stupid, be a smarty, come and join the Nazi party!" Brooks likes nothing more than to push a stereotype to such an extreme that the lie behind it

becomes hilarious. In the conformist hell of Leo Bloom's accounting firm—given a light, Expressionist touch by Robin Wagner's
design—a black accountant with a deep bass voice suddenly breaks
into Leo's litany of woe: "Oh I debits all de mornin' / An' I credits all
de eb'nin' / Until dem ledgers be rightttt." This left-field approach
also applies to the dialogue. At one point, when the zaftig blond
Swedish bimbo secretary (the effective Cady Huffman) brushes up
against Leo and he moves away sharpish, she asks, "Vhy Bloom go so
far downstage right?"

The performing centerpiece of the show is Nathan Lane, as the
flamboyant huckster Bialystock, who, when he's not producing shows
like "The Breaking Wind" or "The Kidney Stone" and its sequel,
"This Too Shall Pass," is seducing old ladies for their little "check-
ees," which are always made out to a show called "Cash." "Please,
let's play one game with absolutely no sex," the exhausted Bialystock
says to one rapacious old biddy. "Let's play the Jewish Princess and
her husband." Lane is expert at delivering these tart wisecracks,
and he has an astute sense of timing that pays off best in caterwaul-
ing song—for instance, when he takes up residence under a ladder,
breaks a mirror, and throws a black cat around by the tail to invoke
bad luck. He's a noisy, comic whirlwind, and he works well against
Broderick's cunning, droll underplaying. As good as he is, Lane can't
quite find the oily desperation that Zero Mostel brought to the film
role or escape the shadow of Mostel's comic genius. Empty vessels
make the most noise; and even when he's knockin' 'em dead, shouting his gonif wisdom into Bloom's ear—"NEVER PUT YOUR OWN
MONEY IN THE SHOW!"—there's something undefined in Lane,
whose bravado, unlike Brooks's, seems to mask rather than reveal.
Nonetheless, Lane's kind of high-amperage panache is in limited
supply these days, and both he and Broderick deliver the mail. In
that, there is gallantry as well as grace.

As a foot soldier tromping through Germany at the end of the

Second World War, Brooks was the platoon cutup; he sang all the time and was never one to brood about the dead bodies around him, or the prospect of becoming one of them. In a *New Yorker* Profile in the late seventies, he mentioned to Kenneth Tynan that he used to tell the troops, "Nobody dies—it's all made up." He explained, "Otherwise we'd all get hysterical, and that kind of hysteria—it's not like sinking, it's like slowly taking on water, and that's the panic. Death is the enemy of everyone . . . death is more of an enemy than a German soldier." If our president won't sign up for the Kyoto agreement to protect the atmosphere, we can still sign up for the Brooks agreement, which is sure to protect our inner environment. The pact goes like this: We are polluted by grief and greed; let's acknowledge it, defy it, meet the inevitable vulgar annihilation with careless vulgar rapture, and, with the last measure of our energy and imagination, refuse darkness its dominion. That is the comic's bargain with the public. Laughter makes you light-headed, but it also brings light. It's intoxicating. It works. I've signed on; and I can say without fear of contradiction that there are millions of other heartbroken souls in line right behind me. ▪

—May 7, 2001

16

MIKE NICHOLS

Once, in the early seventies, Mike Nichols was sitting in a commercial jet as it took off from JFK. Moments after it was airborne, the plane went into what Nichols recalls as "an unnervingly steep bank. Everybody looked at each other. Nobody knew what it meant." The pilot came on the intercom. "We are experiencing—" he began in his best *Right Stuff* drawl. Then, suddenly, he said, "Just a minute!" The mike went dead. In the long silence that followed, the people on the airplane started to panic. A woman a few rows in front of Nichols turned around and looked squarely at him. "What do we do now, Mr. Success?" she said.

Nichols, who has a sharp American wit but courtly European manners, bit his tongue. "All those 'Mr. Success' years would have been hard to explain to anybody if I tried," Nichols, now sixty-eight, says. "What I really wanted to say to that envious woman was 'Don't worry. There's still nothing happening inside me. I'm not experiencing success or anything much.' "

But feelings aren't facts. From the moment Nichols made his name, in the late fifties, as the lanky deadpan half of the comedy team Nichols and May, he took up residence in success. As early as 1961, a letter addressed to "Famous Actor, Mike Nichols, USA" reached him. And, by the seventies, Nichols represented the high-water mark in not just one but three areas of American entertainment. As a comedian, he improvised routines with Elaine May,

which are among the treasures of American humor; as a stage director, beginning in the early sixties, he had a string of commercial hits
that made him the most successful Broadway director since George
Abbott; as a film director, he made the bold, intelligent *Who's Afraid
of Virginia Woolf?* (1966) and *The Graduate* (1967). The latter, for
which he won an Academy Award and which both summed up and
influenced his generation, got him off the Hollywood blocks perhaps
faster than any director since Orson Welles.

Nichols has made seventeen films in the last three decades. Success, however, as Winston Churchill said, is never final. On May 3,
1999—just one day short of sixty years since Nichols, then Michael
Igor Peschkowsky, the son of a White Russian émigré and a German
beauty, arrived in New York by boat from Germany—he found himself at one of those occasions he likes to call a "ratfuck," at Lincoln
Center's Avery Fisher Hall, where more than three thousand citizens had gathered to celebrate his lifetime achievement in film.
The first part of the evening was a cinematic homage. Just before it
began, Nichols and his wife, Diane Sawyer—the most observed of all
observers—took their seats in the front row of a box just beside the
stage and surveyed the illustrious guests below, among them Richard Avedon, Steve Martin, Itzhak Perlman, Stephen Sondheim, Caroline Kennedy Schlossberg, and Barbara Walters. Nichols assumed
the runic crooked smile Elizabeth Taylor describes as "that smile
that tilts up at one end, that you can read so much into—a shared
joke, a certain skepticism." Then, one by one, various grandees of
American popular culture—Meryl Streep, Paul Simon, Elaine May,
Harrison Ford, Buck Henry, Nora Ephron, Candice Bergen, Art Garfunkel, Matthew Broderick, Nathan Lane—filed into the box, too,
and flanked the evening's sovereigns. They were part of Nichols's
story; later in the ceremony, in their encomiums from the stage,
they would individually swear allegiance to him like courtiers to a
king—which, in a way, he is.

"He knows that all the Versailles stuff is bullshit," says the screen-writer Buck Henry, a close friend who has scripted three of Nichols's films, including *The Graduate*. "He knows when his ass is being kissed, and he knows when it isn't, although it is most of the time. He casts a baleful eye on all of it, but in his heart he wants it and needs it." In its deluxe panoply, the Lincoln Center extravaganza fulfilled one of Nichols's life-long fantasies. "He's on an island that belongs to him, manned on the turrets by men with machine guns," another close friend, Richard Avedon, explains. "People can only get in with a passport, and then only his friends." The need for a seamless armor is the legacy of Nichols's friendless, despairing ref-ugee childhood. When he arrived from Berlin, at the age of seven, he was totally bald; he'd been permanently denuded of all body hair at the age of four, a reaction to a defective whooping-cough vaccine. He knew just two English sentences—"I do not speak English" and "Please do not kiss me." He'd lost his homeland, his language, his class pedigree, and, by the age of twelve, he would also lose his father. "I was a zero," Nichols says now. He adds, "In every way that mat-tered, I was powerless." Nichols sought something to counteract his paralyzing sense of inadequacy and to disarm a world that he saw, and still sees, as predatory and cruel. "The most useful thing is if your enemy doesn't know he's your enemy," Nichols told me, setting out the rule of dissimulation by which, over the years, he has kept the world in his thrall. "Never let people see what you want, because they will not let you have it. Never let anybody see what you feel, because it gives them too much power. You're probably better off not show-ing weakness whenever you can avoid it, because they'll go for you." With its aspects of detachment, generosity, and control, the impe-rial posture has served him well.

On the night of Nichols's gala, Elaine May couldn't resist a wink at his jerry-built crown. "So he's witty, he's brilliant, he's articulate, he's on time, he's prepared, and he writes," she said. "But is he perfect? He knows that you can't really be liked or loved if you're perfect. You have to have just enough flaws. And he does. Just the right perfect flaws to be absolutely endearing. And my three minutes are up, but if I had another four seconds I'd tell you every one of those flaws."

Nichols is a purveyor of aplomb, a rare commodity these days. He lives like a pasha and long ago took up the kingly pastime of breeding Arabian horses. (In 1972, he had the national-champion stallion and mare, Elkin and Elkana.) Over the years, Nichols, who calls himself "a Dionysian who gets tired easily," has also been romantically linked to a variety of goddesses—goddesses of literature (Robert Graves's Black Goddess, Margot Callas, who was Nichols's second wife), goddesses of glamour (Suzy Parker), activism (Gloria Steinem), society (Jackie Onassis), and the media (Sawyer, who became the fourth Mrs. Nichols, in 1988). Well before Nichols grew into his grandiosity, his hauteur had him typecast in college plays as the Dauphin and the emperor. With his long Russian nose, he emits a kind of mandarin snottiness—what Woody Allen calls "his superb contumely," adding, "It's supercilious in the way we all wish we had the genius for. He's a nice version of George Sanders in *All About Eve*." At a dinner party in the sixties, Nichols corrected Norman Mailer, who had declared that his favorite line of poetry was Dylan Thomas's "Do not go quietly into that good night." "Actually, it's 'gentle,'" Nichols said. "'Quietly' wouldn't scan, would it?" Mailer rounded on Nichols, calling him a "royal baby," a put-down that Nichols thought was "pretty good." (In jollier circumstances, Sawyer has been known to refer to her husband as "His Royal Cuteness.")

At the finale of the gala, Nichols had planned to go onstage and say to the assembled, "Well, that's all very well and good, but what about my humanity? What about my *fucking* humanity?" But Art Garfunkel scuppered the joke by speaking earnestly to that very point. So when Nichols stepped before his audience—a tall man with big, gnarly hands and an indulged belly that precedes him by some inches—he resorted to another gripe. "Where the hell is Dustin Hoff-man?" Nichols said. "He was nothing when I found him." His straight face caught the audience off guard and made the joke ambiguous. "It's like the monster not showing up at the tribute for Dr. Franken-stein," he continued. "Actually, I suspect that his not showing up is related to my not going to his AFI tribute, although that was all the way across the country. . . . Well, it's all blood under the bridge now."

But blood has a way of sticking to things; even the solvent of Nichols's wit can't wipe out certain dark spots. In his movie career, things have not all gone Nichols's way. There was a string of flops in the mid-seventies: *Catch-22* (1970), *The Day of the Dolphin* (1973), *The Fortune* (1975), and *Bogart Slept Here*, which Nichols closed down in production; there followed a seven-year hiatus before his next film, the excellent *Silkwood* (1983). Some of his later movies—*Heartburn* (1986), *Regarding Henry* (1991), *Wolf* (1994)—were more or less rumbled by the critics. In 1995, after Nichols had shown the final cut of *The Birdcage* (which went on to gross more than $180 million worldwide) to his editing team on Martha's Vineyard, he sat down with them for a celebratory meal. "I was very emotional and very angry. I couldn't speak all through lunch," Nichols told a friend. "The film was so good, so strong. I realized I'd had no inkling of my anger at the people who had written me off. My reaction, instanta-neously, was 'Fuck you, bastards. You thought I couldn't do this any-more. Well, look at this.'"

So, here at his retrospective, Nichols both masked and displayed his vindictive triumph. As a parting shot, he announced that he was leaving the next day for Los Angeles, to go into preproduction on his new film—a comedy called *What Planet Are You From?* And he left the audience with a slightly altered version of W. H. Auden's acid envoi—a ruler's deadpan rebuke to those young upstarts "who think they could do it better" and who might dismiss the proceedings as merely "geezer aggrandizement":

> *Death takes the innocent young,*
> *As poets have frequently sung,*
> *The rolling-in-money,*
> *The screamingly funny,*
> *And even the very well-hung.*

In mid-July, I caught up with Nichols in his current kingdom, Sound Stage 15, at Culver Studios, in Culver City, where a broken ankle and crutches—the result of a spill on the set—in no way impeded his show of good spirits. "Life is difficult and fucked up and complicated," Nichols says. "The cutting room isn't." At the studio, his power is absolute. "I really need to control it. Every aspect of it, every nuance of the reading. How long every second of every shot is," he says. "Partly because that's the job, and partly because I just have to. I'm happy when I'm controlling it and uncomfortable when I'm not and crazed when it's out of control."

On the set, Nichols's wit serves him well both as a social lubricant and as an equalizer. In conversation, he lays out his colorful word hoard like a vendor at a bazaar—a delightful abundance of erudition, playfulness, and surprise, which helps take the odor off his Eeyore-like nature. His voice, which is nasal and comes from the back of his throat, can wring all sorts of sardonic music from the sounds of words. "A retreat? How *moving*. It's not a sweat lodge, is it?" he says, taking a call on his portable phone as the crew prepares for a scene with Garry Shandling and Ben Kingsley. "Come and see me. We can have a *tiny* retreat in my trailer."

While the shot is being set up, Nichols hobbles away toward his trailer, which is parked opposite the sound stage; the makeup man standing at the shadowy threshold of the building cautions Nichols about the ledge he's standing on. "Thank you, Roy," Nichols says. "Where were you when I fell in that hole?" Among the myriad problems facing Nichols on this particular cerulean day, as he clambers up the steps to his trailer, is what to get the cast as an end-of-production present. "My assistant came up with a silver—what do you call it—vibrator," he says. "I'm not sure. Maybe if it has *Ars Gratia Artis* on it." Inside, the trailer is dominated by photos of his handsome children—Daisy, thirty-five, who dubs movies into French; Max, twenty-five, who is a record-company A&R man; and Jenny, twenty-three, a student at Brown—and by food (See's Candies, jelly beans, nuts, chocolate-chip cookies). Nichols, who has never met a calorie he didn't like, is, as Candice Bergen says, "a poster child for unhealthy living." Because he's currently immobilized and can't climb up onto the space-station set, a gizmo called a "god box" has been installed in his trailer, just opposite the sofa. A microphone allows Nichols to talk directly to his players as he watches them. "It's annoying," he says. "It's like wearing a condom. You're there and you're not there."

What Planet Are You From? is about an alien, played by Shandling, who, as part of a plan to dominate the universe, is sent to earth to impregnate as many women as possible and take over the planet from within. Nichols inspects a replay of the just completed scene in which Ben Kingsley, the leader of Shandling's planet, taps him for the procreative mission. "The success of our planet's domination of the universe rests in your hands," Kingsley says, in his gravest British Received Pronunciation. "Now, if you'll come this way we'll arrange your transfer and attach your penis." A big, chesty laugh rumbles through Nichols's body. "Kingsley was put on earth to say that line," he says, and laughs some more. Nichols has as many kinds of laughs as he does ironic inflections, but his high-pitched Big Laugh is like no other. His eyes widen, his body stiffens, his pale skin reddens as hilarity crashes over him. In that moment of wipeout, all of Nichols's power, self-consciousness, and royal command vanish into childish delight. This wheezy, teary collapse has been captured on record ("Nichols and May at Work"); and anyone who has been in its force field knows the strength of its infectiousness. "It's incredible when you get it," Neil Simon told me. "It inspires you to show him more material to get it again."

In the next shot, which is the movie's finale, Shandling goes into a righteous harangue—"Why are we taking over earth? Is that what it's about? More, more, more?"—and Nichols stops him in mid-flow. "It's a moment from an operetta," he says. "We don't want that gesture. It's too Jewish." Speech, like the portrayal of a character, is in the details; Nichols watches over it with vigilance. "I constantly have to edit the things I want to say," he adds. "Shambling and I get into this kidding thing, but then it gets a little bit out of hand." "He's called 'Shambling,' is he?" I ask. Nichols fixes me with a lidded glance. "Well, now and then," he says. Nichols continues, "He's playing the game of student with the master, which is partly meant to disarm me. He's not without self-knowledge. He knows how to use me to make certain things happen to him in scenes. The game is useful to us both."

But the previous week, for what Nichols said was the first time in his directing career, he had screamed at his star, who is also the film's co-author. Nichols knows that he can be withering. There was a moment during the filming of *The Day of the Dolphin* when Nichols saw himself becoming a tyrannical bastard. "I remember that I told the DP"—director of photography—"toward the end that I was not proud of the way I had treated the guys and I wanted to apologize," he says. "And he—a very mild man—said, 'It's too late for that.' It took my breath away. It made me realize that I had to put the brakes on completely. Because nobody can fight back, the director has an absolute obligation to treat people decently." By his own admission, he had gone "totally nuts" at Shandling, in an outburst that sent people scurrying off the set. He explains, "Garry came in and didn't know the scene, although he'd written it. Annette Bening, of course, knew it perfectly. After it was over, I said something to her about her character." Bening plays a ditzy recovering alcoholic, with no knack for picking Mr. Right. "Garry said, 'I think she should be kooky.' I said, 'You do? Her clothes are kooky, the set is kooky, her lines are kooky—you want her to *act* kooky, too?' I said, 'Why don't you come in prepared and do your own work?' "

"It was mean," Bening told me. "He was attacking Garry inappropriately. It was really out of line." Shandling apologized for being unprepared, and Bening then met with Nichols in his trailer to defend Shandling's right to have a creative conversation, a point that Nichols conceded when he, in turn, apologized to Shandling. In Nichols's remorse, Bening saw a "fierce superego." "He's not as generous to himself as he deserves to be," she says. "He's got a voice in him that's very harsh, and unnecessarily so." In his surprising anger—he now says he was "much angrier than seemed warranted"—Nichols saw "the dim racial memory of rage," that little boy in himself who is still angry and whom he constantly struggles to keep down. "He's the one," Nichols says. "He's somewhere saying, 'Don't fuck with me.' And I can't stop him."

"All the shit was in the beginning," Nichols says of his life. Hitler—or his voice, broadcast from speakers on dockside lampposts—literally saw Nichols and his three-year-old brother, Robert, off to America in 1939. Nichols remembers not being allowed to board the *Bremen*, which was leaving from Hamburg, until the traffic-stopping speech was finished. The brothers, each with ten marks in a purse around his neck, made the journey alone across the Atlantic. Their mother, Brigitte, was ill and stayed behind for a year and a half before rejoining the family; their doctor father, Paul, who had left Russia for Germany after the revolution in 1917, had gone ahead to New York in 1938, just before the Nazi takeover, to set up a practice on the prosperous Upper West Side. On their first night

off the ship, Nichols remembers seeing Hebrew writing on a delica-
tessen and asking his father in German, "Is that allowed?" He also
remembers watching his brother throw a tantrum while his father
"pretended to call the police on the pay phone to deal with him." "He
had no experience as a father," Nichols says. "He had no idea what
to do." Paul saw his boys only intermittently during their first year
in America. He placed them with an English family, some patients
of his who agreed to care for them while he was establishing himself. "They were awful," Nichols says. "They would kiss their own
children good night, then shake our hands. We'd get a spoonful
of milk of magnesia and go to bed." Things didn't improve much
when the Peschkowsky family was reunited. "My parents fought all
the time," Nichols recalls. "They would have divorced if my father
hadn't died—something that my mother immediately forgot." Much
later, Nichols learned that his father "was impotent with her and not
with many other women." Both parents had a series of lovers. "There
were always other people, in Germany and here," he says. "It was just
the way things were."

Nichols felt "landlocked" in the family, trapped in the battle
between his warring parents. A lot of the contention was about him.
"I wouldn't go to school. I wouldn't get up in the morning. I answered
back," Nichols says. He "had a mouth," which made both his school-
mates and his family wary of him. "My father wasn't too crazy about
me," Nichols says. "I loved him anyway. One of the things I regretted
for a long time was that he died before he could see that he would be
proud of me. I was actually more what he wished for than he thought."
He adds, "He could rage." (Nichols still remembers his father, in the
heat of an unhappy family moment, saying to him and his brother,
"I'll be glad to get rid of you two.") "But he also told funny stories, and
he used to dance for us in his underwear. He did routines at parties
that people loved to hear." In later life, Nichols was told by the impresario Sol Hurok, who had been one of Paul's patients, "You're not as

funny as your father." And it's through his father that Nichols feels he understands the stoic bravado of Chekhov's characters. "He was the Russian as entertainer," he says. "What I loved him for—even when he wasn't noticeably loving me—was that he had great vitality and joy of life." Paul never let his darkness show in public. "I feel linked to him in many ways, and that's one of them," Nichols says.

By contrast, Brigitte, who was thirty-four when her husband died, at the age of forty-four, became "a nightmare of accusation," someone who collected injustices. "She was one of those people who would hold you responsible for everything that happened to her and how bad she felt now," Nichols says. He would try to kid her out of her misery. "Everything wounded her," he says. "She was always wounded to the quick. 'I raised you so you could say that to me? Thank you very much, I deserve that.' It went on for hours, days."

Brigitte, who had no profession, no money, no proper English, and only a few friends, would go to the Stanwood Cafeteria, on Broadway, and sit alone for hours. Over the years, she worked in a bakery, a bookshop, even set up a translation agency to support her boys. But after Paul was gone they found themselves plummeting well below the level of middle-class gentility to which they had been accustomed. Although Nichols blocked out the degree of their humiliating poverty, his brother subsequently reminded him of "bug-infested apartments" and of their mother "giving up to the point where she didn't do the laundry. We weren't clean." "She always had some mysterious illness," Nichols adds. When he went home after school to their drab rooms at 155 West Seventy-First Street—"one of those tiny apartment houses with podiatrists on the first floor"—he frequently found Brigitte propped up on her living-room sofa bed (the boys shared the bedroom) with a table of pills, "maybe 150 bottles of medication, and the phone, on which she always was."

In time, Nichols discovered that he could make people laugh by telling stories about his mother. In fact, Nichols and May's definitive sketch "Mother and Son" ("Someday . . . you'll have children of your own. And, honey, when you do, I only pray that they make you suffer the way you're making me. [*Sobs*.] That's all I pray, Arthur. That's a mother's prayer.") was inspired by one of Brigitte's lethal phone calls. As Nichols recalls, it went, " 'Hello, Michael, this is your mother. Do you remember me?' I said, 'Mom, can I call you right back?' Literally. And I called Elaine." He and May were playing at the Blue Angel then. "I said, 'I have a piece for us.' I told her the line. She said, 'We'll do it tonight.' And we did it pretty much the way it is now. She had the identical mother."

Before he found a way to make light of his difficulties, Nichols was swamped by them. From his first day at the Dalton School, on the Upper East Side, the clouds of exclusion and isolation glowered over him. "The kid was as far outside as an outsider can get," says Buck Henry, who was in his class. "He was Igor Peschkowsky when he was at Dalton. He did not speak English. He wore a cap all the time." Nichols says, "I remember being on the school bus in New York and saying, 'What means '*emergency*'?" By the time he reached high school (the progressive school Walden, from which he graduated in 1948), Nichols had mastered English, had a make-do wig, and had learned the idiom and style of his peers, but his assessment of himself during these "searing, painful years" was that he was "the most popular of the unpopular kids." "That was cast in bronze, that's where I was chained in the galaxy forever," he says. "I thought about revenge a lot in those days."

A lazy and lackluster student, Nichols had a quick mind and a formidable intellectual inheritance. (His maternal grandmother, Hedwig Lachmann, did the translation of Oscar Wilde's *Salomé* that Richard Strauss used for his opera; his grandfather Gustav Landauer, among whose best friends were Martin Buber and B. Traven, was a writer turned activist, who was a leader of the German Social Democratic Party, and whose brutal execution by the Nazis had been the reason for the family's exodus.) Nichols filled his solitude with activities that took him out of himself and into exotic other worlds. At sixteen, he went with a date to the second night of Elia Kazan's production of *A Streetcar Named Desire*. "We just sat there," Nichols says. "We didn't talk. We couldn't believe there was such a thing." He adds, "I just wanted to be around theater." He also read voraciously (all of Eugene O'Neill by the age of fourteen, James Joyce's *Ulysses*, E. M. Forster's *A Passage to India*); he was a constant moviegoer; he hung out in Central Park and at the Claremont Riding Academy. "I got to exercise people's horses; sometimes, when people were thrown off, I would catch the horses on the bridle path and ride them back." Animals calmed Nichols; unlike his classmates, they were responsive, unselfconscious, and unable to pass judgment. "The refugee ear is a sort of seismograph for how one is doing," Nichols says. At high school, he explains, "I *heard* what they thought of me—'nebbish,' 'poor boy'—and what they thought of each other. A thousand tiny victories and defeats in an ordinary conversation. I didn't know what to do with it."

To this day, even though Nichols wears a wig, the intrusive, objectifying eyes of others continue to be a threat. "Staring is something that still makes me absolutely nuts," he says. He thinks of the public as "something to be controlled and tamed." "The first person to come up to me at a party is in danger to this day," Nichols says. "My reflex is to attack the first couple of people. I can't stop. Diane is right there, taking off the edges, fixing it. By the third or fourth person, I can be friendly." To Nichols, the audience has always personified Them—the annihilating mob of his childhood, whom he characterizes as "the beast" with "too much power." He says, "I was so impaled on what people thought. I had to train myself away from that. I never had a friend from the time I came to this country until I got to the University of Chicago. I was seventeen."

He ended up there by a fluke: it was one of the only schools in

America that didn't require the College Boards, and Nichols hadn't taken them. "Once I got there, I had a very specific and powerful sense of 'Oh my God, look, there are others like me. There are other weirdos.'" The publisher Aaron Asher, who shared college digs with Nichols, says, "We were all freaks. We were way ahead of the country. There was sex. There was dope. There was a subculture." Asher was just one of Nichols's new friends, who were "refugees or first-generation Jewish intellectual guys." When Nichols mentioned to Asher that his grandmother had written the libretto for Strauss's *Salome*, Asher joked, "Oh, really? Was she Hugo von Hofmannsthal?" Nichols says, "I was looking at somebody who knew who Hofmannsthal was and that he wrote libretti for Strauss. No such thing had ever happened to me before."

The first person Nichols met at registration was Susan Sontag; they struck up a lifelong friendship. "I thought he was terrific," Sontag says. "I adored him from the start. He was totally alive and incredibly verbal. We talked about books, about feelings, about how to get free of our pasts. Because we were interested in theater, we were interested in observing people. I would happily have become his girlfriend physically, except I was intimidated by the hair problem and felt he was untouchable." (Thirty years later, Sontag confessed to Nichols that she couldn't accept the scars from her mastectomy: "I have this thing, and every time I take a bath I'm horrified." He said, "Susan, now you know how I have felt all my life.") Asher characterizes Nichols's look as "something out of a German Expressionist movie," but says that, "despite the strangeness of his appearance, he did very well with the girls. He was courtly, and he was well read, which got you a long way at that university."

Nichols, who had begun therapy, was also deeply depressed. "I would spend long times in my room and just not come out," he says. "Sometimes I would step over all the dishes and the Franco-American spaghetti cans and hang out with some friends, then go back to my lair." Nichols deejayed a popular show of classical music and chat at WFMT, but his depression almost cost him the job. "He was funny and knowledgeable but totally unreliable," says Asher, whose cousin owned the station. "They fired him a number of times."

"I couldn't be a *person* that many hours a day," Nichols explains. "I needed—still need—a lot of time lying on the bed absolutely blank, the way I assume a dog is in front of the fire. A persona takes energy. I just needed a rest from it. Not to be anything in relation to anyone else."

When Nichols did emerge from seclusion, he worked up his losses into a kind of legend. According to one of his theatrical cohorts, quoted in Janet Coleman's *The Compass*, Nichols behaved like "a princeling deprived of his rightful fortune." Nichols was so poor that he took to eating the leftovers from the coffee shop where the director Paul Sills was then a waiter. "He rattled his tin cup," Nichols's friend Hayward Ehrlich, now an associate professor of English at Rutgers, says. "When Mike appeared, you knew that he needed a cup of coffee or a sandwich or something. It became his way of relating to people, to have them sort of help him out of his impoverishment. I think Mike loved to magnify his sense of adversity so that in some way he could triumph over it."

Much to Nichols's surprise, during his sophomore year he found himself "near the center of the in-group" and "a minor celebrity." The theatrical talent pool at the University of Chicago was extraordinary: Sills, Ed Asner, Severn Darden, Anthony Holland, Zohra Lampert, Barbara Harris, Gene Troobnick. Nichols directed his first play, Yeats's *Purgatory*, with Asner, and he performed in a number of plays, among them *Androcles and the Lion*, *St. Joan*, and *La Ronde*. He played Jean the valet in a production of Strindberg's *Miss Julie*, directed by Sills. "He wasn't the working-class man and couldn't come close to it," Sills says now. Nichols agrees; it was, he says, a "pathetic, awful production." He remembers "this evil, hostile girl in the front row staring at me throughout the performance. I was about four feet away from her and she stared at me all through it, and I knew she knew it was shit, and there was no way I could let her know that I knew." A few days later, the show mysteriously got a rave review in the *Chicago Daily News*. Nichols recalls rushing up to Sills on the street with the paper; Sills was with the girl who had unsettled Nichols from the audience. He scoured the review, while the girl read over his shoulder. "Ha!" she said, and walked away. Nichols, who was already toying with the notion of a theatrical career, had just met his future: Elaine May.

Some weeks later, on his way back from his disk-jockey gig, in the spring of 1954, Nichols caught sight of May in the waiting room of the Illinois Central's Randolph Street Station.

Their friendship began with an improvisation. "May I sit down?" he asked. In a thick Russian accent, May replied, "If you *veesh*." "Off she went," Nichols says. "She started us on that." They played out the scene, which Nichols characterized as "half spy, half pickup," all the way home. "I think I went home with her and she made me her specialty, which was hamburger with cream cheese and ketchup—the only thing she cooked," Nichols recalls. "She didn't know conventional dishes. She was utterly a rebel. That was part of the fun of it."

May was also a femme fatale. "Everybody wanted Elaine, and the people who got her couldn't keep her," Nichols says. But, even at their first meeting, which led to a brief romance, he remembers feeling that "we were safe from everyone else when we were with each other. And also safe from each other." He goes on, "I knew somehow that she would not do to me the things she'd done to other guys. I knew she wouldn't lose interest and move on. I knew instantly that everything that happened to us was ours."

May's life had been as painful and complex as Nichols's. "It's almost hard to convey how neurotic we were," Nichols says. Although she had dropped out of high school at fourteen—the only thing she enjoyed there was diagramming sentences—May was, as Edmund Wilson noted in his diary when he fell under her dark-eyed spell in the late fifties, "something of a genius." She had grown up in a nomadic acting family, spending a good part of her childhood playing a little boy named Bennie in a travelling Yiddish theater run by her father, Jack Berlin. According to her second husband, Sheldon Harnick, who wrote the lyrics for *Fiddler on the Roof*, the death of May's beloved father when she was ten left her to a future of apprehensive relations with men. She was married for the first time at sixteen; by eighteen she had a child, Jeannie Berlin, who was about four years old when Nichols met May and was being raised in Los Angeles by May's mother. By the time she reached Chicago, May had studied acting, performed a hillbilly act under the name Elly May, and written advertising copy. May, who saw herself primarily as a writer, was unofficially auditing courses at the University of Chicago and trying to develop a screen treatment of Plato's Symposium. (She once convinced a philosophy class that everyone in the Symposium was drunk and that that was the point of Plato's discourse.) "The only safe thing is to take a chance," May always told Nichols, who was ravished by her daring and her quirkiness.

Nichols and May had talent, but, more important, they had chemistry. They were quick; they were guarded; they were crazy. They were also "insanely judgmental" snobs, bound together, Nichols says, "by tremendous hostility to everyone else but never to each other." (May once said, according to Nichols, "that if somebody told her that I had burned down her house with her whole family in it, she would say, 'Oh, I must ask Michael why he did that.'") "I feel in opposition to almost everything," May, who no longer gives interviews, said in a Profile of the duo published in this magazine in 1961. Like Nichols, she used wit as a pesticide, and her juicy good looks were a particularly disconcerting contrast to her sharp tongue. Once, Nichols recalls, when two men followed her down the street making kissing sounds, May turned on them and said, "What's the matter? Tired of each other?" "Fuck you!" one of them shouted at her. May turned and faced the guy. "With what?" she said.

Nichols dropped out of college in 1953, and, in 1954, he decamped to New York to study the Method with Lee Strasberg. "I have decided that if I don't make it as a nervous young man," he wrote to a Chicago friend, "I will wait and become like Robert Morley, who is clearly the funniest man in the world." But in 1955, with no prospect of work, he returned to Chicago with the promise of twenty-eight dollars a week as part of a new company called the Compass Players, of which Sills and May were founding members. The goal of the Compass, which would evolve into Chicago's legendary Second City, was to do away with conventional plays and make theater by improvisational means. "I was terrified of improvising," Nichols says. "I didn't even know what it was. I hated it, and I was very bad at it." Nichols cried in his scenes for months "because that's what I thought I'd learned from Strasberg. Paul and Elaine kept me going. The fact of Elaine—her presence—kept me doing it."

In the first successful scene they did together, Nichols played a riding instructor, and May his pupil. "We both realized as we got into the middle of the scene that I would get to stand in the middle of the stage and watch her cantering as both horse and rider around me." During the scene, a member of the cast ran into the bar where the other actors were congregated, shouting, "Come quick! Mike has a character!" Nichols reflects, "What is implied in that story—and it was true for the first time in my life—is affection. They had some affection for me. I began to understand that I could be kidded, and people could be fond of me, and that this would all be a pleasurable thing."

As intellectual high-wire acts go, there is no riskier or more astounding enterprise than going out in front of an audience and creating something out of nothing. "You're showing off how smart you are, how good you are," Buck Henry says. "You have the pleasure of having not only performed it but written it at the same time." Improvisation—a process, Nichols says, that "absorbs you, creates you, and saves you"—allowed the actors to stay on the edge of emotion and character without connecting deeply to their interior lives, and this suited both Nichols's and May's private natures. "I would never have been a performer without her, and I don't think she would have without me," Nichols says. "Elaine and I are, in some weird way, each other's unconscious." Nichols made the shapes; May filled them in. "She was shockingly, endlessly inventive. She could go on and on—I couldn't," Nichols says. "I did my jokes, and then I was through."

Within the Compass Players, May could be funny with several different actors, but Nichols could be funny only with her. "I never did a good scene of any kind with anybody else," Nichols told Jeff Sweet, in *Something Wonderful Right Away*, an oral history of the Compass Players. "For me, it depended on a certain connection with Elaine and a certain mad gleam in either her or my eyes when we knew something was starting." The mad gleam meant, as he explained to me, "Oh, fuck, I know where you're going. That's a great idea you've just had, and when you get there I'll be ready." That focus—reminiscent of a parent's empowering gaze—was inspiring. "We had to figure out something or we would disappear, each of us," Nichols adds. (He would later find a similar containing attentiveness in Diane Sawyer. "All of her is available all the time," he says.) With May, Nichols could drop his mask. "*I* interested me when I was with her," he says. "It wasn't only that she was so great but that when I was with her I became something more than I had been."

Onstage, in their own version of Truth or Dare, Nichols and May kept upping the ante on each other. Once, in an improv about an egotistical DJ and a starlet called Barbara Musk, Nichols quizzed May about her next movie. "My latest motion picture is . . . called *Two Gals in Paris*. It is the life story of Gertrude Stein," May said. "What do you play in the picture, sweetheart?" Nichols asked. "Well, I was really just lucky enough to get the part of Gertrude Stein," she said. "I had heard that Gertrude Stein was going to be played by Spencer Tracy," Nichols said, maneuvering her into a tough spot. "Only as a child," May shot back. When the conversation got onto the soundtrack of the movie, May said that she'd recorded the title song. Nichols promptly asked her to sing it. On the spot, May ad-libbed an entire song, which ended:

> *There was dashing Dmitri, elusive Ivan*
> *And Alyosha with the laughing eyes.*
> *Then came the dawn*
> *The brothers were gone*
> *I just can't forget those wonderful guys.*

The University of Chicago proved the perfect place for nurturing their particular ironic and informed voices. "It was the most referential community that I think ever existed in this country," says Nichols, who improvised entire scenes in the style of writers suggested by the audience. "At the Compass, we could drop 'Dostoyevsky' as a name and get a laugh. We were living in the context in which the referential joke was just the highest currency." They were also coming of age in a "safer, quieter place" than New York. "Chicago is not a city of fashion, nor is it full of pride and excitement over its art," Nichols says. "They were very calm about Compass. They came. They laughed. They went home."

Nichols and May were beginning to find resources in themselves that they hadn't known they had, including the ability to make anger work for them. "Rage is the best engine, of course, if you have a tremendous gift to employ it properly," Nichols wrote to a friend. Once, when Nichols was performing a sketch about pretentious snobs at a private party, the actor playing the effete host offered to put on a record. "Would you like to hear *The Four Seasons*?" he asked. "Perhaps just 'Winter,'" Nichols replied. "To freeze his ass was a pleasure," says Nichols, who found that with jokes he could "cow the shit" out of the public. "When a joke comes to you, it feels like it's been sent by God." He adds, "What it is, really, is discovering your unconscious."

There were other discoveries. When Nichols was onstage, even the "curse" of imagining what others thought of him became an asset: "I could hear what the other actors were thinking, where they were going, what the audience was thinking." Nichols also learned "the Aristotelian things" about the building of a scene—conflict, theme, resolution. He and May found ways to "grab the opposite." "There had to be a core to a scene," Nichols told Jeff Sweet. "It didn't matter how clever the lines were. If they weren't hung on a situation, you were only as good as your last line. . . . But if you could grab a situation, whether it was a seduction or a conflict or a fight, once you had that spine, then things could come out of it." And when the jokes were found, Nichols husbanded them. "If there was a laugh to be gotten and Elaine didn't set up the feed line, Mike would work with her until she did," another Compass member, the comedian Shelley Berman, said. "He did everything but lasso her." For a while, according to Janet Coleman, Nichols and May worked with Berman, a trio that May suggested they call "Two Cocksuckers and Elaine." "I actually liked Shelley," Nichols said. "But one day he came offstage and said, 'Hey, guys, Mike had three scenes in that set, and I only had two.' It was a whole new idea in Eden to count. The group was finished in six months."

Nichols and May themselves nearly foundered in 1958, when they were working in St. Louis, where a new Compass Players venue had been launched. Nichols had recently married the Chicago TV personality and singer Pat Scot ("Isn't it a beautiful first wedding?" May said at the ceremony), who joined him on weekends. During the week, on a strictly platonic basis, Nichols and May shared a room, which she vacated when Scot arrived. On those days, May stayed with another company member, Del Close. Nichols was jealous of Close, not for romantic reasons but because May was so much a part of his identity that he couldn't share her. "I persecuted the shit out of Del," Nichols says. "Nothing could stop me. Elaine finally said to the producer, 'I can't stand it anymore—you've got to fire Michael.'" Nichols was summarily fired.

Some weeks later, from New York, where he had gone with Scot (though, as May had predicted, the marriage didn't last much longer), Nichols called to ask May if she'd like to audition with him for the New York agent Jack Rollins. Rollins handled such cabaret talent as Harry Belafonte and Woody Allen. "They were immediately astounding. They were complete," Rollins says, of the first time he set eyes on the team, at his office in the Pierre Hotel. "He is Mr. Practical. She is insanely creative. But Mike is the one that made the act live in this world." By the following Tuesday, Nichols and May were playing the Village Vanguard. "A couple of weeks later, we were on *Steve Allen*," Nichols says. "Then we were on *Omnibus*, and we were very famous. The whole thing took about two months." After the *Omnibus* show, Nichols remembers calling May at 4 a.m. to say, "What do we do now?"

As McCarthyism, the Cold War, and racial unrest made their generation anxious, Nichols and May struck a new disenchanted chord in American life. "Nobody was doing any humor about post–Korean War young people, that urban generation," says the cartoonist and playwright Jules Feiffer, who, when he first heard them, "didn't dare laugh, because I was afraid of missing something." He adds, "Humor was Bob Hope still. When I saw Mike and Elaine, suddenly you felt not just that this is funny but that this is true." Woody Allen, who wanted to write for Nichols and May, says that comedians like them "were touching on some kind of truth—truth of character, social truth, truth of wit. And, suddenly, part of that whole new sense of truth was that they wrote their own material." With Nichols and May, Jewish angst, Freud, literacy, irony, and sex were ushered into the discourse of mainstream comedy. They, along with Mort Sahl, Jonathan Winters, and, later, Lenny Bruce and Woody Allen, were the renegades who led comedy away from the ersatz to the authentic. "The nice thing is to make an audience laugh and laugh and laugh and shudder later," May said. The frisson was the shock of recognition. Nichols and May had the uncanny ability at once to comment on character and to fill it from within. "They were like music," Steve Martin says, referring to the swift intimacy of their overlapping rhythms, the deft interplay of May's soft, breathless voice and the reedy clarity of Nichols's sound. For instance, in their sendup of public outrage over Charles Van Doren and the "Twenty-One" scandal:

NICHOLS: Thank heaven for the investigation.

MAY: Oh, yes.

NICHOLS: When I feel worst I say to myself, "At least the government has taken a firm stand."

MAY: Oh, yes. Well, they can't fool around with this the way they did with integration.

NICHOLS: No.

MAY: This is a . . .

NICHOLS: . . . moral issue.

MAY: Yes.

NICHOLS: A moral issue.

MAY: *Yes! Yes!* It is a moral issue.

NICHOLS: A moral issue.

MAY: And to me that is so much more interesting than a *real*
issue.

"Smart is not necessarily funny," Martin says. "You can go
through a whole evening of smart and have laughed completely per-
functorily." But Nichols and May could be approached from either a
dopey or a smart place. For example, their classic sketch about two
teenagers smoking and making out in the front seat of a car contained two pieces of inspired physical business: May in the middle
of a passionate kiss opening her mouth to breathe and emitting a
puff of smoke (a joke Nichols later used in *The Graduate*), and the
clinching lovers trying to pass a cigarette from one trapped hand
to another.

However, sometimes smart alone could bring down the house.
Nichols began his sendup of Tennessee Williams—a high-pitched,
hard-drinking Southern playwright called Alabama Glass—with
the playwright explaining his newest work to the audience. "Before
the action of the play *begins*," Nichols drawled, "Nanette's husband,
Raoul, has committed *suicide* on bein' unjustly accused of *not* bein'
homosexual."

"Most of the time, people thought we were making fun of others
when we were making fun of ourselves," Nichols says. "Pretentious-
ness. Snobbiness. Horniness. Elaine was parodying her mother, as
I was mine, and a certain girlishness, flirtatiousness in herself."
He adds, "It was utterly freeing." And redeeming. In the teenager
sketch, for instance, Nichols and May were sending up the cheerleader and the football star, those high-school paragons they never
were but now got to play. "We *were* those people, and it healed something, weird as it sounds," Nichols says. Onstage with May, Nichols
felt, "I could be anybody I needed to be. I used to have a mental image
of cracking a whip when I was talking to the audience. I could control

them with jokes." Offstage, the person he presented as Mike Nichols was another version of his stage persona—witty and apparently able to handle everything. " 'We'd like to say a few words about adultery—it's coming back.' That's who I was." He adds, "You start imitating somebody who is calm about all that. You imitate it long enough, and it becomes true."

But, while his public persona stanched old anxieties, success brought new ones. May cared more about process, Nichols more about results. "She was always brave," he says of her desire to improvise. "But I became more and more afraid. I wasn't happy with getting paid a fortune for something and not having tried it out in advance." By the late fifties, Nichols was earning more than half a million dollars a year. He adds, "The audience didn't give a shit whether you were improvising or not. They'd come to see good comedy."

The team's creative differences came to a head in their brilliant Broadway show, *An Evening with Mike Nichols and Elaine May* (1960), which I saw during its yearlong run. "We were irreproachable," Nichols says. "We never got a negative review. We never had an empty seat. Everybody loved us. Everybody felt they had discovered us." But discovery—the fearless adventure of creating in the moment—was gradually being leached out of their performances by the repetition of set routines. May grew increasingly unhappy. "Sometimes she'd be late. What is so difficult? Two hours out of twenty-four. It's a perfect job. It wasn't that way for her," Nichols says. "We had huge fights about it. I never could understand why she found it so difficult."

The most stunning moment of the evening—a kind of augury of their collapse—was a sketch called "Pirandello," a twenty-minute exercise in which Nichols and May began as two little kids, playing at insulting each other like Mom and Dad, then became Mom and Dad yelling at each other, and then turned into a pair of actors having trouble with each other onstage. Suddenly, in a terrifying shift,

Nichols and May were in the middle of some ugly private squabble. At one point, in what Buck Henry characterizes as "a moment of unbelievably intense embarrassment for everyone," Nichols turned to the audience and said, "My partner and I . . ." May said, "Well, screw this," and started to walk offstage. Nichols grabbed at her, ripping May's blouse as she pulled away. She started to cry. "Michael, what do you think you're doing?" she said. "I'm doing 'Pirandello,' " Nichols said. Breaking into smiles, they took their bows. But at one performance Nichols and May actually came to blows: Nichols hit her back and forth across the face, May clawed at his chest until it bled, and the curtain had to be brought down. "We cried together. It didn't happen again," he says. "I think, in many ways, I persecuted her. I went on at her, 'This is too slow, this has to go faster.' "

The end was slow in coming. In October 1962, Nichols took the lead in May's play *A Matter of Position*, which opened in Philadelphia. "It was sort of about me, which she never quite admitted," Nichols says. But, with him on the stage and May in the audience, the balance of their relationship irrevocably shifted. "Suddenly, Elaine was not next to me, doing it with me, but out there judging me," Nichols says. "It was horrendous." The play itself added to the atmosphere of fiasco. As the *Philadelphia Sunday Bulletin* wrote, "Those members of the audience who had not already beat a hasty retreat before the final curtain, as many did, were left with a sensation of numbness that was too far down to be attributed to heartburn." Nichols and May were no longer two against the world. May was looking for a replacement for Nichols, and Nichols was saying to people, "Get her to cut the play or I'm leaving." The play died in Philadelphia; and, although they didn't exactly speak the words, so did their friendship. "It was cataclysmic," Nichols says.

"Mike was in a state of deep depression," says Robby Lantz, Nichols's theatrical agent at the time. "He really wasn't functioning. He went to bed. Period." Nichols was now half of a comedy team. He had lost his best friend, his livelihood, and the scaffolding of his identity. "Mike has no tolerance for failure," says a former collaborator who tried to rally him after May's departure. "I didn't know what I was or who I was," Nichols explains. His predicament was summed up one afternoon on Park Avenue by Leonard Bernstein, a member of the deluxe set he'd become part of. Bernstein put his arm around Nichols. "Oh, Mikey," he said, "you're so good. I don't know at what, but you're so good."

What Nichols was good at, it turned out, was something that his acting classes with Strasberg, his improvising, and his comedy act with May had all been a preparation for: directing. In 1961, in New Jersey, he'd directed a collection of Jules Feiffer cartoon sketches, *The World of Jules Feiffer*, with music by Stephen Sondheim. "It was clear to me that he was extraordinary," Feiffer says. But it was not clear to the producing fraternity or to Nichols. As an apprenticeship, Lantz sent him on what Nichols calls "the lamest possible job," to direct Wilde's *The Importance of Being Earnest* and play the Dauphin in Shaw's *St. Joan*, at a Vancouver theater festival. "Every night at midnight he called and said, 'Get me out of this. I don't want to do this,'" Lantz recalls. "I said, 'This is precisely what the doctor ordered.'" And so it proved. The Broadway producer Arnold Saint-Subber was shopping for a director for Neil Simon's *Nobody Loves Me*. Although Saint-Subber didn't have enough confidence to guarantee the tyro director the Broadway show, he was prepared to let Nichols try out the play in Bucks County, Pennsylvania. Nichols had only seven days to mount *Nobody Loves Me*, which was later retitled *Barefoot in the Park*.

After the first reading at Saint-Subber's house, when none of the actors laughed, the notoriously nervous Simon, known as Doc because of his ability to swiftly rewrite a line and make brilliant comic fixes, wanted to call off the play. Nichols was unruffled. "The play was so light, so sweet, so funny, that my job was to make it real," says Nichols, who impressed Simon with his extraordinary calmness. "I was absolutely confident about what everything should be and where everybody should be." Nichols told his talented cast—Robert Redford, Elizabeth Ashley, Mildred Natwick, Kurt Kasznar—to treat the play as if it were *King Lear*. "Let's do it as though we don't know what's going to happen," Nichols remembers telling the cast. "Let's not let them know it's funny."

But it was Simon who didn't know that his play was funny. At the first Bucks County rehearsal, he sat outside the rehearsal hall. "Suddenly, I heard a roar," Simon says. " 'Thank God, they must be up to a good part.' I went inside. It was Mike telling them a story during the break. Then we went back to the play—no more laughs."

"Doc said, 'Let's call it off. This is not a play. I never thought it was a play,' " Nichols recalls. "I said, 'Let's decide after the first preview. Let's just see how it is with an audience.' Of course, they yelled and screamed and fell out of their chairs. Doc never worried again." Nichols adds, "I had instant maturity."

This marked the beginning of what is probably the most successful commercial partnership in twentieth-century American theater. "We were obsessed in the same way," Nichols says of Simon. "I could wake him up at two in the morning and say, 'I've figured out what's wrong with the third act,' and he would curse me and then come down and meet me in the lobby to listen to it. It was the joy of discovering things together."

As a comedian, Nichols had watched himself become what he calls "a show-biz baby." "I was narcissistic," he says. "I would get mad. I bitched about our billing. I did all the things I dislike. Comedy is the only work in the world in which the work and the reward are simultaneous. Comedians get it on the spot. They get the laugh. It's very corrupting to your character." But as a director Nichols got to play adult instead of baby. "There was something about serving something that wasn't me," Nichols says. Within fifteen minutes of starting rehearsal for *Barefoot in the Park*, he had a life-changing revelation: the experience of taking care of others made him feel taken care of. "I had a sense of enormous relief and joy that I had found a process that both gave me my father back and allowed me to be my father and the group's father," he says.

Nichols's love for his actors was palpable; he created a protective environment for them. "They're giving everyone the right to assess, evaluate, criticize everything about them—their noses, their asses, their intelligence, their worthiness or lack of worthiness," he says. "They're really out there." Nichols was a shrewd father—clever about wielding his authority and about maintaining boundaries. During *Barefoot in the Park*, Redford came to Nichols in a quandary: he was being upstaged by the showy Elizabeth Ashley. "I can't bear it," he told Nichols. "Every night when I kiss Ashley, she kicks her leg up behind her. I feel like I've been used. I'm embarrassed." "Why don't you do it, too?" Nichols suggested. Redford did as he was told and got a huge laugh; Ashley promptly stopped her upstaging.

Some of Nichols's charges could be notoriously bumptious. Sometimes he tamed them with his high-definition humor. Once, during a heated rehearsal of *The Odd Couple*, Walter Matthau looked out at Nichols in the auditorium and said, "Mike, can I have my cock back now?" "Props!" Nichols said. With other wayward actors, like George C. Scott, he knew when to be politic. During the rehearsals of *Plaza Suite*, Scott disappeared for three days. "We're in the middle of a scene, and George walks in. Collar up—it's winter—hands in coat pockets. He's just standing there looking at us," Simon recalls. "I look at Mike, and I'm anxious to hear what he's gonna say. Mike said, 'Hi, George. We're on act 2, page twenty-one.'" On the other hand, Nichols could be strict about certain kinds of behavior. At an early rehearsal of *The Prisoner of Second Avenue*, the cast, which included Peter Falk and Lee Grant, was blocking a scene on the stage of the Plymouth Theatre. "One of the actresses said, 'Mike, if she stands over there, I don't think this part of the house is gonna see me,'" Simon recalls. "Mike turned and whispered to the producer, 'Fire her.'"

Nichols's authority rested, in large part, on his unique understanding of the audience. Onstage, and later in film, his work sought—some would say too eagerly—to speak to the audience in a popular way. At its best, this sensibility produced *The Odd Couple*, one of the century's classic comedies. At its most indulgent, it allowed Robin Williams, as Estragon in *Waiting for Godot* (1988), to break the play's artifice of isolation and ad-lib with the paying customers. "The experience of living in front of the audience for all those years in Chicago did something to me," Nichols says. "It gave me some closeness to them, some trust." His sensitivity to audience reaction was the issue in a dramatic falling-out he had with David Rabe, whose play *Streamers* was probably Nichols's greatest artistic triumph—a beautifully staged and terrifying barracks tale of homosexual baiting. When it came to Rabe's next play, the powerful *Hurlyburly*, Nichols explains, "I was desperate for him to cut. I kept saying, 'I won't do this to the audience.' I could not get him to see the show from the audience; he only saw it from the light booth." Rabe, who finally went mute in protest ("He couldn't reach me. I was not listening," Rabe told me), stayed with the show until it opened but spoke hardly a word to Nichols. Nichols won the argument and the cut play was a success, but it cost him their relationship.

Improvisation had given Nichols another invaluable directorial impulse: "To damn well pick something that would happen in the scene—an Event." As Nichols explains it, the Event in any scene subliminally seeks an agreement with the audience on the human experience. "While you're expressing what happens, you're also saying underneath, 'Do we share this? Are you like me in any way? Oh, look, you are. You laughed!'" The building of this agreement through observation and detailed comic business was Nichols's signature:

Art Carney, in *The Odd Couple*, suddenly single and so nervous on his first date that when he lights the woman's cigarette he closes his Zippo on it; the newlywed Elizabeth Ashley, in *Barefoot in the Park*, who knows nothing about housekeeping, holding a match to a log in the fireplace, or slamming from room to room in a passionate argument with her husband while simultaneously undressing.

Nichols has a gift for making things real. During the tryouts for *Barefoot in the Park*, he and Simon stood at the back of the theater watching a scene in which the bride, after a week of marriage, screams that she wants a divorce. "I said to Mike, 'I don't think we should be watching this,'" Simon recalls. "He said, 'Why not?' I said, 'It's too personal, what they're doing on the stage.' And Mike says, 'Good, I'm glad you like it.'"

Between 1963 and 1984, Nichols chalked up about a dozen Broadway hits in a row, half of them with Simon. "Over and over again, he'd say when everybody was getting nervous, 'It's only a play. They're not going to be waiting for you in front of your house with torches,'" recalls Simon, whose hit play *The Sunshine Boys* was a script that he had abandoned until Nichols encouraged him to complete it. But one thing about theater did make Nichols nervous: seeing his stage business and his contributions to scripts go into movie versions without remuneration. He was the first director to demand, and get, a share of the author's royalties, which, when added to his director's royalty and his piece of the subsidiary rights, quickly made Nichols a very rich man. (According to his accountant, if all his stock and film income were lost, he could still "live comfortably" on his production royalties.) "I wasn't pleased with giving it to him, but I can't argue with it," Simon says. "I would rather have him do it and have the play be great. I never worked with anyone in my life—nor will I ever work with anyone—as good as Mike Nichols. And, when you talk about percentages, what Mike asked for was more than made up for by what I made on *The Sunshine Boys*."

Money played a large part in how Nichols measured his achievement. "He always pushed with agents—I speak for us all: more money, more power, more billing," Robby Lantz says. "Eventually, the demands became cruel. Artists in the theater should not take from each other things that are not necessary." But Nichols, who had almost been wiped out in his first show-biz incarnation, was building an unassailable second career. "The butterflies in my stomach won't stop fluttering until I have thirty million dollars," the producer Lewis Allen overheard Nichols telling Lillian Hellman. "He's ruthless when he wants to be, or sometimes maybe even when he doesn't want to be," Lantz says. "He doesn't let anything stand in his way."

Nichols was also avid for artistic excellence, which he needed power to protect. He learned this lesson in his first taste of Hollywood, in the mid-sixties. Elizabeth Taylor had chosen Nichols to direct her in *Who's Afraid of Virginia Woolf?*, even though she had never seen or read the play: she trusted, she said, Nichols's sense of the tragic, which she'd intuited from their friendship. And it was Taylor whom Nichols invoked when Jack Warner, reversing production plans, insisted on shooting in color. As Nichols recalls, "I said, 'Mr. Warner, it's impossible for several reasons. The sets are built. Elizabeth's thirty-three years old—her makeup will never withstand color. How can she go from thirty-three to fifty-six and have us believe the makeup in color?' " But Warner insisted. The screenwriter and the producer, Ernest Lehman, whom Nichols sardonically nicknamed Slugger, said nothing. "Well, OK, I'll tell you what," Nichols told him. "You make it in color. I'll go home. I like it at home." Warner immediately conceded: "All right, black-and-white," he said. "After that, he treated me very kindly," Nichols says. "Until he threw me off the picture at the end. When it was mixing time, he saved time and trouble and just had his crew mix it."

But even here Nichols had unexpected leverage. Each night from the set, the editor, Sam O'Steen, would play him the sound mix over the phone and Nichols would give him notes on what to change. Finally, Nichols got word to Warner that he wanted to cut a deal. Warner was worried that the film, which was about adultery, drunkenness, and brutal family battles, would not be approved by the powerful Catholic Legion of Decency. In exchange for being allowed back on the set, Nichols came up with a plan to deliver the Legion: "When the Monsignor sees the picture, Jackie Kennedy will sit behind him. When it's over, she will say, 'How Jack would have loved it!' " Jackie Kennedy did as her friend asked; Warner got the Legion's blessing; and Nichols duly finished his film, the first film ever for which all of the four leading players were nominated for Oscars.

Nichols, whose film technique is not showy, is a director's director. "He tends to get actors to give him their finest hours," Steven Spielberg says, citing Kathy Bates's long monologue in *Primary Colors*. For Nichols, who himself gave a tour-de-force performance in Wallace Shawn's *The Designated Mourner*, at London's Royal National Theatre in 1996, the director's job is to help the actors turn psychology into behavior. When Nichols talks to actors and to students at the New Actors Workshop, which he founded with Paul Sills and George Morrison, in 1988, he is generally oblique, offering up examples from his own life to clarify a theatrical moment. "You kind of just free-associate all day long," says the writer-director Nora Ephron, who worked with Nichols on *Silkwood* and *Heartburn*. "Then suddenly you get something that actually is good enough to find its way into the thing you're working on." The veteran director Billy Wilder says, "Mike's scenes have a kind of inner content, which the audience feels and follows. He's very lucid." "What you're looking for every day is one little surprise," Nichols told Charlie Rose about directing. "It's like seeding a cloud and hoping it will rain."

The process requires patience, luck, and a gentle touch. Once, during the casting of *Carnal Knowledge*, Jules Feiffer, who wrote the script, told Nichols that he was worried about putting the twenty-three-year-old Candice Bergen in the lead. "Can she act?" Feiffer asked. "Mike said, 'She'll act for me.' And she did." In his recent biography of Edward Albee, Mel Gussow quotes Richard Burton (who played the harried professor in *Who's Afraid of Virginia Woolf?*) on Nichols. "He appears to defer to you, then in the end he gets exactly what he wants. He conspires with you rather than directs you, to get your best," Burton said.

Nichols's goal is to match the actor to the part. "If I can cast the right people and figure out the things they should be doing in the scene, they don't have to do anything but show up," Nichols says. "Nobody has to act." Over the years, Nichols has made some particularly daring, less than obvious choices—Art Garfunkel in *Carnal Knowledge*, Adrian Lester in *Primary Colors*, Hank Azaria in *The Birdcage*—but the outstanding example of inspired casting is Dustin Hoffman in *The Graduate*, since Hoffman was both unknown and physically wrong for the preppy Benjamin Braddock, a Wasp college athlete who has an affair with one of his parents' friends. "There is no piece of casting in the twentieth century that I know of that is more courageous than putting me in that part," says Hoffman, who considers the film "the most perfect movie I've ever been part of," adding, "I was a paralyzed person. I had come from a paralyzed background—the suffocation of that family. I was not acting."

What Nichols saw in Hoffman—"a dark, Jewish, anomalous presence"—was, of course, himself. Through improvisation, Nichols had learned to "treat yourself as a metaphor"; Hoffman gave him the same opportunity in film. "If the metaphor is powerful, it's always underneath you and you're always surfing it. You're always serving it," says Nichols. Even Hoffman's whimper, Nichols says, "was my little whimper when Jack Warner would tell a joke—in fact, people had to tell me to try not to whimper when he told jokes, that he would notice." Hoffman remembers Nichols taking him aside when he was listless in front of the cameras, a couple of months into the shooting, and saying, "This is the only time you'll ever get a chance to do this scene. It's going to be up there for the rest of your life." Hoffman adds, "He really meant it. It makes me cry, because he had that kind of passion, and it had that importance. I've never forgotten it. Mike worked like a surgeon every second."

Steven Spielberg calls *The Graduate* "a visual watershed," and invokes the moment when Benjamin races home ahead of Mrs. Robinson to tell her daughter Elaine, whom he loves, about his affair with her mother. "All of a sudden, the mother appears in the door behind Elaine, Elaine turns, and the focus racks to the mom. But when Elaine turns back the focus stays—Elaine is actually out of focus—and very slowly comes back until she is sharp and she realizes that Benjamin and her mother have been shtupping. I had never seen long lenses used that way to illuminate a character moment."

In Spielberg's encyclopedic appreciation of Nichols's cinematic innovations, he lists the handheld camera in *Who's Afraid of Virginia Woolf?*, which "further complicated" the anxiety and turned the couple's war into "a dance"; the "brilliant use of light" in *Day of the Dolphin*, when the aquarium lights are turned on and a dead body is discovered floating inside the tank; the way Nichols built, bit by bit, the paranoia and terror in *Silkwood*, which was, for Spielberg, "one of the most frightening and suspenseful things I had ever seen in a movie"; the long opening shot in *Carnal Knowledge*, at the college party, and the way he "made love to Ann-Margret through the lighting." That controversial film, which Nichols considers his darkest, was a coruscating look at predatory sexual chauvinism and at women's suffering, themes that resonated with Nichols's own life at the time. "He was not nice to his girls," says a close friend of those middle years, when Nichols was married to his third wife, the Anglo-Irish novelist Annabel Davis-Goff, who is the mother of two of his children, Max and Jenny. (He had split up with Margot Callas in 1964.) "He was a terrible household tyrant."

Carnal Knowledge dramatized this tyranny. The night before Nichols was to shoot the crucial scene—the bedroom fracas between Jonathan (Jack Nicholson) and the depressed Bobbie (Ann-Margret), in which Jonathan goes berserk trying to force Bobbie out of his house and calls her "a ball-busting, castrating, son-of-a-cunt bitch!"— Feiffer sat with Nichols as Nichols explained why the scene had to go. "It's just so ugly, it's so awful, people are gonna hate it, and they're gonna hate the movie," Feiffer remembers him saying. "We went for a bite," Feiffer adds. "I just sat in the car listening to him go over and over why he couldn't shoot it. Finally, he just looked at me and said, 'No, we've got to do it, because it's true.'"

But after the box-office failures of both *Carnal Knowledge* and the ambitious but misguided *Catch-22*—a story whose surreality was not Nichols's strong suit—Nichols began, by his own admission, to lose his way. Once, during this period, he sat idling in his Rolls-Royce at a Beverly Hills traffic light when a pimp in a flashy car pulled up beside him. "That's a Silver Cloud," the pimp said. "And you, man, are the silver lining." And so it had seemed, until, after his third miscue, with *Bogart Slept Here*, it wasn't. Nichols told the world that he'd lost his appetite for making movies, but what he'd lost was a vital sense of connection to what he was doing and what he wanted to say. "Usually it happens right away, when I'm reading a script—I see a moment, and I know what that moment is, and it's my hook into the whole thing," Nichols says. In the years between closing down *Bogart Slept Here*, in 1975, and starting *Silkwood*, in 1983, those moments of compelling inspiration eluded him. In the interim, besides developing a film version of *A Chorus Line* (which he subsequently abandoned), he produced the musical *Annie* and the one-woman Broadway show that launched Whoopi Goldberg's career.

Then, sometime in the middle of the eighties, visions of an altogether different kind appeared to Nichols: for about six months, he experienced a Halcion-induced psychotic breakdown. He became delusional—he was convinced, for example, that he had lost all his money, and that he'd turned from being "the hero of the story" into the villain. "Because I'd lost the money, I was the bad guy. I'd brought shame and unhappiness to my family," he says. "It was a horrible feeling of abject despair and self-loathing." He was wide-eyed and gaunt. Nothing seemed to help. He called Buck Henry to ask if he'd give him enough sleeping pills to end his life if it was absolutely necessary. "Of course, I said I would," Henry says. "I was lying." At one low point, Nichols sat with the producer John Calley, now the head of Sony Pictures, and tallied up his assets item by item on a foolscap pad. Calley says, "I'd add the numbers up and at the bottom it would have thirteen million six, and I'd say, 'Do you see thirteen six?' He'd say, 'Yes.' I'd say, 'Now, can you accept that?' He'd say, 'The only thing I could accept would be you telling me that when I go into debtors' prison you will take care of the children.' " (Max was then eleven and Jenny was nine.) By the time Halcion was identified as the chemical source of his problem and Nichols stopped taking it, he had learned, he says, "what people are like when you're not so shiny and you don't have your powers." (His marriage to Davis-Goff broke up shortly thereafter.)

His collapse proved cautionary, and his subsequent movies, from Neil Simon's *Biloxi Blues* and *Working Girl* to *Primary Colors* and *The Birdcage*, were an aggressive reassertion of his commercial shine. With the exception of *Primary Colors*, a subtle dissection of power and marriage, the films are crowd-pleasing fables. Nichols's impulse was clearly to build himself as solidly as possible into the Hollywood system. "Every development executive, every studio president, has a list of directors," Spielberg says, "and Mike has never been off the A-list." This puts Nichols's survival at the top of the Hollywood tree at thirty-four years and counting—longer than such legends as Preston Sturges, Billy Wilder, John Huston, and Frank Capra. Spielberg adds, "You want him because you know that he's going to tell the story better than it was told in the screenplay you bought. You're going to be getting basically two scripts for the price of one." Nichols knows the value of stories like *The Remains of the Day*, *All the Pretty Horses*, and *The Reader*; they are works he has produced, or will produce, but wasn't interested in directing. He loved the intellectual showboating of Stoppard's *Arcadia*, a play about chaos theory, and wanted to make it into a film, but he couldn't make the numbers work. "You don't want to take advantage of your friends and say, 'Would you mind doing this at a quarter of your price?' " he says.

"If movies hadn't changed so radically, what Mike would have been, perhaps should have been," Jules Feiffer says, "is the successor to a director like George Cukor—working in romantic comedy with urbane wit and style. But those times passed. So he had to shuffle around to find something to replace that." In choosing his projects, Nichols needs to feel, he says, that "only I can do this." When he picked *What Planet Are You From?*, he thought, Yes, this is for me. I know what to do with it. Nichols's next film, starring Robin Williams and with a script by Elaine May, will be a remake of the classic Ealing comedy *Kind Hearts and Coronets*. "I can only follow my excitement," Nichols says. "Sometimes I wish it were more high-minded, and sometimes I'm glad that it's not. I have no choice either way. I don't think *The Graduate* and *Carnal Knowledge* were any different from what I'm doing now." But the fact remains that the early pictures said new things in an ironic, challenging way, and the later work ruffles no feathers.

In any case, Nichols's asking price for mainstream movies has gone up: he now gets about $7.5 million just for taking on a film, plus approximately 12 percent of the gross. "So it's hard for him to say no," John Calley says. Some of his friends wish he would. "He knows I don't like a lot of the stuff he does. I think it's beneath him," Buck Henry says. "He should be doing more *Hurlyburlys*." But Nichols, who has heard the arguments, is unmoved. "All movies are pure process," he says. "A commercial movie isn't less process than an art movie. You can't make your decisions about a film on the basis of 'Is it important enough? Is it serious enough?' It's either alive or it's not for me. If it's alive, I want to do it." He adds, "If you're funny, and you stay funny, I think that's already doing pretty good."

In the pale-gray calm of his midtown editing suite, Nichols sits behind his editor, Richie Marks, who works away at an Avid console, tweaking the finale of *What Planet Are You From?* on a triptych of screens. Bening and Shandling—the earthling and the reconstructed alien—stand facing each other to reaffirm their marital vows. Bening is saying, "Harold, meeting you has taught me the universe is one big screwed-up place where everyone's just trying to work out their problems, but I'm honored to work them out with you, because . . . I think . . . I love you." When the lights come on, Nichols says, "I have this experience over and over. I make a movie because it draws me, and when I get it all finished I think, Christ, look, it's about me." The alien, who comes to earth merely to exploit women, has been humanized by love—and he becomes, as Nichols points out, "simultaneously the leader of his planet." In Nichols's eyes, his marriage to Diane Sawyer has wrought the same miracle. "True love made Pinocchio a real boy," Nichols said in a TV interview. "We all sort of feel like we're contraptions, like we pasted ourselves together—a little bit from here, a little bit from there—and then, if you're very lucky, along comes someone who loves you the right way, and then you're real."

"Mike spent many years without happiness. I mean, there were dark years where it wasn't quite working in relationships," Calley says. "He was in them but they weren't giving him a lot of joy. With Diane, he doesn't have to pretend not to be who he is to make a partner comfortable." Intimacy requires equality; and Sawyer, who has her own constituency, checkbook, and clout, is in every way an equal to Nichols, whom she first met while waiting to board a Concorde flight from Paris. Even today, if asked to shut her eyes and picture him, Sawyer sees Nichols as she did that first day: "All that light in his eyes and some sort of invitation. He's just full of invitation. It's like, 'Let's be young together. Let's see things for the first time and tell each other the absolute truth, want to?' " After their chance meeting, Sawyer approached Nichols for a TV interview: "I just had this idea of wild intelligence and that there'd be some surprise there," she says. The surprise was, she says, "that there was no end to the surprises."

Nichols and Sawyer live on the seventh floor of a handsome Fifth Avenue apartment building with a view of the Metropolitan Museum of Art from their library. Most of Nichols's art collection was sold off at bargain-basement prices in his Halcion panic; at one point he owned six paintings by Balthus, including the infamous *The Guitar Lesson*, which hung over his bed. ("I had to get rid of it," he says. "It pissed off too many women.") But there is still a Stubbs, a Fischl, and a beautiful Morandi study of bottles whose hard-won peace echoes the current mood of its owner. He is on record as saying that the best definition of happiness appears in Tom Stoppard's *The Real Thing*. "Happiness is equilibrium," the main character says. "Shift your weight." "It's good, and it's true," Nichols continues Stoppard's thought. "You have to stay light on your feet and remember what's important and what's not." These days, Nichols teaches; he attends meetings of Friends in Deed, an outreach charity for people with AIDS and other life-threatening diseases, which he founded with the actress Cynthia O'Neal; and he keeps up a proliferating e-mail correspondence. He visits his horses, and he even cooks now: his specialties include lemon pasta, risotto with smoked mozzarella, and sour-cream-peach ice cream. Sawyer leaves notes on the floor beside their bed when she slips off to the network every day at 4 a.m. to anchor *Good Morning America*; before going back to sleep, according to Sawyer, Nichols "opens one eye and says, 'Tell it like it is.'"

On the chaise longue in the bedroom is an embroidered pillow with words that play on a line from one of Nichols's favorite movies, *Lawrence of Arabia*, in which an Arab tells Lawrence to abandon a straggler in his party. "It is written," the Arab says. The cushion gives Lawrence's answer: "Nothing Is Written." It seems an apt motto for Nichols's journey. Nichols, who keeps no diaries and few mementos of his extraordinary life, is still all future. "He can go on and on until he chooses not to go on anymore," Spielberg says of Nichols's movie-making career. But the greatest of Nichols's mise-en-scènes is himself: he has created a person who lives well in the world.

At the end of our time together, he sat back on the sofa and declared himself pleased with the conversation. "I do well with the fundamentally inconsolable," I said. The words seemed to surprise Nichols and to press him back in his seat. His eyes fluttered shut for a moment, then opened. "We get a lot done, you know," he said. ∎

—February 21, 2000

Death of a Salesman

In the first beat of Arthur Miller's *Death of a Salesman* (now in a luminous revival, directed by Mike Nichols, at the Ethel Barrymore), the salesman Willy Loman (Philip Seymour Hoffman) trudges up the path to his Brooklyn house, sample cases in hand. He has returned home after falling asleep at the wheel of his car. Inside, he slouches in a kitchen chair, like a tire deflating. "Oh boy, oh boy," he says, thrumming the table with his stubby fingers, dimly aware that something in him is going terribly wrong. He is losing his concentration, his sales mojo, his salary, his temper, and, given his unmooring visions, maybe even his mind. "I have such thoughts, I have such strange thoughts," he confides to Linda, his long-suffering wife (the tender and compelling Linda Emond). Willy has arrived at a kind of bewildering tipping point. "They seem to laugh at me," he tells Linda about the buyers, adding, "I don't know the reason for it, but they just pass me by. I'm not noticed." Willy has begun to feel posthumous, or, as he puts it later, "I still feel kind of temporary about myself."

A blowhard of pluck and positivity ("Be liked and you will never want" is one of his mantras), Willy has always wanted to seize victory from the world and to claim the kingdom of self, to be a somebody—which is both the promise and the imperative of American individualism. In his grandiosity, he inflates the facts and figures of his hapless life; and he puffs the same optimistic smoke into his two adult sons, Biff (Andrew Garfield) and Happy (Finn Wittrock), who bear the scars of his delusional expectations. As a father, Willy basks in a nostalgic glow, remembering the boys' idolatry of him. But those bright-eyed youngsters have turned into ordinary, confused adults, each in his own way an enemy of promise—a fact that alternately perplexes and enrages Willy, whose idealization of Biff puts a fire wall of fantasy between him and his furious disappointment. "You got a greatness in you, Biff . . . ; you got all kindsa greatness," he insists, force-feeding hope to his reluctant son.

The revelation of this production—drawn out by Nichols's seamless and limpid orchestration of Willy's disconcerting flights of imagination (Miller's original title for the play was *The Inside of His Head*)—is that Willy, for all his fervent dreams of the future and his fierce argument with the past, never, ever, occupies his present. Even as he fights, fumes, and flounders, he is sensationally absent from his life, a kind of living ghost. It is existence, not success, that eludes him. He inhabits a vast, restless, awful, and awesome isolation, which is both his folly and his tragedy.

Willy is defined by the spirit of competition and by its corollary, invidious comparison. Envy is the gasoline on which American capitalism runs; it also runs Willy, driving him crazy. His "powerful strivings," as Miller calls them, are his way of battling a corrosive sense of inadequacy. When Willy's neighbor Charley (Bill Camp) shows him some generosity—he offers Willy work after he is crushed by the loss of his sales job—Willy's bumptious, confounding ingratitude underlines Charley's surplus and his own pathetic emptiness. The best defense against toxic self-loathing is to become the object of envy, which is why the gospel of achievement is Willy's fundamentalist faith. He lives by the metric of success, constantly measuring the imagined distance between himself and others. "You are going to be five times ahead of him," he says to his boys about Bernard (Fran Kranz), Charley's nerdy son, who gets good grades. "I thank Almighty God you're both built like Adonises," he tells them when they are teenagers. "Because the man who makes an appearance in the business world . . . is the man who gets ahead." If Willy can never actually make a killing, he can live within the lingo and the fantasy of vindictive triumph. "Knocked 'em cold in Providence, slaughtered them in Boston," he brags to his boys, who, as adults, are flummoxed by their inability to rise in the world. Biff's problem with petty theft and Happy's misogynistic penchant for ruining the virginal brides-to-be of the higher-ups in his company ("I just have an overdeveloped sense of competition or something," he says) are testimony to their own envious desires. In their ruthless quest to rob others of their power, the boys act out the message they learned at their father's knee.

Nichols's satisfying production emphasizes this dynamic, giving his staging of the play a particularly shocking subliminal punch. And Hoffman, an eloquent package of virulence and vulnerability, finds all the crazy music in Willy's disappointment. Gravity seems to hang on his lumpy body like a rumpled suit, tethering him to the shaky ground he stands on. Willy is "tired to the death": his exhaustion is spiritual, not just physical—the result of a soul-sapping struggle to face down humiliation in a world that keeps telling him he's a failure.

The night he kills himself, Willy walks outside to plant some seeds in his garden. He has reared his children—his own seed—in the contaminated soil of delusion. "Dad, you're never going to see what I am, so what's the use of arguing," Biff says, in their final, blistering confrontation. He goes on, "Pop, I'm a dime a dozen and so are you!" "I am not a dime a dozen!" Willy roars back. "I am Willy Loman, and you are Biff Loman!" Willy has never actually known his boys—he knows only his dream of them. He has never reflected back a true picture of them; he has never let the truth be spoken. As a result, the family has lived a collective lie, which endures even after it is denounced. When Biff, crying and broken, begs his father, "Will you let me go, for Christ's sake? Will you take that phony dream and burn it before something happens?," it's a searing moment—and Garfield, as Biff, makes the heartbreak sing. But Willy, on seeing tears in his son's eyes, announces, with astonishment and elation, "Isn't that . . . isn't that remarkable? Biff! He likes me!" At a stroke, he eliminates the negative: hate becomes love, and suicide becomes a father's heroic sacrifice in order to jump-start Biff's success with an insurance payout. "That boy . . . that boy is going to be . . . magnificent," Willy says, "choking with his love." The love is pure; it's the fantasy that's perverse. The greatest loss is the loss of an illusion; Willy goes to his grave with his mad, destructive dream intact.

Cast to a T, and beautiful in all its scenic dimensions (with Jo Mielziner's original, 1949 set design), this staging of *Death of a Salesman* is the best I expect to see in my lifetime. ■

—*Mar 26, 2012*

ACKNOWLEDGMENTS

When I was a little boy, I dreamed of having a magic pen. I would grab the pen with both hands, and it would write like fury, making perfect sentences in an elegant script. To acquire fluency, all I had to do was hold on. In reality, writing never came easily. I struggled with the mysteries of vocabulary, punctuation, grammar, and rhythm. The obsession with better expression never went away; it became an unending study. I have spent a lifetime trying to learn how to write better sentences. This pursuit takes time, application, and help.

The New Yorker has been my literary luck. Down the decades, I have collaborated with extraordinary editors: Charles McGrath, Deborah Garrison, and Deborah Treisman, who has been my editor for the last fifteen years. While giving the pieces their fine filigree, these mentors and friends have also given me unwitting tutorials in style. I may not have had that magic pen, but, with them behind me, it sometimes felt like I did. Through the many iterations of these pieces, grammarians (Mary Norris, Ann Goldstein, David Remnick, Carol Anderson), fact-checkers, and, of course, my editor-in-chief and executive editor, Dorothy Wickenden, have provided forensic notes that have greatly improved them. Although this editorial rub-down is not without its pain, it is a bracing, exciting process. The experience is rather like the lavabo that Dorothy and her beleaguered crew experience before entering Oz: "Clip clip here / Clip clip there."

Since I wrote my first profile in 1994, Ty Baldwin has transcribed every taped interview I've conducted. He has been my sidekick on these biographical adventures. His intelligence and gifts as a writer have made his service much more than secretarial. I can't imagine doing these profiles without his proficient backup.

I am grateful to John Glusman, the editor-in-chief of W. W. Norton and my editor, for his support of my theatrical enterprise and for putting my *New Yorker* writing so handsomely between hard covers. Over the decades, my wife, Connie Booth, has lived these profiles with me, as they've taken shape; she has shed her special light both on them and on me.

INDEX

Abarbanel, Jonathan, 129
Abbott, George, 500
Åberg, Ulla, 451
Abraham, F. Murray, 133
Accident (film), 221
Acheson, James, 313
Ackerman, Peter, 348
Acorn Theatre, New York, 207, 277
Adler, Renata, 236, 242
Adler, Richard, 346, 347
Adolphson, Kristina, 323
Adorno, Theodor W., 87
Ahlstedt, Börje, 319
Ahmanson Theatre, Los Angeles, 99
Ahrens, Lynn, 470, 476
Aidem, Betsy, 234
Akalaitis, JoAnne, 103
Åkerblom, Anna, 434–35
Albee, Edward:
  Me, Myself & I, 365–69
  Who's Afraid of Virginia Woolf?, 500, 530–31, 532, 533
Alda, Alan, 151
Alexander, Robert, 31
Ali, Muhammad, 30, 44
All About Eve (film), 502
Allen, Lewis, 530
Allen, Woody, 236, 441, 469–70, 484, 489, 491–93, 502, 520, 521

All the Pretty Horses (film), 536
Almeida Theatre Company, 226, 312
Almqvist, Jonas Love, 317–18, 323
Altman, Robert, 103, 288
Ambassadors Theatre, London, 144
American Airlines Theatre, New York, 346
American Gangster (film), 325
American Repertory Theater, Boston, 55
American Theatre Wing, 483
Andersson, Bibi, 318, 439, 443–44, 445
Andersson, Harriet, 444
And the World Goes 'Round (revue), 481
Annie (film/musical), 277, 496, 534
Annis, Francesca, 316
Ann-Margret, 534
Anouilh, Jean, 438
Ansari, Sakina, 49, 68
Antonioni, Michelangelo, 285
Appleman, Hale, 198
Arbus, Diane, 232
Aristotle, 160, 470
Armstrong, Louis, 30
Aronov, Michael, 191
Aronson, Letty, 484, 492

Arquette, Rosanna, 157
Artaud, Antonin, 402
Arthur, Owain, 418–19, 420
Asher, Aaron, 512
Ashley, Elizabeth, 366, 405, 526,
    527, 529
Asner, Ed, 513
Astaire, Fred, 470, 477–78, 480, 482
Atkins, Eileen, 249
Atkinson, Brooks, 383
Atlantic Theater Company, 124,
    126, 281
Auden, W. H., 219, 503–4
August, Pernilla, 319, 444
Autumn Sonata (film), 447
Avedon, Richard, xix, 240, 500,
    501
Avenue Q, 99
Avery Fisher Hall, New York,
    500–501, 502
Axelrod, George, 441
Azaria, Hank, 532

Bacon, Jenny, 168
Bailey, Pearl, 336
Baitz, Robbie, 95
Balanchine, George, 482
Baldwin, Alec, 117
Baldwin, James, 32, 36, 38, 46
    *The American Dream and the
    American Negro,* 61, 62
Balliett, Whitney, 243
Balthus, *The Guitar Lesson,* 538
Banes, Lisa, 344
Bankhead, Tallulah, xv
Baraka, Amiri, 30
Barnett, Samuel, 423
Barry, B. H., 247
Barrymore Theatre, New York, 359,
    539
Bartlett, Mike, 410
Barton, Anne, 302

Barton, Floyd (Schoolboy), 68
Barton, John, 298–311
    The Hollow Crown, 302
    Tantalus, 302, 303
    The Wars of the Roses, 302
Bassett, Angela, 30–31
Bates, Kathy, 531
Beach, Gary, 496
Bean, Richard, 407, 414, 420
    England People Very Nice, 418
Beardon, Romare, 50–51, 57
    The Prevalence of Ritual, 50
Beatles, 256
Beatty, John Lee, 23, 352
Beckett, Samuel, 79, 133, 219, 293,
    307, 369
    Endgame, 251
    Krapp's Last Tape, 209
    Waiting for Godot, 336, 401, 528
Bedford, David, 40
Beerbohm, Max, 167
Beethoven, Ludwig van, Ninth Sym-
    phony, 450
Belasco Theater, New York, 65, 188,
    312
Bening, Annette, 506–7, 537
Benjamin, Walter, 87
Bennett, Alan, 416–17
    The History Boys, 407, 417,
    422–24
    The Madness of George the Third,
    407, 409
    One Man, Two Guvnors, 407,
    414, 417–20
    Untold Stories (prose collection),
    423
Bennett-Warner, Pippa, 331
Benson, George, 36
Bergen, Candice, 500, 505, 532
Bergman, Dag, 432
Bergman, Daniel, 449
Bergman, Erik, 428–30, 432, 433

Bergman, Eva, 449

Bergman, Ingmar, 317–23, 403–4, 425–68
  films of, *see specific films*
  Images: My Life in Film (memoir), 426, 427, 439
  Kasper's Death, 437
  The Magic Lantern (autobiography), 429, 435, 446
  Sunday's Children (autobiog. novel), 430, 431–32

Bergman, Ingrid, 447

Bergman, Karin, 430, 432, 433–34, 435, 450

Bergman, Mats, 443, 465

Berkeley, Busby, 482

Berlin, Irving, 471

Berlin, Jack, 515

Berlin, Jeannie, 515

Berman, Shelley, 519

Bernstein, Leonard, 525

Berry, Chuck, 45

Best, Eve, 222, 223

Best Intentions, The (film), 319

Bettelheim, Bruno, *The Uses of Enchantment*, 136

Beyond the Fringe (revue), 422

Big Fish (musical), 471, 475

Billington, Michael, 217, 221

Birdcage, The (film), 503, 532, 535

Bishop, André, 483

Bishop, Elizabeth, 165

Bishop's Company Repertory Players, 281

Björk, Anita, 434, 444, 455

Black Horizons Theater, Pittsburgh, 49

Blake, Marsha Stephanie, 67

Blanchett, Cate, 488

Blazing Saddles (film), 494

Bliven, Bruce, 244

Bliven, Naomi, 243, 244

Bloom, Harold, 77, 100

Bloomgarden, Kermit, 22

Blue Jasmine (film), 488

Blumberg, Kate, 233

Boevers, Jessica, 371

Bogart, Anne, 161, 162

Bogart Slept Here (film), 503, 534

Bohon, Justin, 372

Bond, Christopher, 363

Booth, Zachary, 366

Boublil, Alain, 409

Bouma-Moore, Debbie, 477, 478–79

Boyle, Peter, 125

Brackman, Jacob, 242, 245

Bradley, Scott, 68, 165

Braff, Zach, 485, 490, 492

Brand, Daniel, 211

Brando, Marlon, 279, 380, 381, 404

Brantley, Ben, 76

Brasseur, Pierre, 217

Brearly, Joe, 217–18

Brecht, Bertolt, 19, 362
  A Short Organum for the Theatre, 87

Breen, Patrick, 234

Brenman-Gibson, Margaret, *Clifford Odets, American Playwright,* 175, 187

Brice, Fanny, xvii

Brigham Young University, 267, 269, 272, 273–74

Broadhurst Theatre, New York, 42

Broderick, Matthew, 496, 497, 500

Brodin, Helena, 454

Bronnenberg, Mark, 88

Brook, Peter, 402–3

Brooklyn Academy of Music (BAM), 75, 298, 303, 317, 328, 331, 453, 461

Brooks, Mel, 5, 470, 471, 474, 484, 493–98

Brown, Blair, 342, 344

Brown, Brennan, 233
Brown, Carlisle, 31
Brown, Michael Henry, 31
Brubeck, Dave, 476
Bruce, Lenny, 521
Brustein, Robert, 55–56
Brynolfsson, Reine, 318
Buffett, Warren, 79
Bullets over Broadway (film/musi-
    cal), 469–70, 473, 484–93
Bullins, Ed, 30
    Twentieth-Century Cycle, 52
Burley, Charley, 29–30
Burley, Julie, 37
Burns, Robert, 474
Burstein, Danny, 191
Burton, Brenda, 49, 68
Burton, Kate, 298, 308
Burton, Richard, 532
Burton, Tim, 471
Bush, George W., 80, 94
Bush, Laura, 101
Bybee, Jay S., 101
Byron, George Gordon, Lord, 343
Byström, Margaretha, 454

Callas, Margot, 502, 533
Calley, John, 535, 536, 537
Calvino, Italo, *Six Memos for the
    Next Millennium,* 154
Camp, Bill, 162–63, 541
Campbell Moore, Stephen, 422
Cannavale, Bobby, 207
Cape Fear (film), 277
Capra, Frank, 535
Carlson, Jeffrey, 170
Carnal Knowledge (film), 128,
    531–32, 533, 534, 536
Carney, Art, 529
Catch-22 (film), 503, 534
Catholic Legion of Decency, 531
Cats (musical), 370, 394, 482

Center Avenue Poets Theater Work-
    shop, Pittsburgh, 49
Center Stage (film), 476
Cerveris, Michael, 363
Chad, Harrison, 110
Chaikin, Joseph, 285, 290
Chaplin, Ben, 349
Chaplin, Charlie, 402
Charuvastra, Tony, 153
Chase, Chevy, 244
Chekhov, Anton, 34, 157, 416, 509
Chicago (musical), 480
Chisholm, Anthony, 61
Chorus Line, A (musical), 534
Christmas Carol, A (musical), 470
Churchill, Winston, 500
Church of the Latter-Day Saints,
    263, 269, 270, 273, 274, 277
Circle in the Square, New York, 295
Civic Repertory Theatre, New York,
    179
Clapp, Gordon, 151
Clark, Victoria, 374, 377
Clarke, Larry, 199
Clarkson, Patricia, 101
Classic Stage Company, New York, 77
Claxton, Richard, 145
Clayburgh, Jill, 206
Clinton, Bill, 93–94, 263
Close, Del, 520
Clueless (film), 236
Clurman, Harold, 173, 178, 179, 180
Cobb, Lee J., 21
Cocteau, Jean, 438
Cohn, Roy, 91, 102, 105–6, 107–9
Coleman, Chad L., 66
Coleman, Janet, *The Compass,* 513,
    519
Coleridge, Samuel Taylor, 327
Collins, Pat, 107
Compass Players, Chicago, 516, 517,
    518, 519–20

Conklin, John, 104
Connick, Harry Jr., 346–49
Contact (musical), 475–76, 483–84
Conte, Bob, 139
Cook, Ralph, 282–83
Cook, Ron, 332
Cooper, Dominic, 423
Coppola, Michael (Trigger Mike), 486
Corden, James, 417
Cordero, Nick, 485, 492
Cork, Adam, 328
Corneille, Pierre, 97
Cornford, Frances, 423
Corthron, Kia, 31
Cort Theatre, New York, 23, 210, 222
Costabile, David, 111–12
Coward, Noël, 169–70, 209–10, 214
    Hay Fever, 355
    Present Laughter, 355
    Private Lives, 169, 171, 353–58
Cox, Patricia, 128
Cox, Veanne, 112
Crawford, Cheryl, 178
Crazy for You (musical), 470, 471, 473, 475–76, 482–83
Cries and Whispers (film), 434, 442
Crisis (film), 437, 438
Cristofer, Michael, 24
Crivello, Anthony, 191
Crouse, Lindsay, 118, 134–35, 136
Crouse, Russel, 134
Crowley, Bob, 145, 227, 380, 390, 393, 413, 423
Crucible, The (film), 409
Crudup, Arthur (Big Boy), 68
Crudup, Billy, 342
Cukor, George, 536
Cusack, Joan, 157
Cusack, John, 157

Dahlbeck, Eva, 444
Darden, Severn, 513
Dass, Ram, 201
David, Keith, 70
Davidson, Gordon, 91, 103
Davies, Howard, 354, 357–58
Davis, Maudie Lee, 76
Davis, Paul, xix
Davis, Viola, 70
Davis-Goff, Annabel, 533, 535
Davison, Peter J., 314
Day, Doris, 441
Day of the Dolphin, The (film), 503, 506, 533
Dean, James, 195, 206, 391
Dean, Phillip Hayes, 30
Dee, Janie, 392
Degas, Edgar, *Blue Dancers,* 478
de la Tour, Frances, 414, 424
de Mille, Agnes, 393
Dench, Dame Judi, 302
De Niro, Robert, 117
Dennehy, Brian, 8
Dent, Alan, 218
De Palma, Brian, 138
Descartes, René, 81
DeTullio, N. Joseph, 253
Deutscher, Martha, 81, 85
Dial M for Murder (film), 277
Dirty Pretty Things (film), 325
Dixon, Willie, 68
Dizzia, Maria, 165
Donaldson, Walter, 471
Don Giovanni (opera), 481
Donmar Warehouse, London, 324, 331, 380
Donne, John, 237–38, 249, 254, 256
Donnellan, Declan, 92
Dostoyevsky, Fyodor, 101, 518
Douglas Fairbanks Theatre, New York, 264

Doyle, John, 359, 361, 362, 364
D'Silva, Darrell, 386
Duncan, Lindsay, 145, 149, 354, 356–58
Duncan, Robert, 49
  "My Mother Would Be a Falconress," 85
Dundas, Jennifer, 340, 344
Dunnock, Mildred, 21
Durden, Richard, 380
Dutton, Charles S., 30
Dylan, Bob, 284, 285
Dymling, Carl Anders, 438

Ealing Studios, 536
Ebb, Fred, 480, 481
Eckhart, Aaron, 262, 263, 271, 273, 274, 275
Eckstine, Billy, 36
Edblad, Stina, 455–56
Edgar, David, 414
Edge, The (film), 116–17, 142
Edwards, Stacy, 268, 275
Eisenberg, Deborah, 240, 253, 255
Ejiofor, Chiwetel, 325
Ekmanner, Agneta, 454–55, 466
Elan, Erica, 169
Eldard, Ron, 264
Elder, Lonne, 30
Eliot, T. S., 214, 219, 234
Elizabeth II, queen of England, 421–22
Elliott, Scott, 208
Ellis, Scott, 198, 481, 482
Ellison, Ralph, 47
Emond, Linda, 540
Endre, Lena, 444, 462, 465
English National Opera, 409, 416
Enquist, Per Olov, *The Image Makers,* 426
Enter Laughing (film), 156
Ephron, Nora, 95, 500, 531

Equity Library Theatre, New York, 480
Erlich, Hayward, 513
Erté, 485
Escoffier, Jean Yves, 267
Esparza, Raúl, 223, 360
Essandoh, Ato, 199
Eugene O'Neill Theatre, New York, 75, 98, 362, 363
Eureka Theater, San Francisco, 89, 91
Euripides, 442
  The Bacchae, 427, 453
  Medea, 312
Eustis, Oskar, 89, 91, 93, 96, 107
Evans, Walker, 153
Everage, Dame Edna, xv, 336
Eyre, Peter, 315
Eyre, Richard, 408–9, 413, 414

Fairley, Michelle, 326, 327
Falk, Peter, 527
Falls, Robert, 8
Fanny and Alexander (film), 319, 427, 430, 433, 442, 450
Fargo (film), 127
Farina, Dennis, 129
Fay, Jimmy, 294
Feast, Michael, 330
Feiffer, Jules, 520–21, 525, 531–32, 534, 536
Feuer, Donya, 320, 321, 442, 449, 453, 462
Fiddler on the Roof (musical), 389, 515
Fielding, Emma, 344, 356
Fielding, Susannah, 386
Fiennes, Ralph, 312–14, 316
Fishburne, Laurence, 31, 324
Fitzgerald, Tara, 315
Flaherty, Stephen, 476
Flamberg, James, 266

Flanner, Janet, 243
Fleetwood, Kate, 329
Fleischer, Brad, 200
Fleming, Renée, 476
Flinck, Thorsten, 462
Flockhart, Calista, 264
Flora the Red Menace (musical), 481
Flournoy, Nicholas, 48
Flynn, Kimberly, 87–89
Ford, Gerald R., 94
Ford, Harrison, 500
Forster, E. M., *A Passage to India*, 511
Fortune, The (film), 503
Fosse, Bob, 346, 471, 480
Foy, Eddie Jr., 346
Fragonard, Jean Honoré, 483
Frain, James, 222
Frances (film), 293
Frank, Anne, 83
Frank, Robert, 285
Franklin, Marcus Carl, 113
Fraser, Antonia, 221
Frears, Stephen, 325
Freeman, K. Todd, 108
Freeman, Morgan, 266, 267
French Lieutenant's Woman, The (film), 133, 211
Friends in Deed, 95, 538
Fry, Christopher, 219
Fugitive Kind, The (film), 380
Furman, Roy, 485
Furth, George, 359

Gabrielle, Josefina, 371
Garber, Victor, 343
Garfield, Andrew, 540, 542
Garfunkel, Art, 500, 502, 532
Garland, Judy, 496
Garlin, Jeff, 157
Garner, Erroll, 36

Garvin, Casey, 486
Gates, Henry Louis Jr., 34
Gehry, Frank, 29
Gershwin, George and Ira, 470
Gershwin Theatre, New York, 370
Giamatti, Paul, 342
Gianino, Gian-Murray, 167
Gibbs, Wolcott, xix
Gillespie, Dizzy, 284
Ginsburg, Ruth Bader, 79
Glover, Keith, 31
Go-Between, The (film), 221
Godley, Adam, 356
Goffman, Erving, 464
Goldberg, Whoopi, 534
Goldoni, Carlo, *The Servant of Two Masters*, 407, 417–18
Gombrowicz, Sitold, *Princess Ivona*, 431
Goodman Theatre, Chicago, 8, 56, 61, 130, 168, 374
Goodspeed Musicals, Connecticut, 479
Goold, Rupert, 328, 329, 330
Gore, Al, 86
Gore, Lisa, 263, 272–73, 274, 277
Gotti, John, 316
Graduate, The (film), 404, 500, 501, 522, 532, 533, 536
Graham, Martha, 478
Grandage, Michael, 324, 331, 332
Grant, Lee, 527
Graves, Robert, 502
Grayson, Bette, 185
Green, Paul, 32
Greene, Graham, 438
Gregory, André, 239, 240, 241, 242, 246, 251, 255–56, 257, 260
Alice in Wonderland, 402
Griffin, John, 345
Griffiths, Richard, 422
Gross, Alan, 129

Group Theatre, New York, 22, 173, 174, 177–79, 182–83, 184, 187, 188, 378
Gruen, John, 246
Guare, John, 134
Guettel, Adam, 374, 376, 378
Gurira, Danai, 68
Gussow, Mel, *Edward Albee: A Singular Journey,* 365, 532
Guys and Dolls (musical), 410

Hairspray (musical), 76
Hall, Lee, 410
Hall, Peter, 210, 212, 216, 219, 298, 302, 408
Halliday, Richard, 369
Hamburger, Philip, 243, 245
Hamilton, LisaGay, 62
Hamlett, Dilys, 217
Hammerstein, Oscar II, 396
    Carousel, 388–89, 390, 393, 394, 395
    The Desert Song, 388
    Oklahoma!, 369–70, 373
    Rose-Marie, 388
    Show Boat, 388
    see also Rodgers and Hammerstein
Hampton, Christopher, *The Philanthropist,* 339
Haney, Carol, 346
Hansberry, Lorraine, *A Raisin in the Sun,* 30, 52, 63
Hanzon, Thomas, 463
Harden, Marcia Gay, 101
Hardy, Thomas, 423
Hare, David, 209, 214, 237, 251
Harelik, Mark, 377
Harnick, Sheldon, 515
Harris, Barbara, 513
Harris, Mark, 98, 100
Harrison, Howard, 260, 328

Hart, Lorenz, 388, 423
Harting, Carla, 167
Hatley, Tim, 356, 411, 412
Hawke, Ethan, 207
Hawthorne, Nathaniel, 104
Hayden, Michael, 391–92
Hayworth, Rita, 478
Hazlitt, William, 139
Heaney, Seamus, "Fosterling," xviii
Heartburn (film), 503, 531
Heavey, Lorna, 328
Hecht, Jessica, 24
Heely, Allan, 365
Hellman, Lillian, 136, 530
Hello, Dolly! (musical), 336, 389
Helsingborg City Theatre, Sweden, 438
Henriksson, Krister, 319
Henry, Buck, 500, 501, 510, 517, 524, 535, 536
Hensley, Shuler, 372
Hertzberg, Hendrik, 245
Herzog, Werner, 267
Heyward, Dubose, 32
Hiddleston, Tom, 326
Higgins, Clare, 256
Hines, Earl (Fatha), 36
Hiss, Tony, 245
Hitchcock, Alfred, 277, 438
Hitler, Adolf, 507
Hit the Deck (musical), 479
Hobbs, William, 316
Hodge, Douglas, 230
Hoffa, Jimmy, 124
Hoffman, Dustin, 117, 404, 503, 532–33
Hoffman, Philip Seymour, 295, 539, 541
Hofmannsthal, Hugo von, 512
Holder, Donald, 491
Holland, Anthony, 513
Hollis, Tommy, 71

Holloway, Stanley, 415
Holm, Ian, 229, 303
Homicide (film), 124
Hootkins, William, 382
Hope, Bob, 86
Hopkins, Anthony, 116
Hopper, Edward, 161, 190
Horkheimer, Max, 87
Horne, Lena, 36
Horovitz, Israel, *Indian Wants the Bronx, The,* 336
Hour of the Wolf, The (film), 425
House of Games (film), 117, 135, 136
Howard, Arliss, 67
Hudson, Ernie, 66–67
Huffman, Cady, 497
Huffman, Felicity, 137
Hughes, Langston, 45
Hughes, Ted, 328
Hugo, Victor, 177
Hull House Theater, Chicago, 125
Humphries, Barry (Dame Edna), xv, 258–59, 336
Hunt, Helen, 298, 305
Hurok, Sol, 508
Hurston, Zora Neale, 32, 47, 62, 110–11, 114
Huston, John, 277, 535
Hyman, Earle, 232
Hytner, Benet and Joyce, 415
Hytner, Nicholas, 380, 382, 383, 390–93, 395–96, 404, 407–24

Ibsen, Henrik, 34, 269, 438, 442
   Hedda Gabler, 448
   Peer Gynt, 246, 453
Illich, Ivan, 208
Inge, William, 441
In the Presence of a Clown (TV), 443, 451
Ionesco, Eugene, *The Bald Soprano,* 156

It Rains on Our Love (film), 437
It's a Wonderful Life (film), 184
Ivey Long, William, 485–86, 488, 493
Izzard, Eddie, 145

Jackson, Samuel L., 30
Jacobi, Derek, 331–32
Jaeck, Scott, 169
Jamal, Ahmad, 36
James, Peter Francis, 304, 309–10
Jay, Ricky, 135
Jelks, John Earl, 61
Jerry Springer: The Opera (musical), 410
Johansson, Scarlett, 24, 25
Johnson, O-Lan (Jones), 286, 293
Johnson, Dr. Samuel, 4, 326
Johnston, J. J., 129–30
Jones, Bill T., 93
Jones, James Earl, 43
Jonson, Ben, *Bartholomew Fair,* 87
Josephson, Erland, 436–37, 443, 445, 447–48, 450–51
Joyce, James, 234, 244, 339
   Ulysses, 511
Joyce Theatre, New York, 476
Jujamcyn Theaters, 103, 485

Kafka, Franz, 461
   The Trial, 226
Kander, John, 480, 481
Kant, Immanuel, 470
Kasznar, Kurt, 526
Katz, Jonathan, 117, 135
Kaye, Danny, 480
Kazan, Elia, 26–27, 53, 173–74, 179, 180, 183, 185, 401–2, 403, 404, 511
   Elia Kazan: A Life (autobiography), 8, 21–22, 23, 178
Kazin, Alfred, 181

Keaton, Diane, 236

Keel, Howard, 391

Keenan-Bolger, Celia, 374

Keene, Donald, 453

Kelley, Sam, 31

Kelly, Gene, 391

Kelly, George, *The Torch-Bearers*, 168

Kelly, Glen, 490

Kendal, Felicity, 344

Kennedy, Arthur, 21

Kennedy, Jacqueline [Onassis], 502, 531

Kennedy, John F., 112, 302

Kennedy Center, Washington DC, 476

Kent, Jonathan, 312, 314–15, 316

Keyser, David de, 237

Kind Hearts and Coronets (film), 536

King, Jeffrey, 105

King, W. D., *Writing Wrongs*, 237

King of Marvin Gardens, The (film), 242

Kingsley, Ben, 504, 505

Kissinger, Henry A., 106, 240

Kittel, Fritz, 38–40, 43

Klein, Robert, 125

Kline, Kevin, 298, 300–302, 303, 308

Klinga, Elin, 443, 444

Knotts, Don, 267

Koren, Ed, 115

Koroly, Charles, 454, 457, 464–65

Kramer, Larry, 93
  The Normal Heart, 91, 101

Kranz, Fran, 541

Kroll, Jack, 104

Kulle, Jarl, 462

Kushner, Eric, 82

Kushner, Lesley, 81–82, 84

Kushner, Sylvia, 80–83, 84–86, 100, 103

Kushner, Tony, 5, 75–114
  Angels in America, 75, 76, 77, 78, 80, 86, 88, 90–93, 96–97, 102–10, 410
  A Bright Room Called Day, 78, 85, 89
  Caroline, or Change, 75, 76, 77, 78, 79, 88, 97, 98–99, 110–14
  Homebody/Kabul, 75, 78, 79, 88
  Hydriotaphia, or the Death of Dr. Brown, 78
  The Illusion, 96
  La Fin de la Baleine: An Opera for the Apocalypse, 78, 88
  Millennium Approaches, 88, 90, 91–92, 102, 105–7, 108
  Only We Who Guard the Mystery Shall Be Unhappy, 101
  Perestroika, 75, 91, 92, 102, 107–9
  Thinking about the Longstanding Problems of Virtue and Happiness, 79

Kushner, William, 81–83, 100

Kustow, Michael, 303

Kwei-Armah, Kwame, *Elmina's Kitchen,* 410–11

LaBute, Marian, 270, 271, 272

LaBute, Neil, 261–80
  Bash, 263–64, 277
  Filthy Talk for Troubled Times: Scenes of Intolerance, 261, 268
  In the Company of Men, 261–62, 263, 268, 270, 273, 274, 275
  Lepers, 262, 273
  The Mercy Seat, 277–80
  Your Friends and Neighbors, 262, 263, 266, 267–68, 269–70, 274

LaBute, Richard, 270–71, 272

LaBute, Richard Jr., 271
Lachmann, Hedwig, 510, 512
Lage, Jordan, 151
Lagerlöf, Selma, 426
Lahr, Bert, xix, 4, 336, 401, 402
Lahr, Chris, 211
Lahr, John, *Prick Up Your Ears,* 243
Lamarr, Hedy, 234
Lampert, Zohra, 513
Landauer, Gustav, 510–11
Landesman, Heidi, 103
Landesman, Rocco, 103, 494
Lane, Nathan, 497, 500
Lang, Fritz, 18
Lange, Jessica, 293
Langrishe, Go Down (film), 221
Lansky (TV movie), 139
Lansky, Meyer, 130
Lantz, Robby, 524, 525, 530
Larsson, Carl, *The Birth of Drama,* 318
Lasdun, Denys, 408
Laura Pels Theatre, New York, 198
Laurenson, James, 316
Lawrence, Megan, 348
Lawrence of Arabia (film), 539
Laws, Heather, 360
Lawson, John Howard, *Success Story,* 181
Ledbetter, Huddie (Leadbelly), 118
Lee, Ang, 5
Lee, Eugene, 63, 222, 253, 260
Lee, Stewart, 410
Lehman, Ernest, 530
Lehman, Ross, 171
Leibman, Ron, 105–6
Leigh, Amari Rose, 66
Lenin, V. I., 339
Leon, Kenny, 61
Leonard, Robert Sean, 345
Les Misérables (musical), 370
Lester, Adrian, 532

Leveaux, David, 227, 228
Lewis, Jerry Lee, 284
Lichtenstein, Roy, 86
Lincoln Center Repertory Theater, New York, 173, 335, 378
Lincoln Center Theater, New York, 173, 188, 191, 285–86, 483
Lindblom, Gunnel, 444
Lindh, Irene, 318
Lindsay, Howard, 134
Lindsay and Crouse, *Life with Father,* 134
Linkletter, Art, *People Are Funny,* 37
Linson, Art, 137, 138, 139
Lion, Margo, 103
Lithgow, John, 349
Little Dancer (musical), 476
Little Richard, 45, 256, 283
Loesser, Frank, *How to Succeed in Business without Really Trying,* 369
Löfgren, Lars, 446–47, 451
London Evening Standard, 92, 102
Loquasto, Santo, 469, 485–86, 488, 490
Love and Death (film), 441
Lucas, Craig, 377
Ludwig, Ken, 482
Lumet, Sidney, 135, 137–38, 380
LuPone, Patti, 363–64
Lupone, Robert, 296
Lymon, Frankie, and the Teenagers, 45
Lyttleton Theatre, London, 390, 408, 421

Mace, Cynthia, 106
Mackendrick, Alexander, 182
MacLaine, Shirley, 346
MacMillan, Sir Kenneth, 393–94
MacRae, Gordon, 391

Macy, William H., 127, 129, 137
Magic Flute, The (film), 453
Magician, The (film), 441
Magnani, Anna, 380
Magnuson, Benjamin, 364
Mailer, Norman, 502
Malick, Terrence, 240
Malle, Louis, 240, 251
Malloy, Matt, 268, 275
Mamet, Bernie, 118–21, 123–25
Mamet, Clara, 118, 141, 143
Mamet, David, 3, 5, 33, 115–51, 209,
   214, 219, 226, 255, 267, 268
   American Buffalo, 124, 130–31,
      132, 138–39, 337
   *The Cabin: Reminiscence and
      Diversions,* 144
   Camel, 126–27
   The Cryptogram, 117–18, 120,
      133, 141, 143–50
   Edmond, 124, 135
   Glengarry Glen Ross, 116, 125,
      132, 134, 151
   Jolly, 121
   The Old Neighborhood, 121, 126
   Oleanna, 121, 137, 226
   "The Rake," 122, 144
   Sexual Perversity in Chicago,
      115–16, 126, 127, 128, 129, 133,
      267
   Speed-the-Plow, 140
   Three Uses of the Knife, 118
   True and False, 133
Mamet, Judy, 119, 123
Mamet, Leonore (Lee), 118–21, 123
Mamet, Lynn, 117, 119, 120–21,
   122–23, 140, 144
Mamet, Willa, 118, 132
Mamet, Zosia, 118
Mandvi, Aasif, 371
Manhattan (film), 236
Manis, David, 344

Mann, Emily, 366
Månsson, Claes, 465
Mantegna, Joe, 131
Mantello, Joe, 105, 151
Marcuse, Herbert, 87
Marks, Richie, 537
Mark Taper Forum, Los Angeles, 91,
   92, 102, 103, 110
Marshall, Kathleen, 346
Martin, Andrea, 371
Martin, Mary, 369
Martin, Steve, 95, 117, 137, 500, 521,
   522–23
Marx Brothers, 402
Massey, Anna, 229
Mastrogiorgio, Danny, 189
Matthew, Walter, 527
May, Elaine, 96, 404, 499–500,
   501–2, 506, 509–10, 514–25,
   536
   A Matter of Position, 524
Mayer, Michael, 79, 80, 100
Mazzie, Marin, 490, 492
McClinton, Marion, 30, 31, 55, 56,
   57, 60
McCormick, Carolyn, 234
MCC Theater, New York, 277
McDonagh, Martin, *The Cripple of
   Inishmaan,* 407
McDonnell, Emily, 259
McGinley, Sean, 293–94
McGregor, Ewan, 325, 327
McKay, Claude, *Home to Harlem,*
   48
McKean, Michael, 222, 348
McKellen, Sir Ian, 303
McLane, Derek, 346
McLaughlin, Ellen, 107
McPherson, Conor, 410
McShane, Ian, 223
Meehan, Thomas, 496
Meisner, Sanford, 126

Melville, Herman, 461
  Mardi and a Voyage Thither, 77–78
  Moby-Dick, 104
Menken, Alan, 470
Merchant, Vivian, 217, 221, 223
Merlo, Frank, 383–84
Merrison, Clive, 424
Merry Widow, The (opera), 476
Metropolitan Opera, New York, 476
Metten, Charles, 269, 272, 273, 274
Meyer, Michael, 438, 448
Meyerhold, Vsevolod, 402
Michaels, Lorne, 273
Mielziner, Jo, 21, 542
Milestone, Lewis, 188
Miller, Arthur, 7–27, 33, 34, 185, 403
  After the Fall, 173
  All My Sons, 7, 13, 27, 272
  Death of a Salesman, 7–11, 12–13, 14, 15, 16–17, 19–23, 27, 35, 56, 83, 179, 539–42
  "In Memoriam," 13
  Timebends (autobiography), 8, 12, 14, 183
  A View from the Bridge, 23–27
Miller, Augusta, 13
Miller, Isidore, 12
Miller, Mary, 7
Milner, Ron, 30
Minnelli, Liza, 481
Mirren, Helen, 302, 380, 381, 408, 414
Mishima, Yukio:
  "Icarus," 452
  Madame de Sade, 317, 452–60, 461
Miss Saigon (musical), 390, 409
Mitchell, Cameron, 21
Mitchell, Joseph, 244

Molière, *The Misanthrope,* 317, 443, 446, 460–68
Molina, Lauren, 364
Molnár, Ferenc, *Liliom,* 388, 391, 393, 394, 395
Monk, Thelonious, 284
Monroe, Marilyn, 26
Monsef, Ramiz, 167
Montgomery, Mark L., 168
Moore, Archie, 29
Moore, Bonnie, 394
Morath, Inge, 11
Mordden, Ethan, *Broadway Babies,* 359
Mordecai, Ben, 33, 52, 54
Mordern, Sir Michael, 303
Mörk, Lennart, 318
Morley, Robert, 516
Morrison, Bill, 258
Morrison, George, 531
Mosher, Gregory, 23, 26, 123, 128, 130, 131, 133, 145
Mostel, Zero, 497
Mozart, Leopold, 124
Mulligan, Gerry, 284
Munch, Edvard, *The Dance of Life,* 320
Murray, Brian, 366
Music Box Theater, New York, 210, 407
Music in Darkness (film), 437–38
Music Man, The (musical), 476
My Dinner with André (film), 236, 240, 245, 251, 256

National Actors Theatre, 303
Natwick, Mildred, 526
Navasky, Victor, 185
Neighborhood Playhouse, Chicago, 126
New Group, New York, 206, 207
Newman, Abby, 14, 16

Newman, Buddy, 14

Newman, Manny, 13–14, 15

New York City Ballet, 470–71, 482

New York City Opera, 481

New York Theatre Workshop, 88

Nichols, Brigitte, 507–8, 509–10

Nichols, Mike, 76, 80, 90, 92,
    95–96, 128, 136, 204–5, 237,
    238, 240, 251, 403, 404–5,
    499–542

Nichols, Paul, 507–9

Nichols, Robert, 507, 508, 509

Nicholson, Jack, 242, 534

Nicholson, William:
    Gladiator (co-auth.), 352
    Shadowlands, 352
    The Retreat from Moscow,
      349–53

Nijinsky, Vaslav, *L'Après-Midi d'un*
    Faune, 246

Nilsson, Maj-Britt, 444

Nixon, Richard M., 94

Noble, Adrian, 299

None but the Lonely Heart (film),
    184–85

Nottage, Lynn, 31

Numrich, Seth, 189

Nunn, Trevor, 340, 370, 373, 408,
    414

Nurse Betty (film), 263, 264–66,
    276–77

Object of My Affection, The (film),
    409

Ockrent, Mike, 473–74, 475, 481–82,
    483

O'Connor, Flannery, 157

Odets, Clifford, 173–91
    Awake and Sing!, 173–74, 177,
      179, 181, 182, 188
    The Big Knife, 174, 177, 184, 186
    The Country Girl, 174, 184

    The Flowering Peach, 185, 186
    Golden Boy, 174, 177, 184,
      188–91
    Humoresque, 184
    Night Music, 174, 185–86
    910 Eden Street, 177
    Paradise Lost, 177
    Rocket to the Moon, 177
    The Time Is Ripe, 174
    Waiting for Lefty, 174, 179–81,
      182, 188

Odets, Genevieve, 175

Odets, Lou "L.J.," 175–77, 183–84

Odets, Nora, 185, 186

Odets, Pearl Geisinger, 174–75, 183

Odets, Walt, 185, 186

Odland, Bruce, 252

O'Hara, Kelli, 347, 348

Old Vic, London, 408

Oliver, Judy, 49

Oliver, Mary, 335

Olivier, Sir Laurence, 324, 408, 415,
    448

Olivier Theatre, London, 408, 410,
    421

Olympic Games (Munich 1972), 79

Onassis, Jacqueline Kennedy, 502,
    531

O'Neal, Cynthia, 538

O'Neill, Eugene, 32, 33, 34, 74, 511
    The Iceman Cometh, 19, 244
    Long Day's Journey into Night,
      35, 244

O'Neill Playwrights Conference,
    51–52, 53

On the Waterfront (film), 26

Open Theater, 285

Oram, Christopher, 327, 331

Orbach, Jerry, 480

Orton, Joe, 209, 226, 243

Osborne, John, 214

Oscar, Brad, 496

O'Steen, Sam, 530
O'Toole, Peter, 303
Ovid, 160

Pacino, Al, 5, 76, 307, 336, 403
Pajama Game, The (musical), 346–49
Pakledinaz, Martin, 346
Pan, Hermes, 482
Papp, Joseph, 197, 205–6, 246
Paramount Theater, New York, 470
Parker, Charlie, 29
Parker, Jamie, 423
Parker, Suzy, 502
Parks, Joseph, 165
Parks, Suzan-Lori, 31
Passion of Anna, The (film), 425
Pastore, Vincent, 487–88, 492
Payne, Natalia, 368
Paz, Octavio, 165
Peil, Mary Beth, 232
Penny, Rob, 40, 48, 49, 51
Penry-Jones, Rupert, 315
Perlman, Itzhak, 500
Persona (film), 435–36
Pevner, Stephen, 270, 271, 272
Phantom Carriage, The (film), 426
Picasso, Pablo, 341
Pidgeon, Rebecca, 118, 139–41, 143
Pimlott, Steven, 384
Pine, Larry, 253
Pinkins, Tonya, 98, 110, 113
Pinter, Harold, 125, 133, 136, 209–35, 416
    American Football, 225
    Betrayal, 212, 226
    The Birthday Party, 211–12, 215, 225, 226
    The Caretaker, 212, 226
    Celebration, 232, 233–35
    The Homecoming, 210–12,
213–14, 215–23, 226, 229, 231, 337
    Moonlight, 221, 225–31
    Mountain Language, 227
    The New World Order, 227
    No Man's Land, 226
    Party Time, 227
    The Room, 232–33
Pittsburgh Public Theater, 55
Pittu, David, 234
Piven, Joyce, 157
Piven Theatre, Evanston, Illinois, 157
Places in the Heart (film), 134
Plato, Symposium, 515
Playing Shakespeare (TV), 302
Playwrights Horizons, New York, 152, 161, 366
Poe, Edgar Allan, 259
Pontiac Correctional Center, 130
Poor, Bray, 167
Porter, Cole, 75, 103, 173
Port of Call (film), 437
Powell, Eleanor, 480
Prebble, Lucy, 410
Prenger, Jodi, 419
Primary Colors (film), 531, 532, 535
Prince, Hal, 346, 358, 470, 481
Princess Bride, The (film), 236
Prison (film), 437
Producers, The (musical), 470, 471, 474–75, 493–98
Propaganda Films, 266
Pryce, Jonathan, 311
Public Theater, New York, 75, 76, 89, 97, 103, 110, 197, 246
Pullman, Philip, *His Dark Materials,* 407
Purdy, Claude, 50

Quiller Memorandum, The (film), 221

Rabe, David, 192–208
  The Basic Training of Pavlo Hummel, 196–97
  Casualties of War, 193
  Dinosaurs on the Roof, 207
  Goose and Tomtom, 201–2, 205–6
  Hurlyburly, 193, 202–5, 207–8, 528, 536
  I'm Dancing as Fast as I Can, 193
  In the Boom Boom Room, 193
  The Orphan, 205
  Sticks and Bones, 193, 197–98
  Streamers, 192–93, 198–200, 204–5, 528
  Those the River Keeps, 193–94
Rabe, Marsha, 194–95
Rabe, William, 194
Racine, *Phèdre,* 408
Radio City Music Hall, New York, 481
Rafelson, Bob, *The Postman Always Rings Twice* (remake), 134
Rainer, Luise, 176, 188
Rainey, Ma, 32, 47, 50, 52
Raitt, John, 347, 391
Rake's Progress, The (opera), 262
Randall, Tony, 298
Rashad, Phylicia, 62, 63
Rattigan, Terence, 214
Rea, Stephen, 293
Reader, The (film), 536
Redford, Robert, 405, 526, 527
Redgrave, Vanessa, 101, 380
Reeves, Keanu, 80
Reeves, Saskia, 382
Regarding Henry (film), 503
Rehnquest, William, 101
Reilly, John C., 295
Reilly, Kelly, 325, 326
Reisz, Karel, xix, 133, 211
Remains of the Day, The (film), 536
Rich, Claude, 217

Rich, Frank, 89, 92, 104, 248, 363, 482
Richard, Keith, 284
Richard Rodgers Theatre, New York, 354
Richards, John C., 266
Richards, Lloyd, 52–55, 59, 74
Richardson, Marie, 444, 457
Richardson, Miranda, 237, 258
Rickman, Alan, 303, 354, 356–58
Riding, Joanna, 392
Rigby, Terence, 314, 315
Rigg, Diana, 312
Right Stuff, The (film), 282
Rite, The (film), 451
Riva, Emmanuelle, 217
Rivera, Chita, 480
Robbins, Jerome, 471
Robinson, Charles Shaw, 167
Robinson, Roger, 72
Robinson, Sugar Ray, 29
Rock, Chris, 264, 265–66, 267
Rodgers, Mary, *The Light in the Piazza,* 374–78
Rodgers, Richard:
  Carousel, 388, 391, 394, 413
  Musical Stages (memoir), 373
  Oklahoma!, 369–70, 374
Rodgers and Hammerstein:
  Carousel, 387–97, 407, 410, 413–14
  Oklahoma!, 369–74, 388, 495
  The Sound of Music, 369
  South Pacific, 410
Rodgers and Hart:
  By Jupiter, 388
  Pal Joey, 388
Rogers, Ginger, 477, 478, 480
Rogers, Paul, 216
Rogers, Roxanne, 288
Rogers, Sam Shepard Jr., 287, 288–90, 291

Rogers, Sandy, 288
Rollins, Jack, 520
Romero, Constanza, 28, 40, 59–60, 63
Romyn, Ann, 437
Ronconi, Luca, *Orlando Furioso*, 402
Roosevelt, Franklin D., 189
Rosander, Oscar, 438
Rose, Anika Noni, 111
Rose, Charlie, 531
Rosen, Ingrid von, 449, 451
Rosenberg, Ethel, 106, 108
Ross, Jerry, 346, 347
Roth, Philip, 251
Rothko, Mark, 145
Roudané, Matthew, 286
Roundabout Theatre Company, New York, 192, 206, 346
Rousseau, Jean-Jacques, 470
Routledge, Patricia, 394
Rowe, Clive, 392–93
Royal Court Theatre, London, 226, 247, 256
Royal Dramatic Theatre (Dramaten), Stockholm, 317, 404, 426, 431, 437, 446, 451, 453, 460, 461
Royale Theatre, New York, 151
Royal Exchange, Manchester, 408–9, 416
Royal National Theatre, London, 22, 92, 102, 134, 140, 237, 250, 370, 383–84, 387, 390, 393, 404, 407–11, 414, 416, 418, 422, 448, 531
Royal Shakespeare Company, 299, 302, 303, 409
Rudd, Paul, 264
Ruhl, Kate, 155, 156
Ruhl, Kathleen, 156
Ruhl, Patrick, 155–56

Ruhl, Sarah, 5, 152–64
    The Clean House, 152, 153, 160
    Dead Man's Cell Phone, 152, 161–63
    Death in Another Country, 153
    Dog Play, 152, 157
    "Dream," 158
    Eurydice, 152, 155, 159, 165–68
    Melancholy Play, 152, 155, 162
    Passion Play, 152, 158, 159–60, 163
    Stage Kiss, 168–72
Russell, Hilary, 271, 274
Russell Beale, Simon, 411–12, 420
Ryan, Thomas Jay, 232, 234

Sacco, Nicola, 310
Sade, Marquis de, *Justine,* 459–60
Sadleir, Preston, 368
Sageworks, 33
Sahl, Mort, 521
St. James Theatre, New York, 469, 485, 488, 492, 494
St. Louis Repertory Theatre, 88
St. Nicholas Company, Chicago, 128–29
Saint-Subber, Arnold, 525
Salinger, J. D., 157
Sanders, George, 502
Santiago-Hudson, Ruben, 31, 64, 70–71, 298, 305
Saturday Night and Sunday Morning (film), 133
Sawyer, Diane, 500, 502, 517, 537–39
Saxe, Gareth, 222–23
Scalia, Antonin, 80
Scenes from a Marriage (film), 436
Schachter, Steven, 128
Schell, Jonathan, 245
Schenkkan, Robert, *The Kentucky Cycle,* 103
Schlossberg, Caroline Kennedy, 500

Schlossberg, Julian, 492
Schneider, Alan, 401
Schönberg, Michel, 409
Schopenhauer, Arthur, 470
Schreiber, Liev, 24, 26, 151, 277
Schubert, Franz, 443
Science Museum of Minnesota, 50
Scorsese, Martin, 33–34, 277
Scot, Pat, 520
Scott, George C., 527
Scott, Ridley, 325
Scott-Reed, Christa, 234
Scottsboro Boys, The (musical),
   473–74
Second City, Chicago, 125, 516
Second Stage, New York, 165
Seigel, Lee, 93
Sendak, Maurice, 78
Seneca, *Letters from a Stoic,* 142
Serpent's Egg, The (film), 441
Seventh Seal, The (film), 438, 441
Shakespeare, William, 23, 86–87,
   154, 156, 201, 211, 298–332,
   442
  As You Like It, 298
  Barton and, 298–311
  Coriolanus, 412
  Hamlet, 299, 311–16, 412, 415
  Henry V, 300–302, 303, 306
  Julius Caesar, 305
  King John, 306
  King Lear, 304, 307, 331–32,
   418
  Macbeth, 328–30
  Measure for Measure, 304–5
  The Merchant of Venice, 437
  A Midsummer Night's Dream,
   402–3
  Much Ado about Nothing, 420
  Othello, 309–10, 324–27
  Richard II, 301, 307–8
  Richard III, 307

Sonnet No. 147, 319, 320
  Timon of Athens, 411–13
  Twelfth Night, 305
  The Winter's Tale, 317–23, 461
Shalhoub, Tony, 190
Shandling, Garry, 504, 505–7, 537
Sharian, John, 199
Shaw, George Bernard, xvi
  St. Joan, 525
Shawn, Allen, 243
Shawn, Wallace, 236–60, 268–69
  Aunt Dan and Lemon, 237, 240,
   247, 254, 256, 269
  The Designated Mourner,
   237–38, 240, 248–49, 250–56,
   259–60, 337, 410, 531
  The Fever, 237, 239, 240, 243,
   247–48, 249–50, 256, 257
  Grasses of a Thousand Colors,
   256–60
  Marie and Bruce, 237
  A Modest Proposal, 248
  Our Late Night, 246
  A Thought in Three Parts,
   246–47
Shawn, William, 238, 242, 243, 244,
   245–46, 247, 253, 257
Shay, Michele, 68
Sheen, Michael, 230
Shepard, Jesse Mojo, 286
Shepard, Matthew, 93
Shepard, Sam, 281–97
  Ages of the Moon, 281, 293–94
  Angel City, 285
  Buried Child, 287, 290, 291
  Curse of the Starving Class, 282,
   287
  Fool for Love, 288, 293
  Forensic & the Navigators, 284,
   286
  The Holy Ghostly, 284, 288, 289
  Kicking a Dead Horse, 293

The Late Henry Moss, 290
A Lie of the Mind, 287, 289, 290, 292
Motel Chronicles (memoir), 287
Operation Sidewinder, 284, 285–86
Seven Plays, 287
Stalking Himself (TV), 285, 287, 292
Starving Class, 289, 290, 291, 292
The Tooth of the Crime, 282, 284
True West, 287, 289, 290–91, 292, 294–97
Sher, Bartlett, 65, 188, 191, 375
Shewey, Don, *Sam Shepard,* 288
Show Boat (musical), 470
Shubert Theater, New York, 482, 494
Shultz, George, 106
Sickinger, Bob, 125
Silence, The (film), 433, 441
Silkwood (film), 503, 531, 533, 534
Sills, Paul, 513–14, 516, 531
Simmons, Jean, 415
Simon, John, 93
Simon, Neil:
    Barefoot in the Park, 405, 525–27, 529
    Biloxi Blues, 535
    The Odd Couple, 527, 528, 529
    Plaza Suite, 527
    The Prisoner of Second Avenue, 527–28
    The Sunshine Boys, 168, 529
    Working Girl, 535
Simon, Paul, 500
Simone, Nina, 284
Simpson, Alan, 86
Sjöberg, Alf, 437
Sjöström, Victor, 426, 438
Skinner, Claire, 227

Slap Shot (film), 134
Sledge, Percy, 46
Slover, Tim, 273
Smiles of a Summer Night (film), 438
Smith, Bessie, 46, 490
Smith, Charles, 31
Smith, Maggie, 448
Smith, Patti, 284
Softley, Peter, 408
Sondheim, Stephen, 396, 495–96, 500, 525
    Assassins, 363
    Company, 358–61, 495
    A Little Night Music, 410
    Pacific Overtures, 363
    Sunday in the Park with George, 363
    Sweeney Todd: The Demon Barber of Fleet Street, 359, 361–64, 389
Sontag, Susan, 512
Sophocles, *Oedipus Rex,* 142
Sound of Music, The (musical), 134, 369
Spanish Prisoner, The (film), 117, 137, 141
Spector, Morgan, 25
Spencer, Elizabeth, *The Light in the Piazza,* 374, 376
Spielberg, Steven, 79, 107, 421, 531, 533, 535–36, 539
Spinella, Stephen, 86, 106, 298, 304
Spinoza, Baruch, 470
Stafford-Clark, Max, 246
Stander, Lionel, 183
Stanislavsky, Konstantin:
    An Actor Prepares, 195
    Method Acting, 178–79, 195, 402, 516
Stanley, Elizabeth, 360
Starr, Nick, 414

Stebbins, Emma, 77

Stein, Gertrude, 518

Steinberg, David, 125

Steinem, Gloria, 502

Stepping Out at Radio City (revue), 481

Stewart, Jon, 79

Stewart, Patrick, 328, 329

Stewart, Rod, 284

Stiller, Ben, 262

Stinton, Colin, 140

Stoll, Corey, 25

Stoppard, Tom:
  Arcadia, 339–45, 536
  Jumpers, 339
  Lord Malquist and Mr. Moon, 339
  The Real Thing, 538
  Rosencrantz and Guildenstern Are Dead, 339
  The Invention of Love, xx–xxi
  Travesties, 339

Strahovski, Yvonne, 189–90

Strand, Mark, 161

Strasberg, Lee, 178, 182–83, 516, 525

Strauss, Richard, 510, 512

Stravinsky, Igor, 81

Streep, Meryl, 76, 500

Strindberg, August, 317, 438, 442, 444, 448
  A Dream Play, 450
  Miss Julie, 513

Stritch, Elaine, xix, 336, 361

Stroman, Charles, 476–77

Stroman, Corky, 476, 479

Stroman, Debbie, 477

Stroman, Ella, 476

Stroman, Frances, 476

Stroman, Susan, 372, 404, 469–98
  Double Feature, 471

Stroszek (film), 267

Sturges, Preston, 535

Sullivan, Daniel, 210, 351

Sultan, Donald, 140

Summer Interlude (film), 439

Summer with Monika (film), 439

Sunday's Children (film), 431–32, 434, 449

Sunset Boulevard (musical), 370

Sweet, Jeff, *Something Wonderful Right Away,* 517, 519

Sweet Smell of Success (film), 174, 176, 182, 185

Swift, Jonathan, "A Modest Proposal," 255

Taccone, Tony, 107

Takazauckas, Albert, 115

Take Five, More or Less (musical), 476

Tambor, Jeffrey, 151

Tate, Kevin Ricardo, 113

Tayler, Edward, 86–87

Taylor, Elizabeth, 500, 530–31

Tchassov, Stanislav, 394

Teresa, Saint, 397

Tesori, Jenine, 97–98, 110, 112

Testament of Dr. Mabuse, The (film), 18

Thacher, Molly Day, 22

Theatre Genesis, New York, 283

Theatre Guild, 378

Theatre of Cruelty, 402

Thebus, Jessica, 168

Things Change (film), 130

Thirst (film), 437

Thomas, Dylan, 45, 502

Thomas, Richard, 410

Thompson, David, 473, 474, 481, 482

Thompson, Mark, 340, 384

Through a Glass Darkly (film), 441

Thulin, Ingrid, 444

Tilly, Jennifer, 259
Tinguely, Jean, *Rotozaza,* 346
Tocqueville, Alexis de, 105
Tolin, Tom, 84
Torment (film), 437
Town Hall, New York, 55
Townsend, Stuart, 380–81, 414
Tracy, Spencer, 518
Trading Places (musical), 480–81
Trinity Repertory Company, Providence, 158
Trixie the Pomeranian, 492
Troobnick, Gene, 513
Trow, George, 245
Truffaut, François, 434, 438, 444
Tubb, Ernest, 293
Tubman, Harriet, 280
Tynan, Kenneth, 494, 498

Ullmann, Linn, 449
Ullmann, Liv, 425, 434, 435, 439, 444, 445–46, 447, 449–50
University of Chicago, 511–14, 515, 518
Untouchables, The (film), 130, 138

Vance, Courtney, 30
Van Doren, Charles, 521
Van Ryker, Patricia, 54
Vanstone, Hugh, 380
Vanya on 42nd Street (film), 236, 251, 256
Vanzetti, Bartolomeo, 310–11
Veazey, Jeff, 480–81
Veblen, Thorstein, 116, 462
Vera Ellen, 480
Verdict, The (film), 134, 135, 138
Verdon, Gwen, 480
Vietnam War, 195–96, 198–200, 201, 206, 311, 495
Vivian Beaumont Theatre, New York, 339

Vogel, Paula, 157–58
    Baltimore Waltz, 158

Wagner, Arthur, 178, 181
Wagner, Robin, 497
Wag the Dog (film), 117
Walker, Joseph, 30
Walsh, Barbara, 361
Walsh, Enda, 410
Walter, Harriet, 344
Walter Kerr Theatre, New York, 61, 68
Walters, Barbara, 500
Wanamaker, Zoë, 384, 386, 420
Warchus, Matthew, 295
Ward, Anthony, 328
War Horse (film), 407, 421–22
Warner, David, 311
Warner, Jack, 530–31, 532
Waters, Les, 165
Waterston, Sam, 298, 303, 308
Watteau, Jean-Antoine, *La Partie Quarrée,* 461
Waugh, Evelyn, 357
Weaver, Sigourney, 277
Weber, Carl, 87
Weisberg, Steven, 475
Weiss, Nadja, 467
Welch, Sheila, 124, 134
Weller, Frederick, 151
Welles, Orson, 500
Welty, Eudora, 157
Wernick, Morris (Moishe), 220–21
Wesker, Arnold, 214
Wesley, Richard, 30
Weston, Celia, 297
What Planet Are You From? (film), 503–4, 505–7, 536, 537
Wheeler, Hugh, 362–63
Whiting, Jeff, 490
Whitman, Walt, 180
    Democratic Vistas, 294–95

Wilbur, Richard, 463
Wilcox, Wayne, 375
Wilde, Oscar, 339
  The Importance of Being Earnest, 525
  Salomé, 510, 512
Wilder, Billy, 531, 535
Wild Strawberries (film), 426, 438, 439, 441
Wilhoite, Kathleen, 265
Williams, Chawley, 43, 45, 48
Williams, Heathcote, 209, 226
  AC/DC, 337
Williams, J. D., 199
Williams, Robin, 528, 536
Williams, Tennessee, 5, 33, 34, 53, 100, 116, 410, 522
  Battle of Angels (later *Orpheus Descending*), 378–80, 382
  Cat on a Hot Tin Roof, 185
  The Glass Menagerie, 17–18, 35, 109, 379
  Orpheus Descending, 378, 380–83, 414
  The Rose Tattoo, 383–87
  A Streetcar Named Desire, 17–18, 179, 279, 383, 401, 404, 511
  Summer and Smoke, 383
Wilson, August, 5, 28–74
  The Coldest Day of the Year, 50
  Fences, 31, 43, 53, 57–58, 74
  Gem of the Ocean, 61–65
  Jitney, 31, 51, 54–55
  Joe Turner's Come and Gone, 31, 33, 34, 47, 51, 63, 65–68
  King Hedley II, 29, 30, 31, 33, 46, 56–58, 62
  Ma Rainey's Black Bottom, 30, 31, 47, 52
  "Morning Statement," 49
  "Muhammad Ali," 44

The Piano Lesson, 31, 34, 51, 53, 54, 59, 74
  "Poem for the Old Man," 43
  Radio Golf, 65
  Seven Guitars, 31, 33, 34, 37, 52, 68–74
  Two Trains Running, 31, 46, 47–48, 58, 62, 63
Wilson, Azula, 28, 34, 59, 60–61
Wilson, Chandra, 111
Wilson, Daisy, 37–38, 39, 40, 42–43, 46
Wilson, Donna, 37, 38, 40
Wilson, Edmund, 451, 515
Wilson, Edwin, 37
Wilson, Freda, 37, 38, 39–40, 44, 59
Wilson, Linda Jean, 37, 39, 41, 42, 43, 49
Wilson, Patrick, 370
Wilson, Richard, 37
Winchell, Walter, 173, 177, 188
Wing-Davey, Mark, 163–64
Winnicott, D. W., *Thinking about Children,* 142
Winter Light (film), 430
Winters, Jonathan, 521
Wittrock, Finn, 540
Wolf (film), 503
Wolfe, George C., 75, 96–97, 98, 110, 113
  Jelly's Last Jam, 103, 389
Woolf, Henry, 220, 221
Wopat, Tom, 151
World of Jules Feiffer, The (musical), 525
Worters, Danny, 145
Wright, Richard, 45
Wriothesley, Henry, 319
Wycherley, William, *The Country Wife,* 262

Yale Repertory Theatre, New Haven, 52, 163
Yeager, Chuck, 282
Yeargan, Michael, 66
Yeats, W. B., 227
Purgatory, 513
Youmans, Vincent, 479
Young Frankenstein (film), 494

Zeisler, Mark, 166
Zellweger, Renée, 265, 266
Zigler, Scott, 126
Zindel, Paul, *Effect of Gamma Rays on Man-in-the-Moon Marigolds, The,* 83
Zollo, Fred, 132, 134, 138–39, 141